The History of the Reformation of the Church of England: the Third Part: Being a Supplement to the Two Formerly Published
by Gilbert Burnet

Address:
HardPress
8345 NW 66TH ST #2561
MIAMI FL 33166-2626
USA
Email: info@hardpress.net

THE

HISTORY OF THE REFORMATION

OF THE

CHURCH OF ENGLAND

BY

GILBERT BURNET, D.D.

BISHOP OF SALISBURY.

A NEW EDITION CAREFULLY REVISED, AND THE RECORDS
COLLATED WITH THE ORIGINALS,

BY

NICHOLAS POCOCK, M.A.

LATE MICHEL FELLOW OF QUEEN'S COLLEGE.

VOL. III.

OXFORD

AT THE CLARENDON PRESS

MDCCCLXV

THE THIRD PART.

BEING A SUPPLEMENT TO THE TWO FORMERLY PUBLISHED.

TO THE KING'.

SIR,

THIS work, which is designed to finish the History of our Reformation, seems reserved to be laid at your MAJESTY's feet; who, we trust, is designed by God to complete the reformation itself.

To rectify what may be yet amiss, and to supply what is defective among us; to oblige us to live and to labour more suitably to our profession; to unite us more firmly among ourselves; to bury, and for ever to extinguish, the fears of our relapsing again into popery; and to establish a confidence and correspondence with the protestant and reformed churches abroad.

The eminent moderation of the most serene house from which your MAJESTY is descended, gives us auspicious hopes, that as God has now raised your MAJESTY, with signal characters of an amazing providence, to be the head and the chief strength of the reformation; so your MAJESTY will, by a wise and noble conduct, form all these churches into one body; so that though they cannot agree to the same opinions and rituals with us in all points, yet they may join in one happy confederacy, for the support of the whole, and of every particular branch of that sacred union.

[George I.]

BURNET, PART III.   B

May this be the peculiar glory of your MAJESTY's reign; and may all the blessings of heaven and earth rest upon your most august person, and upon all your royal posterity.

This is the daily prayer of him, who is with the profoundest respect,

SIR,

Your MAJESTY's

most loyal, most obedient, and most

devoted subject and servant,

GI. SARUM.

THE PREFACE.

I HAD in my Introduction to this volume, which I published a year[2] ago, said all that then occurred to me in the way of preface: but some particulars coming to my knowledge since that time, give me an occasion to add a little to what was then copiously deduced.

I begin with M. Le Grand, who I understand is now in a considerable post in the court of France. He, being lately at

[2] [The author had published in the previous year a small volume entitled, 'An Introduction to the Third Volume of the History of the Reformation of the Church of England, by the Right Reverend Father in God, Gilbert Lord Bishop of Sarum.' It contained the following preface addressed to his publisher:

'Mr. Churchill,
'Your care in putting so many advertisements in the Gazettes has been of very great use to me; but because I would gladly have the History of our Reformation to be as full and perfect as may be, I do now send you the *Introduction to the Third Volume*, that is almost ready to be put in the press; which I desire you to print in a smaller form; hoping it will give such public notice of my design, that it may come into the hands of those who perhaps look not into the advertisements in Gazettes, and so may move them that can furnish me with other materials to help me to finish this work with great advantage; for which I am ready to make

them all the returns that are in my power. I desire you will prefix to this a passage out of Livy which does so perfectly agree with my present thoughts, that I cannot express them better nor more truly than those words do.
'I am, Sir,
'Your most humble servant,
'G. SARUM.
'Salisbury, Sept. 26, 1713.'

The pamphlet passed into a second edition in the same year. The passage of Livy was inserted on the title page, and was as follows, *Hoc laboris pretium petam uti me a conspectu malorum, quæ nostra tot per annos vidit ætas, tantisper certe dum prisca illa totâ mente repeto, avertam: omnis expers curæ quæ scribentis animum, etsi non flectere a vero, solicitum tamen efficere possit.*— Livii Hist. lib. i. The book itself is reprinted in the Third Volume as Introduction, varying only in the spelling of a few words and in one or two passages where the variation is noticed at the foot of the page.]

B 2

Geneva, explained himself to my friends in these terms; "that
" he was young when he wrote against me, and that the heat
" of youth had carried him to some expressions, from which
" he would abstain, if he were to write now : he was glad to
" hear that I was upon the reviewing the History of the Re-
" formation;" and named to them a Life that he had seen in
Spain of Bartholomew Carranza, archbishop of Toledo, who
was king Philip's confessor, and went with him to England;
and was particularly employed in reforming (as they called it)
the universities : and, as he said, he died when he was to be
delivered out of the prison of the inquisition. He added, that
he had also seen a collection of cardinal Pole's letters, with an
account of what passed in England after the death of king
Edward, which he believed I had not seen, and that could
inform me of many particulars; but that he himself had other
employments than to think of the affairs of England. If I
had received this civil message from M. Le Grand before I
had published my Introduction, I would have said nothing at
all with relation to him; but what is past cannot be recalled;
so I hope he will accept of this for all the reparation I can
now make him.

As for Anthony Harmer, some have doubted if he could be
capable of making three capital errors[3] in one line : and since ii
Mr. Strype has suggested to me that, in which I was under
some reserve before, as having it from another hand, I am
now free to set it down. For *capitulum ecclesiæ cathedralis*,
he has printed, *epistolam conventûs ecclesiæ catholicæ*[4]. If
the abbreviations may seem to excuse the reading *epistolam*
for *capitulum*, and *catholicæ* for *cathedralis*, nothing can
excuse the adding the word *conventus*, which he thought
wanting to make a complete title, having read the others as
he did : so I hope I have reason to have no regard to any
thing that comes from him upon his bare authority. The
weak and ill-natured attempts that some among ourselves have
of late made upon me, give me no sort of concern, unless it is
to pray for those who have despitefully used me.

There was also a great poem[5] lately prepared, and, I sup-

[3] [See Introduction, p. xxvi.]
[4] [See Anglia Sacra, vol. i. p.
772. l. 20.]

[5] [Ward (Thomas). England's
Reformation, from the time of king
Henry VIII. to the end of Oates's

pose, designed to be published, when that which our enemies hoped was near accomplished should have been effected. It was written in imitation of Hudibras, and so was a mock poem on the reformation, composed by one Thomas Ward, of whom I can give no other account, but that it is said he is a priest. In it, Sanders' work was made the plot of the fable : it was full of impious abuse, put in a strain apt enough to take with those who were disposed to divert themselves with a show of wit and humour, dressed up to make the reformation appear both odious and ridiculous ; not doubting of equal success with Butler's admired performance. It was no wonder, if, upon such a design, my History was treated with all the characters of scorn and contempt. This was what I might justly expect from those of that side : but I was sorry to find so much censure from those from whom I had no reason to expect it, and which seemed to be the effect only of envy and ill-nature : God forgive them for it.

I must say a little more, with relation to a learned and copious writer of our ecclesiastical history[6], who finds my History often in his way : he treats me decently as to his expressions, but designs all through to set such remarks on my work, as, if they were well grounded, must destroy the credit that it has hitherto obtained. I will first give some instances to shew what the spirit, the principles, and the design of that writer must be : I will name but four out of a great many.

When he sets forth king Henry the Eighth's proceedings against the memory of Thomas Becket, he has these words; " And though his conduct in this dispute was not altogether " defensible, he was far, however, from being guilty of that " gross mismanagement with which he is charged." I will leave the judgment that must be passed upon this period to all who are in any sort acquainted with the history of that time.   P. 150. vol. ii. col. 1.

When he gives the character of king Edward the Sixth, immediately before he tells of his death, it is in these words: p. 332. col. 2. " His conscience was not always under a serviceable direction ;" (the meaning of this dark expression I do not reach ;) he was " tinctured with Erastian principles, and under wrong pre-

---

plot, a poem in four cantos, London, 1716, 8vo.]
[6] [Jeremy Collier, whose Ecclesiastical History was published in two volumes folio, Lond. 1708-14.]

" possessions as to church government; he seems to have had
" no notion of sacrilege;———and, which is somewhat remark-
" able, most of the hardships were put upon ecclesiastics in
" the latter end of his reign, when his judgment was in the
" best condition :" and without adding one word of his good
qualities, or to correct those severe reflections, he concludes
with the account of his death.

p. 601.
col. 2. He gives a very different account of the death of Mary
queen of Scots, in these words ; " Her fortitude and devotion
" were very remarkable : she supported her character with
" all imaginable decency : she died like a Christian, and like
" a queen."

And, to mention no more, when he comes to queen Elizabeth's death and character, he runs a parallel between the two
p. 671.
col. 2. sisters, Mary and Elizabeth, in these words ; " The one made
" martyrs, the other made beggars : the one executed the
" men, and the other the estates : and therefore, reserving the
" honour of the reformation to queen Elizabeth, the question
" will be, Whether the resuming the first-fruits and tenths,
" putting many vicarages in a deplorable condition, and settling
" a perpetuity of poverty on the church, was not much more
" prejudicial than fire and fagot ? Whether destroying bishop-
" rics was not a much greater hardship than the destroying
" bishops ? because this severity affects succession, and reaches
" down to future ages. And lastly, Whether, as the world
" goes, it is not more easy to recruit bishops, than the revenues
" to support them ?" These words give such an indication of
the notion that the author has of the happiness or misery of a
church, that they want no commentary.

Hist. of the
Reform.
Part 2.
Book i.
p. 149. I will add this one remark of a fact upon a passage that I
had writ concerning the book of Ordination, published in the
third year of king Edward, which was in these words : " An-
" other difference between the ordination-book set out at that
" time, and that we now use, was, that the bishop was to lay
" his one hand on the priest's head, and with his other to give
" him a Bible, with a chalice and bread in it, saying the words
" that are[7] now said at the delivery of the Bible. In the con-
" secration of a bishop, there is[8] nothing more than what is
" yet in use, save that a staff was put into his hand with this

---

[7] [*that are*, om. Edd.]   [8] [*was*, Edd.]

" blessing, *Be to the flock of Christ a shepherd.*" Upon this his remark is in these words : " But here, as it happens, this P. 290. col. 2. " learned person has been led into a mistake ; for the two first " editions of the Ordinal made in king Edward's reign have " none of the different rites mentioned by this gentleman." I was indeed surprised when I read this, and went to look into the first edition of that Ordinal which I knew was in the Lambeth library[9] : for, by archbishop Sancroft's order, I had the free use of every thing that lay there. There I went to examine it, and I found indeed a small variation from my History. The whole is in these words : In the ordination of a priest, after the imposition of hands, with the words still used, follows this rubric; " Then the bishop shall deliver to every one of " them the Bible in the one hand, and the chalice, or cup, with " the bread, in the other hand, and say, *Take thou authority,* " &c." In the consecration of a bishop, this rubric is ; " The " elected bishop, having upon him a surplice and a cope, shall " be presented by two bishops, being also in surplices and " copes, having their pastoral staves in their hands." And after the form of the consecration this rubric follows ; " Then " shall the archbishop lay the Bible upon his neck, saying, " *Give heed to reading.*" The next rubric is, " Then shall " the archbishop put into his hand the pastoral staff, saying, ᵥ " *Be to the flock of Christ a shepherd ;*" on to the end of the " charge, now given all together, but then divided in two. This book was printed by Richard Grafton, the king's printer, in March 1549 ; or by the Roman account, 1550[10]. I have

[9] [The form and manner of making and consecrating of Archbishops, Bishops, Priests and Deacons, anno Domini MDXLIX, has been printed from Lambeth MS. Nº. 885, by the Parker Society. The author has been guilty of some verbal inaccuracies. There is no *then* before the first rubric quoted, and in the last the words are 'give heed *unto* reading,' &c.]

[10] [The title is as follows :

THE FORME
and maner of makyng
and consecrating of
Archebishoppes

Bishoppes
Priestes
and
Deacons
M.D.XLIX.

At the end is the name of the printer thus :
RICHARDVS GRAFTON
typographus Regius
excudebat

Mense Martii
A. M.D.XLIX.
Cum priuilegio ad imprimendum solum.]

given this full account of that matter in my own justification:
I am sorry that I cannot return this learned person his compliment to myself, *that he was led into a mistake.*

. The next, and indeed the last particular, that out of many
more I will mention, is, the setting down the explanation, that
was made upon the order for kneeling at ·the sacrament in
king Edward's time, wrong in a very material word : for in
p. 310.
ool. 2. that the words were, " That there was not in the sacrament
" any real or essential presence of Christ's natural flesh and
" blood;" but he instead of that puts, " corporal presence[11]."
It seems in this he only looked at the rubric, as it is now at
the end of the communion service, upon a conceit that it stands
now as it was in king Edward's book, though it was at that
D. P. G.[12] time changed: and we know who was the author of that
change, and who pretended that a *corporal presence* signified
such a presence as a body naturally has, which the assertors
of transubstantiation itself do not, and cannot pretend is in
this case ; where they say the body is not present corporally,
but spiritually, or as a spirit is present. And' he who had the
chief hand in procuring this alteration had a very extraordinary subtilty, by which he reconciled the opinion of a real
presence in the sacrament with the last words of the rubric,
" That the natural body and blood of Christ were in heaven,
" and not here ; it being against the truth of Christ's natural
" body to be at one time in more places than one." It was
thus : a body is in a place, if there is no intermediate body
but a *vacuum* between it and the place ; and he thought, that,
by the virtue of the words of consecration, there was a *cylin-
der* of a *vacuum* made between the elements and Christ's body
in heaven: so that, no body being between, it. was both in
heaven and in the elements. Such a solemn piece of folly as
this can hardly be read without indignation. But if our author
favours this conceit, yet, when he sets down that which was vi
done in king Edward's reign, he ought not to have changed

[11] [This is part of a rubric of
king Edward's second prayer book :
the words are, ' lest yet the same
kneeling might be thought or taken
otherwise, we do declare that it is
not meant thereby that any adora-
tion is done or ought to be done
either unto the sacramental bread
or wine there bodily received, or to
any real and essential presence there
being of Christ's natural flesh and
blood.']

[12] [The initials here mean Dr.
Peter Gunning, bishop of Ely.]

the word, especially such an important one. I shall say no more of that work, but that there appeared to me, quite through the second volume, such a constant inclination to favour the popish doctrine, and to censure the reformers, that I should have had a better opinion of the author's integrity, if he had professed himself not to be of our communion, nor of the communion of any other protestant church.

But as I thought myself bound to give this warning to such as may have heard of that work, or that have seen it ; so there is another History lately written in French, and which, I hope, is soon to appear in our own language, which I cannot recommend more than it deserves. It is M. L'Enfant's History of the Council of Constance[13] ; in which that excellent person has with great care, and a sincerity liable to no exception, given the world, in the history of that council, so true a view of the state of the church, and of religion, in the age before the reformation, that I know no book so proper to prepare a man for reading the History of the Reformation, as the attentive reading of that noble work. He was indeed well furnished with a collection of excellent materials, gathered with great fidelity and industry by the learned doctor Vander Hordt, professor of divinity in the university of Helmstadt ; and procured for him by the noble zeal and princely bounty of that most serene and pious prince Rodolph August, the late duke of Brunswick Wolfenbuttle, who set himself with great care, and at a vast charge, to procure from all places the copies of all papers and manuscripts that could be found, to give light to the proceedings of that great assembly : that collection amounted to six volumes in folio. From these authentic vouchers the history of that council is now happily compiled. And if that learned author can find materials to give us as full and as clear a history of the council of Basle, as he has given of that of Constance, I know no greater service can be done vii the world : for by it, popery will appear in its true and native colours, free from those palliating disguises which the progress of the reformation, and the light which by that has been given the world, has forced upon those of that communion. We

---

[13] [Histoire du Concile de Constance, 2 vols. 4to. Amst. 1727. An English translation made by Stephen Whatley came out in two vols. 4to. London, 1730.]

have the celebrated History of the Council of Trent, first published here at London, written with a true sublimity of judgment, and an unbiassed sincerity ; which has received a great confirmation, even from cardinal Pallavicini's attempt [14] to destroy its credit, and a much greater of late from that curious discovery of Vargas' Letters [15]. But how well and how justly soever the history that P. Paolo gave the world of that council is esteemed, I am not afraid to compare the late History of the Council of Constance even to that admired work ; so far at least, as that if it will not be allowed to be quite equal to it, yet it may be well reckoned among the best of all that have written after that noble pattern, which the famous Venetian friar has given to all the writers of ecclesiastical history.

Since I published my Introduction, I fell on many papers concerning the reformation in Scotland, which had escaped the diligence of that grave and judicious writer archbishop Spotswood ; of which I have given a full account, and have used the best endeavours I could to be furnished with all the other materials that I could hear of. It is true, I never searched into a lately gathered famous library in this place ; but yet I had from some, on whose good judgment and great care I might well depend, who had carefully looked through it, every thing that they found material to my purpose.

No curiosity pleased me more than that noble record of the legate's proceedings in the matter of king Henry's divorce ; of which I had the free use, as of every thing else that was in the library of my learned and dear brother, the late bishop of Ely [16]; in whose death the church and all his friends, and none more than myself, have had an invaluable loss. I read that record very carefully twice or thrice over, and gave a full abstract of it, but did not then reflect on what has occurred to me since ; for though, upon the credit of so noble a record, I viii have said that the king and queen were never together in

[14] [Pallavicino (Card. Sforza). Istoria del Concilio di Trento, Roma, 2 vols. fol. 1656–62.]

[15] [Lettres et Mémoires de François de Vargas, de Pierre de Malvenda et de quelques Evêques d'Espagne, Touchant le Concile de Trente. Traduits de l'Espagnol, avec des Remarques, par M. Michel Le Vassor, Amst. 1700, 8vo.]

[16] [John Moore, who was translated from Norwich to Ely in 1707, and died July 31, 1714.]

court, yet I find the contrary is affirmed by that king himself, in a letter bearing date the 23rd of June, to his ambassadors at Rome, in these words; " Both we and the queen appeared " in person:" and he sets forth the assurances the cardinals gave of their proceeding without favour or partiality; " yet " she departed out of court, though thrice called to appear, " and was denounced contumacious." The only reconciling of this apparent contradiction seems to be this ; that they were indeed together in the hall where the court sat, but that it was before the cardinals sat down, and had formed the court : for as it is not to be imagined that in the record so material a step could have been omitted, so highly to the honour of the court; so it is not likely that the queen, after her appeal, would have owned the court, or have appeared before those judges : therefore the most probable account of that particular is this, that the king intending to appear in the court, the queen went thither after him, and made that speech to him in the open hall, that I mentioned in my former work : but all this was over, and they were both gone, before the court was opened, or that the cardinals had taken their places ; so that their appearance could be no part of the record of the court.

I am now to give an account of some papers that I add as an Appendix, for they relate to the former volumes. The first of these was sent me by one Mr. Thomas Granger[17], of whom I can give no other account, but that I understood he was a clergyman. He dated his letter from Lamerton, near Tavistock in Devon, the seventh of February 168¾. I wrote him such a civil answer, as so kind a censure deserved : and I promised that I would make my acknowledgments more publicly to him whensoever I reviewed that work. Upon my settling at Salisbury, I inquired after him, but I was told he was dead : so I lost the occasion of returning my thanks to him in a more particular manner, which I now express thus publicly.

ix   I had another letter, writ in another strain, full of expostulation, from Anthony (who affected to write himself) à Wood. He thought it incumbent on him to justify himself, since I had reflected on him : so he gave this vent to it. I wrote short remarks on it ; one of these I find is in the bishop of Wor-

[17] [These notes are printed at the foot of the page with the initial [G.]]

cester's hand: they were sent to bishop Fell, to be communicated to him; but whether they were, or not, I cannot tell. The thing has escaped my memory, but the paper still remains with me; and therefore I have thought it a justice to Mr. Wood's memory, and to his writings, to insert it here[18].

The third paper was drawn by me at Paris, in the year 1685. My History being then translated into French, was much read; and as to the main conduct of our reformation, it was approved by some men of great name. At that time there was an embroilment between the court of Rome and that of Versailles; and the propositions that passed in the year 1682 seemed to threaten a greater rupture to follow. Upon that, the scheme of the English reformation was a subject of common discourse; and that was so much magnified by those who were called the *Converters*, that the hope of a reformation in France was one of the artifices that prevailed on some, who knew not the *depths of Satan*, and were easily wrought on to make their court by changing their religion, in hope that a great reformation of abuses among them was then projected. But one of the learnedest men that ever I knew of that communion said then to myself, that all that was only done to fright pope Innocent the Eleventh, who was then in the interests of the house of Austria; but that whensoever they should have a pope in the interests of France, their court would not only declare him infallible in points of doctrine, but even in matters of fact: and he added, that it was an abuse that people put upon themselves, to imagine, that with what pomp or zeal soever the court seemed to support those articles passed in the assembly of the clergy, that this could have any other effect but to bring the court of Rome into their interests. He said, this had been cardinal Mazarine's practice during his whole ministry: when he could not carry matters to his mind x at Rome, he shewed such favour to the Jansenists, as let many of them into great dignities; but when he had brought that court to what he designed, he presently changed his conduct towards them.

A person of distinction at Paris, finding my History so much liked, wrote a censure upon it. This ran through many hands,

[18] [This paper is printed at p. 571, as an Appendix to Part I.]

but was never printed : it fell into M. Auzout's hands, and from him I had it. I wrote an answer to it, and got it to be translated into French : it was favourably received by many in Paris. I do not find the copy of that censure among my papers ; but I have still the copy of my remarks on it, from which the substance of that censure may be gathered : so I have thought fit to add this to my Appendix [19].

The fourth paper is a large collection of many mistakes (descending even to literal ones) in both the volumes of my History, and in the Records published in them, which a learned and worthy person has read with more exactness than either my amanuensis or myself had done. I publish these sheets, as that unknown [20] person sent them to me ; whom I never saw, as far as I remember, and who will not suffer me to give any other account of him, but that he lives in one of the universities. His copy of my work being of the second edition, only some very few of the errors marked that had crept into the second, but that were not in the first edition, are struck out. In several particulars I do not perfectly agree with these corrections : but I set them down as they were sent me, without any remarks on them ; and I give my hearty thanks in the fullest manner I can, to him who was first at the pains to make this collection, and then had the goodness to communicate it to me in so obliging a manner : for he gave me a much greater power over these papers than I have thought fit to assume.

The next paper is a much shorter one : it is indeed the abstract of a larger paper, but I have taken out of it only that which relates to my History, and have not meddled with some remarks made on Harmer's Specimen, and many more made xi on the Rights of an English Convocation. These did not be-

[19] [This paper is printed at the end of the text of Part I. p. 575 of this edition.]

[20] [This was the celebrated antiquary Thomas Baker, whose notes have been transferred from the Appendix to the foot of the page, and may be recognised by the initial [B] being added to them. These notes, if they were all sent at one time to the author, must have been forwarded after the separate publication of the following Introduction, for one of the corrections alludes to a passage in the Introduction. (See p. xli.) Several other corrections made by Baker have been printed in the British Magazine, vol. xxxvi. by the Rev. J. B. Mayor ; these have not been printed in this edition, though the editor has frequently made use of them.]

long to my subject ; so I have not copied them out. The writer has not let me know his name; he sent the sheets to me in an unsubscribed letter, to which I wrote an answer by the conveyance that he marked out to me : but I have heard no more of him.

The sixth and last paper was sent me by the sincere and diligent Mr. Strype, who has descended to such a full and minute correction, both of my History, and of my copies of the Records, that I confess it gave me great satisfaction. Many of his corrections may seem so inconsiderable, that it may be suggested that they were not worth the while : but my whole concern in writing being to deliver the transactions of a former age faithfully down to posterity, nothing could please me more than to have every error I had fallen into discovered ; and it was no small satisfaction to me, to find that a writer, who has been now above thirty years examining all that passed in that age, and has made great discoveries of many secrets hitherto not known ; and who was so kind as to pass over nothing, how small and inconsiderable soever it may appear to be, that was liable to correction ; yet did not touch upon any one thing that is of any moment in my whole work. This I look on as a very authentic confirmation of it all, except in the places thus censured, by one who has searched into all the transactions of that time with so much application and success.

This work was composed above a year ago, and after it was read and corrected by some proper judges, it was put in the press, and was printed off to the end of king Edward's reign, before the first of August last : nor has any thing been added to it since that time, except some very few particulars in the last book relating to Scotland.

[Aug. 1. 1714.]

I cannot conclude this Preface, and so dismiss this work out of my hands, without some reflections on what has appeared among us of late, but too evidently, in a course of some years. Many who profess great zeal for the legal establishment, yet seem to be set on forming a new scheme both of religion and government ; and are taking the very same methods, only a little diversified, that have been pursued in popery, to bring the world into a blind dependence upon the clergy, and to draw the wealth and strength of the nation into their hands. xii

The opinion of the sacrament's being an expiatory sacrifice, and of the necessity of secret confession and absolution, and of the church's authority acting in an independence on the civil powers, were the foundations of popery, and the seminal principles out of which that mass of corruptions was formed. They have no colour for them in the New Testament, nor in the first ages of Christianity; and are directly contrary to all the principles on which the reformation was carried on, and to every step that was made in the whole progress of that work: and yet these of late have been notions much favoured, and written for with much zeal, not to say indecency; besides a vast number of little superstitious practices, that in some places have grown to a great height, so that we were insensibly going off from the reformation, and framing a new model of a church totally different from all our former principles, as well as from our present establishment: to all which they have added that singular and extravagant conceit of the invalidity of baptism, unless ministered by one episcopally ordained; though this not only cuts off all communion with the foreign protestant churches; of which, perhaps, they make no great account; but makes doubtings to arise with relation to great numbers, both among ourselves, and in the Roman communion.

This I lament; not that I think that there is such a sacredness in any human constitution, that it is never to be called in question, or altered: for if we had the same reasons to alter any thing established at the reformation, that our fathers had to alter the former establishment in the times of popery, I should acknowledge we had now as good grounds to change the present, as our ancestors had then to change the former constitution. The scriptures are the only sure foundation of our faith that is unalterable; all other constitutions being always to be governed by that perfect declaration of God's holy will with relation to mankind. But it gives a just indignation, to see the same men make wide steps to great alterations on the one hand, and yet make heavy complaints where there is no just occasion given, and that about points of mere speculation; whereas the other relate to matters of practice, which had been in former ages so managed, that the whole complex of the Christian religion was totally depraved by them.

We have also rules and rubrics for worship that are our standards, fixed by law : and yet we see a humour of innovation making a great progress in these, without the least complaint, by the same persons who are apt to make tragical outcries on the smallest transgressions on the other hand.

Both are very culpable : but of the two, we find the growth of superstition has been so spreading, as well as so specious, that the extremes of that hand may be justly reckoned the more dangerous ; one of the worst effects of superstition being that with which our Saviour charged the pharisees of his time, that while they were exact in *tithing mint, anise, and cummin, they omitted the weightier matters of the Law, judgment, mercy, and faith* in opposition to which, he gives a standing rule, applicable to all such cases ; *These things ye ought to have done, and not to leave the other undone.* This relates to practices of a lower order, but such as are commanded ; whereas voluntary and assumed ones, like the washings among the Jews in our Saviour's time, eat out the sense of the great duties of religion : instead of which, some trifling performances are set up and are highly magnified, while the others are spoken of more coldly. Nor does any thing feed a censorious and uncharitable temper more than these voluntary and distinguishing practices, which as they are the badges of different parties, so they are engines to keep up that wrath, emulation, and hatred, that has made such havoc among us of the great and indispensable duties of *peace, brotherly kindness, and charity.*

These have been but too visibly the arts of Satan to divide xiv and distract us, and have oftener than once brought us near the brink of ruin. God has often rescued us, while the continuance and progress of these evil dispositions have as often made us relapse into a broken and disjointed state. Oh that we may at last *see the things that belong to our peace,* and *follow after those things that make for peace, and the things wherewith we may edify one another.* In this prayer I will continue as long as I live, and I hope to end my days with it. We must ask it of God, and of him only : it is in vain to ask it of some men, who, when we *speak to them of peace, make them ready to battle :* we must look for it only to him who said, *Peace I leave with you, my peace I give unto you ; not as the world giveth, give I unto you.* The world will only give it to those of their own knot and party : but *the wisdom that is from above is first pure, then peaceable, gentle, and easy to be entreated ; full of mercy and good fruits, without partiality, and without hypocrisy : and the fruits of righteousness are sown in peace of them that make peace*[21].

[21] [At the end of the Preface in the original edition is given a very imperfect list of Errata in the History and in the Collection of Records.]

THE INTRODUCTION.

I COME, after a long interval of three and thirty years[22], to give all the finishing to the History of our REFORMATION, that I have been able to collect, either from new discoveries that have come in my own way, or the kind advertisements of friends, and the severe animadversions of critics ; of which I have endeavoured to make the best use that I could. It has been objected to me, that I wrote in haste, and did not reflect enough on the matters I wrote about. That may be very true ; and I will give an account how it happened to be so. When Sanders' History was published in France, it had so ill an effect there, that some of our best divines were often called on to hasten such an answer to it, as might stop the course of so virulent a book. Those to whom these advices were sent thought me a proper person to be engaged in it.

The ancient, the learned, and the pious bishop of Worcester[23] is the only person now alive that was concerned in the choice : and he having read all the printed books that he could hear of relating to those times, had taken the dates of every remarkable thing that passed out of them ; which he caused to be copied out for me : they are about eight sheets of paper. Upon this stock I set out, and searched all the public offices about the town with a labour and diligence, that was then looked on as no contemptible performance. I marked every thing as exactly as I could. I might in such a variety make some mistakes, for which men of candour will make just allowances. But when I had gone through all that lay thus open to me, I knew what treasures were still in the Cotton library.

[22] [This Introduction appeared in 1713, thirty-three years after the completion of the writing of the second part of the History of the Reformation.]

[23] [William Lloyd, who was translated from Lichfield and Coventry to Worcester in 1699, and died on the 30th of August, 1717, aged 90.]

The present bishop of Worcester [24] carried me to sir John Cotton, to ask admittance: but a great prelate [25] had been beforehand with us, and had possessed him with such prejudices against me, as being no friend to the prerogative of the crown, nor to the constitution of our church, that he said, (as he was prepared,) that unless the archbishop of Canterbury and a secretary of state would recommend me, as a person fit to have access to his library, he desired to be excused: and though that worthy prelate said, he would be answerable for the use that I should make of it, yet he could not be prevailed on to depart from the answer that he had made us. Nor could that reverend person prevail with archbishop Sancroft to interpose. And though I offered to deliver up all the collections I had made to any person that would undertake the work, yet no regard was had to that: so I saw it was resolved on, either not to let that work go on; or, at least, that I should not have the honour to be employed in it.

ii With this we were at a full stop, when, accidentally meeting with sir John Marsham the younger, I told him how I was denied access to the Cotton library: but he told me he was by marriage a nephew to the family, and that for many years he had free access to it, and he might carry with him whom he pleased. So I, with a copier, went thither under his protection; and we were hard at work from morning to night for ten days: but then the owner, with his family, coming to town, I could go no further. In that time, and in the haste we were in, I did make such a progress, that the good bishop, together with the late archbishop of Canterbury, Tillotson, and the late bishop of Worcester, Stillingfleet, thought I was sufficiently furnished with materials for composing the first volume. Every part of it, as I wrote it, passed through their hands, and under

[24] [See note [23].]
[25] [Dolben, bishop of Rochester. The author says in his History of his Own Time: 'I got for some days into the Cotton library. But duke Lauderdale, hearing of my design, and apprehending it might succeed in my hands, got Dolben bishop of Rochester to divert Sir John Cotton from suffering me to search into his library. He told him I was a great enemy to the prerogative, to which Cotton was devoted even to slavery. So he said I would certainly make an ill use of all I had found. This wrought so much on him that I was no more admitted till my first volume was published. And then when he saw how I had composed it, he gave me free access to it.' Vol. i. p. 396.]

their censure; and I submitted to their judgment in every particular.

I have been told, one that was much practised in that library[26], who is now dead, has censured me for not comparing what my copier wrote carefully with the originals. To this all I can say is, that, as my copier by much practice was become pretty exact, so I made him read all over to me, having the originals in my hands. I cannot say, in such dull, though necessary work as the collating those things, I carried along with me all the attention that was requisite; but I did it as well as I could: and when I was lately in the Cotton library, I read over several of the originals, but found no material differences from the copies I had printed. One indeed runs through all those in the English language, which might perhaps offend a severe critic, that the old spelling is not every where exactly copied. I did recommend it to my copier, and he observed it often; but he said, when he wrote quick, it was impossible for him to carry an antiquated spelling along with his pen.

The first volume lay a year after I wrote it before it was put in the press, and was offered to be read and corrected by all who were willing to give themselves that trouble. When it was brought to secretary Coventry for his license, he was pleased to say, that he dipped into it out of curiosity; but added, that he found such an entertainment in it, that he could not part with it till he had read it quite through. The earl of Nottingham, lord chancellor, took time to read and examine it, and to add many remarks in several parts of it; in all which I submitted to his censure: and some smaller matters coming in my way, they were added. So when those, under whose direction I made every step in it, advised me to put it in the press, I went on with it.

[26] [Probably Dr. Thomas Smith, of whom Baker says, that he had compared most of our author's copies with the originals in the Cotton Library, and had left his observations in Mr. Hearne's hands. The following is his remark quoted by Hearne in his preface to Leland's Collectanea, p. xxv. 'Interea tamen, quod non malo animo sed ex solo veritatis amore et reverentiâ a me dici profiteor, non possum quin damnem sive Auctoris, sive amanuensium in exscribendis schedis Cottonianis sive inscitiam, sive socordiam qui aut male intelligendo, aut verba mutando et integras sententias omittendo eas a vero sensu perverterunt.']

It happened to come out a few months after the discovery of the popish plot ; and the ferment of that working powerfully over all the nation, the work was favourably received : and as I had the thanks of both houses of parliament for it, with a desire to finish what I had begun : so those who were the most zealous against popery pressed me to make all possible haste with the second volume, when they understood that I had made considerable discoveries with relation to queen Mary's reign. By that time sir John Cotton, seeing the good use I had made of his library, was pleased to acknowledge the injustice of the suggestions that had been made to my prejudice, iii and allowed me free liberty to examine every thing in it [27] : in which I ought to have been more exact than I was, in searching into the matters set forth in my first volume ; but the repeated importunities of my friends for my publishing the second volume so far prevailed, that I only examined what belonged to that period. I took indeed some papers relating to the former reign, that accidentally fell in my way, and inserted them. I had also other materials brought me from several hands, upon the public notice that I gave of my design in the first volume.

That primitive bishop, Fell, of Oxford, engaged an acquaintance of his, Mr. Fulman, to make remarks on it ; which he did with a particular acrimony of style : for which the bishop had prepared me. I bore it, and drew out of it all that was material ; and sent it to him, to see if he did not find in it the substance of all his remarks on the first at the end of the second volume. It has been published over and over again, that he complained that I did not print a full account of his censure. The fact was thus : I sent it to him by the carrier, and begged of him, that, if he had any exception to the abstract I had made of his remarks, he would return it back to me as soon as was possible ; for the press was to be stopped till it

[27] [The author of Speculum Sarisburianum observes (p. 6) : ' But after all, the access to the library by Sir John's leave at last obtained which the bishop mentions, was owing solely to the recommendation of Archbishop Sancroft (whatever the motive to it was) as I have been lately informed by some of the family, who are ready to attest it ; and that he was received most obligingly in Sir John's family whilst he had occasion to make use of the library, and that this happened within a very short time after his first repulse, and not after so long a time as his lordship insinuates.']

came. I stayed for it till the second return of the carrier; and when no answer came, I reckoned he acquiesced in my abstract: so I put it in the press. But before it was printed off, his answer came by the third return of the carrier; and I, finding that he excepted to some few parts of my paper, was at the charge of reprinting it exactly to his mind: and he afterwards received the present that I made him, without any insinuation of any complaint.

Thus this work was sent abroad into the world: nor do I yet see what more I could have done to procure me better information, nor what other steps I could have made. It took quiet possession of the belief of the nation at home, and of a great part of Europe abroad, being translated into four languages; and for some years I heard of neither censure nor answer.

When I went to Paris in the year 1685, I found there was a censure going about, written, but not printed. It came into my hands, and I presently wrote an answer to it, which I got to be put into French; and all who read both papers seemed fully satisfied with my answer: which will be found at the end of this volume. I was told, that it was writ by M. Le Grand; who had given out in many companies, that he had great objections ready to be made to my History. Upon that, two learned and worthy men, M. Auzout and M. Thevenot, designed to bring us together, and to hear what M. Le Grand had to object. We dined at M. Thevenot's; and after dinner, for the space of three hours, M. Le Grand proposed his objections, and I answered them on the sudden, far from charming them with my eloquence; which M. Le Grand must certainly mean as a jest, for I pretend to no more French, than to be understood when I speak it. What he said was mean and trifling; and yet it was so fully answered by me, that we parted civilly, and (as I thought) good friends: and when he was gone, both Thevenot and Auzout said, they were ashamed to hear such iv poor things objected, (*pauvretés* was their word,) after the noise that M. Le Grand had made. But two days after, M. Auzout came to me, both in his own name and in M. Thevenot's, and desired me not to speak of that matter to any person. The court was then so set on extirpating heresy, that they apprehended any thing said by me might bring me into trouble:

they would do me justice, so I needed not be concerned to do it to myself.

I must also add, that M. Le Grand said, after he had offered his objections, that, as to the main of my History, he could furnish me with many materials to support it : and he made me a present of a very valuable book, published by Camusat at Troyes, 1613, with the title of *Mélanges Historiques*[28]; of which I have made good use in the following work[29]. The matter rested thus till the year 1688, that M. Le Grand published the History of King Henry the Eighth's Divorce : and soon after that, two other volumes of his appeared : one was a severe invective against me and my History; the other was a collection of letters, by which his history was justified[30]. In this last there are some very valuable ones, to which I have had occasion oftener than once to refer my reader. In the two first of these tomes, M. Le Grand thought fit to lay aside all sort of good manners, and to treat me more in the style of an angry monk, than of one that had lived long in the company of well-bred men. I imputed this to a management he was under by some of the court of that unfortunate prince, who soon after felt the tragical effects of such unhappy counsellors as had then the ascendant. To these I did believe M. Le Grand had dedicated his pen : and that drew from me a severe postscript to a censure that I published upon the bishop of Meaux's Book of Variations ; for which I am heartily sorry, and ask his pardon[31].

The truth is, the first paper in his third tome seemed to justify any thing that could have been said, to expose a man that could offer such an abstract as he gave of it in his History,

[28] [Camusat (Nic.) Meslanges Historiques. Troyes, 1619, 8vo.]

[29] [The Introduction, as originally published, had *of which I shall have occasion to make good use.*]

[30] [Histoire du divorce de Henry viii Roy d'Angleterre et de Catherine d'Arragon ; avec la défense de Sanderus ; la refutation des deux premiers livres de l'histoire de la réformation de M. Brunet : et les preuves. The work was printed at Paris in three small 12mo volumes

in 1688 ; the title of the third volume being ' Preuves de l'histoire du divorce : de la défense de Sanderus : et de la refutation de M. Burnet.]

[31] [A letter to Mr. Thevenot containing a censure of Mr. Le Grand's history of King Henry the 8th's divorce, with a censure of Mr. de Meaux's History of the variations of the Protestant Churches. London, 1689, 4to.]

and them that judged so ill as to think fit to print that letter, that does plainly contradict the sense he gave of it. The letter is writ by Pace, dean of St. Paul's, to king Henry, (*said by him to be written in the year* 1526[32]; *but in that he is mistaken, as will appear afterwards,*) on the subject of the divorce. He owns that he writ the book, which had been brought to the king the day before, by the advice and assistance of Dr. Wakefield; who was ready to defend it all, either in writing, or in a public disputation. "[33] And since he heard " from the king, that some of his learned counsellors wrote, " that Deuteronomy abrogated Leviticus, he shews him how v " false that was. It was only a recapitulation of the Mosaic " Law. It seems they thought this was the importance of the " Greek word *Deuteronomy,* (or a second Law;) but he shews, " that it imported only a repetition of the former Law, and " the book had another title in the Hebrew. Then he says, " that Wakefield desired him to let him know, whether the " king had a mind to know the truth in that matter, whether " it stood for him, or against him. To this Pace answered, " that the king desired nothing but what became a noble and " a virtuous prince ; and that he would do a most acceptable " thing to him, if he would take pains to let him know what " was the pure verity. Then he, being under some fear, said " he could not set about it, unless his majesty would enjoin " and command it ; but when he received his commands, he " would set forth such things both against him, and for him, as

[32] [The Introduction had *to king Henry in the year* 1526 *on the subject.*]

[33] Et quoniam majestas tua mihi significavit, nescio quos e suis literatis consiliariis scripsisse Deuteronomium abrogare Leviticum, diligenter perquisivi quid id sibi vellet; et tandem inveni id indubitato falsum esse : est compendium, ac repetitio, seu, ut ita dicam, recapitulatio Legis Mosaicæ. Et illud Græcum nomen *Deuteronomium,* quantum ad sensum rei attinet, illud idem significat quod habetur in Hebræo; id est, liber, in quo continetur secunda Lex, vel repetitio primæ Legis. Post meum a majestate tuâ discessum, D. R. Wakefeldus unice me rogavit, ut sibi significarem, an placeret tibi veritatem hâc in re intelligere, utrum staret a te an contra te ? Ei ita respondi, Te nihil velle quod esset alienum a nobili principe, et singularibus virtutibus prædito ; illum majestati tuæ rem gratissimam facturum si laboraret ut puram veritatem tibi declaret. Tum ille nescio quo ductus timore negavit se hoc posse facere, nisi majestas tua id sibi injungeret et mandaret; et si mandares se producturum in medium tam contra te quam pro te illa quæ nemo alius in hoc tuo regno producere posset.

" no other person within his kingdom could do." There is nothing here but what is honourable both for the king, for Pace, and for Wakefield.

M. Le Grand has made a very particular abstract of this. He says : " Pace, designing to flatter his prince's passion, " thought they should not stand either on the Vulgar, or the " LXX translators, but have recourse only to the Hebrew, " which he maintained was more favourable to the king. He " had written to Wakefield, and shewed him the trouble the " king was in, and desired he would clear up the matter. " Wakefield, ravished to be thus employed, said he would jus- " tify all that Pace had said to the king : but then, appre- " hending that Pace might deceive him, or be deceived himself, " or perhaps that the king might change his mind, he desired " that the king himself would let him know what he would " have him to do ; whether he should defend the one side or " the other : and he would do according to the orders he " should receive, and make such discoveries for or against it as " should pass the capacity of all Englishmen. Thus (ends he) " Wakefield, who had more vanity than religion, was driving a " traffic with his sentiments[34]."

I have put in the margin the Latin of Pace's letters, and the account that M. Le Grand gives of it in French, that the reader may judge what can be thought of a man that represents things vi so unfairly, and makes such inferences from them. I confess this raised in me too much indignation to be governed as it ought to have been : I therefore thought such a writer de- served not to be followed in every step. I likewise employed

[34] Nous avons la lettre de ce dernier, (Pace,) qui cherchant à flatter la passion de son prince, vouloit que sans s'arrêter ni à la Vulgate ni à la Traduction des Septante, on eût recours au texte Hébreu ; qu'il soutenoit luy estre plus favorable. Il en écrivit à Robert Wakefield, et luy découvrit l'embarras où le roy se trouvoit, le priant de luy vouloir éclaircir cette matière. Wakefield, ravy de travailler pour le roy, repondit d'abord, qu'il appuieroit ce que Pace avoit dit à Henry. Puis faisant réflexion que Pace pouvoit le trom- per ou se tromper luy même, ou que le roy changeroit peut estre, il alla trouver Pace, et luy témoignoit, qu'il souhaitroit que sa majesté luy ecrivît elle même, ce qu'elle vouloit qu'il fît, et si il devoit défendre le pour ou le contre, et qu'alors selon les or- dres qu'il recevroit, il donneroit des éclaircissemens ou pour ou contre, qui passeroient la capacité de tous les Anglois. C'est ainsi que Wake- field, qui avoit plus de vanité que de religion, trafiquoit de ses senti- ments.

at several times some who went to Paris, to try in what esteem that performance was; and if I was not much deceived in the accounts sent me from thence, the book had lost the esteem of all persons there, so that it was no more talked of, nor read. I cannot therefore bring myself to examine it minutely; yet where any matter of weight requires it, I shall either justify or retract what I had delivered in my History. I shall say no more of that work in this place, save only that the original judgment of the Sorbonne, about which M. Le Grand seemed to be chiefly concerned, both in the conference I had with him, and in his book, is now found by Mr. Rymer, among the other judgments of the universities, in the secret treasury, out of which that laborious searcher into our original treaties has already published fifteen great volumes in folio [35]. Of this I shall give a more particular account in its proper place.

The next attack that was made on my work was in the year 1693, under the title of, *A Specimen of some Errors and Defects in the History of the Reformation of the Church of England; by Anthony Harmer.* It is well known that was a disguised name, and that the author was Mr. Henry Wharton, who had published two volumes with the title of Anglia Sacra [36]. He had examined the dark ages before the reformation with much diligence, and so knew many things relating to those times beyond any man of the age. He pretended that he had many more errors in reserve, and that this specimen was only a hasty collection of a few out of many other discoveries he could make. This consisted of some trifling and minute differences in some dates of transactions of no importance, upon which nothing depended: so I cannot tell whether I took these too easily from printed books, or if I committed any errors in my notes taken in the several offices. He likewise follows me through the several recapitulations I had made of the state of things before the reformation, and finds errors and omissions in most of these: he adds some things out of papers

---

[35] [The fifteenth volume of the first edition of Rymer's Fœdera was published in 1713.

The second edition, which is always referred to in the notes to these volumes, came out in 1727.]

[36] [Anglia Sacra, sive Collectio historiarum partim antiquitus, partim recenter scriptarum de archiepiscopis et episcopis Angliæ, a primâ fidei Christianæ susceptione ad annum 1540, nunc primum in lucem editarum, 2 voll. fol. Londini, 1691.]

I had never seen. The whole was writ with so much malice
and such contempt, that I must give some account of the man,
and of his motives. He had expressed great zeal against
popery in the end of king James' reign, being then chaplain
to archbishop Sancroft, who, as he said, had promised him the
first of those prebends of Canterbury that should fall in his
gift. So when he saw that the archbishop was resolved not
to take the oaths, but to forsake his post, he made an earnest
application to me, to secure that for him at archbishop Tillotson's hands. I pressed him in it[37] as much as was decent for
me to do; but he said he would not encourage these aspiring
men, by promising any thing before it should fall; as indeed
none of them fell during his time. Wharton upon this answer
thought I had neglected him, looking on it as a civil denial,
and said he would be revenged; and so he published that
specimen. Upon which I, in a letter that I printed, addressed
to the present bishop of Worcester[38], charged him again and
again to bring forth all that he pretended to have reserved at
that time; for, till that was done, I would not enter upon the
vii examination of that specimen. It was received with contempt;
and Tillotson justified my pressing him to take Wharton under
his particular protection so fully, that he sent and asked me
pardon: he said he was set on to it, and that, if I would procure any thing for him, he would discover every thing to me.
I despised that offer; but said, that I would at any price buy
of him those discoveries that he pretended to have in reserve:
but Mr. Chiswel (at whose house he then lay, being sick) said,
he could draw nothing of that from him, and he believed he
had nothing. He died about a year after: so I will say no [March.5,
more of him, only this, that where I see a voucher for any ¹695.]
thing that he objects, I will submit and own my error; but I
have no reason to take any thing on his word. I have a work
lying on my table, which shows how little regard is due to his
collections. It was sent me by a worthy person in one of the
universities, and is a collating of ten pages of his Anglia Sacra
with the manuscript that he vouches: it swells indeed to a

[37] [Introduction had *I pressed it.*]
[38] [Letter to the bishop of Litch-
field and Coventry concerning a
book called, Specimen of some
errors and defects in the History of
the English Reformation, Lond.
1693, 4to.]

book.   Wharton omits the most material passage of an instrument that blemished one of his heroes.   In some places there are errors in every line; and there are three capital errors in one line[39], and about fifty in that small compass.   I have shewed the book to a great many persons, and will shew it to any who desire to see it; but do not descend here to further particulars, for that perhaps might discover the author, and expose him to the malice of an ill-natured cabal.   Since that time, a writer of a greater name has with abundance of ill-natured scorn pretended to undervalue my work.   I name him not, for I love not to transmit the remembrance of such things to posterity.   Where he gives such vouchers as can be come at, I will be ready to retract; but when he appeals to some nameless manuscript in his own possession, I will have no regard to this: for a writer that has been found too faulty in citing such vouchers as can be examined, ought not to expect belief when he has recourse to such as are kept by him as secrets, not to be communicated but to a few confidants; nor entirely to these, as I have been informed.   All that has been hitherto objected to me, though with airs of great assurance and scorn, has been so trifling, that some good judges have thought I shewed them too much respect to take any notice of them: they thought it was enough to mark down such small mistakes as I saw had been made by me, without so much as mentioning those who made such reflections.   I would have complied with their advice, if I had not a just zeal to maintain the credit of that work: which I cannot do better than by acknowledging the discoveries that had been made, even in the minutest matters, though with all the indecency and contempt possible.

A very worthy[40] person in one of the universities has sent me a copious collection of remarks on both my former volumes, but upon condition not to name him; which I will observe religiously, because I promised it, though it is not easy to myself, since I may not own to whom I owe so great an obligation: but I suppress none of them, and give them entirely as he offered them to me.   I have had assistance from some other

---

[39] [See Preface.]
[40] [This was the celebrated antiquary Thomas Baker, of St. John's college.]

hands, which I will gratefully own as I come to mention them in their proper places.

viii I have chosen rather to publish all that is of new offered to me in a volume apart, than to reprint my former volumes with these corrections, as some have advised me to do. There are some thousands of the former impressions abroad in the nation, that would be of little value, if any such new edition should appear. I have ever looked on such new enlarged editions as little less than a robbing the public : besides that in so doing I should only drop those errors of my former work, without that formal disowning and retracting of them, which I think I owe the public. I have ever looked on falsehoods in history, when fallen into deliberately, as the worst sort of lying ; both the most public, and the most lasting. But if they are more innocently committed, and are yet persisted in after a discovery, they are as bad as when done on design. I writ before as well and as carefully as I could : and if, in so great a variety of materials, some are spurious, and others appear doubtful ; and if, in the haste in which the circumstances of that time almost forced me to publish that work, without looking out for more aid, and without waiting for further discoveries, there are some inconsiderable errors and defects in the less important parts of my work, that relate not to the main of things ; I hope the world will be so just and so favourable, as to make fair allowances for them, and to accept all the reparation I can make for past errors, when I own my failing, and set my readers right.

I come next to give an account of the reasons that moved me to set about this work at this time. The reasons of my engaging in it at first seemed now to return upon me, and have determined me to delay the doing of it no longer. The danger of a popish successor then in view, and the dreadful apprehensions we had of the power of France, and of the zeal with which the extirpating that which some called the *pestilent heresy, that had so long infested those northern kingdoms,* was then driven on, made it seem a proper time to awaken the nation, by shewing both what popery, and what the reformation was ; by shewing the cruelty and falsehood of the former, and what the patience and courage of our reformers was : and the work had generally so good an effect then, that, if the like dangers seem to revert, it may not be an improper attempt to try once more to awaken a nation that has perhaps forgot past dangers, and yet may be nearer them than ever.

If there is any difference between the present state of things, and that we were in above thirty years ago, it is, that we are now more naked and defenceless, more insensible and stupid, and much more depraved in all respects than we were then. We are sunk in our learning, vitiated in principle ; tainted, some with atheism, others with superstition ; both which, though by different ways, prepare us for popery. Our old breaches are not healed ; and new ones, not known in former times, are raised and fomented with much industry and great art, as well as much heat : many are barefacedly going back to that misery, from which God with such a mighty hand rescued us, and has hitherto preserved us with an amazing chain of happy providences ; but *the deaf adder stops her ear, let the charmer charm never so wisely.*

All books relating to those controversies lie dead in shops, ix few calling for them ; many of them (as men of the trade have told me) being looked on as waste paper, and turned to paste-board[41]. There are, after all, some real and sensible arguments, that may perhaps have some effect on those, who let not themselves be moved with matters of dry speculation, or with cold reasoning. I have made many discoveries, that may awaken some, on whom the clearest demonstrations will perhaps make no impression.

In queen Mary's time, beside all that scene which I had formerly opened, of a perfidious breach of solemn promises, of the corrupting and packing of parliaments, and of that unrelenting cruelty, which was pursued to the end of that reign without intermission ; I have had occasion to see much further

---

[41] ["His lordship is mistaken here ; for not to mention Dr. Hickes' Apologetical Vindication of the Church of England, &c., and his Controversial Letters, and Mr. Spinckes' Answer to the Essay for Catholic Communion, a late book, viz. The case stated between the Church of Rome and the Church of England, hath been called for so fast, that in a little time it hath passed a fourth impression, and several thousands of them have been sold ; and which is more, no book written against popery for several years past hath made such a noise, and more raised the visible displeasure of the English Romanists." — Speculum Sarisburianum, p. 30.]

into the spirit which then prevailed. I have had the perusal of the original Council-Book, that went from the beginning of her reign to the last day of the year 1557; in which such a spirit of cruelty and bigotry appears through the whole course of that reign, that I was indeed amazed to find a poor harmless woman, weak though learned, guilty of nothing but what her religion infused in her, so carried to an indecence of barbarity, that it appears that Bonner himself was not cruel enough for her, or at least for her confessor. She believed herself with child, and when the time came, in which she expected to be delivered, she continued looking for it every day above a month : then a conceit was put in her head, that she could not bear her child as long as there was a heretic left in the kingdom.

It was a great part of the business of the council, to quicken the persecution every where. Letters were writ to the men of quality in the several counties, to assist at the execution of those who suffered for heresy, and to call on all their friends to attend on them. Letters of thanks were writ to such officious persons as expressed their zeal, ordering them to commit all to prison who came not to the service, and to keep them in prison till the comfort of their amendment appeared. Directions were given to put such as would not discover others to the torture. Thanks were in a particular style sent to some [June 27, gentlemen, who (as it is expressed) came so *honestly, and of* 1555. themselves, to assist the sheriffs at those executions*[43]. Pre- Book, p. tences of conspiracies were every where under examination : 273.] many were committed, and tried for words. Letters were writ to corporations, about the elections of mayors ; and the lords had many letters, to look carefully to the elections of parliament-men, and to engage the electors to reserve their voices for such as they should name. Sheriffs began to grow backward, and to delay executions, in hopes of reclaiming persons so condemned : but they were ordered to do so no more.

[43] [' A letter to the lord Riche, wherein he is required, on the king and queen's highness' behalf, to render thanks unto Edward Bery, gentleman, and divers other of the hundred of Rocheforde in Essex, for coming so honestly and of themselves to Colchester and other places in the shire, and assisting the sheriff at the said executions.']

[July 28,
1557, p.
660.]

Letters were on one day [44] wrote to the sheriffs of Kent, Essex,
Suffolk, and Staffordshire, and to several mayors, to signify
what had moved them to stay the executions of such persons
as had been delivered to them by the ordinaries, being condemned for heresy.   One letter, of a more singular strain,

[Jan. 14,
1555-6.
Ibid. p.
356.]

was wrote to the lord mayor and the sheriffs of London, to
give substantial orders [45], (I give the words in the Council-
Book,) "that when any obstinate man, condemned by order
" of the law, shall be delivered to be punished for heresy,
" there be a good number of officers and other men appointed x
" to be at the execution; who may be charged to see such as
" shall misuse themselves, either by comforting, aiding, or
" praising the offenders, or otherwise use themselves to the
" ill example of others, to be apprehended and committed to
" ward: and, besides, to give commandment that no house-
" holder suffer any of his apprentices or other servants to be
" abroad, other than such as their masters will answer for:
" and that this order be always observed in like cases here-
" after."   Such pains were taken to extinguish all the impressions of humanity, or at least to punish every expression
of it.   And this was so constantly pursued, that three men
and two women were burnt at Canterbury on the tenth of
November, a week before her death; for she died on the 17th.

Cox's His-
tory of Ire-
land. [vol.
i. p. 308 46.]

Nor were they satisfied with all these arts of cruelty in
England: but hearing that there were some of that sort in
Ireland, one Cole was sent over with a commission to set
a persecution on foot there.   When he was at Chester, the
corporation waited on him, in respect to his being sent by
the queen: he shewed them his powers and letters to the
government of Ireland; but leaving his papers on the table,
when he went, in respect to this body, to conduct them down
stairs, the mistress of the house, being secretly a zealous

44 [At Richemounde the 28th of
July. ' Letters to the sheriffs of Kent,
Essex, Suffolk, and Stafforde, the
mayor of Rochestre, and the baliffs
of Colchester to signify hither what
hath moved them to stay such persons as have been condemned for
heresy from execution, who have
been delivered unto them by the
ordinary.']

45 [The Introduction had in the
margin here 14 Jan. 1555-6.]

46 [Cox (Richard). 'Hibernia
Anglicana; or the History of Ire-
land from the conquest thereof by
the English to this present time.'
In two parts.   The second edition,
London, fol. 1692.]

woman, did with a particular address make up a packet like his, in which she put a pack of cards, the knave of clubs being turned uppermost: and so she took away his papers, putting this instead of them. He suspecting nothing, nor looking into them, went over to Dublin, and delivered his message and packet to the council there; which was certainly received with scorn and indignation. He came back to London, and got new powers, a few days before the queen's death; for the news of it overtook him before he had his passage. The levity of this story made me at first suspect it, till I found it in several books, in which it is said that the woman had for this service a pension from queen Elizabeth.

I have in my former History shewed what steps were made in that reign towards the setting up an inquisition in England; which was very probably suggested by king Philip and some of his Spaniards as the only sure method to extirpate heresy: but I have since seen some further steps made towards it. Ratcliffe, earl of Sussex, was in high favour; and he, who saw what was the method to secure and advance it, moved, that, instead of the dilatory proceedings in the ordinary courts, such offenders should be proceeded against by martial law. To this the council wrote answer; They [Sept. 4, commended his zeal, and acknowledged that such persons 1556, deserved to be so used: yet it was not thought the best way; Book, p. but they were to be punished as the laws did order. But 506.] when they had had their punishment, he was ordered to keep them in prison and in irons, till they came to know themselves and their duty. I have also found what he did towards the setting up an inquisition. I did formerly print the instructions that were sent to the county of Norfolk: of these the sixth did run thus; "They shall procure to have in every parish, Hist. of the "or part of the shire, as near as may be, some one or more part ii. "honest men, secretly instructed to give information of the book 2. xi "inhabitants amongst or about them." I find in a register of Numb. 19. the earl of Sussex, that to the sixth article it is agreed, "That "the justices of the peace, in every of their limits, shall call "secretly before them one or two honest and secret persons, "or more, by their discretions, and such as they shall think "good; and command them by oath, or other ways, as the

" same justices shall think good, that they shall secretly learn
" and search out such person or persons, as shall evil behave
" themselves idly at church ; or despise openly by words the
" king and queen's proceedings ; or go about to make or move
" any stir, commotion, or unlawful gathering together of the
" people ; or that shall tell any seditious or lewd tales, rumours,
" or news, to move or stir any person or persons to rise, stir,
" or make any commotion or insurrection, or to consent to any
" such intent or purpose.   And also, that the same persons, so
" to be appointed, shall declare to the same justices of the
" peace, the ill behaviour of lewd, disordered persons, whether
" it shall be for using unlawful games, idleness, and such other
" light behaviour of such suspected persons, as shall be within
" the same town, or near thereabouts.   And that the same
" information shall be given secretly to the justices : and the
" same justices shall call such accused persons before them,
" and examine them, without declaring by whom they be ac-
" cused.   And that the same justices shall upon their examin-
" ations punish the offenders, according as their offences shall
" appear to them upon the accusement and examination, by
" their discretion, either by open punishment, or good aber-
" ring [47]." Here are sworn spies appointed, like the familiars of
the inquisition : secret depositions not to be discovered ; and upon
these further proceedings are ordered.   If this had been well
settled, what remained to complete a court of inquisition would
have been more easily carried.

Here is that, which those who look towards a popish successor must look for, when that evil day comes.   All this will
make little impression on those, who have no fixed belief
of any thing in religion themselves, and so may reckon it
a small matter to be of any religion that comes to have the law
and the government on its side ; and resolve to change with
every wind and tide, rather than put any thing to hazard
by struggling against it.   Yet some compassion to those who
have a more firm belief of those great truths might be expected
from men of the same country, kindred, and who have hitherto

[47] [*Abering*, Introduction. To
which is added, ' I do not understand the importance of this word.'
The word is in common use in the
Council Book of the period, and is
spelled *abearing*, and corresponds
to our *bearing*.]

professed to be of the same religion. The reviving the fires in Smithfield, and from thence over the whole nation, has no amiable view, to make any haste to it ; and least of [48] all to those, who, if they have any principles at all, must look for nothing less than the being turned out of their livings, or forced to abandon their families, and upon every surmise or suspicion to be hunted from place to place, glad if they can get out of the paw of the lion into parts beyond the seas : and then they may expect to meet with some of that haughty contempt, with which too many have treated foreigners who took sanctuary among us.

But when this fatal revolution comes upon us, if God for our sins abandons us into the hands of treacherous and bloody men, whither can we hope to fly ? For, with us, the whole reformation must fall under such an universal ruin, that, humanly speaking, there is no view left beyond that.

xii

Yet since that set of men is so impiously corrupted in the point of religion, that no scene of cruelty can fright them from leaping into it, and perhaps from acting such a part in it, as may be assigned them ; there are other considerations of another sort, arising from some papers, (put in my hands since I wrote the History,) that may perhaps affect them deeper, because they touch in a more sensible part.

It is well known, how great and how valuable a part of the whole soil of England the abbey-lands, the estates of the bishops, of the cathedrals, and the tithes are. I will not enter into any strict computation of what the whole may amount to. The resumption of these would be no easy matter to many families : and yet all these must be thrown up ; for sacrilege in the church of Rome is a mortal sin. And therefore cardinal Pole, even in that pretended confirmation of the grants that were then made, laid a heavy charge on those who had the goods of the church in their hands, to remember the judgments of God that fell on Belshazzar for profaning the holy vessels, though they had not been taken by himself, but by his father. It is true, this may be supposed to relate only to church-plate ; though there is no reason to restrain such a solemn charge to so inconsiderable a part of what had been taken from the

---

[48] [*of* om. Introduction.]

church : no doubt, he had the whole in his view. And this
shewed, that, though he seemed to secure them from any claim
that the church might have, or any suit or proceeding upon
that account, yet he left the weight of the sin on their consciences ; which a dextrous confessor might manage so as
to make the possessors yield up their rights, especially when
they themselves could hold them no longer : the thing was
still a sin, and the possession was unjust. And to make it
easy to restore in the last minutes, the statute of Mortmain
was repealed for twenty years : in which time, no doubt, they
reckoned they would recover the best part of what they had
lost. Besides that, the engaging the clergy to renew no leases
was a thing entirely in their own power ; and that in forty
years' time would raise their revenues to be about ten times
their present value.

But setting all this aside, it has appeared evidently to me,
from some papers sent me some years after I wrote my History,
that all that transaction was fraudulent, and had so many
nullities in it, that it may be broke through, whensoever there
is a power strong enough to set about it. In the first powers
that are in that collection, all the grace and favour that the
pope intended to the possessors of those lands was, to indemnify
them for the mean profits they had received, and for the goods
that had been consumed : *They restoring first (if that shall
seem expedient*[49]*) the lands themselves that are unjustly
detained by them.* This was only the forgiving what was past ;
but the right of the church was insisted on for the restitution
of those lands. The reservation in these words, (*if that shall
seem expedient to you,*) can be understood in no other sense,
but that it was referred to his discretion, whether he should
insist to have the restitution first made before he granted the
indemnity for the mean profits, or not.

It is true, the council in England, who were in that supported xiii
by the emperor, thought these powers were too narrow, and
insisted to have them enlarged. That was done ; but in so
artificial a manner, that the whole settlement made by Pole
signified nothing, but to lay the nation once asleep, under a
false apprehension of their being secured in those possessions,

[49] [*to you,* Introduction.]

when no such thing was intended : nor was it at all granted, even by the latest powers that were sent to cardinal Pole. For in these, after the pope had referred the settling that matter to him, that he might transact it with such possessors for whom the queen should intercede, and dispense with their enjoying them for the future without any scruple, a salvo is added, by which the whole matter is still reserved to the pope for his final confirmation, in these words ; *Salvo tamen, in his quibus propter rerum magnitudinem et gravitatem hæc sancta sedes merito tibi videretur consulenda, nostro et præfatæ sedis beneplacito et confirmatione :* " Saving always in such things, in " which for their greatness and importance it shall appear " to you that this holy see ought in reason to be consulted, " our and the said see's good pleasure and confirmation." By these words it is very plain, that as in the powers granted they seemed to be limited to a few, to such for whom the QUEEN should intercede, since it is not expressed that the pope thought that she should[50] intercede for all that possessed them ; so they were only provisional : and therefore, since no bull of confirmation was ever obtained, all these provisional powers were null and void when the confirmation was asked and denied ; as all the historians of that time agree it was : and this was so suitable to pope Paul the Fourth's temper and principles, that no doubt is to be made of his persisting stedfastly in that resolution.

I know there was a mercenary writer[51] found in king James' reign, who studied to lay all people asleep, in a secure persuasion of their titles to those lands. He pretends there was a confirmation of all that Pole did, sent over to England. He brings indeed some proof that it was given out and believed ; which might be a part of the fraud to be used in that matter : but as no such thing appears in the Bullary, so he

---

[50] [*would*, Introduction.]

[51] [*Secretary of State*, Introduction. Sir William Coventry, one of the commissioners appointed in June, 1667, to execute the office of lord treasurer of England. Wood says (Ath. Oxon. ii. 795.) that he published in 1685, London, 4to. ' a letter written to Dr. Gilbert Burnet, giving an account of cardinal Pole's secret powers, from which it appears, that it was never intended to confirm the alienation which was made of the abbey lands. To which are added two breves that cardinal Pole brought over, and some other of his letters that were never before printed.' He died in 1686.]

does not tell us who saw it, or where it was laid up. He indeed
supports this by an argument that destroys it quite : for he
tells us, that two years after this, secretary Petre had a particular bull, confirming him in his possession of some church-
lands.   This shews, that either that person, who was secretary
of state, knew that no confirmation was sent over, so that it
was necessary for him to procure a particular bull for securing
his own estate ; or, whatever might be in Pole's powers, he
might think such a general transaction, which the necessity of
that time made reasonable, would be no longer stood to, than
while that necessity continued.

General treaties and transactions have had such a fate, that
few will trust to them : the spirit of the church, as well as the
spirit of a treaty, will be preferred to the words of all transactions.   Have not we seen, in our own days, an edict that was
passed with all solemnity possible, and declared perpetual and
irrevocable ; yet recalled with this very preamble, that it was
made in compliance to the necessity of that time, and on
design to bring those that were promised to be for ever
tolerated by it into the bosom of the church? There is so
much in the canon-law against all sacrilege, and all alienations xiv
of what is once dedicated to God, that though some canonists
may have carried the plenitude of the papal power so far as to
reach even to this, which this hired writer builds on ; yet
there is so much affirmed to the contrary by others, that it is
certain, whensoever the papacy has strength enough to set
aside all the settlement then made, they will find sufficient
grounds in law to proceed to the overturning all that was then
done.   The princes of Germany, whose settlements he appeals
to, do not trust to any treaty with either emperor or popish
princes, with relation to the church-lands, of which they
possessed themselves ; but to the treaties and guarantees into
which they entered with one another : and so they are engaged
by their faith and by their mutual interests to maintain one
another and themselves in their possessions.   Nor does it
appear that a papal bull was ever obtained to confirm them :
on the contrary, the pope's legates protested against them ;
and, as will appear afterwards, Charles the Fifth's confessor
refused to give him absolution for his consenting to edicts
of that sort.   If the necessity of the time makes it necessary

to maintain that settlement, so long it will be maintained, and no longer.

But to put this matter out of all doubt, that same pope did, soon after our ambassadors were sent to him, by a bull dated the twelfth of July 1555, within three weeks after the English ambassadors had their audience, condemn all the alienations of church-lands, and even all leases for one or more lives, or for a term longer than three years. This he extends to all cathedrals, monasteries, and hospitals; and annuls all leases, grants, exchanges, mortgages, and obligations of lands, castles, towns, and cities, even though made by popes themselves, or by their authority and order, and by the presidents, prelates, or rectors of churches, monasteries, or hospitals, of what rank and dignity soever, cardinals by name being expressed, that were done to the prejudice of the church, the solemnity [52] by law required not being observed: and that which was null in the first making, but supplied by subsequent contracts, in what form soever made, though by proofs upon oath, and by what length of time soever it may claim prescription, is all rescinded, and made void and null: and the detainers of goods upon those titles are required to quit possession, and to make full satisfaction for what they have received; and to be thereto compelled, if they obey not, both by ecclesiastical censures and pecuniary punishments.

It is true, in all this England is not expressly named; and perhaps the pope had the recovering from the family of the Farnese, that which Paul the Third had alienated to it, chiefly in his eye: but the words of this bull do plainly take in the late settlement in England; for though the English ambassadors were then newly come to Rome, demanding the confirmation of what Pole had done, yet no exceptions are made for England: so, it seems, it was intended by these general words, put in on design, to overthrow it. Now because this matter is of such great concern, and every one has not a Bullary to examine into this bull, I will begin my Collection of Records with it, as no small piece of instruction to all who are possessed of any estate so alienated from churches, monasteries, or hospitals.

xv Upon the conclusion of this head, I cannot but take notice

[52] [*solemnities*, Introduction.]

of one insinuation, that I hear some are not ashamed to make; that such a resumption may be indeed a prejudice to the laity, but that the clergy will be enriched by it. If this had been brought me by an ordinary hand, I should not have thought it worth mentioning: but since some have the impudence to set it on foot, I must add, that these are vain hopes, as well as they are suggested on black designs: for though the church, take it in the bulk, has immense riches in the Roman communion; yet in no church that ever I saw are the parochial clergy kept poorer, and made more despicable; they are as the hewers of wood and drawers of water, kept at hard labour on a very poor subsistence. The several orders among them, the governing clergy, and the outward magnificence of their churches and services, devours all that treasure: so that the poor clergy, even in that state of celibate, have scarce necessary sustenance, unless it be in some[53] capital cities, and in very vast parishes in them; they are starved, to maintain the luxury and vanity of others. This was the true occasion of all the poverty of the parochial clergy among us; to which some remedies have been sought for, and to some degree found, ever since the reformation was first settled among us.

But none of these things will move an insensible and degenerate race, who are thinking of nothing but present advantages; and so[54] they may now support a luxurious and brutal course of irregular and voluptuous practices, they are easily hired to betray their religion, to sell their country, and to give up that liberty and those properties, which are the present felicities and glories of this nation. The giving them up will be a lasting infamy on those who are guilty of it, and will draw after it the heaviest curses of posterity on such perfidious betrayers of their trust: by this they will bring slavery on themselves, (which they well deserve, being indeed the worst sort of slaves,) and entail it on the succeeding generation.

I return to prosecute the account of my design in this work. I went through those volumes in the Cotton library, of which I had only a transient view formerly, and laid together all that I thought necessary to complete it. I saw a great and a fair prospect of such a change ready to be made in France, as king Henry had made in England. Mr. Le Vassor has, out of an

[53] [*some few*, Introduction.]   [54] [*that*, Introduction.]

invaluable collection of original papers that are in sir William Trumball's hands, published instructions sent by the duke of Orleans to the princes of Germany; by which, as he declared himself a protestant, so he gave in general words good hopes of his father Francis. I found also, both in papers and printed books, that king Henry often reproached Francis for not keeping his word to him; and in a long despatch of a negotiation that Paget was employed in with the admiral of France, I saw further evidence of this. I was by these indications set on to see how far I could penetrate into that secret.

I was by the favour of the earl of Dartmouth admitted to a free search of the Paper-Office, which is now in much better order and method than it was above thirty years ago, when I saw it last: and there, among other very valuable papers, I found the copy of that solemn promise that Francis made to Henry, minuted on the back by Cromwell's hand as a true copy, in these words; *An instrument devised from the French king, for his justification and defence of the invalidity of the king's highness' first marriage, and the validity of the second.*

xvi " By this, he in express words condemns the pope's bull dis-
" pensing with the marriage with queen Catharine, which he,
" by the unanimous consent of those learned men whom he
" had appointed to examine it, condemns as incestuous and
" unlawful; and reputes the daughter born in it spurious and
" illegitimate: and that the second marriage with Anne, then
" queen, was lawful and just; and that [55]queen Elizabeth, born
" of it, was lawfully born: and he promises to assist and main-
" tain the king in this against all the world. In this instru-
" ment he owns king Henry to be, under God, the supreme
" head of the church of England: and he affirms, that many
" of the cardinals, in particular the late cardinal of Ancona,·
" and even pope Clement the Seventh himself, did, both to his
" ambassador, and to himself at Marseilles, plainly confess,
" that the pope's bull, and the marriage made upon it, were
" null and void; and that he would have given a definitive
" sentence, if some private affections and human regards had
" not hindered it." This makes me conclude, that he gave other instruments of a further extent to king Henry; for failing in which, I find he was often reproached, though this single

[55] [*queen*, om. Introduction.]

[Herbert,
p. 552.]

instrument is all that I could find out : but the lord Herbert reckons among the chief causes of king Henry's last rupture with Francis, that he had not deserted the bishop of Rome, and consented to a reformation, as he once promised.

I saw, when I passed through Zurich, a volume of letters that passed between Bullinger and those English divines that had been so kindly entertained by him in that noble canton : and by the interposition of my learned, judicious, and pious friend, Mr. Turretin of Geneva, Mr. Otto, a worthy professor there, has taken such care, that copies of them are procured for me ; in which we may see the sense of those who revived our reformation in queen Elizabeth's time. Men who had been abroad, and had seen all things about them in a true light, that saw in what the strength of popery lay, and what fortified or weakened the body of the reformed, were liker to have truer views than can be expected from retired or sullen men, who have lived in a corner, and have but a small horizon.

It has been objected to me, that I have said little of proceedings in convocation, and of the struggle that the clergy made before they were brought to make the submission, which brought[56] those bodies under restraints, that seem now uneasy to the advocates for church power. I must confess I have been very defective here : I understood that the books of convocation were burnt : none of those great men, under whose direction that work went on, knew any thing of those discoveries that have been of late made ; so no wonder if I passed over what was then so little known. Yet now I have examined all that I could find of those matters, I confess I am not inclined to expect much from the assemblies of clergymen. I have seen nothing in church history to incline me to depart from Gregory Nazianzen's opinion of those assemblies ; what has happened among ourselves of late has not made me of another mind : and I will not deny, but that my copiousness on these matters is, in my own opinion, one of the meanest parts of my work. The wisest and worthiest man in that convocation, archbishop Warham, was the person that promoted the submission the most : it was no wonder if a corrupt clergy, that made such ill use of their power, had no mind to part with any branch of it.

[56] [*has brought*, Introduction.]

Yet since these things have been of late such a subject of
xvii debate among us, I have taken what pains I could to gather
all that is left of those times in such copies, or rather abstracts,
as have been of late found in private hands : only I will set
down the opinion of sir Thomas More, the best man of the
popish side in that age, of those meetings. " It is true," he More's
says, " the clergy's assembling at the convocation was called Apol.
" by the name of confederacies[57]. But," he adds, " if they fol. 241.
" did assemble often, and there did such things, for which such
" assemblies of the clergy in every province through all Christ-
" endom from the beginning were instituted and devised, much
" more good might have grown thereof than the long disuse
" can suffer us now to perceive. But all my days, as far as I
" have heard, nor (I suppose) a good part of my father's
" neither, they came never together to convocation, but at the
" request of the king ; and at such their assemblies, concerning
" spiritual things have very little done. Wherefore that they
" have been in that necessary part of their duty so negligent,
" whether God suffer to grow to an unperceived cause of di-
" vision and grudge against them, God, whom their such negli-
" gence hath, I fear me, sore offended, knoweth."

The affinity of the matter has led me to reflect on a great 1532.
transaction, with relation to the church of France, which was
carried on, and finally settled, in the very time that king
Henry was breaking with the court of Rome. It was the concordat, that Francis the First made with pope Leo the Tenth :
the king and the pope came to a bargain, by which they divided the liberties of the Gallican church between them, and
indeed quite enslaved it. There are so many curious passages in the progress of that matter, that I hope the opening

---

[57] [He calls the clergy's assembling at the convocation by the name
of Confederacies. If they did assemble often, &c., Introduction.]
In the Introduction Sir Thomas
More is quoted as calling Convocations Confederacies. It is not that
he calls them so, but the penman
whom he answers ; for the words
that go before shew this very clearly. ' But, I suppose he calleth those

assemblies at the Convocations by
the name of Confederacies. For,
but if he do so I wot nere what he
meaneth by that word. And so on
the tother side if he do so, for ought
that I see he giveth a good thing
and an wholesome an odious heinous name. For if they did assemble often, &c. Apol. p. 241. 2nd
Edit. 1533. [B.]

these will be a very acceptable entertainment to the nation :
and the rather, because in it this nation will see, what it is to
deliver up the essential liberties of a free constitution to a
court, and to trust to the integrity and firmness of courts of
justice, when an assembly of the states is no more necessary to
the raising of money, and the support of the government.   I
know nothing writ in our language with relation to this matter,
besides that account I gave of it in a book concerning the
regale [58].   It was taken from a very exact history of that
transaction, that was written by Mr. Pinsson [59], printed anno
1666 ; and that seemed to some very proper judges to relate
so much to our affairs, that, as they thought, it very probably
disposed the nation more easily to throw off the papal authority : they saw what a filthy merchandise the court of Rome
had made of the liberties of the neighbouring church, taking
care only to secure their own profits, and delivering up the
rest to the crown.   The best writers of that church have, on
many occasions, lamented the loss of their liberties by that
detestable bargain, into which Francis' necessities, wrought on
by the practices of the court of Rome, drew him.   " By this
" the church of France, from being a queen, became" (as
bishop Godeau expresses it) a slave : " and he adds, " Our
" fathers have groaned, and all that love the order of the
" house of God will still groan, as long as elections continue to
" be put down ; so that we must needs enter into the sanctuary
" by the way of the court."   In another place, " These promo-
" tions have been always fatal to the church ; and the bishops
" that the court has made have been ordinarily the chief
" advancers of schisms, heresies, and of the oppression of the
" church."   And he concludes, " One cannot read Nazianzen's
" verses of the prelates of his time, without being struck with
" horror, and forced to acknowledge, that a secular temper is
" entirely contrary to the episcopal spirit."   Of this a Greek xviii
writer makes a severe remark, in the history of Andronicus'

---

[58] [A collection of letters and instruments that have passed during
the late contests of France concerning the Regale. London, 8vo, 1681.]

[59] [Caroli Septimi Francorum Regis Pragmatica Sanctio, cum glossis
D.Cosmæ Guymier,Parisini,&c. Ac-
cedunt Historia Pragmaticæ Sanc-
tionis et Concordatorum, Annota-
tiones Marginales et veterum in-
strumentorum supplementa, operâ
et studio Francisci Pinssonii Bitu-
rici, Advocati Parisiensis. Parisiis,
1666, fol.]

reign, which may perhaps be as justly applied to other reigns, telling what sort of bishops were then made : " Princes choose " such men to that charge, who may be their slaves, and in all " things obsequious to what they prescribe ; and may lie at " their feet, and have not so much as a thought contrary to " their commands." This change in their constitution has put an end, not only to national, but even to provincial synods in that kingdom. Some were indeed held, upon the progress that Luther's doctrine was beginning to make in France ; and others, during the civil wars, in order to the getting the council of Trent received in France : but now in the space of ninety years last past, these are no more brought together. The assemblies of the clergy meet only to give subsidies, and to present their grievances ; but do not pretend to the authority of a regular synod : and though in the year 1682 they drew up some articles, yet these had their authority only from the severity of the king's edict, till by a transaction with the court of Rome that was let fall.

I have now gone over all the matters that do properly fall within this Introduction : it remains, that I leave the sense of the subject of this, and of my two former volumes, upon the consciences of my readers. Can it be possible, that any are so depraved, as to wish we had no religion at all ; or to be enemies to the Christian religion ? Would these men reduce us to be a sort of Hottentots ? And yet this must grow to be the effect of our being without all religion. Mankind is a creature, by his make and frame disposed to religion ; and if this is not managed by true principles, all the jugglings of heathenism would again take possession of the world. If the principles of truth, justice, temperance, and of universal love, do not govern men, they will soon grow curses and plagues to one another ; and a crew of priests will grow up, who will teach them to compound for all crimes, and to expiate the blackest practices by some rituals.

Religion has so much to struggle with, that if it is not believed to be revealed by God, it will not have strength enough to resist those ill inclinations, those appetites and passions, that are apt to rise up in our minds against its dictates. What is there in the true and unsophisticated Christian religion that can give a colour to prejudices against it ? The whole complex of that rule of life which it prescribes is so plainly suited to our composition, both in our souls and their faculties, and in our bodies, with relation to good health, to industry and long life; and to all the interests of human society, to the order and peace of the world, and to the truth and love that are the cements and securities of the body politic; that, without any laboured proof of its divine original, these are such characters, that they may serve to prove, it is sent into the world by a lover of mankind, who knew our nature, and what was proper both to perfect it, and to render it not only safe, but happy.

But when to all this we add the evidence that was given at its appearing in the world; that he who was the first Author of it, and those whom he employed first to propagate it, did upon many occasions, in full daylight, and in the sight of great multitudes, do things so far above the powers of nature, in such uncontested miracles, that by these it evidently appeared they were assisted by somewhat superior to nature, that could command it at pleasure; here is the fullest ground of conviction possible. These things were written, published, and received in the age in which they were transacted: and those xix writings have been preserved with great care, and are transmitted down to us, at the distance of above sixteen ages, pure and uncorrupted. In these we have the fixed standard of our religion; and by them we can satisfy ourselves concerning all such practices as have been made upon it, or such inferences as are drawn from it. I wish those, who take to themselves the name of free-thinkers, would consider well, if they think it is possible to bring a nation to be without any religion at all; and what the consequences of that may prove; and then see, if there is any religion so little liable to be corrupted, and that tends so much to the good of mankind, as the true Christian religion reformed among us.

As for those that do truly believe this religion, and have an ingenuous sense and taste of liberty, can they admit a comparison to be made between a religion restrained to a fixed standard, (into which every one is admitted to examine the sense of it in the best method he can,) and that which sets up another uncertain standard, of which they pretend to be the depositaries; I mean, traditions: and pretend further, they are the infallible expounders of it; and that the true standard itself is not to be exposed to common view? that God is to be worshipped in a language not understood; that, instead of a competent provision to those who labour in this work, the head of them is to become a great prince, and may pretend to a power to dispose of kingdoms and states, to pardon sins, and to redeem sinners out of the miseries of a future state; and that the character derived from him is so sacred, that, in defiance to sense and reason, a priest by a few words can work a miracle, in comparison to which the greatest of miracles is nothing; and who by these means have possessed themselves of an immense wealth and a vast authority?

These are all things of so strange a nature, and so contrary to the genius and design of the Christian religion, that it is not easy to imagine how they could ever gain credit and success in the world. But when men's eyes have been once opened; when they have shaken off the yoke, and got out of the noose; when the simplicity of true religion has been seen into, and the sweets of liberty have been tasted; it looks like charm and witchcraft, to see so many looking back so tamely on that servitude, under which this nation groaned so heavily for so many ages. They may soon see and know what our happy condition is, in the freedom we enjoy from these impositions; and what their misery is that are condemned to them. It is not enough for such as understand this matter to be contented in their own thoughts with this, that they resolve not to turn papists themselves; they ought to awaken all about them, even the most ignorant and the most stupid, to apprehend their danger, and to exert themselves with their utmost industry to guard against it, and to resist it: they ought to use all their efforts to prevent it, and earnestly to pray to God for his blessing upon them. If, after all men's endeavours to prevent it, the corruption of the age, and the art and power of our enemies, prove too hard for us, then, and not till then, we must submit to the will of God, be silent, and prepare ourselves for all the extremities of suffering and of misery; and if we fall under a persecution, and cannot fly from it, we must resolve to glorify God by bearing our cross patiently. Illegal sufferings are no more to be borne than the violences of a robber: but if the law comes once to be in the hands of those wicked men, who will not only revive the repealed laws against heretics, but, if they can, carry their cruelty up to the height of an inquisition, then we must try by *the faith and patience of the saints to go through fire and through water*, and in all things to be *more than conquerors*.

I know some, who are either apt to deceive themselves, or hope to deceive others, have this in their mouths, that popery is not what it was before the reformation; things are much mended, many abuses are detected, and things are not so gross xx as they were then: and they tell us, that further corrections might be expected, if we would enter into a treaty with them; in particular, they fancy they see the error of proceeding severely with heretics; so that there is no reason to apprehend the return of such cruelties as were practised an age and a half ago.

In answer to this, and to lay open the falsehood of it, we are to look back to the first beginning of Luther's breach. It was occasioned by the scandalous sale of pardons and indulgences, which all the writers of the popish side give up, and acknowledge it was a great abuse; so in the countries where the reformation has got an entrance, or in the neighbourhood of them, this is no more heard of: and it has been taken for granted, that such an infamous traffic was now no more practised. But of late, that we have had armies in Spain and Portugal, we are well assured that it is still carried on there in the most barefaced manner possible. It is true, the proclaiming a sale is forbid by a bull; but there is a commissary in every place, who manages the sale with the most infamous circumstances imaginable. In Spain, by an agreement with the pope, the king has the profits of this bull; and it is no small branch of his revenue. In Portugal, the king and the pope go shares. Dr. Colbatch[60] has given a very particular account of the managing the bull there: for as there is nothing so impudent, that those men are ashamed to venture on; so they may safely do what they please, where the terror of the inquisition is so severe a restraint, that men dare not whisper against any thing that is under that protection.

A notable instance of this has appeared lately, when, in the year 1709, the privateers of Bristol took the Galleon, in which

[60] [Account of the court of Portugal under the reign of Don Pedro II, 1700, 8vo.]

they found 500 bales of these bulls, and 16 reams were in a bale; so that they reckoned the whole came to 3,840,000. These bulls are imposed on the people, and sold, the lowest at three rials, a little more than 20d. but to some at fifty pieces of eight, about 11l. of our money; and this to be valued according to the ability of the purchaser, once in two years : all are obliged to buy them against Lent. Besides the account given of this in the cruising voyage, I have a particular attestation of it by captain Dampier; and one of the bulls was brought me printed, but so that it cannot be read. He was not concerned in casting up the number of them; but he says, that there was such a vast quantity of them, that they careened their ship with them.

As for any changes that may be made in popery, it is certain, infallibility is their basis; so nothing can be altered where a decision is once made. And as for the treatment of heretics, there has been such a scene of cruelty of late opened in France, and continued there now almost thirty years without intermission, that even in the kingdom where popery has affected to put the best face on things possible, we have seen a cruel course of severity, beyond any thing in history. I saw it in its first and sharpest fury, and can never forget the impression that made on me.

A discovery lately made, shews what the spirit of those at Rome, who manage the concerns of that religion, is, even in a mild reign, such as Odeschalci's was; and we may well suppose, that, because it was too mild, this was ordered to be laid before him, to animate him with a spirit of persecution. When the abbey of St. Gall was taken in the late war in Switzerland, a manuscript was found, that the court of Propaganda ordered their secretary to prepare for Innocent the Eleventh's own use; which after his death came into the hands of cardinal Sfondrato, who was abbot of St. Gall, and so at his death left this book there. It gives a particular account of all the missions they have in all the parts of the world, and of the rules and instructions given them; with which I hope those worthy persons, in xxi whose hands this valuable book is now fallen, will quickly acquaint the world. The conclusion of it is an address to the pope, in which they lay his duty before him, from two of the words in the New Testament, directed to St. Peter. The first was, *Feed my sheep ;* which obliged him not only to feed the flock that was gathered at that time, but to prosecute the constant increase of it, and to bring those sheep into it that were not of that fold.   But the other word was addressed to him by a voice from heaven, when the sheet was let down to him full of all sorts of beasts, of which some were unclean, *Rise, Peter, kill and eat ;* to let all see that it is the duty of the great pontiff to rise up with apostolical vigilance, to kill and to extinguish in the infidels their present life, and then to eat them, to consubstantiate their false and brutal doctrine into the verity of our faith.   There is an affectation in these last words suitable to the genius of the Italians.   This application of these two passages, as containing the duties of a pope, was formerly made by Baronius, in a flattering speech to encourage pope Paul the Fifth in the war he was designing, against the Venetians.

By this we see, that how much soever we may let the fears of popery wear out of our thoughts, they are never asleep, but go on steadily prosecuting their designs against us.   Popery is popery still, acted by a cruel and persecuting spirit : and with what caution soever they may hide or disown some scandalous practices, where heretics dare look into their proceedings, and lay them open ; yet even these are still practised by them, when they know they may safely do it, and where none dare open their mouth against them ; and therefore we see what reason we have to be ever watching, and on our guard against them.

This is the duty of every single Christian among us ; but certainly those peers and commoners, whom our constitution has made the trustees and depositaries of our laws and liberties, and of the legal security of our religion, are under a more particular obligation of watching carefully over this sacred trust, for which they must give a severe account in the last day, if they do not guard it against all danger, at what distance soever it may appear.   If they do not maintain all the fences and outworks of it, or suffer breaches to be made on any of them ; if they suffer any part of our legal establishment to be craftily undermined ; if they are either absent or remiss on critical occasions ; and if any views of advantage to themselves prevail on them to give up or abandon the establishment and security of our religion ; God may work a deliverance for us another way, and, if it seem good in his eyes, he will deliver us : but they and their families shall perish, their names will rot and be held in detestation ; posterity will curse them, and the judgments of God will overtake them, because they have sold that which was the most sacred of all things, and have let in an inundation of idolatry, superstition, tyranny, and cruelty upon their church and country.

But, in the last place, those who are appointed to be the *watchmen*, who ought to give warning, and to *lift up their voice as a trumpet*, when they see those wolves ready to break in and devour the flock, have the heaviest account of all others to make, if they neglect their duty ; much more if they betray their trust. If they are so set on some smaller matters, and are so sharpened upon that account, that they will not see their danger, nor awaken others to see it, and to fly from it ; the guilt of those souls who have perished by their means *God will require at their hands*, if they, in the view of any advantage to themselves, are silent when they ought to cry out day and night : they will fall under the character given by the prophet of the watchmen in his time ; *They are blind, they are all ignorant, they are all dumb dogs that cannot bark, sleeping, lying down, loving to slumber ; yea, they are greedy dogs, which can never have enough : and they are shepherds that cannot understand ; they all look to their own way, every one for his gain from his quarter ; that say, Come, I* xxii *will fetch wine, and we will fill ourselves with strong drink ; to-morrow shall be as this day, and much more abundant.*

This is a lively description of such pastors as will not so much as study controversies, and that will not know the depths of Satan ; that put the evil day far off, and, as the men in the days of Noah or Lot, live on at their ease, satisfying themselves in running round a circle of dry and dead performances ; that do neither awaken themselves nor others. When the day of trial comes, what will they say ? to whom will they fly for help ? Their spirits will either sink within them, or they will swim with the tide : the cry will be, The church, the church, even when all is ruin and a desolation. I hope they will seriously reflect on the few particulars that I have, out of many more, laid together in this Introduction, and see what

weight may be in them; and look about them to consider the
dangers we are in, before it is too late.   But what can be said
of those, who are already going into some of the worst parts
of popery?   It is well known, that in practice the necessity of
auricular confession, and the priestly absolution, with the conceit of the sacrifice of the mass, are the most gainful parts of
popery, and are indeed those that do most effectually subdue
the world to it.   The independence of the church on the state
is also so contended for, as if it were on design to disgrace our
reformation.   The indispensable necessity of the priesthood to
all sacred functions is carried in the point of baptism further
than popery.   Their devotions are openly recommended, and
a union with the Gallican church has been impudently proposed[61] : the reformation and the reformers are by many daily
vilified; and that doctrine, that has been most universally
maintained by our best writers, I mean the supremacy of the
crown, is on many occasions arraigned.   What will all these
things end in? and on what design are they driven?   Alas! it
is too visible.

God be thanked, there are many among us that stand upon
the *watch-tower*, and that give faithful warning; that stand in
the *breach*, and make themselves a *wall for their church and
country; that cry to God day and night, and lie in the dust
mourning before him*, to avert those judgments that seem to
hasten towards us.   They search into the mystery of iniquity
that is working among us, and acquaint themselves with all
that mass of corruption that is in popery.   They have another
notion of the worship of God, than to dress it up as a splendid
opera.   They have a just notion of priesthood, as a function
that imports a care of souls, and a solemn performing the
public homage we owe to God; but do not invert it to a political piece of craft, by which men's secrets are to be discovered,
and all are subdued by a tyranny that reaches to men's souls
as well as to their worldly concerns.   In a word, they consider

[61] [" *The devotions openly recommended*, every one will know, are
the reformed ones by Dr. Hickes,
which have passed through a fourth
edition with great applause, in a
protestant country, and are ready
for a fifth (unless he means some
others too, published by his brother
the dean of Canterbury ;) and by
the *Union with the Gallican church
being impudently proposed*, he must
understand the *Regale and Pontificate*, by Mr. Lesley."—Speculum
Sarisburianum, p. 9.]

religion in the soul as a secret sense of divine matters, which purifies all men's thoughts, and governs all their words and actions : and in this light they propose it to their people, warning them against all dangers, and against all deceivers of all sorts ; watching over them as those that must give an account to the *great Bishop of souls, feeding the flock over which the Holy Ghost has made them overseers*, ready to lay down their lives for them, looking for their crown from the *chief Shepherd, when he shall appear.*

May the number of these good and faithful servants increase daily more and more ; may their labours be so blessed, that they may see the travail of their soul, and be satisfied : and may many by their means and by their example be so awakened, that they may resist even to blood, striving against sin, and against the man of sin : and may I be of that number, labouring while it is day ; and ready, when the night comes, either to lie down and rest in the grave ; or, if God calls me to it, to seal that doctrine, which I have been preaching now above fifty years, with my blood ! May his holy will be done, so I may but glorify him in my soul and body, which are his !

THE HISTORY

OF

THE REFORMATION

OF

THE CHURCH OF ENGLAND.

PART III.—BOOK I.

Of matters that happened in the time comprehended in the First Book of the History of the Reformation.

BEFORE I enter on the affairs of England, I have thought it would be of great use to prepare the reader for what relates to them, by setting before him the progress of that agreement into which the French king's affairs carried him ; by which he delivered up one great part of the liberties of the Gallican church to the pope, and invaded the rest himself. This was carried on in a course of many years ; and the scene lying next us, and it being concluded in the very time in which the breach of this nation was far carried on, in the year 1532, I thought it would not be an improper beginning of my work to set out that matter very copiously ; since it is highly probable that it had a great influence on all who were capable to reflect on it.

2 The greatest transaction that happened in this period being the setting up the *concordat*, in the room of the pragmatic sanction, by Francis the First, it will be necessary, in order to

the clear opening of the matter, to look back into the former ages.

The progress the papacy had made from pope Gregory the Seventh to pope Boniface the Eighth's time, in little more than two hundred and thirty years, is an amazing thing. The one began the pretension to depose kings; the other, in the jubilee that he first opened, went in procession through Rome, the first day attired as pope, and the next day attired as emperor, declaring, that all power, both spiritual and temporal, was in him, and derived from him: and he cried out with a loud voice, *I am pope and emperor, and have both the earthly and heavenly empire;* and he made a solemn decree in these words, *We say, define, and pronounce, that it is absolutely necessary to salvation for every human creature to be subject to the bishop of Rome.* The holy war, as it was called, was a great part of the business of that interval; by which the authority and wealth of the papacy received no small addition. It is true, the removal of the popes to Avignon, and the schism that followed upon the popes' return to Rome, did put no small stop to that growing power, and to the many and great usurpations and inventions, not known to former ages, which were set on foot to draw all people into a servile dependence on the popes.

This long schism between the popes that sat at Rome and Avignon was the best conjuncture the bishops could ever have hoped for to recover their authority; which had been for some ages oppressed, and indeed trodden under foot by the papacy. And if that had happened in a less ignorant age, it is very probable there would have been more effectual provisions made against it. The bishops that met at Constance did not apprehend that the continuance of that breach was that in which their strength lay: they made too much haste to heal it; but they soon found that when all was again united, none of the regulations that they made could restrain a power that pretended to know no limits. The greatest security of the church, as they thought, was in the act for perpetual general councils, which were to meet after short intervals; and in the act for subjecting the popes to the councils, requiring them to call them and the council to meet at the end of ten years, whether the pope summoned it or not.

The progress of the papal usurpations.

1300.

The schism in the papacy.

[A.D. 1414.]

But these proved feeble restraints: yet the council of Basle The council
did sit, pursuant to the decree made at Constance; and the of Basle.
[A.D. 1431.]
bishops who met there endeavoured, as much as their low size
of learning could direct them, to set forward a reformation of
those abuses that were brought into the church, and that supported that despotic power which the popes had assumed.
They reckoned, a regulation of the elections of bishops was
the laying a good foundation, and the settling of pillars and
bases, upon which the fabric of the church might securely rest.
Many bishops were made by papal provisions; these they
simply condemned: others were promoted by the power and
favour of princes, to which ambitious men recommended themselves by base compliances and simoniacal bargains; in opposition to these, they restored elections to the chapters, with as
good provisions as they could contrive, that they should be
well managed.

A contest falling in upon their proceedings between them The pope
and pope Eugenius the Fourth, they addressed themselves to and council
quarrel.
Charles the Seventh, king of France, for his protection. They
sent him the decrees they had made against *annates*, that is,
first-fruits; a late device of pope Boniface the Ninth, then
about fifty years standing, pretending to carry on a war against
the Turk by that aid. They also condemned *gratias expecta-
tivas*, or the survivances of bishoprics, and other benefices;
with all clauses of reservations in bulls, by which popes reserved to themselves at pleasure such things as were in a
bishop's collation. They appointed elections to be confirmed
by the metropolitan, and not by the pope. They condemned
all fees and exactions upon elections, except only a salary for
the writer's pains; and all appeals, except to the immediate
superior; with all appeals from a grievance, unless it was such
that the final sentence must turn upon it: and when the
appeal rose up by all intermediate steps to the pope, it was to
be judged by delegates appointed to sit upon the place where
the cause lay, or in the neighbourhood; only the causes
marked expressly in the law, as *greater causes*, were reserved
to the pope. Provision was made for the encouragement of
learning, and of the universities, that the benefices that fell in
any collator's gift should be, in every third month of the year,
given to men that had been, during a limited number of years,

bred in them; and had upon due trial obtained degrees in them. If a bishop had ten benefices in his gift, the pope might name to one; and if fifty, to two; but to no more. Some of the provisions relate to the discipline and order of the cathedral churches : but the main thing of all was, their declaring the council to be above the pope; that the pope was bound to submit to it, and that appeals lay to it from him.

[Pinsson, p. 716.]

The first breach between the pope and the council was made up afterwards by the interposition of Sigismond the emperor : the pope recalled his censures, confessed he had been misled, and ratified all that the council had done. But that lasted not long : for, upon the pretence of treating a reconciliation with the Greek church, some moved for a translation of the council

[Ibid. p. 717.]

to Ferrara; but the majority opposed it : yet the pope did translate it thither. Upon which the council condemned that bull, and proceeded against Eugenius. He on the other hand declared them to be no council, and excommunicated them : they on their part deposed him, and chose another pope, Amedee duke of Savoy, who took the name of Felix : he had retired from his principality, and upon that they again begged the protection of France.

The pragmatic sanction made in France. [July 7.] 1438.

The king being thus applied to by them, summoned a great assembly to meet at Bourges; where the dauphin, the princes of the blood, many of the nobility, and many bishops, met. They would not approve the deposition of the pope, nor the new election of Felix : but yet they rejected the meeting of Ferrara, and adhered to that at Basle. The decrees passed at Basle were by them reduced into the form of an edict; and published under the title of the pragmatic sanction : which the 4 king declared he would have to be inviolably observed; and he resolved to moderate matters between the pope and the council.

The effects it had.

There are very different relations made of the effects that this edict had : some say, that the church of France began to put on a new face upon it, and that men were advanced by merit, and not, as formerly, by applications to the court of Rome, nor solicitations at the court of France : " others give a " most tragical representation of elections, as managed by " faction, indirect arts, the solicitations of women, and si- " moniacal bargains; and in some places by open violence, out

" of which many suits were brought into the courts of law.
" The treasure of the church was, as they said, applied to
" maintain these; the fabric was let go to ruin; and bishops'
" houses dilapidated.   Pope Leo the Tenth, in his bull that
" abrogates this sanction, enumerates many evils that arose
" out of these elections; and that, in particular, simony and
" perjury prevailed in them, of which he says he had undeni-
" able evidence, in the many absolutions and reabilitations that
" were demanded of him."   This might be boldly alleged, because it could not be disproved, how false soever it might be.

There might be some instances of faction, which were no
doubt aggravated by the flatterers of the court of Rome : for
the profits which came from France being stopped by the
pragmatic, all arts were used to disgrace it.

Æneas Silvius was counted one of the ablest men of that
time.   He was secretary to the council of Basle, and wrote
copiously in defence of it against the pope ; but he was gained
over to the interests of the court of Rome : he had a cardinal's
hat, and was afterwards advanced to the popedom, and reigned
by the name of Pius the Second.   He retracted all his former
writings, but never answered them : yet he was so barefaced
in setting himself to sale, that, when he was reproached for
changing sides, he answered, the popes gave dignities, abbeys,
bishoprics, and red hats to their creatures ; but he asked, how
many of such good things did the council give. *(The pope condemns it, [Ibid. p. 720.])*

He distinguished himself, as deserters are apt to do, by
railing at all that the council of Basle had done, and against
the pragmatic sanction.   He branded it as a *heresy* : and, in a
council that he held at Mantua, twenty years after, he inveighed severely against it.   He said, bishops thought to have
established their power, but on the contrary their authority
was ruined by it; for ecclesiastical causes were brought into
the secular courts, and all things were put into the king's
hands : yet that sanction was observed in France till the king's
death ; and though some were persuaded to go to Rome, and
to procure bulls, these were esteemed no better than traitors
and enemies to the country.   It is true, upon this the courts of
parliament took upon them to judge in all ecclesiastical matters,
and to examine whether the ecclesiastical courts had proceeded
according to the laws of the church or not : and that the sen- *(In a council at Mantua. 1458.)*

tences of the temporal courts might be executed, they ordered the revenues of bishops, if they stood out in contumacy, to be seized into the king's hands, and their persons to be arrested.

When Danesius the attorney general heard how pope Pius 5 had arraigned the pragmatic sanction, and that he was designing to proceed to censures against the king and his ministers, he protested against all he had said, referring the decision of the matter to a general council.

Louis the Eleventh abrogates it.

Upon that king's death, he was succeeded by Louis the Eleventh ; and the bishop of Arras having great credit with him, the pope gained him, by the promise of a cardinal's hat, to use his endeavours to get the king to abrogate the sanction : and because he thought that which might work most on the king was, the apprehension that much money, which was now kept within the kingdom, would upon the laying it aside be carried to Rome ; this expedient was offered, that there should be a legate resident in France, with powers to grant such bulls as was necessary : though this was never done, and it seems it was only offered as a specious concession to gain their point. King Louis the Eleventh's character is given us so fully by Philip de Comines[1], who knew him well, that none who have read him will wonder to find, that, when he needed any favour from the court of Rome, he made the fullest submission that any king perhaps ever made. He, in a letter that he wrote to

Councils, tom. xiv. p. 97. [ed. Labbe, 1671.]

the pope, owns *the pope to be God's vicar on earth, to whose words he will always hearken and obey : and therefore, though the pragmatic sanction was received, upon long deliberation, in a great assembly, and was now fully settled, yet since the pope desired that it might be abrogated, and since the bishop of Arras had put him in mind of the solemn promise that he had made by him, before he came to the crown ; he, reckoning that obedience was better than all sacrifice, since that sanction was made in a time of sedition and schism, so that by it his kingdom was not conform to other kingdoms, though many men studied to maintain it, yet he resolved to follow and obey the pope's orders ; therefore*

[1] [This book had been translated into English by Uvedale, and published three years before the appearance of this third part of the History of the Reformation, in 2 vols. 8vo. Lond. 1712.]

he abrogates it entirely, and does of his own accord, not com-
pelled in any sort, restore him to the authority that Martin
the Fifth and Eugenius the Fourth did exercise in former
times ; and bids him use the power given him by God at his
pleasure : and promises, on the word of a king, that he will
take care that all his commands shall be executed within his
kingdom, without opposition or appeal ; and that he will
punish such as are contumacious, as the pope shall direct.

Here was an entire submission, penned no doubt by the aspiring cardinal. It was received at Rome with no small joy ; the pragmatic was dragged about the streets of Rome, the pope wept for joy, and at mass on Christmas-eve he consecrated a sword with a rich scabbard, to be sent to the king. The title of the *Most Christian King* had been given by former popes to some kings of France ; but pope Pius was the person who upon this high merit made it one of the titles of the crown : such as read de Comines' History will not find any other merit in that king to entitle him to so glorious a compellation. *To the pope's great joy.*

The court of parliament of Paris interposed ; they made a noble remonstrance to the king, in which they pressed him to maintain the pragmatic sanction, which had its original from a general council ; and they affirmed, that the king was obliged to maintain it. Yet afterwards, that king's project of engaging the pope to assist his son-in-law to recover Sicily, then possessed by the bastard of Arragon, did miscarry, the pope refusing to concur in it ; upon which the king was offended, and carried his submissions no further ; only he suffered bulls of reservations and survivances to take place again. *The parliament of Paris oppose it.*

6

This matter was taken up again six years after by pope Paul the Second. A new minister was gained, by the same bait of a cardinal's hat, to procure the revocation : so the king's edict was sent to the court of parliament of Paris, to be registered there, in vacation time. The court ordered the attorney general to examine it. St. Romain was then attorney general, and he behaved himself with such courage, that he was much celebrated for it. " He opposed the registering it, and spoke " much in the praise of the pragmatic sanction. He shewed " the ill consequences of repealing it : that it would let in upon *The honest courage of the attorney general.*

" them abuses of all sorts, which were by it condemned ; all
" affairs relating to the church would be settled at Rome ; many
" would go and live there, in hopes of making their fortunes by
" provisions. He set forth, that ten or twelve bulls of sur-
" vivances were sometimes obtained upon the same benefice ;
" and, during three years in pope Pius' time, (in which the
" exact observation of the pragmatic sanction was let fall,)
" twenty-two bishoprics happening to fall void, five hundred
" thousand crowns were sent to Rome to obtain bulls ; and
" sixty-two abbeys being then vacant, a like sum was sent for
" their bulls ; and a hundred and twenty thousand crowns
" were sent to obtain other ecclesiastical preferments. He
" added, that for every parish there might be a bull of a
" *gratia expectativa,* or survivance, purchased at the price of
" twenty-five crowns ; besides a vast number of other graces
" and dispensations. He insisted, that the king was bound to
" maintain the rights and liberties of the church in his king-
" dom, of which he was the founder and defender."

For which
he was
turned out.
The aspiring cardinal, offended with this honest freedom of
the attorney general, told him he should fall under the king's
displeasure, and lose his place for it. He answered, " the king
" had put him in the post freely ; he would discharge it faith-
" fully as long as the king thought fit to continue him in it,
" and he was ready to lay it down whensoever it pleased the
" king; but he would suffer all things, rather than do any
" thing against his conscience, the king's honour, and the good
" of the kingdom." The favourite prevailed to get him turned
out, but the crafty king gave him secretly great rewards ; he
esteemed him the more for his firmness, and restored him
again to his place.

The university of Paris also interposed ; and the rector told
the legate, that, if the matter was farther prosecuted, they
would appeal to a general council : but this notwithstanding,
and though the court of parliament stood firm, yet the king
being under the apprehensions of some practice of his brother's
of Rome, whom he hated mortally, in order to the defeating
those, renewed his promises for abrogating the pragmatic
sanction ; and it was for many years let fall into desuetude.
Towards the end of this reign, an assembly was held at

7 Orleans, in order to the reestablishing the pragmatic sanction, and the hindering money to be carried to Rome. The king [Aug. 30.] died 1483.

Upon Charles the Eighth's succeeding, an assembly of the states was held at Tours, in which the observation of the pragmatic sanction was earnestly pressed; the third estate insisted on having it entirely restored. The prelates, who had been promoted contrary to it under king Louis, opposed this vehemently; and were in reproach called the court-bishops, unduly promoted; and were charged as men that aspired to favour at Rome. St. Romain, now again attorney general, said, he knew no ecclesiastical law better calculated to the interest of the kingdom than the pragmatic sanction was; and therefore he would support it. The king saw it was for his advantage to maintain it, and so was firmly resolved to adhere to it. The courts of parliament not only judged in favour of elections made by virtue of that sanction, but, by earnest remonstrances, they pressed the king to prohibit the applications made to the court of Rome for graces condemned by it.

The prag-matic sanc-tion reesta-blished.

Innocent the Eighth continued by his legates to press the entire repeal of the pragmatic; yet, notwithstanding all opposition, it continued to be observed during Charles the Eighth's reign. Louis the Twelfth did, by a special edict, appoint it to be for ever observed. Thus it continued till the council of Lateran, summoned by pope Julius the Second; to which Silvester bishop of Worcester, and sir Robert Wingfield, were commissioned by king Henry the Eighth to go " in his name, " and on behalf of the kingdom, to conclude every thing for " the good of the catholic church, and for a reformation both " in the head and in the members: and to consent to all " statutes and decrees for the public good; promising to ratify " whatever they or any of them should do." The king's empowering two persons in such a manner seems no small invasion of the liberties of the church; but it was in the pope's favour, so it was not challenged.

But it was still com-plained of by the popes.

1499.

[1511.]

Rymer, tom. xiii. [p. 325. Ap. 1, 1512.]

This council was called by that angry pope, chiefly against Louis the Twelfth: and the pragmatic sanction was arraigned in it; both because it maintained the authority of the council to be superior to the pope, and because it cut off the advantages that the court had made by the bulls sent into France.

The pope brought Louis the Eleventh's letters patents, by which it was abrogated, into the council; and the advocate of the council, after he had severely arraigned it, insisted to have it condemned. So a monition was decreed, summoning all who would appear for it to come and be heard upon it within sixty days. The pope died in February thereafter.

[Feb. 21, 1513.]
Condemned by the council in the Lateran.

Pope Leo the Tenth succeeded, and renewed the monitory letters issued out by his predecessor. But the personal hatred with which Julius prosecuted Louis being at an end, things were more calmly managed. Some bishops were sent from the Gallican church to assist in the council: but, before any thing could be concluded, king Louis dying, Francis succeeded. He understood that the pope and the council were intending to proceed against the pragmatic sanction, so he resolved to bring the matter to an agreement; in which some progress was made, in an interview that he had with the pope at Bologna. It was concluded by a sanction called the concor- 8 dat, between the cardinals of Ancona and of *Sanctorum qua-tuor* on the pope's side, and chancellor Prat for the king. Some small differences remained; which were all yielded as the pope desired: and in the month of December the pope's bull, condemning the pragmatic sanction, was read, and approved by that council, such as it was.

1516.

The *concordat* put instead of it.

The *concordat* was put instead of it. The truth was, Francis was young; and was so set on pursuing his designs in Italy, in which he saw the advantage of having the pope on his side, that he sacrificed all other considerations to that, and made the best bargain he could. " The king and the pope divided " the matter between them. When any bishopric became " vacant, the king was within six months to name to it a " doctor, or one licensed in divinity, of the age of twenty- " seven. If the pope did not approve of the nomination, the " king had three months more to nominate another; but if he " failed again, the pope was to provide one to the see. The " pope had reserved to himself the providing of all that became " vacant in the court of Rome: (a pretension the popes had " set on foot, in which by degrees they had enlarged the ex- " tent of it to very great and undetermined bounds; and did " thereby dispose of many benefices.) And the king was " limited in his nomination by some conditions, with relation

" to the person so nominated ; yet the want of these was not
" to be objected to the king's kindred, or to other illustrious
" persons. The king was also to nominate to all abbeys a
" person of twenty-three years of age. *Gratiæ expectativæ*,
" or survivances and reservations in bulls, were never to be
" admitted : only one benefice might be reserved from a col-
" lator of ten, and two from one of fifty. Causes of appeals
" were to be judged *in partibus*, in the parts where the
" matters lay ; excepting the causes enumerated in the law as
" *greater causes*. It was also provided, that in all bulls that
" were obtained, the true value of the benefice was to be ex-
" pressed ; otherwise the grace was null and void." No mention was made of *annates ;* and, in other particulars, the
articles in the pragmatic sanction were inserted. The pope
promised he would send a legate to France, to tax the value
of all ecclesiastical benefices. All former excommunications
were taken off, with an indemnity for all that was past.

The king having the two instruments, the one abrogating
the pragmatic sanction, and the other establishing the *con-*
cordat, sent in great pomp to him, in order to their being
registered in parliament ; resolved only to offer the latter, as
that in which the other was virtually comprehended. So he
went in person to the court of parliament, to which many
great men, divines, and other persons of distinction, were
called. The chancellor set forth the hatred pope Julius bore
king Louis the Twelfth, and the violence with which he had
proceeded against him : the king succeeding when the council
of the Lateran was assembled ; which was composed chiefly of
members of the court, or of dependers on the court of Rome,
who were all engaged against the pragmatic sanction, as that
which diminished their profits. The king saw it was in vain
9 to insist in defending it : but apprehending, if it were simply
condemned, all the old oppressions would again take place, he
being then engaged in a most dangerous war in Italy, saw
no better way to gain the pope than by agreeing to the
concordat.

The ecclesiastics who were present said, by their mouth the
cardinal of Boisi, that the *concordat* did so affect the whole
Gallican church, that without a general consent it could not be
approved. The king upon this said with some indignation,

[margin note: King Francis carried it to the parliament of Paris.]

[margin note: It was there opposed by the ecclesiastics of that court.]

that he would command them either to approve it, or he would send them to Rome to dispute the matter there with the pope. The president answered in the name of the court, that he would report the king's pleasure to the court; and they would so proceed in that matter, as to please both God and the king. The chancellor replied, the court were wise: the king said, he did enjoin them to obey without delay. Then letters patents were made out, setting forth the *concordat*, and requiring the court of parliament, and all other judges, to observe it, and to see it fully executed.

Opposition made to it by the king's learned council.

Some days after that, the chancellor, with some of the officers of the crown, came and brought the whole courts together, and delivered them the king's letters patents, requiring them to register the *concordat*. They upon that appointed the king's council to examine the matters in it. The advocate-general did in the chancellor's presence represent the inconvenience of receiving the *concordats*, by which the liberties of the Gallican church were lessened; and said, that by the paying of *annates*, much money would be carried out of the kingdom: so he desired they would appoint a committee to examine it. Four were named; who, after they had sat about it ten days, desired more might be added to them; so the president of the *enquêtes*, or inquisitions, and four more, were joined to them. A week after that, the advocate-general moved the court to proceed still to judge according to the pragmatic, and not to receive the revocation of it, against which he put in an appeal. Four days after this, the bastard of Savoy, the king's natural uncle, came into the court with orders from the king, requiring them to proceed immediately to the publishing the *concordats*; appointing him to hear all their debates, that he might report all to the king. He told them how much the king was offended with their delays: they on the other hand complained of his being present to hear them deliver their opinions. They sent some of their number to lay this before the king: it looked like a design to frighten them, when one, not of their body, was to hear all that passed among them. The king said, there were some worthy men among them; but others, like fools, complained of him, and of the expense of his court: he was a king, and had as much authority as his predecessors. They had flattered Louis the

Twelfth and called him the *Father of Justice*: he would also
have justice done with all vigour. In Louis' time some were
banished the kingdom because they did not obey him ; so, if
they did not obey him, he would send some of them to Bor-
deaux, and others to Toulouse, and put good men in their
places : and told them, he would have his uncle present during
their deliberation. So they were forced to submit to it.

10   On the 13th of June they began to deliver their opinions,   1517.
and that lasted till the 24th of July : and then they concluded   They re-
that the court could not, and ought not to register the *con-*   solve not to
cordats ; but that they would still observe the pragmatic
sanction : and that the university of Paris, and all others that
desired to be heard, ought to be heard. Therefore, they said,
they must appeal from the abrogation of the pragmatic sanction ; and if the king would insist to have the *concordat*
observed, a great assembly ought to be summoned, such as
Charles the Seventh had called to settle the pragmatic. They
also charged the Savoyard to make a true report to the king
of their proceedings.

      Upon this the king wrote to them, to send some of their   The king
body to give him an account of the grounds they went on :   was highly
two were sent, but it was long before they were admitted to   this.
his presence ; the king saying, he would delay their despatch,
as they had delayed his business. When they were admitted,
they were ordered to put what they had to offer in writing.
This they did, but desired to be likewise heard. But being
asked if they had any thing to offer that was not in their
paper, they said they had not, but desired the king would
hear their paper read to him : the king refused it. They
were a body of one hundred persons, and had been preparing
their paper above seven months, but the chancellor would
answer it in less time : and the king would not suffer them to
have a verbal process against what he had done. He told
them, there was but one king in France : he had done the
best he could to bring all to a quiet state, and would not suffer
that which he had done in Italy to be undone in France ; nor
would he suffer them to assume an authority like that of the
senate of Venice. It was their business to do justice, but not
to put the kingdom in a flame, as they had attempted to do

in his predecessor's time.   He concluded, he would have them
approve the *concordats ;* and if they gave him more trouble,
he would make them ambulatory, and to follow his court : nor
would he suffer any more ecclesiastics to be of their body.
They were not entirely his subjects, since he had no authority
to cut off their heads : they ought to say their breviary, and
not to meddle in his affairs.

They answered him, that these things were contrary to
the constitution of their court.   He said, he was sorry his ancestors had so constituted it ; but he was king as well as they
were, and he would settle them on another foot : so he bid
them be gone early the next morning.   They begged a short
delay, for the ways were bad ; but the great master told them
from the king, that, if they were not gone by such an hour,
he would put them in prison, and keep them in it six months,
and then he would see who would move to set them at liberty :
so they went to Paris.   The duke of Tremouille was sent after
them to the parliament, to let them know that the king would
have the *concordats* to be immediately published, without any
further deliberation.   They must obey the king as became
subjects : he told them, the king had repeated that ten times
to him in the space of a quarter of an hour ; and concluded, that
if they delayed any longer to obey the king, the king would
make all the court feel the effects of his displeasure.

The king's learned council oppose it no longer.   The court called for the king's learned council : but they 11
said, they had received positive orders from the king by Tre-
mouille to consent to the *concordats ;* otherwise the king
would treat them so, that they should feel it sensibly.   The
advocate general said, he was sorry for the methods the king
took ; but he wished they would consider what might follow, if
they continued to deny what was so earnestly pressed on them :
the publishing this could be of no force, since the church that
was so much concerned in it, was neither called for, nor heard ;
the thing might be afterwards set right, for Louis the Eleventh
saw his error, and changed his mind.   He offered two things
to soften that which was required of them : one was, to insert
in the register, that it was done in obedience to the king's
commands often repeated ; the other was, that they should
declare that they did not approve the abrogation of the prag-

matic sanction, but were then only to publish the *concordats*; and that they might resolve in all their judiciary proceedings to have no regard to that ; and in particular to that clause, that all bulls were void, if the true value of the benefice was not expressed in them.　On the 18th of March they came to this resolution, that their decree of the 24th of July, for observing the pragmatic, was by them fully confirmed : but, in obedience to the king's commands, they published the *concordats*; adding a protestation, that the court did not approve it, but intended in all their sentences to judge according to the pragmatic sanction.

1.518.

The court made these protestations in the hands of the bishop of Langres, a duke and peer of France, setting forth, that their liberty was taken from them ; that the publication of the *concordats* was not done by their order, but against their mind, by the king's express order ; and that they did not intend to approve it, nor to be governed by it in their judgments, but to observe the pragmatic sanction.　They ordered likewise an appeal to be made from the pope, to the pope better advised, and to the next general council ; upon all which the bishop of Langres made an authentic instrument : so it was resolved to proceed to publication on the 22nd of March.　But on the 21st the rector of the university of Paris, accompanied by some of that body, and by some advocates, appeared, desiring to be heard before they should proceed to such publication.　The court received his petition, and promised to consider it ; but said, if they made the publication, it should not prejudice any of their rights, for they were resolved to judge as formerly, notwithstanding that : yet they required him not to publish this.　The dean of Notredame came on the 22nd to the court, and said, they heard they were going to publish the *concordats*, which both implied their condemning the councils of Constance and Basle, and tended to the destruction of the liberties of the Gallican church, which the popes had always envied them.　He desired they would not proceed to it till the whole Gallican church was consulted in the matter ; and protested, that what they were about to do should not be to the prejudice of the church.　After this was received, they proceeded to the publication, as they had promised, adding these words to it ; *Read, published, and registered by the*

The parliament publishes it, but with a protestation.

order and command of the king often repeated to us, in the 12
presence of the lord of Tremouille, his first chamberlain,
specially sent to have it done. And on the 24th of March
they renewed their protestation, that they did not approve of
it; that they insisted in their former appeals, and were resolved to proceed in all their judgments without regard to it.

The university and clergy op-pose it.

On the 27th of March the rector of the university ordered a
mandate to be affixed, prohibiting their printers to print the
concordats: he likewise appealed from the pope to a general
council, lawfully assembled, sitting in a safe place, and in full
freedom. This was printed and affixed: and great reflections
were made by some preachers in their sermons, both on the
king and on the chancellor. The king being informed of this,
wrote to the first president, complaining both of the rector,
and of the preachers: he ordered them to take informations of
all those matters, and to get the *concordats* to be printed as
soon as was possible, and to punish the authors of sedition.
But the court said, they knew nothing tending that way; for
their business took them up so entirely, that they could not
attend on sermons. The king complained likewise severely of
the appeal they had made; he was monarch, and had no
superior to whom an appeal could lie: he also sent an order to
inhibit all meetings in the university.

The exceptions to the *concordat* by the parliament.

In the *concordat* it was provided, that, if it was not published within six months in France, it should be null and void:
but the delays that had been made put the king on getting
that term prolonged a year longer. " The three chief excep-
" tions that the parliament had to the *concordats* were, first,
" the declaring bulls void if the true value of the benefices was
" not set forth in them, which might put the obtainers of them
" to great charge, and many suits: the second was, the carry-
" ing the *greater causes* to be judged at Rome: the third was
" concerning elections. The first of these was given up, and
" was no further urged by the court of Rome; but it was not
" settled what those *greater causes* were. By the pragmatic
" they were restrained to bishoprics and monasteries; but the
" *concordats* held the matter in general words: so the number
" of these causes was indefinite, and on all occasions it would
" increase as the canonists pleased. They condemned that
" device of the court of Rome, of granting provisions for all

" that was held by any who died in the court, considering the
" great extent to which that had been carried.   They also
" found that by the *concordats* all nunneries were left to the
" pope's provision ; and likewise all inferior dignities, such as
" deaneries and provostships.   All churches that had special
" privileges were exempted from the king's nomination ; and
" at Rome exceptions might be unjustly made to the per-
" sons named by the king.   But above all, they stood on
" this ; that the right of electing was founded on the law of
" God, and on natural right : that this was established by the
" authority of general councils, by the civil law, and by many
" royal edicts, during all the three races of their kings.   This
" right was now taken away without hearing the parties con-
" cerned to set it forth.   If there had crept in abuses in elec-
" tions, these might be corrected : but they thought the king
13 " usurped that which did not belong to him, on this pretence,
" that the pope granted it to him ; which was contrary both to
" the doctrine and practice of the Gallican church.   They
" found many lesser exceptions in point of form to the method
" of abrogating the pragmatic sanction : one was, that the
" council of the Lateran did forbid all persons that held lands
" of the church to observe or maintain that sanction, under
" the pain of forfeiting those lands ; which was a plain invasion
" of the king's prerogatives, who is supreme lord of all those
" lands within his dominions.   The pope also took upon him to
" annul that sanction, that then subsisted by the royal au-
" thority : this might be made a precedent in time to come for
" annulling any of their laws.   They likewise thought the
" taking away the pragmatic sanction, which was made upon
" the authority of the councils of Constance and Basle, and
" had declared the subjection of the pope to the council, did
" set aside that doctrine, and set up the pope's authority above
" the council, though the pragmatic was made while the pope
" was reconciled to the council : and the breach upon which
" Eugenius was deposed happened not till almost a year after
" that ; it being published in July 1438, and his deposition
" was not till June 1439 : besides that, ten years after that,
" pope Nicolas the Fifth confirmed all the decrees made at
" Basle.   They likewise put the king in mind of the oath he
" took, at his coronation, to maintain all the rights and liberties

"of the Gallican church. So they moved the king, either
"to prevail with the pope to call a general council, or that he
"would call a national one in France, to judge of the whole
"matter : and as for the threatenings given out, that the
"pope would depose the king, and give away his kingdom, if
"he did not submit to him ; they said the king held his crown
"of God, and all such threatenings ought to be rejected with
"scorn and indignation."

These were answered by the chancellor. To all these the chancellor made a long and flattering answer ; for which he had the usual reward of a cardinal's cap. He set forth the danger the king was in, being engaged in the war of Italy ; the pope threatening him with censures : for the pragmatic sanction was then condemned by the pope, and that censure was ratified by the council in the Lateran ; upon which he would have reassumed all the old oppressions, if the king had not entered into that treaty, yielding some points to save the rest. He said, the kings of the first race nominated to bishoprics : for which he cited precedents from Gregory of Tours. So the kings of England did name, and the popes upon that gave provisions : the kings of Scotland did also name, but not by virtue of a right, but rather by connivance. He said, elections had gone through various forms ; sometimes popes did elect, sometimes princes with the people, sometimes princes took it into their own hands, sometimes the whole clergy without the people, and of late the canons chose without the concurrence of the clergy. That the king being in these difficulties, all those about him, and all those in France who were advised with in the matter, thought the accepting the *concordats* was just and necessary. Pope Leo repented that he had granted so much : and it was not without great difficulty that he brought the cardinals to consent to it. He went very copiously as a canonist through the other heads, softening 14 some abuses, and shewing that others had a long practice for them, and were observed in other kingdoms.

The matter finally settled. And thus was this matter carried in the parliament of Paris ; in which, as the court shewed great integrity and much courage, which deserve the highest characters with which such noble patriots ought to be honoured ; so in this instance we see how feeble the resistance even of the worthiest judges will prove to a prince, who has possessed himself of the whole legislative

authority ; when he intends to break through established laws
and constitutions, and to sacrifice the rights of his crown, and
the interest of his people, to serve particular ends of his own.
In such cases, the generous integrity of judges, or other ministers, will be resented as an attempt on the sovereign authority : and such is the nature of arbitrary power, that the most
modest defence of law and justice, when it crosses the designs
of an insolent and corrupt minister, and an abused prince, will
pass for disobedience and sedition.

If the assembly of the states in France had maintained their
share of the legislative power, and had not suffered the right
they once had to be taken from them, of being liable to no
taxes but by their own consent, these judges would have been
better supported : and the opposition they made upon this
occasion would have drawn after it all the most signal expressions of honour and esteem, that a nation owes to the trustees
of their laws and liberties, when they maintain them resolutely,
and dispense them equally. And the corrupt chancellor would
have received such punishment as all wicked ministers deserve,
who for their own ends betray the interest of their country.

The court of parliament shewed great firmness after this: The parliament still
and it appeared that the protestation that they made, of judg- judged by
ing still according to the pragmatic, was not only a piece of the pragmatic sanc-
form to save their credit. The archbishop of Sens died soon tion.
after ; and the king sent to inhibit the chapter to proceed to [Feb. 11,
an election. It was understood, that he designed to give it to 1518.
Pinsson,
the bishop of Paris ; so the chapter wrote to that bishop not p. 746.]
to give such a wound to their liberties as to take it upon the
king's nomination : but seeing that he had no regard to that,
they elected him, that so they might by this seem to keep up
their claim. The bishop of Alby died soon after that ; the
king named one, and the chapter chose another : upon that
Alby being within the jurisdiction of Toulouse, the court of
parliament there judged in favour of him who was elected by
the chapter, against him who had obtained bulls upon the
king's nomination ; at which the king was highly offended.
The archbishopric of Bourges falling void soon after, the king
nominated one, and the chapter elected another. The chapter
pretended a special privilege to elect ; so the pope judged in
their favour. Some years after this, the king carried on his 1524.

wars in Italy, leaving his mother regent of France: so the court of parliament made a remonstrance to her, setting forth the invasions that had been made upon the rights of the Gallican church, desiring her to interpose, that the pragmatic sanction, and the liberty of elections, might again have their full force; but that had no effect.

Upon the king's being a prisoner, the *concordat* was more condemned. [Pinsson, p. 747.]

Soon after this, the king was taken prisoner by the army of 15 Charles the Fifth at the battle of Pavia: and upon that his mother declared, that she looked on her son's misfortunes as a judgment of God upon him, for his abolishing the pragmatic sanction; and though she would not take it upon her to make any alteration during her son's absence, yet she promised, that, when he should be set at liberty, she would use her utmost endeavours with him to set it up again, and to abolish the *concordats*. This was registered in the records of the court of parliament, yet it had no effect upon the king's return out of Spain. He, finding the parliament resolved to maintain all elections, ordered that matter to be taken wholly out of their cognizance; and he removed all suits of that sort from the courts of parliament to the great council, upon some disputes that were then on foot concerning a bishopric and an abbey given to chancellor Prat, then made a cardinal in recompense of the service he had done the court of Rome: so by that an end was put to all disputes.

These matters removed from the parliament to the great council.

The parliament struggled hard against this diminution of their jurisdiction: they wrote to the dukes and peers of France to move the regent not to proceed thus to lessen their authority: on the other hand she said, they were taking all things into their own hands in prejudice of the king's prerogative. But the king confirmed that, and settled the chancellor in the possession of the see and abbey; and the proceedings of the parliament against him were annulled, and ordered to be struck out of their registers. And it appearing that some chapters and abbeys had special privileges for free elections;

1532.

the king obtained a bull from Clement the Seventh, suspending all those during the king's life. The court of Rome stood long upon this, and thought to have gained new advantages before it should be granted: but the pope was at that time in a secret treaty with the court of France, which was afterwards accomplished at Marseilles; so he was easier in this matter,

and the bull was registered in parliament in May thereafter.
And upon this the chancellor, pretending that he would see and
examine those privileges, called for them all; and when they
were brought to him, he threw them all into the fire.

But to lay all that I have found of this matter together;
the clergy of France, in a remonstrance that they made to
king Henry the Third, affirmed, that Francis at his death
declared to his son, that nothing troubled his conscience more,
than his taking away canonical elections, and his assuming to
himself the nomination to bishoprics. If this was true, his son
had no regard to it, but went on as his father had done. Upon
his death, when the cardinal of Lorraine pressed the parliament to proceed in the vigorous prosecution of heresy, they
remonstrated, that the growth of heresy flowed chiefly from
the scandals that were given by bad clergymen and ill bishops:
and that the ill choice that had been made by the court, since
the *concordats* were set up, gave more occasion to the progress
that heresy made than any other thing whatsoever. The
courts were so monstrously corrupt during that and the two
former reigns, that no other could be expected from them.

Remon-
strances
made by
the clergy
against
this.
[1585.
Pinsson,
p. 759.]

1560.

16   An assembly of the states was called in the beginning of
Charles the Ninth's reign. In it the first estate prayed, that
the pragmatic sanction might again take place, particularly in
the point of elections; they backed this with great authorities
of councils ancient and modern: with them the two other
estates agreed. The court tried to shift this off, promising to
send one to Rome to treat about it: but that did not satisfy;
so a decree was drawn up to this effect, that an archbishop
should be chosen by the bishops of his province, by the chapter
of his cathedral, and twelve persons of the chief of the laity;
and a bishop by the metropolitan and the chapter. The court
of parliament opposed this: they thought the laity ought to
have no share in elections, so they pressed the restoring the
pragmatic sanction without any alteration; yet, in conclusion,
the decree was thus amended: an archbishop was to be chosen
by the bishops of the province, and the chapter of the see;
but a bishop was to be chosen by the archbishop, with the
bishops of the province, and the chapter, and by twenty-four
of the laity to be thus nominated: all the gentry were to be
summoned to meet, and to choose twelve to represent them at

[Ibid.
p. 756.]

[Ibid.
p. 757.]

the election, and the city was to choose other twelve. All these were to make a list of three persons to be offered to the king, and the man named by the king was to have the see. Thus they designed to bring this matter into a form as near the customs mentioned in the Roman law as they could. But this design vanished, and was never put in practice.

[April, 1561. Pinsson, p. 758.]

The clergy still called for restoring the elections: president Ferrier was sent to Rome to obtain it. He in a long speech shewed, that neither the Gallican church, nor the courts of parliament, had ever received the *concordats*, that shadow of approbation given to it by the parliament of Paris being extorted from them by force; and he laid out all the inconveniences that had happened since the *concordats* were set up. But that court felt the advantages they had by them too sensibly, to be ever prevailed with to give them up. And thus that great affair was settled in the view of this church and nation, at the time that king Henry broke off all correspondence with it. It may be very reasonably presumed, that inferences were made from this, to let all people see what merchandise the court of Rome made of the most sacred rights of the church, when they had their own profits secured: and therefore the wise men in this church at that time might justly conclude, that their liberties were safer while they remained an entire body within themselves, under a legal constitution; by which, if princes carried their authority too far, some check might be given to it by those from whom the public aids were to be obtained for supporting the government, than while all was believed to belong to the popes, who would at any time make a bargain, and divide the spoils of the church with crowned heads; taking to themselves the gainful part, and leaving the rest in the hands of princes.

An apology, with the reasons for this digression.

I hope, though this relation does not belong properly to the history of the reformation; yet since it is highly probable it had a great influence on people's minds, this digression will be easily forgiven me. And now I turn to such of our affairs as fall within this period.

Sept. 16, 1513. Queen Catharine's letter to king Henry

The first thing that occurred to me, in order of time, was a 17 letter of queen Catharine's to king Henry, who, upon his crossing the sea, left the regency of the kingdom in her hands; the commission bears date the 11th of June 1513. King James

the Fourth of Scotland having invaded England with a great upon the death of the king of Scotland.
army, was defeated and killed by the earl of Surrey. The
earl gave the queen the news in a letter to her, with one to
the king; this she sent him with a letter of her own; which [Rymer, tom. xiii. p. 370.]
being the only one of hers to the king that I ever saw, I have
inserted it in my Collection. The familiarities of calling him Collect. Numb. 2.
in one place *My husband*, and in another, *My Henry*, are not
unpleasant. She sent with it a piece of the king of Scots'
coat to be a banner: she was then going to visit, as she calls
it, our lady of Walsingham.

I will next open an account of the progress of cardinal Wol- The progress of Wolsey's rise.
sey's fortunes, and the ascendant he had over the king. The
first step he made into the church was to be rector of Lyming-
ton in the diocese of Bath and Wells; then, on the 30th of
July 1508, he had a papal dispensation to hold the vicarage of
Lyde, in the diocese of Canterbury, with his rectory. There
is a grant to him as almoner, on the 8th of November 1509. [Rymer, tom. xiii. p. 267.]
The next preferment he had was to be a prebendary of
Windsor: he was next advanced to be dean of Lincoln. A [Ibid. p. 293.]
year after that, pope Leo having reserved the disposing the [Ibid. p. 390.]
see of Lincoln to himself, gave it to Wolsey, designed in the
bulls dean of St. Stephen's, Westminster. But no mention is
made of the king's nomination. This is owned by the king in
the writ for the restitution of the temporalities. On the 14th July 14, 1514, [Ibid. p. 404.]
of July that year, cardinal de Medici, afterwards pope Clement
the Seventh, wrote to king Henry, that, upon the death of
cardinal Bambridge, he had prayed the pope not to dispose of
his benefices till he knew the king's mind, which the pope out
of his affection to the king granted very readily. Perhaps
the king did recommend Wolsey; but no mention is made of Ibid. [p. 412.]
that in his bulls. The king granted the restitution of the August 5.
temporalities of York before his instalment; for in the writ
he is only called the *elect archbishop:* and it is not expressed that he had the king's nomination. He had Tournay
in commendam, but resigned it into the hands of Francis, who
for that gave him a pension of twelve thousand livres during July 31, 1518. [Ibid. p. 610.]
life: at the same time prince Charles, afterwards Charles the
Fifth, gave him a pension of three thousand pounds. It seems
he afterwards desired to have it better secured: so in the end Dec. 16, 1518.
of that year prince Charles lodged a pension of five thousand

March 29,
1520.
[Rymer,
tom. xiii.
p. 714.]
[Ibid.
p. 725.]
[Ibid.
p. 769.]
Nov. 18,
1525. [tom.
xiv. p. 100.]
ducats to him on the bishopric of Pace in Castile. Above a year after that, pope Leo gave him a pension of two thousand ducats out of Palencia, instead of that which was charged on the bishopric of Pace. Besides all this, when Charles the Fifth was in London, he gave him another pension of nine thousand crowns, dated the 8th of June 1522. It seems he had other pensions from France; for, five years after this, there was an arrear stated there as due to him of a hundred and twenty-one thousand, eight hundred and ninety-eight crowns. He had also pensions from other princes of a lower

Rymer,
tom. xiii.
[p. 525.]
order. The duke of Milan's secretary did, by his master's express order, engage in the year 1515 to pay Wolsey ten thousand ducats a year; he on his part engaging, that there should be a perpetual friendship settled between the kings of England and France with that duke.

Decemb. 2,
1524.
[tom. xiv.
p. 29.]
The French king being a prisoner, his favour was necessary 18 in that distress; so the regent engaged to pay it in seven years time. But whatever may be in Wolsey's provisions when the bishopric of Salisbury was given to cardinal Campeggio by a bull, mention is expressly made in it of the king's letters interceding humbly for him.

King Henry's book of the Seven Sacraments.
When king Henry wrote this book of the Seven Sacraments, it seems it was at first designed to send it over in manuscript; for Wolsey sent one to the king finely dressed, that was to be presented to the pope: and he writes, that he was to send him more, which were to be sent about with the

Collect.
Numb. 3.
pope's bulls to all princes and universities: one in particular, as he writes, was far more excellent and princely. He also sent with it the choice of certain verses, to be written in the king's own hand in the book that was to be sent to the pope, and subscribed by him, to be laid up in the archives of the church to his immortal glory and memory. The matter was

[Rymer,
tom. xiii.
p. 756.]
so laid, that the book was presented to the pope on the 10th of October; and the very day after, the bull giving him the title of Defender of the Faith bears date: and in a private letter that pope Leo wrote to him, he runs out into copious strains of flattery, affirming, *That it appeared that the Holy Ghost assisted him in writing it*[2].

---

[2] [*Ut Sanctum affuisse Spiritum appareat.* [Rymer, tom. xiii. p. 759.]

The king was so pleased with the title, that Wolsey directed
his letters to him with it on the back, as appears in a letter of Collect.
Numb. 4.
his, that sets forth the low state of the affairs of Spain in Italy.
It appears it was written (for the year is not added in the
date) after that Luther wrote his answer to the king's book,
at least after letters came from him on the subject; the original of which he desires might be sent him, that he might
send it to the pope : and he intended to send copies both of
those and of the king's answers to the cardinal of Mentz and
to George duke of Saxony.

After the king's interviews both with the emperor and the Wolsey
sent to
king of France were over, new quarrels broke out, by which Charles
the emperor and Francis engaged in hostilities: but king the Fifth,
gained by
Henry, pretending to be the umpire of their differences, sent him.
Wolsey over to compose them.   He came to Calais in the 1521.
beginning of August.   From Dover he wrote to the king, and Collect.
Numb. 5.
sent two letters to him, which the king was to write in his own
hand to the emperor, and to the lady regent of Flanders,
which he desired the king would send to him; for he would
move slowly towards him.   Thus he took the whole ministry
into his own hands, and prepared even the king's secret letters
for him.   He was with the emperor thirteen days, who gave
him a singular reception ; for he came a mile out of town to
meet him.   The town is not named, but it was Bruges; for in
one of Erasmus' letters[3], he mentions his meeting Wolsey in [Erasmi
Epp. p.661.
that town, he being then with the emperor.   The cardinal ed. Lugd.
returned by the way of Gravelines; and from thence, beside Bat. 17c6.]
the public letter in which he gave the king an account of his
negotiation, he wrote a private one to him with this direction
on it, *To the King's Grace's own hands only.*   It seems he Collect.
Numb. 6.
had no private conversation with the emperor formerly ; " for
" in this he observes, that for his age he was very wise, and
19 " understood his affairs well.   He was cold and temperate in
" speech ; but spoke to very good purpose.   He reckoned
" that he would prove a very wise man: he thought he was
" much inclined to truth, and to the keeping of his promises :

---

[3] [The letter is addressed to archbishop Warham, and is dated ' Brugis,
22 Augusti, anno 1521.']

" he seemed to be inseparably joined to the king; and was
" resolved to follow his advice in all his affairs, and to trust
" the cardinal entirely.   He twice or thrice in secret promised
" to him, by his faith and truth, to abide by this; he promised
" it also to all the rest of the privy-council that were with the
" cardinal, in such a manner, that they all believed it came
" from his heart, without artifice or dissimulation.   So Wolsey
" wrote to the king, that he had reason to bless God that he
" was not only the ruler of his own realm, but that now by
" his wisdom Spain, Italy, Germany, and the Low Countries
" should be ruled and governed."   Whether the emperor did
by his prudent and modest behaviour really impose upon
Wolsey; or whether, by other secret practices he had so
gained him, as to oblige him to persuade the king to such a
confidence in him, I leave it to the reader to judge.

It passes generally among all the writers of that age, that
he aspired to the popedom : and that the emperor then promised him his assistance; in which he failing to him afterwards, Wolsey carried his revenges so far, that all the change
of counsels, and even the suit of the divorce, is in a great
measure ascribed to it.   I went into the stream in my history, and seemed persuaded of it; yet some original letters of
Wolsey's, communicated to me by sir William Cook of Norfolk,
which I go next to open, make this very doubtful.   The first
was upon the news of pope Adrian's death, upon which he immediately wrote to the king, " that his absence from Rome
" was the only obstacle of his advancement to that dignity:
" there were great factions then at Rome : he protests before
" God, that he thought himself unfit for it, and that he desired
" much rather to end his days with the king; yet, remember-
" ing that at the last vacation (nine months before) the king
" was for his being preferred to it, thinking it would be for his
" service, and supposing that he was still of the same mind, he
" would prepare such instructions as had been before sent to
" Pace, dean of St. Paul's, then ambassador at Rome, and send
" them to him by the next :" with this he also sent him the letters
that he had from Rome.   The next day he sent the letters and
instructions, directed to the king's ambassadors, who were, the
bishop of Bath, Pace, and Haniball, for procuring his prefer-

Wolsey's
practices to
be chosen
pope.

Collect.
Numb. 7.
Sept. 14.
Sept. 30.

Collect.
Numb. 8.
Octob. 1.

ment; or, that failing, for cardinal de Medici : these he desired the king to sign and despatch.   And that the emperor
might more effectually concur, though, pursuant to the conference he had with the king on that behalf, he verily supposed
he had not failed to advance it, he drew a private letter for the
king to write with his own hand to the emperor, putting to it
the secret sign and mark that was between them.

The despatch, that upon this he sent to the king's ambassa- Part ii.
dor at Rome, fell into my hands when I was laying out for Coll. Re-
materials for my second volume : but though it belonged in the Numb. 48.
order of time to the first, I thought it would be acceptable to p. 192.
the reader to see it, though not in its proper place.   In it, after
20 some very respectful words of pope Adrian, which, whether he
wrote out of decency only, or that he thought so of him, I
connot determine, " he tells them, that, before the vacancy, Wolsey's
" both the emperor and the king had great conferences for his designs to
" advancement, though the emperor's absence makes that he pope.
" cannot now join with them ; yet the regent of the Nether-
" lands, who knows his mind, has expressed an earnest and
" hearty concurrence for it : and by the letters of the cardinals
" de Medici, Sanctorum Quatuor, and Campeggio, he saw their
" affections.   He was chiefly determined by the king's earnest-
" ness about it, though he could willingly have lived still where
" he was ; his years increasing, and he knew himself unworthy
" of so high a dignity : yet his zeal for the exaltation of the
" Christian faith, and for the honour and safety of the king
" and the emperor, made him refer himself to the pleasure of
" God.   And in the king's name he sends them double letters :
" the first to the cardinal de Medici, offering the king's assist-
" ance to him ; and if it was probable he would carry it, they
" were to use no other powers : but if he thought he could not
" carry it, then they were to propose himself to him, and to
" assure him, if he was chosen, the other should be as it were
" pope.   They were to let the other cardinals know what his
" temper was, not austere, but free : he had great things to
" give, that would be void upon his promotion : he had no
" friends nor relations to raise, and he knew perfectly well the
" great princes of Christendom, and all their interests and
" secrets.   He promises he will be at Rome within three
" mouths, if they choose him ; and the king seems resolved to

BURNET, PART III.   G

" go thither with him : he did not doubt, but, according to the
" many promises and exhortations of the emperor to him, that
" his party will join with them.

" The king also ordered them to promise large rewards and
" promotions, and great sums of money to the cardinals ; and
" though they saw the cardinal de Medici full of hope, yet they
" were not to give over their labour for him, if they saw any
" hope of success : but they were to manage that so secretly,
" that the other may have no suspicion of it." This was dated
at Hampton-Court the 4th of October.

, To this a postscript was added in the cardinal's own hand to
to the bishop of Bath : he tells him, " what a great opinion the
" king had of his policy ; and he orders him to spare no rea-
" sonable offers, which perhaps might be more regarded than
" the qualities of the person. The king believed all the im-
" perialists would be with him, if there was faith in the em-
" peror : he believed the young men, who for most part were
" necessitous, would give good ear to fair offers, which shall
" undoubtedly be performed. The king willeth you neither to
" spare his authority, nor his good money or substance ; so he
" concludes, praying God to send him good speed." But all
this fine train of simony came too late ; for it found a pope
already chosen.

Collect.
Numb. 9.
Decem. 17.

His next letter upon that subject tells the king, " that, after
" great heat in the conclave, the French party was quite
" abandoned ; and the cardinals were fully resolved to choose
" cardinal de Medici or himself : that this coming to the know- 21
" ledge of the city of Rome, they came to the conclave windows,
" and cried out what danger it would be to choose a person
" that was absent ; so that the cardinals were in such fear,
" that, though they were principally bent on him, yet, to avoid
" this danger, they, by the inspiration of the Holy Ghost, (so
" he writes,) did on the 19th of November choose cardinal de
" Medici, who took the name of Clement the Seventh : of
" which good and fortunate news the king had great cause to
" thank Almighty God ; since as he was his faithful friend, so
" by his means he had attained that dignity : and that for his
" own part he took God to record, that he was much gladder
" than if it had fallen on his own person." In these letters
there is no reflection on the emperor, as having failed in his

promise at the former election : nor is that election any way
imputed to him, but laid on a casualty ordinary enough in con-
claves ; and more natural in that time, because pope Adrian's
severe way had so disgusted the Romans, that no wonder if
they broke out into disorders upon the apprehension of another
foreigner being like to succeed. If it is suspected, that though
Wolsey knew this was a practice of the emperor's, he might
disguise it thus from the king, that so he might be less suspected in the revenge that he was meditating, the thing must
be left as I find it ; only though the emperor afterwards
charged Wolsey as acting upon private revenge for missing
the popedom, yet he never pretended that he had moved himself in it, or had studied to obtain a promise from him ; which
would have put that general charge of his aspiring, and of
his revenging himself for the disappointment, more heavily
on him.

The king and the cardinal continued in a good correspondence both with that pope and the emperor till the battle of
Pavia, that Francis' misfortune changed the face of affairs, and
obliged the king, according to his constant and true maxim, to
support the weaker side, and to balance the emperor's growing
power, that by that accident was like to become quickly superior to all Christendom. It has been suggested, that the
emperor wrote before to Wolsey in terms of respect scarce
suitable to his dignity, but that he afterwards changed both
his style and subscription : but I have seen many of his letters,
to which the subscription is either your *good* or your *best
friend;* and he still continued that way of writing. His letters
are hardly legible, so that I could never read one complete
period in any of them, otherwise I would have put them in my
Collection.

The king of France taken prisoner.

But having looked thus far into Wolsey's correspondence
with the king, I shall now set him in another light from a very
good author, the lord Burghley, who, in that memorial[5] pre-

Lord Burghley's character of Wolsey.

---

[5] [' There was also a *Memorial,*
as it was called, highly injurious to
the cardinal, printed in the year
1706, under the borrowed name of
Cecil Lord Burghley ; wherein however this honourable attestation has
been given to him by the author,
whoever he was, that 'his decrees in
chancery were equitable and just.'
Fiddes' Life of Wolsey, p. 531.   It
was reprinted in ' The Prince's Cabala or Mysteries of State. Written
by king James the First and some
Noblemen in his reign and in Queen

pared for queen Elizabeth against favourites, probably intended
to give some stop to the favour she bore the earl of Leicester,
has set out the greatness of Wolsey's power, and the ill use he
[The
Prince's
Cabala,
p. 105.] made of it. " He had a family equal to the court of a great
" prince. There was in it one earl, and nine barons, and about
" a thousand knights, gentlemen, and inferior officers. Besides
[p. 106.] " the vast expense of such a household, he gave great pensions
[p. 107.] " to those in the court and conclave of Rome ; by whose 22
" services he hoped to be advanced to the papacy. He lent
" great sums to the emperor, whose poverty was so well known,
" that he could have no prospect of having them repaid ; (pro-
" bably this is meant of Maximilian.) Those constant expenses
" put him on extraordinary ways of providing a fund for their
[p. 108.] " continuance. He granted commissions under the great seal
" to oblige every man upon oath to give in the true value of
" his estate ; and that those who had fifty pound, or upwards,
" should pay four shillings in the pound. This was so heavy,
" that, though it had been imposed by authority of parliament,
" it would have been thought an oppression of the subject : but
" he adds, that to have this done by the private authority of a
" subject, was what wants a name. When this was represented
" to the king, he disowned it ; and said, no necessities of his
" should be ever so great, as to make him attempt the raising
" money any other way but by the people's consent in parlia-
[p. 109.] " ment. Thus his illegal project was defeated ; so he betook
" himself to another not so odious, by the way of benevolence :
" and, to carry that through, he sent for the lord mayor and
" aldermen of London, and said to them, that he had pre-
" vailed with the king to recal his commissions for that heavy
" tax, and to throw himself on their free gifts. But in this he
" was likewise disappointed ; for the statute of Richard the
" Third was pleaded against all benevolences : the people ob-
" stinately refused to pay it ; and though the demanding it
" was for some time insisted on, yet the opposition made to it

Elizabeth's, &c., London, 1715,' of
which volume it forms the fourth
pamphlet, with the title, ' A Memorial Presented to Queen Elizabeth against her Majesty's being
engrossed by any particular favourite. Written by William Cecil Lord
Burleigh, then Lord High Treasurer
of England. London, printed in the
year 1714.' It occupies pp. 97–111.
The passage in the text contains,
though not very exactly expressed,
the substance of the original.]

" being like to end in a civil war, it was let fall." All this I drew from that memorial. I found also a commission to the Cott.Libr.[6] archbishop of Canterbury, the lord Calham, and others, setting forth the great wars that the king had in France, in which the duke of Bourbon, called one of the greatest princes in France, was now the king's servant : they are by it required to practise with all in Kent, whose goods amounted to four pound, or above, and whose names were given to a schedule, to anticipate the subsidy granted in parliament. This is all that has occurred to me with relation to Wolsey's ministry. I will in the next place set out what he attempted or did in ecclesiastical matters, with the proceedings in convocation during this period. When king Henry called his first parliament, by a writ tested Wolsey's proceedings as legate. October 17, 1509, to meet at Westminster the 21st of January following, he did not intend to demand a supply ; so there appears no writ for a convocation : but the archbishop of Canterbury summoned one, as it seems by his own authority ; yet [Jan. 26, 1510.] none sat then at York. The house of lords was sometimes adjourned by the lord treasurer ; because the chancellor (Warham) and the other spiritual lords were absent, and engaged in convocation : but it does not appear what was done by them.

In the year 1511, on the 28th of November, a writ was sent His insolence to Warham. to Warham to summon a convocation, which met the 6th of February : they had several sessions, and gave a subsidy of [viginti-trium. twenty-four thousand pounds, but did nothing besides with relation to matters of religion. There was some heat among Wilkins' Concilia, vol. iii them on the account of some grievances and excesses in the p. 652.] archbishop's courts. A committee was appointed of six persons, [Reg. Exon. Old- the bishops of Norwich and Rochester, the prior of Canterbury, ham, fol. 23 the dean of St. Paul's, and an archdeacon, but without addition 44, ap. Wilkins' of his place : these were to examine the encroachments made Conc. iii. by the archbishop's courts, and the inhibitions sent to the in- 653.] ferior courts ; but especially as to the probates of wills, and the granting administrations to intestate goods, when there was any to the value of five pound in several dioceses : an estimate first settled by Warham, for which he had officials and apparitors in every diocese, three or four in some, and five or six in others, which was looked on by them as contrary to law.

<hr>

[6] [The editor is unable to say whether this reference is a mistake. He has been unable to find it the commission amongst the Cotton MSS.]

[Wilkins'
Conc. iii.
p. 654.]
Cardinal Morton is said to be the first who set up this pretence of prerogative : against these the bishops alleged the
Constitutions of Ottobonus and of archbishop Stratford : it is
also set forth, that when Warham was an advocate, he was
[ibid. p.
655.]
employed by Hill, bishop of London, in whose name he appeared against them, and appealed to pope Alexander against
these invasions made by the archbishop on the rights of his
see.   And when Warham was promoted to the see of London,
he maintained his claim against them, and opposed them more
than any other bishop of the province, and sent his chancellor
to Rome to find relief against them.   But when he was advanced to be archbishop, he not only maintained those practices, but carried them further than his predecessor had done.
[ibid. p.
656.]
All this, with thirteen other articles of grievances, were drawn
up at large in the state of the case between the archbishop and
the bishops ; and proposals were made of an accommodation
between them about the year 1514 : but the event shewed that
this opposition came to nothing.   This must be acknowledged
to be none of the best parts of Warham's character.   In the
year 1514, they were again summoned by writ : they met and
gave subsidies, but they were not to be levied till the terms of
paying the subsidies formerly granted were out.   In the year
1518, Warham summoned a convocation to meet at Lambeth
to reform some abuses ; and in the summons he affirmed, that
Reg. Heref.
Booth, fol.
37. ap.
[Wilkins'
Concilia,
vol. iii. p.
660.]
he had obtained the king's consent so to do.   At this Wolsey
was highly offended, and wrote him a very haughty letter : in
it he said, " it belonged to him, as *legate a latere*, to see to the
" reformation of abuses : and he was well assured, that the
" king would not have him to be so little esteemed, that he
" should enterprise such reformation to the derogation of the
" dignity of the see apostolic, and otherwise than the law will
Wake's
State of the
Church 7,
Append.
p. 208.
[Nᵒ. 132.]
" suffer you, without my advice and consent."   And he in
plain words denies that he had any such command of the king,

7 [' The State of the Church and
Clergy of England in their Councils, Synods, Convocations, Con-
ventions, and other public assemblies ; historically deduced from the
Conversion of the Saxons to the
present times, with a large appendix of original writs and other documents by William Wake, D. D.,
Dean of Exeter and Chaplain in
Ordinary to her Majesty. Occasioned by a book entitled, The
Rights, Powers, and Privileges of
an English Convocation &c.' London, 1703, folio.]

but that the king's order was expressly to the contrary. So
he orders him to come to him, to treat of some things concerning his person.   This it seems Warham was required to send
round his suffragan bishops: so he recalled his monitions in
expectation of a legatine council: the pestilence was then
raging, so this was put off a year longer; and then Wolsey
summoned it by a letter, which he transmitted to the bishops:
that to the bishop of Hereford is in his register.   He desires Reg.Heref.
him to come to a council at Westminster for the reforming the Booth, fol.
clergy, and *for consulting in the most convenient and soundest* [Wilkins'
way, of what we shall think may tend to the increase of the Concilia,
faith.   He hoped this letter would be of as much weight with 661.]
him as monitories in due form would be.

24   It appears not by any record I could ever hear of, what A legatine
was done in the legatine synod thus brought together, except synod.
by the register of Hereford, in which we find that the bishop ref. Booth,
summoned his clergy to meet in a synod at the chapter-house, fol. 43. ap.
to consult about certain affairs, and the articles delivered by Concilia,
Wolsey as legate in a council of the provinces of Canterbury 681.]
and York, to the bishops there assembled, to be published by
them.   All that is mentioned in this synod is concerning the
habits of the clergy, and the lives and manners of those who
were to be ordained; which the bishop caused to be explained
to them in English, and ordered them to be observed by the
clergy: and these being published, they proceeded to some May 5,
heads relating to those articles: and he gave copies of all that 1519.
passed in every one of them.

The next step he made was of a singular nature.   When 1523.
the king summoned the parliament in the fourteenth year of
his reign, Warham had a writ to summon a convocation of his
province, which did meet five days after, on the 20th of April.
The cardinal summoned his convocation to meet at York almost He called
a month before, on the 22nd of March; but they were imme- the convo-
diately prorogued to meet at Westminster the 22nd of April. Canter-
The convocation of Canterbury was opened at St. Paul's; but bury to sit
a monition came from Wolsey to Warham, to appear before [Reg. He-
him with his clergy at Westminster on the 22nd: and thus fol. 93. ap.
both convocations were brought together.   It seems he in- Wilkins'
tended that the legatine synod, thus irregularly brought to- vol. iii. p.
gether, should give the king supplies: but the clergy of the 700.]

province of Canterbury said, their powers were only directed
to the archbishop of Canterbury, and these would not warrant
them to act in any other manner than in the provincial way :
so the convocation of Canterbury returned back to St. Paul's,
and sat there till August, and gave the supply apart ; as did

Reg.Heref.
fol. 84. ap.
[Wilkins'
Concilia,
vol. iii. p.
701.]
also that of York.   But Wolsey, finding those of Canterbury
could not act under him, by the powers that they had brought
up with them, issued out, on the 2nd of May, monitory letters
to the bishops of that province to meet at Westminster the 8th
of June[8], to deliberate *of the reformation of the clergy, both
of seculars and regulars, and of other matters relating to it.*
In this he mentions Warham's summoning a convocation, which
he had brought before him ; but upon some doubts arising,
because the proctors of the clergy had no sufficient authority
to meet in the legatine synod, he therefore summoned them to
meet with him, and to bring sufficient powers to that effect by
the 2nd of June : but it does not appear that any assembly of
the clergy followed pursuant to this ; so. it seems it was let fall.
This is the true account of that matter.   I gave it indeed differently before, implicitly following some writers that lived in

Antiq.Brit.
[p. 469.]
that time ; more particularly that account given of it by either
archbishop Parker or Josceline, a book of such credit, that the
following it deserved no hard censure.   The grant of the subsidy is indeed in the name of the province of Canterbury : but
the other relation of that matter being too easily followed by
me, it seemed to me that it was a point of form for each province to give their subsidy in an instrument apart, though it
was agreed to, they being together in one body.   It was
indeed an omission not to have explained that ; but now, upon 25
better evidence, the whole matter is thus fully opened.   I find
no other proceedings of Wolsey's, as legate, on record, save
that he took on him, by his legatine authority, to give institutions at pleasure into all benefices in the dioceses of all bishops,
without so much as asking the bishop's consent.   In the register

Reg. Tun-
stall, fol.31.
of London, an institution given by him to South Wickington,
on the 10th of December 1526, is entered with this addition ;
that the cardinal had likewise given seven other institutions in
that diocese, without asking the consent of the bishop: and on the

[8] [The monitory letter to Long-   May 7, and the summons is for the
land, bishop of Lincoln, is dated   2nd of June.]

margin it is added, that the giving and accepting such institutions by the legate's authority, being papal provisions, involved the clergy into the *praemunire*, from which they were obliged to redeem themselves. Wolsey did also publish a bull, condemning all who married in the forbidden degrees; and he sent mandates to the bishops to publish it in their several dioceses: he also published pope Leo's bull against Luther, and ordered it to be every where published: he also required all persons, under the pain of excommunication, to bring in all Luther's books that were in their hands: he enumerated forty-two of Luther's errors; and required a return of the mandate to be made to him, together with such books as should be brought in upon it, by the 1st of August. The date of the mandate is not set down; and this is all that I find in this period relating to Wolsey. Fisher's Regist. fol. 127. Reg.Heref. fol. 66.

This last shews the apprehensions they were under of the spreading of Luther's books and doctrine. All people were at this time so sensible of the corruptions that seemed by common consent to be as it were universally received, that every motion towards a reformation was readily hearkened to every where: corruption was the common subject of complaint; and in the commission given to those whom the king sent to represent himself, and this church, in the council of the Lateran, the *reformation of the head and members* is mentioned as that which was expected from that council.

This was so much at that time in all men's mouths, that one of the best men in that age, Colet, dean of St. Paul's, being to open the convocation with a sermon, made that the subject of it all; and he set forth many of those particulars to which it ought to be applied. It was delivered, as all such sermons are, in Latin; and was soon after translated into English. I intended once to have published it among the papers that I did put in the Collection; but those, under whose direction I composed that work, thought, that, since it did not enter into points of doctrine, but only into matters of practice, it did not belong so properly to my design in writing: yet since it has been of late published twice [9] by a person distinguished by his Colet's sermon before a convocation.

---

[9] ['The rights, powers, and privileges of an English Convocation, Stated and vindicated, in answer to a late book of Dr. Wake's &c. By Francis Atterbury, Preacher at the Rolls, and Chaplain in Ordinary to

controversial writings on this subject, I will here give a translation of all that he thought fit to publish of it [10].

[Rom. xii. 2.]
His text was, *Be ye not conformed to this world, but be ye
transformed in the renewing of your mind.* He told them,
" he came thither that he might admonish them to apply their
" thoughts wholly to the reformation of the church." He

Rights of
an English
convoca-
tion, in both
editions.
[p. 291. ed.
1701.]
goes on thus : " Most of those who are dignitaries, carry
" themselves with a haughty air, and manner; so that they 26
" seem not to be in the humble spirit of Christ's ministers, but
" in an exalted state of dominion : not observing what Christ,
" the pattern of humility, said to his disciples, whom he set,
" over his church, *It shall not be so among you ;* by which
" he taught them, that the government of the church is a
" ministry ; and that primacy in a clergyman is nothing but
" an humble servitude.

" O covetousness ! from thee come those episcopal, but
" chargeable visitations, the corruptions of courts, and those
" new inventions daily set on foot, by which the poor laity are
" devoured.   O covetousness ! the mother of all wickedness ;
" from thee springs the insolence and boldness of officials, and
" that eagerness of all ordinaries in amplifying their jurisdic-
" tion : from thee flows that mad and furious contention about
" wills, and unseasonable sequestrations ; and the superstitious
" observing of those laws that bring gain to them, while those
" are neglected that relate to the correction of manners.

" The church is disgraced by the secular employments in
" which many priests and bishops involve themselves: they
" are the servants of men more than of God ; and dare neither
" say nor do any thing, but as they think it will be acceptable
[Ibid.
p. 292.]
" and pleasant to their princes : out of this spring both igno-
" rance and blindness ; for being blinded with the darkness of
" this world, they only see earthly things.

her Majesty. The second edition,
much enlarged, 8vo. London, 1701.'
The first edition was published in
1700, without the author's name.]
[10] [It was first printed in 4to.
1511, with the following title : *Oratio habita a D. Joanne Colet, Decano
Sancti Pauli ad Clerum in Convocatione, anno* MDXI. A translation of
it was afterwards published in 8vo.

without date, entitled, *Sermon of
conforming and reforming made to
the convocation in S. Paul's church,
on Rom.* xii. 2, *an.* 1511. This was
reprinted at Cambridge in 1661.
This sermon has also been printed
in the Appendix to Knight's Life of
Colet, p. 239, ed. Oxon. 1823, followed by a reprint of the old English translation, ibid. p. 251.]

" Therefore, O ye fathers, ye priests, and all ye clergymen !
" awaken at last out of the dreams of a lethargic world ; and
" hearken to Paul, who calls upon you, *Be ye not conformed*
" *to this world.*   This reformation and restoration of the
" ecclesiastical state must begin at you, who are our fathers :
" and from you must come down to us your priests.   We look
" on you as the standards that must govern us : we desire to
" read in you, and in your lives, as in living books, how we
" ought to live : therefore if you would see the motes that are
" in our eyes, take the beams first out of your own.

" There is nothing amiss among us, for which there are not
" good remedies set out by the ancient fathers : there is no
" need of making new laws and canons, but only to observe
" those already made.   Therefore, at this your meeting, let
" the laws already made be recited.   First, those that admonish
" you fathers, not to lay hands suddenly on any : let the laws
" be recited which appoint that ecclesiastical benefices should
" be given to deserving persons, and that condemn simoniacal
" defilement.   But above all things, let those laws be recited
" that relate to you our reverend fathers, the lords bishops,
" the laws of just and canonical elections, after the invocation
" of the Holy Ghost.

" Because this is not done in our days, and bishops are
" chosen rather by the favour of men than by the will of God ;
" we have sometimes bishops who are not spiritual, but worldly
" rather than heavenly ; and who are led by the spirit of the
" world, rather than by the Spirit of Christ.   Let the laws be [Ibid.
" recited for bishops residing in their dioceses.   Last of all, p. 293.]
" let those laws be recited for frequent councils, which appoint
27 " provincial councils to be more frequently called, for the re-
" formation of the church ; for nothing has happened more
" mischievous to the church, than the not holding of councils,
" both general and provincial.

" I do therefore, with all due reverence, address myself to
" you, O fathers ! for the execution of laws must begin at you :
" if you observe the laws and transform your lives to the rules
" set by the canons, then you shine so to us, that we may see
" what we ought to do, when we have the light of excellent
" examples set us by you : we seeing you observe the laws,
" will cheerfully follow your steps.   Consider the miserable

" face and state of the church, and set about the reforming it
" with all your strength.   Do not you, O fathers, suffer this
" famous meeting to end in vain, and in doing nothing : you
" do indeed meet often ; but (by your favour suffer me to say
"what is true) what fruit has the church yet had of all your
" meetings?   Go then with that Spirit which you have prayed
" for, that, being assisted by his aid, you may contrive, esta-
" blish, and decree such things as may tend to the advantage of
" the church, to your own honour, and to the glory of God."

Colet's character.

This Colet had travelled through France and Italy ; and,
upon his return, he settled for some time at Oxford, where he
read divinity lectures without any obligation, or reward for it.
His readings brought about him all the learned and studious
persons in the university.   He read not according to the custom that prevailed universally at that time, of commenting on
Thomas Aquinas, or on Scotus, but his readings were upon

[May, 1505.]

St. Paul's Epistles.   He was brought afterwards to the deanery
of St. Paul's, where old Fitz-James, then bishop of London,
was his enemy ; but he was protected both by Warham and
by the king himself.   He did in one of his sermons reflect on
bosom-sermons, which Fitz-James took as a reflection on himself, for he read all his sermons.   He did not recommend himself at court by strains of flattery : on the contrary, he being
to preach there when the king was entering on a war,
preached on Christians fighting under the banner of Christ,
whom they ought to make their pattern in all the occasions of
quarrel that they might have, rather than imitate a Cæsar or
an Alexander.   After sermon, the king sent for him, and told
him, he thought such preaching would dishearten his military
men : but Colet explained himself so, that the king was well
satisfied with him, and said, Let every man choose what doctor

[Sept. 16.]

he pleased, Colet should be his doctor.   He died in the year
1519.

It seems this sermon was preached in the year 1513, though
it is printed as preached in the year 1511 [11] ; for the mention
that he made in it of the immunities of the clergy, and of those

[11] [There are two different editions, both without date, one in 8vo.
and one in 4to.   The title of the
8vo. edition is, *Orationes duæ ad
Clerum in Convocatione, an.* 1511.

The 4to. edition, of which there is
a copy in the Bodleian Library, is
entitled, *Oratio habita a D. Joanne
Colet, Decano Sancti Pauli ad Clerum in Convocatione, anno* MDXI.]

words, *Touch not mine anointed*, seems to relate to the opposition that the clergy made to the act that passed in parliament in the year 1512, against the immunity of the inferior
orders of the clergy. It is true, in the translation I have
given, there are no such words ; but I find them in the reflections that I made on that sermon, when I intended to have
printed it : so I took it for granted, that the sermon was not
fully printed in the book, out of which I was forced to make
my translation, the copy that I had of it being mislaid, or lost.

28 It had been but a reasonable [12] thing for that writer, either to
have printed the whole sermon, or to have told the reader that
only some passages were taken out of it, since the title given
to it would make him think it was all printed. I could not
find either the Latin sermon, or the English translation of it,
that was printed near that time ; and I cannot entirely depend
on a late impression of the English translation : yet I will add
some few passages out of it, which deserved to be published by
him that picked out a few with some particular view that it
seems he had. Before the first period printed by him, he has
these words :

" How much greediness and appetite of honour and dignity
" is seen nowadays in clergymen ! How run they (yea almost
" out of breath) from one benefice to another ; from the less
" to the greater, from the lower to the higher ! Who seeth
" not this ? And who seeing sorroweth not ? "

Before the next period, these words are to be found ;
" What other things seek we nowadays in the church but fat
" benefices, and high promotions ? And it were well if we
" minded the duty of those, when we have them. But he that
" hath many great benefices, minds not the office of any small
" one. And in these our high promotions, what other things
" do we pass upon, but only our tithes and rents ? We care

---

[12] [There was no reason to find
fault with the author of 'The rights,
&c. of an English Convocation,' as
he expressly says, p. 290. 'The
passages .... I shall take notice of
are in pieces not easy to be met
with ; and should therefore my
transcripts from thence be somewhat large, I hope they will not be
thought tedious. Moreover, it was
impossible to mistake the extracts
for the whole sermon, as they do
not occupy quite three pages, and
are detached passages quoted from
the original, with the pages from
which they are taken, marked.']

" not how vast our charge of souls be : how many or how
" great benefices we take, so they be of large value."

In the next period, these remarkable words are omitted :
" Our warfare is to pray devoutly ; to read and study scrip-
" tures diligently ; to preach the word of God sincerely ; to
" administer holy sacraments rightly ; and to offer sacrifices
" for the people."

A little before the next period, he has these words : " In
" this age we are sensible of the contradiction of lay people.
" But they are not so much contrary to us, as we are to our-
" selves.　Their *contrariness* hurteth not us so much, as the
" *contrariness* of our own evil life, which is contrary both to
" God and to Christ."

After Colet had mentioned that of laying hands suddenly on
none, he adds, " Here lies the original and spring-head of all
" our mischiefs : that the gate of ordination is too broad ; the
" entrance too wide and open.　Every man that offers himself
" is admitted every where, without putting back.　Hence it is
" that we have such a multitude of priests that have little
" learning, and less piety.　In my judgment it is not enough
" for a priest to construe a collect, to put forth a question, to
" answer a sophism ; but an honest, a pure, and a holy life, is
" much more necessary : approved manners, competent learn-
" ing in holy scriptures, some knowledge of the sacraments ;
" but chiefly above all things, the fear of God, and love of
" heavenly life."

A little after this, " Let the canons be rehearsed that com-
" mand personal residence of curates (rectors) in their churches :
" for of this many evils grow, because all offices nowadays are
" performed by vicars and parish priests ; yea, and these
" foolish, and unmeet, oftentimes wicked."

At some distance from this, but to the same purpose, he 29
adds, " You might first sow your spiritual things, and then ye
" shall reap plentifully their carnal things.　For truly that
" man is very hard and unjust who will reap where he never
" did sow, and desires to gather where he never scattered."

These passages seemed proper to be added to the former, as
setting forth the abuses and disorders that were then in this
church.　I wish I could add, that they are now quite purged

out, and appear no more among us.   Colet was a particular [Erasmi Epp. pp. 1572, 1789.] friend of Erasmus, as appears by many very kind letters that passed between them.

To this account of the sense that Colet had of the state of Sir Thomas More's thoughts of religion in his Utopia. religion at that time, I will add an acount of sir Thomas More's thoughts of religion.   Those of the church of Rome look on him as one of their glories, the champion of their cause, and their martyr.   He in this period wrote his Utopia: the first edition that I could ever see of it was at Basle in the year 1518[13]; for he wrote it in the year 1516; at which time it may be believed that he dressed up that ingenious fable according to his own notions.   He wrote that book probably before he had heard of Luther; the Wycliffites and the Lollards being the only heretics then known in England.   In that short, but extraordinary book, he gave his mind full scope, and considered mankind and religion with the freedom that became a true philosopher.   By many hints it is very easy to collect what his thoughts were of religion, of the constitutions of the church and of the clergy at that time : and therefore, though an observing reader will find these in his way, yet, having read it with great attention, when I translated it into English[14], I will lay together such passages as give clear indications of the sense he then had of those matters.

Page the 21st, when he censures the enclosing of grounds, The references are to the pages of my translation. he ranks those *holy men* the abbots among those *who thought it not enough to live at their own ease, and do no good to the*

---

[13] [De optimo reipublicæ statu, deque novâ insulâ Utopiâ libellus vere aureus, nec minus salutaris quam festivus clarissimi disertissimique viri THOMÆ MORI, inclytæ civitatis Londinensis, civis et Vice-comitis.   Basileæ, apud Joannem Frobenium Mense Novembri, an. MDXVIII.   There was however an earlier edition without date, published probably in 1517, with the title ' Libellus vere aureus nec minus salutaris quam festivus de optimo reipublicæ statu, deque nova insula Utopia, authore clarissimo viro THOMA MORO, inclytæ civitatis Londinensis cive et vice-comite, cura Petri Ægidii Antuerpiensis, et arte Theodorici Martini Alustensis Typographi almæ Louaniensium Academiæ nunc primum accuratissime editus.   Cum gratia et privilegio.' 4to.   A copy of this exists in the British Museum.]

[14] [UTOPIA ; Written in Latin by Sir Thomas More, Chancellor of England: Translated into English, London, 8vo. 1684.   It has been reprinted several times.   The name of the translator is not given, but the new edition of 1751, corrected by Thomas Williamson, ascribes it to Burnet.   A full account of all the editions of the original as well as translations, is given in Dibdin's edition, 2 vols. 8vo. Lond. 1808.]

public, but resolved to do it hurt instead of good : which
shews that he called them *holy men* in derision. This is yet
more fully set forth, page 37, where he brings in cardinal
Morton's jester's advice to send all the beggars to the Benedic-
tines to be lay-brothers, and all the female beggars to be nuns,
reckoning the friars as vagabonds that ought to be be taken
up and restrained : and the discourse that follows, for two or
three pages, gives such a ridiculous view of the want of breeding, of the folly and ill nature of the friars, that they have
taken care to strike it out of the later impressions. But as I
did find it in the impression which I translated, so I have

Collect.
Numb. 10. copied it all from the first edition, and have put in the Collection that which the inquisitors have left out. From thence it
is plain, what opinion he had of those who were the most eminent divines and the most famed preachers at that time. This
is yet plainer, page 56, in which he taxes the preachers of that
age for *corrupting the Christian doctrine, and practising
upon it : for they, observing that the world did not suit their
lives to the rules that Christ has given, have fitted his doctrine as if it had been a leaden rule to their lives, that some
way or other they might agree with one another*. And he
does not soften this severe censure, as if it had been only the 30
fault of a few, but lets it go on them all, without any discrimination or limitation.

Page 83, he taxes the great company of *idle priests,* and of
those that are called *religious persons,* that were in other
nations ; against which he tells us, in his last chapter, how
carefully the Utopians had provided :⁻ but it appears there,
what just esteem he paid to men of that character, when they
answered the dignity of their profession ; for as he contracts
the number of the priests in Utopia, page 186, so he exalts
their dignity as high as so noble a function could deserve : yet
he represents the Utopians *as allowing them to marry*, page
114. And, page 130, he exalts *a solid virtue much above all
rigorous severities*, which were the most admired expressions
of piety and devotion in that age. He gives a perfect scheme
of religious men, so much beyond the monastic orders, that it
shews he was no admirer of them.

Page 152, he commends the Europeans for " observing their
" leagues and treaties so religiously ; and ascribes that to the

" good examples that popes set other princes, and to the
" severity with which they prosecuted such as were per-
." fidious." This looks like respect ; but he means it all ironi-
cally : for he who had seen the reigns of pope Alexander the
Sixth, and Julius the Second, the two falsest and most perfidious persons of the age, could not say this but in the way of
satire : so that he secretly accuses both popes and princes for
violating their faith, to which they were induced by dispensations from Rome. Page 192, his *putting images out of the
churches of the Utopians*, gives no obscure hint of his opinion
in that matter. The opinion, page 175, that he proposes,
doubtfully indeed, but yet favourably, of the first converts to
Christianity in Utopia, who (there being no priests among
those who instructed them) were inclined to choose priests that
should officiate among them, since they could not have any
that were regularly ordained ; adding, that they seemed resolved to do it : this shews that in cases of necessity he had a
largeness of thought, far from being engaged blindfold into
the humours or interests of the priests of that time ; to whom
this must have appeared one of the most dangerous of all
heresies.

And whereas persecution and cruelty seem to be the indeli-
ble characters of popery ; he, as he gives us the character
of the religion of the Utopians, *that they offered not divine
honours to any but to God alone*, page 173 ; so, page 177, he
makes it one of the maxims of the Utopians, *that no man
ought to be punished for his religion :* the utmost severity
practised among them being banishment, and that not for dis-
paraging their religion, but for inflaming the people to sedition ; a law being made among them, that *every man might
be of what religion he pleased*, page 191. And though there
were many different forms of religion among them, yet they all
agreed in the main point of " worshipping the Divine Essence ;
" so that there was nothing in their temples, in which the
" several persuasions among them might not agree."

" The several sects performed the rites that were peculiar
" to them in their private houses ; nor was there any thing in
" the public worship that contradicted the particular ways of
31 " the several sects :" by all which he carried, not only tolera-
tion, but even comprehension, farther than the most moderate

of our divines have ever pretended to do.   It is true, he represents all this in a fable of his Utopians : but this was a scene
dressed up by himself, in which he was fully at liberty to frame
every thing at pleasure : so here we find in this a scheme of
some of the most essential parts of the reformation,   " He
" proposes no subjection of their priests to any head ; he
" makes them to be chosen by the people, and consecrated by
" the college of priests ; and he gives them no other authority
" but that of excluding men that were desperately wicked
" from joining in their worship, which was short and simple :
" and though every man was suffered to bring over others to
" his persuasion, yet he was obliged to do it by amicable and
" modest ways, and not to mix with these either reproaches or
" violence ; such as did otherwise were to be condemned to
" banishment or slavery."

These were his first and coolest thoughts ; and probably, if
he had died at that time, he would have been reckoned among
those, who, though they lived in the communion of the church
of Rome, yet saw what were the errors and corruptions of that
body, and only wanted fit opportunities of declaring themselves
more openly for a reformation.   These things were not writ
by him in the heat of youth ; he was then thirty-four years of
age, and was at that time employed, together with Tunstall, in
settling some matters of state with (the then prince) Charles ;
so that he was far advanced at that time, and knew the world
well.   It is not easy to account for the great change that we
find afterwards he was wrought up to : he not only set himself
to oppose the reformation in many treatises, that, put together,
make a great volume ; but, when he was raised up to the chief
post in the ministry, he became a persecutor even to blood ;
and defiled those hands, which were never polluted with bribes,
by acting in his own person some of those cruelties, to which
he was, no doubt, pushed on by the bloody clergy of that age
and church.

He was not governed by interest ; nor did he aspire so to
preferment, as to stick at nothing that might contribute to
raise him ; nor was he subject to the vanities of popularity.
The integrity of his whole life, and the severity of his morals,
cover him from all these suspicions.   If he had been formerly
corrupted by a superstitious education, it had been no extra-

ordinary thing to see so good a man grow to be misled by the
force of prejudice. But how a man who had emancipated
himself, and had got into a scheme of free thoughts, could be
so entirely changed, cannot be easily apprehended; nor how
he came to muffle up his understanding, and deliver himself up
as a property to the blind and enraged fury of the priests. It
cannot indeed be accounted for, but by charging it on the in-
toxicating charms of that religion, that can darken the clearest
understandings, and corrupt the best natures: and since they
wrought this effect on sir Thomas More, I cannot but conclude,
that *if these things were done in the green tree, what shall be
done in the dry.*

His friend Tunstall was made bishop of London by the Reg.Tunst.
pope's provision; but it was upon the king's recommendation fol. 1.
[17 Feb.
signified by Hannibal, then his ambassador at Rome. Tunstall 1522.]
32 was sent ambassador to Spain, when Francis was a prisoner
there. That king grew, as may be easily believed, impatient
to be so long detained in prison: and that began to have such
effects on his health, that the emperor, fearing it might end in
his death, which would both lose the benefit he had from
having him in his hands, and lay a heavy load on him through
all Europe, was induced to hearken to a treaty, which he pretended he concluded chiefly in consideration of the king's mediation. The treaty was made at Madrid, much to the em- [Jan. 14,
peror's advantage: but because he would not trust to the faith 1526.
Rymer,xiv.
of the treaty, Francis was obliged to bring his two sons as p. 308.]
hostages for the observance of it. So he had his liberty upon
that exchange. Soon after, he came back to France, and [Nov. 29,
then the pope sent him an absolution in full form from the 1529.]
faith and obligation of the treaty. It seems his conscience
reproached him for breaking so solemn an engagement, but
that was healed by the dispensation from Rome: of which the
original was sent over to the king; perhaps only to be showed
the king, who upon that kept it still in his secret treasure;
where Rymer found it. The reason insinuated in it is, the Rymer.
king's being bound by it to alienate some dominions that be- [xiv. p.
352.]
longed to the crown of France. For he had not yet learned a
secret, discovered, or at least practised since that time, of
princes declaring themselves free from the obligations of their
treaties, and departing from them at their pleasure.

THE HISTORY

OF

THE REFORMATION

OF

THE CHURCH OF ENGLAND.

PART III.—BOOK II.

---

*Of matters that happened during the time comprehended in
the Second Book of the History of the Reformation.*

1525.   I WILL repeat nothing set forth in my former work, but
suppose that my reader remembers how Charles the Fifth had
sworn to marry the king's daughter, when she should be of
age, under pain of excommunication, and the forfeiture of one
hundred thousand pounds[1] : yet when his match with Portugal
was thought more for the interests of the crown, he sent over
to the king, and desired a discharge of that promise. It has
been said, and printed by one who lived in the time, and out of
him by the lord Herbert, that objections were made to this in
Spain, on the account of the doubtfulness of her mother's
marriage[2]. From such authors I took this too easily; but in
a collection of original instructions[3] I have seen that matter in
a truer light.

Lee, afterwards archbishop of York, was sent ambassador to
Spain, to solicit the setting Francis at liberty ; and, in reckon-

*Hall. [p.
711,
Herbert,
p. 171.]*

*Among the
manu-
scripts of
the bishop
of Ely.*

---

[1] [See part i. p. 5.]
[2] [See part i. p. 39.]
[3] [No. 234 in the printed catalogue (Oxon. 1697. folio) of bishop
Moore's books, now E e iv. 27. Art

2 a—19 in the Catalogue of MSS.
in the Public Library at Cambridge,
pp. 137—142. (Cambridge, 1857,
8vo.)]

ing up the king's merits on the emperor, his instructions men- Many am
bassadors
in Spain.
tion, " the king's late discharge of the emperor's obligation to
" marry his dearest daughter, the princess Mary; whom,
" though his grace could have found in his heart to have be-
" stowed upon the emperor, before any prince living, yet for
" the more security of his succession, the furtherance of his
" other affairs, and to do unto him a gratuity, his grace hath
" liberally, benevolently, and kindly condescended unto it[4]."
There are other letters of the 12th of August[5], but the year is
not added, which set forth the emperor's earnest desire to be
with all possible diligence discharged of his obligation to marry
the princess.   At first the king thought fit to delay the granting it till a general peace was fully concluded, since it had been
agreed to by the treaty at Windsor; but soon after, a discharge in full form under the great seal was sent over by an
express to Spain: but from some hints in other papers[6], it
seems there were secret orders not to deliver it; and king
Henry continued to claim the money due upon the forfeiture,
as a debt still owing him.   The peace was then treated, chiefly

[4] [This passage is on the fifth page
of Instructions, and is as follows :
" In whiche matier they shal ex-
tende the glad and towarde mynde,
that the kingis highnes is of, alwaies
to do unto themperour honour and
pleasure, and amongis othre in his
late discharge of the mariage with
his derest doughter the princesse,
whiche though his grace coude
have founde in his hert to have
bestowed her upon themperour bi-
fore any prince lyving, yet for the
more suretie of his succession, the
furtherance of his other affaires, and
to do unto him gratuite, his grace
hathe liberally, benevolently, and
kindely condescended unto."

[5] [This date is a mistake for Sept.
21, 1525.   It is a copy of a letter,
which was given to Lee, together
with his Instructions, addressed by
the king to Tunstall and Sampson.
At the commencement of the letter
the king acknowledges the receipt
of letters from the ambassadors by
two messengers ' who bothe togider

arrived here the 12th day of this
monethe,' i. e. September.   The original of this letter, the copy of which
is without date, was dated Ampthill
21st Sept. as appears from the reply printed in State Papers, Part
V. N⁰. 127, which is dated from
Toledo, Dec. 2.   In it the king
speaks of five points in the ambassador's letters which require an
answer.   Of these the third is :
' Thirdly in themperours con-
tynual desire to be discharged of
the said mariage with our derest
doughter the princesse, not abiding
the conclusion of the peax there.']

[6] [This also is a mistake.   The
next paper in the Collection is a
letter from the king to Lee, dated
17 July, and belongs to 1526, long
after the emperor had been discharged from the marriage.   Questions of the emperor's obligations
in money were going on for a long
time after the question of the marriage was settled.]

with a view to resist the Turk, and to repress heresy, that was then much spread both through Germany and Poland[7].

Another original letter was writ after Francis was at liberty, "setting forth that the nobles and courts in France would not "confirm the treaty that Francis had signed to obtain his "liberty; and therefore earnest persuasions were to be used "to prevail with the emperor to restore the hostages, and to 34 "come into reasonable terms, to maintain the peace, and to "call his army out of Italy." By these it appears, that the league against the emperor was then made, of which the king was declared the protector; but the king had not then accepted of that title. He ordered his ambassadors to propose a million of crowns for redeeming the hostages, to be paid at different times; yet they were forbid to own to the emperor, that if the offices, in which the king interposed, were not effectual, he would enter into the league[8].

Wolsey's letter to them.

There are in that collection some of Wolsey's letters[9]; by one of the 17th of July[10] he claims his pensions of 7,500 ducats upon the bishoprics of Palentia and Toledo; besides 9000 crowns a year, in recompense for his parting with the bishopric of Tournay, and the abbey of St. Martin's there; for which there was an arrear of four years due. On the 29th of September[11] he wrote over a severe charge to be laid before the

---

[7] [This is quoted from the king's letter to Lee, of July 17, 1526, alluded to in the last note. The original is as follows: — 'We doubt not, but that our mynde, studies and zeale to the furtherance of quiete, tranquillite and repose in Christendome, the resistence of the malice of the turkis enemyes unto Cristis religion .... and also unto the repressing of the most pernicious and dampnable heresies as wel of martyn luther as of other his fautours and adherentis nowe in late daies suscitate and spred both thorough Germany and also in the Realme of Pologne.']

[8] [This is not from another original letter as stated in the text, but from the same letter dated July 17, from Oking. It consists of two parts, the first more open and the

second more private. A French translation of the first part was enclosed, which might be shewn to the emperor and his council in case Lee's French or Latin should fail in readiness or clearness. The 'million of crowns' the ambassadors were to suggest if asked, but not voluntarily to propose.]

[9] [These are the next letters in the Collection, and are all addressed to Lee, one from the More, Sept. 29, and the two others from Westminster, October 21. All belong to the year 1526.]

[10] [This is a mistaken date, which belongs to the previous letter of Henry to Lee. The true date is Sept. 29.]

[11] [This also is a mistaken date belonging to the preceding letter. The true date is Oct. 21, 1526.]

emperor for the sack of Rome, the indignities put on the person of the pope, the spoiling the church of St. Peter, and other churches, and the ignominious treating the ornaments of them : all the blame was cast on the cardinal Colonna, and Hugo de Moncada, they being persuaded that it was done without the emperor's knowledge or order. He proposes the king to be mediator, as a thing agreed on by all sides : he uses in this that bold way of joining himself with the king, very often saying, *the king and I :* and on the 20th of October [12] he presses with great earnestness the mediating a peace between France and the emperor ; in all which, nothing appears either partial or revengeful against the emperor. The true interest of England seems to be pursued in that whole negotiation.

There was then in the emperor's court a very full embassy from England : for in one or other of these letters mention is made of the bishops of London, Worcester, and of Bath ; of Dr. Lee and sir Francis Bryan [13]. But since the dismal fate of Rome and of pope Clement is mentioned in these letters, I must now change the scene.

Pope Clement, as soon as he could after his imprisonment, wrote over to Wolsey an account of the miserable state he was in, which he sent over by sir Gregory Cassali, who saw it all, and so could give a full account of it. " The pope's only " comfort and hope was in Wolsey's credit with the king, and " in the king's own piety towards the church and himself, now " so sadly oppressed, that he had no other hope but in the " protection he expected from him." There were many other letters written by the cardinals, setting forth the miseries they were in, and that in the most doleful strains possible ; all their eyes being then towards the king, as the person on whose protection they chiefly depended. Upon this, Wolsey went over to France in a most splendid manner, with a prodigious and magnificent train, reckoned to consist of a thousand persons ; and he had the most unusual honours done him, that the court of

(margin:) Collect. Numb. 11.

(margin:) The sack of Rome.

---

[12] [The date of this letter is Oct. 21.]

[13] [This passage is full of mistakes. It is not sir Francis Bryan, but sir Francis Poyntz. Clerk, bishop of Bath, was not in Spain at all, but at Paris, and Poyntz was ordered to call upon him at Paris for information. The bishop of London and Sampson returned in January, 1526. The former was succeeded by Ghinucci, bishop of Worcester, in Jan. 1527, and Lee went out in the autumn of 1527, to take the place of Sampson.]

France could invent, to flatter his vanity. , He was to conclude
a treaty with Francis for setting the pope at liberty, and to
determine the alternative of the marriage of the princess Mary,
either to the king of France, or to the duke of Orleans, his 35
second son, and to lay a scheme for a general peace. He
came to Compiegne in the end of September[3], and from thence

Sept. 16.
he wrote the first motion that was made about the divorce to
the pope; for the first letter that I found relating to that
matter begins with mentioning that which he wrote from Compiegne. M. Le Grand told me, he had seen that despatch, but
he has not printed it.

The cardi-
nals write
to the pope
for a full
deputation.
Le Grand,
tom. iii.
numb. 2.
[p. 4.]
[Ibid. p. 7.]

[Ibid. p. 9.]

From that place Wolsey, with four cardinals, wrote to the
pope, " setting forth the sense that they had of the calamity
" that he was in, and their zeal for his service, in which they
" hoped for good success: yet fearing lest the emperor should
" take occasion from his imprisonment to seize on the territories
" of the church, and to force both him to confirm it, and the
" cardinals now imprisoned with him to ratify it, which they
" hoped neither he nor they would do; yet, if human infirmity
" should so far prevail, they protested against all such aliena-
" tions: they also declare, that if he should die, they would
" proceed to a new election, and have no regard to any election,
" to which the imprisoned cardinals might be forced. In con-
" clusion, they do earnestly pray, that the pope would grant
" them a full deputation of his authority: in the use of which
" they promise all zeal and fidelity; and that they would invite
" all the other cardinals that were at liberty to come and con-

[Ibid. p.
13.]

Collect.
Numb. 12.

" cur with them." This was signed by Wolsey, and by the
cardinals of Bourbon, Salviati, Lorraine, and cardinal Prat.
Wolsey wrote to the king[4], expressing the concern he had for
him, with relation to his great and secret affair; it seems, expecting a general meeting of cardinals that was to be called
together in France, which he reckoned would concur to the
process that he intended to make: but apprehending that the
queen might decline his jurisdiction, he would use all his en-

---

[3] [The author must mean August.
Wolsey was at Calais July 16th, at
Abbeville July 24th, at Amiens
during nearly the whole of August.
He was at Compiegne Sept. 5, where
he received through Knight, Sept.
10, his letters of recall. He wrote
to the king, stating that he left

Compiegne on Sept. 17.]
[4] [This letter was written from
Abbeville July 29th, and is printed
in State Papers, vol. i. p. 230. The
copy from which the author printed
Number 12 of the Collection is only
a draft which was considerably altered before the letter was sent.]

deavours to bring the king of France to agree to the emperor's
demands as far as was reasonable; hoping the emperor would
abate somewhat, in consideration of the king's mediation : but
if that did not succeed, so that the pope was still kept a prisoner, then the cardinals must be brought to meet at Avignon,
and thither he intended to go, and to spare no trouble or
charge in doing the king service. When he was at Avignon,
he should be within a hundred miles of Perpignan; and he
would try to bring the emperor and the French king's mother
thither, if the king approved of it, to treat for the pope's deliverance, and for a general peace. This is the substance of
the minute of a letter writ in the cardinal's hand.

The king at this time intended to send Knight, then secre- *Knight sent to Rome.*
tary of state, to Rome, in point of form to condole with the
pope, and to prevent any application that the queen might
make by the emperor's means in his great matter : so he ap-
pointed the cardinal to give him such commissions and instruc- *Collect. Numb. 13.*
tions as should seem requisite, with all diligence ; and he
pressed the cardinal's return home, with great acknowledgments of the services he had done him. By this letter it
appears, that the queen then understood somewhat of the
king's uneasiness in his marriage. The king of France sent
from Compiegne a great deputation, at the head of which
Montmorency, then the great master, was put to take the
36 king's oath confirming the treaties that Wolsey had made in *25th Sept.*
his name; one in the commission was Bellay, then bishop of
Bayonne, afterwards of Paris, and cardinal.

When that was done, the king's matter, that had been *Pace wrote to the king of his di- vorce.*
hitherto more secretly managed, began to break out. M. Le
Grand had published a letter that Pace wrote to the king, as *Le Grand, Tom. iii. numb. 1.*
he says, in the year 1526; but no date is added to the letter.
The substance of it is, " that the letter and book, which was
" brought to the king the day before, was writ by him; but
" by the advice and help of doctor Wakefield, who approved it, *[p. 2.]*
" and was ready to defend every thing in it, either in a verbal
" disputation, or in writing. The king had told him, that
" some of his learned counsellors had written to him, that
" Deuteronomy abrogated Leviticus : but that was certainly
" false; for the title of that book in Hebrew was the two first
" words of it : it is a compend and recapitulation of the Mo-
" saical law; and that was all that was imported by the word

" Deuteronomy. He tells the king, that, after he left him,
" Wakefield prayed him to let him know, if the king desired
" to know the truth in that matter, whether it stood for him
" or against him. To whom Pace answered, that the king
" desired nothing but what became a noble and a virtuous
" prince; so he would do him a most acceptable thing, if he
[p. 3.] " would set the plain truth before him. After that, Wakefield
" said, he would not meddle in the matter, unless he were
" commanded by the king to do it; but that, when he received
" his commands, he would set forth such things both for and
" against him, that no other person in his kingdom could do
" the like." The letter is dated from Sion, but I have reason
to believe it was written in the year 1527; for this Wakefield
(who seems to have been the first person of this nation that
was learned in the oriental tongues, not only in the Hebrew,
the Chaldaic, and the Syriac, but in the Arabic) wrote a book
for the divorce. He was at first against it, before he knew
that prince Arthur's marriage with queen Catharine was consummated: but when he understood what grounds there were
to believe that was done, he changed his mind, and wrote a
book on the subject. And in his own book, he with his own
hand inserts the copy of his letter to king Henry, dated from
Sion 1527; which it seems was written at the same time that
Pace wrote his: for these are his words, (as the author of
[Wood, *Athenæ Oxonienses* relates, who says he saw it,) *He will defend*
Athenæ *his cause or question in all the universities of Christendom:*
Oxoni- but adds, " that if the people should know that he, who began
enses, vol.
i. col. 46. " to defend the queen's cause, not knowing that she was car-
sub an " nally known of prince Arthur, his brother, should now write
1537.] " against it, surely he should be stoned of them to death; or
" else have such a slander and obloquy raised upon him, that
" he would die a thousand times rather than suffer it."

He was prevailed on to print his book in Latin, with an
Hebrew title[5]; in which he undertook to prove, that the marrying the brother's wife, she being carnally known of him, was
contrary to the decrees of holy church, utterly unlawful, and
forbidden both by the law of nature and the law of God, the

---

[5] [Wakfeldus (Robertus)] Kotser   illicitum omnino, inhibitum inter-
Codicis [quo præter ecclesiæ sacro-   dictumque esse. 4to. London.—exc.
sanctæ decretum, probatur conju-   Tho. Berthelet, 1528.]
gium cum fratriâ carnaliter cognitâ

laws of the gospel, and the customs of the catholic and orthodox church.

37   It appears from the letters writ in answer to those that
Knight carried to Rome, that the pope granted all that was
desired.   This was never well understood till Mr. Rymer, in
his diligent search, found the first original bull[6], with the seal
in lead hanging to it : he has printed it in his 14th volume,
p. 237. and therefore I shall only give a short abstract of it.
It .is directed to cardinal Wolsey, and bears date the ides of
April, on the 13th day, in the year 1528.   " It empowers
" him, together with the archbishop of Canterbury, or any
" other English bishop, to hear, examine, pronounce and de-
" clare concerning the validity of the marriage of king Henry
" and queen Catharine, and of the efficacy and validity of all
" apostolical dispensations in that matter, and to declare the
" marriage just and lawful, or unjust and unlawful, and to give
" a plenary sentence upon the whole matter ; with license to
" the parties to marry again, and to admit no appeal from
" them.   For which end he creates Wolsey his vicegerent, to
" do in the premises all that he himself could do, with power
" to declare the issue of the first as well as of any subsequent
" marriage legitimate : all concludes with a *non obstante* to all
" general councils and apostolical constitutions."

This rare discovery was to us all a great surprise, as soon
as it was known : but it does not yet appear how it came about
that no use was ever made of it.   I am not lawyer enough to
discover, whether it was that so full a deputation was thought
null of itself, since by this the pope determined nothing, but
left all to Wolsey ; or whether Wolsey, having no mind to
carry the load of the judgment on himself, made the king
apprehend that it would bring a disreputation on his cause,
if none but his own subjects judged it ; or whether it was
that Wolsey would not act in conjunction with Warham, or
any under the degree of a cardinal.   I leave the reasons of
their not making use of the bull, as a secret, as great as the
bull itself was, till it was found out by Rymer.   Another bull

Side notes:
1528.
A bull sent to Wolsey to judge the marriage. [Rymer, tom. xiv. p. 237.]

[Ibid. p. 238.]

It was not made use of.

---

[6] [This document is said to be *Ex origine*, and is headed in Rymer thus, *Bulla Commissionis ad cognoscendum in causa Matrimoniali inter Regem et Catherinam Reginam.* Registrata in Camera Apostolica de Mandato Serenissimi Domini nostri Papæ.   B. Motta.]

was after that desired and obtained, which bears date the 8th of

Rymer.
[tom. xiv.
p. 295.]

June (*sexto idus*) from Viterbo. This I take from the license granted under the great seal to the legates to execute the commission of that date : but it seems they did not think they had the pope fast enough tied by this ; and therefore they obtained from him, on the 23rd of July following, a solemn promise, called in their letters *pollicitatio,* by which he promised, in *the word of a pope,* that he would never, neither at any person's desire, nor of his own motion, inhibit or revoke the commission he had granted to the legates to judge the matter of the king's marriage. This I did not publish in my

[Herbert,
p. 249.]

former work, because the lord Herbert had published it : but since that history is like to be confined to our own nation, and this may probably go further, I put it in the Collection ; and the rather, because the lord Herbert, taking it from a copy, as I do, seems in some doubt concerning it : but probably he had not seen the letter that Wolsey wrote to Gardiner, in which he mentions the pollicitation that he had in his hands, with

Collect.
Numb. 15.

several other letters that mention it very frequently. The copy that I publish was taken from a transcript attested by a notary, which is the reason of the oddness of the subscription.

The bishops think the king's scruples reasonable.

In the meantime Warham called such bishops as were in town to him, and proposed to them the king's scruples ; which being weighed by them, a writing was drawn up to this purpose : that, having heard the grounds of the king's scruples

Rymer.
[tom. xiv.
p. 301.]

relating to his marriage, they all made this answer, that the causes which gave the king the present agitation and disturbance of conscience were great and weighty ; and that it did seem necessary to them all for him to consult the judgment of

1529.

their holy father the pope in that matter. This was signed by Warham, Tunstall, Fisher, and the bishops of Carlisle, Ely, St. Asaph, Lincoln, and Bath, on the 1st of July, 1529. And I incline to think, that this was the paper of which Cavendish,

Life of
Wolsey.
[Vol. i.
p. 157.]

whom I followed too implicitly in my former work[7], gave a wrong account, as brought out when the legates were sitting on the king's cause. There is no reason to doubt of Fisher's signing this : and Cavendish, who wrote upon memory almost thirty years after, might be mistaken in the story ; for the false account that he gives of the battle of Pavia shews how

[7] [See part i. p. 73.]

little he is to be depended on. At this time the pope in a letter to Wolsey offered to go in person to Spain, or to any place where an interview should be agreed on, to mediate a general peace. This Wolsey wrote over to the king's ambassadors at Rome on the 19th of December: and in the same letter he orders them to offer the guard to the pope in the name of the two kings; and adds, that Turenne should command that part of it which was to have their pay sent from France, and sir Gregory Cassali that which the king was to pay. Cotton lib.. Vitell. B. 11.[1]

In prosecuting the history of the divorce, I must add a great deal out of some French authors. Bellay, the Sieur de Langey, has writ memoirs of that time with great judgment, and very sincerely. I find also many letters relating to those transactions both in the *Mélanges Historiques*, and in Le Grand's third tome. These I shall follow in the series in which things were transacted, which will be found to give no small confirmation, as well as large additions, to what I formerly published in my History. The first of these was much employed in embassies, and was well informed of the affairs of England, both his brothers being at different times employed to negotiate affairs in that court. John in particular, then bishop of Bayonne, afterwards of Paris, and cardinal Le Grand, as lord Herbert had done before, has given the relation of the answer that the emperor gave by word of mouth, and afterwards in writing, to Clarencieux, when he came with a French king at arms to denounce war in the name of the two kings to the emperor. Page 38. [Herbert, p. 217.]

Demand was made of great debts that the emperor owed the king; among these, the sum forfeited for his not marrying the princess Mary is one. To that the emperor answered, that, before he was married, he required the king to send her to him, which was not done: and by letters that he intercepted, he saw that the king was treating a marriage for her with the king of Scoland long before the emperor was married. It was further said to that herald, that a report went current, that the king designed a divorce, and upon that to marry another wife. "The emperor said, he had in his hands ample 39 " dispensations for the marriage : nor could the king go on in " that design without striking at the pope's authority ; which Jan. 27, 1528. The emperor's answer to the king by Clarencieux. [Herbert, p. 220.]

" would give great scandal, and occasion much disturbance,
" and give the emperor just cause of war.   This would shew
" what faith, what religion, what conscience, and what honour
" the king had before his eyes.   He had offered his daughter
" to him in marriage, and was now going to get her declared
" a *bastard* : he ascribed all this to the ill offices done by the
" cardinal of York, who was pushed on by his ambition and
" avarice, because he would not order his army in Italy to
" force the electing him to the popedom ; which, he said, both
" the king and the cardinal desired of him in letters that they
" wrote to him on that occasion : and, because he had not in
" that satisfied his pride, he had boasted that he would so
" embroil the emperor's affairs, though England should be
" ruined by it, that he should repent his using him so."   This
seems to be much aggravated ; for it may be easily supposed,
that the king and Wolsey might, in the letters that they wrote
to the emperor at the last conclave, desire him to order his
troops to draw near Rome to keep all quiet, till, if he was
chosen, he might get thither.   Yet it is not probable that they
could desire so barefaced a thing as the emperor here fastened
on them.   He in that, perhaps, was no truer, than when he
said he had in his hands ample dispensations for the king's
marriage ; though it appears these were forged : for the date
of the breve being the same with the bull, both bearing date

[Rymer,
xiv. pp.
294, 353.]
the 26th of December 1503, it was plainly false.   For Rymer
has printed one attestation from Rome, that the year in the
breves begins on Christmas-day : so, if had been a true piece,
it must have had the date 1504.   He has likewise published
[Ibid.
p. 296.]
an authentic attestation, signed by the cardinal chamberlain,
that, in the register of the breves, there was none to be found
relating to the king's dispensation for his marriage, but one
dated the 6th of July 1504, and another the 22nd of February
1505.

Le Grand,
p. 64.
[No. 9.]
Jan. 2,
1528.
A proposi-
tion to de-
pose the
emperor.
The bishop of Bayonne made a bold proposition to Wolsey :
he thought it might be a proper method to engage the pope
to depose the emperor for such enormous felony as he had
committed against him, which would secure that see from all
such attempts for the future.   The cardinal, after a little reflection on it, swore to him that he would pursue that thought ;
but, it seems, it was let fall.

When Gardiner and Fox were sent to Rome, they passed through France, with letters from Wolsey to Montmorency for his assisting them.   It seems the people were expressing their uneasiness upon these steps made in order to the divorce, of which the bishop of Bayonne wrote to the court of France; which was upon his letters so talked of at Paris, that Wolsey reprimanded him for it; though in his own excuse he writes, that the bishop of Bath had said it more openly than he had written it.   *Le Grand, p. 102. [No. 14.] May 24.*

On the 8th of June, it seems, matters went not well at Rome; for Wolsey complained to the bishop of Bayonne of the pope, for not doing them justice, who had served him so well, both before his advancement, and ever since.   They also appre-
40 hended, that Campeggio, then named to come over as legate, who was subject to the gout, would by that pretence manage matters so as to keep them long in suspense.   *[Ibid. p. 136.]*

At that time the sweating-sickness raged so, that the court was in dread of it.   It broke out in the legate's house; some died of it: he upon that stole away privately, without giving notice whither he went.   The king made his last will, and received all the sacraments: he confessed himself every day, and received the sacrament every holyday.   The queen did the same; and so did Wolsey.   *Ibid. p. 144. June 30.*   *[Ibid. p. 152.]*

In another letter, without date, Bayonne gives an account of a free conference he had with Wolsey; who told him, " he " had done many things against the opinion of all England; " upon which many took occasion to reproach him, as being " wholly French : so he must proceed warily.   The French " would feel their loss, if his credit were lessened ; therefore " it was necessary that the bishop should make the king and " his council here apprehend, that this alliance was not to their " prejudice.   The king had of late (as Bayonne had from " good hands) said some terrible words to the cardinal, appre- " hending that he was cold in his matter.   Wolsey said to " him, that if God gave him the grace once to see the hatred " of the two nations extinguished, and a firm friendship settled " between the two kings, and that he could get the laws and " customs of the nation a little changed, the succession se- " cured, and, upon the king's second marriage, an heir male " born, he would immediately retire, and serve God all the   *[Aug. 20. Ibid. p. 157.]*   *[p. 158.]*   *[p. 164.]*   *[p. 165.]*

" rest of his life." Here were many things to be done before his retirement : yet the bishop did believe he indeed intended, upon the first good occasion, to retire from all affairs; for he could not but see, that his credit must lessen upon the king's

[p. 166.]

second marriage. He was also making haste to furnish his episcopal palaces, and to finish his colleges; and he seemed to him to prepare for a storm. Gardiner was at this time advanc-

Part ii.
Coll. Rec.
Numb. 26.
p. 297.

ing the king's business all that was possible at Rome. I did, in my second volume, publish among the Records a letter of his that was written in April after his coming to Rome. The substance of it is, " He had acquainted the pope with the " secret message that the princes of Germany had sent the " king, to see if that would work on his fears; for he says, the " pope was a man of such a nature, that he is never resolved " in any thing, but as he is compelled by some violent affec- " tion. He assures the king, the pope will do nothing that " may offend the emperor: nor was it reasonable for him to " do it, except he would remove his see to some other place ; " for while he was at Rome he was in the emperor's power. " By his words and manner, the pope seemed to favour the " king; but he was confident he would do nothing. He be- " lieved, if the cause were determined by the legates, they at " Rome would be glad of it: and if the emperor should begin " a suit against that, they would serve him as they now did " the king, and drive off the time by delays: so he put the " king on getting Campeggio to judge for him, which should " be a short work; and he assures him, nothing was to be ex- " pected from Rome but delays. They had put the king's 41 " cause, if it should be brought to Rome, in the hands of two " advocates; (the same that pleaded for the king afterwards " in the excusatory plea.) The pope would hear no disputa- " tion about his power of dispensing : but, so the pope did not " decide upon that ground, he would not care whether the " king's cause were decided upon it or not; and he believed " the pope was resolved to meddle no more in the king's mat- " ter, but to leave it with the legates. He desired his letter " might not be shewed to either of the legates. With that " bearer he sent over the pope's promise, in which he had got " some words to be put, that he thought favoured the king's " cause as much, and more, than if the decretal commission,

" that was in Campeggio's hands, should be shewed; so he
" thought the pope ought to be no more moved in that matter."
The words he mentions are, *Cum nos justitiam ejus causæ
perpendentes; We considering the justice of his cause.* These
are in the promise, or pollicitation, which I do now publish[8]; [Collect.
and they prove this to be a true copy, since we have an au- Numb. 15.]
thentic proof of the very words that seemed the greatest
ground to doubt of its truth.

About a fortnight after this, Gardiner wrote another letter
to the king, which will be found in the Collection. A motion Collect.
was then made at Rome for recalling the powers sent to Numb. 14.
the legates; but he did not think it was made in earnest,
but only to stop the ambassadors in their other suits. The
pope told them, that the emperor had advertised him that the
queen would do nothing in the matter but as the king should
command her; therefore he would look after the cause the
more earnestly. This the pope seemed to tell them, that they
should not inquire who was the queen's proctor. The ambassadors were amazed to see, by Campeggio's letters that
were shewed them, that neither he nor Campanus had made
any promise in the pope's name to the king, but only in general terms; considering that they had mentioned the *plenitude
of the pope's power*, which they trusted he would use in that
cause. He writes, he did not succeed in that which he was
ordered to move, which he did indeed apprehend could not be
obtained : he lays the blame on the pope, or some other, but it
became not him to fasten that on any, (perhaps this pointed at
Wolsey;) the rest relates to the bulls, probably demanded by
the cardinal for his colleges : this was dated the 4th of May.
He had a letter writ to him a month before this by Anne
Boleyn, in which she expresses a great sense of the service he
was doing her : it seems by it, that at his first coming to Rome
he had great hopes of success; but these were then much
abated.

At this time king Henry was writing every day letters full of King Hen-
passion to that lady. Some way or other, they fell into the to Anne
hands of those who carried them to Rome, where they lie in the Boleyn.
library of the Vatican. I saw them there, and knew king Henry's

---

[8] [This which should have been Number 14 in the Collection has been
placed after Gardiner's Letter, and been numbered 15.]

hand too well, not to be convinced at first sight that they were
writ by him.   I did not think it fit for me to copy them out,
but I prevailed with my worthy friend Dr. Fall to do it for me.
They were very ill writ, the hand is scarce legible, and the
French seems faulty : but, since our travellers are encouraged
to look on them, I gave a copy of them to the printer, to be 42
printed apart ; for I could not think it proper to put them in
the Collection.   Objections lay in my way, even as to this :
they were trifling letters ; some insinuations are not very
decent, and little wit occurred in them to season them in any
sort ; yet they carry the characters of an honourable love,
directed all to marriage ; and they evidently shew that there
was nothing amiss, as to the main point, in their commerce.
So, since those at Rome make so ill an use of them, as to
pretend that they are full of defilement, and in derision call
them the true original of our reformation, all these considerations prevailed on me to suffer them to be printed apart[9] ; for
I did not think it fitting that such stuff should be mixed with
graver matters.   So I ordered them to be printed exactly
from the copy ; and to take no other care about them, but to
give them as I had them.   But since I mention that lady, I
must add some passages out of a relation made by a son of sir
Thomas Wiat's, of his father's concerns, marked on the back
by a hand very like lord Burghley's.   He shews how false that
story must be, of his father's pretending to king Henry that
he had corrupted her.   He was then esquire of the body,
and did continue still about his person in that post, except
when he was employed in embassies abroad.   This shews how
incredible that fiction of Sanders was ; since, if he had pretended to make any such discovery, he must have fallen either
under the king's jealousy, or the queen's power ; or, to avoid
both, he would have withdrawn himself : and probably he
would have been afterwards set up a witness to disgrace her at
her trial.   That relation adds, that she was secretly tried in

Ex M. V.
Gul. Petyt.

---

[9] ['Love Letters from King Henry
the VIIIth to Anne Boleyn : and
two Letters from Anne Boleyn to
Cardinal Wolsey, with her last to
Henry the eighth,' 1714, 8vo. They
have been reprinted many times,
e. g. by Hearne, in the Harleian
Miscellany, and the Pamphleteer,
and in Tierney's edition of Dod's
Church History, and at Paris 1826
and 1835, under the title, ' Lettres
de Henri VIII a Anne Boleyn avec
la traduction, précedées d'une notice
historique sur Anne Boleyn.']

the Tower. Some of the lords declared, that her defence did fully clear her; none of the women that served her were brought to witness the least circumstance against her: and all the evidence upon which she was convicted was kept so secret, that it was never known. This I know is put here out of its place, but the thread of other things led me into it. I shall have occasion to mention this paper again in queen Mary's reign.

The bishop of Bayonne writes, that, even after Campeggio came into England, both king and queen did eat at one table, and lodged in one bed. The queen put on so good a counte- nance, that, to see them together, one could discern no breach between them. He tells in that letter, that the earl of Angus, who was married to the queen of Scotland, king Henry's sister, was come up, being banished out of Scotland, because the queen had taken another husband, who was a handsomer man than he was; (*plus beau compagnon que lui.*) In his next letter he writes, that Wolsey said to him, that the general of the Cordeliers, that good prophet, then a cardinal, had capitu- lated with the pope in the emperor's name, when the pope was set at liberty. That Cordelier cardinal was then to sail to Spain: he wished the French would set out some vessels to seize on him, and draw from him the particulars of that treaty; for they knew that, in the articles of that treaty, the reason that obstructed the king's matter would appear. Upon this, after some expostulation, that the king of France did not help them in it as he might, Wolsey added, that the first project of **43** the divorce was set on foot by himself, to create a perpetual separation between England and the house of Burgundy: and he had told the king's mother at Compiegne, that, if she lived a year to an end, she would see as great a union with them, and as great a disunion from the other, as she could desire; and bid her lay that up in her memory.

In his next he writes, that both the legates had been with the king and queen. In Campeggio's speech to the king, he set forth his merits upon the apostolic see with great pomp. Fox answered him decently in the king's name. The queen answered them more roundly: she spoke with respect to Cam- peggio, but said, " she thanked the cardinal of York for the " trouble she was put to: she had always wondered at his

Oct. 16.
The king
and queen
seemed to
live well
together.
Le Grand,
p. 170.

[Ibid. p.
174.]
Oct. 21.
Ibid. p.
178.

[Ibid. p.
179.]

[Ibid. p.
186.]

[Oct. 28.]
The legates
go to the
king and
queen.
Ibid. p.
188.
[Ibid. p.
189.]

The queen
treats Wol-
sey very
severely.
Vitellius,
B. xii.
[fol. 52.]

" pride and vainglory ; she abhorred his voluptuous life and
" abominable lewdness, and little regarded his power and
" tyrrany : all this rose from his malice to her nephew the
" emperor, whom he hated worse than a scorpion, because he
" would not satisfy his ambition, and make him pope. She
" blamed him both for the war in which the king was engaged,
" and for the trouble he put her to by this new-found doubt."
The cardinal blushed, and seemed confounded : he said, " he
" was not the beginner nor the mover of the doubt ; and that
" it was sore against his will that the marriage was brought
[fol. 52 b.] " into question : but since the pope had deputed him as a judge
" to hear the cause, he swore upon his profession he would
" hear it indifferently."

Le Grand,
p. 192.

[p. 195.]
[p. 196.]

On the 1st of November the bishop writes, that the queen
had chosen for her council the archbishop of Canterbury, the
bishops of London, Bath, Rochester, Ely, and Exeter, with the
dean of the chapel : but of these, the bishops of London and
Rochester, and the dean of the chapel, were the only persons
that in their opinion were of the queen's side. She expected
an advocate, a proctor, and a counsellor from Flanders. It
was not allowed her to bring any over from Spain, for there
was then war between England and Spain ; but the Netherlands had a neutrality granted them.   " The bishop reckoned
" that the marriage must be condemned ; for, though the pope
" and all the cardinals had approved it, they could not main-
" tain it, if it was proved, as he was told it would be, that her
" former marriage was consummated ; for in that case God
" himself had determined the matter."

Ibid.
p. 197.
The bishop
of Bay-
onne's
opinion of
the pope's
dispensa-
tion.
Ibid. [p.
200.]

On the 8th of November he writes, " that Wolsey had asked
" him, if he could say nothing to invalidate the pope's dispensa-
" tion, and to prove the marriage unlawful, so that the pope
" could not dispense in that case ; since nothing could unite
" the two kings so entirely, as the carrying on the divorce
" must do : he heard he was a great divine, so he prayed him
" to speak his mind freely. The bishop excused himself ; but
" being very earnestly pressed, he put his thoughts in writing,
" referring for these to his last letter : he sent over a copy of
" it to Montmorency, and desired he would shew it to the
[p. 202.] " bishop of Bourges, who would explain it to him. Wolsey
" desired that the king's mother would write earnestly to Cam-

" peggio in favour of the king's cause.   The bishop makes
" great excuses for giving his opinion in the matter : he did
" not sign it : and he gave it only as a private person, and not
" as an ambassador."

44   On the 27th[10] of November the bishop writes, that he had Le Grand,
p. 209.
been with Campeggio, and had talked of the pope's dispensa-
tion.   Campeggio would not bear to have the pope's power [p. 216.]
brought into debate : he thought his power had no limits, and Apprehen-
sions of
so was unwilling to let that be touched ; but he was willing to disorders
hear it proved that the dispensation was ill founded. He gives on the
in that letter a relation of the king's sending for the lord mayor queen's
account.
of London, to give the citizens an account of the scruples he [p. 217.]
had concerning his marriage : and he writes, that he had said
the bishop of Tarbes was the first person that made him entertain them ; nor does the bishop of Bayonne pretend to call the
truth of that in question.

The same bishop, in his letter of the 9th of December, writes, p. 231.
" that Anne Boleyn was then come to court, and was more
" waited on than the queen had been for some years : by this
" they prepared all people for what was to follow. The people
" were uneasy, and seemed disposed to revolt. It was resolved
" to send all the strangers out of the kingdom ; and it was
" reckoned there were above fifteen thousand Flemings in [p. 232.]
" London : so the driving all these away would not be easily
" brought about.   Care was taken to search for arms, and to
" keep all quiet.   Wolsey, in a great company, above an hun-
" dred persons of quality being present, reported, that the
" emperor had said he would drive the king out of his king-
" dom by his own subjects: one only of all that company ex-
" pressed an indignation at it.   The advocates that the queen [p. 240.]
" expected from Flanders were come, but had not yet their
" audience."

In one of the 20th of December the bishop writes, " that the p. 245.
" king had shewed him what presumptions there were of the
" forgery of the breve that they pretended was in Spain ; and [p. 252.]
" upon that he went through the whole matter so copiously
" with him, that he saw he understood it well, and indeed
" needed no advocate : he desired that some opinions of learned

---

[10] [The book is very inaccurately   the letter itself, but the margin as-
printed. This is the date given in   signs it to November 17th.]

" men in France might be got, and be signed by them, if it
" could be obtained."

Le Grand,
p. 259.
Endea-
vours to
gain Cam-
peggio.
[p. 260.]
By the letter of the 25th of December, it appears there was
an argument of more weight laid before Campeggio, for he was
offered Durham instead of Salisbury.   He said to them who
offered it, that the pope was about to give him a bishopric of
that value in Spain ; but the emperor would not consent to it.
The lawyers that came from the Netherlands had an audience
of the king, in which they took great liberties : for they said to
[p. 261.]
him, they wondered to see him forsake his ancient friends, and
to unite himself to his mortal enemies.   They were answered
very sharply.   They applied themselves to Campeggio with
respect, but neglected Wolsey : and after that they had lodged
such advices as were sent by them with the queen, they returned home.

p. 295.
Wolsey's
credit is
shaken.
On the 25th[11] of January the bishop of Bayonne writes, " that
" the court, apprehending the pope was changing his measures
" with relation to the king's affair, had sent Gardiner to Rome
" to let the pope know, that, if he did not order Campeggio to
" proceed in the divorce, the king would withdraw himself
" from his obedience : he perceived Wolsey was in great fear ;
" for he saw, that, if the thing was not done, the blame would
" be cast wholly on him, and there it would end.   Sir Thomas 45
" Cheyney had some way offended him, and was for that dis-
" missed the court : but by Anne Boleyn's means he was
" brought back ; and she had upon that occasion sent Wolsey
" a severe message.   The bishop had, in a letter sent him from
p. 299.
" Paris, a list of the college of the cardinals, by which they
" reckoned fifteen of them were imperialists ; and Campeggio
[p. 301.]
" is reckoned among these : eighteen were of the contrary
" party ; three had not declared themselves, but might be
[p. 302.]
" gained to either side; and six were absent.   This canvassing
" was occasioned by the pope's sickness : and it was writ as
[p. 306.]
" news from France, that an Englishman, passing through and
" going to Spain, had reported with joy that there would be no
" divorce ; that Campeggio served the pope well ; that this
" was very acceptable to all the great men of England, and
" that the blame of all was laid on Wolsey, whose credit with

[11] [There is no date either in the   between one of the 28th January
letter or in the margin.   It comes   and another of the 2nd of February.]

" the king was sinking; that he was not at the feast of St.
" George, for which the king had chid him severely, he being
" the chancellor of the order."

In a letter of the 22nd of May he writes, " that Wolsey _{Le Grand,}
" was extreme uneasy. The dukes of Norfolk and Suffolk, _{p. 313.}
" and others, made the king believe, that he did not advance _{of Norfolk}
" his affair so much as he could: he wishes that the king _{folk his}
" of France and his mother would make the duke of Suffolk _{enemies.}
" desist, for he did not believe that he, or the other duke,
" could be able to manage the king as Wolsey had done. They
" at court were alarmed at the last news from Rome, for the
" pope seemed inclined to recal the commission: upon which
" Bennet was sent thither, to use either promises or threaten-
" ings, as he should see cause. They pressed the pope to
" declare the breve from Spain null; but he refused to do it.
" He adds, that in the breve lay one of the most important [p. 314.]
" points of the whole matter:" (probably that was, that the
consummation of the former marriage was expressly affirmed
in it.) " Wolsey had pressed the bishop very earnestly to
" move his master to concur zealously to promote the king's
" cause; upon which he pressed on Montmorency, that the
" king of France should send one to the pope to let him know
" that he believed the king's cause was just, and that both
" kingdoms would withdraw from his obedience, if justice was
" denied on this occasion. To this were to be added, all sorts
" of promises when it should be done; which Wolsey pro-
" tested, such was his love to the king, he would value much
" more, than if they made him pope. The point then to be [p. 321.]
" insisted on was, to hinder the recalling the commission."

By letters of the 30th of June it appears, that Gardiner _{p. 333.}
was returned from Rome[12], with the proofs of the breves being
a forgery. Campeggio was then forced to delay the matter no [p. 334.]
longer. The bishop of Bayonne had pressed Campeggio to it
by authority from the court of France. On the 13th[13] of July [p. 336.]
Cassali wrote from Rome, that the pope had recalled the king's
cause at the emperor's suit.

But I come now to give an account of the proceedings of the

---

[12] [He wrote from Westminster, June 25th, to Vannes, announcing his safe arrival. The letter is print-ed in State Papers, vol. vii. p. 190.]
[13] [The date given is the 15th of July.]

two legates; in which I must correct the errors of all the writers of that time, whom I had too implicitly followed[14]. I go upon sure grounds; for I have before me the original register of their proceedings, made up with such exactness, that, at the end, the register and clerk of the court do not only attest it with their hands and marks, but reckon up the number of the leaves, with the interlinings that are in every page; and every leaf is likewise signed by the clerk, all in parchment. This noble record[15] was lent me by my reverend and learned brother Dr. Moore, bishop of Ely, who has gathered together a most invaluable treasure, both of printed books and manuscripts, beyond what one can think that the life and labour of one man could have compassed; and which he is as ready to communicate, as he has been careful to collect it.

The proceedings of the legates.
[Cotton MSS. Vitell. B. xii. fol. 47 b.]

The legates sat in a room called *the parliament chamber*, near the church of the Black Friars. Their first session was on the 31st of May. The bishop of Lincoln presented to them the bull, by which the pope empowered them to try and judge the cause concerning the king and queen's marriage, whether it was good or not, and whether the issue by it was legitimate or not. The legates, after the reading of the bull, took it into their hands, and saw it was a true and untouched bull; so they took upon them to execute it: and they ordered the king and queen to be cited to appear before them on the 18th of June; and appointed, that the bishop of Lincoln should cite the king, and the bishop of Bath and Wells the queen.

[Ibid. fol. 58.]

On the 18th the form of the citation was brought before them, in which the bull was inserted at full length, and the two bishops certified, that they had served the citation both on the king and queen on the 15th; and Sampson, dean of the chapel, and Dr. Bell, appeared, with a proxy from the king in due form: but the queen appeared personally, and read an instrument, by which she declined the legates, as not competent judges, and adhered to an appeal she had made to the pope. Upon reading this, she withdrew; and though she was required to return, she had no regard to it. Upon which they pronounced her contumacious; and on the 21st of June they ordered the bishop of Bath and Wells to serve her with a moni-

[14] [See part i. p. 73.]
[15] [This is not now amongst bishop Moore's MSS.]

tion and a peremptory citation, certifying, that if she did not
appear, they would proceed in the cause. And on the 25th of
June the bishop certified upon oath, that he had served the
citation, but that the queen adhered to her protestation; so
she was again judged contumacious: and as she never came
more into the court, so the king was never in it. And from
this it is clear, that the speeches that the historians have made
for them are all plain falsities.

The next step made was, that the legates exhibited twelve
articles, setting forth the whole progress of the queen's first
and second marriage, and of the dispensations obtained from
Rome, all grounded upon public fame; and the queen was [Rymer,
ordered to be cited again on the 28th of June. The bishop xiv. p.299.]
certified upon oath, that he had served the queen with the
citation; but she not appearing, was again judged contuma-
47 cious, and witnesses were sworn to prove the articles. The
king's answer to the articles was laid before them; in which,
by his answer to the seventh, it appeared, that he was married
to the queen by virtue of a papal dispensation.

On the 5th of July, the king's proctors brought the bull of
pope Julius, dispensing with the impediments in the marriage,
as likewise the copy of the breve, of which the original was in
Spain, but attested very solemnly from thence. The legates
ordered more witnesses to be sworn on the 9th of July. In
another session, additional articles were offered; in which it
was set forth, that impediments lay against the marriage, as
being prohibited both by the divine and the ecclesiastical laws:
so that it could not be maintained by the dispensations, and
that they were of no force, but were null and void. Then
they set forth all the objections formerly made against the
bull; by which it appeared, that the pope was surprised by
the false suggestions made to him, on which he had granted
it; and in particular, that there was no war, nor appearance
of war, between England and Spain at that time. They did
also set forth the presumptions, on which they concluded that
the breve was not a genuine, but a forged piece. On the 12th
of July, commission was given to examine the witnesses. On
the 14th, additional articles were brought in; and on the 16th
of July, the king's proctors were required to bring all instru-

ments whatsoever relating to the articles before the legates; and another commission was given to examine some absent witnesses.

On the 19th of July publication was made of the depositions of the witnesses: by which it appears, that Warham in his examination said, he referred the matter of the lawfulness of the king's marriage to divines; but that he himself believed, that it was contrary both to the laws of God, and to the ecclesiastical laws; and that otherwise, there was no need of a dispensation from the pope. He confesses, there were great murmurings against the marriage; for nothing of that sort had ever been heard of in this kingdom before; and that he himself murmured against it, and thought it detestable and unnatural; and that he had expostulated with the bishop of Winchester for his advising it, but he acquiesced when the pope's dispensation was obtained. The bishop of Ely deposed, that he doubted concerning the consummation of the queen's marriage with prince Arthur; for the queen had often, upon her conscience, denied it to him: yet many witnesses were brought to prove the consummation; some, because the prince and the queen constantly lodged in the same bed; and that prince Arthur continued in a state of good health till the beginning of Lent: some inferred it from what they themselves had done when they were of his age. Some swore to words that he spake next morning after his marriage, not decent enough to he repeated. Other witnesses were brought to prove, that there was no war between England and Spain when the dispensation was granted; but that a free intercourse had been kept up between these nations for many years. It was likewise proved, that the matter set forth in the preamble **48** of the bull was false; and that the breve was a forgery. On the 21st, the protestation the king had made, that he did not intend to marry the queen, was read and proved. With that, the king's council closed their evidence, and demanded a final sentence: so the 23rd of July was assigned for concluding the cause.

On that day, the king's proctor moved, that judgment should be given; but cardinal Campeggio did affirm, on the faith of a true prelate, that the harvest vacation was then begun in

Rome; and that they were bound to follow the practice of the
consistory: so he adjourned the court to the 28th of September.

At the end of every session, some of the men of quality then
present are named; and at this time, the duke of Norfolk and
the bishop of Ely are only named; which seems to contradict
what is commonly reported of the duke of Suffolk's being there,
and of what passed between him and cardinal Wolsey[16]. This
record is attested by Clayberg the register, and Watkins the
clerk of the court. And four years after that, on the 1st of
October, anno 1533, it is also attested by Dr. Wotton; which
he says he does, being required to attest it by Clayberg and
Watkins. How this came to be desired, or done at that time,
is that of which I can give no other account, but that this is
affixed to the register. By this extract that I have made of
this great record it appears, that Campeggio carried on this
cause with such a trifling slowness, that if the king had not
thought he was sure of him, he could never have suffered such
delays to be made; by which the cardinal had a colour from
the vacation, then begun in the consistory in Rome, to put off
the cause, on the day in which a present sentence was expected. It is very natural to think, that, as the king was
much surprised, so he was offended out of measure, when he
found he was treated with so much scorn and falsehood.

On the 23rd of August a sad embroilment happened upon [Le Grand,
the duke of Suffolk's returning from France. Wolsey com- p. 337.]
plained to the king that he had done him ill offices at that
court. Suffolk denied it; the cardinal said he knew it by the
bishop of Bayonne: upon which Suffolk came and challenged
him: the bishop denied he had said it. Suffolk confessed in- [p. 338.]
deed he had said some things to his disadvantage; but the
bishop prayed him that the matter might be carried no further: yet he offered to deny, in Wolsey's presence, that which
was charged on him. But he saw the duke of Suffolk intended
to oblige him to deny it in the king's presence. The bishop,
apprehending the ill effects this might have, resolved to keep
out of the king's way for some time, and he hoped to avoid
the being further questioned in the matter. He found both
the king and Wolsey desired that he might make a journey to

[16] [See part i. p. 77.]

Paris, to get the opinions of the learned men in the king's cause: he would not undertake it till he knew whether the king of France approved of it or not: he desired an answer might be quickly sent him; adding, that if it was not agreed to by France, it would increase the jealousies the king had of that court. He saw they designed to hold a parliament in England, and they hoped by that to make the pope feel the effects of his injustice.

[Le Grand, p. 342.]

p. 354.

By the bishop's letter of the 18th of September, it appears 49 that Campeggio, having got his revocation, " resolved to go to " court, that he might have his audience of leave; where it *[P. 355.]* " was thought best to dismiss him civilly: in the mean while, " Wolsey, who seemed full of fear, pressed the bishop to get " the matter to be examined by the divines; and though he " disguised his fears, yet he could not quite cover them. Some " had left him, whom he had raised: probably this was Gar- " diner; for he united himself to the duke of Norfolk in all " things. The bishop of Bayonne desired leave to go over, on " the pretence of his father's old age and weakness, but really " to know the sense of the French divines; and also desired, " that his brother, William Du Bellay, might be sent to the " court of England during his absence."

p. 364.

On the 4th of October he writes, " that he saw the parlia- " ment was set to ruin Wolsey. Campeggio was [17] well treated " by the king, and had good presents at parting; and the " king desired that they would use him well, as he passed " through France; and particularly, that they would suffer " him to resign an abbey he had there, in favour of his son. *[p. 369.]* " He was stopped at Dover; for it was suspected that he was " carrying over Wolsey's treasure."

p. 370.
The cardi- nal's dis- grace.

On the 17th of October he describes the cardinal's fall: " The bishop thought it was the greatest example of fortune · " that could be seen: both heart and voice failed him; he " wept, and prayed that the king of France and his mother " would pity him, if they found that he had been true in all " that he had promised to them. His visage was quite altered; " and the disgrace was so sudden and heavy, that even his " enemies pitied him. The bishop saw he would be hotly pur-

---

[17] [This is in a letter of the 12th of October, and not in that of Oct. 4.]

" sued, and that nothing but intercessions from France could
" save him ; he did not pretend to continue either legate or
" chancellor ; he seemed ready to quit all to his shirt, so he
" might recover the king's favour again. He was capable of no
" comfort. He proposed, that the French king and his mother [Le Grand,
" should write to the king to this purpose : that they heard P. 373.]
" of his disgrace, and of the design to ruin him ; that they
" prayed him not to proceed too suddenly : he had been a
" good instrument between them ; if there was just cause for
" it, his power might be lessened ; but that they prayed the
" king would not carry things to extremity. The bishop lays
" this before Montmorency, without presuming to give advice
" in it ; only he thought this could do no hurt. Whatsoever
" was done, must seem to be of their own motion, and not as
" coming from a desire of the cardinal ; for that would precipi-
" tate his ruin. It seems, he had received great presents from
" the king's mother, of which he hoped she would say nothing
" that might hurt him. It was intended, as he thought, on
" his ruin, to destroy the state of the church, and seize on
" their lands, which had been openly talked at some tables.
" If the king of France intended to interpose in his favour, no
" time was to be lost. Anne Boleyn, as it was believed, had [p. 375.]
" got a promise of the king, that he would not admit him to a
" private audience, lest that might beget some pity in him."

50   On the 22nd of October he wrote, " that all his goods were p. 377.
" seized on, and that his spirit was quite sunk. It was not All his goods seiz-
" known who should have the great seal ; it was believed it ed on.
" would no more be put into a priest's hands ; but he saw
" Gardiner was like to have a great share in affairs. The
" cardinal's goods that were seized on were valued at five hun- p. 379.
" dred thousand crowns. More, who had been chancellor of
" the duchy of Lancaster, was made lord chancellor. The see
" of York was to be left in his hands ; and some of his goods [p. 380.]
" were to be sent back to him. The bishop did apprehend,
" that if the new ministry did not agree, which he believed
" they would not do long, he might be brought back to
" court again[18]."

18 [See a very interesting letter   printed in French with an English
from Chapuys, the emperor's am-   translation, in Bradford's 'Corres-
bassador in London, to Charles V,   pondence of the Emperor Charles V,'

\

I have given the relation of this great transaction more particularly than was perhaps necessary : but finding so clear a
thread in those letters, I thought it not improper to follow
them closely ; the rather to shew, that none of the papers that
M. Le Grand has published do in the least contradict, but
rather establish, all that I had written : and so punctual a
relation being laid before me, by those who bore no good-will
to me nor to my work, seemed an invitation to me to enlarge
further than perhaps was necessary.   I will end therefore all
that relates to cardinal Wolsey at once.

Wolsey's
good con-
duct in his
diocese.
Upon his going to York, he behaved himself much better
than he had done in the former parts of his life.   In a book
that was printed in the year 1536, entitled *A Remedy for
Sedition*[19], writ by one that was no friend to popery, this

pp. 265, 290. It is dated from London, Oct. 25, 1529, and describes
the writer's interview with the duke
of Norfolk on the 21st and with the
king on the following Sunday, adding an account of the cardinal's
downfall, and attributing the opening of Campeggio's baggage to a
suspicion that Wolsey had attempted to send some of his goods out of
the country. He states also that
More had received the seals that
day. The letter contains a postscript written two days later, stating
that Wolsey had been declared
guilty of high treason for obtaining
his legatine authority in opposition
to the authority of the king and the
privileges of the realm. In another
letter dated Feb. 6, 1530, he alludes
to the king having granted his pardon, and the hopes entertained of
his restoration to office.—Ibid. p.
309.]

[19] [A remedy for sedition, wherein are conteyned many thynges
concernyng the true and loyall
obeysance that commēs owe unto
their prince and soueraygne lorde
the kynge, anno MDXXXVI. Londini in Ædibus Thomæ Bertheleti
Regii Impressoris Cum privilegio.
The only copy of this book which

the editor has been able to find is
in the Lambeth library, xxix. 3. 17.
The whole passage is as follows :
' Who was less beloved in the north
than my lord cardinal, God have
his soul, before he was among them?
Who better beloved after he had
been there awhile ? We hate oft-
times whom we have good cause to
love.   It is a wonder to see how
they were turned, how of utter enemies they became his dear friends.
He gave bishops a right good en-
sample how they might win men's
hearts.   There was few holy days,
but he would ride five or six mile
from his house, now to this parish
church, now to that; and there
cause one or other of his doctors to
make a sermon unto the people.
He sat amongst them, and said mass
before all the parish.   He saw why
churches were made.   He began to
restore them to their right and proper use. If our bishops had done
so, we should have seen that preaching of the gospel is not the cause of
sedition, but rather lack of preaching of it.   He brought his dinner
with him, and bade divers of the
parish to it.   He enquired whether
there was any debate or grudge between any of them ; if there were,

character is given of the last part of Wolsey's life : " None
" was better beloved than he, after he had been there a while.
" He gave bishops a good example, how they might win men's
" hearts. There was few holydays but he would ride five or
" six miles from his house ; now to this parish church, now to
" that ; and there cause one of his doctors to make a sermon
" unto the people : he sat among them, and said mass before
" all the parish. He saw why churches were made, and began
" to restore them to their right and proper use. If our bishops
" had done so, we should have seen, that preaching the gospel
" is not the cause of sedition ; but rather lack of preaching it.
" He brought his dinner with him, and bade divers of the
" parish to it. He inquired if there was any debate or grudge
" between any of them ; if there were, after dinner he sent
" for the parties to the church, and made them all one.''

I had, in my work[20], mentioned the concluding character
that I found Cavendish gave of him, that was left out in the
printed editions ; which made me vouch the manuscript from
which I had it : but the last edition agreeing with that copy, I
need say no more to justify my quotation, for it will be found
in it.

It may seem strange, that when the bishop of Bayonne first
suggested to Wolsey, that, if the king's marriage was against
the law of God, the pope's dispensation could be of no force ;
yet no inferences were made from this. All our writers give
Cranmer the honour of having started that first ; and they
make that the foundation of his advancement. I can see no
51 other way to reconcile all this, but that it may be supposed
Wolsey, as true to the interests of the papacy, was unwilling
to let it be moved in public ; and that he kept this between the
bishop of Bayonne and himself, without communicating it to
the king. Now the cause was called away to Rome, and so a
new process followed with a very slow progress : delays upon
delays were granted, and yet all was precipitated in conclusion.

In the mean while, the king sent his question to the faculties
of law and divinity in the several universities of Europe : and

The king consults the universities.

after dinner he sent for the parties
to the church and made them at
one. Men say well that do well.
God's laws shall never be so set by

as they ought before they be well
known.'—Signat. E. 2.
[20] [See part i. p. 82.]

understanding that Martin Du Bellay, the elder brother of the bishop of Bayonne, distinguished by the title of sieur de Langey, had great credit in the universities, both in France, Italy, and Germany, he engaged him to procure their opinions upon the point of the unlawfulness of his marriage; who, in the view of this service, prevailed with the king to lend the king of France a hundred and fifty thousand crowns[21], being to be advanced as a part of the two millions that he was to pay for the redemption of his sons, which was to be repaid to king Henry in five years. Besides, he assigned over to him the forfeiture due by the emperor, for not marrying his daughter; and he sent in a present to his godson Henry, afterwards king of France, a jewel, with some of that which was believed to be the true cross, that had been left in pawn with the king by Philip, Charles' father, for fifty thousand crowns: so ready was the king to engage the king of France into his interest, at no small charge to himself.

I come next to open the transactions in the convocation that was summoned to meet on the 5th of November 1529, two days after the opening of the parliament. At their first meeting, a reformation of abuses was proposed; and with that an inquiry was made concerning heretical books. A committee of bishops was appointed with relation to heretics. On the 19th of December secrecy was enjoined; and that was again a second time enjoined under the pain of excommunication: then the prolocutor came up, and had secret conference with the upper house. They remitted to the king the loan that they had made him; and they put an end to that work on Christmas-eve, a week after the parliament was risen.

The bishops were much offended at the translations of the New Testament by Tyndale, Joye, and others; and proceeded severely against those who read them: yet it was not easy to put a stop to the curiosity and zeal of the people. The king came to the star-chamber, and conferred with the bishops and other learned men on this subject: the bishops said, these translations were not true, and complained of the prologues set before them, So the king commanded, by a proclamation issued and printed in June 1530[22], that these translations

Mart. du Bellay's Memoirs, p. 282. [fol. 91. b.]

Proceedings in convocation. [Wilkins' Conc. iii. 717.]

[May 24. Translation of the scriptures condemned. [Ibid. p. 727.]

[21] [This is a mistake for 950,000 crowns.]

[22] [A copy of this proclamation exists in the Collection of the Society

should be called in, and promised that a new one should be made. On this occasion it is not unfit to mention what doctor Fulke writes, that he heard Miles Coverdale say in a sermon he preached at Paul's Cross. After he had finished his translation, some censured it: upon which king Henry ordered divers bishops to peruse it. After they had it long in their hands, he asked their judgment of it: they said, there were many faults in it. But he asked upon that, if there were any heresies in it: they said, they found none. Then said the king, In God's 52 name, let it go abroad among my people. The time is not marked when this was said, therefore I insert it here: for in the beginning of the following year the king ordered a Bible of the largest volume to be had in every church; but it does not appear to me by whom it was translated.

On the 19th[23] of September 1530, another proclamation [Sept. 12.] was made aganst all who should purchase any thing from the   1530.

of Antiquaries at Somerset House. It is headed,

' Mense Junii anno regni metuendissimi domini nostri regis Henrici Octavi xxii. A proclamation made and diuysed by the kyngis highnes with the aduise of his honorable counsaile, for dampning of erronious bokes and heresies, and prohibitinge the hauing of holy scripture, translated into the vulgar tonges of englisshe, frenche, or duche, in suche maner, as within this proclamation is expressed.'

The effect of the proclamation is to condemn the books called 'the wicked Mammona, the obedience of a Christen man, the Supplication of beggars, the revelation of Antichrist, the Summary of Scripture, and other books printed beyond seas.' It also speaks of the translation of the Scriptures as tending to the continuance and increase of errors, and adds, 'All be it if it shall here after appere to the kynges highnes that his saide people do utterly abandon and forsake all peruerse, erronious and sedicious opinyons, with the newe testament and the olde, corruptly translated into the englisshe tonge, nowe beinge in printe: And that the same bokes and all other bokes of heresy, as well in the frenche tonge as in the duche tonge, be clerely extermynate and exiled out of this realme of Englande for euer : his highnes entendeth to prouyde, that the holy scripture shall be by great lerned and catholyke persones, translated into the englisshe tonge, if it shall than seme to his grace conuenient so to be.' The proclamation does not speak of bishops having been consulted, but only the primates and other learned persons. It ends—And God saue the kynge. Thomas Bertheletus regius impressor excusit. Cum priuilegio.]

[23] [The editor has not seen a printed copy of this proclamation. A MS. copy is in the volume from which the preceding proclamation was described. It is dated Sept. 12, an. xxii. H. viii. and is entitled, 'A proclamation prohibiting the purchasing of any Bulles from the Court of Rome.']

court of Rome, contrary to the king's prerogative, or to hinder his intended purposes. The convocation was again brought together about the 7th of January : their greatest business was to purchase their pardon ; for as the cardinal had fallen under a *præmunire,* by the act of the 16th of Richard the Second, so they were generally involved more or less in the same guilt : the sum was soon agreed to, with the consent of the lower house ; a hundred thousand pounds was to be their ransom.

[Wilkins' Conc. iii. p. 742.]

The steps in carrying the king's being declared head of the church.

On the 7th of February some of the king's counsellors and judges came and conferred with them about some words that were proposed to be put in the preamble of the bill of subsidy, which were these ; *The king, who is the protector, and the only supreme head of the church and clergy of England.* Upon this the prolocutor and clergy were called up to confer about i : the lord chief justice with others came into the convocation, and conferred with the archbishop and his brethren. The next day the prolocutor desired a further time, and the archbishop assigned them one o'clock : then the archbishop had some discourse with them concerning the king's pardon. Some of the judges came and communicated to them a copy of the exceptions in the act of grace : this was in the 23rd session. In the 24th session there was yet further talk about the king's supremacy.

The judges came and asked them whether they were agreed upon the exceptions ; and added, that the king would admit of no qualifications. When these were gone, the prolocutor came up, and asked yet more time ; the archbishop appointed two o'clock the same day : a long debate followed. The next day the archbishop had a secret conference with the bishops ; and Cromwell came and had some discourse with him. When he went away, the bishops resolved to send the bishops of Lincoln and Exeter to the king ; it seems, to soften him : but they came back, and reported that the king would not speak with them. The judges told them, they had no orders to settle the king's pardon till they did agree to the supremacy. They were prorogued till the afternoon ; and then there was so great a variety of opinions, that no agreement was like to follow. The lord Rochford, Anne Boleyn's father, was sent by the king with some expedients. The archbishop directed them to consider of these; and that when they were come to a resolution upon them, that they should send three or four of each house to treat with the king's council, and with the judges: but the king would admit of no treaty, and asked a clear answer. It was put off a day longer; and on the 11th of February the article was thus conceived in Latin: *Ecclesiæ et cleri Anglicani singularem protectorem et unicum et supremum dominum, et quantum per Christi legem licet, etiam* 53 *supremum caput, ipsius majestatem recognoscimus.* In English thus; *We recognise the king's majesty to be our only sovereign lord, the singular protector of the church and clergy of England, and, as far as is to be allowed by the law of Christ, likewise our supreme head.*

The form being thus agreed on, the archbishop offered it to the whole body: all were silent; upon which he said, Whosoever is silent seems to consent: to this one answered, Then we are all silent. The meeting was put off till the afternoon; and then, after a long conference, all of the upper house agreed to it, none excepted. Fisher is expressly named as present. And in the evening the prolocutor came and signified to the archbishop, that the lower house had also consented to it: and thus the bill of subsidy was prepared and offered to the king on the 1st of April. Thus this matter was carried, by adding this limitation, which all parties understood according to their different notions.

The limitation added to it:

Though these words of limitation had not been added, the nature of things required that they should have been supposed; since among Christians all authority must be understood to be limited by the laws that Christ has given: but those who adhered to their former notions understood this *headship* to be only a temporal authority in temporal matters; and they thought, that by the laws of Christ the secular authority ought not to meddle in ecclesiastical matters: whereas others of the new learning, as it was then called, thought that the magistrate had a full authority even in ecclesiastical matters; but that the administration of this was so limited to the laws of the gospel, that it did not warrant him to command any thing but what was conform to these. So that these words were equivocal, and differently understood by those who subscribed, and afterwards swore them.

And ac-
cepted by
the king.

It seems the king thought it was of great advantage to him to have this matter settled with any limitation ; for that in time would be dropt and forgotten ; as indeed it was. This no doubt was intended to terrify the court of Rome ; since it was published over all Europe, that it went unanimously in the convocation of this province.

Tunstall was now translated to Durham ; and, being a man of great probity, he could not at first approve of a thing in which he saw a fraudulent management and an ill design ; so he protested against it. He acknowledged the king's headship

[Wilkins'
Conc. iii.
p. 745.]

in temporal matters, but did not allow it in spirituals : but the king, who had a particular friendship for him, wrote him a letter, which from the printed title to it I too hastily thought was directed to the convocation at York[24] ; but it was writ only to Tunstall ; and it seems it so far satisfied him, that he took the oath afterwards without any limitation.

The pro-
ceedings of
the clergy
against
heretics.

I shall now go through the rest of the abstract of that convocation, by which it will appear, what was the spirit that prevailed among them. In the forty-ninth session, after all had agreed to the preamble of the bill of subsidy, the bishop of London laid before them a libel against the clergy. In the

[Ibid.
p. 725.]

next session, Crome, Latimer, and Bilney were examined upon 54 some articles : it does not appear whether the libel was laid to their charge or not ; only their examination following the other motion so soon, gives ground to apprehend that it might be the matter under examination. In the fifty-fifth session the king's pardon was read to them ; and it seems exceptions being taken to some things in it in the fifty-eighth session, the emendations that the king's council had made were read to them, in which it seems they acquiesced, for we hear no more of it.

Complaints
of Tracy's
Testament.

After that, there was a long conference with relation to Crome's errors : but the matter was referred to the prolocutor and the clergy. The prolocutor had in the forty-fifth session complained of Tracy's Testament ; but no answer being made, he renewed his complaint in the sixty-second session, and desired that it might be condemned, and that Crome should be proceeded against ; as also that Bilney and Latimer might be cited : but, for some reasons not expressed, the archbishop thought fit to delay it. In the sixty-fourth session the prolo-

[24] [See part i. p. 112.]

cutor repeated his motion for condemning Tracy's Testament; so in the sixty-sixth session, on the 23rd of March, the archbishop gave judgment against it.   Tracy's son was examined about it : he said, it was all written in his father's own hand; and that he had never given a copy of it to any person, except to one only.   In the sixty-ninth session, the archbishop examined Lambert (alias Nicolson, who was afterwards burnt) before two notaries; and in the seventieth session the sentence [Ibid. p. condemning Tracy's Testament was publicly read : and after 746.] two other sessions, the convocation was prorogued to October.

It appears from all this, that the convocation was made up of men violently set against our reformation.   But I turn now to another scene.   The king, seeing no hope left of succeeding in his suit at the court of Rome, resolved to try the faculties of divinity in the several universities.   His chief reliance was [Le Grand] upon France, and on those three brothers formerly mentioned. p. 383. He began to suspect there was some secret negotiation between the court of Rome and the king of France; yet, though he opened this to the bishop of Bayonne, he did on all other occasions express an entire confidence in that king : and, the new ministry seemed zealous in the interests of France, and studied to remove all the jealousies that they apprehended Wolsey might have given of them.

At this time the bishop of Tarbes, then cardinal Grammont [25], The king's was with the pope, and had a particular charge sent to him to proceedings at assist the English ambassadors.   He wrote to the French king Rome. on the 27th of March, " that he had served Boleyn, then lord p. 399. " Rochford, all he could; that he had pressed the pope to shew " the regard he had to the king of France, as well as to the " king of England : he writes, that the pope had three several [p. 400.] " times said to him in secret, that he wished that the marriage " had been already made in England, either by the legate's " dispensation, or otherwise, provided it was not done by him, " nor in diminution of his authority, under the pretence of the " laws of God."   He also wrote, " that the emperor had [p. 402.]

[25] [Anno Domini 1530. Pontificatus 7, 6 Idus Junii, Papa Clemens vii. creavit Cardinalem unum; is fuit Gabriel de Acromonte, Gallus, Episcopus Tarbiensis, orator regis Francorum, Presbyter Cardinalis, tt. S. Cæciliæ.   Onuphrii Panvinii Pontifices et Cardinales &c. ed. Ven. 1557.]

" pressed the pope to create some new cardinals upon his
" recommendation : but that the pope complained, that, when
" he was a prisoner, he had made some cardinals who were a
" disgrace to the college. The emperor said, he was sorry for 55
" it; but it was not by his order. The pope said, he knew
" the contrary ; for he saw the instructions sent to the cardinal
" Cordelier, signed by the emperor, in which they were named :
" so the pope refused to give the two caps that he desired."

p. 411.
There was an Italian, Joachim sieur de Vaux, at the court
of England, who was an agent of France : he, in a letter to the
king of France, March the 15th, writes, that the king thought,
that by his means he might have the opinion of the faculty at
Applica-
tions made
to divines
and law-
yers.
p. 418.
Paris in his cause. On the 4th of April he writes, that the
king expected no good from the pope, and seemed resolved to
settle his matter at home, with the advice of his council and
parliament. He looked on the pope as simoniacal, and as an
ignorant man, and not fit to be the universal pastor ; and
resolved not to suffer the court of Rome to have any advantage
from the benefices in his kingdom, but to govern it by a provincial authority, and by a patriarch ; and he hoped other
kingdoms would do the same.

An opinion
given by
some in
Paris,
p. 421.
After some interval, the bishop of Bayonne's letters are
again continued. In one of the 29th of December he writes,
" that the king was marvellously well pleased with the account
" his ambassadors wrote to him of what the divines of Paris
" had done ; though he undertands there is one Beda, a dan-
" gerous person, among them. That declaration which their
" divines had made was such, that all other things were for-
" given in consideration of it."

[p. 425.]
The next letter is from his brother William ; who writes,
" that the good answer that came from the doctors and uni-
" versities of Italy made the king wonder that those of Paris
" were so backward. It was suspected in England, that the
" king of France or his counsellors had not recommended the
[p. 426.]
" matter effectually to them. He had a letter from one Ger-
" vais, a doctor there, who had much advanced the king's
" affairs, for which Montmorency had made him great acknow-
" ledgments. He shewed this letter to king Henry ; who upon
" that carried him to his closet where his books lay, and there
" he entertained him four hours : he told him, he was in such

" perplexity, that it was not possible for him to live longer
" in it."

This Du Bellay was to go to Paris to talk with the doctors ; Bishop of
therefore he prayed Montmorency, that he might find a letter Bayonne
from the king, empowering him so to do, that so he might not Paris.
seem to act without his orders : and he promised to manage
the matter with discretion.

In a letter that the bishop of Bayonne wrote from Lusignan p. 427.
on the 13th of April, where he was then with the French king,
he writes, that the matter of the divorce was entirely despatched
at Paris, as it had been before that done at Orleans, by his
brother's means.   But he adds, some represented to the king,
that he had shewed too much diligence in procuring it, as if he
was serving two masters.   Joachim had before that, on the
15th of February [26], written to the king, that king Henry p. 442.
thanked him for his commands to the doctors in Paris in his
56 matter, which he laid to heart more than all other things ; and
desired they would give their opinions in writing, that they
might be laid before the pope.

It does not appear that the pope took any other pains to be Cardinal
well informed in the matter, but by consulting cardinal Caje- opinion
tan, who was then justly esteemed the learnedst man of the against the
college. He, when he wrote commentaries upon Thomas' Sum, 2da 2dæ
though that father of the schoolmen thought, that the laws in Quæst. 159.
Leviticus, concerning the degrees of marriage that are pro- Art. 9.
hibited, were moral, and of eternal obligation ; Cajetan, in his
Commentary, declares himself to be of another mind, but takes
a very odd method to prove it : for, instead of any argument
to evince it, he goes only on this ground, that they cannot be
moral, since the popes dispensed with them ; whereas they
cannot dispense with a moral law.   And for that he gives an
instance of the marriage of the king of Portugal; to which he
adds, the present queen of England had likewise consummated
her marriage with the late brother of the king of England,
her husband.   By which, as it appears that they took it then
for granted at Rome, that her first marriage with prince Arthur
was consummated, so he departed only from Aquinas' opinion,
because the pope's practice of dispensing in such cases could

[26] [The date in the margin is 15, and 18 Feb. That at the end of the
letter is Feb. 18.]

not be justified, unless he had forsaken his master in that particular.   And here he offers neither reason nor authority to
maintain his opinion, but only the practice of the court of
Rome ; which is in plain words to say, that what opinion soever
is contrary to the practice of the popes must for that reason be
laid aside : for he offers no other argument, but three modern
instances, of which this of the queen of England is one, of
popes dispensing with those laws.   But now, being required by
the pope to consider the present case more particularly, he, on
the 13th of March this year, gave his opinion in writing to

Ad an.
1530.
Numb. 193.
[sqq.] him.   Raynaldus has inserted it in his Annals.   In it, after he
had compared the laws in Leviticus and Deuteronomy together,
he concludes, " that the marrying a brother's wife was simply
" unlawful ; but that in some circumstances it might have been
" good, if a much greater good should follow on such a marriage
" than that provided for in Deuteronomy, of continuing the

[Numb.
197.] " name of a brother dead without children.   Now he argues,
" that the reason of a provision made in a private case would
" be much stronger in a case of a public nature : so that a
" marriage being made to keep peace between two nations,
" must be held lawful, since a dispensation was obtained for it.
" This was not only good in itself, but it was warranted by

[Numb.
198.] " the apostolical authority.   He confesses that the pope cannot
" in the least alter or derogate from the laws of God or of
" nature : but in doubtful cases he may determine with relation

[Numb.
199.]
[Numb.
201.] " to the laws of God and of nature.   He insists chiefly upon
" England's being delivered from a war by the marriage.   He
" acknowledges that both councils, popes, and holy doctors,
" have condemned such marriages, as contrary to the laws of
" God and of nature ; but they do not condemn them when
" other circumstances accompany them, when it is for the good
" of both parties, and for a common good ; and therefore he 57

Ad. an.
1503.
Numb. 22. " justifies pope Julius' dispensation :" who, as the same Raynaldus tells us, did it with the view of the advantages that Spain
and England would have ; but chiefly, because it was hoped,
that, by this conjunction of force, they would be able to depress
the French [27].

----

[27] [Nam ex eâ affinitate Hispanus   confirmandasque adversum eos vires
et Anglus maxima commoda, tum   communes se consecuturos spera-
præcipue ad deprimendos Gallos   bant.]

This opinion of so great a man was sent over to king Henry, signed by himself, bearing date the 27th of January 1534; but this date is perhaps only the date of his signing that copy. It had not the effect they expected from it; especially because it was defective in that way of writing that was then the most cried up against heretics.   For he brought no authority from any ancienter writer to confirm his opinion: so that he argued, from his private way of commenting on scripture, against the streams of tradition, which was called the heretics' way of writing.

Cotton lib. Vitell. B. xiv. [perhaps burnt.]

The pope made a new step on the 7th of March; for he sent a breve to the king, setting forth a complaint made by queen Catharine, "that king Henry intended to proceed to a " second marriage; he therefore prohibited that, under the " pain of the severest censures, threatening to put the whole " kingdom under an interdict; and charged the king, in the " solemnest manner, to live with the queen as formerly." This was granted at Bologna, upon the emperor's pressing instances. This had been attempted before, but was afterwards disowned by the pope: for when the avocation was sent over to England, there was sent with it an inhibition, to proceed further in the matter; threatening censures and punishments in case of disobedience.   But complaint being made of this, the pope did by a bull, dated the 5th of October 1529, declare, that the censures threatened in the inhibition were added against his mind: so he annuls them, and suspends the cause to the 25th of December.

The pope's first breve against the divorce.

Rymer, tom. xiv. [p. 346.]

In a letter that the cardinal Grammont wrote to Montmorency, he tells him, that the emperor said he would have the matter of the marriage carried through: if it was judged unlawful, he would not support his aunt; but if otherwise, he would support her.   And when Boleyn once offered to answer him, he stopped him, and said he was a party, and ought not to speak in the matter.   The cardinal told Boleyn, he had orders from the king of France to solicit that matter as if it was his own: but Boleyn thought it was best to look on for some time, to see how matters went; for if the pope and the emperor should fall into new quarrels, then they might hope to be better heard.

[March 28.] Le Grand, p. 454.

On the 12th of June [28], Bellay wrote to the king a long

p. 458. The proceedings of

[28] [The letter was written on the 9th of June and a postscript added on the 12th.]

the Sor-
bonne.
account of his proceedings with the doctors of the Sorbonne;
by which, it seems, what is formerly mentioned of their giving
opinion in the king's favour was only as private doctors, and
not in a body as a faculty. " The young princes of France
" were yet detained in Spain; so it was necessary to proceed
" with such caution as not to irritate the emperor. He had
" delayed moving in it for some days, but the English am-
" bassadors were impatient. He complains, that there were
" few honest men in the faculty; but, apprehending the incon-
" venience of delaying the matter any longer, he presented
[p. 459.]
" the king's letters to them. The assembly was great; the
" bishop of Senlis, several abbots and deans, the guardians of 58
" the four mendicant orders, and many others, were present:
" so that of a great while there had not been so numerous an
" assembly. The proposition was made on king Henry's part
[p. 460.]
" with great advantage: an express law in the scripture was
" quoted; the four great doctors of the church, eight councils,
" and as many faculties or universities, were of his side: so, in
" respect to them, the king desired they would determine the
" matter in the doctrinal way. The emperor, on the other
[p. 461.]
" hand, who was likewise the king's ally, opposed the divorce,
" the queen of England being his aunt; for he thought
" himself bound to interpose on her account. So the king,
" being pressed by two allies, who both were resolved to be
" governed by the laws of God, and of right reason, laid
" the whole matter before them, who were now assembled in
" an extraordinary manner, and enjoined them to recommend
[p. 462.]
" themselves to God, and, after a mass of the Holy Ghost, to
" consider that which was to be laid out to them, without fear
" or favour; and, after full consideration, to determine it as
" God should inspire their consciences. This was the substance
" of Bellay's speech. Beda spoke next: he said, they all knew
" how much the king studied to please the king of England.
" Many strangers that were of the faculty seemed to applaud
[p. 463.]
" this. Bellay replied, there was certainly a great friendship
" between the two kings: the emperor was likewise the king's
" ally. But they ought to have God only before their eyes,
" and to search for the truth. And having said that, he with-
" drew.

Great heat
in their
debates.
　　" Those who spoke first thought the king's desire was rea-
" sonable, and that therefore they ought to examine the matter:

" this could not be refused, if asked on the behalf of the mean-
" est person.   Others said, the faculty was subject to the
" pope, from whom they had their privileges : and since this
" question related to his power, they ought not to speak to it
" till they sent' to know his mind ; or, at least, till they sent
" to know how the king approved of it, and if he would ask
" the pope's leave to suffer them to debate about it.   Another [p. 464.]
" party moved, that, while their letters were despatched to
" that purpose, they should proceed to examine the question,
" but suspend the coming to a final resolution till an answer
" was brought them.   They said, they thought that they had
" their privileges from the king, as well as from the pope ;
" and that it was a reflection on the pope, to imagine he would
" be offended, if they should examine a case in which the
" conscience of a Christian was disquieted ; and that even an
" order from the pope to the contrary ought not to restrain
" them from examining the matter.   Upon these different [p. 465.]
" opinions, the beadle began to gather their votes ; whether
" they ought to proceed to examine the question, or not.   But
" one of the doctors rose from his place, and plucked the scroll
" out of the beadle's hands, and tore it in pieces : and so they
" all rose up in a tumult, crying out, that nothing ought to be
" done, without writing first to the king and to the pope. Thus
" the meeting broke up in confusion.   The English ambassa-
59 " dors were near enough to see and hear all this.   They said
" they knew this was laid by Beda and his party : Bellay did [p. 466.]
" not then think so, and prevailed with them not to write to
" England till he tried what might be done.   He went to
" Lizet, the first president of the court of parliament, to whom
" the king in especial manner had recommended the managing
" of that affair.   Lizet sent for Beda, and other his complices,
" and prevailed with them to meet again the next day, and to
" proceed according to the third opinion ; which was, to discuss
" the question provisionally, and to seal up their conclusion,
" and send it to the king : so next morning they met, and ap-
" pointed to begin the Monday following to examine the [p. 467.]
" question.
    " This did not satisfy the English ambassadors ; they thought The jea-
" this was only an artifice to gain time : and indeed they had lousy of the
" just ground of suspicion from what several of the doctors did France ;

" openly talk. Bellay therefore desired the king would write
" to the dean, that he would cut off impertinent digressions,
" and bring the matter to as speedy a conclusion as was possi-
" ble : for some said they would make it last a year. Beda
" did give it out, that he knew that what he did was for the
[p. 468.] " king's service : of this he made no secret. Bellay complain-
" ing of this to Lizet, he sent for Beda, and spake so earnestly
" to him, that he swore very positively he would be so far
" from hindering the doctors from obeying the king's com-
" mands, that he would employ himself, as if it were for the
" saving of his life, to get the matter to pass without noise
[p. 469.] " or scandal : but Bellay saw that the president trusted him,
" so he did acquiesce, though he knew, that, by the noise he
" had already made, he had broke a promise which he had
" made to Montmorency. The bishop of Senlis was very sen-
" sible of the disorder of that body : it appearing that the
" English ambassadors did suspect the court of France was
" dealing doubly in the matter; the bishop of Senlis was re-
" solved to go to the king, and to let him see how matters
" were managed in that faculty, and to shew him the necessity
" of reforming them."

[June 18.]
P. 471.
Upon the
changing
the divines'
opinions.
    At this time the duke of Norfolk wrote to Montmorency,
that they wondered to find the faculty was so much altered;
that before this time fifty-six doctors were in their opinion on
the king's side, and there were only seven against him; but
that in the late congregation thirty-six were against it, and
[p. 472.] twenty-two only were for it. The king of England had reason upon this to suspect some underhand dealing; therefore
he hoped they would so manage the matter as to clear all
suspicions.

[Aug. 15.]
P. 473.
    The next letters of Du Bellay did certainly give the progress
of the deliberations of the Sorbonne : but we find nothing of that
in Le Grand's Collection. It is somewhat strange, and may
be liable to suspicion, that, after so close a series of letters
concerning that affair, no letter is produced from the 12th of
June to the 15th of August; thus we have no account given
us of the deliberations of the Sorbonne, and yet it is not to be
doubted, but that a very particular relation was written to the
court of every step that was made in it. The producing no
letters for these two months must leave a very heavy suspicion

60 of unfair dealing somewhere ; for the first letter of Du Bellay's that is published by him, after that of the 12th of June, is of the 15th of August.

Rymer has published the original decision of the Sorbonne on the 2nd of July 1530, but he adds, *avulso sigillo* ; yet after that, he publishes an attestation of the notaries of the court of Paris (*curiæ Parisiensis*) of the authenticalness of this original decision. The attestation of the notaries, dated the 6th of July, mentions both seal and subscription, free from all blemish, and liable to no suspicion. It is probable this precaution was thought necessary, in case the messenger that was to carry it to England had fallen into the hands of any of the emperor's parties in their way to Calais, who, no doubt, would have destroyed this instrument : but this notarial attestation would have been a full proof of it ; for the difficulties in obtaining it might make those who had conducted the matter think it would be no easy thing to procure a new instrument from the Sorbonne itself. How it came that the seal was pulled from the instrument itself, must be left to conjecture ; perhaps it was pulled from it in queen Mary's time.

The decision of the Sorbonne.
Rymer, tom. xiv. [p. 393.]
[Ibid. p. 394.]

" Bellay, in his letter of the 15th of August, writes, that he " had moved Lizet to send for Beda, and to let him know the " king's intentions. Beda talked as a fool ; he would not say " as an ill man : but the president was possessed with a good " opinion of him. The king of France had, at the earl of " Wiltshire's desire, ordered an examination to be made of his " behaviour. He had also ordered the president to demand " of the beadle an authentic copy of an act that Beda had " once signed ; but then wished he had not signed it : but " Lizet would not command the beadle to do this, till he had " the consent of the faculty to give it, though he had an order " from the king to require it. So Bellay having got the " king's letter, went to the president, and delivered it to him : " he promised he would execute it, and get the authentic copy " into his hands. Towards the evening he went to the presi- " dent to see what he had done ; he said the beadle told him, " he could not give it without the consent of the faculty : upon " which Bellay said, that might be a rule in case a private " person asked it ; but when the prince demanded it, he " thought it was no just excuse. The act which was demanded

[Le Grand, p. 473.] Lizet, the president, seemed to work against it. [p. 474.]
[p. 475.]
[p. 476.]

[Le Grand, p. 477.] "was approved by the faculty, by the dean, and the students,
"and by all concerned in it. The beadle pretended that it
"might be said, that he had falsified the act: Bellay an-
"swered, that was the reason why they desired the act: he
"was present when it passed, and had minuted it; but since
"Beda and his complices repented that they had signed it,
"and that the minute they had signed was in some places
"dashed and interlined, they might make new dashings and
"interlineations, therefore he prayed the president to com-
"mand the beadle to bring him the minute that he said was
[p. 478.] "conform to the original. For an hour together the presi-
"dent would do no more but desire the beadle to do it; at
"last he commanded him, but so mildly, that the beadle did
"not think fit to obey him: upon which Bellay said to him,
"if he suffered himself to be so treated, he was unworthy of
"the character that he bore. This quickened Lizet so, that
"he commanded the beadle, all excuses set aside, to obey him. 61
"The act was brought and read, and he promised to bring
"him a copy of it by the next morning. The president
"thought that Bellay had spoken too boldly to him, and he
"would not let him have it, but sent it directly to the king.
[p. 479.] "Lizet had that esteem for Beda, that he thought him a saint,
"and he would not believe him capable of the faults that he
"saw him guilty of, which were such, that Bellay wrote, that
"if he had been to be charged with them, and had a dozen
"of heads, he had deserved to lose them all. He writes, that
"Beda was not the only bad man of the faculty; he had
"many companions, who seemed to desire an occasion to pro-
"voke the king to do that to them, which would make them
"pass for martyrs among the people. He had often heard
"of their wicked designs, under the hypocritical disguise of
"sincerity, but could not have believed the tenth part, if he
"had not seen it."

p. 480.
[Aug. 15.] His letter
of that
whole
matter.   Next to this, we have in Le Grand's Collection the letter
that Lizet wrote to Montmorency of the same date, "men-
"tioning, that, according to the king's letters to him, he had
"procured the copy of the act, which the king of England
"desired: for though the bishop of Bayonne asked it of him,
"that he might carry it to that king, yet that not being
"ordered in the king's letters to him, he therefore thought

" it his duty to send it directly to the king himself : and s
" touching the examination that the king had ordered to be
" made of the conduct of that matter ; he desired it may be
" delayed till he was heard give an account of it : for that in-
" formation would perhaps be a prejudice, rather than a ser-
" vice, to the king of England.   In it he desires to know the
" king's pleasure, that he might follow it as carefully as was
" possible."

The bishop of Bayonne gives a further account of this
matter ; and writes, " that after the assembly of the Sorbonne
" was dismissed by the dean, and that the bishop of Senlis,
" with many abbots, and nine or ten, either generals, provin-
" cials, guardians, or priors of the chief convents of the king-
" dom, and others of great rank and credit, were gone, Beda
" and his complices did by their own private authority meet,
" and study to overturn that which had been settled in so
" great an assembly.   He writes, that this disease was of a
" long continuance, and was still increasing.   This company,
" pretending they were a capitular congregation, sent an order
" to the bishop of Senlis, who was gone into his diocese, and
" had carried the original act of the determination with him,
" requiring him, under the pain of disobedience, to send it to
" them.   He wrote in answer to them, that he had orders to
" deliver it to none but to the king : he was resolved to obey
" the king's orders, and advised them to do the same.   Upon
" which, they moved to deprive him as a rebel to the faculty :
" he was not frightened with this, but wrote to them, that he
" was bound to obey the faculty as his mother, but to obey
" the king as his father : yet they resolved to proceed farther
" after the feasts.   In this letter he tells what pains his bro-
" ther had taken to prevent the scandal that such proceedings
" would give, which were better hindered than punished : but
62 " he complains, that those who had authority to restrain such
" insolences did secretly encourage them."   By which it is
clear, he means Lizet.   The date of this letter is printed the
14th of August[29] : but it is more probable it was the 14th of
July, some days after the determination was made ; for this
matter has no relation to the business of the former letter,

A design to make a contrary decree.
[Le Grand, p. 491.]

[p. 492.]

[p. 493.]

[29] [It is printed twice 14th of August : once in the margin, and once
in the letter itself, so there can hardly be any mistake.]

that was written by his brother a day after this, if it is the true date.

It is plain from this, that there were two instruments : the one was the act of the determination, which at the time of the writing this letter was in the bishop of Senlis' hands : the other was a minute signed by them all, to which the former letter relates, and that might have had rasures and glosses in it, which are not to be imagined could be in the authentic act. It seems the English ambassadors desired both.

[Le Grand] p. 500. There is another letter on the 15th of August, of the bishop of Bayonne's to Montmorency ; in which " he complains that " the faction was going to make a determination contrary to " the former ; and had made an order that none of the faculty " might sign against the marriage, but left it free for any to " sign for it : but that the king had ordered that the determi- " nation already made should remain entire. The bishop had " pressed the president to obey the king's orders : he had " promised him to do it ; but Beda promised the contrary to " his party. Bellay feared the king of England would sus- " pect that the king did not act sincerely. He confessed, that, " from the appearances of things, he should do so himself, if " he had not seen the concern that the king was in upon this " occasion. When he pressed Lizet to obey the king's orders, " he spoke two or three hours to him in bad Latin, (he calls
[p. 501.] " it the Latin of Auvergne,) but he could not understand what " he meant. He says the beadle pretended there was one
[p. 502.] " little fault in the act, upon which he might be accused of " forgery. Upon this the bishop suspected Beda's practice " more than he had done ; and he had required the president " to obey the king's orders, otherwise he would protest if he " did not : and he secretly told him, he did say that to justify " him at their hands, whom he saw he was resolved not to " offend. The president then promised him the act that night ; " but then delayed it till next morning at five : when he sent " for it, sometimes the gate was not opened, and the key was
[p. 503.] " lost ; sometimes the president was asleep ; and then it was " said, that he had taken physic, and that the bishop must " have patience : but he understood that he had gone out by a " back door to the abbey of St. Germain's ; thither he followed " him, and asked for the act : but he said he had sent it to

" the king.   He reckons many other impertinences, that gave
" a mean character of Lizet."

But while this matter was transacted thus at Paris, though [Le Grand,]
the university of Angers had determined against the marriage, p. 507.
yet the faculty of divinity there did on the 7th of May 1530, vided ; the
determine "that it was lawful for a Christian to marry his university
" brother's widow, he dying without children, but having con- vorce, and
" summated the marriage ; that such marriage was not con- the divines
" trary to the laws of God and of nature, and therefore the against it.
63 " pope might upon reasonable grounds dispense in that case."
This was the judgment of the faculty ; but that university did p. 508.
in a body, on that same day, decree the quite contrary, without any mention of this opinion of the divines ; so, it seems,
that was kept secret.

Thus I have fully opened all that M. Le Grand has thought
fit to publish concerning the divines of France.   By the relation given of the proceedings in the Sorbonne, it appears, that
in the opinion of the bishop of Bayonne, and his brother, that
body was then much corrupted ; that a few incendiaries influenced many there, so that it was far from deserving the high
character that it had in the world.   It is highly probable, they
apprehended that the carrying on the divorce might open a
door to let in that which they called heresy into England ;
which, considering the heat of that time, was enough to bias
them in all their deliberations.

I turn next homeward, to give a more particular account of Collect.
the proceedings both in Cambridge and Oxford.   I begin with The king's
the former, because it was first ended there ; and I have a letters to
sure ground to go on.   A worthy person[30] found among the sity of Ox-
manuscripts of Benet college a manuscript of Dr. Buckmaster, ford.
then the vice-chancellor, in which there is a very particular
relation of that affair.   It was procured to that house in queen
Elizabeth's reign by Dr. Jegon, then head of that house, and
was by him given to that college : for there is nothing remaining in the registers of the university relating to it, as that
learned person has informed me.

The vice-chancellor was then a fellow of Peter-house, of
which Dr. Edmunds was head, who was then a vicar and pre-

[30] [This was the famous antiquary Baker, of St. John's College, Cambridge.]

bendary in the diocese and cathedral church of Salisbury.

Collect.
Numb. 16.
The whole will be found in the Collection. " It begins with a
" short introductory speech of the vice-chancellor's, upon which
" he read the king's letter to them. It set forth, that many
" of the greatest clerks in Christendom, both within and with-
" out the realms, had affirmed in writing, that the marrying
" the brother's wife, he dying without children, was forbidden
" both by the law of God, and by the natural law : the king
" therefore, being desirous to have their minds, to whom he
" had shewed a benevolent affection, did not doubt but they
" would declare the truth, in a case of such importance, both
" to himself and to the whole kingdom. For this end, he sent
" Gardiner and Fox to inform them particularly of the circum-
" stances of the matter ; and he expected their answer under
" the seal of the university." The king's letter is dated the
16th of February.

" After this was read, the vice-chancellor told them, they
" saw what the king desired of them. They were men of free
" and ingenuous tempers ; every one of their consciences
" would dictate to them what was most expedient. After this
" follows the form of the grace that was proposed and granted,
" that the vice-chancellor and ten doctors, and the two proc-
" tors, with seventeen masters of arts, should have full au-
" thority to determine the question proposed, and to answer it
" in the name of the whole university. And whatsoever two
" parts in three of these persons should agree in, that, without
" any new order, should be returned to the king as the answer **64**
" of the university : only the question was to be disputed pub-
" licly ; and the determination that they should make was to
" be read in the hearing of the university.

" On the 9th of March, at a meeting of the university, the
" vice-chancellor told them, that the persons deputed by them
" had with great care and diligence examined the question,
" and had considered both the passages in the scriptures, and
" the opinions of the interpreters ; upon which they had a
" public disputation, which was well known to them all : so
" now, after great labours, and all possible industry, they came
" to the determination then to be read to them. Then follows
" the determination ; in which they add to the question pro-
" posed to them these words after *brother's wife, She being*

" *carnally known by her former husband :*" so, after above a
fortnight's study or practice, this was obtained of them : " The
" vice-chancellor came to Windsor, and on the second Sunday
" of Lent, after vespers, he delivered it to the king.   Of this
" he gave an account to Dr. Edmonds in a letter ; in which he
" tells him, he came to court while Latimer was preaching :
" the king gave him great thanks for the determination, and
" was much pleased with the method in which they had ma-
" naged it with such quietness.   The king praised Latimer's
" sermon ; and he was ordered to wait on the king the next
" day.   Dr. Butt brought twenty nobles from the king to
" him, and five marks to the junior proctor that came with
" him ; scarce enough to bear their charges," and far from
the price of corruption ; and gave him leave to go when he
pleased.   But after dinner the king came to a gallery, where
Gardiner and Fox, with the vice-chancellor, Latimer, and the
proctor were, and no more, and talked some hours with them.
He was not pleased with Gardiner and Fox, because the other
question, *Whether the pope had power to dispense with such
a marriage ?* was not likewise determined.   But the vice-
chancellor said, he believed that could not have been obtained.
But the king said, he would have that determined after Easter.
It appears by his letter, that there was a great outcry raised
against Cambridge for that which they had done.   The vice-
chancellor was particularly censured for it ; and he had lost a
benefice that the patron had promised him, but had upon this
changed his mind.   Those who did not like Latimer were not
pleased with his preaching.

   He heard, those of Oxford had appointed a select number
to determine the king's question ; and that Fox, when he was
there, was in great danger.   But a more particular account of
the proceedings in that university I take from three of king
Henry's letters to them, communicated to me by my learned
friend Dr. Kennet ; which, since they have not yet been
printed, will be found in the Collection.

   In the first letter that the king wrote to the university, he Collect.
sets forth, " That, upon certain considerations moving his con- Numb. 17.
" science, he had already consulted many learned men, both
" within the kingdom and without it ; but he desired to feel
" the minds of those among them who were learned in divinity,

" to see how they agreed with others : therefore he hoped 65
" they would sincerely and truly declare their consciences in
" that matter, and not give credit to misreports. He requires
" them, as their sovereign lord, to declare their true and just
" learning in that cause : therefore, in a great variety of ex-
" pressions, mixing threatenings with promises, if they should
" not uprightly, according to divine learning, handle them-
" selves, he leaves the declaring the particulars to the bishop
" of Lincoln, his confessor, to whom they were to give entire
" credit.

" By the second letter, the king tells them, he understood
" that a great part of the youth of the university did in a
" factious manner combine together, in opposition to the wise
" and learned men of that body, to have a great number of
" regents and non-regents to be joined in a committee of the
" doctors, proctors, and bachelors of divinity, for the deter-
" mination of the king's question : this he believed had not
" been often seen, that such a number of men of small learning
" should be joined with so famous a sort, to stáy their seniors
" in so weighty a cause. The king took that in very ill part,
" since they shewed themselves more unkind and wilful than
" all other universities had done : he hoped they would bring
" those young men into better order, otherwise they should
" feel what it was to provoke him so heinously.

" By his third letter, he complains that they delayed to
" send him their determination. He tells them the university
" of Cambridge had in a much shorter time agreed upon the
" manner of sending their answer ; and had sent their answer
" under their common seal. He would have more easily borne
" with a delay in making the answer, if they had so far obeyed
" him as to put the matter in a method. He therefore, being
" unwilling to proceed to extremities, had sent his counsellor
" Fox to them, hoping that the heads and rulers would con-
" sider their duty, in granting his request ; which was only,
" that they would *search the truth*, in a cause that so nearly
" concerned both himself and his people. And therefore he
" desired, that the numbers of private suffrages might not
" prevail against their heads, their rulers, and sage fathers ;
" but that they would so try the opinions of the multitude, as
" the importance of the matter did require. Hoping that their

" constitution was such, that there were ways left to eschew
" such inconveniences when they should happen : as he trusted
" they would not fail to do, and so to redeem the errors and
" delays that were past[31]." In conclusion, the matter was
brought into the method set forth in my History.

Here is no threatening them, by reason of any determination they might give ; but, on the contrary, all the vehemence in those letters is only with relation to the method of proceeding : and it was certainly a very irregular one, to join a great number of persons, who had not studied divinity, with men of the profession, who could only by a majority carry the point against reason and argument.

66   Here I shall insert some marginal notes that Dr. Creech wrote in his own book of my History, which is now in my hands. He says, that in the determination of Oxford they added the words of the brother's wife, (*ab eodem carnaliter cognitam,*) *that the first marriage was consummated ;* though this was not in the question sent to the university by their chancellor, archbishop Warham. He says further, that they mention the king's letters, in which it is written, that an answer was already made by the universities of Paris and Cambridge. This of Paris, though not in the king's letter, might have been written to them by their chancellor ; for it has appeared, from the letters published by Le Grand, that though the decision of the Sorbonne was not made till July, yet

[31] [In the same volume with the three letters referred to in the text, immediately following them is a letter by the king, dated 6 March, 21 regni, introducing Dr. Bell to the university. This is followed by another from Warham of the 15th of March, stating that he is informed, that ' the universities of Paris and Cambridge have already declared their resolute mind in this matter,' and recommending the appointment of thirty persons to determine the matter according to God's law, and accounting for his letter being in English instead of Latin, as in times past, on the ground that nothing might be interpreted otherwise than he meant.

The next letter is signed Willielmus Cantuar. Chancellor of the University of Oxford, and complains of the conduct of the regents and non-regents towards the heads of colleges ; and again recommending them to appoint some doctors and bachelors of divinity to determine the matter quickly. This is dated from Canterbury the 27th of March, 1530. The last letter on the subject is from the king (fol. 106 d), thanking them for the decision. This is dated from Windsor the 13th day of April, and reflects on the perverse conduct of some whom he recommends to be punished accordingly.]

several months before, the doctors of Paris had given their opinions for the divorce.   He also writes, that a letter came from their chancellor, Warham, to remove all the masters of arts out of the convocation, as unfit to determine so weighty a question.   Warham also, as he says, made the proposal of choosing thirty, to whom the question might be referred.   In another place he quotes the book that was published for the divorce ; which affirms, that the determinations of the universities were made without any corruption.   The questions were

[Rymer,
tom. xiv.
pp. 391—
401.]

not proposed to all the universities in the same terms : for to some, as to the faculty of the canon law at Paris, and to those of Angers and Bourges, the consummation of the marriage is expressly asserted in it.   And in the book in which the determinations of the universities are printed, those of the universities in England are not mentioned.   These are all the strictures he wrote on this part of my History.

Some more particulars are given us by Rymer concerning the determination of the foreign universities.   A copy of that

The decision made
at Bologna.

made at Bologna was carried to the governor : upon which five doctors swore before Croke that they had not carried it to him ; and that they had kept no copy of it.   This is attested

[Ibid.
p. 396.]

by a notary ; and the clerks and notaries swore the same, and that they did not know who carried it.   By this, it seems, Croke had engaged them to secresy ; and that the matter coming some way to the governor's knowledge, they took these oaths to assure him that they had not broken their word to him.

And at
Padua.
[Ibid.
p. 399.]

The decree in Padua was made July the first, and was attested by the podesta, and afterwards by the doge of Venice, on the 20th of September ; who affirm, that eleven doctors were present ; and that the determination was made with the

[Ibid.
p. 400.]

unanimous consent of the whole body.   And this is attested by notaries.

But now the scene must be removed to Rome for some time. The pope had ordered a citation to be made of the king to appear before him, to hear his cause judged.   The king would not suffer any such citation to be intimated to him ; so it was affixed at some churches in Flanders, at Tournay and Bruges. The king treated this with contempt ; while the emperor and his ministers were pressing the pope to proceed to censures.

The king of France interposed to obtain delays; in considera-
67 tion of whom, several delays were granted : and the pope said,
if king Henry would proceed no further in the matter of the
supremacy, he would yet grant a further delay. And whereas
the French king pressed for a delay of four months; the pope
said, if the king of England would own him as his judge, he
would give not only the time that was asked, but a year or
more.

Here I shall give an account of a long letter that the king
wrote to the pope ; there is no date put to it in the copy from
which I took it, but the substance of it makes me conclude it
was writ about this time.   It will be found in the Collection. Collect.
Numb. 18.

  " In it he complans, that no regard was had neither to his Among
" just desires, nor to the intercession of the most Christian Rymer's
MSS.32
" king : that the prayers of his nobility were not only despised, The king
" but laughed at.   All this was far contrary to what he ex- writes fully
to the pope.
" pected ; and was indeed so strange, that he could scarce
" think the pope was capable of doing such things, as he cer-
" tainly knew he was doing.   The pope, against what all men
" thought just, refused to send judges to come to the place
" where the cause lay.   The holy councils of old had decreed,
" that all causes should be determined there where they had
" their beginning : for this he quotes St. Cyprian among the
" ancients, and St. Bernard among moderns; who were of that
" mind.   The truth would be both sooner and more certainly
" found out, if examined on the place, than could possibly be
" at a distance.   The pope had once sent legates to England,
" and what reason could be given why this should not be done
" again ? But he saw the pope was so devoted to the emperor,
" that every thing was done as he dictated.   The queen's
" allegation, that England was a place so suspected by her,
" that she could not expect to have justice done her in it,
" must be believed, against the clearest evidence possible to
" the contrary.   The king bore with the liberties that many
" took who espoused her cause, more than was fitting ; nor
" did he threaten any, or grow less kind than formerly, to
" those who declared for the marriage ; and yet the pope pre-

32 [For an account of Rymer's   amongst the Sloane MSS. in the
MSS. see the end of the 17th   British Museum.]
volume of the Foedera.   They are

" tended he must give credit to this, and he offered no other
" reason for his not sending judges to England.   This was to
" fasten a base reflection upon the king, and an injustice, which
" he must look on as a great indignity done him. ·

" He further complains, that the pope took all possible
" methods to hinder learned men from delivering their opinion
" in his cause ; and though, after long and earnest applica-
" tions, he did give leave by his breves to all persons to give
" their opinion in it ; yet his own magistrates did, in his name,
" threaten those that were against the power of dispensing
" with the laws of God : this was particularly done at Bologña.
" The emperor's ministers every where, in contempt of the
" permission granted by the pope, terrified all who gave their
" opinion for the king ; at which the pope connived, if he did
" not consent to it.   The pope's nuncio did in France openly,
" and to the king himself, declare against the king's cause, as
" being founded neither on justice nor on reason : he still ex-
" pected, that the pope would have regard to the prerogative
" of his crown, and to the laws of England, which are as
" ancient as the pope's laws are ; and that he will not cite him 68
" to answer out of his kingdom, nor send any inhibitions into
" it : for he will suffer no breach to be made on the laws
" during his reign.   He was resolved to maintain that which
" was his own, as he would not invade that which belonged
" to another : he did not desire contention ; he knew the ill
" effects such disputes would have : upon all which, he ex-
" pected the pope's answer."   This had no effect on the pope ;
so far from it, that, upon a representation made to him, in
queen Catharine's name, that king Henry seemed resolved
to proceed to a second marriage, the pope sent out a second
breve on the 5th of January 1531, declaring any such marriage to be null, and the issue by it to be illegitimate ; de-
nouncing the severest censures possible against all that should
be any ways assisting in it, and requiring the king to live with
the queen in all conjugal affection till the suit was brought to
a conclusion.

The pope's second breve against the king's marrying another wife.

Something was to be done to stop proceedings at Rome ; or
upon this an immediate rupture must follow.   This brought
on the sending an *excusator* in the name of the king and
kingdom, to shew that the king was not bound to appear

Pleadings by an *excusator*.

upon the citation; nor yet to send a proctor to appear in his name. Sigismund Dondalus, and Michael de Conrades, two eminent advocates, were brought to Rome to maintain the plea of the *excusator*. They sent over the substance of their pleadings, which was printed at London by Berthelet. The sum of it was, Capisucci, dean of the rota, had cited the king to Rome to answer to the queen's appeal: the chief instructions sent by Carne were, to insist on the indignity done the king, to cite him to come out of his kingdom: but it seems that was a point that the advocates thought fit to leave to the ambassadors; they thought it not safe for them to debate it, so they pleaded on other heads.

They insisted much on that, (*de loco tuto*,) that no man ought to be cited to a place where he was not in full safety. It could not be safe, neither for the king nor the kingdom, that he should go so far from it. They shewed likewise, that, to make a place safe, all the intermediate places through which one must pass to it must be likewise safe. The pope therefore ought to send delegates to a safe place, either (*in partibus*) where the cause lay, or in the neighbourhood of it. It was said against them, that a cause once received in the court of Rome could never be sent out of it: but they replied, the pope had once sent delegates into England in this cause, and upon the same reason he might do it again; indeed the cause was never in the court, for the king was never in it. But it was said, the king might appear by a proctor: they answered, he was not bound to send a proxy where he was not bound to appear in person, but was hindered by a just impediment: nor was the place safe for a proxy. In a matter of conscience, such as marriage was, he could not constitute a proctor; for by the forms he was to impower him fully, and to be bound by all that he should do in his name. It is true, in a perpetual impediment, a proctor must be made: but this was not perpetual; for the pope might send delegates.

69   An *excusator* was to be admitted in the name of the king and kingdom, when the impediment was clear and lasting; they confessed, if it was only probable, a proctor must be constituted. There was no danger to be apprehended in the king's dominions. The queen's oath was offered, that she could not expect justice in that case. They shewed this ought

not to be taken, and could not be well grounded; but was only the effect of weak fear: it appearing evidently, that not only the queen herself, but that all who declared for her, were safe in England.　They did not insist on this, that the court ought to sit (*in partibus*) in the place where the cause lay: it seems they found that would not be borne at Rome: but they insisted on a court being to sit in the neighbourhood.　They shewed, that though the *excusator's* powers were not so full as to make him a proxy; yet they were not defective in that which was necessary for excusing the king's appearance, and for offering the just impediments, in order to the remanding of the matter.　The book is full of the subtleties of the canon law, and of quotations from canonists.

The French king obtains many delays.
p. 319.
Melange Hist. Lettres du Roy, fol. 1.[33]

Thus this matter was pleaded, and, by a succession of many delays, was kept on foot in the court of Rome above three years; chiefly by the interposition of Francis: for Langey tells us, that the king of France wrote once or twice a week to Rome, not to precipitate matters.　That court, on the other hand, pressed him to prevail with king Henry not to give new provocations.　He wrote to Rome from Arcques in the beginning of June 1531[34], and complained of citing the king to Rome: he said, learned persons had assured him that this was contrary to law, and to the privilege of kings, who could not be obliged to leave their kingdom; adding, that he would take all that was done for or against king Henry as done to himself.

[Jan. 10.]

fol. 8.

There is a letter writ from the cardinal of Tournon to king Francis, but without a date, by which it appears, " that the " motion of an interview between the pope and the king of " France was then set on foot: and he assures the king, that " the pope was resolved to satisfy him at their meeting; that " he would conduct king Henry's affair so dextrously, that " nothing should be spoiled: he must, in point of form, give " way to some things that would not be acceptable to him, " that so he might not seem too partial to king Henry; for " whom, out of the love that he bore to king Francis, he would " do all that was in his power, but desired that might not be " talked of."

[Ibid. fol. 8. b.]

On the 4th of May he wrote to him, that the emperor

---

[33] [The ' Lettres du Roy' begin with a new foliation after fol. 73.]　　[34] [Escript à Arcques le 10. Janvier 1531.]

threatened, that, if king Henry went on to do that injury to
his aunt, he would make war on him by the king of Scotland :
bot they believed he would neither employ his purse nor draw
his sword in the quarrel.　Langey reports the substance of
king Henry's letters to Francis ; he complained of the pope's
citing him to answer at Rome, or to send a proxy thither.　In
all former times, upon such occasions, judges were sent to the
place where the cause lay.　Kings could not be required to
go out of their dominions : he also complained of the papal
exactions.

70　Now there were two interviews set on foot, in hopes to make
up this matter, that seemed very near a breach.　Francis had
secretly begun a negotiation with the pope for the marriage of
the duke of Orleans, afterwards king Henry the Second, and
the famous Catharine de Medici : Francis, whose heart was
set on getting the duchy of Milan above all other things, hoped
by this means to compass it for his second son.　He likewise
pretended, that, by gaining the pope entirely to his interests,
he should be able to make up all matters between king Henry
and him.　But to lay all this matter the better, the two kings
were to have an interview first, in the neighbourhood of Calais,
which the bishop of Bayonne, who was now again in England,
was concerting.　King Henry pressed the doing it so, that he Le Grand,
might come back by All-Saints to hold his parliament.　The p. 553.
bishop saw king Henry would be much pleased if Francis [p. 554.]
would desire him to bring Anne Boleyn over with him, and if [p. 555.]
he would bring on his part the queen of Navarre.　The queen
of France was a Spaniard, so it was desired she might not
come ; he also desired that the king of France would bring his [p. 556.]
sons with him, and that no imperialists might be brought, nor
any of the Railleurs, (Gaudisseurs,) [35] for the nation hated that
sort of people,　Bayonne writes, he had sworn not to tell from
whom he had this hint of Anne Boleyn : it was no hard thing
to engage Francis into any thing that looked like gallantry ;
for he had writ to her a letter in his own hand, which Montmorency had sent over.　At the interview of the two kings, a An inter-
perpetual friendship was vowed between them : and king view be-
Henry afterwards reproached Francis for kissing the pope's two kings.
foot at Marseilles, which, he affrms, he promised not to do ;

[35] [ceux qui ont la reputation d'estre mocqueurs et gaudisseurs.]

nor to proceed to marry his son to the pope's niece, till he gave the king of England full satisfaction ; and added, that he promised, that if the pope did proceed to final censures against Henry, he would likewise withdraw himself from his obedience ; and that both the kings would join in an appeal to a general council.

The king marries Anne Boleyn.

Soon after that the king returned from this interview, he married Anne Boleyn ; but so secretly, that none were present at it but her father and mother, and her brother, with the duke of Norfolk. It went generally among our historians, that Cranmer was present at the marriage ; and I reported it

[Letter xiv. p. 244.]

so in my History [36] : but Mr. Strype saw a letter of Cranmer's to Hawkins, then the king's ambassador at the emperor's court, in which he writes, *Notwithstanding it hath been reported throughout a great part of the realm, that I married her, which was plainly false ; for I myself knew not thereof a fortnight after it was done : and many other things be reported of me, which be mere lies and tales*. In the same letter, he says it was about St. Paul's day. This confirms Stow's relation. But to write with the impartial freedom of an historian : it seems, the day of the marriage was given out wrong on design. The account that Cranmer gives of it cannot be called in question. But queen Elizabeth was born, not, as I put it,

[Letter lxxxiii. p. 274.]

on the 7th, but as Cranmer writes in another letter to Hawkins, on the 13th or 14th of September [37] : so there not being full eight months between the marriage and that birth, which would have opened a scene of raillery to the court of Rome, it seems the day of the marriage was then said to be in November. And in a matter that was so secretly managed, it was no hard thing to oblige those who were in the secret to silence. This seems to be the only way to reconcile Cranmer's letter to the reports commonly given out of the day of the marriage.

71

Cotton libr. Vitell. B. [xiv. fol. ? perhaps burnt.]

The news of this was soon carried to Rome. Cardinal Ghinuccius wrote to the king, "that he had a long conversation " with the pope, when the news was first brought thither. The " pope resolved to take no notice of it ; but he did not know " how he should be able to resist the instances that the em- " peror would make. He considered well the effects that his

[36] [See part i. p. 126.]   [37] [See part i. p. 134, and the note there.]

" censures would probably have.   He saw, the emperor in-
" tended to put things past reconciliation ; but it was not
" reasonable for the pope to pass censures, when it did not
" appear how they could be executed.   He could not do any
" thing prejudicial to the king, unless he resolved to lay out a
" vast sum of money ; which he believed he would not do, the
" success being so doubtful.   And he concludes, that they
" might depend upon it that the emperor could not easily
" bring the pope to pass those censures that he desired."

At this time, the third breve was published against the king,
on the 15th of November[38] : but it seems it was for some time
suppressed ; for it has a second date added to it, on the 23rd
of December in the year 1532 : " in which, after a long ex-
" postulation upon his taking Anne as his wife, and his putting
" away the queen, while the suit was yet depending ; the pope
" exhorts him to bring back the queen, and to put Anne away,
" within a month after this was brought to him ; otherwise he
" excommunicates both him and Anne :" but the execution of
this was suspended.   Soon after this, Bennet wrote a letter to
the king, all in cipher ; but the deciphering is interlined.   He
writes, " the pope did approve the king's cause as just and
" good ; and did it in a manner openly.   For that reason, he
" did not deliver the severe letter that the king wrote upon
" this breve, lest that should too much provoke him.   The
" emperor was then at Bologna, and pressed for the speedy
" calling a general council ; and, among other reasons, he gave
" the proceeding against the king for one.   The king's am-
" bassadors urged the decree of the council of Nice, that the
" bishops of the province should settle all things that belonged
" to it ; so by this, he said, the pope might put the matter out
" of his hands.   But the pope would not hear of that."   He
writes further, " that an old and famous man, who died lately,
" had left his opinion in writing, for the king's cause, with his
" nephew, who was in high favour with the pope.   The em-
" peror was taking pains to engage him in his interests, and
" had offered him a bishopric of 6000 ducats a year, likely soon
" to be void.   The king's ambassadors had promised him, on
" the other hand, a great sum from the king : they upon that

[38] [It is printed at length in Le Grand, vol. iii. p. 558.]

"ask orders about it speedily, lest too long a delay might
"alienate him from the king."

There is also a long letter, but without a date, written by
one who was born in Rome, but was employed to solicit the
king's cause. He told the pope, and was willing to declare it 72
to all the cardinals in the consistory, "that if they proceeded
"further in the king's cause, it would prove fatal to the see.
"They had already lost the Hungarians, with a great part of
"Germany; and would they now venture to lose England,
"and perhaps France with it? The king thought his marriage
"with queen Anne was firm and holy, and was resolved to
"prosecute his cause in that court no more. The king said,
"he was satisfied in his own conscience; but yet, if the pope
"would judge for his present marriage, both he and his minis-
"ters said, it would be agreeable to him."

Langey,
p. 317.
The cardinals of France pressed the king of France to use
all endeavours to bring king Henry with him to the interview
at Marseilles, or one fully empowered to put an end to the
p. 338.
matter of the divorce. Langey was sent to propose it to king
Henry; but that king told him, since he saw such a train of
dissimulation in the pope's proceedings, and delays upon delays,
that had quite disgusted him: he had now obtained a sentence
in England of the nullity of his marriage, in which he acquiesced: and upon that he was married, though secretly.
He was resolved to keep it secret till he saw what effects the
interview had; if the pope would not do him justice, he would
deliver the nation from that servitude.

Rymer,
[tom. xiv.
p. 416.]
June 22,
1531.
He had obtained the judgment of some universities concerning the citation to Rome. The university of Orleans gave
their opinion, that he was not bound to appear at Rome, neither
in person nor by proxy; and that the citation was null; but
that there ought to be a delegation of judges in the place
June 14,
1531. [ibid.
p. 419.]
Aug. 19,
1531.
where the cause lay. Many advocates in the court of parliament of Paris gave their opinions to the same purpose. The
canonists in Paris thought, that the king could not be cited to
go to Rome; but that judges ought to be sent to determine
the matter in some safe place.

King Hen-
ry opposes
King Henry wrote to his ambassadors [39] with the king of

[39] [This letter, addressed by Hen-
ry to Norfolk, Rochford, Brown and
Brian, has been printed in State
Papers, vol. vii. p. 473. It was

France, to divert him from the interview with the pope, as a the inter-
view with
the pope
in vain.
Rymer,
MSS. thing too much to the pope's honour.　And whereas the king of France wrote, that his chief design in it was to serve the king : he wrote upon it, that he was so sure of his nobility and commons, that he had no apprehension of any thing the pope could do.　He therefore desired him to write to the cardinals of Tournon and Grammont, and to his ambassadors at Rome, to press the admitting the *excusator's* plea ; for that was a point in which all princes were concerned.

King Francis pretended, that the breaking off the project of the interview could not be done : it had now gone too far, and his honour was engaged.　He was very sorry that the *excusator's* plea was rejected ; yet he did not despair but that all things might be yet set right ; which made him still more earnest for the interview.　And he was confident, if the king would come to the meeting, all would be happily made up : but since he saw no hope of prevailing with the king for that, 73 he desired that the duke of Norfolk might be sent over, with some learned persons, who should see the good offices he would do.

The duke of Norfolk was sent over upon this, and he found The duke
of Norfolk
sent to
France ; the king of France at Montpelier in the end of August[40] ; but told him, that upon the last sentence that was given at Rome, the king looked on the pope as his enemy, and he would resent his usage of him by all possible methods.　He studied to divert the interview, otherwise he said he must return immediately. King Francis answered, that the sentence was not definitive ; but though he could not break the interview, that was concerted by king Henry's own consent, he promised he would espouse the king's affair as his own.　He pressed the duke of Norfolk so earnestly to go along with him, that once he seemed

written some time in June, 1533, and alludes to Norfolk's letter from Amiens of the 6th of that month.]

[40] [There is a mistake in this date.　Norfolk had been sent over at the end of May, and was one of the ambassadors to whom the above letter was written.　He was at Calais May 30, at Amiens June 6, at Paris June 18, and at Briere June 23.　Rochford had been sent home some time before the beginning of August, for in the king's letter to Norfolk, of Aug. 8, 1533, a previous letter sent by Rochford is alluded to (State Papers, vii. 493).　This letter is entirely concerned with dissuading the interview between Francis and the pope, and recalling Norfolk, not allowing him to be present at it.　The dates are given correctly also by Herbert.]

convinced that it might be of good use in the king's cause, and a memorial was given him of the method of settling it: he upon this sent the lord Rochford to the king, to see if he would change the orders he had given him; and he stayed only a few days after he had despatched him. But he said his orders for his return were positive: if a change of orders should come, he would quickly return; if not, he would get some learned men to be sent, to see what might be devised at Marseilles.

But soon recalled.

The king of France wrote to his ambassador with king Henry, that if the duke of Norfolk could have been allowed to go with him to Marseilles, much might have been done; and he sent with that a part of the cardinal of Tournon's last letter to him of the 17th of August, in which he wrote, "that he " had spoke fully to the pope, as the king had ordered him, " about the king of England's affair: the pope complained " that king Henry had not only proceeded to marry contrary " to the breve he had received, but that he was still publishing " laws in contempt of his see; and that Cranmer had pro- " nounced the sentence of divorce as legate. This gave the " cardinals such distaste, that they would have been highly " offended with the pope, if he had done nothing upon it. He " therefore advised the king to carry the duke of Norfolk with " him to Marseilles; for if king Henry would but seem to " repair the steps he had made in the *attentates*, as they called " them, and do that which might save the pope's honour, he " assured him, such was his love to him, that for his sake he " would do all that was desired, with all his heart. But he " feared expedients would not be readily found, if the duke of " Norfolk went not to Marseilles."

The king of France was to have been god-father, if queen Anne had brought a son.

The king of France sent such messages to king Henry by the duke of Norfolk, and such compliments to queen Anne, as highly pleased them: for his ambassador wrote to him, that, since the duke of Norfolk's coming, king Henry expressed his confidence and friendship for him in a very particular manner. King Henry had asked him, if he had no order to stand god-father in the king of France's name, in case the queen should be delivered of a son. He answered, he had none; but he would write to the king upon the subject. The duke of Nor-folk said, he had spoke to the king of France about it; who agreed to it, that either the ambassador, or some other sent

express, should do it. The child's name was to be Edward or Henry ; (but the birth proving a daughter, this went no far-
74 ther.)   He adds in his letter, that Gardiner, then bishop of Winchester, was sent to Marseilles. The king of France sent from Arles on the 17th of September an order for the christening.

But now the next scene is at Marseilles : where, after the ceremonies were over, the king of France set himself, as he writes, with great zeal to bring the pope to be easy in the king's matter : he protested he minded no business of his own, till he should see what could be done in the matter of the king's divorce. The pope said, he left the process at Rome ; so that nothing could be done in it. The French ambassador wrote to his master, that king Henry charged him with this, that he himself brought over instructions, with promises that Francis would not proceed to the marriage of his son, till the king's matter was done: the ambassador denied this, and offered to shew his instructions, that it might appear that no such article was in them. King Henry insisted that the French king had promised it both to himself and to the queen ; and if he failed him in this, he could depend no more on his friendship. When the ambassador told the duke of Norfolk how uneasy this would be to the king of France, who had the king's concerns so much at heart, and that all the interest that he could gain in the pope would be employed in the king's service ; for if he should break with the pope, that must throw him entirely into the emperor's hands : the duke of Norfolk confessed all that was true ; but said, that the king's head was so embroiled with this matter, that he trusted no living man, and that both he and the queen suspected himself.

The bishop of Auxerre, the French ambassador, had wrote from Rome, " that the pope would do all that they asked, and " more if he durst or could : but he was so pressed by the " emperor's people, that though it was against God and reason, " and the opinion even of some of the imperial cardinals, he " was forced to do whatsoever cardinal Dosme demanded." In a letter to cardinal Tournon, the bishop of Auxerre complains, that the king of England was ill used ; and in a letter to the pope's legate in France, he writes, " that the pope was " disposed to grant king Henry's desire, yet he was so pressed

Marginal notes:

The interview at Marseilles.

Mel. Hist. fol. 142.

[Nov. 7, 1533. Ibid. fol. 142 b.]

[fol. 143.]

[Feb. 7.] Mel. Hist. p. 174. Great promises made by the pope.

[Feb. 7. Ibid. fol. 174 b.]
[Feb. 7. Ibid.]

" by the imperialists, that he expected no good from him, un-
" less in the way of dissembling : he firmly believed he would
" do well if he durst : his answer to the king of France was as
" good as could be wished for, he hoped the effects would

Mel. Hist.
p. 175.

" agree to it : cardinal Farnese, the ancientest cardinal, (after-
" wards pope Paul the Third,) was wholly for them : the car-
" dinal of Ancona, next to him in seniority, was wholly im-
" perialist.   He writes, that the ambassadors had an audience
" of three hours of the pope, when they delivered the king of
" France's letters on the king of England's behalf : the pope
" said he was sorry that he must determine the matter : for he
" should have small thanks on both sides.   The thing had
" been now four years in his hands, he had yet done nothing :
" if he could do as he wished, he wished as they all wished :
" and he spake this in such a manner, that they were much
" mistaken, if he spoke not as he thought.   The pope asked
" them what made the king of France to be so earnest in this
" matter : they answered, that the two kings were so united,
" that they were both more touched with the affairs each of 75
" the other, than with their own."

[July 13.
Ibid. fol.
176 b.]

In another letter to Montmorency he writes, " that there
" was a new delay granted for four months. The pope, upon
" his granting it, pressed him to write to the king, to prevail
" with king Henry to send a proxy.   He answered, he be-
" lieved that would not be done, unless assurance was given

[fol. 177.]

" that the cause should be remitted.   If the matter had been
" then put to the vote, the ancient and learned cardinals would
" have judged for the king of England ; but they were few,
" and the number of the others was great ; so that the cause
" would have been quite lost."

Cottonlibt
Vitell. B.
xii. [?]
Practices
upon r-
dinals

At the same time, the cardinal of Ancona proposed to Bennet,
and to Cassali, that if a proxy were sent to Rome, they should
have not only justice, but all manner of favour : for both the
pope and the cardinals did very positively promise, that a commission should be made to delegates to hear the witnesses in
England, reserving only the final sentence to the pope.   Cassali was upon this sent to England ; but his negotiation had no
effect : only he seems to have known well the secret method of
practising with the cardinals.   For, upon his return, he met
the king of France at Compiegne, with whom he had much

discourse about managing the cardinals : particularly cardinal
de Monte, (afterwards pope Julius the Third.) The king of
France had sent forty thousand crowns to be distributed in the
court of Rome ; upon which, he offers some very prudent suggestions. The letter to the king from thence seemed so con- [Nov. 16.]
siderable, that I have put it in the Collection.   Collect.
These were the preparations on all hands for the meeting at Numb. 19.
Marseilles ; where Francis protested that he set himself so
earnestly to get satisfaction to be given to Henry, that he
minded no business of his own till he should see what could be
done in that. The pope said indeed, that he had left the
process at Rome ; but they wrote over, that they knew this
was false : yet by that they saw the pope intended to do nothing in it. Francis indeed complained, that there was no
proxy from the king sent to Marseilles : if there had been one,
he said, the business had been ended. It was also reported, Mel. Hist.
that the king of France had said to the duke of Norfolk, he fol. 19.
would be the king's proxy ; (here, in the margin, it is set
down, *The duke of Norfolk denies he said this*[41] ;) but the
king of France knew, that the king would never constitute a
proxy, that being contrary to the laws of his kingdom. The
pope confessed that his cause was just : all the lawyers in
France were of that mind. But the pope complained of the [fol. 19 b.]
injuries done the see by king Henry. Francis answered, the
pope began doing injuries : but king Henry moved, that,
setting aside what was past, without asking reparation of either
side, justice might be done him ; and if it was not done, he
would trouble himself no more about it.

He afterwards charged king Francis, " that in several par-
" ticulars he had not kept his promises to him. He believed,
" that if he had pressed the pope more, he would have yielded. [fol. 20.]
76 " It was said, king Henry was governed by his council ;
" whereas, he said, he governed them, and not they him.
" Upon this audience, the duke of Norfolk seemed troubled
" that the king was so passionate : he had advised the king,
" but in vain, to let the annates go still to Rome." This is
put in the margin[42].

[41] [Apostile portant ces mots
*Nota que Mr. de Norfort dict n'en
avoir du tout tant dict.*]

[42] [This occurs in the margin,
and is called *Apostile sur l'original*,
Mr. de Norfort sur ce propos m'a

M 2

fol. 21. In another memorial, set next to the former, and, as it seems, writ soon after it, it is said, that the emperor had sent word to the queen and her daughter not to come to Spain till he had first got right to be done them : and that the people were in a disposition to join with any prince that would espouse their quarrel.   This is said to be the general inclination of all sorts of people: for they apprehended a change of religion, and a war that would cut off their trade with the Netherlands ; so that the new queen was little beloved.

The con-
vocation
meets. But now I must return, and set out the progress of matters that provoked the pope and court of Rome so much.   I shall give first the several proceedings of the convocation.

The parliament had complained of the oath *ex officio*, by which the ordinaries obliged persons to answer to such accusations as were laid to their charge upon oath : and as they answered, charging themselves, they were obliged either to abjure or to burn [43]. To this they added some other grievances. When they presented them to the king, he told them he could give no answer till he heard what the clergy would say to [capp. 5, 6,
13. Sta-
tutes, vol.
iii. pp. 285,
288, 292.] them. They also passed acts about some points that the clergy thought belonged to them ; as mortuaries, plurality of benefices, and clergymen taking farms.

The first motion made by the lower house was concerning Tracy's testament; who had left his soul to God through Jesus Christ, to whose intercession alone he trusted, without the help of any other saint: therefore he left no part of his goods to any that should pray for his soul. This touching the clergy very sensibly, they began with it; and a commission was given for the raising his body.

[Wilkins'
Concilia,
vol. iii. p.
747.] In a following session, the prolocutor complained of another testament, made by one Brown of Bristol, in the same strain. So, to prevent the spreading of such an example, it was ordered, that Tracy's body should be dug up and burnt.   In the eighty-fourth session, the house being thin, an order was made, that all the members should attend, for some constitutions were at that time to be treated of.

In the ninety-first session, which was in the end of February,

---

dict qu'il à prié et conseillé au Roy son maistre de laisser aller les Annates à Rome, mais il ne luy à encores l'accordé.]

[43] [See part i. p. 116.]

the prolocutor came up with a motion, that those who were
presented to ecclesiastical benefices should not be obliged by
their bishops to give any bond, obliging them under temporal
punishment to residence : but to this no answer was given, nor
was any rule made against it.   There had been complaints
made of clerks nonresidents in the former session of parliament; and it seems some bishops thought, the surest way to
stop that clamour was to take bonds for residence. And though
this complaint shews the ill temper of the lower house, since
77 they did not offer any other better remedy ; yet the upper
house offering no answer to it, seems to imply their approving
of it.

They treat
concerning
residence.
[92nd ses-
sion, March
5, ibid.]

In the ninety-third session, Latimer, who had been thrice
required to subscribe some articles, refused to do it : he was
excommunicated, and appointed to be kept in safe custody in
Lambeth. Session ninety-six, it was resolved, that if Latimer
would subscribe some of the articles, he should be absolved.
Upon that he submitted, confessed his error, and subscribed
all the articles except two.

[March 11,
ibid.]

[March 21,
ibid.]

In the ninety-seventh session, on the 12th of April 1532, the
archbishop proposed to them the preparing an answer to the
complaints that the commons had made to the king against
the proceedings in their courts.

An answer
to the com-
plaints of
the com-
mons.
[Wilkins'
Concilia,
vol. iii. p.
748.]
[April 15.]

In the ninety-eighth session, the preamble of that complaint
was read by Gardiner, with an answer that he had prepared
to it.   Then the two clauses of the first article, which answers
to them, were also read and agreed to, and sent down to the
lower house. Latimer was also brought again before them,
upon complaint of a letter that he had written to one Green-
wood, in Cambridge.

In the ninety-ninth session, an answer to the complaint of
the commons was read and agreed to, and ordered to be laid
before the king ; with which he was not satisfied. Latimer
being called to answer upon oath, he appealed to the king, and
said, he would stand to his appeal.

[98th ses-
sion, ibid.]

Peto and Elstow, two brethren of the house of the Observants in Greenwich, accused Dr. Curren for a sermon preached
there : but the archbishop ordered them to be kept in custody,
with the bishop of St. Asaph, till they should be dismissed.

Pro-
ceedings
against
heretics.

In the hundredth session, the king sent a message by Gar-

diner, intimating, that he remitted Latimer to the archbishop :
and upon his submission, he was received to the sacraments.
This was done at the king's desire : but some bishops protested, because this submission did not import a renunciation
usual in such cases.   After this, four sessions were employed
in a further consideration of the answer to the complaints of
the house of commons.

In the hundred and fifth session, the prolocutor brought up
four draughts concerning the ecclesiastical authority, for making
laws in order to the suppressing of heresy : but declared, that
he did not bring them up as approved by the house ; he only
offered them to the bishops, as draughts prepared by learned
men.   He desired they would read them, and choose what
was true out of them : but added, that he prayed, that, if they
prepared any thing on the subject, it might be communicated
to the lower house.   Some of these are printed : I shall therefore only insert one in my Collection, because it is the shortest
of them, and yet does fully set forth their design.   It was
formed in the upper house, and agreed to in the lower, with
two alterations.   In it they promise the king, that " for the
" future, such was the trust that they put in his wisdom, good-
" ness, and zeal, and his incomparable learning, far exceeding
" the learning of all other princes that they had read of, that
" *during his natural life,* they should not enact, promulge, or
" put in execution, any constitution to be made by them, un-
" less the king by his royal assent did license them so to do.
" And as for the constitutions already made, of which the
" commons complained, they would readily submit the consi-
" deration of these *to the king only :* and such of these as the
" king should judge prejudicial and burdensome, they offered
" to moderate or annul them according to his judgment.
" Saving to themselves all the immunities and liberties granted
" to the church, by the king and his progenitors, with all such
" provincial constitutions as stand with the laws of God, and
" *holy church,* and of the realm, which they prayed the king
" to ratify : providing that, till the king's pleasure should be
" made known to them, all ordinaries might go on to execute
" their jurisdiction as formerly."   This did not pass easily ;
there was great debating upon it : but upon adding the
words, *during the king's natural life,* which made it a tem-

Rights of
an English
Convoca-
tion. [pp.
521, sqq.]
Collect.
Numb. 20.
The peti-
tion to the
king.
[Ibid.
p. 534.]

78

porary law ; and by adding the words *holy church* after the
laws of God, which had a great extent ; this form was agreed
to : but what effect this had, or whether it was offered to the
king, does not appear.   The alterations that were afterwards
made will appear to any who compares this with the submission ; of which a particular account will be found in my
History.

The bishop of London, presiding in the absence of the [Wilkins'
archbishop, told them, that the duke of Norfolk had signified Concilia,
to him, that the house of commons had granted the king a 749.]
fifteenth, to be raised in two years; so he advised the clergy
to be as ready as the laity had been to supply the king.   The
prolocutor was sent down with this intimation : he immediately
returned back, and proposed that they should consider of an
answer to be made to the king, concerning the ecclesiastical
authority; and that some might be sent to the king, to pray
him that he would maintain the liberties of the church, which
he and his progenitors had confirmed to them : and they desired, that the bishops of London and Lincoln, with some
abbots, the dean of the king's chapel, and Fox, his almoner,
would intercede in behalf of the clergy ; which they undertook
to do.

In the hundred and sixth session, which was on the 10th The sub-
of May, the archbishop appointed a committee to go and made to
treat with the bishop of Rochester at his house upon that the king,
matter.   In the hundred and seventh session, the 13th of only dis-
May, the archbishop appointed the chancellor of Worcester to senting.
raise Tracy's body : then they agreed to the answer they
were to make to the king.   In the hundred and eighth session, on the 15th of May, the writ for proroguing the convocation was brought to the archbishop : at the same time,
the duke of Norfolk, the marquis of Exeter, the earl of Oxford, the lord Sandys, lord chamberlain, and the lord Boleyn,
and lord Rochford, were in a secret conference with the archbishop and bishops for the space of an hour ; when they withdrew, the prolocutor and clergy came up.   The archbishop
asked, how they had agreed to the schedule; which, as appears, was the form of the submission.   The prolocutor told
him, how many were for the affirmative, how many for the
negative, and how many were for putting off the three articles

(of the submission). The archbishop said, he expected those
lords would come back to him from the king, and so sent them
back to their house.   These lords came back to the chapter- 79
house, and, after some discourse with the bishops, they retired.
After dinner, the schedule was read in English; and the archbishop asked, if they agreed to it; they all answered they did
agree to it, only the bishop of Bath dissented.   Then he sent
it down by his chancellor, to propose it to the lower house.
After that, on the 15th of May, it seems the schedule was sent
back by the lower house, though that is not mentioned in the
abstract that we have remaining : for that day the convocation was prorogued, and the next day the archbishop delivered
it to the king, as enacted and concluded by himself and others.
The convocation was prorogued to the 5th of November.

And thus this great transaction was brought about in little
more than a month's time ; the first motion towards it being
made on the 12th of April, and it was concluded on the 15th
of May.   It appears, by their heat against Tracy's testament,
and against Latimer, that they who managed the opposition
that was made to it were enemies to every thing that looked
towards a reformation.   It seems Fisher did not protest : for
though, by their sending a committee to his house, it may be
supposed he was sick at that time, yet he might have sent a
proxy, and ordered a dissent to be entered in his name : and
that not being done, gives ground to suppose that he did not
vehemently oppose this submission. By it, all the opposition
that the convocations would probably have given to every step
that was made afterwards in the reformation was so entirely
restrained, that the quiet progress of that work was owing
chiefly to the restraint under which the clergy put themselves
by their submission : and in this the whole body of this reformed church has cheerfully acquiesced, till within these few
years, that great endeavours have been used to blacken and
disgrace it.

[Wilkins'
Conc. vol.
iii. p. 748.]
I have seen no particular account how this matter went in
the convocation at York, nor how matters went there; save
only that it was agreed to give a tenth.   I have seen a letter
of Magnus, one of the king's chaplains, who was required by
The pro-
ceedings at
York. Cromwell to go thither, where Dr. Lee was to meet him.
There is no year added in the date of the letter ; but since he

mentions the last convocation, that had given a great sum of money, and owned the king to be the supreme, that fixes it to this session. He dates it from Marybone the 21st of April, as it will be seen in the Collection. "He was then in an ill state *Collect.* "of health, but promises to be at York soon after the begin- *Numb.* 21. "ning of their convocation. He complains, that he had no "assistance at the last meeting; and that the books, which "the king had promised should be sent after him, were not "sent: which made the king's cause to be the longer in treat- "ing, before it came to a good conclusion. The prelates and "clergy there would not believe any report of the acts passed "at London, unless they were shewed them authentically, "either under seal or by the king's letters. He hopes both "these things, which had been neglected formerly, would be "now done; otherwise the clergy in those parts would not "proceed to any strange acts: so he warns him, that all "things may be put in order."

80　Whatsoever it was that passed either in the one or the other convocation, the king kept it within himself for two years; for so long he was in treating terms with Rome: and if that had gone on, all this must have been given up. But when the final breach came on, which was after two years, it was ratified in parliament.

Before the next meeting, Warham died. He had all along [Aug. 23.] concurred in the king's proceedings, and had promoted them in convocation; yet in the last year of his life, six months before his death, on the 9th of February 1531, he made a pro- 1532. testation of a singular nature, not in the house of lords, but at [24 Feb. Lambeth; and so secretly, that mention is only made of three *Wilkins'* notaries and four witnesses present at the making of it. It is *Conc. vol.* iii. p. 746.] to this effect; *that what statutes soever had passed, or were to pass in this present parliament, to the prejudice of the pope, or the apostolic see; or that derogated from, or lessened the ecclesiastical authority, or the liberties of his see of Canterbury, he did not consent to them; but did disown and dissent from them.* This was found in the Longueville library, and was communicated to me by Dr. Wake, the present bishop of Lincoln. I leave it with the reader, to consider what construction can be made upon this; whether it was in the decline of his life put on him by his confessor, about the time of Lent, as a penance for what he had done; or if he must be looked on as a deceitful man, that, while he seemed openly to concur in those things, he protested against them secretly. The instrument will be found in the Collection. Upon his death, the prior and convent of Christ's Church of Canterbury deputed the bishop of St. Asaph to preside in the convocation. On the 20th of February, in the fourth session, the bishop of London moved, that the two universities should be exempted from paying any part of the subsidy: the same was also desired for some religious orders; and it was agreed to, Gardiner only dissenting as to the exemption of the religious orders. It may reasonably be supposed, that his opposing this was in compliance with the king, who began to shew an aversion both to the monks and friars, seeing they were generally in the interests of queen Catharine; and Gardiner was the most forward in his compliances of all the clergy, Bonner only excepted, though the old leaven of popery was deep in them both.

Collect.
Numb. 22.
Proceedings during the vacancy of Canterbury.
[Wilkins' Conc. vol. iii. p. 749.]

[Ibid. p. 756]

In the eleventh session, on the 26th of March, Latimer was again brought before them: and it was laid to his charge, that he had preached, contrary to his promise. Gardiner inveighed severely against him; and to him all the rest agreed. When the prolocutor came up, the president spoke to him of the subsidy: then the matter of the king's marriage was brought before them. Gardiner produced some instruments, which he desired them to read: they were the judgments of several universities. Some doubted if it was safe to debate a matter that was then depending before the pope; but the president put an end to that fear, by producing a breve of the pope's in which all were allowed to deliver their opinions freely in that matter: so he exhorted them to examine the questions to be put to them carefully, that they might be prepared to give their opinions about them

The convocation judges against the king's marriage.

In the twelfth session, the president produced the original 81 instruments of the universities of Paris, Orleans, Bologna, Padua, Bourges, and Toulouse; (Angers and Ferrara are not named;) and, after much disputing, they were desired to deliver their opinions as to the consummation of the marriage. But because it was a difficult case, they asked more time. They had till four o'clock given them; then there were yet

more disputings: in conclusion, they agreed with the universities. This was first put to them; though in the instrument
made upon it, it is mentioned after that which was offered to
them in the next session.

On the 2nd of April 1533, Cranmer being now consecrated, [April 5.]
and present, two questions were proposed, and put to the vote. Rymer.
The first was, *Whether the prohibition to marry the brother's* [tom. xiv.
wife, the former marriage being consummated, was dispen- p. 454.]
sable by the pope? Or, as it is in the minutes, *Whether it was*
lawful to marry the wife of a brother dying without issue,
but having consummated the marriage? And if the prohibi-
tion of such a marriage was grounded on a divine law, with
which the pope could dispense, or not? There were present
sixty-six divines, with the proxies of an hundred and ninety- [Ibid. p.
seven absent bishops, abbots, and others: all agreed to the 455.]
affirmative, except only nineteen.

The second question was, *Whether the consummation of*
prince Arthur's marriage was sufficiently proved? This belonged to the canonists; so it was referred to the bishops and
clergy of that profession, being forty-four in all, of whom one
had the proxy of three bishops[45]: all these, except five or six,
affirmed it: of these, the bishop of Bath and Wells was one.
Of all this a public instrument was made.

In the account I formerly gave of this matter[46], I offered a
conjecture concerning the constitution of the two houses, that
deans and archdeacons, who sat in their own right, were then
of the upper house; which I see was without any good ground.
I likewise committed another error through inadvertence: for
I said, the opinions of nineteen universities were read; whereas
only six were read. And the nineteen, which I added to the
number of the universities, was the number of those who did
not agree to the vote[47].

These questions were next sent to the convocation of the The arch-
province of York; where there were present twenty-seven bishop,
divines, who had the proxies of twenty-four who were absent: Cranmer,
gives sen-
tence a-
gainst it.

[45] [The bishop of Winchester had
the proxies of the bishop of Chichester, Bangor and Worcester.]

[46] [See part i. p. 129.]

[47] [The whole mode of proceeding, with all the names for and a-

gainst are in Fiddes' Wolsey, pp.
195–204. It is apparently taken
from Wharton's MSS. The date is
April 5, 1533. Amongst the 19 dis-
sentients are the bishops of Rochester and Llandaff.]

and all these, two only excepted, agreed to the first question. There were likewise forty-four canonists present, with the proxies of five or six: to them the second question was put; and all these were for the affirmative, two only excepted. The whole representative of the church of England, in the convocation of the two provinces of Canterbury and York, did in this manner give their answer to the two questions put to them; upon which Cranmer wrote to the king on the 11th of April, complaining that the great cause of his matrimony had depended long: and upon that, he desired his license to judge it; which the king readily granted. So he gave sentence, condemning it on the 23rd of May: and then the king openly owned his second marriage; for the new queen's big belly 82 could be no longer concealed.

With that the court of Rome was highly offended.

This was highly resented at Rome, as an open attempt upon the pope's authority; and these steps, in their style, were called the *attentates:* so, considering the blind submission to the popes, in which the world had been kept for so many ages, it was no wonder to find the imperialists call upon the pope, almost in a tumultuary manner, to exert his authority to the full, when he saw it so openly affronted. And it is very probable, that if the pope had not, with that violent passion, that Italians have for the advancing their families, run into the proposition for marrying his niece to the duke of Orleans, he would have fulminated upon this occasion: but he, finding that might be broke off, if he had proceeded to the uttermost extremities with king Henry, was therefore resolved to prolong the time, and to delay the final sentence; otherwise the matter would have been ended much sooner than it was.

Gardiner, Brian, and Bennet were sent as ambassadors to the king of France, to Marseilles. Bonner was also sent thither on a more desperate service; for he was ordered to go and read the king's appeal from the pope to a general council, in the pope's own presence, at such time and in such a manner

Cotton lib. Vitell. B. xiv. [burnt.] Collect. Numb. 23.

as the king's ambassadors should direct. Of the execution of this he gave the king a very particular account, in a letter to him, bearing date at Marseilles the 13th of November 1533: which the reader will find in the Collection, copied from the original. In it he tells the king,

" That, being commanded by his ambassadors to intimate

" to the pope in person the provocations and appeals that he Bonner intimates the
king's ap-
peal to the
pope.
" had made to a general council; he carried one Penniston,
" who it seems was a notary, with him, to make an act con-
" cerning it.   They came to the pope's palace on the 17th of
" November, in the morning. He found some difficulty in
" getting access; for he was told that the pope was going to
" hold a consistory, so that no other business was to inter-
" pose: yet he got into the pope's chamber, where the pope
" was with the two cardinals De Medici and Lorraine; the
" pope being apparelled in his stole to go to the consistory.
" The pope quickly observed Bonner, for he had prayed the
" datary to let the pope know he desired to speak with him:
" the datary said it was not a proper time, but Bonner was
" resolved to go immediately to him; so he told the pope of
" it; who upon that dismissed the cardinals, and, going to a
" window, he called him to him. Upon that Bonner told him
" the message he had from the king to read before him,
" making such apology, first in the king's name; and then in
" his own, as was necessary to prepare him for it.   The pope
" cringed in the Italian way, but said, he had not·time then
" to hear those papers; but bade him come again in the after-
" noon, and he would give him a full audience. When he
" came again, he was, after some others had their audience,
" called in; Penniston following him, whom the pope had not
" observed in the morning. So Bonner told him, that it was
" he who had brought over his commission and orders; upon
83 " that the pope called for his datary, and for Simonetta and
" Capisucci.   Till they came in, the pope in discourse asked
" both for Gardiner and Brian, seeming not to know that they
" were at Marseilles; and he lamented the death of Bennet:
" he complained of the king's using him as he did. Bonner,
" on the other hand, complained of his unkind usage of the
" king; and that he had, contrary to his promise, avocated
" the cause, when it was brought to the point of giving sen-
" tence; and had now retained the cause to Rome, whither
" the king could not come personally, nor was he bound to
" send a proctor: and he urged the matter very close upon
" the pope. He also complained, that, the king's cause being
" just, and esteemed so by the best learned men in Christen-
" dom, yet the pope kept it so long in his hands. The pope

" answered, that had not the queen refused the judges as sus-
" pect, and taken an oath that she expected no justice in the
" king's dominions, he would not have avocated the cause: but
" in that case, notwithstanding his promise, he was bound to
" do it; and the delay of the matter lay wholly at the king's
" door, who did not send a proctor. While Bonner was reply-
" ing, the datary came in, and the pope cut him short; and
" commanded the datary to read the commission: which he
" did. The pope often interrupted the reading it with words
" that expressed a high displeasure: and when the appeal was
" read to the next lawful general council to be held in a proper
" place, he expressed with some rage his indignation; but re-
" strained himself, and said, all that came from the king was
" welcome to him: but by his gesture and manner it appeared
" he was much discomposed. Yet after that, he shewed how
" willing he was to call a council, but that the king seemed to
" put it off; he ordered the datary to read it quite through:
" in the end mention being made of the archbishop of Canter-
" bury's sentence, he spake of that with great contempt. He
" also observed, that the king in words expressed respect to
" the church and to the apostolic see, yet he expressed none
" to his person. While they were thus in discourse, the king
" of France came to see the pope, who met him at the door.
" That king seemed to know nothing of the business, though
" Bonner believed he did know it. The pope told him what
" they were about; they two continued in private discourse
" about three quarters of an hour, and seemed very cheerful:
" then that king went away, the pope conducted him to the
" door of the antechamber. When the pope came back, he
" ordered the datary to read out all that remained: the pope
" often interrupting him as he read. When the first instru-
" ment was read to an end, Bonner offered the two appeals
" that the king had made to a general council: these the pope
" delivered to the datary, that he might read them.

It was re-
jected by
the pope.

" When all was read, the pope said he would consider with
" the cardinals what answer was to be given them; and
" seemed to think that the writings were to remain with him:
" but Bonner pressing to have them again, he said he would
" consider what answer he was to give to that. So the pope
" dismissed him, after an audience that lasted three hours.

" The datary told Bonner, there was to be a consistory next
" day ; after that he might come to receive his answer.   On
84 " the 10th, a consistory was held ; in the afternoon, the pope
" was long taken up with the blessing of beads, and admitting
" persons of quality of both sexes to kiss his foot.   When that
" was over, he called Bonner in, and the pope began to ex-
" press his mind towards the king, that it was to do him all
" justice, and to please him all he could ; and though it had
" not been so taken, yet he intended to continue in the same
" mind : but, according to a constitution of pope Pius, that
" condemned all such appeals, he rejected the king's appeal·
" to a general council, as frivolous and unlawful.   As for a
" general council, he would use all his diligence to have it
" meet, as he had formerly done : but the calling it belonged
" wholly to him.   He said he would not restore the instru-
" ments ; and told Bonner, that the datary should give him
" his answer in writing.   Bonner went to the datary's cham-
" ber, where he found the answer already written, but not
" signed by him : next day he signed it, adding the *salvo* of
" answering it more fully and more particularly, if it should
" be thought meet.

" The pope left Marseilles the next day, and went towards
" Rome.   Bonner concludes that the French knew of their
" design, and were willing it should be done two or three days
" before the pope's departure ; yet when it was done, they
" said it had spoiled all their matters, and the king's likewise."
He says nothing of any threatening of bad usage to himself.
The king of France indeed, when he expostulated upon the
affront done the pope while in his house, said, that he durst
not have done that in any other place : this makes it probable
that the pope told him how he would have used Bonner, if he
had served him with that appeal in his own territories.   So
whether this came to be known afterwards from the court of
France, or whether Bonner might have spread it in England
at his return, to raise the value of that piece of service, which
he was capable of doing, cannot be determined.   It is certain
it was reported in England so, that in the Answer to Sanders Anti-
it is set down ; and from him I took it: but I will leave it with Sanderus.
the reader to consider what credit may be due to it.

At the same time Cranmer, hearing the pope designed to

proceed against him, did by the king's order appeal likewise
to a general council, and sent the instrument, with a warrant
to execute it, to Cromwell, that it might be sent to the bishop
of Winchester, to get it to be intimated to the pope in the best
manner that could be thought of: he therefore, by the king's
command, sent this to him in a letter dated the 22nd of November, which will be found in the Collection; but it does not
appear to me what was done upon it.

Collect.
Numb. 24.

I shall in the next place give an account of the instructions
that the king of France sent by Bellay, then translated from
Bayonne to Paris, whom he despatched immediately after he
came back from Marseilles, as the person in the kingdom that
was the most acceptable to the king.   The substance of them
is, "that Francis had at the interview studied nothing so much
" as to advance Henry's matters: yet he heard that he com-
" plained of him as having done less than he expected, which
" he took much amiss.   It was agreed by the two kings, that
" a proposition should be set on foot for the duke of Orleans
" marrying the pope's niece;   which had not been before 85
" thought of.   The matter was so far advanced, and the inter-
" view so settled, that Francis could not afterwards put it off
" with honour; all being done pursuant to their first agree-
" ment at Calais.   The pope promised to make no new step in
" king Henry's matter, if he would do the same.   But king
" Henry did innovate in many particulars; yet, contrary to
" all men's expectations, he had effectually restrained the pope
" from shewing his resentments upon it.   And he was in a fair
" way to have engaged the pope against the emperor, if king
" Henry would have given him any handle for it.   Once
" Francis hoped to have brought Henry to Marseilles; but he
" judged that was not fit for him, and promised to send the
" duke of Norfolk in his stead: for notwithstanding the sen-
" tence passed at Rome, a remedy was proposed, if a person
" was sent with full powers, as was expected.   When Gardiner
" came to Marseilles, he said he had orders to do whatsoever
" Francis should direct him; but indeed he brought no such
" powers.   The pope was resolved to do all that he could
" advise him for Henry's satisfaction; and Francis would enter
" upon none of his own affairs till that was first settled: he
" still waited for powers from England, but none were sent.

Le Grand,
p. 571.
Bellay sent
over to the
king by
king Fran-
cis.

[p. 572.]

[p. 573.]

[p. 576.]

[p. 577.]

[p. 578.]

" This might have provoked Francis to have been less zealous,
" but it did not: instead of sending what Francis expected,
" there was an appeal made from the pope to a general [Le Grand,
" council, which so highly provoked the pope, that what he p. 580.]
" had been labouring to do a whole week, was pulled down in
" one hour. It was also an injury to Francis to use the pope
" ill without his knowledge, when he was in his house, doing
" that there which they durst not have done any where else.
" This gave great joy to the Spaniards ; and though the pope [p. 581.]
" offered to put Leghorn, Parma, and Piacenza, with other
" places of greater importance, into Francis' hand, yet upon
" the rupture with Henry he would treat of nothing ; so he
" concluded the marriage, with no advantage to himself from
" it : and yet for all this zeal and friendship that he had ex-
" pressed to king Henry, he had no thanks, but only com-
" plaints. He saw he was disposed to suspect him in every
" thing, as in particular for his treating with the king of Scot- [p. 584.]
" land, though by so doing he had taken him wholly out of the
" emperor's hands. He proposes of new to king Henry, the
" same means that were proposed at Marseilles, in order to
" the reconciling him to the pope, with some other motions,
" which he will see are good and reasonable ; and upon that
" all that passed would be easily repaired. He perceived
" plainly at Marseilles, that the king's ambassadors had no
" intentions to bring matters to an agreement; and when he [p. 583.]
" told them that he saw there was no intention to make up
" matters, they only smiled. It touched the king of France
" very sensibly, to see all his friendship and good offices to be
" so little understood and so ill requited. He was offered the
" duchy of Milan if he would suffer the emperor and the pope [p. 585.]
" to proceed against the king of England : but he was now to
" offer to king Henry, if he would reconcile himself to the
" pope, a league between the pope and the two kings offensive
" and defensive. But if king Henry would come into no such [p. 586.]
" agreement, yet he was to assure him, that he would still
86 " continue in a firm and brotherly friendship with him ; and if
" by reason of his marriage, and the censures that might be
" passed on that account, any prince should make war upon
" him, that he would assist him according to their treaties :
" and that he would so manage the king of Scotland, that he [p. 587.]

BURNET, PART III.   N

" should engage him into a defensive league with him. In
" conclusion, he desired that some other better instruments
" than the bishop of Winchester might be employed; for he
" thought he had no good intentions, neither to the one nor
" the other of them."

There is some reason to suspect that these instructions are
not fully set forth by Le Grand; for the best argument to
persuade the king to come to terms of reconciliation, was to
tell him what the pope had said to him of the justice of his
cause. It is certain that Francis owned that on other occasions: this makes it highly probable that it was set forth in
these instructions; so that I cannot help suspecting that some
part of them is suppressed.

Cotton libr.
Nero B. vi.
[fol. 85.]
A repre-
sentation
made to
the em-
peror.

At this time, the king, in a letter to his ambassador that
was at the emperor's court, after he had ordered him to lay
open the falsehood of the reports that had been carried to the
emperor, of queen Catharine's being ill used; and to complain
of her obstinate temper, and of her insisting on her appeal to
the pope, after the law was passed against all such appeals:
he adds, that, as he had told the emperor's ambassador at his
court, the pope had to the French king confessed that his
cause was just and lawful; and that he had promised to him
at Marseilles, that, if the king would send a proxy, he would
give sentence for him in his principal cause: which the king
refused to do, looking on that as a derogation from his royal
dignity. The pope, it seems, looked on his refusing to do this
as a contempt, and pronounced sentence against him, notwithstanding his appeal to a general council, that had been personally intimated to him. This the king imputed to his malice,
and his design to support his usurped authority.

Mémoires
de Bell.[48]
[fol. 133.]
p. 414. He
prevailed
much on
the king to
submit.
A letter of
the king's
to his am-
bassadors

The bishop of Paris coming to London, had very long and
earnest conferences with the king: in conclusion, the king
promised, that if the pope would supersede his sentence, the
king would likewise supersede the separating himself entirely
from his obedience: upon that, though it was in winter, he
went immediately post to Rome. At the same time the king
sent a letter to his ambassadors at Rome: he tells them,
" that, after the interview at Marseilles, he had heard both by

[48] [Les Mémoires de Mess. Martin du Bellay, Seigneur de Langey. A
Paris, 1569, fol.]

" Bonner and sir Gregory, that the pope had in a lively man-
" ner spoken to the emperor in favour of the king's cause, and
" seemed more inclined than formerly to do him justice. He
" had proposed, that the king should send a mandate, desiring
" his cause might be tried in an indifferent place; upon which
" he would send a legate and two auditors to form the process,
" reserving the judgment to himself: or, that the king of
" France and he would concur to procure a general council,
" by concluding a truce for three or four years; upon which
" he would call one, and leave the king's cause to be judged
" in it. The same overtures were made to the king by the
" pope's nuncio. He pretended that sir Gregory had made
" them to the pope in the king's name; and that the pope
" had agreed to them: yet the king had never sent any
87 " such orders to sir Gregory, but rather to the contrary.
" Yet since the pope in these overtures shewed better inclina-
" tions than formerly, which indeed he was out of hope of, he
" ordered thanks to be given him in his name. The king
" asked nothing in return for all the service he had done him
" and the see, but justice according to the laws of God, and
" the ordinances of the holy councils; which if he would now
" do speedily, setting aside all delays, he might be sure that
" he and his kingdom would be as loving to him and his see,
" as they had been formerly accustomed to be: but for the
" truce, how desirous soever he was of outward quiet, yet he
" could not set himself to procure it till he had first peace in his
" own conscience, which the pope might give him; and then
" he would use his best endeavours for a general peace with
" the king of France, from whom he would never separate
" himself. He therefore charges them to press the pope to
" remit the fact, to be tried within the kingdom, according to
" the old sanctions of general councils. If the pope would
" grant his desire, he would dispose all his allies to concur in
" the service of that see. He could not consent to let his cause
" be tried out of the realm: it was contrary both to his prero-
" gative and to the laws of his kingdom; and by his corona-
" tion oath he was bound to maintain those. So, without the
" consent of his parliament, he could not agree to it; and he
" was sure they would never consent to that. He hoped the
" pope would not compel him to do things prejudicial to the

at Rome.
Rymer,
MSS.
Collect.
Numb. 2¡

N 2

" papal dignity, as it was then exercised, which, unless he
" were forced to it by the pope's conduct towards him, he had
" no mind to do.   The pope had said to sir Gregory, that, by
" their laws, the pope could not dispense in such a marriage
" unless there was an urgent cause pressing it : and the clear-
" ing this point he thought would more certainly advance the
" king's cause, than the opinion of lawyers and divines, that
" the pope could not dispense with it.   The emperor had said
" to the pope, that there was an extreme bloody war at that
" time between England and Spain ; for the pacifying which,
" the dispensation allowing the marriage was granted : whereas
" in the league signed by his father, and by Ferdinand and
" Isabella, upon which the dispensation was obtained, no such
" thing was pretended ; the marriage was agreed to for the
" continuance and augmentation of their amity, and upon the
" account of the good qualities of the queen : it was also plainly
" expressed in that league, that her former marriage was con-
" summated.   So the dispensation was granted without any
" urgent cause : and therefore, by the pope's own concession,
" it could not be valid.   He sent to Rome an attested tran-
" script of that league : so if the pope would refer the judging
" in this matter to the church of England, and ratify the sen-
" tence given in it, he will not only acquire the obedience of
" us and of our people, but pacify the disputes that have been
" raised, to the quiet of all Christendom.   He concludes, that
" if the pope seemed disposed to be benevolent to the king,
" they were not to declare all this as his final answer, but to
" assure him, that he would study by all honourable ways to
" concur with the pope's towardly mind, if he will earnestly
" apply himself and persevere in such opinion as may be for 88
" the acceleration of the said cause."   This is all that I can
find of the submission that he offered ; but how much further
his promises sent by the bishop of Paris went, does not appear
to me.

Duke of
Norfolk's
letter to
Montmo-
rency.

Le Grand,
p. 588.

To quicken the court of France to interpose effectually with
the pope, to bring this matter to the conclusion that all the
papists of England laboured earnestly for, the duke of Norfolk
wrote on the 27th of January a very full letter on the subject
to Montmorency.   " He was glad that the bishop of Paris was
" sent to Rome, with instructions expressing the entire union

" that was between the two kings.   He wished he might suc-
" ceed ; for if the pope would persist in his obstinacy to favour
" the emperor, and to oppress the king in his most just cause,
" an opposition to his authority would be unavoidable : and it
" would give occasions to many questions, greatly to his pre-
" judice, and against his usurpations.   It began to be believed, [p. 589.]
" that the pope had no authority out of Rome, any more than
" any other bishop has out of his diocese : and that this
" usurped authority grew by the permission of princes, blinded
" by popes ; who, contrary to the laws of God, and the good
" of the church, had maintained it.   To support this, many
" clear texts of Scripture were brought, with reasons founded
" on them : and many histories were alleged to prove, that [p. 590.]
" popes themselves were made by the emperors ; and that
" their authority was only suffered, but not granted nor con-
" firmed by emperors or kings.   Of all this the bishops, and
" other doctors, had made such discoveries, that he himself,
" and other noblemen, as well as the body of the people, were
" so convinced of it, that, if the king would give way to it,
" (which, if no interposition saves it, probably he will do,)
" this present parliament will withdraw from the pope's obe-
" dience ; and then every thing that depends on it will be
" hated and abhorred by the whole nation : and other states [p. 591.]
" and kingdoms may from thence be moved to do the same.
" He, out of the friendship that was between them, gave him
" this advertisement.   He apprehended some ill effects from
" the readiness the king of France had expressed to favour the
" pope, even to the prejudice of his own authority : for he had [p. 592.]
" taken a bull to do justice in his own kingdom ; as if he had
" not full authority to do that without a bull.   The pope and
" his successors might make this a precedent for usurping on
" the royal authority.   He also complains, that though their
" king had promised to the earl of Rochford, that Beda, who
" had calumniated the king so much, and was his enemy in
" his just cause, should be banished, not only from Paris, but
" out of his kingdom ; yet he was now suddenly recalled.   He [p. 593.]
" wishes these things may be considered in time ; he does not
" propose that the king of France should turn the pope's
" enemy ; but if there came a rupture between the king and
" the pope, that he would not so favour the pope, as to give

[p. 594.]

" him more boldness in executing his malice against the king,
" or his subjects : and that they might not be deceived by his
" promises, as if he would enable Francis to recover his do- 89
" minions in Italy, if he should be thereby engaged to lose the
" friendship of the king and his allies."

Cotton lib.
Vitell. B.
xiv.[burnt.]
The pope
was in great
anxiety.

This came in time to quicken the court of France; for, by a
letter writ from Rome on the 20th of February, it appears,
that the pope was at that time in great anxiety. He was
pressed hard by the imperialists on the one hand, and he saw
the danger of losing England on the other hand. To some
about him he expressed a great inclination to be reconciled to
the king : he sent secretly for some great lawyers; they
were positive that the king's cause was just, and that his
second marriage was good. But now the matter being
brought to a crisis, I shall give it in the words of Du Bellay,
who no doubt had his information from his brother. " King

Mem. de
Bellay, p.
414, 415,
416.
[fol. 133.]

" Henry, upon the remonstrances that the bishop of Paris
" made to him, condescended, that, if the pope would super-
" sede the sentence till he sent judges to hear his matter, he
" would supersede the executing that which he was resolved to
" do ; which was, to separate himself entirely from obedience
" to the see of Rome. And the bishop of Paris offering to

[fol. 134.]

" undertake the journey to Rome, he assured him, that when
" he obtained that which he went to demand there, he would
" immediately send him sufficient powers to confirm that which
" he had promised; trusting in him, by reason of the great
" friendship that he had for so long a time borne him; for he
" had been ambassador in his court for two years.

" It was a very severe winter ; but the bishop thought the
" trouble was small, so he might accomplish that which he

Bellay was
to go to
Rome, in
hopes to
make up
the breach.

" went upon. So he came in good time to Rome, before any
" thing was done ; and, in an audience in the consistory, he
" gave an account of that which he had obtained of the king
" of England, for the good of the church. The proposition
" was judged reasonable, and a time was assigned him for
" getting the king's answer : so he despatched a courier to
" the king, with a charge to use such diligence, that he might
" return within the time limited.

The final
sentence
given in
great haste.

" The day that was set for the return of the messenger
" being come, and the courier not come back, the imperialists

" pressed in consistory, that the pope should give sentence.
" The bishop, on the other hand, pressed both the pope in
" particular, and all the cardinals, that they would continue
" the time only for six days ; alleging, that some accident
" might have happened to the courier : the sea might not be
" passable, or the wind contrary ; so that, either in going or
" coming, the courier might be delayed : and since the king
" had patience for six years, they might well grant him a
" delay for six days.   He made these remonstrances in full
" consistory ; to which many of those who saw the clearest,
" and judged the best of things, condescended : but the greater
" number prevailed over the lesser number of those, who con-
" sidered well the prejudice that was like to happen to the
" church by it ; and they went on with that precipitation, that
" they did in one consistory that which could not be done in
" three consistories ; and so the sentence was fulminated.

90   " Two days had not passed, when the courier came with The courier
" the powers and declarations from the king of England, of came two
" which the bishop had assured them.   This did much con- late.
" found those who had been for the precipitating the matter.
" They met often, to see if they could redress that which they
" had spoiled ; but they found no remedy.   The king of
" England, seeing with what indignity he was used, and that
" they shewed as little regard to him as if he had been the
" meanest person in Christendom, did immediately withdraw
" himself and his kingdom from the obedience of the church
" of Rome ; and declared himself to be, under God, the *head*
" *of the church of England.*"

We have a further account of this transaction in the letters Le Grand,
that M. Le Grand has published.   On the 22nd of February, p. 630.
Raince, the French ambassador, wrote from Rome a letter full proofs of
of good hopes : and it seems the bishop of Paris wrote in the the matter.
same strain ; but his letter of the 23rd of March is very differ- [p. 631.]
ent from that : it was on the same day that the consistory
was held.   " There were two and twenty cardinals present
" when sentence was given ; by which king Henry's marriage
" with queen Catharine was declared good and valid, and the
" issue by it lawful.   Upon hearing the news of this, he went
" and asked the pope about it, who told him it was true ; but
" that though some would have had it immediately intimated, [p. 632.]

" he had delayed the ordering that till after Easter. He,
" with the other French ambassadors, made no answer to the
" pope : only the bishop of Paris told him, he had no other
" business there ; so he must return home again. They did
" not put the pope in mind of the promises and assurances he
" had given them to the contrary, when they saw it was to no
" purpose ; and it was not easy to say such things as the occa-
" sion required : but the bishop intended to speak more plainly
" to the pope when he should take his leave of him, which
" would be within three or four days. He adds, that, for
" some reasons, which he would tell the French king, they
" were in doubt whether that which was done was not conform
" to a secret intention of the king's, that was not made known

[p. 633.]

" to them. He apprehended, if he stayed longer there, it
" might give the king of England cause of suspicion : for he
" had by his last letters to him given him assurances, upon
" which perhaps he had dismissed his parliament ; for which
" he would be much displeased with the bishop. He desires
" the king will give advice of this with all diligence to king
" Henry ; and then all the world would see, that the king had
" done all that was possible for him to do, both to serve his

[p. 634.]

" friend, and to prevent the great mischief that might follow
" to the Church, and to all Christendom : for there was not
" any one thing omitted that could have been done. The im-
" perialists were running about the streets in great bodies,
" crying, *Empire and Spain,* as if they had got a victory ;
" and had bonfires and discharges of cannon upon it. The
" cardinals Trevulce, Rodolphe, and Pisane were not of that
" number ; others had not behaved themselves so well as was
" expected. Raince, one of the ambassadors, said, he would
" give himself to the Devil if the pope should not find a way
" to set all right that is now spoiled : he pressed the other am- 91

[p. 635.]

" bassadors to go again to the pope for that end, it being a
" maxim in the canon law, that matrimonial causes are never
" so finally judged but that they may be reviewed : they were
" assured that the pope was surprised in this, as well as he
" had been in the first sentence passed in this matter. The
" pope had been all that night advising with his doctors how
" to find a remedy, and was in great pain about it : upon the
" knowledge of this they were resolved to go to him, and see

" if any thing was to be expected. In a postscript, he tells
" the king that he ought not to think it strange, if in their
" last letters they gave other hopes of the opinions of the car-
" dinals, than appeared now by their votes : they took what [April 16.]
" they wrote to him from what they said, which they heard ; fol. 177.
" and not from their thoughts, which they could not know."
By a letter that Pompone Trevulce wrote from Lyons to the
bishop of Auxerre, it appears, that the bishop of Paris passed
through Lyons in his return on the 14th, two days before.
" In it he gave him the same account of the final sentence,
" that was formerly related : the bishop said to him, it was not
" the pope's fault, for he was for a delay ; and if they had
" granted a delay of six days, the king of England would have [fol. 177 b.]
" returned to the obedience of the apostolic see, and left his
" cause to be proceeded in according to justice ; but the im-
" perialists and their party in the consistory pressed the matter
" so, that they would admit of no delay : but when after a day
" the courier came, the imperialists themselves were confounded.
" He adds one thing that the bishop told him of his brother
" the cardinal, that he pressed the delay so earnestly, that he
" was reproached for it, and called a Frenchman : he avowed
" that he was a servant to the most Christian king, and that
" the king of France, and his predecessors, had never done
" any thing but good to the apostolic see."

And now I have laid together all the proceedings in the Reflections
matters relating to the king's divorce, and his breach with on this
breach.
the court of Rome. In opening all this, I have had a great
deal of light given me by the papers that M. Le Grand has
published, and by the book that he gave me ; for which, whatever other differences I may have with him, I return him in
this public way my hearty thanks. There appears to have
been a signal train of providence in the whole progress of this
matter, that thus ended in a total rupture. The court of
Rome, being overawed by the emperor, engaged itself far at
first ; but when the pope and the king of France were so entirely united as they knew they were, it seems they were
under an infatuation from God to carry their authority so far
at a time, in which they saw the king of England had a parliament inclined to support him in his breach with Rome. It
was but too visible, that the king would have given all up, if

the pope would have done him but common justice. But when the matter was brought so near a total union, an entire breach followed, in the very time in which it was thought all was made up. Those who favoured the reformation saw all their hopes, as it seemed, blasted ; but of a sudden all was revived again. This was an amazing transaction ; and how little 92 honour soever this full discovery of all the steps made in it does to the memory of king Henry, who retained his inclinations to a great deal of popery to the end of his life ; yet it is much to the glory of God's providence, that made the persons most concerned to prevent and hinder the breach, to be the very persons that brought it on, and in a manner forced it.

The sentence was given at Rome on the 23rd of March, on the same day in which the act of the succession to the crown of England did pass here in England : and certainly the parliament was ended before it was possible to have had the news from Rome of what passed in the consistory on the 23rd of March ; for it was prorogued on the 30th of March. So that if king Henry's word had been taken by the pope and the consistory, he seems to have put it out of his power to have made it good, since it is scarce possible to think, that a parliament that had gone so far in the breach with Rome, could have been prevailed on to undo all that they had been doing for four years together.

All in England concur to renounce the pope's authority. [Wilkins' Conc. iii. p. 769. negantes 34, dubitans unus, affirmantes 4.]
Nothing material passed in convocation before the 31st of March, and then the actuary exhibited the answer of the lower house to this question, *Whether the bishop of Rome has any greater jurisdiction given him by God in the holy scriptures, within the kingdom of England, than any other foreign bishop ?* There were thirty-two for the negative, four for the affirmative, and one doubted. It was a thin house, and no doubt many absented themselves on design : but it does not appear how this passed in the upper house, or whether it was at all debated there ; for the prelates had by their votes in the house of lords given their opinions already in the point. The

[ibid. p. 782.]
convocation at York had the same position, no more made a question, put to them on the 5th of May : there the archbishop's presidents were deputed by him to confirm and fortify this. After they had examined it carefully, they did all unanimously, without a contrary vote, agree to it ; upon which an

instrument was made by the archbishop, and sent to the king, which will be found in the Collection, and it was taken out of the register of York. Collect. Numb. 26.

The king sent the same question to the university of Oxford, and had their answer. That part of the king's letter that relates to this matter, and the university's answer, were sent me, taken from the archives there, by the learned Mr. Bingham ; which will be found in the Collection. The king required them to examine the question sent by him to them, concerning the power and primacy of the bishop of Rome, and return their answer under the common seal, with convenient speed ; according to the sincere truth. Dated from Greenwich the 18th day of May. The answer is directed to all the sons Collect. Numb. 27. [ap. Wood, Hist. et Antiq. Univ. Oxon. lib. i. p. 258.] [May 23.] of their mother-church, and is made in the name of the bishop of Lincoln their chancellor, and the whole convocation of all doctors, and masters regents, and non-regents. " It sets forth, " that whereas the king had received the complaints and peti- " tions of his parliament against some intolerable foreign exac- " tions ; and some controversies being raised concerning the " power and authority of the bishop of Rome, the king, that 98 " he might satisfy his people, but not break in upon any thing " declared in the scriptures, (which he will be always most " ready to defend with his blood,) had sent this question to " them, (setting it down in the terms in which it was proposed " to the convocation.) They upon this, to make all the re- " turns of duty and obedience to the king, had brought to- " gether the whole faculty of divinity : and for many days " they had searched the scriptures, and the most approved " commentators ; and had collated them diligently, and had " held public disputations on the matter : and at last they had " all unanimously agreed, that the bishop of Rome has no " greater jurisdiction given him by God, in the holy scriptures, " in this kingdom of England, than any other foreign bishop. " This determination, made according to the statutes of their " university, they affirm and testify as true, certain, and agree- " ing to the holy scriptures." Dated on the 27th of June 1534. Here was a long deliberation ; it lasted above five weeks after the king's letter, and was a very full and clear determination of the point.

To this I shall add the fullest of all the subscriptions, instruments, and oaths that was made, pursuant to these laws and decrees of convocation. I have seen several others to the same purpose; of which Rymer has published many instruments, all from page 487 to page 527, of *ecclesiastics*, *regulars* as well as *seculars*, *mendicants* and *carthusians*: but that from the prior and chapter of Worcester being much the fullest of them all. I shall only insert it in my Collection, and leave out all the rest, that I may not weary the reader with a heavy repetition of the various forms, in which some expatiated copiously, to shew their zeal for the king's authority, and against the papacy; which was looked on then as the distinguishing character of those who designed to set on a further reformation : whereas those who did adhere to their former opinions, thought it enough barely to sign the proposition, and to take the oath prescribed by law.

Collect.
Numb. 28.

There was likewise an order published, but how soon it does not appear to me; Strype says, in June 1534; it was before queen Anne's tragical fall, directing the bidding prayers for the king, as the only and supreme head of this catholic church of England; then for queen Anne, and then for the lady Elizabeth, daughter to them both, our princess; and no further in the presence of the king and queen: but in all other places they were to pray for all archbishops and bishops, and for the whole clergy, and such as shall please the preacher to name of his devotion; then for all the nobility, and such as the preacher should name; then for the souls of them that were dead, and such of them as the preacher shall name. Every preacher was ordered to preach once, in the greatest audience, against the usurped authority of the bishop of Rome; and he was left after that to his liberty : no preachers were in the pulpit to inveigh against, or to deprave one another; if they had occasion to complain, they were to do it to the king, or the bishop of the diocese. They were not to preach for or against purgatory, the honouring of saints, that faith only justifieth, to go on pilgrimages, or to support miracles : these things had occasioned great dissensions, but those were then well pacified. 94 They were to preach the words of Christ, and not mix with them men's institutions, or to make God's laws and men's laws of equal authority; or to teach that any man had power to dispense with God's law. It seems there was a sentence of ex-

An order for the bidding of prayers and preaching.
[Strype's Cranmer, p. 25.]
[Wilkins' Concilia, vol. iii. p. 783.]
[*daughter and heir.*]

communication with relation to the laws and liberties of the church published once a year, against all such as broke them; this was to be no more published. The collects for the king and queen by name were to be said in all high masses: they were likewise to justify to the people the king's last marriage, and to declare how ill the king had been used by the pope in all that matter, with the proofs of the unlawfulness of his former marriage; and a long deduction was made of the process at Rome, and of all the artifices used by the pope to get the king to subject himself to him, which I need not relate: it contains the substance of the whole cause, and the order of the process formerly set forth: I have put it in the Collection. All that is particular in it is, that the king affirms, that a decretal bull was sent over, decreeing, that if the former marriage was proved, and if it did appear, that as far as presumptions can prove it, that it was consummated, that marriage was to be held unlawful and null. This bull, after it was seen by the king, was, by the bishop of Rome's commandment, embezzled by the cardinals. He adds another particular, which I find no where but here; that the pope gave out a sentence in the manner of an excommunication and interdiction of him and his realm : of which complaint being made, as being contrary to all law and right, the fault was laid on a new officer lately come to the court; who ought to have been punished for it, and the process was to cease: but though this was promised to the king's agents, yet it went on, and was set up in Flanders. Perhaps the words in the bishop of Paris' last letter, that the pope was surprised in the last sentence, as he had been in the first, are to be explained and applied to this. He also mentions the declarations that the pope had made to the French king and his council, of what he would gladly do for the king, allowing the justness of his cause; and that he durst not do it at Rome for fear of the emperor, but that he would come and do it at Marseilles; and there he promised to that king to give judgment for the king : so he would send a proxy, which he knew before that he would not do, nor was he bound to do it.

Thus the king took care to have his cause to be fully set forth to all his own subjects: his next care was to have it rightly understood by all the princes of Europe. I have found the original instructions that he gave to Paget, then one of

Collect.
Numb. 29.

the clerks of the signet, whom he sent to the king of Poland, and the dukes of Pomerania and Prussia, and to the cities of Dantzig, Stettin, and Konigsberg; and it is to be supposed, that others were sent to other princes and cities with the like instructions, though they have not come in my way. I have put them in the Collection. By these,

Collect.
Numb. 30.
Instruc-
tions given
to Paget
sent to
some
northern
courts.

" Their old friendship was desired to be renewed; the " rather, because the king saw they were setting themselves " to find out the truth of God's word, and the justice of his " laws; and the extirpation of such corrupt errors and abuses, " by which the world has been kept slaves under the yoke of 95 " the bishop of Rome, more than the Jews were under the " ceremonies of Moses' law. The king orders Paget to let " them undestand his great desire to promote not only a friend- " ship with them, but the common good of all Christendom: " he orders him to give them an account of the whole progress " of his cause of matrimony, with the intolerable injuries done " him by the bishop of Rome, and the state in which that " matter then stood. He was first to shew them the justice " of the king's cause, then to open the steps in which it had " been carried on. Here all the arguments against his mar- " riage are stated, to make it appear to be contrary both to " the laws of God, of nature, and of men. In this the king " did not follow his own private opinion, nor that of the whole " clergy of his realm; but that of the most famous universities " of Christendom: and therefore, by the consent of his whole " parliament, and by the sentence of the archbishop of Can- " terbury, he has, for the discharge of his own conscience, and " the good of his people, and that he might have a lawful suc- " cessor to rule over them, separated himself from the princess " dowager, and was then married to queen Anne; of whom " follows a very exalted character, setting forth the purity of " her life, her constant virginity, her maidenly and womanly " pudicity, her soberness, her chasteness, her meekness, her " wisdom, her descent of noble parentage, her education in all " good and lawful shows and manners, her aptness to procrea- " tion of children, with her other infinite good qualities, which " were more to be esteemed than only progeny. If any should " object to this second marriage, as contrary to the pope's " laws; he asserts, that every man's private conscience is to

" him the supreme court for judgment : so the king was satis-
" fied in his own conscience, that, being enlightened by the
" Spirit of God, and afterwards by the means formerly set
" forth, he was judged to be at liberty from his former mar-
" riage, and free to contract a new one.   The king also took
" great pains to satisfy the world, by long travail and study,
" with inestimable cost and charges, though he had no fruit
" from it all.   Upon this head, Paget was to set forth the
" pope's ungodly demeanour in the whole progress of the
" king's cause ; keeping him off by delays for seven years and
" more.   At first the pope, instead of judging the matter him-
" self, sent a commission to England to try it, with full powers,
" pretending that it could not be judged at Rome.   He gave
" with these, a decretal bull, in which he pronounced sentence
" that the king might (*convolare ad secundas nuptias*) *marry*
" *another wife;* yet he gave the legate secret directions not
" to proceed by virtue of the decretal bull, nor to give sen-
" tence.   He wrote a letter to the king with his own hand,
" in which he approved of the king's cause, and promised to
" the king, on the word of the pope, that he would not avocate
" the cause, but leave it in its due course ; yet afterwards,
" contrary to his conscience and knowledge, he decreed several
" citations against the king to appear at Rome, to the subver-
" sion of the royal dignity : or to send a proxy, which cannot
" be justified by any colour of reason.   He cites the councils
96 " of Nice, Africa, and Milevi, against appeals to remote places.
" It was not reasonable to send original instruments, and other
" documents, to a distant place ; nor, in a matter of con-
" science, could a man give such a power to a proxy, by which
" he was bound to stand to that which he should agree to.   It
" was fit that all princes should consider what an attempt this
" made upon their dignity, for the pope to pretend that he
" could oblige them to abandon their kingdoms, and come and
" appear before him ; by which he might depose kings, or
" rule them according to his own pleasure : so that all this
" was not only unjust, but null of itself.   Dr. Carne being then
" at Rome, as the king's subject, he offered a plea excusatory ;
" yet this was not regarded by the dean of the Rota, who in
" that acted as he was directed by the pope : pretending he
" had no powers from the king, which by law was not neces-

" sary for an *excusator*.   Carne had appealed to the pope : to
" this Capisucci gave an ambiguous answer, promising to give
" a more determinate one afterwards, which yet he never did ;
" but upon a second appeal the cause was brought into the
" consistory, and there it was judged that Carne, could not be
" heard, unless he had a proxy from the king : and when
" Carne objected that such proceeding was against law, the
" pope answered, that he might judge all things according to
" his own conscience ; and so they resolved to proceed in the
" main cause.   At that time the king's ambassadors at Rome
" shewed the pope the determination of the universities of
" Paris and Orleans, with the opinions of the most learned
" men in France and Italy, condemning the pope's proceedings
" as unjust and null ; the words of their opinion being inserted
" in the instructions : yet the pope still went on, and sent out
" slanderous breves against the king, and designed to excom-
" municate him.   To prevent that, the king did order a pro-
" vocation and appeal to be made from the pope to a general
" council, and caused it to be intimated to the pope, but he
" would not admit it ; and pretended, that, by a bull of pope
" Pius', that was condemned : and that he was superior to all
" general councils.   He rejected it arrogantly, saying, they
" were heretics and traitors to his person who would appeal
" from him to any general council.   It appeared evidently
" that the pope, for the defence of his own glory and ambi-
" tion, regarded not what injuries he did to Christian princes :
" so they were all obliged now to be on their guard against
" such invasions of their authority.   For these reasons the
" king was resolved to reduce that exorbitant power which the
" pope had assumed, within due limits : so that in his domin-
" ions he shall exercise no other jurisdiction than what is
" granted to him by express words of scripture.   Paget was
" to open all these things to those princes and states, desiring
" that they would adhere to the king in this matter, till it
" should come to be treated of in a general council : and in
" the mean time to give him their best assistance and advice,
" especially in some articles, of which a schedule was to be
" given him, signed with the king's hand, which he was to
" communicate to them as he should find it convenient.   They
" related to some abuses and customs which seemed necessary

97 " to be reformed : and if they would propose any other, Paget
" was to receive their mind, and to assure them, that the king,
" as he desired their assistance in his causes and quarrels, so
" he would kindly admit of whatsoever they should propose,
" and would endeavour to extirpate all abuses against God's
" word and laws ; and to do all that lay in him for the refor-
" mation thereof, for the maintenance of God's word, the faith
" of Christ, and the welfare of Christendom."

But because the king did not know what the mind of those
princes might be, nor how far they were devoted to the pope,
Paget was to try to find out their inclinations, before he should
deliver the king's letters to them ; and so to proceed according to his discretion, to deliver, or not to deliver his letters, or
to show his instructions to them. What followed upon this,
and how it was executed, does not appear.

The judicious and diligent Seckendorf, in his History of
Lutheranism, gives an account of a negotiation of Paget's two
years before this.   Cranmer, who was then the king's ambassador at the emperor's court, met with John Frederic, elector
of Saxony, at Nuremberg, who had secretly left the diet of
Ratisbon ; and there he delivered letters from the king, both
to the elector, to the duke of Lunenburg, and to the prince of
Anhalt ; which contained only a general offer of friendship.
Cranmer came the next day to the elector, who had two of his
ministers about him and, and, asked him many questions concerning their agreement with the state of religion, the Turkish
war, and the church lands, which (as they heard) they had
seized on.   He said great things of the king, and of the aid
he had offered the emperor against the Turk, in conjunction
with the French king.   He asked where Paget was, whom
the king had sent to the elector.   General answers were made
to all his questions ; and for Paget, he had been with the
elector the - former year.   This passed on the 15th of July
1532.   Four days after this, he came privately to Spalatin,
one of the elector's secretaries, and assured him, that both the
king and the French king would assist the elector and his
allies in the matter of religion.   In August after that, Paget
came to the elector, who proposed many things to him concerning religion : but the princes had then come to an agreement with the emperor ; so they could enter into no treaty at

Margin note: L.iii.sect.6.
§.16. Add.
[p. 41.]
Negotia-
tions in
Germany.

that time. Only John Frederic did, in a writing under his own hand, offer the scheme of that which was afterwards proposed in their name to the king.

Advices offered the king.
All these negotiations were set on foot, pursuant to a paper of advices offered to the king by Cromwell; in which there are divers marginal notes writ in the king's own hand, which will be found in the Collection. " First, all the bishops were Collect. Numb. 31. " to be sent for, especially those nearest the court, to examine " them, Whether they can prove, that the pope is above the " general council, or the council above him? And whether, by " the law of God, he has any authority in England? Next, " they are to be charged to preach this to the people; and to " shew, that the pope's authority was an usurpation, grown up " by the sufferance of princes. This ought to be preached 98 " continually at Paul's Cross; and the bishop of London was " to suffer none to preach there but those who will set this " forth. The same order was to be given to all other bishops, " and to the rulers of the four orders of friars, particularly to " the friar observants, and to all abbots and priors. The king's " appeal was also to be set up on every church door in Eng- " land, that so none may pretend ignorance; as also the act " against appeals to Rome. It was also proposed, that copies " of the king's appeal might be sent to other realms, particu- " larly to Flanders. A letter was also proposed, complaining " of all the injuries done the king by the pope; to be written " to him by all the lords spiritual and temporal. The king writes " on the margin, *Not yet done; nor can it well be done be- " fore the parliament.* To send spies into Scotland, to see " what practices were there: on the margin the king's orders; " *Letters to be written to the lord Dacres, the duke of Nor- " folk, and sir Thomas Clifford.* To send to the kings of " Poland and Hungary, the dukes of Saxony and Bavaria, the " landgrave of Hesse, and the three ecclesiastical electors: on " the margin the king writes, *In the king's arbitrement.* " This, it sems, gave the occasion of sending Paget. The like " proposed for the Hanse towns: on the margin, in the king's " hand, *To know this of the king.* To remember the mer- " chant-adventurers, chiefly those of Brabant: on the margin, " *This is already done.* Then it is proposed, that an order " be given for establishing the princess dowager's house, and

" the lady Mary's, and for my lady princess' house : this was
" Elizabeth's. To this, on the margin, it is written by the
" king, *The order is taken."*

In June, in the year 1535, after the parliament had settled
every thing demanded of them, the king published a circular
letter, which will be found in the Collection, taken from the
original. " In which, after he had set forth that both clergy
" and temporalty had abolished the bishop of Rome's usurpa-
" tions, and had united to the crown the dignity of *supreme*
" *head in earth of the church of England ;* which was also
" approved in convocation, and confirmed by their oaths and
" subscriptions : he adds, that, considering what quiet would
" follow in the nation, if the bishops and clergy would sin-
" cerely, and without dissimulation, publish the many and
" great abuses of the pope's usurpation ; he had sent letters
" to all bishops, charging them, not only in their own persons,
" but by their chaplains, to preach the true and sincere word
" of God to the people, and to give warning to all ecclesiastical
" persons to do the same ; and to cause the pope's name to be
" razed out of all the books of divine service. He had also,
" required the justices of peace to examine whether the bishops
" and clergy did this sincerely ; or whether they did it coldly,
" or feignedly ; or used any addition or gloss to it. Upon
" all this, the king requires them, at their assizes and ses-
" sions, to make diligent search, whether the bishops and
" clergy do their duty sincerely. Likewise, at their meetings,
" they were to set the same forth to the people ; and also
99 " declare the treasons committed by the bishop of Rochester
" and sir Thomas More, who by divers secret practices in-
" tended to breed among the people most mischievous opin-
" ions ; for which they, with some others, had suffered as they
" deserved. He requires them, if they found any fault or
" dissimulation in any person, that they should immediately
" signify it to the king and his council, as that which was of
" the greatest moment to the quiet of the kingdom ; threaten-
" ing such punishment of those who were negligent in this, as
" would make them examples to all others : and he charges
" them upon their allegiance to obey all this punctually."

But it seems this had not the effect that was expected ;
therefore in April after this, a new letter or proclamation was

Collect.
Numb. 32.
A letter of
the king's
to the jus-
tices, to ob-
serve the
behaviour
of the
clergy.

Collect.
Numb. 33.

writ to some of the nobility, setting forth that he had heard
that some, both *regulars* and *seculars,* did secretly extol the
authority of the bishop of Rome, praying for him in the pulpit, and making him a god, preferring his power and laws to
God's most holy laws.   The king therefore, out of his desire
to maintain unity and quiet among his people, and to bring
them to the knowledge of the truth, and to be no more blinded
with superstition and false doctrine, required them, that wheresoever they found any person spreading such pernicious doctrines, to the exaltation of the bishop of Rome, to cause them
to be apprehended and put in prison without bail or mainprise.

The arch-
bishop of
York is
suspected
to favour
the pope.
Among the bishops, all were not equally honest, nor zealous.
Lee, archbishop of York, and Gardiner, were those in whom
the old leaven had the deepest root: so the king being informed that Lee, though he had given in his profession, subscribed and sealed by him, yet did not his duty in his diocese
and province, neither in teaching himself, nor causing others
to teach the people, conform to what was settled both in convocation and parliament, sent him orders both to preach these
things, and to order all other ecclesiastical persons in his province to do the same.   Upon this he wrote a long vindication
of himself in June 1535, which will be found in the Collection.

Collect.
Numb. 34.
He justifies
himself.
" He sets forth in it the complaints that the king signified
" had been made of him, with the orders that he had received
" from the king, and then sets out his own conduct.   He ac-
" knowledges he had received, at the end of the last parlia-
" ment, a book sent from the archbishop of Canterbury, as a
" book of orders for preaching : (probably that which is the
" 28th paper in the Collection.)   Upon his receiving it, he
" went on Sunday next to York, and there he set forth the
" cause of the king's marriage, and the rejecting the pope's
" authority, very fully : and, that this might be done the more
" publicly, he had caused it to be published at York the Sun-
" day before that he would be there, and so took care to have
" a full audience : so that there was a great multitude there.
" His text was, *I have married a wife, and therefore I can-*
" *not come :* and he so declared the king's matters, that all
" seemed satisfied.   It is true he did not touch the title of the
" king as the supreme head, for there was no order given as
" to that, for it was thus only ordered to have it named in the

100 " prayer.   It is true he did not use to bid prayers, for the
" greater haste to utter his matter.   But upon the receipt of
" that book, he commanded his officers to make out a great
" number of them, to be sent to every preacher in his diocese:
" and by all that he ever heard, every one of his curates fol-
" lowed that book, and has done their duty in every particular
" enjoined in it: he took care that all who preached in their
" churches should follow the rules prescribed in it.   He also
" sent a book to every house of friars.   And for the religious,
" when any such person came to him, naming particularly the
" Carthusians and the Observants, for counsel, he told them
" what he had done himself, and advised them to do the same.
" On Good-Friday last, he had ordered the collect for the
" pope to be left out; and also the mentioning him in other
" parts of the service: he desired the king would examine
" these things, and he would find he was not so much in fault
" as he imputed it to him.   He had been hitherto open and
" plain, and had never deceived the king.   He had also sent
" letters to the bishops of Durham and Carlisle, pursuant to
" the letters that he had from the king: and had charged his
" archdeacons to see that all obedience might be given to the
" king's orders.   He had, since he received the king's last
" letters, on the Sunday following, declared to the people every
" thing comprised in them.   He refers himself to Magnus and
" Lawson, two of the king's chaplains, who heard him, to make
" report of what they thought of it.   Whatever he promised
" to the king he would fulfil it; and he had done every thing
" as the king commanded, and would still do it, so God were
" not offended by it.   He besought the king not to believe
" any complaints of him till he have heard his answer.   Some
" thought it was a high sacrifice, when they could bring such
" a poor priest as he was under the king's displeasure: but he
" trusted God would continue in him a gracious mind to his
" priests and chaplains, and that he would give their enemies,
" who studied to provoke him against them, better minds for
" the future."

I have no particulars to add to the relation[48] I gave of the
sufferings of Fisher and More.   There are heavy things laid to
their charge; but except Fisher's being too much concerned in

Of the sufferings of Fisher and More.

[48] [See part i. p. 158.]

the business of the Nun of Kent, which was without doubt managed with a design to raise a rebellion in the nation, I do not find any other thing laid to his charge : and it does not at all appear that More gave any credit or countenance to that matter. Yet I have seen that often affirmed. In our own days, when things have happened both together, though the one did not by any sort of proof appear to be connected with the other, yet they have been represented as done in concert : so the conspiracy of the Nun, and those who managed that imposture, was given out both at home and abroad as having its rise from Fisher, who indeed knew of it, and seemed to give credit to it ; and from More, though he had no share at all in it.

The king of France was not satisfied with this way of proceeding : he thought it too violent, and that it did put things past all possibility of a reconciliation. He had answered for the king to the pope at Marseilles, and he was in such a concern for him, that the wrong steps he made reflected on himself. He told the king's ambassador, that he advised the banishing of all such offenders, rather than the putting them to death. That king confessed there had been extreme executions and cruelty lately exercised in his own kingdom : but he was now putting a stop to it, and resolved to call home all those that had fled out of his kingdom. He had seen a relation of More's sufferings, by which it appeared that he exhorted his daughter to all duty and respect to the king, which made the proceedings against such a man to be the more censured. 101

Collect. Numb. 35. Rymer, MSS. An expostulation with the court of France.

The ambassadors wrote this to the king soon after More's death. The king wrote, on the 23rd of August, an answer from Thornbury to this purpose ; " If the king of France had " answered for the king, and had justified his cause, he had " done what was just and suitable to their friendship : the con- " spiracies of Fisher and More to sow sedition, and to raise " wars, both within and without the kingdom, were manifestly " proved to their face ; so that they could not avoid, nor deny " it. The relation he had seen concerning More's talk with " his daughter at his death was a forged story ; the king took " it in ill part that king Francis should so lightly give ear and " credit to such vain tales. This ungrateful behaviour shewed " that the king of France had not that integrity of heart that

" the king deserved, and might expect from him. Then follows
" a vindication of the laws lately made, which indeed were only
" old laws revived. The banishing of traitors was no ways
" convenient: that was to send them in places where they
" might more safely and conveniently execute their conspira-
" cies. Upon all which the ambassador was ordered to ex-
" postulate plainly, but discreetly, both with the king and with
" the great master. There appears a strain of coldness in the
" whole intercourse between the two courts of France and
" England, ever from the interview at Marseilles to this time."

Pope Clement was now dead, with whom the king of France *The king of France engages himself to adhere to and defend the king in his second marriage.* was more closely united: and he found the king's friendship was yet so necessary to him, that he resolved to remove all jealousies: so, to give the king a full assurance of his firmness to him, he sent him a solemn engagement to adhere to him [49]. It is true, I have seen only a copy of this; but it is minuted on the back by Cromwell's hand [50], and is fairly writ out. There is no date set to it, but it was during queen Anne's life, and after pope Clement's death; so probably it was sent over about this time. It will be found in the Collection. *Collect. Numb. 36.*

It begins thus; " That both friendship and piety did require
" that he should employ his whole strength and authority to
" maintain the justice of his dearest friend. The king of Eng-
" land, defender of the faith, lord of Ireland, and, under God,
" supreme head of the church of England, had by a dispensa-
" tion, granted by pope Julius, contracted a marriage in fact
" with Catharine of Spain, relict of the king's elder brother
" Arthur, and had one daughter yet living of that marriage:
" that king, upon great and weighty reasons, well known to
" king Francis, had withdrawn himself from that marriage:
102 " and had lawfully and rightfully married Anne, now his
" queen, of whom he hath issue the princess Elizabeth: and a
" debate had arisen concerning the dispensation, and the first

---

[49] [This declaration of Francis I. in French is printed in State Papers, vol. vii. p. 602, with the marginal corrections made by Henry VIII. It is in the State Paper Office, and is endorsed, ' A devise in Frenshe to be confirmed by the Frenshe king for the adnullacion and revocacion of the Bisshop of Romes sentences agenst the kinges Highnes.']

[50] [It is not in Cromwell's hand. See State Papers, vol. vii. p. 602.]

" marriage, and the legitimacy of the issue by it ; in which
" king Francis by many arguments did perceive, that the pope
" himself had not a due regard to equity ; and that what by
" the iniquity of the times, what by ill practice against all law
" and right, many things were done. The king therefore
" consulted the men of the greatest integrity in his kingdom,
" and the most learned both in divinity and in the laws of the
" church ; whom he charged to make a report to him ac-
" cording to their consciences, as in the sight of God, having
" first conferred among themselves fully upon the whole mat-
" ter : he does therefore, upon all their unanimous opinion,
" clearly perceive that the dispensation granted by the pope
" was in itself null, both by reason of the surprise put on him
" by the grounds pretended in it for obtaining it, but chiefly
" because the pope could not dispense in that case ; since such
" marriages are contrary to the laws of God and of nature :
" for the pope has no authority to dispense in that case; so
" that the marriage between king Henry and queen Catharine
" was incestuous and null, as contrary to the laws of God and
" man ; and by consequence the lady Mary, born of that mar-
" riage, was illegitimate. And further, that the marriage the
" king has contracted with Anne, now his queen, was holy,
" lawful, and good : and that Elizabeth, born of that marriage,
" and all the other issue that might come of it, was lawful, and
" ought so to be esteemed. He adds, that many of the cardi-
" nals, naming particularly the late cardinal of Ancona, and
" even the late pope Clement himself, did declare their own
" positive opinion to himself personally at Marseilles, and fre-
" quently to his ambassadors, that the dispensation granted by
" pope Julius, upon which the first marriage was made, was
" null and void : and the pope would have declared this by a
" final and definitive sentence, if private affections and human
" regards had not stood in his way. All which that king did
" solemnly declare. He therefore, looking on that dispensa-
" tion as null and void, and by consequence, on the marriage
" contracted by that authority as unlawful and incestuous, and
" on the lady Mary as incapable to succeed, being born in it ;
" did judge and affirm, that the marriage with queen Anne,
" and the issue come, or to come from it, was lawful and valid ;
" and that the just right of succeeding to the crown was vested

" in the issue of that marriage : and that all judgments and
" censures either by the late pope Clement, or by any other
" judge, that were made and published, or that might hereafter
" be made or published, were, and are null and void, unjust,
" and unlawful. And he promised on the word and faith of a
" king, and under the forfeiture of all his goods, and of all the
" goods of his subjects, in the form of a contract of guaranty,
" both for himself and his heirs successors, that he, at all
" times, and in all places, particularly in all synods or general
" councils, and before all persons, and against all men whatso-
" ever that should oppose it, of what rank or condition soever
103 " they might be, he would both by himself, and by his sub-
" jects, maintain and defend it, and (if need were) justify it,
" by a strong hand, and with all his forces. Nor would he
" ever, for the future, publicly or privately, directly or indi-
" rectly, go against it, or so much as attempt it, nor suffer it
" to be attempted by any other, as much as in him lay."

    Here was as positive an assurance, as could be put in words. From
And though princes have in former times, as well as in our which he
own days, made bold with their promises and treaties ; and parted.
have very easily thrown them off, or broke through them,
without any appearance of great remorse or shame ; yet it
must be confessed, that Francis did never, even in the war that
he afterwards had with king Henry, depart from, or falsify
this engagement.

THE HISTORY

OF

THE REFORMATION

OF

THE CHURCH OF ENGLAND.

PART III.—BOOK III.   104

Of what happened during the time comprehended in the Third
  Book of the History of the Reformation; from the year
  1535, to King Henry's death, anno 1546—7.

1535.
The king
was much
pleased
with the
title of Su-
preme
Head
[cap. 1.
Statutes,
vol. iii.
p. 492.]

KING Henry seemed not a little pleased with his title of the
Supreme head of the Church of England; of which it was
enacted, in the session of parliament that sat after the breach
was made with Rome, that it should be for ever joined to
the other titles of the crown, and be reckoned one of them.
He ordered an office for all ecclesiastical matters, and a seal to
be cut; which, in an inhibition sent to the archbishop, in order
to a royal visitation of the whole clergy of all England, is, for
aught I know, first mentioned. It is dated the 18th of
September, 1535; and, at the end, these words are added;
" Under our seal that we use in ecclesiastical matters, which
" we have ordered to be hereunto appended."

The arch-
bishop of
Canter-
bury's title
changed.

The archbishop of Canterbury's title was also in convocation
ordered to be altered: instead of the title of legate of the
apostolic see, he was to be designed metropolitan, and primate.
This last was one of his ancient titles. In that session, there

was some discourse concerning heresy, and of some English
books; in particular, of Tyndale's books. And there was a book
laid before them, with the title of a Primer; of which there is
no other account given, but that, from the rubrics of it, they
suspected it was a book not fit to be published. This, it seems,
produced a petition to the king, that he would command all
heretical books to be called in, within a time limited; and that
he would appoint the scripture to be translated in the vulgar
tongue; but that, though the laity might read it, yet they were
to be required not to dispute concerning the catholic faith.

[Wilkins, Conc. iii. 769.]
[Dec. 11, 1534. ibid.]

It is very probable, that a breach was upon this occasion
begun between Cranmer and Gardiner. The sharpness against
heresy was probably supported by Gardiner; as the motion
for the translation of the Bible was by Cranmer. But when
Cranmer, in order to an archiepiscopal visitation of the whole
province, having obtained the king's license for it on the 28th
of April, sent out his inhibition according to form, to the ordinaries during the visitation; upon this, Gardiner complained
to the king of it, for two reasons. He thought the title of
primate of England did derogate from the king's power. The
105 other was, that since his diocese had been visited within five
years last past, and was now to pay for ever tenths to the king,
it ought not to be charged with this visitation. Of this
Cromwell gave Cranmer notice. He on the 12th of May wrote
a vindication of himself; which will be found in the Collection.

Cranmer and Gardiner oppose one another.

[April 20.]

Collect. Numb. 37. Cranmer vindicates himself.

" He believed that Gardiner (who wanted neither law, in-
" vention, nor craft to set out his matters to the best advantage)
" studied to value himself upon his zeal for the king's supre-
" macy, that so he might seem more concerned for that than
" for himself. Cranmer laid himself, and all his titles, at the
" king's feet; but he wrote, why did not Gardiner move this
" sooner? for he had received his monition on the 20th of
" April. The pope did not think it lessened his supremacy,
" that he had many primates under him : no more did his title
" lessen the king's supremacy. Gardiner knew well, that if
" the pope had thought those subaltern dignities had weakened
" his supreme one, he would have got all the bishops to be put
" on the level; there being many contentions concerning juris-
" diction in the court of Rome. But if all the bishops of the
" kingdom set no higher value on their styles and titles than he

[April 24.]

" did, the king should do in those matters what he pleased:
" for if he thought that his style was in any sort against the
" king's authority, he would beg leave to lay it down. He
" felt in his heart, that he had no sort of regard in his style or
" title, further than as it was for the setting forth of God's word
" and will; but he would not leave any just thing at the plea-
" sure of the bishop of Winchester, he being no otherwise
" affectionate to him than he was. In the apostles' days, there
" was a Diotrephes, who loved the preeminence; and he had
" more successors than all the other apostles; from whom all
" glorious titles, and much pomp, was come into the church.
" He wished that he, and all his brethren, might leave all their
" styles, and call themselves only the apostles of Jesus Christ;
" so that they took not the name vainly, but were such indeed;
" and did order their dioceses, so that not parchment, lead, or
" wax, but the conversation of their people, might be the seals
" of their office; as St. Paul said the Corinthians were to him."
He answers the other part very fully; but that will be found
in the letter itself, it not being of that importance to deserve,
that any abstract should be made of it.

Bishops
proceed
against
those who
desired a
reforma-
tion.

It was soon observed, that there was a great faction formed
against any reformation in doctrine or worship; and that those
who favoured and promoted it were ill used by the greater part
of the bishops: of which I shall give one instance, and by it
one may judge of the rest; for I have seen many complaints
to the same purpose. Barlow was, by queen Anne's favour,
made prior of Haverfordwest, in Pembrokeshire. He set himself
to preach the pure gospel there, and found many were very
desirous to hear it; but he was in danger of his life daily by
reason of it: and an accusation being brought against him by
a black friar there, set on by Rawlins then bishop of St. David's,
who both rewarded him for it, and recommended him to the
arches: for Barlow had appealed to the king. He owns, that, 106
by Cromwell's favour, their design against him was defeated;
but he having sent a servant home about business, the bishop's
officers cited him to their courts, and ransacked his house;
where they found an English Testament, with an exposition of
the sermon on the mount, and of some other parts of the New
Testament. Upon this, they clamoured against him as a heretic
for it. They charged the mayor of the town to put him and

some others in prison, seeking by all means to find witnesses
against them ; but none appearing, they were forced to let them
go, but valued themselves upon this their zeal against heresy.
He sets forth the danger that all were in, who desired to live
according to the laws of God, as became faithful subjects : for
in that multitude of monks, friars, and secular priests, that was
then in those parts, there was not one that sincerely preached
the word of God, and very few that favoured it. He complains
of the enormous vices, fraudulent exactions, and heathenish
idolatry, that was shamefully supported under the clergy's jurisdiction ; of which he offered to make full proof, if it should
be demanded and received : but that being done, he desired
leave to remove from thence ; for he could neither go home,
nor stay there safely, without a special protection. This letter Collect.
Numb. 38.
will be found in the Collection.

Barlow was that year made bishop of St. Asaph, and the [Jan. 16.
year afterwards was translated to St. David's ; and was after 1536.]
[April 10.]
that removed to Wells, but driven out by queen Mary ; and [Feb. 3.
was made bishop of Chichester by queen Elizabeth, in which 1547.]
[Dec. 20.
he lived ten years. 1559.]

The secret opposition that the bishops gave to the steps The arch-
made towards a reformation, obliged Cromwell to send many bishop of
York much
agents, in whom he trusted, up and down the nation, to observe suspected.
all men's tempers and behaviour. Legh, among others, being
sent to York, did (in January) enjoin the archbishop, by an
order from the king, to preach the word of God, and to set
forth the king's prerogative. He also enjoined him to bring up
to the king all the foundations of his see, and all commissions
granted to it. In these he did not doubt but they would find
many things fit to be reformed : and he advised, that every
bishop might be so ordered, that their dioceses might be better
instructed and edified. That would establish them in their
fidelity to the king, and to his succession : but the jurisdictions
might be augmented, or diminished, as should seem convenient.
This letter, which will be found in the Collection, opens a Collect.
design, that I find often mentioned, of calling in all the pope's Numb. 39.
bulls, and all the charters belonging to the several sees, and
regulating them all. But perhaps the first design being the
suppressing the monasteries, it was not thought fit to alarm
the secular clergy till that was once done : yet the order for

sending up all bulls was at the same time generally executed.
There is a letter of Tunstall's writ soon after this to Cromwell,
put in the Collection, in which he mentions the king's letters to
all the bishops, to come up immediately after the feast of the pu-
rification, with all the bulls they had obtained from Rome at
any time.   But the king, considering that Tunstall had gone
down but late, ordered Dr. Layton to write to him, that he
needed not come up; but advised, that he should write to the 107
king that he was ready to do as other bishops did, and to deliver up all such bulls as the king desired of him.   Layton
wrote to him, that Cromwell, as his friend, had assured the
king that he would do it.

Collect.
Numb. 40.

In answer to this, Tunstall thanked him for his kindness on
that, and on many other occasions.   "He did not understand
" to what intent these bulls were called for, (and it seems he
" apprehended it was to have all the bishops give up their
" right to their bishoprics,) yet he had sent them all up to be
" delivered at the king's pleasure.   He adds, that he hoped by
" this demand the king did not intend to make him leave his
" bishopric, and both to turn him out of his living, and to ruin
" all his servants, that had their living only by him; in which,
" he wrote, he could not be thought either ambitious or un-
" reasonable : so he desired to know what the king's pleasure
" was, not doubting but that the king would use him as well as
" he used the other bishops in the kingdom, since, as he had
" obtained these bulls by him, he had renounced every thing
" in them that was contrary to his prerogative.   He had but
" five bulls, for the rest were delivered to those to whom they
" were addressed : so he commits himself to the king's good-
" ness, and to Cromwell's favour;" dating his letter from
Auckland the 29th of January, which must be in the year
1535–6.

Tunstall might be under more than ordinary apprehensions
of some effect of the king's displeasure; for as he had opposed
the declaring him to be the supreme head, in the convocation
of York ; so he had stuck firmly to the asserting the lawfulness
of the king's marriage to queen Catharine.   Before the meeting of the parliament, in which that matter was determined,
he, with the proxy that he sent to the bishop of Ely, wrote
him a letter, of which Mr. Richard Jones saw the original

which he had inserted in his voluminous Collections, that are
in the Bodleian library[1], in which these words are, after he
had told him that he had given him full power to consent or
dissent from every thing that was to be proposed : he adds,

"Yet nevertheless, I beseech you, if any thing harmful or
"prejudicial in any point to the marriage between the king's
"highness and the queen's grace shall be proposed, wherein
"our voices shall be demanded ; in your own name say what
"you will, and what God putteth in your mind : but I desire
"you, and on God's behalf I require you, never in my name
"to consent to any such hing proposed, either harmful or pre-
"judicial to the marriage aforesaid ; but expressly to dissent
"unto the same : and for your discharge on that behalf, ye
"may shew, when you think it requisite, this my particular
"declaration of my mind, made unto you therein ; and what I
"have willed and required you to do in my name in this point,
"praying your lordship not to do otherwise in my name, as
"my singular trust is in you, that ye will not."   Dated from
Auckland in January, but neither day nor year are mentioned.

The session of parliament, in which the act of the succession
passed, by which the king's marriage with queen Catharine
was condemned, meeting in January, this letter seems to be [Jan. 15,
108 written before that session ; and yet no opposition was made 1534.]
to that act in the house of lords, either by the bishop of Ely,
or by the bishop of Bath, whom he had made his second
proxy, as appears by the same letter, in which he is also
named.   The act passed so soon, that it was read the first [Journals
time on the 20th of March, and passed on the 23rd in the pp. 77, 78.
house of lords, without either dissent or protest.   It is also
certain that Tunstall afterwards took the oath enjoined by
that act.   But how these bishops came to be so silent upon
that occasion, being so solemnly required to do otherwise by
Tunstall : and how he himself came to change, and to take the
oath, is that of which I can give no account.   It is certain
king Henry had a very particular regard for him ; but yet by

[1 This is apparently a mistake. of Sunningwell. Neither can the
The Collection alluded to contains letter mentioned in the text be found
sixty three MSS., and was left to there now.]
the Bodleian by Henry Jones, vicar

this letter it appears, that he had some fears of a severity aimed at himself: but he was afterwards in all things very compliant, even to the end of king Edward's reign.

Complaints of the monks and friars.

There came up, from all parts of the kingdom, many complaints of the ill behaviour and bad practices of the monks and friars; of the last chiefly, for the mendicant order being always abroad begging, they had many more occasions to shew themselves: and though the monks had not those occasions to be in all public places, yet it was very visible that they were secretly disposing people to a revolt. So it was resolved to proceed against them all by degrees: and, after the visitations and injunctions, which had no great effect, they began with the smaller houses, that were not above 200*l.* a year: this swept away at once all the mendicants, who were the most industrious, and by consequence the most dangerous.

The archbishop of York clears himself.

[April 23.] Collect. Numb. 41.

The archbishop of York was much suspected: and if many apologies look like intimations of some guilt, he had a great deal; for he took many occasions to justify himself. Upon the act for taking all the lesser monasteries into the king's hands, he expressed great zeal in serving the king, which appears in a letter of his to Cromwell in April 1536. He gave a strict commandment to his archdeacons to warn all in the monasteries within the act, not to embezzle or convey away any thing belonging to the house: and if they had done any such thing, to restore it. He ordered them to give warning to all others not to meddle with any such goods. He had also warned the mayor of York and his brethren, and the master of the mint there, to receive none of the goods or plate of these monasteries. Having thus expressed his care in that matter, he made an earnest suit for two places that were of the patronage of his see. The one was St. Oswald's, which was a free chapel; the prior was removable at the archbishop's pleasure, and he might put secular priests in it, if he pleased. The other was Hexham, upon the borders of Scotland, which was once an episcopal see; and there not being a house between Scotland and that lordship, if that house should go down, there would be a great waste that would run far into the country. Whether he obtained these suits or not, does not appear to me. After that he adds, that he had given order that no preachers should be suffered that preached no-

velties, and did sow seeds of dissension. Some, after that they
were forbid to preach, did go on, and preach still.   He had
109 ordered process against them ; some of them said they would
get the king's license: if that were done, he must be silent;
but he hoped Cromwell would hinder that, and give him notice
if they had obtained the king's license.   Some said they had
the archbishop of Canterbury's license : but none of these
should be obeyed there ; none but the king's licenses, and his.

Upon the many complaints of preachers of all sorts, king
Henry wrote a circular letter to all the bishops on the 12th of
July, letting them know, that, considering the diversity of
opinion in matters of religion, he had appointed the convocation to set forth certain articles of religion, most catholic :
but, to prevent all distraction in the minds of his people, he
ordered, that, till that was published, no sermon should be
preached till Michaelmas, unless by the bishop, or in his presence, or in his cathedral, where he is to take care to furnish
such as he can answer for : every bishop is therefore required
to call in all his licenses for preaching, and to publish this in
the king's name.   He is also required to imprison all those
who acted against this order; and not to suffer any private
conventicles or disputations about these matters.   To this is
added, a direction for the *bidding of prayers ;* that they
should pray for departed souls, that God would grant them
the fruition of his presence: and a strict charge is laid on
curates, that when the articles of religion shall be sent them,
they should read them to their people, without adding or di-
minishing; excepting only such to whom he shall under his
seal give power to explain them.

The blind bishop of Norwich, Nix, was condemned in a
præmunire, and put out of the king's protection, for breaking
through a custom that the town of Thetford had enjoyed past
all memory, that no inhabitant of that town could be brought
into any ecclesiastical court, but before the dean of that town :
yet that old and vicious bishop cited the mayor before him,
and charged him, under the pain of excommunication, not to
admit of that custom.   Upon this, judgment was given in the
temporal courts against the bishop : but he was now received
into the king's protection.   In the pardon, mention is made of
his being convicted upon the statute of provisors.   Stokesley

Reg. Heref.
Fox. fol. 6.
All preach-
ing is for
some time
prohibited.

bishop of London was charged with the breach of the same
statute, for which he took out a pardon.

Rymer.
[tom. xiv.
p. 569 et
alibi.]
During these years, Cromwell carried no higher character
than that of secretary of state : but all applications were made
to him in ecclesiastical matters ; so whether this was only by
reason of his credit with the king, or if he was then made
vicar-general, does not appear to me.   But as the king took
care to keep all things quiet at home, so he set himself to cul-
tivate a particular friendship with the princes of the empire of
the Augsburg Confession ; hoping by their means to be able
to give the emperor a powerful diversion, if he should go about
A treaty
with the
Lutheran
princes.
[Sleidan,
fol. 145.]
to execute the pope's censures.   The king of France had been
for some time endeavouring to beget a confidence of himself in
the minds of those princes ; pretending that he was neither for
the divine nor the unbounded authority that the popes had
assumed ; but only he thought it was reasonable to allow them
a primacy in the church, and to set limits to that.   Langey
was the person most employed in the managing of this matter.
But when the king came to understand that the king of 110
France had sent for Melancthon, being then at Langley, he
ordered the duke of Norfolk and the lord Rochford to write
to Cromwell, commanding him to despatch Barnes immediately
to Germany ; and to use such diligence, that if it was possible,
he might meet Melancthon before he was gone into France ;
and to dissuade his going thither, since the French king was
then persecuting those who did not submit to the pope's
usurped authority.   He was to use all possible arguments to
divert him from going, and to persuade him all he could to
come over to England ; shewing him the conformity of the
king's opinions with his own, and setting forth the king's noble
and generous temper : but if he was gone into France, Barnes
was to go on to the princes of Germany, and Cromwell was to
send a messenger with him, to be sent back with an account
of the state of matters among them.   He was to engage the
princes to continue firm in the denial of the pope's authority ;
in which their honour was deeply concerned : and they might
depend upon the king in that matter, who had proceeded in it
with the advice of the most part of the great and famous
clerks in Christendom, from which he would never vary, nor
alter his proceedings.   Barnes was to carry over a book written

on that subject, and some sermons of the bishops, and to put the princes on their guard as to the French king; for he assured them, that both he and his council were altogether papists.

Barnes was likewise directed to send Heynes (afterwards *Barnes sent* dean of Exeter) and Christopher Mont (an honest German, *to them.* who was long employed by the crown of England) to sir John Wallop, the king's ambassador in France, on pretence that they went as his friends to visit him. If Melancthon was in France, they were to go secretly to him, to dissuade his stay long there, or his altering his opinion in any particular. Some copies of the book, and the sermons, were to be carried by them to France. If it is true that the king of France was so set to maintain the pope's supremacy, Wallop was to represent to him, how contrary that was to his honour, to subject himself to the pope, and to persuade others to do the same; and to charge him that he would remember his promise to maintain the king's cause and proceedings: and since the king did not move the subjects of any other prince, why should the French king study to draw the Germans from their opinion in that matter; which the king thought himself much concerned in, since it was so much against the king's interest and his own promise? Wallop was to use all means to incline him rather to be of the king's opinion. They also ordered Cromwell to write to the bishop of Aberdeen, that the king took it very unkindly that his nephew, the king of Scotland, was suing to marry the duke of Vendome's daughter without his advice: he had proposed it to him before, and then he would not hearken to it. This negligence the king imputed to that bishop, and to the rest of the Scottish council: the letter concludes, that Barnes should not be stayed for further instructions from the bishop of Canterbury. These should be sent afterwards by the almoner, (Fox.) This letter will be found in the Collection. *Collect. Numb. 42.*

111　　This came soon enough to stop Melancthon's journey to *Melanc-* France. The great master, and the admiral of France, did not *thon's going to* think of any thing with relation to Germany, but of a civil *France pre-* league, to embroil the emperor's affairs. They were against *vented.* meddling in points of religion; and so were against Melanc- *Paper* thon's coming to France. They were afraid that the French *Office.* divines and he would not agree; and that might alienate the *[State Papers, vol. vii. p. 622.)*

German princes yet more from the court of France. Heynes and Mont wrote this over from Rheims, on the 8th of August 1535. It is true, Langey was sent to bring him, hoping to meet him at Wirtemberg : but he was not come thither; only the heads of their doctrine were sent to him. With these he came back to France. The king's divines made some emendations ; which, Langey said to Mont, he believed the Germans would submit to : and so he was sent back with a gold chain, and letters to bring Melancthon, and six other eminent German divines, with him. Of this Mont gave the king advice the 7th of September in that year.

[State Papers, vol. vii. pp. 625 and 627.

The French king fluctuates.

This whole matter came to nothing ; for Francis' sister, the queen of Navarre, was the person who pressed him chiefly to it ; hoping by this, once to engage him in some point of doctrine, which, as she hoped, might draw on a rupture with Rome ; but his ministers diverted him from all thoughts of engaging in doctrinal matters ; and they put him on entering into a league with the princes of the empire only with relation to their temporal concerns. Nor were the German princes willing to depart in a tittle from the Augsburg Confession, or enter upon new treaties about points that were settled already among them ; which might give occasion to new divisions among themselves. And no doubt, the king's interposing in the matter with such earnestness had great weight with them ; so he was delivered from the alarm that this gave him. But to go on with our king's affairs in Germany.

Seck. lib. iii. sect. 13. § 39. [p. 111.]

Fox sent to Germany.

Fox, with Heath, (on whom Melancthon set a high value,) was sent, soon after Barnes, to negotiate with the Germans. He had many conferences with some of their divines, and entered into a large treaty about several articles of religion with those of Wittenberg, which lasted three months, to the elector's great charge, and the uneasiness of the Germans.

Melancthon had dedicated his Commentary on the Epistles[2] to the king ; who sent him (upon it) a present of two hundred crowns, and wrote a letter to him, full of particular expressions of esteem, and assurances that he would always assist him in

---

[2] [Seckendorf says that Melancthon sent to the king a copy of his Commentary on the epistle to the Romans. The second edition of it had lately been published, Haganoæ, 1535. The first edition appeared at Wittenberg in 1532. Neither edition is dedicated to the king.]

those his pious labours; dated from Winchester the 1st of
October 1535. Fox seemed to assure them, that the king would
agree with them in all things : and told them that the king had
already abolished the popish superstitions, which he called the
Babylonish tyranny; calling the pope Antichrist. They of
Wittenberg insisted on the abuses of the mass, and on the
marriage of the clergy; and took notice, that the king had
only taken away some smaller abuses, while the greatest were
still kept up. So that Melancthon wrote on the margin of their
paper, at this part of it, in Greek, *Nothing sound*. All this
was sent over to the king; but did not at all please him. For,
112 in an answer written by Cromwell, these words are a part of it :
" The king knowing himself to be the learnedest prince in
" Europe, he thought it became not him to submit to them;
" but he expected they should submit to him." They, on the
other hand, saw the great advantage of his protection and assistance : so that they brought Luther to make an humble
submission to him, asking him pardon for the manner of his
writing against him; which I find intimated, though it never
came in my way. They studied also to gain both upon his
vanity, offering him the title of the *defender* or *protector of
their league;* and on his interest, by entering into a close confederacy with him.

It was an opinion common enough in that time, that the
emperor was the sovereign of Germany. Gardiner, in several
of his letters, seems to be of that mind : and upon that account,
he endeavoured to possess the king with a prejudice against
his treating with them, that it was to animate subjects to revolt
against their prince : whereas, by the constitution and laws of
the empire, the princes had secured to themselves the right of
coining, fortifying, arming, and entering into treaties, not only
with one another, but with foreign princes, for their defence.
A homage was indeed due to the emperor; and a much greater
submission was due to the diet of the empire : but the princes
were sovereigns in their own territories,.as the Hanse towns
were free states. Fox pressed them to approve of all that the
king had done in the matter of his divorce, and of his second
marriage. To which they gave the answer that I had inserted
in my History, among the transactions of the year 1530 [3] : but

[3 See Part i. p. 94, and Records, p. 94.]

the noble Seckendorf shews, that it was sent in the year 1536.
In their answer, as they excused themselves from giving their
opinion in that matter till they were better informed, they
[Ibid.
p. 112.]
added, (which, it seems, was suppressed by Fox,) " Though we
" do agree with the ambassadors, that the law against marry-
" ing the brother's wife ought to be kept, yet we are in doubt
" whether a dispensation might not take place in this case ;
" which the ambassadors denied. For that law cannot oblige
" us more strictly than it did the Jews : and if a dispensation
" was admitted to them, we think the bond of matrimony is
" stronger."   Luther was vehemently against the infamy put
on the issue of the marriage. He thought the lady Mary was
cruelly dealt with, when she was declared a bastard. Upon
queen Catharine's death, they earnestly pressed the restoring
her to her former honour. So true were they to that which
was their principle, without regarding the great advantage they
saw might come to them from the protection of so great a king.

His ambassadors, at that time, gave these princes an advertisement of great importance to them, that was written over to
the king by Wiat, then his ambassador in Spain ; that the emperor had, in a passionate discourse with him, called both the
elector and the landgrave his enemies, and rebels. The truth
was, the elector did not entirely depend on all that Fox said to
him. He thought the king had only a political design in all
this negotiation ; intending to bring them into a dependence
on himself, without any sincere intentions with relation to reli- 113
gion.   So he being resolved to adhere firmly to the Augsburg
Confession, and seeing no appearance of the king's agreeing to
it, he was very cold in the prosecution of this negotiation. But
the princes and states of that Confession met at this time at
Smalcald, and settled the famous Smalcaldic league ; of which
the king's ambassadors sent him an authentic copy, with a
translation of it in English ; which the reader will find in the
Collect.
Numb. 43.
Collection.
" By it, John Frederick, elector of Saxony, with his brother
" Ernest ; Philip, Ernest, and Francis, dukes of Brunswick ;
" Ulric, duke of Wirtemberg ; Philip, landgrave of Hesse ; the
" dukes of Pomerania ; four brothers, princes of Anhalt ; two
" brothers, counts of Mansfield ; the deputies of twenty-one free
" towns ;" which are not named in any order, for Hamburg

and Lubeck are the last save one; but, to avoid disputes,
they were named in the order in which they came, and produced their powers.   " All these did, on behalf of themselves
" and their heirs, seeing the dangers of that time, and that
" many went about to disturb those who suffered the sincere
" doctrine of the gospel to be preached in their territories;
" and who, abolishing all abuses, settled such ceremonies as
" were agreeable to the word of God; from which their
" enemies studied to divert them by force and violence; and
" since it was the magistrate's duty to suffer the sincere
" word of God to be preached to his subjects, and to provide
" that they be not violently deprived of it : therefore, that
" they might provide for the defence of themselves and their
" people, which is permitted to every man, not only by the
" law of nature, but also by the written laws, they entered
" into a Christian, lawful, and friendly league ; by which they
" bound themselves to favour all of their body, and to warn
" them of any imminent danger, and not to give their enemies
" passage through their territories.   This was only for their
" own defence, and not to move any war.   So if any of them
" should be violently assaulted for the cause of religion, or on
" any pretence, in which the rest should judge that religion
" was the true motive, the rest of the confederacy were bound,
" with all their force and power, to defend him who was so
" assaulted in such a manner, as for the circumstances of the
" time shall be adjudged : and none of them might make any
" agreement or truce, without the consent of the rest.   And,
" that it might not be understood that this was any prejudice
" to the emperor their lord, or to any part of the empire, they
" declare, that it was only intended to withstand wrongful vio-
" lence. They also resolved to receive all into this confederacy
" who received the Augsburg Confession, and desired to be
" joined to it.   And whereas the confederacy made six years
" before was to determine on the *Sunday invocavit* of the fol-
" lowing year, in which the princes of Wirtemberg, Pomerania,
" and Anhalt, and six of the cities, were not comprehended ;
" they received them into this confederacy, which was to last
" for ten years after the *Sunday invocavit :* and if any war
" should be begun, but not finished within these ten years, yet
114 " it shall be continued till the war is brought to an end ; but at
" the end of the ten years, it shall be lawful to the confederates

" to prolong it further. And they gave their faith to one an-
" other, to observe this religiously, and set their seals to it."

On the same day, the king's answer was offered to the demands the princes had made : both which are in the Paper
Office ; and both will be found in the Collection. Their demands were, " that the king would set forth the true doctrine
" of Christ, according to the Augsburg Confession ; and that
" he would defend that doctrine at the next general council, if
" it be pious, catholic, free, and truly Christian : and that nei-
" ther the king, nor the princes and states of that union, should
" without mutual consent agree to any indiction of a general
" council made by the bishop of Rome ; but that if such a
" council should be called, as they had desired in their answer
" to Vergerius, the pope's ambassador, it should not be refused :
" and that if a council shall be celebrated, to which the king
" and these princes do not agree, they shall (to their power)
" oppose it : and, that they will make protestations against it,
" that they will not obey any constitution made in it, nor suffer
" any decrees made in it to be obeyed ; but will esteem them
" null and void, and will make their bishops and preachers
" declare that to their people. That the king will associate
" himself to the league, and accept the name of the defender
" or protector of it. That they will never suffer the monarchy
" of the bishop of Rome to take place ; nor grant that it is ex-
" pedient that he should have preeminence before all other
" bishops, or have any jurisdiction in the dominions of the
" king, and of the princes. That upon these grounds they
" enter into a league with one another. And in case of any
" war, either for the cause of religion, or any other cause what-
" soever, that they should not assist those who begin any
" such war. That the king shall lay down a hundred thousand
" crowns ; which it shall be lawful to the confederates to make
" use of, as a moiety of that which they themselves shall con-
" tribute : and if need be, in any cause of urgent necessity, to
" contribute two hundred thousand crowns ; they joining as
" much of their own money to it. And if the war shall end
" sooner than that all the money is employed in it, what re-
" mains shall be restored to the king. And they assured him,
" that they should not convert this money to any other use,
" but to the defence of the cause of religion, together with
" their own money. And since the king's ambassadors were to

Collect.
Numb. 44.

" remain some time in Germany, disputing with their learned
" men about some points; they desire, that they may know
" the king's mind, and that he will signify it to the elector of
" Saxony, and the landgrave of Hesse : and then the princes
" will send their ambassadors, and a learned man with them,
" to confer with the king about the articles of doctrine, and
" the ceremonies of the church."

To these the king sent two different answers, one after
another. The first, that will be found in the Collection, was, Collect.
" That the king intended to set forth the true doctrine of Numb. 45.
" Christ, which he was ready to defend with life and goods :
115 " but that he being reckoned somewhat learned, and having
" many learned men in his kingdom, he could not think it
" meet to accept at any creature's hand what should be his
" faith, or his kingdom's; the only ground of which was in
" scripture, with which he desired they would not be grieved :
" but that they would send over some of their learned men, to
" confer with him and his learned men to the intent that they
" might have a perfect union in faith. He would also join
" with them in all general councils, that were catholic, free,
" and held in a safe place, for the defence of the true doctrine
" of the gospel : and as for ceremonies, there may be such
" a diversity in these used through the whole world, that
" he thought that ought to be left to the governors of the
" several dominions, who know best what is convenient for
" themselves. He agreed that neither he nor they should
" accept of the indiction of a general council, but by all their
" mutual consent ; but that if such a free council may be held
" in a safe place, it shall not be refused. The king did not
" think fit to accept the title offered by them till first they
" should be thoroughly agreed upon the articles of doctrine :
" but that being once done, he would thankfully accept of it.
" To that of a defensive league, he added one clause, that they
" should not suffer any of their subjects to serve those who set
" on them in any such war : he thought it not reasonable that
" he should bear any share of the wars already past, (which
" it seems was secretly mentioned, though not expressed in their
" demands ;) but for the future, he was willing to contribute
" a hundred thousand crowns as they desire. Upon further con-

Collect.
Numb. 46.

" sidering their demands, the king sent a second and fuller
" answer, which will be likewise found in the Collection.
" It begins with very tender expressions of the sense the
" king had of their benevolence to him, and of their constancy
" in adhering to the truth of the gospel: he acknowledges the
" goodness of God in giving them such steadfastness and
" strength. Their wondrous virtues had so ravished the king,
" that he was determined to continue in a correspondence of
" love with them on all occasions." Then follow some ex-
planations of the former memorial, but not very important, nor
differing much from it: only he lets them know, " that it was
" not for any private necessity of his own, that he was moved
" to join in league with them; for by the death of a woman
" all calumnies were extinct, (this is meant of queen Anne,) so
" that neither the pope nor the emperor, nor any other prince,
" had then any quarrel with him: yet, that they might know
" his good affection to them, he would contribute the sum they
" desired, and upon the terms they proposed; only on his part
" he demanded of them, that in case any prince invaded his
" dominions on the account of religion, that they would furnish
" him, at their expense, with five hundred horsemen completely
" armed, or ten ships well arrayed for war, to serve for four
" months: and that it should be at the king's choice, whether
" horse or ships: and that they should retain at the king's
" charge such a number of horse and foot as the king should
" need, not exceeding the number of two hundred horse, and
" five thousand foot: or instead of the foot, twelve ships in
" order, with all things necessary, which the king might keep 116
" in his service as long as he pleased: and last of all, that the
" confederates will promise in all councils, and every where
" else, to promote and defend the opinion that Dr. Martin, (so
" they named Luther,) Justus Jonas, Cruciger, Pomeran, and
" Melancthon had of his marriage." This negotiation sunk to
a great degree upon queen Anne's tragical fall: and as the
king thought they were no more necessary to him, so they
saw his intractable humour, and had no hope of succeeding
with him, unless they would have allowed him a dictatorship
in matters of religion. Yet, to end all this negotiation at once,
  The elector of Saxony and the landgrave of Hesse wrote a

letter to the king, which will be found in the Collection, taken Collect. Numb. 47.
from the original, occasioned by pope Paul the Third's sum-
moning " a general council to meet at Mantua on the 23rd of
" May, upon which the emperor had sent messengers to them,
" to give them notice of it, and to require them to come to it,
" either in person or by their proctors : but though they had
" always desired a council for the reforming of those abuses
" that had continued so long, by the negligence or corruption
" of popes and prelates ; yet in this bull the pope clearly in-
" sinuates that he will not suffer the restoring of true doctrine,
" or the correcting of abuses, to be treated of, but that their
" doctrine .without any examination was to be condemned with
" infamy. He also endeavoured to oblige all, by the receiving of
" his bull, without taking cognizance of the matter, to extirpate
" and destroy the doctrine they professed : so that if they had
" accepted the bull, they had seemed to be involved in that
" design. . They therefore told the emperor's minister, that
" they looked on that bull as unjust and pernicious : and they
" desired he would let the emperor know that they could not
" accept of it.   They did not doubt but the pope, or his party
" about the king, would upon this occasion pretend, that the
" pope had done his duty, and would study to load them with
" ill characters : so they thought it necessary to justify them-
" selves to the king and other princes on this occasion.
    " They sent over with this a full vindication of their pro-
" ceedings, which they desired the king would read, and that
" he would consider not only the present danger of the Ger-
" mans, but the common concern of the whole church, in which
" it was visible that all good discipline was lost, and that great
" and worthy men had wished and desired that some received
" abuses, that could not be denied, might be amended : there-
" fore they recommend the cause of the church, and their own
" cause, to his care."   This is dated the 25th of March 1537.
    I have in my other work[3] given an account of the ambassa-
dors whom they sent into England, of the representations they
made, and of a full paper that they offered to the king : to all
which I have nothing now to add, but that I have found a
letter of Cranmer's to Cromwell, which I have put in the Col- Collect. Numb. 48.
lection, in which he complains of the backwardness of the

_____
    [3] [See part i. p. 255.]

bishops. The ambassadors had been desired to tarry one
month, that their book might be considered: but though he
moved them to treat about it, as they had done upon other
articles, they answered him, they knew the king had taken it 117
on himself to answer them; and that a book to that end was
already devised by him: therefore they would not meddle with
the abuses complained of. The bishops desired that the archbishop would go on to treat of the sacraments of matrimony,
orders, confirmation, and extreme unction, in which they knew
certainly that the Germans would not agree with them, except
only in matrimony. "He saw the bishops were seeking an
" occasion to break the concord: and that nothing would be
" done, unless there came a special command from the king.
" They saw they could not defend the abuses, and yet they
" would not yield that point: he complains likewise that the
" ambassadors were very ill lodged; multitudes of rats were
" running in their chambers day and night, and their kitchen
" was so near their parlour, that the smell was offensive to all
" that came to them. He wishes that a more convenient house
" might be offered them."

It is true, the king used them with a particular civility, and
spoke to them before all his court in a most obliging manner;
and often wished that Melancthon might be sent over to him.
Cranmer and Cromwell used them with all possible kindness.
Cranmer wrote often by them to the elector, exhorting him to
continue firm and zealous for the truth and purity of the
gospel; but under all the shows of the king's favour, they understood that his heart was turned from them. He wrote, when
he dismissed them, to the elector, in terms full of esteem for
their ambassadors; " not doubting but good effects would follow
" on this beginning of conferences with them: but the matter
" being of the greatest importance, it ought to be very maturely
" considered. He again desired that Melancthon might be sent
" over to him, that he might treat with him; promising that
" he would apply himself wholly to what became a Christian
" prince to pursue." Dated the 1st of October 1538. During
this embassy, there was an anabaptist seized by the landgrave
of Hesse: in whose papers they found that he had some followers in England, that he had hopes of great success there,
and was designing to go thither, but he said he was forbidden

Seck. lib.
iii.
[Sect. 17.
§ 66. p. 18.]

by the Spirit: upon this they wrote an account of all they found to the king, and gave him a description of the anabaptists of Germany. They were much spread through Frisia and Westphalia, and in the Netherlands; chiefly in those places where none of their preachers were tolerated. The not baptizing infants was the known character of the party; but with this, they were for a community of goods: they condemned all magistracy, and all punishing of crimes, which they thought was a revenge forbidden by Christ. They condemned all oaths, and were against all order and government. They seemed to be Manichæans in religion: they despised the scriptures, and pretended to particular illuminations; and allowed both polygamy and divorce at a man's pleasure: and wheresoever their numbers increased, they broke out into sedition and rebellion. They wrote all this to the king in a letter, that by the style is believed to be penned by Melancthon, both to let him see how far they themselves were from favouring such corruptions, and to put the king on his guard against them.

Here ends this negotiation; for I find no mark of any
118 farther commerce between them: and though this ran out far beyond the year 1535 in which it was begun, yet I thought it best to lay it all together, and so to dismiss it. The unlooked for accidents that happened in England had wrought much on the king's temper; his own inclinations were still biassing him to adhere to the old opinions and practices; and the popish party watched and improved all advantages, of which a very signal one happened soon, to their great joy. [Jan. 7. 1536.]

Queen Catharine, or, as she was called, the princess dowager, Cott. libr. 4 died first. I have nothing to add concerning her, but that I Otho. C. x. fell on a report of a conversation that sir Edmund Beding- [fol. 199, field and Mr. Tyrrel had with her, in which she solemnly pro- 203, 206.] tested to them, that prince Arthur never knew her carnally, and insisted much on it; and said, many others were assured of it. But on the contrary, Bedingfield urged very fully all the probabilities that were to the contrary: and said, that, whatever she said on that subject, it was little believed, and it seemed not credible. The tragedy of queen Anne followed soon

[4 This part of the volume is in- Harleian Collection, from which
jured by fire, but there is a copy of they have been reprinted in State
two of the articles referred to in the Papers, vol. i. pp. 397–404.]

after this : it broke out on the first of **May 1536**, but it seems it was concerted before ; for a parliament was summoned, at least the writs were tested, the 27th of April before.

Meteren, Hist. des Pays Bas, lib. I. fol. 21 sqq.

There is a long account of her sufferings given by Meteren, in that excellent history that he wrote of the wars in the Netherlands, which he took from a full relation of it, given by a French gentleman, Crispin, who was then in London, and, as Meteren relates the matter, wrote without partiality. He begins it thus ; " There was a gentleman who blamed his " sister for some lightness that appeared in her behaviour : " she said the queen did more than she did, for she admitted " some of her court to come into her chamber at undue hours ; " and named the lord Rochford, Norris, Weston, Brereton, " and Smeaton the musician. And she said to her brother, that " Smeaton could tell much more : all this was carried to the " king."

When the matter broke out on the first of May, the king, who loved Norris, sent for him, and said, if he would confess those things, with which the queen was charged, he should neither suffer in his person nor his estate ; nor so much as be put in prison : but if he did not confess, and were found guilty, he should suffer the extremity of the law. Norris answered, he would much rather die than be guilty of such falsehood ; that it was all false, which he was ready to justify in a combat against any person whatsoever : so he was sent with the rest to the Tower. The confession of Smeaton was all that was brought against the queen. He, as was believed, was prevailed on to accuse her ; yet he was condemned contrary to the promise that had been made him : but it was pretended that his crime was, that he had told his suspicions to others, and not to the king ; and when it was alleged, that one witness was not sufficient, it was answered, that it was sufficient. He adds, that the queen was tried in the Tower ; and that she defended her honour and modesty in such a way, as to soften the king, (for she knew his temper,) by such humble deportment, to favour her daughter. She was brought to her trial without having any advocate allowed her ; having none but her maids about her. A chair was set for her, and she looked to all her judges with a cheerful countenance, as she made her curtsies to them without any fear : she behaved herself as if she had 119 been still queen; she spoke not much in her own defence; but the modesty of her countenance pleaded her innocence, much more than the defence that she made; so that all who saw or heard her believed her innocent. Both the magistrates of London, and several others who were there, said, they saw no evidence against her; only it appeared, that they were resolved to be rid of her.

She was made to lay aside all the characters of her dignity; which she did willingly: but still protested her innocence. When she heard the sentence, that she was to be beheaded, or burnt, she was not terrified, but lifted up her hands to God, and said, "O Father! O Creator! Thou, who art the " way, the truth, and the life; thou knowest that I have not " deserved this death." And turning herself to her judges, (her uncle, the duke of Norfolk, being the lord high steward,) she said, " My lords, I will not say that your sentence is unjust, " nor presume that my opinion ought to be preferred to the " judgment of you all. I believe you have reasons and occa- " sions of suspicion and jealousy, upon which you have con- " demned me: but they must be other than those that have " been produced here in court, for I am entirely innocent of " all these accusations; so that I cannot ask pardon of God " for them. I have been always a faithful and loyal wife to the " king. I have not, perhaps, at all times shewed him that humi- " lity and reverence, that his goodness to me, and the honour to [p. 21 b. " which he raised me, did deserve. I confess I have had " fancies and suspicions of him, which I had not strength nor " discretion enough to manage; but God knows, and is my " witness, that I never failed otherwise towards him: and I " shall never confess any other, at the hour of my death. Do " not think that I say this on design to prolong my life; God " has taught me to know how to die, and he will fortify my " faith. Do not think that I am so carried in my mind as " not to lay the honour of my chastity to heart; of which " I should make small account now in my extremity, if " I had not maintained it my whole life long, as much as ever " queen did. I know these my last words will signify nothing, " but to justify my honour and my chastity. As for my " brother, and those others, who are unjustly condemned, I " would willingly suffer many deaths to deliver them: but

" since I see it so pleases the king, I must willingly bear with
" their death, and shall accompany them in death, with this
" assurance, that I shall lead an endless life with them in
" peace." She said all this, and a great deal more ; and then,
with a modest air, she rose up, and took leave of them all.
Her brother, and the other gentlemen, were executed first.
" He exhorted those who suffered with him to die without
" fear ; and said to those who were about him, that he came to
" die, since it was the king's pleasure that it should be so.
" He exhorted all persons not to trust to courts, states, and
" kings, but in God only. He had deserved a heavier punish-
" ment for his other sins ; but not from the king, whom he
" had never offended : yet he prayed God to give him a long
" and a good life. With him, all the rest suffered a death,
" which they had no way deserved. Mark Smeaton only con- 120
" fessed, he had deserved well to die : which gave occasion to
" many reflections.

    " When the queen heard how her brother and the other
" gentlemen had suffered, and had sealed her innocence with
" their own blood ; but that Mark had confessed he deserved
" to die : she broke out into some passion, and said, Has he
" not then cleared me of that public shame he has brought me
" to ? Alas ! I fear his soul suffers for it, and that he is now
" punished for his false accusation. But for my brother and
" those others, I doubt not but they are now in the pre-
" sence of that Great King, before whom I am to be to-
" morrow."

    It seems that gentleman knew nothing of the judgment that
passed at Lambeth, annulling the marriage ; for it was transacted secretly. It could have no foundation or colour, but
[p. 57 sqq.] from that story mentioned in Cavendish's Life of Wolsey, of
the lord Percy's addresses to her. He was now examined upon
that : but it will appear, from his letter to Cromwell, that he
solemnly purged both himself and her from any precontract ;
being examined upon oath by the two archbishops : and that
he received the sacrament upon it, before the duke of Norfolk,
and some of the king's council that were learned in the
spiritual law ; assuring them by his oath, and by the sacrament
that he had received, and intended to receive, that there was
never any contract, or promise of marriage, between her and

him. This he wrote on the 13th of May, four days before
the queen's execution; which will be found in the Collection. Collect.
Numb. 49.
This shews plainly, that she was prevailed on, between fear
and hope, to confess a precontract, the person not being
named.

The French gentleman gives the same account of the man-
ner of her death, and of her speech, that all the other writers [Hall, p.
of that time do. "When she was brought to the place of 819. Stow,
p. 573.
" execution, within the Tower, he says her looks were cheer- Archæolo-
" ful; and she never appeared more beautiful than at that gia, vol.
xxiii. p.65.]
" time. She said to those about her, Be not sorry to see me
" die thus; but pardon me from your hearts, that I have not
" expressed to all about me that mildness that became me;
" and that I have not done that good that was in my power to
" do. She prayed for those who were the procurers of her
" death. Then, with the aid of her maids, she undressed her
" neck with great courage, and so ended her days."

This long recital I have translated out of Meteren; for I
do not find it taken notice of by any of our writers. I leave
it thus, without any other reflections upon it, but that it seems
all over credible.

Thevet, a Franciscan friar, who, for seventeen or eighteen
years, had wandered up and down Europe to prepare materials
for his Cosmography [5], (which he published in the year 1563,) Cosmog.
says, that many English gentlemen assured him, that king lib. xvi.
[vol. ii. fol.
Henry expressed great repentance of his sins, being at the 657 b.]
point of death; and, among other things, of the injury and
the crime committed against queen Anne Boleyn, who was
121 falsely accused, and convicted of that which was laid to her
charge. It is true, Thuanus has very much disgraced that
writer, as a vain and ignorant plagiary : but he, having been
of the order that suffered so much for their adhering to queen
Catharine, is not to be suspected of partiality for queen Anne.
We must leave those secrets to the great day.

It may be easily believed, that both the pope and the emperor, as they were glad to be freed from the obligation they

---

[5] [La Cosmographie Universelle
d'André Thevet, Cosmographe du
Roy. Illustrée de diverses figures
des choses plus remarquables veues
par l'auteur et incogneues de noz
anciens et modernes; 2 vols.; fol.
Par. 1575.]

[Cotton
MSS.
Vitell.
B. xiv.
fol. 215.]

seemed to be under to protect queen Catharine, so queen
Anne's fall gave them a great deal of ill-natured joy. The
pope, upon the first news of her disgrace, sent for Cassali,
expressing a great deal of pleasure upon the queen's imprisonment; and, at the same time, spoke very honourably of
the king. " He hoped, upon these emergents, all matters
" would be brought to a good agreement; and that the king
" would reconcile himself to the see, by which he would be-
" come the arbiter of all Europe. He told Cassali, that he
" knew how good an instrument he was in pope Clement's
" time; and what pains he took, both with the pope and the
" emperor, to prevent the breach. He added, that the nam-
" ing of Fisher to be a cardinal was so pressed on him, that he
" could not decline it. He desired Cassali would try how any
" messenger that he might send to the king would be received;
" for, as soon as he knew that, he would send one immedi-
[May 27.] " ately." Of all this Cassali wrote an account to the king.

[April 12.]
Cotton
Lib. Vitell.
B. xiv.
[fol. 177.]

At the same time, Pace[6] gave him an account of a long conversation he had with the emperor on the same subject: for
he was then the king's ambassador in that court. " The em-
" peror excused his adhering to his aunt, whom he could not
" in honour forsake : but at the same time, he said, he abhorred
" the pope's bull for deposing the king; and he was so far
" from any thoughts of executing it, that he commanded it to
" be suppressed in his dominions; nor did he encourage, as was
" suspected, the king of Scotland to undertake to execute it.
" He imputed the breach that had been made between him
" and the king to the French king; who, he said, was like an
" eel in a man's hand, ready to forsake him, *and even to re-*
" *nounce God, who, he believed, had given him over to a*
" *reprobate mind.* He was resolved now to return to his old
" friendship with the king; and he would not hearken to inti-
" mations given him by the agent of France, that the king
" had poisoned his aunt. He pressed him to legitimate the
" princess Mary. He might do that, without owning the
" lawfulness of the marriage; which was a point in which he

[6] [The author has mistaken Richard Pate, archdeacon of Lincoln,
for Richard Pace, dean of St. Paul's,
who died in 1532. It is Pate who
was the king's ambassador with
the emperor, and who is referred to
in this and the following pages.
Lord Herbert makes the same mistake.]

" would stir no more.   She was born in a marriage in fact,
" and *bonâ fide;* and in many cases, in which marriages had
" been dissolved, yet the legitimacy of the issue was often
" secured."

Of all this Pace gave the king an account; and pressed,
with some vehemence, the legitimating the princess.   The emperor was then going to Rome; so king Henry intended to
join Cassali with Pace in his embassy to the emperor.   Pace
begged that might not be done; expressing a great aversion
to him, as being a base and perverse man.   It is plain, Pace
pressed the king much to think of being reconciled to the
122 pope.   Cardinal Ghinucci offered his service again to the king,
with expressions full of zeal.   Granvelle also entered with Cassali upon the same subject: but Cassali wrote to the king, that
he did not at all meddle in that matter.   The emperor went
to Rome, and Pace followed him thither.   The king sent a Paper
despatch to Pace, which will be found in the Collection, telling Office.
him of the motion that the emperor's ambassador made to him Numb. 50.
for returning to the old friendship with their master.   They
also made him some overtures in order to it.   First, the emperor would be a mean to reconcile him to the bishop of Rome:
he also hoped that the king would contribute towards the war
against the Turk; and that, since there was an old defensive
league between them, and since it seemed that the French
king intended to invade the duchy of Milan, he expected the
king would assist him according to that league.

To all this the king answered, " that the interruption of The king
" their friendship proceeded from the emperor, who had made answered
" him ill returns for the services he had done him.   For he
" pretends he made him first king of Spain, and then emperor.
" When the empire was at his disposition, he had furnished
" him with money; so that he ought to thank the king only
" for all the honour he was advanced to: but in lieu of that,
" he had shewed great ingratitude to the king, and had not
" only contemned his friendship, but had set on all the ill
" usage he had met with from the bishop of Rome; which, as
" he understood, he owed chiefly to him.   Yet, such was the
" king's zeal for concord among Christian princes, and such
" was his nature, that he could continue his displeasure against
" no man, when the cause of it was once removed: so if the

" emperor would desire him to forget all that was past, and
" would purge himself of all particular unkindness to him, he
" would be willing to return to their old friendship ; but he
" having received the injuries, would not sue for a reconcilia-
" tion, nor treat upon the foot of the old leagues between
" them, till the reconciliation should be first made, and that
" without any conditions : when that was done, he would
" answer all his reasonable desires.

He refuses
any treaty
with the
pope.　　　" But as for the bishop of Rome, he had not proceeded on
" on such slight grounds, that he could in any sort depart
" from what he had done ; having founded himself on the
" laws of God, of nature, and honesty, with the concurrence
" of his parliament. There was a motion made to him from
" that bishop for a reconciliation, which he had not yet em-
" braced, nor would he suffer it to be compassed by any other
" means ; and therefore he would not take it in good part, if
" the emperor would insist in that matter, for the satisfaction
" of the bishop of Rome, that was his enemy ; or move him to
" alter that, which was already determined against his au-
" thority. When there was a general peace among Christian
" princes, he would not be wanting to give an aid against the
" Turk ; but till the friendship between the emperor and him
" was quite made up, he would treat of nothing with relation
" to the king of France : when that was done, he would be a
" mediator between them. This was the answer given to the
" emperor's ambassador ; which was communicated to Pace, 129
" that, in case he had any discourse with the emperor on the
" subject, he should seem only to have a general knowledge
" of the matter, but should talk with him suitably to these
" grounds ; encouraging the emperor to pursue what he had
" begun, and extolling the king's nature and courage, with his
" inclination to satisfy his friends, when he was not too much
" pressed : that would hurt and stop good purposes. And he
" orders him to speak with Granvelle of it, of whom it seems
" he had a good opinion, and that he should represent to the
" emperor the advantage that would follow, on the renewing
" their old friendship, but not to clog it with conditions ; for
" whatever the king might be afterwards brought to upon
" their friendship, when made up, the king would not suffer it
" to be loaded with them ; for the king had suffered the injury :

" but he was ordered to say all this as of himself, and Pace was
" ordered to go to court, and put himself in Granvelle's way,
" that he might have occasion to enter upon these subjects
" with him." Thus that matter was put in a method; so that
in a little time the friendship seemed to be entirely made up.

The king would never hearken to a reconciliation with the Proceed-
ings in
convoca-
tion. pope. On the contrary, he went on in his design of reforming
matters in England. In the convocation in the year 1536,
Cromwell came and demanded a place as the king's vicar-
general: the archbishop assigned him the place next above
himself. On the 21st of June, the archbishop laid before the [Wilkins'
Conc. iii.
803.] house the sentence definitive of the nullity of the king's marriage with queen Anne, which Cromwell desired they would
approve. It was approved in the upper house, and sent down
to the lower, in which it was also approved. On the 23rd of
June, the prolocutor, with the clergy, offered a book to the
upper house in which they set forth a collection of many ill
doctrines that were publicly preached within the province. On
the 28th of June, the confirmation of the decree concerning the
king's last marriage was subscribed by both houses. On the
11th of July, the book concerning the articles of faith, and the
ceremonies, was brought in by the bishop of Hereford, and was
signed by both houses. These were also signed by the arch-
bishop of York, and the bishop of Durham. On the 20th of [Fuller, lib.
v. p. 223.] July, the bishop of Hereford brought another book, containing
the reasons why the king ought not to appear in a council, sum-
moned by the pope to meet at Mantua: this was likewise agreed
to, and subscribed by both houses. I have nothing new to add
to the account I have given in my History of the other proceedings in matters of religion this year; in which no convocation sat at York. There are several draughts of these articles
that are in several places corrected by the king's own hand;
some of the corrections are very long and very material: of
these only it was that I meant, and not of the engrossed and
signed articles themselves, when I said they were corrected [Atterbury,
p. 188.] by the king; as I have been misunderstood.

By these steps it appearing clearly that the king had no Pole made
a cardinal. thoughts of a reconciliation with Rome, the pope on his part
resolved to create him as much trouble as he could. Pole had
124 been sent over from England to Paris while the suit of divorce
was in dependence: he was particularly recommended by the

bishop of Bayonne, in one of his letters to Montmorency, as a person of great hopes, and much favoured by the king : he came after that to England ; for he tells himself that he was in England while the point of the supreme headship was in
[Atterbury, p. 84.]
debate.   He says he was then absent, which shows that at that time he was contented to be silent in his opinion, and that he did not think fit to oppose what was doing.   He was afterwards suffered to go and settle at Padua, where the gravity of his deportment, that was above his age, and the sweetness of his temper, made him be very much considered.   He was still supported from England ; whether only out of his deanery of Exeter, or by any farther special bounty of the king's, is not certain.   In several letters from Padua, he acknowledges the king's bounty and favour to him, and in one he desires a farther supply.   He being commanded by the king to do it, wrote over his opinion concerning his marriage : the king sent it to Cranmer before his being sent out of England : for that faithful and diligent searcher into the transactions of those times,
[Strype's Cranmer, Appendix, Number I.]
Mr. Strype, has published the letter that he wrote upon it ; the year is not added, but the date being the 13th of June, it must be before he was sent out of England, this being writ before he was consecrated ; for he subscribes *Cranmer*, and upon his return he was consecrated long before June.   It is
Mar. 30. 1533.]
written to the earl of Wiltshire : he mentions Pole's book, and commends both the wit and eloquence of it very highly ; he thinks, if it should come abroad, it would not be possible to stand against it.   Pole's chief design in it was, to persuade the king to submit the matter wholly to the pope.   In it,

He wrote first against the divorce.
" He set forth the trouble that might follow upon the di- " versity of titles to the crown, of which the wars upon the " titles of Lancaster and York had given them a sad warning. " All that was now healed, and therefore care should be taken " not to return to the like misery.   He could never agree to " the divorce, which must destroy the princess' title, and ac- " cuse the king of living so long in a course of incest, against " the law of God and of nature.   This would increase the " hatred the people began to bear to priests, if it should " appear that they had so long approved that which is found " now to be unlawful.   As for the opinions of the universities, it " was known they were often led by affections ; and that they " were brought over with great difficulty to declare for the king :

" but he sets in opposition to them, the king's father and his
" council, the queen's father and his council, and the pope and
" his council. It could not be expected that the pope would con-
" demn the act of his predecessor, or consent to the abridging
" his own power, and do that which would raise sedition in many
" kingdoms, particularly in Portugal.   He next shews the em-
" peror's power, and the weakness of France; that the prohibit-
" ing our trade to the Netherlands would be very ruinous, and
" that the French were never to be trusted.   They never kept
" their leagues with us; for neither do they love us, nor do we
" love them: and if they find their aid necessary to England, they
125 " will charge it with intolerable conditions."   This is the substance of that letter.   So that at this time Pole wrote only to
persuade the king by political considerations to submit wholly
to the pope's judgment.   The matter rested thus for some
time: but when the breach was made, and all was past reconciling, then Cromwell wrote to him, by the king's order, to
declare his opinion with relation to the king's proceedings.
Upon this reason only he wrote his book, as he set forth in a
paper of instructions given to one to be shewed to the king,
which will be found in the Collection.   In which he writes, Collect.
" that he thinks, if it had not been for that, he had never Numb. 51.
" meddled in the matter, seeing so little hope of success; and Sends one
" that he had reason to think that what he should write with in-
" would not be acceptable.   They had sent unto him from structions
" England the books written on the contrary part: but he
" said he found many things suppressed in these; and all the
" colours that could be invented were set upon untrue opinions.
" Besides, what had followed was grievous, both in the sight
" of God, and in the judgment of the rest of Christendom:
" and he apprehending yet worse effects, both with relation to
" the king's honour, and the quiet of his realm, did upon that
" resolve to employ all the wit and learning that God had
" given him to set forth the truth, and to shew the conse-
" quences of those ill opinions.   He hoped that what he wrote
" on the subject would fully satisfy all that would examine it.
" This he did, in hopes that the king, whom God had suffered
" to be carried away from those opinions that he had the
" honour formerly to maintain, would yet by the goodness of
" God be recovered out of the evil way he was then in.
    " There were great instances of such cases in scripture, in

" the stories of David and Solomon; the last particularly,
" who, notwithstanding the gift of wisdom that he had from
" God, yet fell into idolatry. So, though the king was not
" fallen from the true doctrine of Christ, yet as David, when
" in a state of sin, was by a prophet, sent to him from God,
" brought to true repentance, and restored to the favour of
" God, he hoped he might, by the grace of God, be an instru-
" ment to bring the king to a better sense of things. There-
" fore, as he set himself to study the matter, so he prayed
" earnestly to God to manifest the truth to him : in which he
" hoped God had heard his prayer; so he looked for good
" success. And that he might make the king apprehend the
" danger he was in, both from his own people, who hated in-
" novations in religion, and from other princes, to whose
" honour it belongs to defend the laws of the church against
" all other princes who impugn them; and to make the king
" more apprehensive of this, he had as in his own person
" brought out all such reasons as might provoke people or
" princes against him, since he was departing from the course
" in which he had begun. These reasons, if read apart, with-
" out considering the purpose he proposed, of representing to
" the king the danger to which he was exposing himself, might
" make one think, from his vehemence of style in that argu-
" ment, that he was the king's greatest enemy; but the reading
" the whole book will shew what his intent in it all was. The
" book was too long for the king to read; he desired there-
" fore that he would order some learned and grave man to 126
" read it, and to declare his judgment upon it, he being bound
" with an oath of fidelity, first to God, and then to the king,
" to do it without affection on either part. He named parti-
" cularly Tunstall, bishop of Durham, whom he esteemed both
" for learning and fidelity to the king above any other he
" knew. After Tunstall had first examined it, the king may
" refer the further examination of it to such other persons as
" he may think fit; he was likewise resolved that his book
" should never come abroad till the king had seen it.

" In these instructions, he mentions that he had sent another
" book to the king concerning his marriage; but in that he
" was disappointed of his intent, as the bearer might inform
" him, who knew the whole matter. And since God had de-
" tected her, who had been the occasion of all the errors the

" king had been led into, it was the hope of all who loved him,
" that he would now come to himself, and take that discovery
" as a favourable admonition of God to consider better the
" opinion of those who dissented from that marriage, as seeing
" the great dishonour and danger like to follow on it.   He
" wished the king would look on that as a warning to return
" to the unity of the church : he was sensible nothing but the
" hand of God could work a change in the king's mind : and
" when that should be done, it would be one of the greatest
" miracles that the world had seen for some ages ; with the
" most signal characters of God's favour to him, which would
" deliver him out of those very great dangers, that must fol-
" low upon the meeting of a general council : whereas, if he
" should return to the unity of the church, no prince would
" appear in that assembly with more honour than would be
" paid to him, if he should return ; even his fall would prove
" a great blessing to the church, and tend to the reformation
" of the whole, and to the manifestation of the honour of God.
" It would then appear that God had suffered him to fall, to
" make him rise with more honour ; to the greater wealth,
" not only of his own realm, but of the whole church besides.
" With these instructions he sent a private letter to Tunstall
" from Venice, dated Corpus Christi Eve."

When his book against the divorce came first to England, [Cotton
he was written to in the king's name to come over and explain MSS.
some things in it ; but he excused himself : he pretended the Cleop. E.
love of retirement, and of the noble company with whom he vi. fol. 334.
lived in an easy and learned friendship there.   Eloquence ap. Strype's
seems to be that which he turned his mind most to ; for in Mem. Ec-
every thing he wrote there is much more of declamation than cles. vol. i,
of argument. p. 199.]

Tunstall being thus provoked by Pole, and commanded by
the king, wrote a full and solid answer to him, on the 13th of
July 1536, which will be found in the Collection.   " He Collect.
" acknowledged he had received his letter, as the king has Numb. 52.
" received his book ; in which he desired that the reading of
" it might be first put upon him : he had read both his letter
" and his long book, and was truly grieved as he read it ; Tunstall
" seeing both the vehemence of his style, and that he misre- writes co-
" presented the whole matter, as if the king was separated him.
" from the church.   He wished he had rather written his

" opinion privately in a letter to the king, which might have 127
" been read by himself, and not have enlarged himself into so
" great a book, which must be communicated and seen of others.
" What stupidity was it to send so long a book so great a
" way, by one who might have miscarried in it ; and so the book
" might have fallen into the hands of those who would have
" published it, to the slander of the king and the kingdom,
" but most of all to his own, for his ingratitude to the king,
" who had bred him up to that learning, which was now used
" against him, in whose defence he ought to have spent both
" life and learning : he advised him to burn all that he had
" written on that subject. There appeared a strain of bitter-
" ness in his whole book, that was very unbecoming him. He
" then comes to the argument, to shew that the king, by the
" title of the supreme head, did not separate himself nor his
" church from the unity of the whole body. The king did not
" take upon him the office belonging to spiritual men, the
" cure of souls ; nor that which belongs to the priesthood, to
" preach the word of God, and to minister the sacraments. He
" knew what belonged to his own office as king, and what be-
" longed to the priest's office : no prince esteemed spiritual men,
" that were given to learning and virtue, more than he did. His
" only design was, to see the laws of God sincerely preached,
" and Christ's faith (without blot) observed in his kingdom ;
" and to. reduce his church out of the captivity of foreign
" powers (formerly usurped) into the state in which all the
" churches of God were at the beginning ; and to put away all
" the usurpations that the bishops of Rome had by undue
" means still increased, to their own gain, but to the impo-
" verishing of the kingdom. By this he only reduced things
" to the state that is most conformable to the ancient decrees
" of the church, which the bishops of Rome solemnly promise
" to observe at their creation ; naming the eight general
" councils ; and yet any one, who considers to what a state the
" bishop of Rome had brought this church, would soon see the
" diversity between the one and the other. At Venice he
" might see these in Greek, and they were already published
" in Latin : by which it appears, that the bishop of Rome had
" then no such monarchy as they have usurped of late.
    " If the places of scripture which he quoted did prove it,
" then the council of Nice did err, which decreed the contrary ;

" as the canons of the apostles did appoint, that the ordinations
" of priests and bishops should be made in the diocese, or at
" most in the province, where the parties dwelt. These canons
" Damascen reckoned holy scriptures.   Nor can it be thought
" that the four general councils would have acted as they did,
" if they had understood those passages of scripture as he
" did ; for above a thousand years after Christ the customs were
" very contrary to those now used by the bishop of Rome :
" when the blood of Christ and of the martyrs were yet fresh,
" the scriptures were then best understood, and the customs
" then used in the church must be better, than those that
" through ambition and covetousness had crept in since. Light
" and darkness may be as well reconciled, as the worldly
128 " authority in temporal things now usurped can be proved
" from St. Peter's primacy, in preaching the word of God.
" He refers him to cardinal Cusa's second book, in which he
" will find this well opened.

" The king going to reform his realm, and to reduce things
" to the state in which they were some ages ago, did not
" change, but establish those laws, which the pope professes to
" observe.   If other princes did not follow him in this, that
" ought not to hinder him from doing his duty : of which he
" did not doubt to be able to convince him, if he had but one
" day's discourse with him, unless he were totally addicted to
" the contrary opinion. Pole wrote in his letter, that he thought
" the king's subjects were offended at the abolishing the pope's
" usurpations : but Tunstall assured him, that in this he was
" deceived ; for they all perceived the profit that the kingdom
" had by it, since the money that was before carried over to
" Rome was now kept within the kingdom.   That was become
" a very heavy burden, and was daily increasing ; so that if
" the king would go about to restore that abolished authority,
" he would find it more difficult to bring it about, than any
" thing he had ever yet attempted in his parliament. Pole had
" in his letter blamed Tunstall for fainting in his heart, and
" not dying for the authority of the bishop of Rome.   He as-
" sures him, that from the time that he understood the progress
" of Christ's church from the beginning, and had read ecclesi-
" astical history, he never thought to shed one drop of blood
" in that cause. None of those who had advantage by that
" authority would have lost one penny of it to have saved his

" life : he would do what in him lay to cool that indignation
" which his book had raised in the king. He desired him not
" to fancy (from what he saw in Italy, or in other places) that
" it was so from the beginning. The councils would show him
" how that dignity was given to the bishops of Rome. The
" emperors called those councils, and the dignity that was
" given him was because he was bishop of the chief city of the
" empire, and not for the sake of Peter and Paul. The second
" place was given to the patriarchs of Constantinople ; because
" it was called New Rome, and so was preferred to Antioch,
" where St. Peter was bishop, and where the name *Christian*
" first began ; and it was set before Alexandria, and likewise
" before Jerusalem, where Christ himself preached ; and the
" whole college of the apostles after him, and where James
" (the brother of our Lord) was the first bishop. That church
" was called the mother of all the churches. It was also set
" before Ephesus, where St. John wrote his Gospel, and died.
" To all these Constantinople was preferred : and yet this was
" fully settled in the council of Chalcedon, where 630 bishops
" met. If he read the Greek fathers, Basil, Nazianzen, Chry-
" sostom, and Damascen, he would find no mention of the mo-
" narchy of the bishop of Rome. He desired him to search
" farther into this matter, and he would find that the old
" fathers knew nothing of the pope's late pretensions and usur-
" pations. He wished therefore that he would examine these
" matters more carefully, which had been searched to the
" bottom in England. The learned men here thought, they 129
" were happily delivered from that captivity, to which he en-
" deavours to bring them back. He tells him how much all his
" family and kindred would be troubled, to see him so much
" engaged against his king and his country ; whom he might
" comfort, if he would follow the establishment of the whole
" church of God from the beginning, and leave the supporting
" of those usurpations. He refers him to Gregory the Great,
" who wrote against the bishop of Constantinople, pretending
" to the like monarchy. St. Cyprian writes, that all the apostles
" were of equal dignity and authority : which is also affirmed
" by the third council of Ephesus. He begged him not to trust
" too much to himself, but to search further, and not to fancy
" he had found out the matter already. He prayed him to
" burn all his papers ; and then he hoped he should prevail

" with the king to keep that which he had sent him secret.
" He concludes all with some very kind expressions."

This I have abstracted the more fully, for the honour of
Tunstall's memory; who was a generous and good-natured, as
well as a very learned man.   Pole, who was then a cardinal,
wrote no answer[4] to this that I could find; but he wrote a long
letter, either to Tunstall or to Cromwell, in May 1537, which
will be found in the Collection.

" He begins it with protestations of his affection to the king, Collect.
" though the king had taken such methods to destroy him, as Numb. 53.
" the like had not been known in Christendom, against any Pole's vin-
" who bore the person that he did at that time; yet he still himself.
" maintained a deep affection to him.   He knew well all that
" the king had designed against him; which, if he bore the
" king a small degree of love, would be enough to extinguish
" it.   He saw what he did for the best was taken in the worst
" part.   He did not think it possible, that the king should
" conceive such indignation against him, as to break through
" all laws to have him in his hands, and to disturb the whole
" commerce of nations rather than not have his person in his
" power.   But he still adhered to his former principles, and
" maintained his former temper towards the king.

" Upon his arrival in France, he was ashamed to hear that,
" he coming thither in the quality of an ambassador and legate,
" one prince should desire of another to betray him, and deliver
" him into the king's ambassador's hands.   He himself was so
" little disturbed at it, when he first heard of it, that he said
" upon it, (to those who were about him,) that he never felt
" himself in full possession of being a cardinal till then, since
" he was now persecuted by him whose good he most earnestly
" desired.   Whatever religion men are of, if they would observe
" the law of nations, the law of nature alone would shew how
" abominable it was to grant such a request; and it was no
" less to desire it.   So that if he had the least spark of an
" alienation from the king in him, such proceedings would blow

---

[4] [The answer dated August 1,
from 'a place in the country near
Padua,' is in Cleopatra, E. vi. fol.
337, the same volume from which
the author extracted Tunstall's letter.
It has been printed from the original in Strype's Memorials, vol. i.
Appendix, pp. 206-218.   Pole was
not cardinal at the time of writing
this letter, but was created with
eleven others, Dec. 22, 1536, by
Paul III.   See Onuphrii Panvinii
Pontifices et Cardinales, p. 377. ed.
Ven. 1557.]

" it up into a fire. He might upon this be justly tempted to
" give over all commerce with the king, and to procure (by all
" honest ways) the means to repay this malignity, by doing
" him the utmost damage he could devise: but he did not for **130**
" that abstain from trying to do all he could for the king's
" honour and wealth. He acknowledges that the bishop of
" Verona was sent by him to the court of France, to intimate
" that the pope (for the common good of Christendom) had
" committed some affairs to him, to treat with the king. That
" bishop passed through Abbeville when the bishop of Win-
" chester and Mr. Brian were there : so he could not but wonder
" at the king's acting towards him ; the whole design of his
" legation being for the king's honour. Upon which that bishop
" desired to confer with the king's ambassadors, that he might
" declare to them the whole truth of the matter, which was
" made known to them. They, it is true, had no communication
" with him ; but they sent their secretary, after the bishop had
" declared the effect of his legation, as far as it related to the
" king, to him.

" It seemed visible to all, that the king (in what he had
" done against him) was abused by false reports, and by the
" false conjectures of some ; so it was hoped, that, the matter
" being once cleared, the king would have changed his mind.
" All this he understood from the bishop of Verona at his re-
" turn ; and he readily believed it. That bishop had been the
" king's true servant, and had shewed (when he was in a ca-
" pacity to serve him) the sincere love that he bore him. He
" had been also Pole's particular acquaintance ever since he
" came out of England. He would have been ready, if the
" king had consented to it, to have gone and given the king
" full satisfaction in all things. For, the chief reason of his
" being sent into France was, the pope's intending to gain the
" king, knowing the friendship that was between him and the
" French king : so the bishop of Verona was thought the fittest
" person to be first employed, who had great merits on both
" kings, for the services he did them when he was in office :
" and being esteemed the best bishop in Italy, it was designed
" that he should accompany Pole, as well as he was sent before,
" to prepare matters for his coming ; which he, out of his zeal
" to do God and the king service, undertook very willingly ;
" and resolved to try how he could get access to the king's

" person : so now, having fully explained himself, he hoped it
" would not be thought possible that he had those designs, of
" which the king's proceeding against him shewed he sus-
" pected him, (which was, that he came on purpose to animate
" the people to rebel.)

" Upon his first coming to Rome, he acquainted the king
" with the design, for which he was called thither : and he had
" acquainted him with the cause of his legation. These were
" not the methods of those who intended to rebel. He had
" then procured a suspension, in sending forth the censures,
" which at that time might have caused the king more trouble :
" and he sent his servant purposely with the offer of his assist-
" ance, animating the chief of his kindred to be constant in the
" king's service. If any had been at Rome, in the king's pay,
181 " to do him service, they could not have done more than he
" did ; so that some began to reflect on him, because he would
" not consent to divers things that would have been uneasy to
" him : and particularly, because he had the censures in his
" hand, which were instantly called for by those who had au-
" thority to command : yet they never came into their sight,
" nor hands ; and to that hour he had suppressed them. He
" would go no further in justifying himself, if what he had al-
" ready done, and what the bishop of Verona had said, did not
" do it ; he would take no more pains to clear himself: he ra-
" ther thought he had been faulty in his negligence in these
" matters. But there was nothing now left to him, but to pray
" for the king."

This letter is dated from Cambray : for upon the king's
message to the French king, to demand him to be delivered
into his hands, Francis could in no sort hearken to that, but he
sent to him not to come to his court, but to go with all convenient haste out of his dominions : so he retired to Cambray, as
being then a peculiar sovereignty. The king had a spy, one
Throckmorton, secretly about Pole, who gave him an account
of all his motions : but, by what appears in his letters, he was
faithfuller to Pole than to the king. He wrote over, that his
book was not then printed, though he had been much pressed
to print it by those at Rome ; but he thought that would hinder
the design he went on : he believed indeed, that, upon his returning thither, he would print it. He tells him, that he had
procured the suspensions of the pope's censures, to try if it was

possible to bring about a reconciliation between the pope and
the king : and he adds, that many wondered to see the king so
set against him, and that he did not rather endeavour to gain
him.   He intended to have stayed some time in Flanders, but
the regent sent him word, that it could not be suffered.   He

[Cotton
MSS.
Cleop. E.
vi. fol. 372.]
went from thence and stayed at Liege, where he was on the
20th of August ; for the last of Throckmorton's letters is dated
from thence.   He writes, that the pope had called him back,
having named him to be his legate to the council that he had
summoned to meet the 1st of November ; though it did not
meet for some years after this.

The king
was recon-
ciled to the
emperor.
[Nott's
Surrey and
Wyatt, vol.
ii. pp. 311–
337.]
The king's indignation upon his advancement, and for his
book, carried him to a great many excesses, and to many acts
of injustice and cruelty ; which are not the least among the
great blemishes of that reign.   Wiat was then the king's ambassador at the emperor's court ; and by his letters to the king[5]
it seems an entire confidence was then settled with the emperor.
The king pressed him much not to suffer the pope to call a
council, but to call one by his own authority, as the Roman
emperors had called the first general councils ; and he proposed Cambray as a proper place for one : but he saw he was
not like to succeed in that, so he only insisted on a promise
that the emperor had made, that nothing should be done in
the council, whensoever it should meet, against him or his
kingdom.

[April,
1538.
State Pa-
pers, vol.
viii. p. 23.]
The king was at this time under much uneasiness, for he **132**
sent both Bonner and Heynes over to the emperor's court in
conjunction : the one seems to have been chosen to talk with
those who were still papistical ; and the other had great credit
with the protestants.   Our merchants in the emperor's dominions
were threatened by the inquisition for owning the king as supreme head of this church.   Upon this Wiat complained to the
emperor.   But though that prince vindicated the inquisitors,

---

[5] [Dr. Nott has published Wiat's
Instructions together with several
despatches from Cromwell to Wiat,
but the editor has been unable to discover any letters from Wiat to the
king written at this period.   There
are four letters to the king from Wiat
written in Dec. 1539 (vol. ii. pp. 350–
365), and several others of the following year, ibid. pp. 368–420.   The
same volume contains sixteen letters
from the king to Wiat (461–518),
after which is printed (518–523),
Wiat's Memorial of his letter to the
king upon the interview had with
the emperor in company with sir
John Dudley, Nov. 1537.]

he promised to give such order, that they should not be disquieted on that account : and when Pole applied himself to the emperor for leave to affix the pope's bull against the king in his dominions, he would not consent to it.

I cannot add much to what I wrote formerly with relation to the suppression of the monasteries[5].   There are many letters, setting forth their vices and lewdness, and their robberies, and other ill practices ; and now that the design against them was apparent, many ran beyond sea with their plate and jewels : but I must not conceal, that the visitors give a great character of the abbess and nuns of Pollesworth in Warwickshire.   Dr. London, that was afterwards not only a persecutor of protestants, but a suborner of false witnesses against them, was now zealous even to officiousness in suppressing the monasteries. In the first commission that the visitors had, there was no order for the removing shrines ; yet he in his zeal exceeding his commission had done it : upon which Layton, Legh, and others, desired that a commission for that end might be sent after them, of the same date with their other commissions. He also studied to frighten the abbess of Godstow into a resignation. She was particularly in Cromwell's favour, so she wrote a plain honest letter to him, complaining of " London's violence, of his " artifices to bring them to surrender their house, and of the " great charge he put them to : she writes, that she did not " hear that any of the king's subjects had been so handled. " She insists on her care to maintain the honour of God, and " all truth and obedience to the king ; therefore she was po- " sitively resolved not to surrender her house, but would be " ready to do it whensoever the king's command or his should " come to her, and not till then."   The great character I gave of that abbess and of her house in my former work[7], made me resolve to put this letter in the Collection.

The discovery of the cheats in images, and counterfeits in relics, contributed not a little to their disgrace.   Among these, that of Boxley in Kent was one of the most enormous. Among the papers that were sent me from Zurich, there is a letter written by the minister of Maidstone to Bullinger, that de-

Marginal notes:

Dr. London's violent proceedings in suppressing the monasteries. [Cotton[6] MSS. Cleop. E. iv. fol. 210.]

Collect. Numb. 54. Cheats in images discovered.

---

[5] [See part i. p. 194, and pp. 235 —238.]

[6] [This letter has been printed in the Camden Society's Volume of

Letters relating to the suppression of Monasteries, p. 139.]

[7] [See part i. p. 238.]

Collect.
Numb. 55.

scribes such an image, if it is not the same, so particularly, that I have put it in the Collection. He calls it the Dagon of Ashdod, or the Babylonish Bel. It was a crucifix that sometimes moved the head, the eyes, and did bend the whole body to express the receiving of prayers; and other gestures were at other times made to signify the rejecting them : great offerings were made to so wonderful an image. One Partridge suspected the fraud, and, removing the image, he saw the whole imposture evidently. There were several springs within it, by which all these motions were made. This was brought to Maidstone, and exposed to all the people there; from thence it was carried 1S3 to London, and was shewed to the king and all his court, and in their sight all the motions were performed. The king's council ordered a sermon to be preached at Paul's, by the bishop of Rochester, where this imposture was fully discovered; and after sermon it was burnt.

Upon the birth of prince Edward, matters had a better face : here was an undoubted heir born to the crown :—it is true, the death of his mother did abate much of the joy, that such a birth would have given otherwise; for as she was of all the king's wives much the best beloved by him, so she was a person of that humble and sweet temper, that she was universally beloved on that account : she had no occasion given her to appear much in business, so she had no share of the hatred raised by the king's proceedings cast on her. I fell into a mistake from a letter of queen Elizabeth's, directed to a bigbellied queen, which I thought belonged to her ; but I am now convinced of my error[s], for it was no doubt written to queen Catharine, when, after king Henry's death, she was with child by the lord Seymour. Upon queen Jane's death, Tunstall, being then at York, wrote a consolatory letter to the king, which will be found in the Collection. It runs upon the common topics of affliction, with many good applications of passages of scripture, and seems chiefly meant to calm and cheer up the king's spirit. But the truth is, king Henry had so many gross faults about him, that it had been more for Tunstall's honour, and better suited to his character, if he had given hints to awaken the king's conscience, and to call upon him to examine his ways, while he had that load upon his mind. Either Tunstall did not think him so faulty as certainly he was, or he was very

Tunstall
wrote a
consola-
tory letter
to the king
when
queen Jane
died.
Collect.
Numb. 56.

[s] [See part i. p. 209.]

faulty himself, in being so wanting to his duty upon so great an occasion.

But I go on to more public concerns. The king had by the lord Cromwell sent injunctions to his clergy in the year 1536, as he did afterwards in the year 1538, which I have printed in my former work. There was also a circular letter written to the bishops; that to the bishop of Hereford is dated on the 20th of July 1536, requiring them to execute an order, abrogating some holy-days. The numbers of them were so excessively great, and by the people's devotion, or rather superstition, were like to increase more and more, which occasioned much sloth and idleness, and great loss to the public in time of harvest. It sets forth, that the king, with the advice of the convocation, had settled rules in this matter. The feast of the dedication of churches was to be held every year, on the first Sunday in October : but the feast of the patron of the church was to be no more observed. All the feasts from the first of July to the 29th of September, and all feasts in term-time, were not to be observed any more as holy-days, except the feasts of the apostles, of the blessed Virgin Mary, and of St. George, and those days in which the judges did not use to sit ; but the four quarter-days were still to be offering days. These are all the public injunctions set out about this time. But after the first of these, I find the bishops sent likewise injunctions to their clergy round their dioceses, of which a copy, printed at that time, was given me by my worthy friend Mr. Tate, minister of Burnham. The first was by Lee, archbishop of York, which will be found in the Collection.

Reg. Heref. Fox. fol. 9. Orders about holy-days.

[Wilkins' Conc. iii. 823.]

Collect. Numb. 57. Injunctions given by the archbishop of York.

134

" He begins with the abolishing of the bishop of Rome's au-
" thority, and the declaring the king to be supreme head of the
" church of England, as well spiritual as temporal. He requires
" his clergy to provide a New Testament in English or Latin
" within forty days, and to read daily in it two chapters before
" noon, and two in the afternoon ; and to study to understand
" it. He requires them also to study the book to be set forth
" by the king, of the Institution of a Christian Man. They
" were to procure it as soon as it should be published, that
" they might read two chapters a day in it, and be able to
" explain it to their people. All curates and heads of religious
" houses were required to repeat the Lord's Prayer and the
" Ave-Maria in English ; and at other parts of the service, the

" Creed and the Ten Commandments also in English, and to
" make the people repeat these after them, and none were to
" be admitted to the sacrament at Easter that could not repeat
" them. All parishes were required, within forty days, to pro-
" vide a great Bible in English, to be chained to some open
" place in the church ; that so all persons might resort to it,
" and read it for their instruction.   Priests were forbidden to
" haunt taverns or alehouses, except on necessary occasions.
" The clergy that did belong to any one church were required
" to eat together, if they might, and not to play at prohibited
" games, as cards and dice.   They must discourage none from
" reading the scriptures, exhorting them to do it in the spirit
" of meekness, to be edified by it. They were required to read
" to their people the Gospel and Epistle in English. Rules are
" set for the frequent use of sermons, proportioned to the value
" of their livings : generally four sermons were to be preached
" every year, one in a quarter.   None were to preach but such
" as had license from the king or the archbishop, nor were
" they to worship any image, or kneel or offer any lights or
" gifts to it : but they might have lights in the roodloft, and
" before the sacrament, and at the sepulchre at Easter.   They
" were to teach the people that images are only as books to
" stir them up to follow the saints ; and though they see God
" the Father represented as an old man, they were not to think
" that he has a body, or is like a man.   All images to which
" any resort is used, are to be taken away.   They are to teach
" the people that God is not pleased with the works done for
" the traditions of men, when works commanded by God are
" left undone ; that we are only saved by the mercy of God,
" and the merits of Christ ; that our good works have their
" virtue only from thence.   They were to teach the midwives
" the form of baptism : they were to teach the people to make
" no private contracts of marriage, nor to force their children
" to marry against their wills ; and to open to their people
" often the two great commandments of Christ, *To love God
" and our neighbour*, and to live in love with all people, avoid-
" ing dissension."

The rest relate to the matters set out in the king's injunctions.

Collect.
Numb. 58.   There were about the same time injunctions given by Samp-135
son, bishop of Coventry and Lichfield, for his diocese, which

will be found in the Collection.   He begins with a charge to Injunc-
tions by
the bishop
his clergy, " to instruct the people concerning the king's being
" the supreme head of the church of England, by the word of ofCoventry
and Lich-
" God ; and that the authority used by the bishop of Rome field.
" was an usurpation. Then he charges them to procure by the
" next Whitsuntide a whole Bible in Latin, and also one in
" English ; and to lay it in the church, that every man may
" read in it. Then, with relation to the reading the scriptures,
" and the having sermons every quarter, he gives the same
" charge that Lee gave. As to their sermons, he charges them
" that they be preached purely, sincerely, and according to the
" true scriptures of God. He next requires them in the king's
" name, and as his minister, to teach the people to say the
" Lord's Prayer, and the Ave, and the Creed in English : and
" that four times in every quarter they declare the seven deadly
" sins, and the Ten Commandments.   And because some, out
" of neglect of their curates, and to hide their lewd livings,
" used in Lent to go to confession to friars, or other religious
" houses ; he orders that no testimonial from them shall be
" sufficient to admit one to the sacrament, called by him *God's*
" *board*, till they confess to their own curates, unless upon
" some urgent considerations of conscience, that he or his de-
" puties should grant a special license for it.   That on holy-
" days, and in time of divine service, none should go to ale-
" houses or taverns, nor be received in them : and that the
" clergy should go in such decent apparel, that it might be
" known that they were of the clergy."

The last of the injunctions in that book was given by Shaxton,
bishop of Salisbury, for his diocese, which will be found in the
Collection ; they are said to be given out from the authority Collect.
Numb. 59.
given him by God and the king.

" He begins with provision about non-residents and their And by the
bishop of
Salisbury.
" curates ; in particular, that no French or Irish priest, that
" could not perfectly speak the English tongue, should serve as
" curates.   They were at high mass to read the Gospel and
" Epistle in the English tongue, and to set out the king's su-
" premacy, and the usurpations of the bishop of Rome.   The
" same rules are given about sermons as in the former, with
" this addition, that no friar, nor any person in a religious
" habit, be suffered to perform any service in the church.

" As for reading the New Testament, the clergy are only re-
" quired to read one chapter every day; and that every per-
" son having a cure of souls should be able to repeat without
" book the Gospels of St. Matthew and St. John, with the
" Epistles to the Romans, Corinthians, and Galatians, and the
" Acts of the Apostles, and the canonical Epistles: so that
" every fortnight they should learn one chapter without book,
" and keep it still in their memory: and that the 28th chapter
" of Deuteronomy should be read every quarter instead of the
" general sentence.   He gave the same orders that the others
" gave about images, pilgrimages, and other superstitious ob-
" servances, and for teaching the people the elements of reli-
" gion in English; only he does not join the Ave-Maria, with 136
" the Lord's Prayer, as the others did. He requires the curates
" to exhort the people to beware of swearing and blaspheming
" the name of God, or of Christ's precious body and blood,
" and of many other sins, then commonly practised: he dis-
" pensed with all lights before images, and requires that every
" church should be furnished with a Bible.   He complains
" of the practice of putting false relics on the people, naming
" stinking boots, mucky combs, ragged rockets, rotten girdles,
" locks of hair, gobbets of wood, as parcels of the holy cross,
" of which he had perfect knowledge; besides the shameful
" abuse of such as were perhaps true relics: he prays and
" commands them, by the authority he had under God and the
" king, to bring all these to him, with the writings relating to
" them, that he might examine them, promising to restore such
" as were found to be true relics, with an instruction how they
" ought to be used. He also orders, that the Ave and pardon-
" bell, that was wont to be tolled three times a day, should be
" no more tolled."

These are all the injunctions set out by bishops that have
fallen into my hands.   Here I must acknowlege a very great
omission made in the copy that I printed in the Collection
added to my History, of a very important paragraph, in the
second injunction given by Cromwell, which will be found in
Collect. the Collection, together with an omission of a few lines in bishop
Numb. 60. Bonner's injunctions, that were passed over by a very common
fault of transcribers, who, seeing the words that they wrote last
in the original before them, do not enough examine whether the

same words did not belong to a new portion, and so write on without examining whether there are no words or lines between the one and the other : for *churches and chapels* being in two different places, my copier wrote on from the second place, and so omitted some lines between the one and the other.   I am very ready to correct what I find amiss ; I rather wonder that there is no more occasion for such reprehensions. I know I am not to expect either favour or common civility from some hands. I *do not enter* into faults of a worse nature made by others, but am very ready to confess my own when I see them.

I find nothing to add with relation to the dissolution both of the smaller and the greater monasteries, nor of the several risings that were in different parts of the kingdom ; only I find a letter of Gresham, then lord mayor of London, I suppose he was the father of him who was the famed benefactor to the city; but by the letter which will be found in the Collection, his father was the occasion of procuring them a much greater benefaction.   He began his letter with a high commendation of the king, who, as he writes, "seemed to be the chosen ves-" sel of God, by whom the true word of God was to be set " forth, and who was to reform all enormities.   This encouraged " him, being then the mayor of the city of London, to inform " him, for the comfort of the sick, aged, and impotent persons, " that there were three hospitals near or within the city, that " of Saint George, Saint Bartholomew, and Saint Thomas, and " the New Abbey on Tower-Hill, founded and endowed with

137 " great possessions, only for the helping the poor and impotent, " who were not able to help themselves ; and not for the main-" tenance of canons, priests, and monks, to live in pleasure, not " regarding the poor, who were lying in every street, offending " all that passed by them : he therefore prayed the king, for " the relief of Christ's true images, to give order that the " mayor of London and the aldermen may from thenceforth " have the disposition and rule both of the lands belonging to " those hospitals, and of the governors and ministers which " shall be in any of them.   And then the king would perceive, " that whereas now there was a small number of canons, priests, " and monks in them for their own profit only ; that then a " great number of poor and indigent persons should be main-" tained in them, and also freely healed of their infirmities :

Gresham's letter to the king for putting the great hospitals in the hands of the city. Collect. Numb. 61.

" and there should be physicians, surgeons, and apothecaries,
" with salaries to attend upon them.   And those who were not
" able to labour should be relieved ; and sturdy beggars, not
" willing to labour, should be punished.   In doing this, the
" king would be more charitable to the poor than his progenitor
" Edgar, the founder of so many monasteries ; or Henry the
" Third, the renewer of Westminster ; or Edward the Third,
" the founder of the New Abbey ; or than Henry the Fifth, the
" founder of Sion and Shene ; and he would carry the name
" of the protector and defender of the poor."

How soon after this these hospitals were put under the government of the lord mayor and aldermen of London, will be found
in the history of the city.   But I thought this letter was worth
remembering, since probably it gave the rise.to the putting
those endowments in such hands, in which, to the wonder of all
the world, we see such a noble order and management, and
such an overflowing of charity, that not only all their revenues
are with the exactest management possible applied wholly to
the use for which they were designed ; but that the particular
bounties of those whom God has blessed in the city, that are
annually given to them, do far exceed their stated revenues :
of which there are yearly accounts published in Easter week ;
and which no doubt do bring down great blessings on the
city, and on all its concerns.

The king grows severe against the reformers.
The state of matters began to turn about this time.   The
king seemed to think that his subjects owed an entire resignation of their reasons and consciences to him ; and as he was
highly offended with those who still adhered to the papal authority, so he could not bear the haste that some were making
to a further reformation, before or beyond his allowance.   So,
in the end of the year 1538, he set out a proclamation on the
16th of November[6].

In it he prohibits the importing of all foreign books, or the
printing of any at home without license, and the printing any
parts of scripture, till they were examined by the king and his
council, or by the bishop of the diocese.   He condemns all the
books of the anabaptists and sacramentaries ; and appoints those
to be punished who vented them.   He requires that none may

[6] [A perfect copy of this Proclamation, without any heading, is in the
Collection of the Society of Antiquaries at Somerset House.]

argue against the presence of Christ in the sacrament, under
the pain of death, and of the loss of their goods ; and orders all
to be punished who did disuse any rites or ceremonies not then
138 abolished : yet he orders them to be observed without superstition only as remembrances, and not to repose in them a trust
of salvation by observing them.   He requires that all married
priests should no more minister the sacrament, but be deprived,
with further punishment or imprisonment at the king's pleasure.
What follows after this will be found in the Collection ; for the Collect.
Numb. 62.
whole did not seem so important as to be all set down, it being
very long.   " The king, considering the several superstitions He sets out
a long pro-
clamation.
" and abuses which had crept into the hearts of many of his
" unlearned subjects, and the strife and contention which did
" grow among them, had often commanded his bishops and
" clergy to preach plainly and sincerely, and to set forth the
" true meaning of the sacramentals and ceremonies, that
" they might be quietly used for such purposes as they were
" at first intended : but he was informed that this had not
" been executed according to his expectation ; therefore he
" requires all his archbishops and bishops, that in their own
" persons they will preach with more diligence, and set forth
" to the people the word of God sincerely and purely ; declaring
" the difference between the things commanded by God, and
" these rites and ceremonies commanded only by a lower au-
" thority, that they may come to the true knowledge of a
" lively faith in God, and obedience to the king, with love and
" charity to their neighbours.   They were to require all their
" clergy to do the same, and to exhort the people to read
" and hear with simplicity, and without arrogance, avoiding
" all strife and contention, under the pain of being punished
" at the king's pleasure."

To this he adds, " That it appearing clearly that Thomas An account
set forth by
the king of
Thomas
Becket.
" Becket, sometime archbishop of Canterbury, did stubbornly
" withstand the laws established against the enormities of the
" clergy by king Henry the Second, and had fled out of the
" realm into France, and to the bishop of Rome to procure
" the abrogating of these laws ; from which there arose great
" troubles in the kingdom : his death, which they untruly
" called his martyrdom, happened upon a rescue made by
" him, upon which he gave opprobrious words to the gentle-

" men who counselled him to leave his stubbornness, and
" not to stir up the people, who were risen for that rescue.
" He called one of them bawd, and pulled Tracy by the bosom
" almost down to the pavement of the church.   Upon this
" fray one of the company struck him, and in the throng
" he was slain.   He was canonized by the bishop of Rome,
" because he had been a champion to maintain his usurped
" authority, and a defender of the iniquity of the clergy.
" The king, with the advice of his council, did find there
" was nothing of sanctity in the life or exterior conversa-
" tion of Becket, but that he rather ought to be esteemed a
" rebel and a traitor; therefore he commands that he shall be
" no more esteemed nor called a saint, that his images shall be
" every where put down, and that the days used for his festival
" shall be no more observed, nor any part of that service be
" read, but that it should be razed out of all books.   Adding,
" that the other festivals already abrogated shall be no more
" solemnized, and that his subjects shall be no more blindly
" abused to commit idolatry, as they had been in time past.
" I will leave it to our historians to compare the account here 139
" given of Becket's death with the legends, and to examine
" which of them is the truest."

A circular
letter to
the justices
of peace.

Soon after this, the king, understanding that very malicious
reports were spread about the country, poisoning people's minds
with relation to every thing that the king did; saying they
would be made pay for every thing they should eat, and that
the register of births and weddings was ordered for this end,
that the king might know the numbers of his people, and make
levies, and send, or rather sell them, to foreign service: he
sent in December following a circular letter to all the justices
of England, which will be found in the Collection; in which,
after he had set forth his good intentions for the wealth and
happiness of his people, he added, " that he hoped that all the
" maintainers of the bishop of Rome's authority should have
" been searched for, and brought to justice: and that all the
" inventors and spreaders of false reports, to put the people in
" fear, and so to stir them up to sedition, should have been
" apprehended and punished; and that vagabonds and beggars
" should have been corrected according to the letters he had
" formerly written to them.   The king understood that sundry

Collect.
Numb. 63.

" of them had done their duty so well, that there had been no
" disquiet till of late ; that some malicious persons had by lies
" and false rumours studied to seduce the people; and that
" among these, some vicars and curates were the chief, who
" endeavoured to bring the people again into darkness; and
" they did so confusedly read the word of God and the king's
" injunctions, that none could understand the true meaning of
" them : they studied to wrest the king's intentions in them to
" a false sense.   For whereas the king had ordered registers
" to be kept for shewing lineal descents, and the rights of in-
" heritance, and to distinguish legitimate issue from bastardy,
" or whether a person was born a subject or not; they went
" about saying that the king intended to make new examinations
" of christenings, weddings, and buryings, and to take away
" the liberties of the kingdom : for preserving which, they pre-
" tended Thomas Becket died.   Whereas his opposition was
" only to the punishing of the offences of the clergy, that they
" should not be justified by the courts and laws of the land,
" but only at the bishop's pleasure : and here the same account
" is given of Becket, that was in the former proclamation.
" Becket contended with the archbishop of York, and pre-
" tended, that, when he was out of the realm, the king could
" not be crowned by any other bishop, but that it must be
" stayed till he returned.   These detestable liberties were all
" that he stood for, and not for the commonwealth of the
" realm.   To these lies they added many other seditious de-
" vices, by which the people were stirred up to sedition and
" insurrection, to their utter ruin and destruction, if God had
" not both enabled him by force to subdue them, and afterwards
" move[d] him mercifully to pardon them.   The king there-
" fore required them, in their several precincts, to find out such
" vicars and curates as did not truly declare the injunctions,
" and did confusedly mumble the word of God, pretending that
140 " they were compelled to read them ; but telling their people
" to do as they did, and live as their fathers had done, for the
" old fashion was the best.   They were also required to search
" out all the spreaders of seditious tales, and to apprehend and
" keep them in prison till the justices came about to try them ;
" or till the king's pleasure was known.   The justices of the
" peace are very earnestly pressed to do their duty diligently,

" and to take care likewise that the injunctions and laws against
" the anabaptists and sacramentaries be duly executed." Dated
from Hampton-Court in December, in the 30th year of his
reign.

[Epistolæ
Tigurinæ,
p. 404.]

Among the letters sent me from Zurich[9], I find one written
to Bullinger on the 8th of March in the year 1539, by Butler,
Eliot, Partridge, and Traheron, who had studied for some
time under him, and were then entertained either by the king
or by Cromwell.   They write, " that many of the popish cere-
" monies were still tolerated ; but that new significations were
" put on them : such as, that the *holy water* did put us in mind
" of the blood of Christ, that cleanseth us from all defilement.
" The pax was carried about, to represent our reconciliation to
" God through Christ.   Things that were visible were thought
" fit to be preserved to prevent commotions.   This correction
" quieted some ; but though these rites were ordered to be
" kept up till the king should think fit to alter them, yet some
" preached freely against them, even before the king.

New signi-
fications
put on the
old rites.

Many exe-
cutions in
England.

" They write of the executions of the marquis of Exeter, the
" lord Montacute, and sir Edward Neville, who (they add) was
" a very brave, but a very vicious man.   Sir Nicholas Carew,
" who had been before a zealous papist, when he came to

---

[9] [This letter, which has not been
inserted in the Collection, has been
printed in the ' Epistolæ Tigurinæ,'
p. 404.' It is not addressed to Bullinger, but was sent to him to be
communicated to others. It is headed thus :

*Optimis et eruditissimis viris præ-
ceptoribusque suis in Christo colen-
dis, Conrado Pellicano, Leoni Judæ,
Henrico Bullingero, Theodoro Bibli-
andro, Joannes Butlerus, Nicolaus
Eliottus, Nicolaus Partrigius, Bartholomæus Trehernus optant salutem
per Christum Jesum.* It is dated
from London, March 8, 1539. The
author has not represented the beginning of the letter very accurate-
ly, and has altogether omitted to
notice what the writers say of themselves, viz. :

*Nunc pauca de nostro statu acci-
pite. Joannes Butlerus ad vos ven-*

*turus fuisset, nisi his belli nunciis
retractus fuisset. Eadem causa
Nicolaum Partrigium a nundinis
Francofordiensibus retinuit. Joannes
quidem si vellet, posset honesto loco
esse apud regem : sed musarum a-
more delectatus, ab aulá abhorrere
videtur. Nicolaus Eliottus juri nostro municipali dat operam, regis
munificentiá non parum adjutus. Bartholomæus Trehernus D. Crumwelli
famulus est : Nicolaus Partrigius
docti et pii viri episcopi Sancti Da-
vidis in Walliá. Erit autem a sacris
prælectionibus donec illi melius con-
suli possit. Ab uxoribus adhuc li-
beri sumus omnes. Hæc de nostro
statu.* The direction is as follows :

*Pietatis et eruditionis nomine, cla-
rissimo viro D. Henrico Bullingero,
præceptori suo inprimis observando
dentur hæ literæ. Tiguri. εὐόδωσον
δή.*]

" suffer, exhorted all people to read the scriptures carefully.
" He acknowledged, that the judgments of God came justly
" upon him, for the hatred that he formerly bore to the
" gospel. The king was threatened with a war, in which the
" emperor, the French, and the Scots, would attack him on all
" hands ; but he seemed to despise it, and said, He should not
" sleep the less quietly for all these alarms. The day after
" these tidings were brought in, he said to his counsellors, that
" he found himself moved in his conscience to promote the
" word of God more than ever. Other news came at the same
" time, which might perhaps raise his zeal, that three English
" merchants were burnt in Spain ; and that an indulgence was
" proclaimed to every man that should kill an English heretic.
" Cranmer was then very busy, instructing the people, and pre- [Ibid.
" paring English prayers, to be used instead of the Litany." I p. 406.]
can go no further on these subjects ; but must refer to my
History for the prosecution of these matters.

The foundation of the new bishoprics was now settled. Ry- Tom. xiv.
mer has given us the charters, by which they were founded 717. to p.
and endowed. The new modelling of some cathedrals was next 736 ; and
taken care of. I have found the project that Cromwell sent to to p. 759.
Cranmer for the church of Canterbury. It was to consist of a The project
provost, twelve prebendaries, six preachers ; three readers, ing the
one of humanity and of Greek, another of divinity and of He- church of
141 brew, and another of humanity and divinity in Latin ; a reader bury.
of civil law, another of physic ; twenty students in divinity,
ten to be kept at Oxford, and as many at Cambridge. Sixty
scholars were to be taught grammar and logic, with Hebrew,
Greek, and Latin : for these a schoolmaster and an usher were
to have salaries. Besides these, there were eight petty canons,
twelve singing men, ten choristers, a master of the children, a
gospeller, an epistler, and two sacristans ; two butlers, two
cooks, a caterer, two porters ; twelve poor men, a steward,
and an auditor : in all 162 persons, with the salaries for every
one of these ; together with an allowance for an annual distri-
bution of 100l. for the poor, and as much for reparations ; and Disapprov-
40l. for mending the highways : in all, amounting to about mer.
1900 pound a year. This I have put in the Collection, toge- Collect.
ther with the letter that Cranmer wrote to Cromwell, after he Collect.
had considered of it : though perhaps this will sharpen some Numb. 65.

men's spirits, that are of late much set to decry him, as much as any of his other opinions may have done: but a true historian, that intends to glean all that he could find relating to those transactions, must neither alter nor suppress things, but set them out as he finds them.

" He proposes the altering the prebendaries to somewhat " more useful: for, by all the experience that he had, the " prebendaries had spent their time in much idleness, and their " substance in superfluous living; so he thought it was not a " state to be maintained. Commonly they were neither learned, " nor given to teach others, but only good vianders; they look " to be the chief, and to bear the whole rule; and by their ill " example the younger sort grew idle and corrupt. The state " of prebendaries had been so excessively abused, that, when " learned men have been advanced to that post, they desisted " from their studies, and from all godly exercises of preaching " and teaching: therefore he wished the very name of a pre- " bendary might be struck out of the king's foundations. The " first beginning of them was good, so was that of religious " men; but both were gone off from their first estate: so, " since the one is put down, it were no great matter if both " should perish together. For, to say the truth, it is an estate " which St. Paul did not find in the church of Christ: and he " thought it would stand better with the maintenance of the " Christian religion, that there were in their stead twenty " divines, at 10l. apiece, and as many students of the tongues, " and of French, at ten marks apiece. And indeed, if there " was not such a number there resident, he did not see for " what use there were so many lectures to be read: for the " prebendaries could not attend, for the making of good cheer; " and the children in grammar were to be otherwise employed. " He, in particular, recommends doctor Crome to be dean."

The design of the six articles.

But I leave this invidious subject, to turn now to a very melancholy strain. The king had thrown off all commerce with the Lutherans in Germany, and seemed now to think himself secure in the emperor's friendship: yet he did not break with France, though on many occasions he complained both of the ingratitude and inconstancy of that king. The duchy of Milan seemed to be the object of all his designs; and he was 142 always turned, as the prospect of that seemed to come in view,

or to go out of sight. All the king's old ministers still kept up
his zeal for his admired book of the Sacraments, most particularly for that article of transubstantiation; so that the popish
party prevailed with him to resolve on setting up the six articles, which, they said, would quiet all men's minds, when they
saw him maintain that, and the other articles, with learning
and zeal.   It is certain he had read a great deal, and heard
and talked a great deal more, of those subjects; so that he
seems to have made himself a master of the whole body of divinity. I have seen many chapters of the Necessary Erudition
of a Christian much altered by him, and in many places so interlined with his hand, that it is not without some difficulty
that they can be read; for he wrote very ill.

Upon the carrying the six articles, the popish party were
much exalted.   This appears by the end of a letter, written to
the ambassadors abroad; which will be found in the Collection. Collect.
It sets forth, "how the king had shewed himself in that par- Numb. 66.
" liament so wise, learned, and catholic, that no prince ever did
" the like; so it was no more doubted but the act would pass.
" The bishops of Canterbury, Ely, Salisbury, Worcester, Ro-
" chester, and St. David's, defended the contrary side; yet in
" the end the king confounded them.   The bishops of York,
" Durham, Winchester, London, Chichester, Norwich, and
" Carlisle, shewed themselves honest and learned men.   He
" writes as one of the peers; for he adds, we of the temporalty
" have been all of one opinion.   The lord chancellor and the
" lord privy-seal had been of their side.   Cranmer and all the
" bishops came over; only he adds, that Shaxton continued a
" lewd fool.   For this victory, he writes that all England had
" reason to bless God."

Cromwell, though he complied with the king's humour, yet The king
he studied to gain upon him, and to fix him in an alliance that marries
should certainly separate him from the emperor, and engage Anne of
him again into a closer correspondence with France, on design Cleves.
to support the princes of Germany against the emperor, whose
uneasiness under the laws and liberties of the empire began to
be suspected: and all the popish party depended wholly on
him. I did in my second volume publish a commission to Vol. II.
Cromwell, thinking it was that which constituted him the Coll. Rec.
king's vicegerent, which I, upon reading the beginning of it, book ii. N.
29. p. 303.

took to be so; but that was one of the effects of the haste in which I wrote that work : it does indeed in the preamble set forth, " that the king was then in some sort to exercise that " supreme authority he had over the church of England, under " Christ; since they who pretended that that authority ought " to be lodged with them, did pursue their own private gains, " more than the public good; and had brought matters, by " the negligence of their officers, and their own ill example, " to such a state, that it might be feared, that Christ would not " now own his own spouse. Therefore, since the supreme au- " thority over all persons, without any difference, was given him " from Heaven, he was bound (as much as he could) to cleanse 143 " the church from all briars, and to sow the seeds of virtue in " it. Those who before exercised this authority, thinking " themselves above all censure, had (by their own bad ex- " amples) laid stumblingblocks before the people. He there- " fore, designing a general reformation of his kingdom and " church, resolved to begin with the fountains; for they being " cleansed, the streams would run clear : but since he could " not be personally present every where, he had deputed " Thomas Cromwell, his principal secretary, and master of the " rolls, to be in all ecclesiastical causes his vicegerent and " vicar-general : with a power to name others, to be author- " ized under the great seal. But he being so employed in " the public affairs of the kingdom, that he could not per- " sonally discharge that trust; therefore he deputed, A, B, C, D, " to execute that trust. The king being pleased with this " deputation, did likewise empower them to visit all churches, " both metropolitical, cathedral, and collegiate churches, hos- " pitals and monasteries, and all other places, exempt or not " exempt, to correct and punish what was amiss in them, by " censures of suspension and deprivation, to give them statutes " and injunctions in the king's name, and to hold synods, " chapters, or convocations, summoning all persons concerned " to appear before them, and presiding in them, giving them " such rules as they shall judge convenient : calling such " causes as they shall think fit from the ecclesiastical courts, " to be judged by them; and to force obedience, both by ec- " clesiastical censures and fines, and other temporal punish- " ments;" with several other clauses of a very extended and comprehensive nature. How far this was put in practice, does not fully appear to me. It certainly struck so deep into the whole ecclesiastical constitution, that it could not be easily borne. But the clergy had lost their reputation and credit, so that every invasion that was made on them, and on their courts, seemed to be at this time acceptable to the nation ; one extreme very naturally producing another : for all did acquiesce tamely, in submitting to a power that was now in high exaltation, and that treated those that stood in its way, not only with the utmost indignation, but with the most rigorous severity.

But to return to Cromwell. He, in concurrence with the court of France, carried matters so, that the marriage with Anne of Cleves was made up. This occasioned one of the most unjustifiable steps in all that reign. Among the papers that were sent me from Zurich, there is a long and particular account of many passages in this matter, with some other important transactions of this year, writ by one Richard Hilles, who writes very sensibly and very piously ; and he being zealous for a further reformation, went out of England as a man concerned in trade, which he pursued only as a just excuse to get out of the way : but before he went over, he wrote a long account to Bullinger of the affairs in England. He tells him, "that before Whit-Sunday three persons were burnt "in Southwark because they had not received the sacrament "at Easter, and had denied transubstantiation. There was "after that one Collins, a crazed man, likewise burnt, all by 144 "Gardiner's procurement." A little before Midsummer it began to be whispered about, that the king intended a divorce with Anne, who had been married to him about five months. It was observed that the king was much taken with a young person, a niece of the duke of Norfolk's, (whom he afterwards married ;) Gardiner took care to bring them together to his palace, where they dined once, and had some meetings and entertainments there. This went on some time before there was any talk of the divorce : it was indeed believed that there was an ill commerce between them. Cromwell was newly made earl of Essex : Bourchier, in whom that line was extinct, who had been a severe persecutor, falling from his horse, and breaking his neck, died without being able to speak one word.

He is in love with Catharine Howard.

Sᵉ pᵖ 245

[Epistolæ Tigurinæ, cv. p. 133.]

[p. 134.]

Cromwell's fall.

The king gave Cromwell not only his title, but all that fell to the crown by his dying without heirs: yet he enjoyed not this long; for in the beginning of June he was sent to the Tower. He did not know the secret cause of his fall; it was generally believed it was because he did not flatter the king enough, and that he was against the divorce, as thinking it would neither be for the king's honour nor the good of the kingdom. Some suspected that his late advancement, and great grants the king had given him, was an artifice to make people conclude, when they saw him disgraced after such high favour, that certainly some very black thing was discovered: and it was also thought that the king restored to his son (who was so weak, that he was thought almost a fool) much of his father's estate and goods, (as he made him a baron in December, after his father's death,) on design to make the father more silent, for fear of provoking the king to take from him what he had then given him. Here I stop the prosecuting the rest of the letter, till I have added somewhat more concerning Cromwell.

[Dec. 18. 1540. Rymer, xiv. 708.]

He had many offices in his person; for besides that he was lord vicegerent in ecclesiastical matters, and lord privy-seal, he was lord chamberlain, and chancellor of the exchequer. Rymer has published the grants that the king made of those offices, in which it is said, that they were void upon his attainder; but, which was more, he was the chief minister, and had the king's confidence, for ten year together, almost as entirely as cardinal Wolsey had it formerly. Mont had been sent to Germany to press a closer league defensive against the pope, and any council that he might summon. When the princes did object the act of the six articles, and the severities upon it; he confessed to one of the elector's ministers, that the king was not sincere in the point of religion: he had therefore proposed a double marriage of the king with Anne of Cleves, and of the duke of Cleves with the lady Mary; for he said, the king was much governed by his wives. The elector of Saxony, who had married the other sister of Cleves, had conceived so bad an opinion of the king, that he expressed no heartiness, neither in the marriage, nor in any alliance with England: but he yielded to the importunities of others, who thought the prospect of the advantage from such an alliance was great.

Rymer, xiv. [p. 702.]

A new treaty with the German princes.

There are great remains, that shew how exact a minister

Cromwell was; there are laid together many remembrances of
145 things that he was to lay before the king.   They are too short
to give any great light into affairs; yet I will mention some of
them.   In one, he mentions the abbots of Glastonbury and
Reading, who were then prisoners, and were examined.   The
witnesses, with the council, were ordered to be sent to Berkshire and Somersetshire.   Mention is made of their complices,
who were to be tried, and to suffer with them[6].   To this I
must add, that in one of the Zurich letters it is written to Bullinger[7], that three of the richest abbots in England had suffered for a conspiracy, into which they had entered, for restoring the pope's authority in England.

   The learned Dr. Tanner has sent me the copy of a letter,
that three visitors wrote to Cromwell from Glastonbury, concerning that abbot, on the 22nd of September; but they do
not add the year.   It will be found in the Collection, signed
by Richard Pollard, Thomas Moyle, and Richard Layton.
" They give him an account of their examining the abbot upon
" certain articles.   He did not seem to answer them clearly;
" so they desired him to call to his memory the things which
" he then seemed to have forgot.   They searched his study,
" and found in it a written book against the king's divorce.
" They found also pardons, copies of bulls, and a printed life
" of Thomas Becket; but found no letter that was material.
" They examined him a second time upon the articles that
" Cromwell had given them; and sent up his answer, signed
" by him, to court: in which they write, that his cankered
" and traitorous heart against the king and his succession did
" appear; so with very fair words they sent him to the Tower.
" They found he was but a weak man, and sickly.   Having
" sent him away, they examined the state of that monastery.
" They found in it above 300l. in cash, but had not the cer-
" tainty of the rest of their plate; only they found a fair gold
" chalice, with other plate, hid by the abbot, that had not
" been seen by the former visitors; of which, they think, the
" abbot intended to have made his own advantage.   They
" write, that the house was the noblest they had ever seen of

Marginal notes:
Cotton lib. Tit. B. 1. [fol. 415 sqq.] Some of Cromwell's memoran-dums.

[Epistolæ Tigurinæ, cxlviii. p. 209.]

Collect. Numb. 67.

---

[6] [See also Cleop. E. iv. fol. 99,
133. printed in the Camden Society
volume on the Suppression of the
Monasteries.]

[7] [This is in a letter from Bartholomew Traheron to Bullinger,
dated Feb. 10, 1540.]

" that sort: they thought it fit for the king, and for none
" else." This I set down the more particularly, to demonstrate the falsity of the extravagant account that Sanders
gives of that matter, as if it had been without notice given,
that the abbot was seized on, tried and executed, all of a
sudden. But to return to Cromwell.

In another note, he mentions the determinations made by
Day, Heath, and Thirlby, of the Ten Commandments, of justification, and of purgatory. Another is about Fisher and More.
The judges' opinion was asked, concerning More and the Nun.
Another is, Whether the bishop of Rochester, and the monk,
who wrote the letter as from Heaven, should be sent for ? In
another, that Bocking printed the Nun's book, and took away
five hundred copies, but left two hundred with the printer. In
another, he proposed to send Barnes for Melancthon. In another, he asks who shall be prolocutor in the convocation. In
another, he proposes the making lady Mary a considerable
match for some foreign prince, the duke of Orleans, or some
other. This is all that I could gather out of a vast number of
those notes which he took of matters to move the king in.

Upon Cromwell's imprisonment, the comptroller was sent to
him, and he ordered him to write to the king what he thought
meet to be written concerning his present condition: and, it
seems, with some intimations of hope. Upon that, Cromwell
wrote a long letter to the king, which will be found in the Collection. " He begins it with great thanks to the king for what
" the comptroller had said to him. He was accused of treason ;
" but he protests, he never once thought to do that which should
" displease him, much less to commit so high an offence. The
" king knew his accusers ; he prayed God to forgive them. He
" had ever loved the king, and all his proceedings : he prays
" God to confound him, if he had ever a thought to the con-
" trary. He had laboured much to make the king a great and
" a happy prince ; and acknowledges his great obligations to
" the king. So he writes, that if he had been capable to be a
" traitor, the greatest punishment was too little for him. He
" never spoke with the chancellor of the augmentations (Baker)
" and Throckmorton together, but once : but he is sure, he
" never spoke of any such matter," (as, it seems, was informed
against him.) "The king knew what a man Throckmorton

[Sanders, pp. 137, 8.]

146

The mat-
ters at first
charged on
him, from
which he
clears him-
self.

Collect.
Numb. 68.

" was, with relation to all his proceedings ; and what an enemy
" Baker was to him, God and he knew.　The king knew what
" he had been towards him."　It seems the king had advertised
him of them ; " but God, who had delivered Susan when falsely
" accused, could deliver him.　He trusted only in God, and in
" the king.　In all his service, he had only considered the king ;
" but did not know that he had done injustice to any person :
" yet he had not done his duty in all things ; therefore he
" asked mercy.　If he had heard of conventicles, or other of-
" fences, he had for the most part revealed them, and made
" them to be punished, but not out of malice. He had meddled
" in so many things, that he could not answer them all ; but of
" this he was sure, that he had never willingly offended : and
" wherein he had offended, he humbly begged pardon.　The
" comptroller told him, that fourteen days ago the king had
" committed a great secret to him, which he had revealed : he
" remembered well the matter, but he had never revealed it.
" For, after the king had told him what it was that he misliked in
" the queen ; he told the king, that she often desired to speak
" with him, but he durst not : yet the king bade him go to
" her, and be plain with her in declaring his mind.　Upon which
" he spake privately with her lord chamberlain, desiring him,
" not naming the king, to deal with the queen to behave her-
" self more pleasantly towards the king ; hoping thereby to
" have had some faults amended.　And when some of her
" council came to him for license to the stranger maids to de-
" part ; he did then require them to advise the queen to use
" all pleasantness with the king. Both these words were spoken
" before the king had trusted the secret to him, on design that
" she might render herself more agreeable to the king : but
147 " after the king had trusted that secret to him" (which it
seems was his design to have the marriage dissolved) " he never
" spoke of it but to the lord admiral, and that was by the
" king's order on Sunday last ; who was very willing to seek
" remedy for the king's comfort.　He protests he was ready
" to die to procure the king comfort.　He wishes he were in
" hell if it was not true.　This was all he had done ;" (it seems
the king thought the change in the queen's deportment towards him was the effect of his discovering the secret of the
king's purpose, and in order to prevent it ;) " but for this
" he humbly begs pardon. He understood that it was charged

" upon him, that he had more retainers about him than
" the laws allowed. He never retained any, except his
" household servants, but against his will. He had been pressed
" by many, who said they were his friends; he had retained
" their children and friends, not as retainers, for their fathers
" and friends promised to maintain them. In this, God knows,
" he had no ill intent, but begs pardon if he had offended,"
(for that was represented as the gathering a force about him
to defend himself.) " He concludes, he had not behaved himself
" towards God and the king as he ought to have done: and as
" he was continually calling on God for mercy, for offences
" committed against him, so he begs the king's pardon for his
" offences against him, which were never wilful; and he assures
" him, he had never a thought of treason against him, either in
" word or deed: and he continued to pray for him and the
" prince, ending, indeed, with too abject a meanness."

Reflections on the state of affairs at that time.

[p. 134.]

[p. 135.]

These were all the particulars that were charged on him
upon his first imprisonment: other matters were afterwards
added to throw the more load on him: but it seems they were
not so much as thought on or mentioned at first. But now I
return to the letter writ to Zurich. Hilles adds, that they
heard they once designed to burn Cromwell as a heretic, and
that these considerations made him confess that he had offended
the king. What he said that way at his execution was pronounced coldly by him: upon that the writer runs out very
copiously, and acknowledges that their sins had provoked God
to bring upon them that great change that they saw in affairs.
They had wholly trusted to the learning of some, and to the
conduct of others: but God, by the taking these away, was
calling on them to turn sincerely to him, to trust entirely in
him, and to repent with their whole heart. There was at that
time a great want of sincere labourers, so that from east to
west, and from south to north, there was scarce one faithful
and sincere preacher of the gospel to be found.

Of the king's divorce with Anne of Cleves. [p. 136.]

The act of dissolving the king's marriage did set forth, that
some doubts were raised concerning the king's marriage, which,
as he writes, was manifestly false, for nobody thought of any
doubtfulness in it: nor did they pray, as is in the act, that it
might be inquired into: for nobody spake of it till the king
was resolved to part with the queen, that he might be married
to Mrs. Howard, whom in his bad Latin he calls, *parvissima*

puella, a very little girl. The archbishop of Canterbury, and [p. 134.]
the rest of the bishops, judged she was yet a virgin, which none
that knew the man could believe. Here again I must leave
my letter.

148   There had been no convocation for two years; for the In- What pass-
stitution of a Christian Man was prepared by a commission, ed in con-
given to some bishops of both provinces, and to some arch- vocation.
deacons, but no deans were summoned with them. A convocation sat in both provinces in May, in the year 1539, to which [May 2.]
abbots and priors were summoned; but though there were
eight abbots and nine priors in Exeter diocese, yet the return
from thence says, there were none in the diocese. I do not
know how to reconcile that with the abbot of Tavistock's[8] sit- Journal of
ting in the house of lords, as appears by the Journals of that Lords, p.
parliament.   104.]

Upon this occasion there was a particular summons for both
provinces to meet in a national synod, to judge of the king's
marriage. When I wrote of this in my History[9], I did not at
all reflect on the doctrine of the church of Rome, that makes
marriage a sacrament, in which the two parties are the ministers,
who transfer their persons to one another: and according to
the doctrine of the necessity of the intention in him that
ministers the sacrament, how vile soever this decision in the
matter of the king's marriage may seem to be, yet it was a
just consequence from that doctrine; for without a true, free,
and inward intention, which the king affirmed he had not, the
marriage could be no sacrament: so that the heaviest part of
the shame of that decision falls indeed on that doctrine. When
the news came to France of the king's dissolving his marriage
with Anne of Cleves, king Francis himself asked the ambassadors upon what grounds it went. The cardinal of Ferrara Paper
                                                              Office[10].

---

[8] [The abbot of Tavistock never
took his seat at all in this parliament. His name is mentioned at
the end of the list of abbots on the
first day of the session, but he was
not present, and the name is not
again mentioned. In fact, the abbey
had been surrendered in the previous year and the abbot pensioned
off.]

[9] [See part i. p. 280.]

[10] [This document has not been

printed in ' State Papers.'—Wallop
and Carne ' wrote to the king on the
15th July, reporting discussions
they had had separately with Francis
and with the cardinal of Ferrara,
respecting the divorce of Anne of
Cleves, in neither of which were
they able, though challenged to do
so, to state the grounds of the decree.' The editor speaks of their
despatch as devoid of interest.]

did also send one to ask what was alleged for it by divines and lawyers. Wallop and others were then the ambassadors from England at the court. They sent to the council an account of this; and Wallop wrote over to know what he should say upon the subject. The answer which the council wrote to him was, that the queen herself affirmed, her person had not been touched by king Henry; that a learned convocation had judged the matter; that the bishops of Durham, Winchester, and Bath, were known to be great and learned clerks, who would do nothing but upon just and good grounds; so that all persons ought to be satisfied with these proceedings, as she herself was: and here this matter ended, to the great reproach of that body, that went so hastily and so unanimously into that scandalous decision.

Exceptions in the act of grace.

But to return to my Zurich letter. After he had related the manner of that judgment of those called spiritual, who indeed were very carnal; he mentions the exceptions in the act of pardon: for besides particular exceptions, all anabaptists

[p. 138.]

and sacramentaries were excepted, and all those that affirmed there was a fate upon men, by which the day of their death was unalterably determined.

A design against Crome.
[Cotton MSS. Cleop.E.iv. fol. 302.]

There was at this time a great design against Dr. Crome, whom Cranmer had recommended to be dean of Canterbury, in these words: " I know no man more meet for the dean's " room in England than Dr. Crome, who by his sincere learn- " ing, godly conversation, and good example of living, with " his great soberness, hath done unto the king's majesty as " good service, I dare say, as any priest in England: and yet 149 " his grace daily remembereth all others that doth him service, " this man only excepted, who never had yet, besides his " gracious favour, any promotion at his hands. Wherefore, " if it please his majesty to put him in the dean's room, I do " not doubt but that he should be a light to all the deans and " ministers of colleges in this realm: for I know that when he " was but a president of a college in Cambridge, his house " was better ordered than all the houses in Cambridge be- " sides[11]." Certainly this good opinion that Cranmer had of

[11] [See the Records belonging to this part, No. 65, where this passage occurs, with slight variations. Even in the original edition, there are several slight differences between the record as printed in the text and in the Collection.]

him, made him, in the state in which things were at this time,
to be the worse thought of, and the more watched : so when
he heard that he was to be searched for, he went to the king,
and on his knees begged he would put a stop to the severities
then on foot, and that he would set many then in prison, on
the account of religion, at liberty. The king had such a regard for him, that upon this he ordered a stop to be put to
further prosecutions : and he set those at liberty who were
then in prison, they giving bail to appear when they should
be called for. The king seemed to think that by this small
favour, after some severities, people would be more quiet, and
more obedient. But after the parliament was dissolved, six
persons suffered. Three of these were popish priests, who
suffered as traitors for denying the king's supremacy : and
Barnes, Gerrard, and Jerome were the other three. They [p. 139.]
were tied to one stake, and suffered without crying out, but
were quiet and patient, as if they had felt no pain. He could
never hear any reason given for this their suffering, unless it
was to please the clergy. They were not condemned by any
form of law. They had been so cautious ever since the act of
the six articles passed, that they had not opened their mouths
in opposition to them in public : and by the act all offences
done before it had passed were pardoned. Barnes himself
said at the place of execution, that he did not know for what
cause he was brought thither to be burnt ; for they were attainted by act of parliament, without being brought to make
their answers.

The bishop of Chichester, Sampson, though a man compli- [p. 140.]
ant in all things, and Dr. Wilson, were exempted out of the
general pardon, for no other crime, as he heard, but that, Abel
who suffered for denying the king's supremacy, being in the
greatest extremity of want and misery in prison, where it was
said he was almost eat up by vermin, they had sent him some
alms. From this Hilles goes on to give an account of Crome,
whose constant way had been, when he saw a storm rising, to
preach with more zeal than ordinary against the prevailing
corruption ; so on Christmas-day his enemies, that were watching to find matter to accuse him, framed some articles, which
they carried to the king against him. He had condemned in [p. 141.]
his sermon all masses for the dead ; and said, " if they were

" profitable to the dead, the king and parliament had done
" wrong in destroying the monasteries endowed for that end :
" he also said, that to pray to the saints only to pray for us,
" was a practice neither necessary nor useful. He added,
" You call us the seditious preachers of a new doctrine ; but
" 'tis you are the seditious persons, who maintain the super-
" stitious traditions of men, and will not hear the word of God 150
" himself. The church of Christ will ever suffer persecution,
" as it has done of late among us."

These and some other complaints being carried to the king.
Crome was commanded to answer them : he in his answer ex-
[p.142.] plained, and justified all he had said. The king had no mind
to carry matters further against so eminent a man ; so he
passed a sentence, in which he set forth, that Crome had confessed the articles objected to him ; but the king out of his
clemency intending to quiet his people, appointed Crome to
preach at Saint Paul's, and there to repeat all the articles objected to him, and then to read the judgment that the king
gave in the matter : and it concluded, that, if ever he fell into
the like offence again, he was to suffer according to law. The
king's judgment was, "that private masses were sacrifices pro-
" fitable both to the living and to the dead, but yet that the
" king's majesty, with his parliament, had justly abolished
" monasteries." Upon this Crome preached ; and at the end
of his sermon he told the people he had received an order
from the king to be read to them ; which he read, but said
not one word upon it ; and with a short prayer dismissed the
congregation : whereas the king expected that he should have
applauded his judgment, and extolled his favour to himself, as
Dr. Barnes and his two companions were unhappily prevailed
on to do, and yet were burnt afterwards. Hilles was therefore afraid that Crome might be brought into further trouble.
[p.143.] There was an order sent to him from the king to preach no
more, as he had before forbidden both Latimer and Shaxton
to preach any more. They were not excluded from the general
pardon ; but were still prohibited to preach : and when they
were set at liberty, they were required not to come within ten
miles of either of the universities, or the city of London, or
the dioceses in which they had been bishops. Thus, says he,
faithful shepherds were driven from their flocks, and ravenous

wolves were sent in their stead.   He concludes, hoping that
God would not suffer them to be long oppressed by such
tyranny.   Thus I have given a very particular account of that
long letter, writ with much good sense and piety, but in very
bad Latin ; therefore I do not put it into the Collection.

Sampson, though he fell into this disgrace for an act of
Christian pity, yet hitherto had shewed a very entire compliance with all that had been done.   He had published an explanation on the first fifty Psalms[12], which he dedicated to the
king : in which, as he extolled his proceedings, so he ran out
into a severe invective against the bishop of Rome, and the
usurpations and corruptions favoured by that see ; and he reflected severely on Pole.   Pole's old friend Tunstall did also
in a sermon at Saint Paul's, on Palm-Sunday, in his grave way
set forth his unnatural ingratitude.   But now the popish party,
upon Cromwell's fall, and the exaltation of the duke of Norfolk, by the king's marrying his niece, broke out into their
usual violence ; and they were, as we may reasonably believe,
set on to it by Bonner, who upon Stokesley's death, a year
before, had been brought to London, and immediately upon
151 Cromwell's disgrace changed sides ; and, from having acted a
forced part with heat enough, now came to act that which was
natural to him.

There were so many informations brought in the city of
London, that a jury sitting in Mercers' chapel presented five
hundred persons to be tried upon the statute of the six articles ;
which, as may be easily imagined, put the city under great
apprehensions : but Audley, the lord chancellor, represented
to the king, that this was done out of malice ; so they were
all dismissed, some say, pardoned.   Informations came against
papists, on the other side : a letter was sent from the council
to Cranmer, to send Dr. Benger to the Tower.   Two of Bonner's chaplains were, by order of council, sent to the archbishop, to be examined by him.   A vicar was brought out of
Wiltshire, out of whose offices Thomas Becket's name was not
yet razed : but he was dismissed ; for it was believed to be
the effect only of negligence, and not of any ill principles.

Prosecu-
tions upon
the six
articles.

[Nov. 1.
1540.
Council-
Book,
p. 64.]

---

[12] [Expositio in L. Psalmos pri-   1539.   There is a copy in the Bod-
ores. Lond. Typis Tho. Bertheleti,   leian Library.]

There was a letter of Melancthon's[13], against the king's proceedings, printed in English; (perhaps it was that which I published in the Addenda to my first volume.) Goodrich[14] bishop of Ely's chaplain and servant were examined, and his

[13] [At Hampton-Court the 24th day of December, ' Certain letters were sent from the bishop of Norwich chancellor, and Thomas Godsalve, touching the apprehension of one Thomas Whalpole a seditious fellow, and a setter forth of a naughty book made by Philipp Melanchton against the king's acts of Christian Religion.' Council-Book, p. 88.

[14] Dec. 25.—' Two several letters were written, the one to Dr. Spenser the bishop of Norwiche chancellor, and to Thomas Godsalve, giving them thanks for the apprehension of Thomas Whalpole, being taken for the setting forth of a seditious epistle of Melancton's, and ordering them to send the said Thomas Whalpole up hither. And the other letter was written to sir Gyles Alyngton, knight, sergeaunt Hynd, Philip Parys, and Thomas Megge, esquires, to take a chaplain of the bishop of Elyes called Forfeth or such like name, and one Deryck, a servant of the said bishop, accused for setters forth of the said epistle, and to search their chambers and to send them up hither to the Council; and in case that it appeared certainty to them, that the bishop was of counsel of the translation of the said epistle; they should also search the bishop's study, and charge him to appear before the Council incontinently.' p. 89.

At Hampton-courte the second daye of Januarye.—'Thomas Cottisford, priest, chaplain to the bishop of Elye and Deryck . . . . . . a Flemyng, servant to the said bishop, were brought before the council by sir Gyles Alyngton, knight, and Philip Parys, esquire, accused by one Thomas Whalpole, for the setting forth and publishing of a seditious epistle written by Melancton against the acte of the six articles; and upon their examination, the said Deryck, confessing that he had the copy of the said epistle of the said Cottysford, was committed to the marshal's ward; and Cottysford, confessing that he had the copy of the said epistle of Blages wife, a grocer in chepe in London, was committed to the porter's ward until the matter were further tried; whereupon letters were sent to the recorder of London, and William Lock, mercer, to examine the said Blages wife, and to search her house for the said epistle, and thereupon to send her hither with her confessor, and also the epistle if they could come by it with diligence.' p. 98.

At Hampton-Court the third day of January.—' Richard Banks noted to be the printer of the said Invectives, and examined thereof, denied the same, and laid the fault to Robert Redman deceased, and Richard Grafton, the which Richard Grafton confessing that he had not only printed part of the said Invectives, but also had in his keeping a certain seditious epistle in the English tongue, written by Melancton, contrary to the act of six articles for Christen religion, was committed to the porter's ward.' p. 101.

At Hampton-Courte the 4th day of January.—' The wife of . . . Blage, a grocer in Chepe, appeared, and was examined touching the delivery of a seditious epistle of Melancton's unto Thomas Cottisford, priest, and confessing as well the manner of the delivery of the said epistle to

house was searched for it.   Many were brought into trouble for words concerning the king and his proceedings.   Poor Marbeck of Windsor was imprisoned in the Marshalsea.   Many printers were prosecuted for bringing English books into the kingdom against the king's proceedings.   In one council-day (for all these particulars are taken out of the council-books) five and twenty booksellers were examined as to all books, more particularly English books, that they had sold these last three years.   Heynes, the dean of Exeter, was oft before the council[15]; but particulars are not mentioned.   Articles were

[Council-Book, p. 483. April 25. [Council-Book, pp. 456-8, 480, 490, 521.]

the said priest, as also declaring that she had it of one Richard Grafton a printer, was dismissed.

'Deryck being eftsones examined of the foresaid epistle, and being found, as far as the Council could perceive, not greatly culpable, was dismissed.   Thomas Walpole being sent up by the chancellor of Norwich and Thomas Godsalve, and examined of the having of the foresaid epistle, did confess that he had offended, as well touching the setting forth of the said epistle, as also for conspiring with one Forde of east Deram, touching certain coniuracions.

'A letter was sent to sir Roger Townesende, knight, and Mr. Permor, sheriff of Norfolk to apprehend one Forde, a physician dwelling in east Deram, and to search his house for instruments of conjuration, and to send him up, and such instruments as can be found in his house unto the Council with convenient diligence.' p. 102.

'Thomas Smyth, William George, Richard Grafton, Thomas Walpole, and Thomas Cottisford, priest, were committed to the Fleet there to remain during the king's pleasure.' p.102.]

At Westminster the second day April (this ought to be May).—'The king's pleasure was declared touching the dismissing out of the Tower of Thomas Wiatt, ... Pikering and Thomas Clare, and Grafton, and

Whitchurch, out of the fleet.'

[15] [At Westminster the 15th day of March.—' Letters were sent for Dr. Haynes to repair unto the court and to present himself before the Council the morrow after at two of the clock at after noon.'   16th. 'Doctour Haynes appearing before the council, after certain things objected against him touching his own evil opinions and the maintaining also of sundry parsons, the lyke was committed to the Fleet.'

March 19.—'A letter was sent, signed by the stamp, to the bishop and chapter of Exetre, to certify what they knew touching the evil opinions of doctour Haynes.'

22th day of Aprile.—' It was also this day ordered that a book of articles exhibited against doctor Haynes shall be delivered to the chancellor of the tenthes (Mr. Dacres), the dean of the arches and doctor Oliver ; the said chancellor and Mr. Dacres to call unto them such other of the king's learned counsel as they should think meet for the weighing and considering of the same.'

May 24.—' Item, the bishops of Ely, Sarum, Rochester, and Westminster, to examine doctor Haynes, and they to have deferred unto them all the informations ; and my lord of Westminster to advertise hereof the rest, and to proceed therein with all diligence.'

The fifth day of July.—' Simon

brought against him, and they were referred to the king's learned council. The bishops of Ely, Sarum, Rochester, and Westminster were appointed to examine him, and to proceed with all diligence. He was also sent to the Fleet, for *lewd and seditious preaching*, (the words in the Council-book,) and sowing many erroneous opinions; but, after a good lesson and exhortation, with a declaration of the king's mercy and goodness towards him, he was dismissed, under a recognizance of five hundred marks, to appear (if called for) any time within five months, to answer to such things as should be laid against him.

[1543. Ibid. p. 490.]

On the 4th of May 1542, an entry is made, Cranmer being present, that it was thought good, if the king's highness shall be so content, that a general commission shall be sent to Kent, with certain special articles; and generally, that all abuses and enormities of religion were to be examined. This was

[p. 518.] laid on design to ruin Cranmer; but there is no other entry made in the Council-book relating to this matter, unless this

[1543.] was a consequence of it, that on the 27th of June, Hardds[16] of Canterbury, a prisoner for a seditious libel, was, after a good exhortation, dismissed. And this is all the light that the only Council-book[17] of that reign, for two years, affords as to those matters. Mr. Strype has helped us to more light.

Haynes dean of Exeter having been committed unto the Fleet upon sundry accusations exhibited against him touching lewd and seditious preaching, and the sowing otherwise of many erroneous opinions, was this day called before the Council, and after a good lesson and exhortation with a declaration of the king's mercy and goodness towards him, was dismissed and set at liberty, being bound in recognisance as here ensueth : Simon Haynes clericus . . . domino regi cccc marc. solvend. mens. 5 dno r. etc. The condition of this recognizance is such as if the above bound Simon do at all times within 5 months upon any convenient warning, attend upon the council and answer to all such things as shall there be laid against him ; then etc. ; or else

etc.' p. 521.]

[16] [At Grenewyche the 27th day of June.—' Hardds of Cantorbery having been a certain time in durance for the making of a seditious bill was this day, after a good exhortation, dismissed and set again at liberty.'

[17] [There is but one original Council-book of this reign, the first page of which is as follows : ' The 10th day of August in 32nd year of the reign of our sovereign lord king Henry, the 8. king of England and of France, Defensor of the faith, lord of Ireland, and on earth supreme head immediately under God of the church of England, an order was taken and determined by his majesty, by the advice of his highness' privy council whose names hereafter ensue.'—(Here fol-

152   While Cranmer was visiting his diocese, there were many
presentments made of a very different nature.   Some were
presented for adhering still to the old superstitions condemned
by the king, and for insinuations in favour of the pope's authority.   Others again were, on the other hand, presented for
doctrines, either contrary to the six articles, or to the rites
still practised.   This created a great confusion through that
whole country ; and the blame of all was cast on Cranmer by
his enemies, as if he favoured and encouraged that, which was
called the *new learning*, too much.

A plot was contrived, chiefly by Gardiner's means, with the
assistance of Dr. London, and of Thornden, (suffragan of
Dover, and prebendary of Canterbury,) who had lived in
Cranmer's house, and had all his preferment by his favour.
Several others engaged in it, who had all been raised by him,
and had pretended zeal for the gospel ; but, upon Cromwell's
fall, they reckoned, that, if they could send Cranmer after
him, they would effectually crush all designs of a further
reformation.

They resolved to begin with some of the prebendaries and
preachers.   Many articles were gathered out of their sermons
and private discourses, all terminating in the archbishop ; who,
as was said, shewed so partial a favour to the men of the *new
learning,* and dealt so harshly and severely with the others,
that he was represented to be the principal cause of all the
heat and divisions that were in Canterbury, and in the other
parts of Kent.   These articles went through many hands ; but
it was not easy to prevail with a proper person to present them.
The steps made in the matter are copiously set forth by Mr.
Strype.   At last they came into the king's hands ; and he
upon that passing by Lambeth, where the archbishop stood,
in respect to him, as he passed by, called him into his barge ;

low the names of twenty counsellors.) — ' That there should be a
clerk attendant upon the said Council to write, enter and register all
such decrees and determinations,
letters and other such things as he
should be appointed to enter in a
book to remain always as a leger,
as well for the discharge of the said
counsellors, touching such things

as they should pass from time to
time, as also for a memorial unto
them of their own proceedings, unto
the which office William Paget,
late the queen's secretary, was appointed by the king's highness and
sworn in the presence of the said
council the day and year above
said.']

[Ibid. chap. 27.]
and told him, he had now discovered who was the greatest heretic in Kent. With that, he shewed him the articles against himself and his chaplains. The archbishop knew the falsehood of many particulars; so he prayed the king to send a commission to examine the matter. The king said, he would give him a commission, but to none else. He answered, it would not seem decent to appoint him to examine articles exhibited against himself. The king said, he knew his integrity, and would trust it to no other person: nor would he name above one (though pressed to it) that should be joined in commission with him. And he even then seemed persuaded it was a contrivance of Gardiner's to ruin him.

His great mildness.

The archbishop went down himself into Kent; and then the conspirators, seeing the king's favour to him, were struck with fear. Some of them wept, and begged pardon, and were put in prison; but the rest of the commission, in whose hands the archbishop left the matter, being secretly favourers of that party, proceeded faintly: so it was writ to court, that unless Dr. Legh were sent down, who was well practised in examinations, the conspiracy would never be found out. He was upon that sent down; and he ordered a search to be made, at one and the same time, of all suspected places; and so he discovered the whole train. Some of the archbishop's domestics, 153 Thornden in particular, were among the chief of the informers. He charged them with it. They on their knees confessed their faults, with many tears. He, who was gentle even to excess, said, he did forgive them, and prayed God to forgive them, and to make them better men. After that, he was never observed to change his countenance, or alter his behaviour towards them. He expressed the like readiness to pardon all the rest. Many were imprisoned upon these examinations, but the parliament granting a subsidy, a general pardon set them all at liberty; which otherwise the archbishop was resolved to have procured to them. This relation differs in several particulars from the account that I gave of it in my History: but this seems to be the exacter and the better vouched, and therefore I acquiesce in it[17]. Another instance is given by the same
[Ibid. chap. 28.]
writer of the king's zeal for Cranmer. Sir John Gostwick, knight for Bedfordshire, did in the house of commons charge

[17] [See part i. p. 328.]

him for preaching heresy against the sacrament of the altar,
both at Feversham and Canterbury. The king hearing of
this, did in his rough way threaten Gostwick, calling him
varlet, and charged him to go and ask Cranmer pardon,
otherwise he should feel the effects of his displeasure. The
king said, if he had been a Kentish man, he might have had
some more shadow for accusing him; but being of Bedfordshire, he could have none. Gostwick, terrified with this message, made his submission to Cranmer, who mildly forgave
him, and went to the king, and moved him for his favour;
which he did not obtain without some difficulty.

It appears plainly that the king acted as if he had a mind
to be thought infallible; and that his subjects were bound to
believe as much as he thought fit to open to them, and neither
more nor less. He went on this year, before he took his progress, in finishing the Necessary Doctrine and Erudition of
any Christian Man: a great part of it was corrected by his
own hand, particularly in that article of the Creed, *the ca-*
tholic church, where there are severe reflections added on the
bishops of Rome. Here I found likewise some more of the
answers made to the seventeen queries upon the matter of the
sacraments that I published in my first volume [17]. I set them
out again in my Collection, that by these the reader may
better understand the two following papers, that I print separately, and not intermixed with one another, as I did before;
which I thought to be an ease to the reader: but since that
was made a great offence, I will do it no more. One of these
is only an answer to the queries; the writer of the first is not
named, it is probably Tunstall's; he is plainly of the same
side with the archbishop of York. It will be found in the Collection, as also another paper, with several marginal notes in
the king's hand, by which it appears that the king was much
shaken from his former notions: he asked for scripture in
several particulars that could not easily be brought. On the
margin Cranmer and Barlow are often named, but I do not
understand with what view it was that they and no other
(except Cox once) are named. Over against the 15th article
their names are set down in this order: York, Durham, Carlisle, Corren, Simon, Oglethorp, Edgeworth, Day, Redmayn,

Cott. libr.
Cleop. E. v.
[fol. 53.]
Some steps
made in
setting out
true reli-
gion.

Collect.
Numb. 32.
vol. i.
Reform.

Collect.
Numb. 69.

Collect.
Numb. 70.
Collect.
Numb. 71.

[[17] See part I. Records, p. 201.]

Robinson, Winchester; and a little below, Canterbury, Hereford, Rochester, Davys, (I suppose St. David's,) Westminster, 154 Layton, Tresham, Cox, Crayford; these are writ in a hand that I do not know, but not in the same hand. It seems those lists were made with relation to the different parties in which they stood. The book, thus carefully examined, was finished and published.

Catharine Howard's disgrace.

The king went in progress with his queen, who began to have a great influence on him; and, on what reason I do not know, she withdrew from her uncle, and became his enemy; but, before the king's return, her ill life came to be discovered, which ended fatally to her. It is scarce worth the reader's while to say any more of a matter that is so universally acknowledged; but having found an original account subscribed by herself of one of her examinations, I have put it in

Collect. Numb. 72.

the Collection. It appears there was a particular view in the archbishop of Canterbury's examining her, to draw from her all the discoveries they could make to fasten a precontract with Dereham on her. Many trifling stories relating to that being suggested, she was examined to them all: but though she confesses a lewd commerce with Dereham, she positively denied every thing that could infer a precontract; nor did she confess any thing of that sort done after the king married her,

[Nov. 14. Cotton MSS. Otho, C. x. fol. 250.] Paper Office. Secken. lib. iii. p. 78. A negotiation with the German princes.

which she still denied very positively, even to the last. On the 15th[18] of December letters were written to the king's ambassadors abroad, that contain a severe account of the lewd and naughty behaviour and lightness of her lately reputed for queen, (I give the words of the letter,) at which the king was much troubled.

Upon her disgrace, there was a new negotiation proposed

---

[18] ['The letter sent from divers of the Council to William Paget, our ambassador then in France,' dated Nov. 12, is printed at length in Lord Herbert's History. In a note in State Papers, vol. viii. p. 636, the editor says, that this is probably a mistake, as 'it appears by the Council Register that on the 14th of November letters were addressed to the Deputy of Calais and to the ambassadors in Flanders, in France and with the emperor, declaring the queen's misdemeanor.' The words given by the author in the text do not appear in the letter to Paget, as printed by lord Herbert. The letter has also been printed by sir Harris Nicolas from the original despatch in the British Museum, Otho, C. X. fol. 250. in the Appendix to the Proceedings of the Privy Council, vol. vii. p. 352.]

with the protestant princes of Germany. Mont was again sent over to excuse, as well as he could, the divorce with Anne of Cleves. He said she was treated nobly and kindly in all respects by the king. He renewed the proposition for a league, with relation to their common interests : but they still stood upon this, that they could enter into no alliance with him, unless they agreed in religion, insisting particularly on private masses, the denying the chalice, and the celibate of the clergy. Upon which a conference was proposed in Gelderland, or at Hamburg or Bremen. The king in answer to this wrote, that he would carefully examine all that they laid before him. He expressed great regard to the elector, but complained that some of his learned men had written virulently against him, and misrepresented his proceedings. Cranmer likewise wrote to the elector, and set forth the great things the king had already done in abolishing the pope's authority, the monastic state, and the idolatrous worship of images : he desired they would not be uneasy, though the king in some things differed still from them. He was very learned himself, and had learned men about him : he was quick of apprehension, had a sound judgment, and was firm in what he once resolved on : and he hoped the propositions they had sent over would be well considered.

Lord William Howard, the late queen's uncle, was then ambassador in France : he tells in one of his letters, that the admiral was restored to favour, chiefly by the means of madame D'Estampes, whose credit with that king is well known. There were reports that the emperor and the French 155 king were in a treaty, and that in conclusion they would join to make war on the king : this was charged on the French, but solemnly disowned by that king. It appears the proposition for marrying the lady Mary to the duke of Orleans was then begun : great exceptions were taken to her being declared a bastard ; but it was promised, that, when all other things were agreed to, she should be declared legitimate. Upon queen Catharine Howard's disgrace, lord William was [Sept. 24, recalled, and Paget was sent over in his room[19].　1541.]

There is in the Paper Office an original letter of Paget's to

[19] [The letter recalling Howard, dated Sept. 24, and the instructions given to Paget, are printed in State Papers, vol. viii. p. 611.]

the king, that gives an account of his conversation with the admiral, who was then in high favour, Montmorency being in disgrace. It is very long ; but it contains so many important passages, that I have put it in the Collection, and shall here give an abstract of it. It is dated from Chablais the 22nd of April, in the year 1542.

Collect. Numb. 73.

Paget's negotiation with the court of France.

" He gave the admiral an account of his instructions, and of " what both the king and his council had ordered him to say : " he perceived the admiral sighed and crossed himself often ; " and said, in his answer to him, that he saw the king of " France resolved to enter into some confederacy ; he desired " it might be with the king, and would think of no other " prince till the king refused him. He thought both the kings " were by their interests obliged to stick to one another, " though the marriage had never been spoke of : it is true, " that would fix and strengthen it. But he thought two hun- " dred thousand crowns was a very mean offer for such a " king's daughter to such a prince ; four or five hundred thou- " sand crowns was nothing to the king. The duke of Orleans " was a prince of great courage, and did aspire to great things. " So mean an offer would quite discourage them. The daugh- " ter of Portugal was offered with four hundred thousand " ducats, together with the interest of it since her father's " death, which was almost as much more. At the first motion " of the matter, it was answered, the man must desire the " woman ; now he does desire her, and you offer nothing : " with this he sighed. Paget answered, and fully set out the " personal love that he knew his master had for the French " king : that none of the occasions of suspicion that had been " given could alienate him from it. And he reckoned up many " of these. He acknowledged there was great hopes of the " duke of Orleans ; but he studied to shew that the offer was " not unreasonable, all things considered. Louis the Twelfth " had but three hundred thousand crowns with the king's " sister, and the king of Scots had with the other but one " hundred thousand crowns : but he said, besides the two hun- " dred thousand crowns which he offered to give, they will " also forgive eight hundred thousand crowns that France " owed the king, and discharge the hundred thousand crowns " yearly pension. To this the admiral replied, he counted the

" forgiving the eight hundred thousand crowns for nothing :
" and for the annual pension, they would be at as much charge
" to maintain her and her court. Paget said, the eight hundred
" thousand crowns was a just debt, lent in an extreme necessity ;
" and because it had been long owing, and often respited, must
" that pass for nothing? So he bade him ask reasonably, or
" offer what was proper reciprocally for it. The admiral said,
" the king was rich ; and what was eight hundred thousand
156 " crowns to him, which they were not able to pay? So the
" admiral said, he wished the thing had never been spoke of.
" He fell next to turn the motion to the lady Elizabeth, and he
" proposed a league offensive and defensive against the empe-
" ror : and that whatever should be got from the emperor
" should be the king's in lieu of the pension during life. He
" knew the emperor was practising with the king, as he was
" at the same time with them. Bonner was then sent am-
" bassador to Spain, and had carried over from the king to the
" emperor three horses of value. The emperor might say
" what he will in the way of practice : but he knew he would
" never unite with the king, except he would return to the
" pope ; for so the nuncio told the chancellor, and the chan-
" cellor told it to the queen of Navarre, who fell out with him
" upon that occasion. She told him he was ill enough before ;
" but now, since he had *the mark of the beast*, (for he was
" lately made a priest,) he grew worse and worse ; the empe-
" ror's design was only to divide them. He offered to them
" that the duke of Orleans should be king of Naples, and to
" give Flanders to the crown of France : but in lieu of that,
" he asked the renunciation of Milan and Navarre, and the
" restoring of Piedmont and Savoy : but by this, the father
" and son being so far separate, the emperor would soon drive
" the duke of Orleans out of Naples. He was also studying to
" gain the duke of Cleves, and to restore him Geldern quietly,
" provided that he and his wife would renounce Navarre : but
" he concluded, that they knew the emperor did nothing but
" practise. They knew he offered to the king to reconcile him
" to the pope, without any breach of his honour, for it should
" be at the pope's suit. Paget said he knew nothing of all
" that, but believed it would be hard to reconcile him to the
" bishop of Rome, for virtue and vice cannot stand together in

" one predicament.   Call ye him *vice?* said the admiral; he
" is the very *Devil*, and I trust to see his confusion: every
" thing must have a time and a beginning.   But when begin
" you? said Paget.   The admiral answered, Before it be long,
" the king will give all the abbeys to his lay-gentlemen, and so
" by little and little overthrow him altogether: why may not
" we have a patriarch in France? This the pope's legate began
" to perceive; and though they talked of a general council, he
" believed the pope would as soon be hanged as call one.   Paget
" said he would be glad to see them once begin to do some-
" what.   Ah, said the admiral, I'm ill matched.   He wished
" the entire union of the two kings, and if an interview might
" be between them, it would be the happiest thing that could
" befal Christendom: but he believed some of the king's
" council leaned too much to the emperor, and proposed seve-
" ral advantages from it.   He said the emperor cared not if
" father, friend, and all the world should sink, so his insatiable
" desires might be satisfied.   He suffered two of his brothers-
" in-law to perish for want of fifty thousand crowns: first the
" king of Hungary; and then the king of Denmark, whom he
" might have restored, if he would have given him ten thou-
" sand crowns.   He was then low enough, and they would do
" well to fall on him, now that he was so low, before he took
" breath.   So he pressed Paget to put matters on heartily 157
" with the king: he thought it an unreasonable thing for the
" emperor and his brother to ask aid against the Turk, to
" defend their own dominions, when they kept the king's do-
" minions from him.   Paget gave the king an account of all
" this conversation very particularly, with an humble submis-
" sion to him, if in any thing he had gone too far.   The court
" of France believed the emperor was treating with the king
" for the marriage of the lady Mary; and that for that end
" Bonner was sent to Spain, who was looked on as a man
" throughly imperial.   After Paget had ended his letter,
" written on the 19th of April, he adds a long postscript on
" the 22nd, for the admiral had entered into further discourse
" with him the next day.   He told him how sorry he was to
" see all his hopes blasted: he could not sleep all night for it.
" They had letters from their ambassadors in England, and
" were amazed to find that a king who was so rich stood for so

" small a matter. The pope had offered the duke of Guise's
" son two hundred thousand crowns with his niece : he said ho
" was much troubled at all this ; all that were about the king
" his master were not of one mind, and he had been reproached
" for beginning this matter. They knew the falsehood and
" the lies of the pope and the emperor well enough : he
" wished they would consider well what the effects of an entire
" friendship with the king of France might be : the French
" could do no more than they could do ; within two years they
" would owe the king a hundred thousand crowns, besides
" the hundred thousand crowns during the king's life, and
" fifty thousand crowns for ever after that : but, he said, in
" those treaties many things ought to be done for their own
" defence. At this he was called away by the king, but came
" afterwards to Paget : he said, it was not one hundred thou-
" sand nor two hundred thousand crowns could not enrich the
" one nor impoverish the other king : so, he added, we ask your
" daughter, and you shall have our son : but desired that they
" might carry the matter further into a league, to make war
" on the emperor, defensive, for all their territories.

" He proposed that the king should send ten thousand foot
" and two thousand horse into Flanders, and to pay five thou-
" sand Germans : and the French king should furnish the same
" number of foot and of Germans, and three thousand horse,
" and an equal number of ships on both sides ; and the king of
" France should in some other places fall into the emperor's
" dominions, at an expense of two hundred thousand crowns a
" month. What a thing, said he, would it be to the king to
" have Gravelines, Dunkerque, and all those quarters joining to
" Calais ! Paget answered, they might spend all their money,
" and catch nothing ; and he did not see what ground of quar-
" rel his master had with the emperor : upon which the admi-
" ral replied, Does not he owe you money ? Hath not he
" broken his leagues with you in many particulars ? Did not be
" provoke us to join with the pope and him, to drive your
" master out of his kingdom ? And hath he not now put the
" pope on offering a council to sit at Mantua, Verona, Cam-
" bray, or Metz, (this last place was lately named,) all on de-
" sign to ruin you ! A pestilence take him, said he, false dis-
" sembler that he is ! if he had you at such an advantage as

" you now have him, you should feel it. And he ran out 158
" largely, both against the bishop of Rome and the emperor :
" he desired the war might begin that year, the emperor being
" so low, that, for all his millions, he had not a penny."

On all this the admiral seemed wonderfully set. Paget excused himself from entering further into these matters, and desired that they might be proposed to the king by the French ambassador, then at London ; yet being pressed by the admiral, he promised to lay all before the king ; and he did it very fully, but with many excuses, and much submission. The king's council writ a short answer to this long letter : they expressed their confidence in the admiral, with great acknowledgments for his affection to the king ; but they seemed to suspect the king of France, that all his professions were only to get money from the king. Two hundred thousand crowns seemed nothing when they were willing to forgive him a million ; but by this letter it seems the French ambassadors did still insist on six hundred thousand crowns to be paid down. So this matter was let fall. But to say all that relates to the duke of Orleans at once :

Paper Office.

The duke of Orleans promised to declare himself a protestant. [Lettres et Mémoires de Vargas, p. 26.]

M. Le Vassor has published instructions, of which a collated copy was found among cardinal Granvelle's papers : it is a question that cannot be answered how he came by it ; whether the original was taken with the landgrave of Hesse, or by what other way, is not certain. It bears date at Rheims the 8th of September 1543. " It expresses the great desire that
" he had that the holy gospel might be preached in the whole
" kingdom of France ; but the respect that he owed to the
" king his father, and to the dauphin his brother, made that
" he did not order it to be preached freely in his duchy of
" Orleans, that being under their obedience. But he sent to
" the duke of Saxony, to the landgrave of Hesse, and the
" other protestant princes, to assure them that he was resolved,
" and promised it expressly to them, that he would order that
" the gospel should be preached in the duchy of Luxembourg,
" and in all other places that should belong to him by the
" right of war. He desired to be received into their alliance,
" and to a league offensive and defensive with them. He de-
" sired earnestly that they would grant this request, not to be
" aided by them against any prince, but only on the account

" of the Christian religion, of which he desired the increase
" above all things : that by these means light may be spread
" into other dominions, and into the kingdom of France, when
" the king his father should see him so allied to those princes;
" which will be the cause of making him declare the good
" zeal he has to that matter, and will be able always to excuse
" it to him, and to defend it against all his enemies.   He
" desires therefore, that as soon as he shall give order that
" the gospel shall be preached in the duchy of Luxembourg,
" this league and alliance may begin.   He hopes this will not
" be delayed, from the opinion that they may have that he
" cannot quickly shew what power he has to support the love
" he bears to this cause ; he hopes in a little time to shew, if
" it pleases God, some good effect of it : and he offers at pre-
" sent, not only all his own force, but the whole force of the
" king his father, who has given him authority to employ it in
159 " every thing that he shall judge to be good for them, and in
" every thing that may concern their welfare, their profit, and
" freedom."

It is impossible to read this, and to doubt either of his being
sincerely a protestant, or at least that he was willing to profess
it openly : and it can as little be doubted, that in this he had
his father's leave to do what he did.   The retaking of Luxembourg put an end to this proposition : but it seems the emperor
apprehended that the heat of this young prince might grow
uneasy to him ; therefore he took all methods to satisfy his
ambition.   For on the 18th of December 1544, the ambassadors at the emperor's court writ over, that he was treating a
match between his own eldest daughter and the duke of Orleans ; and that he offered to give with her the ancient inheritance of the house of Burgundy, the two Burgundies, and the
Netherlands : or, if he would marry his brother Ferdinand's
second daughter, to give the duchy of Milan with her.   They [State
also mention in April [20] thereafter, that became to the emperor, Papers,
and stayed some days with him at Antwerp, and then went vol. x. pp
back.   On this they all concluded that the treaty was like to 401–413.

---

[20] [In a letter from Wotton to
the privy council written from Antwerp, April 27, 1545, it is stated,
that ' The duke of Orleans arrived

here Friday the 24th of this present.'
The same fact is stated in a letter
written on the same day by the
same to Paget ; both letters are

go on, but do not mention which of the two ladies he liked best; for there could be no comparison made between what was offered with them.   But all the negotiation, and all the hopes of that prince, vanished on the 11th of September 1545; for Carne[21], the king's ambassador in Flanders, writ over, that on that day he died of the plague.

Practices on him end with his life.

I come next to put together all that I find in the minutes of convocation during this reign.   The Necessary Erudition was never brought in convocation; but it was treated by some bishops and divines of both provinces, and published by the king's authority.   It seems, when the doctrine was thus settled, there was a design to carry on the reformation further.   There was a convocation held in January 1541; in the second session of which, the archbishop delivered them a message from the king, that it was his pleasure that they should consult concerning the reforming our errors: and he delivered some books to them, to be examined by them.   It does not appear what sort of books or errors those were, whether of papists, sacramentaries, or of anabaptists; for of this last sort some had crept into England.   The business of Munster had made that name so odious, that three years before this, in October 1538, there was a commission sent to Cranmer, Stokesley, Sampson, and some others, to inquire after anabaptists, to proceed against them, to restore the penitent, to burn their books, and to deliver the obstinate to the secular arm: but I have not seen what proceedings there were upon this.

Proceedings in convocation.

[Jan. 20.]
[Wilkins' Conc. iii. p. 860.]

In October 1545, there was an order of council published to take away shrines and images: several commissions were granted for executing this; in some, they add bones to images. The archbishop did likewise move the convocation, in the king's name, to make laws against simony, and to prepare a book of Homilies; and also a new translation of the Bible: for, it seems, complaints were made of the translation then printed

A new translation of the Bible designed.

printed in 'State Papers,' vol. x. pp. 401-406, as also one from Carne to Paget of the same date, which mentions his arrival on the 24th of April, and another from Carne to the Council, from Brussels, of May 3rd, stating that he had 'departed herehence toward France yesterday.' Ibid. pp. 407, 413. These are probably the letters alluded to by the author in the text.]

[21] [The fact is mentioned by Thirlby bishop of Westminster, in a letter to Paget written on the same day and printed in 'State Papers,' vol. x. p. 587: the letter from Carne to Paget is mentioned in a note, but has not been printed.]

and set up in churches.   The several books of the Bible were
160 parcelled out, and assigned to several bishops to translate
them.   This came to nothing during this reign; but this same
method was followed in queen Elizabeth's time.   In the fifth
session the persons were named for this translation.   Cranmer
had, some few years before this, parcelled out an old translation of the New Testament to several bishops and divines, to
be revised and corrected by them: but it was then much opposed.   The Acts of the Apostles was assigned to Stokesley
but he sent in no return upon it: so the archbishop sent to
him for it.   His answer was sullen: " He wondered what the
" archbishop meant, thus to abuse the people, by giving them
" liberty to read the scripture, which did nothing but infect
" them with heresy.   He had not looked on his portion; and
" never would : so he sent back the book, saying, He would
" never be guilty of bringing the simple people into error."
Notwithstanding this, Cranmer had published a more correct
New Testament in English, which is referred to in the injunctions that were formerly mentioned: but now he designed a
new translation of the whole Bible.   In the sixth session, which
was on the 17th of February, a statute against simony was
treated of: there was also some discourse about the translating
the Lord's Prayer, the Creed, and the Ten Commandments, in
the vulgar tongue: and it was considered, how some words in
them ought to be translated; but what these were, is not mentioned: only it seems there was a design to find faults in every
thing that Cranmer had done.

Memor. of
Cranmer,
Strype,
chap. viii.
[p. 34, from
Harl. MSS.
422.fol.87.]

On the 24th of February several matters were treated of;
that in particular is named, that none should let leases beyond
the term of twenty-one years.   They treated about many of
the rituals, and of Thomas Becket, and of the adorning of
images, and about reforming some scandalous comedies.   On
the third of March the archbishop told them from the king,
that it was his pleasure that the translation of the Bible should
be revised by the two universities.   But all the bishops, except Ely and St. David's, protested against this : and it seems
they insisted much upon trifles ; for they treated of this,
Whether, in the translation of the Bible, *the Lord* or *our
Lord* should be the constant form.   On the same day the
lord chancellor exhibited to them an act, allowing that the

bishops' chancellors might marry : to this the bishops dissented. Some other matters were proposed; but all was referred to the king. Upon the convocation's being assembled on the 16th of February 1542, some homilies were offered on different subjects; but nothing is marked concerning them. The archbishop also told them, that the king would have the books of the several offices used in churches to be examined and corrected; in particular, that both at matins and vespers one chapter of the New Testament should be read in every parish. Some petitions were offered by the clergy : the first was, for making a body of the ecclesiastical laws. Of this we hear no more in this reign; but we are assured, that there was a digested body of them prepared : probably it was very near the same that was also prepared in king Edward's time. Cranmer, in a letter that he wrote to the king out of Kent, on the 24th of January 1545–6, which I did put in my second

Collection of Records, vol. ii. Numb. 61.

volume, tells him, " That, according to his commands, he had " sent for the bishop of Worcester, (Heath,) to let him know, " that the king's pleasure was, to have the names of such per- 161 " sons sent him as he had formerly appointed to make ecclesi- " astical laws for the realm." The bishop promised with all speed to inquire out their names, and the book which they made, and to bring both the names and the book to the king;

A reformation of the ecclesiastical laws was far advanced.

which, he writes, he had done before that time. By this it appears, that persons had been named for that; and that a commission was granted, pursuant to which the work had been prepared : for things of this kind were never neglected by Cranmer. It seems it had been done some years before, so that it was almost forgotten; but now, in one of king Henry's lucid intervals, it was prepared, as Mr. Strype has published. But how it came to pass, that no further progress was made, during this reign, in so important and so necessary a work, is not easily to be accounted for; since it must have contributed much to the exaltation of the king's supremacy, to have all the ecclesiastical courts governed by a code authorized by him. In the convocation in the year 1543, we have only

[April 24.]

this short word, That on the 29th of April the archbishop

[April 27.]

treated of the sacraments, and on the next day on the article of free-will. This is all that I could gather from the copy of the minutes of the convocations which was communicated to me by my most learned and worthy brother, the lord bishop [Wilkins' Conc. iii. of Lincoln[22], who assured me it was collated exactly with the 868.] only ancient copy that remains, to give us light into the proceedings in the convocations of those times[23].

It does not appear to me what moved Bell, bishop of Worcester, to resign his bishopric. Rymer has printed his resignation; in which it is said, that he did it simply of his own accord. He lived till the year 1556, as his tombstone in Clerkenwell church informs us. Whether he inclined to a further reformation, and so withdrew at this time; or whether the old leaven yet remaining with him made it uneasy for him to comply, does not appear: if his motives had been of the former sort, it may be supposed he would have been thought of in king Edward's time; and if of the latter, then in queen Mary's reign he might again have appeared: so I must leave it in the dark what his true motive was.

Bell, bishop of Worcester, resigned his bishopric. [Nov. 17. 1543.] Rymer, tom. xv. [p. 10.]

Audley, who had been lord chancellor from the time that sir Thomas More left that post, fell sick in the year 1544, and sent the great seal to the king by sir Edward North and sir Thomas[24] Bland. The king delivered it to the lord Wriothesley, and made him lord keeper during the lord Audley's infirmity, with authority to do every thing that the lord Chancellor might do; and the duke of Norfolk tendered him the oaths. It seems there was such a regard had to the lord Audley, that as long as he lived the title of lord chancellor was not given with the seals; but upon his death Wriothesley was made lord chancellor. This seems to be the first instance of a lord keeper with the full authority of a lord chancellor.

Audley, lord chancellor, died. [April 22.] Rymer, tom. xv. [p. 20.] [April 30.]

I have not now before me such a thread of matters as to carry me regularly through the remaining years of this reign; and therefore hereafter I only give such passages as I have gathered, without knitting them together in an exact series. 162 The breach between England and France was driven on by the emperor's means, and promoted by all the popish party: so the king, to prevent all mischief from Scotland during this war with France, entered into an agreement with the earls of Lennox

Practices on some lords of Scotland.

[22 Dr. William Wake, afterwards Archbishop of Canterbury.]

23 [For a fuller account of this convocation see Strype's Memorials

Ecclesiastical, vol. i. p. 377.

24 [This is a mistake for sir Thomas Pope, as appears from the instrument printed in Rymer.]

[May 17.]
Rymer,
[tom. xv.
p. 22.]
and Glencairn, and the elect bishop of Caithness, brother to
the earl of Lennox, in May 1544.   The articles are published:
they promised, "That they should cause the word of God to
" be truly taught in their countries.   2ndly, They should con-
" tinue the king's faithful friends.   3rdly, They should take care
" that the queen be not secretly carried away.   4thly, They
" should assist the king to seize on some castles on the borders."
And they delivered the elect bishop of Caithness to the king,
as an hostage for their observing these things.   On the other
hand, " the king engaged to send armies to Scotland both by
sea and land ; and to make the earl of Lennox, (written in
this, Levenax,) " as soon as he could, governor of Scotland :
" and that he should bestow his niece, lady Margaret Douglas,

[Rymer,
tom. xv.
p. 28.]
[Ibid. p.
47.]
" on him."   There was a fuller agreement made with them,
with more particulars in it, on the 26th of June ; and a pension
of 250l. was assigned to the earl of Glencairn, and 125l. to his
son, both during life.   Those in the castle of St. Andrew's were
also taken into the king's protection : and they promised to
promote the marriage, and the king's interests ; and to deliver
up the castle when demanded.   There were also private agreements made with Norman Leslie, Kircaldy of the Grange, and
some others ; all to be found in Rymer.

Seck. lib. 3.
[Sect. 3.
§ 121.
p. 552.]
Mont sent
to Ger-
many.
The often-cited Seckendorf tells us, that at this time they in
Germany began to have greater hopes of the king than ever.
Mont was again sent to offer an alliance with them.   He excused all the late proceedings : he said, Cromwell had rashly
said, That " he hoped to see the time, that he should strike a
" dagger into the heart of him that should oppose the re-
" formation ;" which his judges thought was meant of the
king.   He said, Barnes had indiscreetly provoked the bishop
of Winchester : he also blamed their ambassadors for entering
into disputes in writing with the king ; he believed Melancthon
and Bucer would have managed that matter with more success.
Buce rseconded Mont's motions, and magnified what the king
had already done ; though there was no complete reformation
yet effected.

This did not move the elector : he looked on the king as an
enemy to their doctrine.   His whole design in what he had
done was, to make himself the head of the church, to which he
was not called of God.   His government was tyrannical, and

his life flagitious; so he looked for no good from him. · The king of France moved him to undertake a mediation between him and the king ; but the elector referred that to a general meeting of those who were engaged in the common Smalcaldic league. The princes in Germany, having their chief dependence on the kings of France and England, saw how much they were weakened, and exposed to the emperor, by the war which was going on between those two kings; so they sent some empowered by them, to try if it was possible to prevent that war, and to mediate a reconciliation between them. To these, when 163 they delivered their message to the king, he complained of the injustice and wilfulness of the French king : he thought their interposition could have no effect, and he used these words in an answer to their memorial : *We give them well to understand, that we do both repose an ampler and a fuller confidence in them than the French king either doth or will do.*

Du Bellay, who, being oft employed, understood those matters well, tells us, that the emperor and king Henry had agreed to join their armies and to march directly into France. He tells in another place, that if king Henry had followed the opinion of his council, which was for his landing in Normandy with thirty thousand men, he would have carried that whole duchy ; and he ascribes his error in that matter to the providence of God, that protected France from so great a danger. The emperor had proposed to the king, that upon the junction of their two armies they should march straight to Paris : for they reckoned that both their armies would have amounted to ninety thousand foot and twenty thousand horse. But after the emperor had drawn the king into his measures, he went on taking some towns, pursuing his own ends; and then made his own peace with France, and left the king engaged in the war : so the king finding the emperor's main army was not like to join him, some bodies out of the Netherlands only coming to act in conjunction with him ; upon that, he sent the duke of Norfolk to besiege Montreuil, and he himself sat down before Boulogne. Marshal Biéz, governor of Boulogne, apprehending the importance of Montreuil, carried a considerable part of the garrison of Boulogne with him, and threw himself into Montreuil : by this means he left Boulogne weak, and in ill hands. In the mean time the emperor took Luxembourg, and some other

A war with France, p. 1094.
[fol. 329.]
p. 1115.
[fol. 333.]

[fol. 330.]

places : so all the project, with which he had amused the king, vanished, and a peace was struck up between him and the king of France.

The French sent an army to raise the siege of Montreuil, and they were moving so as to get between the duke of Norfolk and the king's army ; upon which the duke of Norfolk raised

the siege : but Boulogne was taken ; and that small conquest was out of measure magnified by those who saw their own advantage in flattering their master, though at a vast charge he had gained a place scarce worth keeping.

The emperor had that address, and he had so strong a party about the king, that even all this was excused, and the intercourse between the two courts was not discontinued.

In one point the emperor was necessary to the king, and he kept his word to him.   It is certain the king had great apprehensions of the council that was now sitting at Trent ; and the more, because Pole was one of the legates sent to preside in it : who, as he had reason to apprehend, would study to engage the council to confirm the pope's censure thundered out against the king ; and it was believed he was named legate for that end.   The king of France had offered to Gardiner, that, if the king would join with him, he would suffer no council to meet, but as the king should consent to it : but his fluctuating temper was so well known, that the king trusted in this particular more to the emperor, whose interest in that council he knew must be **164** great ; and the emperor had promised that the council should not at all intermeddle in the matter between the pope and the king.   The effect shewed he was true in this particular.

The king, finding himself so disappointed, and indeed abandoned by the emperor, sent the earl of Hertford, with Gardiner, to him, to expostulate with him.   A letter of the king's was sent by them to the emperor, written in a very severe strain, charging him with perfidy.   The emperor either had the gout, or pretended to have it ; so that he could not be spoke with. His chief ministers at that time, who were Granvelle, and his

son the bishop of Arras, delayed them from day to day, and discovered much chicane, as they wrote : upon which they grew so uneasy, that at last they demanded a positive answer ; and then these ministers told them, that the emperor could not carry on the war longer against France : but he offered to

mediate a peace between England and France. After that they
complain, that they saw the pretence of mediation was managed
deceitfully ; for the emperor's design upon Germany being now
ready, he apprehended those two kings, if not engaged in war
one with another, would support the princes of the empire, and
not suffer the emperor, under the pretence of a religious war,
to make himself master of Germany : therefore he studied to
keep up the war between France and England. I find Maurice
of Saxony was this year, during the emperor's war with France,
in his court ; whether he was then mediating or treating about
his perfidious abandoning the elector, and the other princes of
the Smalcaldic league, I know not.

Before the king went out of England, a great step was made
towards the reforming the public offices. A form of procession
in the English tongue was set out by the king's authority, and
a mandate was sent to Bonner to publish it. The title[24] of it
was, *An Exhortation to Prayer, thought meet by his Majesty
and his Clergy to be read to the People : also a Litany, with
Suffrages to be said, or sung, in the time of the Processions.*
In the Litany they did still invocate the blessed Virgin, the
angels and archangels, and all holy orders of blessed spirits, all
holy patriarchs and prophets, apostles, martyrs, confessors,
and virgins, and all the blessed company of heaven, to pray
for them. After the word *conspiracy* this is added, *from the
tyranny of the bishop of Rome, and all his detestable*[25] *enormities :* the rest of the Litany is the same that we still use,
only some more collects are put at the end, and the whole is
called a *Prayer of Procession.* To this are added some exercises of devotion, called *Psalms,* which are collected out of
several parts of scripture, but chiefly the Psalms : they are
well collected ; and the whole composition, as there is nothing
that approaches to popery in it, so it is a serious and well-
digested course of devotion. There follows a paraphrase on the
Lord's Prayer : on the fourth petition there are expressions

Marginal note: A Litany set out in English, with other devotions.

---

[24] [A Letany with suffrages to be
sayd or sung in time of processions. With an exhortation to prayer
thought meet by the king and his
clergy to be read to the people in
every church, afore processions.
June 16. A.D. 1544.   Berthelet.
BURNET, PART III.

The Litany was inserted in the
Primer which came out in 1545.
See 'Three Primers put forth in the
reign of Henry 8.' Oxford 1834.
p. 480.}
[25] [The word used in the Litany
is *abominable.*]

that seem to come near a true sense of the presence of Christ
in the sacrament; for by *daily bread*, as some of the ancients
thought, the sacrament of the eucharist is understood, which is
thus expressed: *The lively bread of the blessed body of our
Saviour Jesu Christ, and the sacred cup of the precious and
blessed blood which was shed for us on the cross.* This agrees 165
with our present sense, that Christ is present, not as he is now
in heaven, but as he was on the cross: and that, being a thing
past, he can only be present in a type and a memorial.   The
preface is an exhortation to prayer, in which these remarkable
words will be found: "It is very convenient, and much accept-
" able to God, that you should use your private prayer in your
" mother-tongue; that you, understanding what you ask of
" God, may more earnestly and fervently desire the same,
" your hearts and minds agreeing to your mouth and words."
This is indeed all over of a pious and noble strain; and, except the invocation of the saints and angels, it is an unexceptionable composition.   At the same time Catharine Parr, whom
the king had lately married, collected some prayers and medi-
tations, " wherein the mind is stirred patiently to suffer all
" affliction here, to set at nought the vain prosperity of this
" world, and always to long for the everlasting felicity:" which
were printed in the year 1545.[26]

[26] [There is a copy in the British
Museum, of which the title page is as
follows:
PRAYERS OR
Medytacions wherein the
mynd is stirred, paciently to
suffre all afflictions here, to
set at nought the vaine pro-
speritee of this worlde, and
alwaie to longe for the euer-
lastynge felicitee: Collected
out of holy woorkes by
the most vertuous
and graciouse
Princesse
Kathe-
rine
queene of Englande
Fraunce, and
Irelande.
Anno dñi.
1545.
It is not paged or foliated.   It is

of very small size, and consists of
four sheets, A 1 to D 7, and ends:
IMPRINTED AT
London in Fletestrete, in the
house of Thomas
Berthelet
cum priuilegio ad impri-
mendum solum.
The date must be wrong, for at
Signat. D. ii. in 'A praier for the
kynge' occur the words ' kyng Edward the VI.'   In another very di-
minutive and imperfect copy in the
Museum, dated on the title page
1546, the prayer is 'for the king
and the quenes maiesties,' no name
being mentioned. This has no name
of printer, and it does not contain
the three last prayers. From this it
appears that the edition of 1545 is
the second edition, and should have
been dated 1547.]

But so apt was the king, whether from some old and inherent opinions that still stuck with him, or from the practices of those who knew how to flatter him suitably to his notions, to go backward and forward in matters of religion, that though on the 15th of October 1545 he ordered a mandate to be sent to Bonner, to publish the English Procession ordained by him, which was executed the day following; yet, on the 24th of that month, there was a letter written to Cranmer, declaring the king's pleasure for the setting up an image that had been taken down by his injunctions: ordering him at the same time to abolish the use of holy water about St. John's tide, and to take down an image called our *Lady of Pity in the Pew,* for the idolatry that was committed about it. At this time it was discovered, that great indulgences, with all such like favours, were sent from Rome to Ireland; so that generally in that kingdom the king's supremacy was rejected, and yet at the same time it appears that many were put in prison for denying the presence in the sacrament; and a proclamation was set out, both against Tyndale's new Testament and Coverdale's.

Thirlby, bishop of Westminster, was sent ambassador to the emperor; and afterwards secretary Petre was sent to the same court. Mont continued likewise to be employed, but without a character: he seems to have been both honest and zealous; and in many letters, writ both in the year 1545 and 1546, he warned the king of the emperor's designs to extirpate Lutheranism, and to force the whole empire to submit to the pope and the council, then sitting at Trent. The German princes sent over a vehement application to the king, to consider the case of Herman, bishop of Cologne, praying him to protect him, and to intercede for him. They gave a great character of the man, of which Mont makes mention in his letters: but I do not find that the king interposed in that matter. The emperor seemed to enter into great confidences with Thirlby, and either imposed on him, or found him easily wrought on: he told him that the king of France was making great levies in Switzerland, and he was well assured that they were not designed against himself; so he warned the king to be on his guard. This being inquired into, was not only denied by the court of France, but was found to be false, and was looked on as an artifice of the emperor's to keep up a jealousy between

The king neglects the German princes.

166

Paper Office.

U 2

those two courts.   By such practices he prevailed on Thirlby to assure the king, that the emperor did not design to enslave Germany, but only to repress the insolence of some princes, and to give justice a free course : all the news he wrote from thence did run in this strain ; so that Germany was fatally abandoned by both kings.   Yet still the king sent over to the emperor repeated complaints of the ill treatment his subjects met with in Spain from inquisitors ; and that in many courts justice was refused to be done them, upon this pretence, that the king and all who adhered to him were declared heretics, and as such they were excommunicated by the pope, and so were not to be admitted to sue in judicatories : these were sent over to Thirlby, but I do not see what was done upon all those representations.

The elector of Saxony's ill opinion of the king. [Seckend. lib. iii. §. 34, p. 614.]   The last message the king sent to the Germans was in the year 1546, by Mont, with whom one Butler[27] was joined : the German princes, in general terms, prayed the king to insist on rejecting the council of Trent, assuring him that the pope would suffer no reformation to be made.   This letter was agreed to by the greater number of the princes of the union, only the elector of Saxony had conceived great prejudices against the king.   He said, " he was an impious man, with " whom he desired to have no commerce : he was no better " than the pope, whose yoke he had thrown off only for his " own ends : and that he intended out of the two religions to " make a third, only for enriching himself ; having condemned " the principal points of their doctrine in his parliament."

Ferdinand discontented with the emperor.   I find at this time a secret disgust the emperor was in towards his brother Ferdinand : upon which, Ferdinand sent a message to the king, setting forth the just claim he had to his father's succession in Spain ; since, by the agreement of the marriage between Ferdinand of Arragon and Isabel of Castile, a special provision was made, that, whensoever there was a second son issuing from that marriage, the kingdom of Arragon, and all that belonged to it, should be again separated from Castile.   He also pretended, that he ought to have had a larger share in the succession of the house of Burgundy ; and that, instead of those rich provinces, he was forced to accept of

---

[27] [This is a mistake of the author's.   The person who was as-   sociated with Mont was named Bucler. Vid. State Papers x. passim.]

Austria, and the provinces about it, which lay exposed to the Turks, and were loaded with great debts, contracted by his grandfather Maximilian. To this the king sent an answer secretly, and ordered the person (who he was, does not appear; but I think it was Mont) that carried it, to insist on the discourse of his pretensions to the Netherlands, which were then vastly rich. He was particularly required to observe Ferdinand's behaviour, and all that he said on that subject. And it seems that our court, being then in a good understanding with the court of France, communicated the matter to Francis: for he wrote, soon after that, a letter to Ferdinand, encouraging him to stand on his claim, and promising him his assistance to support his pretensions on the emperor. But Ferdinand, not 167 being inclined to trust the court of France with this secret, sent the letter to the emperor: so I see no more of that matter.

The last transaction of importance in this reign was the fall of the duke of Norfolk, and of the earl of Surrey, his son. I find in the council-book[28], in the year 1543, that the earl was accused for eating flesh in Lent without license; and for walking about the streets in the night, throwing stones against windows; for which he was sent to the Fleet: in another letter he is complained of for riotous living. Towards the end of the year 1546, both he and his father were put in prison; and it seems the council wrote to all the king's ambassadors beyond sea an account of this, much aggravated, as the discovery of some very dangerous conspiracy, which they were to

The duke of Norfolk's imprisonment. [April 1. Council Book, p. 465.] [August 1, 1542. Ibid. p. 362.] [Dec. 12.]

[28] [At Saint James' the first day of April.

'The earl of Surrey being sent for to appear before the council was charged by the said presence as well of eating of flesh as of a lewd and unseemly manner of walking in the night about the streets, and breaking with stone bows of certain windows. And touching the eating of flesh, he allowed a licence, albeit he had not so secretly used the same as appertained. And touching the stone bows, he could not deny but he had very evil done therein, submitting himself therefore to such punishment as should to them be thought good, whereupon he was committed to the Fleet, p. 465. At Windesore the 29th of July 'A letter was sent to the Warden of the fleet to repair to the court on Saturday next ensuing of date hereof, and to bring with him the earl of Surrey.' At Wyndesore the first of August. Henricus comes de Surrey...dno regi decem mille marc. solvend. dno regi etc.

The condition of this recognizance is such, as if the above bounden earl of Surrey do neither by himself, his servants, or any other at his procurements, any bodily displeasure other by word or deed to Ro. a Leigh, esquire, or to any of his, then etc. or else etc.]

Collect.
Numb. 74.

represent to those princes in very black characters. I put in
the Collection an account given by Thirlby of what he did
upon it. The letter is long ; but I only copy out that which
relates to this pretended discovery : dated from Hailbron, on
Christmas-day 1546.

" He understood, by the council's letters to him, what un-
" gracious and ungrateful persons they were found to be. He
" professes, he ever loved the father, for he thought him a
" true servant to the king. He says, he was amazed at the
" matter, and did not know what to say. God had not only on
" this occasion, but on many others, put a stop to treasonable
" designs against the king, who (next to God) was the chief
" comfort of all good men : he enlarges much on the subject,
" in the style of a true courtier. The messenger brought him
" the council's letters written on the 15th of December, on
" Christmas-eve ; in which he saw the malicious purpose of
" these two ungracious men : so, according to his orders, he
" went immediately to demand audience of the emperor ; but
" the emperor intended to repose himself for three or four
" days, and so had refused audience to the nuncio, and to all
" other ambassadors : but he said, he would send a secretary,
" to whom he might communicate his business. Joyce, his se-
" cretary, coming to him, he set forth the matter as pompously
" as the council had represented it to him : in particular, he
" spoke of the haughtiness of the earl of Surrey ; of all which
" the secretary promised to make report to the emperor, and
" likewise to write an account of it to Granvelle. Thirlby
" excuses himself, that he durst not write of this matter to the
" king ; he thought it would renew in him the memory of the
" ingratitude of these persons, which must wound a noble
" heart."

Collect.
Numb. 75.
His letter
to the king.

After so black a representation, great matters might be expected : but I have met with an original letter of the duke
of Norfolk's to the lords of the council, writ indeed in so
bad a hand, that the reading it was almost as hard as deciphering ; it gives a very different account of that matter, at
least with relation to the father. He writes, " that the lord
" great chamberlain, and the secretary of state, had examined
" him upon divers particulars. The first was, Whether he had
" a cipher with any man ? He said, he had never a cipher

" with any man, but such as he had for the king's affairs,
" when he was in his service : and he does not remember that
168 " ever he wrote in cipher, except when he was in France with
" the lord great master that now is, and the lord Rochford ;
" nor does he remember whether he wrote any letters then, or
" not ; but these two lords signed whatsoever he wrote.   He
" heard, that a letter of his was found among bishop Fox's
" papers, which being shewed to the bishop of Durham, he
" advised to throw it into the fire.   He was examined upon
" this : he did remember the matter of it was, the setting
" forth the talk of the northern people, after the time of the
" commotions ; but that it was against Cromwell, and not at
" all against the king : (so far did they go back, to find matter
" to be laid to his charge :) but whether that was in cipher, or
" not, he did not remember.   He was next asked, if any per-
" son had said to him, that if the king, the emperor, and the
" French king came to a good peace, whether the bishop of
" Rome would break that by his dispensation ; and whether
" he inclined that way.   He did not remember he had ever
" heard any man speak to that purpose ; but, for his own
" part, if he had twenty lives, he would rather spend them
" all than that the bishop of Rome should have any power
" in this kingdom again.   He had read much history, and
" knew well how his usurpation began and increased ; and
" both to English, French, and Scots, he has upon all occa-
" sions spoken vehemently against it.   He was also asked, if
" he knew any thing of a letter from Gardiner and Knyvet,
" the king's ambassadors at the emperor's court, of a motion
" made to them for a reconciliation with that bishop ; which
" was brought to the king at Dover, he being then there.
    " In answer to this he writes, he had never been with the
" king at Dover since the duke of Richmond died ; but for
" any such overture, he had never heard any thing of it, nor
" did any person ever mention it to him.   It had been said in
" council, when sir Francis Brian was like to have died, as a
" thing reported by him, that the bishop of Winchester had
" said, he could devise a way to set all things right between
" the king and the bishop of Rome : upon which, as he re-
" members, sir Ralph Sadler was sent to sir Francis, to ask
" the truth of that ; but sir Francis denied it : and this was

" all that ever he heard of any such overture. It seems these
" were all the questions that were put to him, to which those
" were his answers. He therefore prayed the lords to inter-
" cede with the king, that his accusers might be brought face
" to face, to say what they had against him; and he did not
" doubt but it should appear he was falsely accused. He de-
" sired to have no more favour than Cromwell had, he himself
" being present when Cromwell was examined. He adds,
" Cromwell was a false man; but he was a true, poor gentle-
" man : he did believe, some false man had laid some great
" thing to his charge. He desired, if he might not see his
" accusers, that he might at least know what the matters
" were; and if he did not answer truly to every point, he
" desired not to live an hour longer.

" He had always been pursued by great enemies about the
" king; so that his fidelity was tried like gold. If he knew
" wherein he had offended, he would freely confess it. On 169
" Tuesday in the last Whitsun-week he moved the king, that
" a marriage might be made between his daughter (the duchess
" of Richmond) and sir Thomas Seymour; and that his son
" Surrey's children might, by cross-marriages, be allied to my
" lord great chamberlain's children; (the earl of Hertford.)
" He appealed to the king, whether his intention in these
" motions did not appear to be honest. He next reckons up
" his enemies : cardinal Wolsey confessed to him at Asher,
" that he had studied for fourteen years how to destroy him,
" set on to it by the duke of Suffolk, the marquis of Exeter,
" and the lord Sandys, who often told him, that if he did not
" put him out of the way, he would undo him. When the
" marquis of Exeter suffered, Cromwell examined his wife
" more strictly concerning him than all other men; of which
" she sent him word by her brother, the lord Mountjoy : and
" Cromwell had often said to himself, that he was a happy
" man that his wife knew nothing against him, otherwise
" she would undo him. The late duke of Buckingham, at the
" bar, where his father sat lord high steward, said, that he
" himself was the person in the world whom he had hated
" most, thinking he had done him ill offices with the king :
" but, he said, he then saw the contrary. Rice, that married
" his sister, often said, he wished he could find the means to

" thrust his dagger in him. It was well known to many ladies
" in the court how much both his two nieces, whom it pleased
" the king to marry, had hated him : he had discovered to the
" king that for which his mother-in-law was attainted of mis-
" prision of treason. He had always served the king faith-
" fully, but had of late received greater favours of him than
" in times past : what could therefore move him to be now
" false to him? *A poor man as I am, yet I am his own near*
" *kinsman. Alas! alas! my lords,* (writes he,) *that ever it*
" *should be thought any untruth to be in me.* He prays them
" to lay this before the king, and jointly to beseech him to
" grant the desires contained in it. So he ends it with such
" submissions, as he hoped might mollify the king."

Here I must add a small correction, because I promised it
to the late sir Robert Southwell, for whose great worth and
virtues I had that esteem which he well deserved. Sir Richard
Southwell was concerned in the evidence against the duke of
Norfolk. He gave me a memorandum, which I promised to
remember when I reviewed my History. There were two
brothers, sir Richard and sir Robert, who were often confounded, an *R* serving for both their christened names. Sir
Richard was a privy counsellor to Henry the Eighth, king
Edward, and queen Mary : the second brother, sir Robert,
was master of the rolls in the time of Henry the Eighth, and
in the beginning of Edward the Sixth. I had confounded
these, and in two several places called sir Richard master of
the rolls[29].

I have now set forth all that I find concerning the duke of
Norfolk : by which it appears, that he was designed to be
destroyed only upon suspicion; and his enemies were put on
running far back to old stories, to find some colours to justify
170 so black a prosecution. This was the last act of the king's
reign; which, happily for the old duke, was not finished, when
the king's death prevented the execution.

Thus I have gone over all those passages in this reign that
have fallen in my way since I wrote my History. I have so
carefully avoided repeating any thing that was in my former
work, that I have perhaps not made it clear enough, into what
parts of it every thing here related ought to be taken in. Nor

A recapi-
tulation of
king Hen-
ry's reign.

[29] [See part ii. pp. 15, 149.]

have I put in my Collection any of those papers that either
the lord Herbert or Mr. Strype had published, one or two only
excepted in each of them: but these I put in it, both because
I copied them from the originals, when I did not reflect on
their being published by those writers, and because they
seemed of great importance to the parts of my History, to
which they belonged.   Some of these being very short, and
the others not long, I thought the inserting them made my
Collection more complete.   I would not lessen the value of
books, to which I have been too much beholden, to make so
ill a return; to the last especially, from whose works I have
taken that which seemed necessary to make the History as
full as might be, but refer my reader to such vouchers as he
will find in them.

His mind
corrupted
by a course
of flattery.

And now having ended what I have to say of king Henry,
I will add a few reflections on him and on his reign.   He had
certainly a greater measure of knowledge in learning, more
particularly in divinity, than most princes of that or of any
age: that gave occasion to those excessive flatteries, which in
a great measure corrupted his temper, and disfigured his
whole government.   It is deeply rooted in the nature of man
to love to be flattered, because self-love makes men their own
flatterers, and so they do too easily take down the flatteries
that are offered them by others; who, when they expect advantages by it, are too ready to give this incense to their
vanity, according to the returns that they expect from it.

Few are so honest and disinterested in their friendship as to
consider the real good of others, but choose rather to comply
with their humour and vanity: and since princes have most to
give, flattery (too common to all places) is the natural growth
of courts; in which, if there are some few so unfashioned to
those places as to seek the real good and honour of the prince
by the plain methods of blunt honesty, which may carry them
to contradict a mistaken prince, to shew him his errors, and
with a true firmness of courage to try to work even against the
grain; while they pursue that, which, though it is the real
advantage and honour of the prince, yet it is not agreeable to
some weak or perverse humour in him; these are soon over-
topped by a multitude of flatterers, who will find it an easy
work to undermine such faithful ministers, because their own

candour and fidelity makes them use none of the arts of a coun-
termine.   Thus the flattered prince easily goes into the hands
of those who humour and please him most, without regarding
either the true honour of the master or the good of the community.

171   If weak princes, of a small measure of knowledge, and a low
capacity, fall into such hands, the government will dwindle into
an unactive languishing; which will make them a prey to all
about them, and expose them to universal contempt both at
home and abroad: while the flatterers make their own advantages the chief measure of the government, and do so besiege
the abused and deluded prince, that he fancies he is the wonder
and delight of all the world, when he is under the last degrees
of the scorn of the worst, and of the pity of the best of his
people.

The course of all courts.

But if these flatterers gain the ascendant over princes of
genius and capacity, they put them on great designs, under
the false representations of conquests and glory; they engage
them either to make or break leagues at pleasure, to enter
upon hostilities without any previous steps or declarations of
war, to ruin their own people for supporting those wars that
are carried on with all the methods both of barbarity and perfidy: while a studied luxury and vanity at home is kept up, to
amuse and blind the ignorant beholders with a false show of
lustre and magnificence.

This had too deep a root in king Henry, and was too long
flattered by cardinal Wolsey, to be ever afterwards brought
into due bounds and just measures; yet Wolsey pursued the
true maxims of England, of maintaining the balance during
his ministry.   Our trade lay then so entirely in the Netherlands, without our seeming to think to carry it farther, that it
was necessary to maintain a good correspondence with those
provinces; and Charles' dominions were so widely scattered,
that, till Francis was taken prisoner, it was visibly the interest
of England to continue still jealous of France, and to favour
Charles.   But the taking of Francis the First changed the
scene; France was then to be supported; it was also so exhausted, and Charles' revenue was so increased, that, without
great sums both lent him and expended by England, all must

Wolsey began it but was a wise minister.

have sunk under Charles' power, if England had not held the balance.

A great occasion of flattery given by his book.

[Seckendorf, lib. i. § cxiv. p. 187.]

It was also a masterpiece in Wolsey to engage the king to own that the book against Luther was written by him, in which the secret of those who, no doubt, had the greatest share in composing it was so closely laid, that it never broke out. Seckendorf tells us, that Luther believed it was writ by Lee, who was a zealous Thomist, and had been engaged in disputes with Erasmus, and was afterwards made archbishop of York. If any of those who still adhered to the old doctrines had been concerned in writing it, probably, when they saw king Henry depart from so many points treated of in it, they would have gone beyond sea, and have robbed him of that false honour and those excessive praises which that book had procured him. It is plain More wrote it not: for the king having shewed it him before it was published, he (as he mentions in one of his letters to Cromwell) told the king, that he had raised the papacy so high, that it might be objected to him, if he should happen to have any dispute with the pope, as was often between princes and popes; and it will be found in the remarks on the former volumes, that he in another letter [30] says, he was a *sorter* of that book. This seems to relate only to the digesting it into method and order.

How far king Henry was sincere in pretending scruples of 172 conscience with relation to his first marriage, can only be known to God. His suit of divorce was managed at a vast expense, in a course of many years; in all which time, how strong soever his passion was for Anne Boleyn, yet her being with child so soon after their marriage was a clear evidence that till then they had no unlawful commerce. It does not appear that Wolsey deserved his disgrace, unless it was, that by the commission given to the two legates they were empowered to act conjunctly or severally; so that, though Campeggio refused to concur, he might have given sentence legally; yet he being trusted by the pope, his acting according to instructions did not deserve so severe a correction: and had any ma-

---

[30] [See part i. p. 31, note 21. The expression does not occur in any letter of More's, but in his life by Roper.]

terial discovery been made to render Wolsey criminal, it may
be reasonably supposed it would have been published.

The new flatterers falling in with the king's passion outdid
and ruined Wolsey.　More was the glory of the age; and his
advancement was the king's honour more than his own, who
was a true Christian philosopher.　He thought the cause of the
king's divorce was just, and as long as it was prosecuted at the
court of Rome, so long he favoured it: but when he saw that
a breach with that court was like to follow, he left the great
post he was in with a superior greatness of mind.　It was a fall
great enough to retire from that into a private state of life:
but the carrying matters so far against him as the king did,
was one of the justest reproaches of that reign.　More's superstition seems indeed contemptible; but the constancy of his
mind was truly wonderful.

Cromwell's ministry was in a constant course of flattery and
submission; but by that he did great things, that amaze one
who has considered them well.　The setting up the king's supremacy instead of the usurpations of the papacy, and the
rooting out the monastic state in England, considering the
wealth, the numbers, and the zeal of the monks and friars in
all the parts of the kingdom, as it was a very bold undertaking,
so it was executed with great method, and performed in so
short a time, and with so few of the convulsions that might
have been expected, that all this shews what a master he was,
that could bring such a design to be finished in so few years,
with so little trouble or danger.

But in conclusion, an unfortunate marriage, to which he advised the king, not proving acceptable, and he being unwilling
to destroy what he himself had brought about, was no doubt
backward in the design of breaking it, when the king had told
him of it: and then, upon no other visible ground but because
Anne of Cleves grew more obliging to the king than she was
formerly, the king suspected that Cromwell had betrayed his
secret, and had engaged her to a softer deportment on design
to prevent the divorce; and did upon that, disgrace and destroy him.

The duke of Norfolk was never till Cromwell's fall the first
in favour; but he had still kept his post by perpetual submission and flattery.　He was sacrificed at last to the king's

[margin: The character of More.]

[margin: Cromwell's ministry.]

jealousy, fearing that he might be too great in his son's infancy; and, being considered as the head of the popish party, might engage in an easy competition with the Seymours during the minority of his son: for the points he was at first examined on were of an old date, of no consequence, and supported by no proof.

173

The king's inconstancy in matters of religion. When the king first threw off the pope's yoke, the reformers offered him in their turn all the flatteries they could decently give: and if they could have had the patience to go no further than as he was willing to parcel out a reformation to them, he had perhaps gone further in it. But he seemed to think, that as it was pretended in popery, that infallibility was to go along with the supremacy, therefore those who had yielded the one ought likewise to submit to the other; he turned against them when he saw that their complaisance did not go so far. And upon that, the adherers to the old opinions returned to their old flatteries, and for some time seemed to have brought him quite back to them: which probably might have wrought more powerfully, but that he found the old leaven of the papacy was still working in them. So that he was all the while fluctuating: sometimes making steps to a reformation, but then returning back to his old notions. One thing probably wrought much on him. It has appeared, that he had great apprehensions of the council that was to meet at Trent, and that the emperor's engagements to restrain the council from proceeding in his matter was the main article of the new friendship made up between them: and it may be very reasonably supposed, that the emperor represented to him, that nothing could secure that matter so certainly as his not proceeding to any further innovations in religion; more particularly his adhering firmly to the received doctrine of Christ's presence in the sacrament, and the other articles set forth by him. This agreeing with his own opinion, had, as may be well imagined, no small share in the change of his conduct at that time.

The dextrous application of flattery had generally a powerful effect on him: but whatsoever he was, and how great soever his pride and vanity and his other faults were, he was a great instrument in the hand of Providence for many good ends: he first opened the door to let light in upon the nation; he delivered it from the yoke of blind and implicit obedience; he put the scriptures in the hands of the people, and took away the terror they were formerly under by the cruelty of the ecclesiastical courts ; he declared this church to be an entire and perfect body within itself, with full authority to decree and to regulate all things, without any dependence on any foreign power ; and he did so unite the supreme headship over this church to the imperial crown of this realm, that it seemed a just consequence that was made by some in a popish reign, that he who would not own that this supremacy was in him, did by that renounce the crown, of which that title was made so essential a part, that they could no more be separated.

He attacked popery in its strong holds the monasteries, and destroyed them all : and thus he opened the way to all that came after, even down to our days.   So that, while we see the folly and weakness of man in all his personal failings, which were very many and very enormous ; we at the same time see both the justice, the wisdom, and the goodness of God, in 174 making him, who was once the pride and glory of popery, become its scourge and destruction ; and in directing his pride and passion so as to bring about, under the dread of his unrelenting temper, a change that a milder reign could not have compassed without great convulsions and much confusion : above all the rest, we ought to adore the goodness of God in rescuing us by his means from idolatry and superstition : from the vain and pompous shows in which the worship of God was dressed up, so as to vie with heathenism itself, into a simplicity of believing, and a purity of worship, conform to the nature and attributes of God, and the doctrine and example of the Son of God.

May we ever value this as we ought ; and may we in our tempers and lives so express the beauty of this holy religion, that it may ever shine among us, and may shine out from us, to all round about us : and then we may hope that God will preserve it to us, and to posterity after us, for ever !

THE HISTORY   175

OF

THE REFORMATION

OF

THE CHURCH OF ENGLAND.

PART III.—BOOK IV.

Of what happened during the reign of King Edward
the VIth, from the year 1547 to the year 1553.

1547. I HAD such copious materials when I wrote of this king,
partly from the original council-book, for the two first years
of that reign, but chiefly from the journal writ in that king's
own hand, that I shall not be able to offer the reader so many
new things in this as I did in the former, and as I may be
able to do in the succeeding reign. Some gleanings I have,
which I hope will not be unacceptable.

A true ac-
count of a
paper of
Luther's
wrong
published
in my
History.

  I begin with acknowledging a great error committed in
copying out a letter of Luther's, that I found among Bucer's
Collections. The noble Seckendorf was the first that admonished me of this; but with a modesty suitable to so great a
man: without that rancour in which some among ourselves
have vented their ill nature against me. I took the sure
method to confess my error, and to procure an exact collated
copy of that paper from that learned body to whose library it

Collect.
Numb. 1.

belongs; which will be found in the Collection. It is an
Original in Luther's own hand; but it could not have been

easily read, if Bucer had not writ out a copy of it, which is bound up in the same volume with the original.   It was an instruction that Luther gave to Melancthon, when he went into Hesse, in the year 1534, to meet and treat with Bucer, upon that fatal difference, concerning the manner of the presence in the sacrament.   " In which it appears, that Luther was so far " from departing from his opinion, that he plainly says, he " could not communicate with those of the Zuinglian persuasion; " but he would willingly tolerate them, in hope that in time " they might come to communicate together.   And as for a " political agreement, he does not think the diversity of reli-" gion ought to hinder that ; no more than it was a bar to " marriage or commerce, which may be among those of dif-" ferent religions."   And now I have, I hope, delivered myself from all the censures, to which the wrong publishing of that paper had exposed me.

I should next enter into the historical passages of king Edward's reign ; but a great discovery, made with relation to the most important foreign transaction that happened both in king Henry and king Edward's reign, (I mean the council of Trent ; the first session of which was in the former reign, and 176 the second in this,) has given me an opportunity of acquainting the world with many extraordinary passages relating to it.

There was a large parcel of original letters writ to Gran-velle, then bishop of Arras, afterwards cardinal, and the chief minister of Charles the emperor, that, when he left the Nether-lands, were in the hands of some of his secretaries ; and were not carried away by him.   About fifty years after that [1], Mr. William Trumbull, then king James the First's envoy at Brussels, grandfather to sir William Trumbull, (a person eminently distinguished by his learning and zeal for religion, as well as by the embassies, and other great employments, he has so worthily borne,) got these into his hands [2] : no doubt, under

(margin) Vargas' letters concerning the council of Trent.

---

[1] [From the preface to the French translation of these letters, it appears that they were brought to England in 1625.]

[2] [Ce fut durant sa résidence à Bruxelles que les mémoires de Vargas lui tombérent entre les mains. Nous ne savons pas bien comment

il trouva quelque chose de si précieux.   Tout ce qu'on peut conjecturer, c'est qu'une grande partie des papiers du Cardinal de Granvelle put demeurer entre les mains de quelqu'un des ses secretaires Flamans, lors que ce Ministre fut obligé de sortir des Pais-bas et que

the promise of absolute secrecy, during the lives of those who
had them : since if they had been then published, it might
have been easily traced from whence they must have come;
which would have been fatal to those who had parted with
them, in a court so bigoted as was that of Albert and Isabella[3].
I have read over the whole series of that worthy gentleman's
own letters to king James the First, and saw so much honesty
and zeal running through them all, that it seems nothing
under some sacred tie could have obliged both father and son
to keep such a treasure so secret from all the world, especially
Padre Paolo's History coming out at that time in London ; to
which these letters, as far as they went, which is from the 7th
of October 1551, to the last of February 1551–2, would have
given an authentic confirmation. I have been trusted by the
noble owner with the perusal of them. It is impossible to
doubt of their being originals : the subscriptions and seals of
most of them are still entire.

Translated
into Eng-
lish by Dr.
Geddes.

These were by sir William deposited in bishop Stillingfleet's
hands, when he was sent to his foreign employments, that such
use might be made of them, when he found a person that was
master of the Spanish tongue, as the importance of the discovery might deserve. Soon after that, my very worthy friend
Dr. Geddes returned from Lisbon, after he had been above ten
years preacher to the English factory there : and since he is
lately dead, I hope I shall be forgiven, to take the liberty of
saying somewhat concerning him. He was a learned and a
wise man : he had a true notion of popery, as a political com-
bination, managed by falsehood and cruelty, to establish a temporal empire in the person of the popes. All his thoughts and
studies were chiefly employed in detecting this ; of which he

M. Trumbull les a eus des héritiers
du secretaire."—Preface to French
translation.]

[3] [" Le zèle ardent que M. Trumbull eut toujours pour sa Réligion
nous fait penser que s'il n'a pas fait
imprimer lui-mesme les lettres et les
mémoires qui concernent le concile
de Trente, c'est qu'il avoit promis
apparemment de les tenir secrets
de peur que ceux, qui l'en faisoient
le maître, ne fussent exposez à quel-

que fâcheuse affaire, pour avoir mis
des papiers de cette conséquence
entre les mains d'un Protestant.
Les troubles du règne de Charles I.
et du commencement de celui de
son successeur, pûrent empescher
que M. Trumbull le fils n'eut le
loisir de mettre en ordre et d'exam-
iner avec plus d'application les papiers que son Pére lui avoit laissez."
—Ibid.]

has given many useful and curious essays in the treatises he wrote, which are all highly valuable. When bishop Stilling-fleet understood that he was master of the Spanish tongue, he put all these papers in his hands[4]. He translated them into English, intending to print the originals in Spanish with them : but none of our printers would undertake that ; they reckoning, that where the vent of the book might be looked for, which must be in Spain and Italy, they were sure it would not be suffered to be sold : he was therefore forced to print the trans-lation in English[5], without printing the originals.

177   Since that time, that learned and judicious Frenchman, And into Monsieur Le Vassor, has published a translation of them in French by M. Le French[6], with many curious reflections : but though he found Vassor. that a complete edition of the letters in Spanish was a thing that the booksellers in Holland would not undertake, yet he has helped that all he could, by giving the parts of the letters that were the most critical, and the most important, in Spanish. Both these books are highly valuable. The chief writer of those letters, Vargas, was a man not only very learned, but of a superior genius to most of that age, as appears both by the letters themselves, and by the great posts he went through. He was specially employed by the emperor, both in the session that was held in the former reign, and in that which sat in

---

[4] [" Ce soin étoit réservé a la diligence de M. le Chevalier Trum-bull, a qui le public est redevable d'une si heureuse découverte. Lors qu'il fut nommé Envoié Extraordi-naire à la Cour de France, il mit les lettres et les mémoires de Vargas et des autres sur le concile de Trente, entre les mains de M. le Docteur Stillingfleet alors Doien de saint Paul de Londres et maintenant Evêque de Worchester. Ce savant Prelat les garda quelque temps avant que de les donner a M. le Docteur Geddis qui les a traduits en Anglois. Enfin M. le Chevalier Trumbull me fit la grace de me les confier l'été dernier."—Le Vassor, Preface.]

[5] [The Council of Trent no free assembly : more fully discovered by a collection of Letters and papers of

the learned Dr. Vargas and other great ministers who assisted at the said synod in considerable posts. Published from the original Manu-scripts in Spanish which were pro-cured by the right honourable Sir William Trumbull's grandfather, envoy at Brussels in the reign of King James the First, &c. by Mi-chael Geddes, LL.D., and Chan-cellor of the Cathedral Church of Sarum. 8vo. Lond. 1697.}

[6] [Lettres et Memoires de Fran-çois de Vargas, de Pierre de Mal-venda et de quelques Evêques d'E-spagne touchant le Concile de Trente. Traduits de l'Espagnol, avec des Remarques, Par Mr. Michel Le Vassor. A Amsterdam, Chez Pierre Brunel, Marchand Libraire, sur le Dam, à la Bible d'Or. M.DCC.]

this reign ; to which only these letters do relate.   He was the
chief of the council that the emperor's ambassadors had, in
matters in which either divinity or canon law (the last being
his particular profession) were necessary : and such a value
was set on him, that the emperor sent him ambassador to the

[Dec. 3,
1563.]
republic of Venice.   And when the last session was held by
pope Pius the Fourth, Philip sent him ambassador to Rome,
as the person that understood best how to manage that court,
with relation to the session of the council.

The fraud
and inso-
lence of the
legate.
I think it may give the reader a just idea of that council,
both of the fraud and insolence of the legate, and of the method
in which matters were carried there, to see some of the more
signal passages in those letters ; that it may both give him
true impressions of what was transacted there, and may move

Octob. 7.
[p. 117.]
him to have recourse to the letters themselves[8].   " He sets
" forth, how much the pope and his ministers dreaded the
" coming of the protestants to the council.   We can plainly
" perceive that they are not themselves, nor in a condition to
" treat about any business, when they are brought to touch on
" that point.——These may, to their mortification, deliver
" their minds freely against abuses, and some other things[7].

[p. 118.]
" ——Whosoever offers any thing that is not grateful to the
" legate, or that doth not suit exactly with some people's pre-
" possessions, he is reported to have spoke ill, and to think
" worse, and to have taken what he said out of I do not know

[p. 119.]
" whom.——There are several matters, which the legate
" ought to treat with more deliberation than he hath hitherto
" handled things : I pray God give him grace to understand
" this."

The pro-
mise that
the empe-
ror made
the pope.
" In the next letter, without date, mention is made of a
" letter that the emperor wrote to the pope ; in which he did
" assure him, that nothing should be done in the council, but
" that which he had a mind should be done in it : and that he
" would oblige the prelates to hold their tongues, and to let
" things pass without any opposition.   The copy of this being

---

[7] [Ils apréhendent de trouver
quelque chose qui les arrête en leur
chemin et de voir ici des gens qui
parleront librement contre les abus,
et qui diront des choses qui ne sont
pas du goût de la cour de Rome.—
p. 117.]

[8] [The quotations have been made
from the English version. The marginal references are to the French.]

" shewed the ambassador, he was astonished at it: but Vargas
" said, it was not to be understood literally; (in the original
" it is *judaically ;*) it was only writ to bring the pope to grant *Judaice.*
" the bull: but that it was not intended by it that the pope [p. 124.]
" should be suffered to do such things as would bring all to
" ruin; but only to do such things as are reasonable.　He
178 " adds in Latin, that the liberty the pope took was not only a
" disease and sickness of mind, but was really grown to a fury
" and a madness."　Here the *spirit* of the promise is set up
against the *letter ;* and a strict adhering to words is counted a
part of the yoke of Judaism, from which some most Christian
princes have thought fit, on many occasions, to emancipate
themselves.

In another letter he sets forth the behaviour of the prelates. Oct. 12.
" The legate never so much as acquaints them with the matter; [p. 125.]
" all things appearing well to them at first sight; and who, [p. 129.]
" knowing nothing of matters until they are just ready to be _{The bi-}shops knew
" pronounced, pass them without any more ado.——I am not what they did.
" willing to let you know how things are carried here, and [p. 131.]
" what the pope's aims are; who seeks to authorize all his own
" pretensions by the council.——There are several other things [p. 131.]
" I am not at all satisfied with, which were carried here with
" the same sleight that pope Paul made use of.——And is not
" this a blessed beginning of a council?——As to the canons [p. 132.]
" of reformation,—they are of so trivial a nature, that several
" were ashamed to hear them; and had they not been wrapped
" up in good language together, they would have appeared to
" the world to be what they are."

In another letter he writes; " I cannot see how either catho- Oct. 28.
" lics or heretics can be satisfied with what is done here.—— [p. 174.]
" All that is done here is done by the way of Rome: for the [p. 175.]
" legate, though it were necessary to save the world from
" sinking, will not depart one tittle from the orders he receives
" from thence; nor indeed from any thing that he has once
" himself resolved on."

" In another he writes; " As for the legate, he goes on Nov. 12.
" still in his old way; consuming of time to the last hour in [p. 200.]
" disputations and congregations concerning doctrines; and
" will at last produce something in a hurry, in false colours,
" that may look plausible: by which means they have no time

" to read, and much less to understand what they are about.
" ———Words or persuasions do signify but very little in this
" place ; and I suppose they are not of much greater force at
" Rome.———By what I can perceive, both God and his majesty
" are like to be very much dishonoured by what will be done
" here : and if things should go on thus, and be brought to
" such an issue as the pope and his ministers aim at, and give
" out, the church will be left in a much worse condition than
[p. 201.] " she was in before.———I pray God the pope may be prevailed
" on to alter his measures ; though I shall reckon it a miracle
" if he is, and shall thank God for it as such."

Nov. 26.
The pride
and impu-
dence of
the legate.
[p. 218.]
In another he writes ; " There are not words to express the
" pride, the disrespect and shamelessness, wherewith the legate
" proceeds.———The success and end of this synod, if God by a
" miracle does not prevent it, will be such as I have foretold.
" I say, by a miracle ; because it is not to be done by any
" human means : so that his majesty does but tire himself in
[p. 219.] " vain, in negotiating with the pope and his ministers.———The
" legate has hammered out such an infamous reformation (for
" it deserves no better epithet) as must make us a jest to the 179
" world.   The prelates that are here resent it highly ; many
" of them reckoning that they wound their consciences by
" holding their tongues, and by suffering things to be carried
" thus."

[p. 220.]
Upon the point of collating to benefices, he writes ; " We
" ought to put them to shew what right the pope has to collate
" to any benefice whatsoever. I will undertake to demonstrate,
" from the principles and foundations of the law of God, and of
" nature, and of men ; and from the ancient usage of the
" church, and from good policy ; that he has no manner of
" right to it : and all this without doing injury to his dignity,
[p. 221.] " and the plenitude of his power.   He advises the leaving
" those matters to a better time, in which God will purge the
[p. 222.] " sons of Levi : which purgation must come, and that with a
" severe scourge ; it being impossible that a thing so violent,
" and so fraught with abuses, should hold long : the whole
" nerve of ecclesiastical discipline being broke, and the goods
" of the church made a perfect trade and merchandise."

No good to
be expect-
ed from a
council.
[p. 213.]
Speaking of general councils, he writes ; " This which is
" now sitting here will totally undeceive the world, so as to

" convince it, that, by reason of the opposition and industry of
" the popes, to engross all to themselves, nothing of reforma-
" tion is ever to be expected from a general council. I would
" not have things, wherein the pope and his court have such
" great interest and pretensions, to be decided or handled [p. 224.]
" here; since it cannot be done but to our great prejudice, and
" to the great detriment of the whole church; which at present
" has neither strength nor courage to resist; and if God do
" not remedy it, I do not see when it will."

Speaking of exemptions, he writes; " The canonists have He com-
" made strange work; having made many jests, as well as the exemp-
" falsehoods, to pass for current truths. When I speak of the tion of
" canonists, I speak as a thief of the family, being sensible of chapters.
" the abuses which have been authorized by them in the
" church. The exemption of chapters ought to have been
" quite taken away, that so there might be something of order
" and discipline, and that they who are the head should not be
" made the feet. It troubles me to see how those matters are
" managed and determined here; the legate doing whatever [p. 235.]
" he had a mind to, without either numbering or weighing the
" opinions of the divines and prelates; hurrying and reserving
" the substance of things, which ought to have been well
" weighed and digested, to the last minute: the major part
" not knowing what they are a doing. I mean before the
" fact; for believing that Christ will not suffer them to err in
" their determinations, I shall bow down my head to them, and
" believe all the matters of faith that shall be decided by them:
" I pray God every body else may do the same. The taking
" no care to reform innumerable abuses has destroyed so many [p. 236.]
" provinces and kingdoms; and it is justly to be feared, that
" what is done in this council may endanger the destroying of
" the rest. I must tell you further, that this council drawing
" so near an end, is what all people rejoice at here exceed-
180 " ingly; there being a great many who wish it never had [p. 237.]
" met: and for my own part, I would to God it had never
" been called; for I am mistaken if it do not leave things
" worse than it found them."

In another of the same date, if there is no error in writing, A decree
" he complains that the decree of the doctrine was not finished amended
" till the night before the session: so that many bishops gave passed.
[p. 243.]

" their *placet* to what they neither did nor could understand.
" The divines of Louvaine and Cologne, and some Spanish
" divines, being much dissatisfied with several of those matters,
[p. 244.] " have publicly declared they were so. This is a very bad
" business : and should things of this nature come once to be
" so public, it must totally ruin the credit of all that has been
" done, or shall be done hereafter ; and must hinder the council
" from being ever received, either in Flanders or in Germany.
[p. 245.] " The bishop of Verdun, speaking to the canons of reformation,
" said, they would be unprofitable, and unworthy of the synod,
" calling it a *pretended reformation ;* the legate fell upon him
[p. 246.] " with very rude language, calling him a boy, an impudent
" raw man, with many other hard names : nor would he suffer
" him to speak a word in his own defence, telling him with
" great heat, he knew how to have him chastised. It is really
" a matter of amazement to see how things appertaining to
" God are handled here ; and that there should not be one to
[p. 247.] " contend for him, or any that have the courage to speak in
" his behalf ; but that we should be all dumb dogs that cannot
" bark."

Nov. 28.   In another he writes, " that the legate himself wished that
[p. 256.] " the decrees were corrected as to some particulars : and in
" another, without date, he tells how the divines were employed
" in correcting them."   This secret was never heard of before :
father Paul knew nothing of it. A decree after it has passed
in council was thus secretly corrected by divines ; so the infallibility was removed from the council, and lodged with the
divines.

Dec. 19.   In another he writes ; " It would have been a happy thing
It had been " that this council had never met ; which is no more than
happy that
the council " what I have often wished and declared : by reason of the
had never
met. " many mischiefs it has already done, and is still doing.   It is
[p. 326.] " to little purpose, either in this, or any following age, to hope
" for any thing of a reformation from a general council ; or to
[p. 330.] " see any better order therein than is in this.   He supposes
" the emperor will still continue to solicit the pope that things
" may not be carried there at such a scandalous rate as they
" have been hitherto : and that he will take care that no occa-
" sion be given to the council for to disperse itself upon the
" prelates speaking their mind freely, or denying their consent

" to such matters as are not convenient; which is a thing that
" may very justly be feared."

In another[9] he writes; " This synod must end tumultuously Jan. 10.
" and ingloriously." In another he writes, " that it was an [p. 402.]
Jan. 19.
" astonishing thing that the legate had foisted in several pas- [p. 429.]
" sages into the doctrine of orders, which must of necessity
" ruin all.   By the brutal violences, pretensions, and obstinacy
" of the legate, things are running into such a state, as must [p. 430.]
181 " in the end, if I am not mistaken, make both himself and the
" whole earth to tremble : or if it does not make him tremble,
" it must be because he is given over to a reprobate sense ; as
" in truth he seems to be abundantly, in every thing that he
" does."

In another he writes; " All they drive at is to get the Jan. 20.
" pope's pretensions established under the doctrine of order ; [p. 431.]
" and so, instead of healing, to destroy and ruin all : those
" being matters which were never so much as proposed or dis-
" puted in the council : neither is it fitting, as things stand
" here, that they, or any thing else of the same nature, should
" be meddled with in this synod."

He enlarges on the authority of bishops being derived from [p. 435.]
Christ, " though subjected to the pope ; and he writes, that
" upon this bottom only the hierarchy of the church can be
" established : to settle it on any other, is in effect to confound
" and destroy it.   Nevertheless, the pope, if he could carry
" this point, though all things else were ruined, and whatever
" was done in the ancient church condemned, would find his
" own account in it : for after that there would be no possi-
" bility of ever having any thing redressed."   The decree of
order, on which the legate had set his heart, is set down at the [p. 437.]
end of this letter ; the translation of it into English runs thus :

" This[10] may be called the new Jerusalem, that comes down The decree
concerning

---

[9] [The writer writing in great haste probably dated this letter Jan. 10 instead of Jan. 11.]

[10] [" Hanc autem veram Hieru-salem de cœlo descendentem merito appellari posse, quod per antiquam Hierusalem veteris Ecclesiæ ordi-natissimam politiam adumbrata, et ad cælestis Hierusalem formam et exemplar exacta fuerit.   Nam ut illa sub uno supremo rectore varios et diversos ministrantium continet ordines, ita visibilis Christi ecclesia summum ipsius Vicarium, pro unico et supremo capite in terris habet cujus dispensatione sic reliquis om-nibus membris officia distribuuntur, ut suis quæque in ordinibus et sta-

the pope's
authority
proposed,
but not
passed.

" from heaven ; which was by the most exactly regulated policy
" of the old Jerusalem, shadowed only as a pattern to re-
" present the heavenly Jerusalem : for as she had many dif-
" ferent orders, under one chief governor, so the visible church
" of Christ has his chief vicar ; for he is the *only* and *supreme*
" *head* in earth, by whose dispensation offices are distributed
" so to all the other members, that, in the several orders and
" stations in which they are placed, they may execute their
" functions to the good of the whole church with the greatest
" peace and union. A deputation of twenty was named to
[p. 439.] " consider of this. The legate and the two presidents making
" three of that number ; it was severely attacked by the bishop
" of Guadix [11]."

The last of
February.
[p. 556.]
In his last letter he writes, "That the legates would one
" way or other bring about the dissolution of the synod : which
" will be certainly done, if they can but get the said clauses
" determined ; because in them they will have gained all that
" they desire : and after that they will never stand in need of
" any more councils for to serve their pretensions. And in
" case they should not be able to carry those points, they will
" then, to rid themselves of this yoke that is upon their neck,
" and of the fears they will be under, when they shall find that
" they are not able to bring the synod to do all the mischief to
" the church, and to the authority of the present and all future
" general councils, that the pope and his ministers would have
" them do, they will then perplex and confound all."

tionibus collocata, munera sua in to-
tius ecclesiæ utilitatem, cum max-
imâ pace et unione exequantur."—
p. 437.]

[11] [The answer given by the bishop of Guadix, when consulted on
the point, was as follows :—Hes-
ternâ nocte perlegi doctrinam ; nam
semel antea legeram. In quâ licet
multa bene dicantur, habet tamen
nonnulla falsa, scatet opinionibus :
ob idque censerem consultius fieri
si dimittatur, ne dubia obtrudantur
pro certis a sanctâ synodo. Upon
the legate's applying for a more
particular explanation of his meaning, he replied, Non est quod mihi
occurrat magis clarum et particu-
lare super doctrinâ quam id quod
dixi ; scilicet mihi non placere ob
causas dictas, quæ sufficientes et
particulares satis videntur, de quibus poterit sacra deputatio judi-
care ; tum etiam, quia cum doc-
trina non sit necessaria ad Syno-
dales determinationes, et vix con-
cludi possit sine offendiculo opinio-
num quæ a Catholicis tenentur, ut
jam experimento didicimus, non
possum non reputare doctrinam
prolixam et hujusmodi periculis ex-
positam, ne dicam obnoxiam.—
p. 438.]

These are very clear discoveries of the zeal and indignation He ex-
which possessed this great statesman during this whole session. presses the same opin-
He shews also the opinion he had of the former session under ion of the
pope Paul, (in which he had likewise assisted,) in the directions former session under
182 he gives concerning the government of a council, and of the pope Paul.
office of an ambassador, which he drew up before the council [p 49.]
was reassembled, in this its second session, in which these
words are:

" In the whole conduct of this council of Trent there does
" not appear the least footsteps of any of the forementioned
" essentials of a general council: on the contrary, the most
" pernicious and effectual methods that can be contrived have
" been taken to destroy liberty totally; and to rob councils of
" that authority, which in case of great storms used to be the
" sheet-anchor of the church: by which means they have cut
" off all hope of ever having any abuses that infest the church
" redressed, to the great disparagement of all past as well as
" future councils; from which no good is ever to be expected.

" The conduct of this council has been of pernicious conse- No shadow
" quence: in which, under the title of directing it, the pope's of liberty in the council.
" legates have so managed matters, that nothing but what they [p. 50.]
" have a mind to can be proposed, discussed, or defined there-
" in; and that too after such a manner as they would have it:
" all the liberty that is here being only imaginary; so that
" their naming it is nothing but cheat and banter: which is so
" notorious, that several of the prelates, even among the pope's
" pensioners, have not the face to deny it.　The clause that [p. 51.]
" they have inserted into the canons of reformation; which is,
" saving in all things the authority of the apostolical see [12];
" is telling the world, in plain terms, that what the pope does
" not like shall signify nothing.　He writes of certain methods [p. 54.]
" that the legates have used in negotiating with people to
" change their minds: this they have done so often, that it is
" now taken notice of by every body: neither can there be
" any course more pernicious, or destructive of the liberty of
" the council.　The legates many times, when they proposed a [p. 55]
" thing, declared their opinion of it first: nay, in the middle
" of voting, when they observed any prelate not to vote as

12 [Salvâ semper in omnibus sedis Apostolicæ auctoritate.—p. 51.]

" they would have him, they have taken upon themselves to
" speak to it, before another was suffered to vote, doing it
" sometimes with soft words, and at other times with harsher ;
" letting others to understand thereby how they would have
" them vote ; many times railing at the prelates, and exposing
" them to scorn, and using such methods as would make one's
" heart bleed to hear of, much more to see.

[p. 56.]   " The common method was, the legates assembled the pre-
" lates in a general congregation the night before the session
" was to be held. Then they read the decrees to them, as
" they and their friends had been pleased to form them. By
" which means, and by their not being understood by a great
" many prelates, some not having the courage to speak their
" minds, and others being quite tired out with the length of
[p. 57.] " the congregation, the decrees were passed. We, who saw
" and observed all these doings, cannot but lament both our
" own condition, and the lost authority of councils [13].

The le- " He shews the legates' drift was to canonize all the abuses 189
gates' way
in correct- " of the court of Rome ; so they never suffered them to be
ing mani-
fest abuses. " treated of freely, but managed them like the compounding
[p. 61.] " of a lawsuit : in all which courses, it is certain the Holy
" Ghost did not assist ; they striving still to authorize abuses,
" and giving the world to understand that the pope is gracious
" in granting them any thing, as if all were his own ; taking
" abuses, though never so pernicious, and splitting them as
" they thought good : by which artifice, that part of the abuse
" which was approved of by the synod becomes perpetual ; and
" for the part that was reprobated, they will, according to their
" custom, find ways to defeat its condemnation.

[p. 62.]   " There is nothing that can be so much as put to the vote
" without the consent of the legates : who, notwithstanding
" that they are (by reason of the great number of pensioners
" which the pope has here) always sure of a majority, do
" nevertheless make use of strange tricks in their conduct of
" the council. Besides, by having made their own creatures
" the secretaries, notaries, and all the other officers of the
" council, they have made it thereby a body, without any

---

[13] [Nos certe qui ea novimus,   Conciliorumque auctoritatem jam
cæteraque observavimus, non pos-   diu deploratam.—p. 57.]
sumus non dolere vicem nostram,

" thing of soul or strength in it : whereas, all those officers
" ought to have been appointed by the council, and especially
" the notaries.

" This is the course that has been hitherto taken in the
" council of Trent, which is employed rather in struggling
" with the pope and his legates, who seek to engross all to
" themselves, than in reforming and remedying the evils under
" which the church groans. I pray God it do not increase [p. 63.]
" them by the course it takes, by artifice and dissimulation, to
" reduce the whole synod to the will of the pope.——It may
" be truly said, we are in a convention of bishops, but not in a
" council [14].——It would have been much better not to have
" celebrated a council at this time, but to have waited till God
" had put the Christian commonwealth in a better disposition ;
" ——rather than to have celebrated one after this manner, with [p. 64.]
" so little fruit, to the great sorrow of catholics, the scorn of
" heretics, and the prejudice of the present and of all future
" councils." So much may serve to shew the sense that Vargas
had of the first as well as of the second session of the council
of Trent.

Malvenda, one of the emperor's divines, that was there,
complains in one letter, " that the decrees, but especially the
" matters of doctrine, were communicated to them very late.
" So that notwithstanding the substance of these decrees may
" be sound, which it is well if it is, nevertheless considering
" that they are to correct them upon a bare hearing them
" read on the eve of a session, that must in my opinion hinder
" them from having that authority and majesty which such
" matters do use to have. I pray God give them grace to
" mend this.——He confesses it was not fit any thing should [Ibid.
" be done without the pope's consent : yet that ought to be P. 159.]
" managed with all possible secrecy, in order to prevent the [p. 160]
" Lutherans, if they should come to know it, from reflecting
" on the liberty of the council, and the freedom that the pre-
184 " lates ought to have ; who might safely enjoy more, without
" having any thing pass to the prejudice of his holiness."

(margin: Malvenda and others made the same complaints. Oct. 12. [Ibid. p. 158]*)*

In another he writes : " As there will not want those that Nov. 22.
" write of this council, so, for my own part, I pray God it may [p. 211.]

---

[14] [Non in concilio, sed in episcoporum conventu.—p. 63.]

"not do more harm than good, and especially to the Germans
"that are here; who, seeing how little liberty it enjoys, and
"how much it is under the dominion of the legate, cannot pos-
"sibly have that respect and esteem for it as is convenient."

There are some letters from the bishop of Orense, written

Oct. 12.
[Ibid.
p. 170.]
in the same strain.   In one he writes, "that for what concerns
"a reformation, the emperor must set himself about it in
"earnest, both with the pope and the fathers: for if he does
"it not, we shall have our wounds only skinned over, but shall
"have the rotten core left, to the corrupting of all quickly
"again.——The prelates here are all very much troubled to
"see with how ill a grace people that say any thing of a re-

Nov. 28.

[p. 260.]
"formation are heard."   In another he writes, "they dis-
"cover here little or no inclination for to do any thing that
"deserves the name of a true reformation.   Several things
"might be done that would be of great advantage to the peo-
"ple, and would be no prejudice to his holiness, or to his
"court.   May God remedy things! under whom, unless his
"majesty and your lordship labour very hard, there will be

[p. 262.]
"no remedy left for the church.   In a postscript, he tells the
"same story that Vargas had told, of the legate's treating
"the bishop of Verdun so ill, for his calling the reformation
"offered, *a pretended reformation:* and he commanded him
"to be silent when he was about to say somewhat in his own
"justification.   The bishop answered, that at this rate there
"was no liberty; and having obtained leave of the emperor,
"by whom he was sent thither, he would be gone.   The legate
"told him he should not go, but should do what he commanded

[p. 264.]
"him.——He writes, that it was a great reproach to the
"bishops, from whom the world expected canons of reforma-
"tion; that in truth they could give them nothing but what

[p. 265.]
"the legate pleases.——It were just with the people, if we do
"not treat about their interest more in earnest than we have
"done hitherto, for to stone us when we return home."

Reflections
upon those
proceed-
ings.
I have set all this out so copiously, that it may appear, from
what those, who were far from being in any sort favourers of
the reformation, who were at Trent, and were let into the
secret of affairs, wrote of the council to the emperor's chief
minister, how little, not only of liberty, but even of common
decency, there appeared in the whole conduct of that council.

This digression is, I hope, an acceptable entertainment to
the reader; and it must entirely free every considering person
from a vulgar but weak prejudice, infused into many by practising missionaries, which was objected to myself by a great
prince, that no nation ought to have reformed itself, in a separation from the rest of the church: but that there ought to
have been a general acquiescing in such things as were com-
185 monly received, till by a joint concurrence of other churches
the reformation might have been agreed and settled in a general council. These letters do so effectually discover the vanity
of this conceit, that at first sight it evidently appears, that
even those abuses and corruptions that could not be justified,
yet could not be effectually reformed at Trent; and that every
thing was carried there, partly by the artifices of the legates,
and partly by the many poor Italian prelates, who were all
pensioners of the court of Rome: so that no abuse, how gross
or crying soever, could be amended, but as the popes for their
own ends thought fit to give it up. This appears so evidently in the letters, out of which I have drawn this abstract,
that I hope any prejudice formed upon the prospect of an universal reformation is by it entirely removed. I turn next to
the affairs of England.

The earl of Hertford, advanced to be duke of Somerset, depended much on Paget's advices. He told him, on the day
that king Henry died, that he desired his friendship; and
promised to him, that he would have a great regard to his
advice. But though Paget put him oft in mind of this[15], he
forgot it too soon. His great success in his first expedition to
Scotland was a particular happiness to him, and might have
established him; but his quarrelling so soon with his brother
was fatal to them both.

Thirlby was still ambassador at the emperor's court: he Thirlby
studied to make his court to the protector, and wrote him a writes of
the *Interim*.
very hearty congratulation upon his exaltation; and added,
that the bishop of Arras seemed likewise to rejoice at it. At
the same time he warned him of the designs of the French
against England. He gave him a long account of the *Interim*,
in which he writes, that Malvenda had secretly a great hand:
he himself seems to approve of it; and says, that it was as high

[15] [See State Papers, Domestic, vol. viii. and Cott. MS. Tit. F. iii. fol. 273.]

an act of supremacy as any in all king Henry's reign ; for by
it, not only many of the doctrines of popery had mollifying
senses put on them, different from what was commonly received, but the sacrament was allowed to be given in both
kinds, and the married priests were suffered to officiate. It is
true, all was softened by this, that it was only a prudent connivance in the *Interim*, till the council should be reassembled,
to bring all matters to a final settlement.

The protector either mistrusted Thirlby, or he called him
home to assist Cranmer in carrying on the reformation. He
sent sir Philip Hobby [16] in his stead. He was a man marked
in king Henry's time as a favourer of the preachers of the
new learning, as they were then called. There was one
Parson, a clerk, known to have evil opinions (so it is entered in
a part of the Council-book for the year 1543) touching the
sacrament of the altar ; who was maintained by Weldon, one
of the masters of the household, and by Hobby, then a gentle-
man-usher, for which they were both sent to the Fleet; but
they were soon after discharged [17].

Hobby was therefore sent over ambassador, as a person on
whose advices the government here might depend, with relation to the affairs of Germany. I have seen a volume of the
letters, writ to him by the protector and council, with copies of
the answers that he wrote.

Hobby sent ambassador to the emperor.

[March 17, Council Book, p. 457.]

[16] ['The "Instructions to sir Philip
Hoby, knight, one of the gentlemen
of his majesty's privy chamber, sent
presently unto the emperor's court,
to reside there as his highness' ambassador in the place of the right
reverend father in God the bishop
of Westminster, whom his majesty
presently revokes," are in the State
Paper Office, and bear date April
15, 1548.]

[17] [" At Westminster the 17th
day of March, Thomas Weldon, one
of the masters of the household,
sent for to appear before the council, being found culpable in the
maintaining of one sir Thomas Parson Parson, clerk, who was known
to be a man of evil opinions touch-

ing the sacrament of the altar, was
committed to the Fleet." " At
Westminster the 18th day of March,
Sternall for like causes avouched
and proved against him, was committed likewise unto the Fleet. The
same day Philippe Hobbye, one of
the gentleman huissiers of the king's
privy chamber, for the maintaining
of the above-named sir Thomas
Parson, &c., was also committed
unto the Fleet." " At Saint James'
the 24th day of March, Phillipp
Hobbye, gentleman of the privy
chamber, was this day sent for from
the Fleet, and discharged from his
imprisonment in the same." There
does not appear to be any entry
about the discharge of Weldon.]

186   His first despatch mentioned a particular. dispute between the emperor and his confessor.   The confessor refused to give him absolution, unless he would recal the decree of the *Interim*, and, instead of favouring heresy, would with the sword extirpate heretics.   The emperor said, he was satisfied with what he had done in the matter of the *Interim*, and that he would do no more against the Lutherans : if the friar would not give him absolution, others would be found who would do it.   So the friar left him. *The emperor's confessor refused him absolution for not persecuting heretics.*

At that time a proposition of a marriage for the lady Mary was made by the emperor, who seemed to apprehend that she was not safe in England.   It was with the brother of the king of Portugal.   He was called at first the prince of Portugal; and it was then hearkened to : but when the council understood he was the king's brother, they did not think fit to entertain it.   And in the same letter mention is made of Geoffrey Pole, who was then beyond sea, and desired a pardon : the council wrote, that he was included in the last act of pardon ; yet, since he desired it, they offered him a special pardon. This letter is signed, T. Cant., Wiltshire, Northampton, Wentworth, T. Ely, T. Cheyne, A. Wyngfield, Herbert, N. Wotton, J. Gage.

The next despatch to him has a particular account of two persons whom the king of France had corrupted to betray one of their forts to him.   The king of France had said to their ambassador, *par la foy de gentilhomme*, by the faith of a gentleman, he would make no war without giving warning first. This he promised on the 20th of July ; yet, hearing of the commotions that were in England, he began hostilities against Boulogne within three or four days after.   This is signed, E. Somerset, T. Cant., R. Ryche Can., W. St. John, W. Paget, W. Petre, T. Smith, E. Wotton.   So long ago did it appear that the *bond fide* of that court was not a thing to be much relied on.   I would have printed these letters, if they were in my power : but having had the originals in my hands about thirty years ago, I did not then copy them out, but contented myself with taking extracts out of them ; to which I shall upon other occasions have recourse. *The perfidy of the French king.*

As for the progress in the reformation at home, Cranmer was delivered from too deep a subjection, in which he had *The progress of the reformation.*

lived to king Henry. The load of great obligations is a weight
on a generous mind : the hope he had of gaining on the king
to carry him to a further reformation, did no doubt carry him
too far in his compliances to him. He did perhaps satisfy
himself, as I have reason to believe many in the Roman communion do to this day, that he did not in his mind, or with
his thoughts, go along in those devotions that they cannot but
think unlawful ; but what through a fearfulness of temper, or
an ill-managed modesty, they do not depart from established
practices, even though they think them unlawful. The compliances that we find in the Apostles, particularly in St. Paul
himself, the Apostle of the Gentiles, in order to the gaining
the Jews, might all meet together to carry him too far in his
submissions to king Henry. This can neither be denied nor
justified ; but the censures passed on it may be much softened
when all these things are laid together. Now he was delivered 187
from that servitude ; so he resolved to set about a further reformation with much zeal, though perhaps still with too great
caution. He studied if it was possible to gain upon Gardiner :
he had reason to believe, from his forwardness in complying
with king Henry, that he had no great scrupulosity in his own
thoughts ; so he tried to draw him to assist, at least not to
oppose, the steps that were to be made ; and, judging that it
was necessary to give the people due instruction, to carry
them to a further measure of knowledge, he set about the
preparing a book of homilies to be read in churches : and, to
give some more light into the meaning of the New Testament,
he chose Erasmus' Paraphrase, as the most unexceptionable
book that could be thought on ; since he had been so much
favoured in England : and as he had written against Luther,
so he lived and died in the Roman communion.

Gardiner at
the head of
the opposi-
tion to it.
Cranmer communicated his designs, with the draught of the
homilies, to Gardiner : but he was resolved to set himself at
the head of the popish party. He had, no doubt, great resentments, because he was left out of the council, which he
imputed to the Seymours. Cranmer tried if the offer of
bringing him to sit at that board could overcome these ; yet
all was in vain. He insisted at first on this, that, during the
king's minority, it was fit to keep all things quiet, and not to
endanger the public peace by venturing on new changes. He

pressed the archbishop with the only thing that he could not [Harl. MSS. 417. fol. 79, well answer; which was, that he had concurred in setting forth the late king's book of *a necessary doctrine:* Gardiner printed in Strype's Cranmer, App. No. 35.] wrote, that he was confident Cranmer was a better man than to do any such thing against his conscience upon any king's account; and if his conscience agreed to that book, which he himself had so recommended, he wished things might be left to rest there. Cranmer pressed him again and again in this matter, but he was intractable. In particular he excepted to the homily of Justification, which was thought to be of Cranmer's own composing: because *justification* was ascribed to *faith* only, in which he thought *charity* had likewise its influence; and that without it *faith* was dead, and a dead thing could not be the cause of *justification.* But the archbishop shewed him his design in that was only to set forth the freedom of God's mercy, which we relying on, had by that the application of it to ourselves; not meaning that *justifying faith* was ever without charity; for even faith did not justify as a meritorious condition, but only as it was an instrument applying God's mercy to sinners. Upon this there was perhaps too much of subtlety on both sides. As for Erasmus' [Cotton MSS. Vesp. D. xviii. fol. 139, printed in Strype's Cranmer, Appendix, No 36.] Paraphrase, Gardiner excepted to it as being in many things contrary to the homilies; so he thought, since they agreed so little together, they ought not to be joined and recommended by the same injunctions: to this it was said, that the Paraphrase was a good and useful book, though in some particulars the homilies differed from it.

But as they had the perverseness of the popish party to deal with, so it was not easy to restrain their own side. Those whose heat could not be well managed, were apt to break out into great disorders; some insulting the priests as they were 188 officiating, others talking irreverently of the sacrament; some defining the manner of the presence, and others asserting the impossibility of it, as it was explained. These disorders gave occasion to two proclamations this year: the first was on the 12th[18] of November, against insolence towards priests, such as the reviling them, tossing them, and taking their caps and [Wilkins, Conc. iv. p. 18.] tippets violently from them; the other was on the 27th of

[18] [Of the existence of this Proclamation, the editor can find no evidence.]

December [19], against irreverent talkers of the sacrament, and against those who in their sermons went to define the manner, the nature and fashion, and the possibility or impossibility of the presence. The visitors went about with their injunctions. They are registered in the books of the dean and chapter of York; where the visitation was held in September. It came not to Winchester till October, for the monition concerning it was made on the 7th of October. Whether the slowness of the visitors coming thither was occasioned by any secret practice with Gardiner, and upon the hopes of gaining him or not, I cannot tell. He it seems had before that refused to receive or obey the injunctions; for which he was put in the Fleet: and when he wrote his letter to the protector, complaining of the proceedings against him, he had been then seven weeks there.

Proceedings in convocation. [Wilkins, Conc. iv. 15.]

I can say nothing new of the parliament that sat this year [20]. When the convocation was opened on the 5th of November, the archbishop told them, that it was with the king and the lords' consent that the prelates and clergy should consult together about settling the Christian religion right, and delivering it to the people. He sent them to choose their prolocutor, and to present him the Friday following. It is set down in the minutes, that the lower house consulted how they might be joined to the lower house of parliament; and about the

[Ibid. p. 16.]

reformation of the ecclesiastical laws. On the 9th of December some were appointed to know if the archbishop had obtained license (in the minutes called indemnity, or immunity) for them to treat of matters of religion. In the fifth session, on the last of November, the prolocutor exhibited an order given him by the archbishop for receiving the communion in both kinds, to which in the next session they agreed, no man

---

[19] [There is a copy of this Proclamation, printed by Grafton, dated Dec. 27, 1547, at Somerset House. It is headed—" ¶ A Proclamacion against the unreuerēt disputers and talkers of the Sacramente of the body and blood of Christ, commonly called the Sacrament of the Aultar, set forth by the Kynges Maiestie with thassente and cōsent of his most deere uncle, Edwarde Duke of Somerset, gouernour of his most royall person, and of hys Realmes, dominiōs and subiectes Protector, and other of hys highnes moste honorable pryuey counsaill, the xxvii. daye of Decembre, in the first yeare of his Maiesties most gratious reigne."]

[20] [See Part ii. p. 39.]

speaking against it: sixty-four agreed to this; Polydore Vergil and Weston being two of them. And in the eighth session, on the 17th of December, a proposition was offered to them in these words: "That all such canons, laws, statutes, decrees, "usages, and customs, heretofore made or used, that forbid "any person to contract matrimony, or condemn matrimony "already contracted, by any person, for any vow or promise "of priesthood, chastity, or widowhood, shall from henceforth "cease, be utterly void, and of none effect." Here it was that Redman's opinion was read, which I had in my History put as read the following year[21]. This proposition went to all monastic vows, as well as to the marriage of priests. The proposition was subscribed by fifty-three, who were for the affirmative; only twenty-two were for the negative; after which a committee was named to draw the form of an act for the marriage of priests. But all that is in the often-cited minutes as to this matter is, *Item* propounded for the marriage of priests; and to it is added, and that the ecclesiastical laws should be promulgated: there is no more in the minutes of the convocations during this reign.

They affirm that it was free for the clergy to marry.

[Wilkins, Conc. iv. 16.]

189   Strype adds to this a particular remark out of the Defence of the Priests' Marriage[22], that divers of those who were for the affimative did never marry; and that some of those who were for the negative yet did afterwards marry. Cranmer went on gathering authorities out of scripture and the fathers against unwritten traditions. He wrote a book on this subject in Latin; but in queen Mary's time it was translated into English[23], and published by an English exile beyond sea. He

[Strype's Cranmer, p. 156.]

Cranmer's labours and zeal.

[21] [See Part ii. p. 92.]

[22] [This book was published in black letter, without any name or date. The title page is as follows: "A defence of priestes mariages, stablysshed by the imperiall lawes of the Realme of Englande, agaynst Ciuilian, namyng hym selfe Thomas Martin doctour of the Ciuile lawes." On the last page is, "Imprinted at London by Richard Jugge, printer to the Queenes *Maiestie.* Cum priuilegio Regiae Maiestatis.]

[23] ["A confutatiõ of unwrittẽ

verities, both bi the holye scriptures and moste auncient autors, and also probable arguments, and pithy reasons, with plaine aunswers to al (or at the least) to the moste part and strongest argumentes, which the aduersaries of gods truth either haue, or can bryng forth for the profe and defence of the same unwritten vanities, verities as they woulde haue them called: made by Thomas Cranmer late Archebishop of Cantorburie, Martyr of god, and burned at Oxford for the defēce of

took a special care to furnish Canterbury with good preachers; but though their labours were not quite without success, yet superstition had too deep a root there to be easily subdued: and in the universities the old doctrines were so obstinately persisted in, that, when some in Cambridge offered to examine the mass by the scriptures and the fathers, and to have a disputation upon it, the vice-chancellor did forbid it. The archbishop had procured a confirmation of their privileges, of Cambridge at least; for Strype only mentions that. The mildness he expressed towards all who opposed him, even with insolence, was remarkable: when one, who thought he carried this too far, told him that if ever it came to the turn of his enemies, they would shew him no such favour; he answered, *Well, if God so provide, we must abide it.*

St. Chrysostom's letter to Cæsarius brought to England.

I did in the account of the arguments against transubstantiation [24] mention a letter of St. Chrysostom's to Cæsarius, of which Peter Martyr brought over a copy in Latin to England. Since that time the popish clergy were sensible that by that letter it appeared plainly that St. Chrysostom did believe that the substance of bread and wine remained still in the sacrament, as the human nature remained in the person of Christ; so that by this, all the other high figures used by that father must be understood so as to reconcile them to this letter: therefore they have used all possible endeavours to suppress it. When the learned Bigot had brought a copy of it from Florence to France, and printed it with other things relating to that father, they ordered it to be cut out in such a manner, that in the printed book it appeared that some leaves were cut out; yet one copy of it was brought to the present learned and pious bishop of Lincoln [25], then chaplain to our ambassador at Paris, who first printed it here in England; as the learned Le Moyne, having another copy sent to him, printed it about the same time in Holland [26].

---

the trewe doctrine of our saviour Christ, translated and set forth by E. P. ¶ The contents whereof thou shalte finde on the next side folowinge." The work was reprinted in 1582.]

[24] [See Part ii. p. 109.]

[25] [Dr. William Wake, afterwards archbishop of Canterbury.]

[26] [It is at p. 530, the end of the first volume of Le Moyne's Varia Sacra, Lugd. Bat. 1685. 2 vols. 4to.

I have nothing to add concerning the tumults of the year 1549 [28], but that the popish clergy were generally at the head of the rebels. Many of these were priests that had complied, and subscribed the new book ; some of them were killed in every skirmish, and very few of the clergy shewed much zeal against them : so that the earl of Bedford could have none but Miles Coverdale to go along with the force that he carried into Devonshire to subdue them [29].

Troubles at Frankfort, p. 195. [27]

[27] " A Brieff discours off the troubles begonne at Franckford in Germany Anno Domini 1554. A-bowte the Booke off common prayer and Ceremonies and continued by the Englishe men theyre to thende off Q. Maries Raigne, in the which discours, the gentle reader shall see the very originall and beginninge off all the contention that hathe byn, and what was the cause off the same." 1575. 4to. This scarce volume was reprinted in 4to. 1642, and again in the Phœnix, 2 vols. 8vo. 1707-8, which was the copy used by Burnet, and again *verbatim et paginatim* in 1846, with an introduction signed J. P. The editor attributes it to Whittingham, and suggests that it was probably printed at Geneva.]

[28] [See Part ii. p. 113.]

[29] [" The greatest traitors and rebells that godly Kinge Edwarde had in the weste partes were priests, and such as had subscribed to the booke, or what so euer by lawe was then in force, but for all their sub-scribings there was no skirmishe where some off those subscribers left not their karkaises in the filde againste God and their prince. Plum-tree and his fellowe priests off the northe, I dowte not but they were conformable and applyable to all orders, and neuer staggered at sub-scriptions. But for all that, time tried their traiterous hartes. " But in all the sturres whiche haue happened either sithens the Queenes

maiestie came to the crowne, or before, I haue not hard off so muche as one (minister or other) that hath lifted up his hande against hir maiestie or state, whom it pleaseth the enuious and malicious men to terme precision, and puritain, in great despite and contempt. In dede, this haue I founde oute and lerned, that euen suche as muste be contente and patiently bear these odious names of puritane, precisian, traitor, and rebell, haue yet bin the men, who moste faithfully (in their callinge) haue serued the queen's maiestie and their country bothe within the realme and withoute the realme, in garnison and in filde, hazardinge their bodies against har-gabuze and cannon, when as those who nowe so furiously charge them both owte off pulpits and other places, durst not or at leste woulde not in anie such seruice off the prince and countrie be seene. For proffe hereoff, yff yow call to re-membrance, who hazarded his liffe with that olde honorable erle off Bedford, when as he was sent to subdue the popish rebells off the weste, yow shall finde that none off the clergie were hastie to take that seruice in hande, but onely olde father Couerdale. When most like-lode was off daunger betweene the Skotts and vs, the preacher to the souldiars was firste Maister Samp-son and afteward Maister Greshopp, when as the right honorable erle off Bedford that nowe is had then the

The lady
Mary de-
nies that
she or her
servants
were con-
cerned in
the risings.
Collect.
Numb. 2.

Upon some information that the lady Mary's servants were active in assisting those commotions, the protector and council wrote to her on the 17th: that letter being delivered to her on the 20th of July, she presently wrote an answer, which I had from sir William Cook, and it will be found in the Collection. In it "she expresses her dislike of those revolts. A "chaplain of hers in Devonshire had been named, but she "writes she had not one chaplain in those parts. Another, that "was named, lived constantly in her house: she justifies all her "servants that had been named; and assured them, that all "of her household were true subjects to the king. The coun- "cil had likewise charged her, that her proceedings in matters "of religion had given the rebels great courage: which, she "wrote, appeared to be untrue; since the rebels in her neigh- "bourhood touched upon no point of religion. She prayed "God, that their new alterations and unlawful liberties might "not rather be the occasion of such assemblies. As for "Devonshire, she had neither lands nor acquaintance in those "parts."

190

In the suppressing these tumults, the protector did visibly espouse the people's interest [30], and blamed the lords for their enclosures, and the other oppressions that had, as he said, occasioned all those disorders. By this he came to be univer-

charge. The erle off Warwick, at his being in Neuehauen, had in dede with him certeine ministers for a time, but after that the cannon came and began to roare, and the plage off pestilence so terrible to rage, then (I weene) not a minister there left but maister Kethe alone. And when as means were made to haue mo ministers oüer, to aide the saied Kethe, (who had so muche to doo, what with preaching and visitinge the poore sick souldiars, which were in no small nombers,) there coulde not be founde (as that right noble erle can uppon his honor testifie) as muche as one whiche coulde be brought | to so muche conformitie as to subscribe to any suche seruice off the queen's ma-

iestie. When sir Henry Sidney had to do with the popishe rebells off Ireland, maister Christopher Goodman shewed his faithfull diligence in that seruice voluntarily with owts all constraynte. And thus it is euidente, that theis with a nomber moo who are now so ill thought off, as iff they were traitors and rebells, haue yet byn so farre off from beinge sedicious, that they haue at all times aduentured their liues againste seditious persons and rebells, when as suche as nowe so hardly charge them bothe by worde and writinge, haue byn right hartely well content to take their ease and reste at home." p. 197.]

[30] [See Part ii. p. 114.]

sally beloved by the people; but, trusting to that, he began to take too much upon him; and was so wedded to his own thoughts, that he often opposed the whole council. Upon which Paget wròte him a long letter, in which, as a faithful friend, he set before him his errors; chiefly his wilfulness, and his affecting popularity too much. He desired to be dismissed the council; for while he was there he was resolved to deliver his opinion according to his reason, and not seek to please another: he had offered him faithful advices, and warned him of the cloud that he saw gathering against him. This he wrote on the 6th of July[31], some months before it broke out. It seems the protector took this freedom well from him, for he continued firm to him to the last. His brother the lord Seymour's fall lay heavy on him; though that lord had almost compassed another design, of marrying the lady Elizabeth: so I find it in the council's letters to Hobby of the 18th of January 1548-9.

[July 7.] Cotton lib. Titus, F. 3 [fol. 274]

As for the other matter with which he was loaded, the entertaining some German troops, I find among sir Philip Hobby's letters a great many orders and letters, signed by the whole council, as well as by the protector, which shew that they all concurred in that matter. The true secret of it on both sides was this: the bulk of the people of England was still possessed with the old superstition to such a degree, that it was visible they could not be depended on in any matter that related to the alterations that were made, or were designed to be made: whereas the Germans were full of zeal on the other side; so that they might well be trusted to: and the princes of Germany, who were then kept under by the emperor, so that they neither durst nor could keep their troops at home, but hoped they might at some better time have an occasion to use them, were willing to put them in the hands of the present government of England. Howsoever, this had an odious name put on it, and was called a ruling by strangers: so that it very much shook the duke of Somerset's po-

The entertaining foreign troops in England.

---

[31] [The copy of this letter occupies six folio pages of close writing in the MS. in the Cotton Library. It is headed, 'To the duke of Somerset, the 7th of July 1549,' and signed W. P. The original is in the State Paper Office, Domestic Series, vol. 8. art. 4. See also vol. 7. art. 5. It is printed in Strype's Memorials, vol. 2. App. p. 109.]

pularity; for though it could not be denied that all the council
had concurred with him in it, yet the load and blame of all was
laid on him.

The popish party was very active in procuring the change
of measures that followed. The council wrote over to the emperor, to let him know that the necessity of their affairs was 191
like to force them to treat for the delivering up of Boulogne to
the French; though this was a secret, not yet communicated
to the whole privy-council.

Bonner's being removed was not much resented, neither at
home nor abroad. He was a brutal man; few either loved or
esteemed him: and Ridley, who came to succeed him, was the
most generally esteemed man of all the reformers. One thing
that made it more acceptable to those who favoured the reformation was, the suppressing the bishopric of Westminster,
and the removing Thirlby to Norwich, where it was thought
he could do less mischief than where he was: for though he
complied as soon as any change was made, yet he secretly
opposed every thing, while it was safe to do it. He had a soft
and an insinuating way with him; which, as was thought, prevailed too much even on Cranmer himself. But Gardiner was
a dextrous man, and much more esteemed, though as little
beloved as Bonner was: so the falling on him gave a greater
alarm to the whole party. He, who was so well known both
in the emperor's court, and in the French court, sent over
tragical accounts of the usage he met with. This was writ
over hither by our ambassador at the court of France: upon
which a very severe character of him is given in a letter,
signed, E. Somerset, T. Cant., R. Rich, C., W. Wiltshire, J. Warwick, J. Bedford, W. Northampton, E. Clinton, W. Petre,
W. Cecyl. In it they gave an account of the proceedings
against him; and add, " he had shewed not only a wilful pride,
" but a cankered heart, guilty of open and shameful lies; by
" which impudent falsehood he shewed himself most unworthy
" to be a bishop, whatsoever strangers may think of him. For
" religion, he is as far from any piety or fashion of a good
" bishop, as a player of a bishop in a comedy is from a good
" bishop indeed."

Whether the protector designed any thing against the constitution of the church, or at least to swallow up the great

[March 30
and April 1,
1550.
Rymer,
xv. pp.
219, 221.]

endowments that were not yet devoured, I cannot tell. But
there is an advice in one of Hobby's letters, dextrously enough
proposed, that gives reason to suspect this might be on design
to broach a business that was to be so cunningly proposed:
and Hobby being a confidant of the protector's, he may be
supposed to have written as he was directed by him. He wrote
it in September 1548. He tells the council, "that the pro-
" testants of Germany hoped that the king, seeing that the
" late wars in Germany happened chiefly by the bishops con-
" tinuing in their princely and lordly estate, would, for pre-
" venting the like, appoint the godly bishops an honest and
" competent living, sufficient for their maintenance, taking
" from them the rest of those worldly possessions and dig-
" nities, and thereby avoid the vainglory that letteth them
" truly and sincerely to do their office, and preach the gospel
" and word of Christ. On the other side he wrote, the papists
" say they doubt not but my lords the bishops, being a great
" number of stout and well learned men, will well enough
" weigh against their adversaries, and maintain still their whole
" estate; which coming to pass, they have good hope that in
" time these princely pillars will well enough resist this fury,
" and bring all things again into the old order."

192   I have no particulars to add concerning the protector's fall, *The popish
and the new scene ; but that soon after, when it appeared that *party de-
the papists were not like to be more favourably dealt with *ceived in
than they were under the duke of Somerset, the bishop of *their hopes
Arras did expostulate upon it with Hobby. He said, they had *on the pro-
been assisting to the pulling down of the duke of Somerset, *tector's fall*
and that hopes of better usage had been given them ; yet
things went worse with them than before : upon that he fell to
rail at Bucer, and said, he believed he inflamed matters in
England as much as he had done in the empire. For at this
time many were forced to come to England for shelter, the
chief of whom were Bucer, Fagius, Peter Martyr, and Bernardin Ochinus : all these were entertained by Cranmer, till
he got good provisions to be made for them in the universities;
which were now most violently set against every step that was
made towards a reformation. Hobby came over to England,
and tried what service he could do to his friend the duke of
Somerset : but the faction was grown too strong to be with-

Council-
book.
[Vol. ii.
p. 14.]

[Ibid.
p. 78.]

[Feb. 17,
ibid. p. 93.]
[Ibid. p.
79.]

[Ibid. p.
100.]
[Ibid. p.
141.]

stood. Upon his submission, the matter went for some time very high against him and his friends. On the 13th[32] of October, sir Thomas Smith, sir Michael Stanhope, sir John Thynne, and Edward Wolfe, called adherents to the duke of Somerset, and the principal instruments of his ill government, were sent to the Tower; and on the 14th[33] he himself was sent thither. No more mention[34] is made of them till the 6th of February, that the duke of Somerset was set at liberty; but bound in a recognizance of ten thousand pounds not to go above four mile from Shene, or Sion, nor to come into the king's presence, unless he was called for by the king and his council. And when he knew that the king was to come within four miles of these houses, he was to withdraw from them. Yet, it seems, his enemies were still in some apprehension of him; and probably some messages went between him and his friends in the Tower: for, on the 18th of February, they were all made close prisoners, and their servants were not suffered to attend upon them. But it seems, upon examination, this was found not to be of a criminal nature: so, on the 22nd, they were dismissed upon their recognizances. And, upon the 10th of

[32] ["At Wyndsour, Sunday the 13th of October, the lords called before them sir Thomas Smyth, sir Michaell Stanhop, sir John Thyn, knight, Edward Wulf, one of his majesty's privy chamber, and William Gray, esquire, adherents of the said duke, and the principal instruments and counsellors that he did use both at this time and otherways also in the affairs of his ill government, whom when they had charged with their offenses, they accorded to send to the tower of London, there to remain until further order were taken with them.

"The same day also sir Thomas Smyth for sundry his misdemeanours and undiscreet behaviour heretofore, being thought unmete to continue any longer of the privy council, was both sequestered from the council, and also deprived from the office of one of his majesty's secretaries."]

[33] ["At Wyndsor, Monday the 13th" (written by mistake for the 14th) "of October 1549, the duke being sent for to appear before their lordships, and charged by them with his faults, was this day with the others before named sent to the tower of London under the conduct of the earls of Sussex and Huntingdon, the lords Gray and Burgayny, sir John Gage, knight of the order, constable of the tower, and certain other gentlemen and their bands. This day also the king's majesty departed from Wyndsour to Hampton Courte."]

[34] [This is not strictly true, as the very next day six noblemen were appointed to be in constant attendance upon the king, considering the duke's being committed to the tower, and Dr. Wotton, dean of Canterbury, was appointed secretary in the room of sir Thomas Smyth.]

April, the duke of Somerset was again brought to the council-board, being that day sworn of the privy-council.

On the 20th of April, Hobby being sent back to the emperor's court, had orders to try if the proposition for a marriage of the lady Mary to the prince of Portugal might be again set on foot ; and, in excuse for its being rejected before, he had orders to say, that few of the council had been made acquainted with it : he was desired therefore to inquire what that prince's estate was.   Whether this flowed from the earl of Warwick's ambitious designs, which might make him wish to have her sent away far out of England ; or, if it flowed from the uneasiness the council was in, by reason of her persisting in the old way of religion, I cannot determine.   Hobby had also orders to represent to the emperor, that they had hitherto connived at her mass, in hopes that she would by that connivance be moved to conform herself to the laws : diversity of rites in matters of religion ought not to be suffered.   The laws were so strict, that no license could be granted in opposition to them : yet they were resolved to connive a little longer, though she abused the king's favour ; for she kept as it were an open church, not only for her servants, but for all her neighbours : they therefore wished that the emperor would give her good advice in this matter.   The letter was signed by Cranmer, by the earls of Wiltshire and Warwick, the marquis of Northampton, the lord Wentworth, and Paget, Petre, Herbert, Darcy, and Mason.   To all this it seems the emperor had little regard : for not long after that, the ambassador wrote over, that, by the emperor's command, an order was served on him, not to have the English service in his house.   The council looked on this as contrary to the privileges of ambassadors, by the law of nations.   So they ordered, that the emperor's ambassador should not have mass in his house, and gave him notice of it. When the emperor knew this, he complained of it, as a high violation of the dignity of that character : but the council-books shew that they stood firm, and would not recal their order till the emperor recalled his order against the new service in the English ambassador's house.   What further proceedings were of either side in this matter does not appear to me.   I find by the council-books, that the carrying on the reformation was cordially espoused and pursued at that board.

Proceed-
ings
against
Gardiner.
Council
Book, vol.
iii. p. 47.]
[Archæ-
ologia, vol.
xviii. p. 135,

[Ibid. p.
136.]

Gardiner had been long a prisoner; and his being detained in the Tower, no proceendigs beng had against him, occasioned a great outcry: so, on the 8th of June 1550, it was resolved to send some to him, to see if he repented of his former obstinacy, and would apply himself to advance the king's proceedings; upon which the king would receive him into favour, and all past errors should be forgiven. So the duke of Somerset, and others, were sent to him. They made report, on the 10th of June, that he desired to see the book of the king's proceedings, and then he would make a full answer. He seemed to them in all things willing to conform himself to it, promising that if he found any thing in it against his conscience, he would open it to none but to the council. So the book was sent him; and he was allowed the liberty of the gallery and gardens in the Tower, when the duke of Norfolk was not in them.

[Council
Book, p.
51.]

On the 13th of June, the lieutenant of the Tower reported, that he had given him back the king's book; and that he said, he would make no answer to it till he was set at liberty; and that then he would speak his conscience: so the

[Council
Book, p.
70.]
[Archæo-
logia, pp.
140, 141.]

lords, who had been with him, were appointed to go to him again. The matter rested till the 8th of July.

In an imperfect book of the minutes of the council, that I have by me, it is set down, that Gardiner did at last subscribe six articles. The two first appear not[35]. The third is, "that

---

[35] ["At Westminster the 10th of July 1550. This day the lord treasurer, lord great master, the master of the horse, and Mr. secretary Petre, made report unto the council that they had not only delivered unto the bishop of Winchester the king's majesty's letter, but also the articles appointed unto all, which articles he subscribed with his own hand, saving to the first, whereunto he wrote his answer in the margin, as hereafter followeth:

The copy of the articles:

Whereas I Stephen, bishop of Winchester, have been suspected as one too much following the bishop of Rome's authority, decrees and ordinances, and as one

The bishop's answer to this article.

that did not approve or allow the king's majesty's proceedings in alteration of certain rites in religion, and was convented before the king's highness' council and admonished thereof. And having certain things appointed for me to do and preach for my declaration, have not done that as I ought to do, although I promised to do the same, whereby I have not only incurred the king's majesty's indignation, but also divers of his highness' subjects have by mine example taken encouragement (as his grace's council is certainly informed) to repine at his majesty's most god-

I cannot in my conscience confess the preface, knowing myself to be of that sort I am indeed and ever have been.

" the Book of Common Prayer was a godly and Christian
" book, to be allowed and observed by all the king's true
" subjects.   4th, That the king, in his young and tender age,
" was a full and entire king : and that the subjects were bound
" to obey the statutes, proclamations, and commands set forth
194 " in this age, as well as if he were thirty or forty years old.
" 5th, That the statute of the six articles was, for just causes,
" repealed by the authority of parliament.   6th, That the
" king, and his successors, had full authority in the churches
" of England and Ireland, to reform and correct errors and
" abuses, and to alter rites and ceremonies ecclesiastical, as
" shall seem most convenient for the edification of his people ;
" so that the alteration is not contrary to the scriptures, and
" the laws of God."   To all this he subscribed his name : but
no date is added in those minutes ; but it is entered, that he
did it in the presence of the council, who also subscribed as
witnesses to it.   Their names are, E. Somerset, W. Wiltshire,
J. Warwick, J. Bedford, W. Northampton, E. Clinton, G. Cobham, William Paget, W. Herbert, William Petre, Edward
North.   It was resolved to carry his submissions further ; so
twenty new articles were drawn up[36]: in which, "the obligation

ly proceedings. I am right sorry
therefore, and acknowledge myself
condignly to have been punished,
and do most heartily thank his majesty that of his great clemency it
hath pleased his highness to deal
with me not according to rigour
but mercy. And to the intent it
may appear to the world how little
I repine at his highness' doings,
which be in religion most godly,
and to the common wealth most
prudent, I do affirm and say freely
of mine own will, without any compulsion, as ensueth :

1. First, that by the law of God
and the authority of scripture, the
king's majesty and his successors are
the supreme heads of the churches
of Englande and also of Irelande.

2. Item, That the appointing of
holidays or fasting days, as Lent,
ymbar days, or any such like, or to
dispense therewith, is in the king's

[July 13,
Council
Book, fol.
78.]

majesty's authority and power : and
his highness as supreme head of the
said churches of Englande and Irelande, and governor thereof, may
appoint the manner and time of the
holy days and fasting, or dispense
therewith as to his wisdom shall
seem most convenient for the honour
of God and the wealth of this realm."
—Council Book, pp. 72, 73.
   The rest is not extracted, being
fairly represented in the text. The
whole has been tolerably correctly
given in Fox, vol. ii. p. 82, and in
Archæologia, vol. xviii. p. 140.]

[36] [" At Westminster the 11th of
July 1550. This day the bishop of
Winchester's case was debated, and
because it appeareth that he sticketh
upon the submission which is the
principallest point considering his
offence that he now goeth about to
defend : to the intent he should
have no just cause to say that he

" to celibacy, and all the vows made by the monks, all images,
" relics, and pilgrimages, are condemned. It is affirmed, that
" the scriptures ought to be read by all: that the mass was
" full of abuse and superstition, and was justly taken away:
" that the eucharist ought to be received in both kinds: that
" private masses were not agreeable to scripture: that the
" sacrament ought not to be adored: that the book of Homi-
" lies was godly and wholesome: that the book of ordaining
" bishops, priests, and deacons ought to be received and ap-
" proved by all; and that the lesser orders were not necessary:

was not mercifully handled: It was agreed that the master of the horse and Mr. secretary Petre should repair unto him again with the same submission: exhorting him to look better upon it, and in case the words seem too sore then to refer it unto himself in what sort and with what words he should devise to submit him; that upon the acknowledging of his fault the king's highness might extend his mercy and liberality towards him as it was determined."—Council Book, p. 75.

" At Westminster the 13th of July 1550. The master of the horse and Mr. secretary Petre made report that they had been with the bishop of Winchester, who stood precisely in justification of himself that he had never offended the king's majesty: wherefore he utterly refused to make any submission at all. For the more surety of which denial, it was agreed that a new book of articles should be devised wherewith the said master of the horse and Mr. secretary should repair unto him again: and for the more authentic proceeding with him they to have with them a divine and a temporal lawyer, which were the bishop of London and Mr. Goderick."—Council Book, fol. 77.

Then follows " The copy of the articles last sent to the bishop of Winchester," twenty in number, occupying three and a half pages, printed in Fox, vol. ii. lib. ix. p. 82.

" At Westminster the 15th of July 1550. Report was made by the master of the horse and Mr. secretary Petre, that they, with the bishop of London and Mr. Goderick, had been with the bishop of Winchester, and offered him the foresaid articles according to the council's order. Whereunto the same bishop of Winchester made answer, that first to the article of submission he would in no wise consent. Affirming as he had done before that he had never offended the king's majesty in any such sort as should give him cause then to submit himself, praying earnestly to be brought unto his trial, wherein he refused the king's mercy, and desired nothing but justice. And for the rest of the articles he answered, that after he were past his trial in this first point and were at liberty, then it should appear what he would do in them. Not being (as he said) reasonable he should subscribe them in prison. Whereupon it was agreed that he should be sent for before the whole council, and peremptorily examined once again whether he would stand at this point or no. Which if he did, then to denounce unto him the sequestration of his benefice and consequently the intimacion, in case he were not reformed within three months, as in the day of his appearance shall appear."—Council Book, p. 82.]

" that the scriptures contained all things necessary to salvation;
" and that Erasmus' Paraphrase was, upon good and godly con-
" siderations, ordered by the king to be put in all churches."

But to this a preface was added, setting forth, " that whereas
" he had been suspected as favouring the bishop of Rome's au-
" thority, and that he did not approve of the king's proceed-
" ings in altering some rites in religion : upon which he had
" been brought before the council and admonished ; and was
" ordered to preach, declaring himself in those things ; but
" though he promised to do it, he had not done this as he
" ought to have done : by which, he had not only incurred
" the king's displeasure, but divers of the king's subjects were
" encouraged by his example (as the king's council was cer-
" tainly informed) to repine at his majesty's proceedings ; for
" which he was very sorry, and confessed that he had been
" condignly punished.   And he thanked the king for his
" clemency, treating him not with rigour, but mercy.   And,
" that it might appear how little he did repine at his highness'
" doings, which in religion were most godly, and to the com-
" monwealth most prudent ; he did therefore of his own will,
" and without any compulsion, subscribe the following articles."
But on the margin of the minutes the bishop's answer to this
is thus set down : " I cannot in my conscience confess the pre-
" face : knowing myself to be of that sort I am indeed, and
" ever have been[37]———."   The rest is torn out.   On the 15th [Council
of July it is entered, that report was made, by those who were Book, p. 82.]
sent to him, that he said he had never offended the king : so he [Archæ-
prayed that he might be brought to his trial, in which he asked ologia, xviii. pp.
195 no mercy, but only justice.   When he had passed his trial, and 142, 143.]
was released, it should then appear what he would do with relation to the articles : but it was not reasonable that he should
subscribe them while he was yet in prison.

Some of the privy counsellors were again sent to him, and [Ibid. p.
they were ordered to carry with them a divine and a temporal 142.]
lawyer ; so they took with them Ridley bishop of London, and
Mr. Goodrick.   His answer was to the same purpose, and was
next council-day reported.   Upon which he was brought before [July 19,
the council, and required to subscribe the paper ; but he still ibid. p. 143.]

37 [The author quotes from the   which have been printed in the
copy of the Council Book in the   18th volume of Archæologia.]
Harleian Collection, extracts from

BURNET, PART III.   z

[Council Book, p. 89.]

[Archæologia, xviii. p. 146.]

refusing to do it, the sentence of sequestration was read, with a denunciation of deprivation, if he did not conform within three months: nevertheless, (it is added in the council-book,) upon divers good considerations, and especially upon hope that within that time he might be yet reconciled, it was agreed, that the said bishop's house and servants should be maintained in their present estate, until the time that this intimation should expire: and the matter in the mean time was to be kept private. These are all the additional passages taken from the council-book relating to Gardiner.

Those steps, in which the reformation was advancing but slowly, occasioned great distractions over most parts of the kingdom; while those who adhered to the old practices and doctrines preached severely against all innovations, and others as severely against all corruptions and abuses. The ill effects of these contradictory sermons had given occasion to a proclamation on the 24th[39] of April 1550, prohibiting all preaching, except by persons licensed by the king or the archbishop of Canterbury: and the disorders occasioned by men's divorcing their wives, or marrying more wives than one, were likewise ordered to be proceeded against by the same proclamation. On the 9th of August there came out another proclamation, prohibiting all plays till Allhallowtide: what the reason of this last was does not appear. That against all preaching was much censured. It was represented, that, by reason of the proclamation against preaching, the people were running into great ignorance and dissoluteness. So letters were ordered to be written to the bishops of Durham and Ely[40]; and eight days

All preaching is forbidden, except by persons especially licensed.

[39] [The date of this proclamation is 1548, as appears from the following heading, which is taken from the printed copy at Somerset House:

"¶ A proclamation set furthe by the kynges maiestie, with the assent and consent of his moste dere uncle, Edward duke of Somerset, governor of his moste royall persone, and of his dominions and subiectes protector, and others of his highnes' priuie counsaill, against false tale tellers, preachers without licence, and suche as putteth awaie their wifes and marieth other, during their wifes lifes or suche as kepeth twoo wifes at once, the xxiii. daie of Aprill in the seconde yere of his maiesties moste gracious reigne.]

[40] [" At Westminster, Sunday the 2nd of February 1549. Letters several to the bishops of Duresme and Ely to appoint in their several dioceses their chaplains, and such parsons, vicars, and curates within the same dioceses to preach as by their discretions they shall think mete, the proclamations and restraints notwithstanding." Council Book, p. 71. " The bishop and learned

after to the bishop of Lincoln, and other bishops, to appoint [Feb. 2, 1550. Council Book, vol. ii. p. 71.] their chaplains, and others by their discretion, to preach in their dioceses, notwithstanding the proclamation against preaching. There was also an order made in council, that some bishops, and other learned men, should devise an order for the creation of bishops and priests. I use the words in the council-book. Twelve were appointed to prepare it. Heath, bishop of Worcester, was one of them. It seems there was a digested Heath refuses to subscribe the book of Ordinations. form already prepared, probably by Cranmer, for that service: for the order was made on the 2nd of February, and on the 28th of it was brought to the council, signed by eleven of the [Council Book, vol. iii. p. 390.] number, Heath only refusing to sign it. He said, as it is entered in the council-book, that all that is contained in the book was good and godly; he also said he would obey it: but added, that he would not sign it. The matter was respited for some days, and great pains was taken by Cranmer and others to persuade him to sign it; but he still refusing it (as the council-book has it) obstinately, he was on the 4th of

196 March[41] sent to the Fleet. He was in September[42] called again [Council Book, vol. iii. p. 390.] before the council, and required to subscribe the book; and divers learned men argued to persuade him that the book was expedient and allowable: his obstinacy was charged on him, for which they said he had deserved a longer imprisonment; but he might still recover the king's favour, if he would subscribe it. He acknowledged he had been very gently used,

whose names be underwritten, appointed by the lords to devise orders for the creation of bishops and priests."—p. 72. No names are added. "In the dining chamber beside the star chamber, Thursday the 13th of February 1549. Letters to the bishops of Lyncoln . . . . to appoint preachers within their dioceses."—p. 90.]

[41] [It is entered in the Council Book of Saturday the 8th of Feb. 1549. "Bishop of Worcester convented before the lords for that he would not assent to the book made by the rest of the bishops and of the clergy appointed to devise a form for the creation of the bishops and priests." On Friday the last of February 1549, there is the following entry: "It is thought convenient by the lords, that seeing the rest appointed to devise the form for consecrating of priests have agreed upon the book, and set their hands to the same, that the bishop of Worcester shall also do the like, specially for that he cannot deny but all that is contained in the book is good and godly."—p. 106. "At Westminster, Tuesday the 4th of March 1549. Bishop of Worcester committed to the Fleet, for that obstinately he denied to subscribe to the book devised for the consecration and making of bishops and priests."—p. 109.]

[42] [This was Sept. 22, 1551.]

rather like a son than a subject. He insisted on what he had
formerly said, that he would not disobey the order set forth in
the book. Every one in the council took pains on him; for it
seemed a contradiction to say he would obey it, and yet not
subscribe it. He was offered more time for conferences. He
said, he knew he could never be of another mind; adding,
that there were other things to which he would not consent, as,
to take down altars, and to set up instead of them tables. The
matter ended with a charge given him to subscribe under the
pain of deprivation. At this time two entries made in the
council-books shew the good effects of Latimer's zealous preaching. On the 10th of March he brought in one hundred and
four pounds, recovered of one who had concealed it from the
king: and a little after three hundred and sixty three pounds
of the king's money: of which, for his attendance in Lent,
fifty pound was allowed to him. I find there was in this reign,
as in the former, a peculiar seal for ecclesiastical matters, which
was in secretary Petre's keeping. Many took out licenses[43]
under this seal for eating meat in Lent; some only for a man
and his wife; and some for four, six, or ten, that did eat with
them; and some for as many as should come to their house.
Licenses of another nature I find were often taken out, for
keeping a number of retainers, above what was allowed by the
statute.

[March 10, 1550. Council Book, vol. ii. p. 115.]

[Rymer, xv. pp. 207, 208, 210, 211, 291, 292.]

---

[43] [Two such licenses are printed at length in Rymer from the patent Rolls; the first to the earl of War-wick, his wife, family, and visitors; the second to the duke of Somerset, in the same terms. These are both dated Feb. 18, 1550. Similar li-censes were granted on the same day to sir William Herbert and his wife; on the 23rd of Feb. to sir Thomas Wrothe; on the 3rd of March to sir Ralph Sadler; on the 4th to sir Anthony Wingfield; on the 6th to lord Fitzwater; on the 17th to sir Thomas Cheney; on the 18th to Dorset and Arundel and Dr. Wotton; and on the 19th to the earl of Worcester; and on the first of June to sir Thomas Chal-loner. Two more are printed at length, that to the archbishop of Can-terbury, bearing date Feb. 28, and that to the bishop of Ely, 18 March. There is also another to Miles Co-verdale, bishop of Exeter, and his wife, with five, or, at the utmost, six guests, dated Sept. 10, 1551; others for sir Philip Hobby and sir John Gates, for himself and any number of guests, dated Nov. 28. Another for the marquis of Winchester, his wife, family, and friends, the guests not exceeding the number of twelve, dated March 13, 1553. Several others bearing different dates in 1551 and 1552 are quoted by Strype in his Memorials Ecclesiastical, vol. ii. pp. 511, 514, 527, 534.]

All endeavours were too weak to overcome the aversion that the people had to the steps that were made towards a reformation. Dr. Cox, the king's almoner and preceptor, was sent to Sussex, to preach and instruct the people there, who were much disturbed (as the council-book has it) by the seditious preaching of Day bishop of Chichester[44], and others. Day denied this: so an order was made in council, that he should bring in writing that which he had preached. The duke of Somerset[45] reported to the council, that Day had been with him, and owned that he had received the order that the council had made for the taking down of altars, and setting tables in their stead; but answered, that he could not in conscience obey it: this seemed indeed unaccountable; but he insisted that he

Day bishop of Chichester in trouble for not removing altars.

[Nov. 8, 1550. Council Book, vol. iii. p. 158.]
[Nov. 30, 1550. Ibid. p. 175.]

[44] [" At Westminster the 8th of November 1550. The bishop of Chichester appeared before the council to answer to the things objected against him for preaching. And because [he denied] the words of his accusations, therefore he was commanded within two days to bring in writing what he preached."—p. 158. "At Westminster the 11th of Nov. 1550. This day the archbishop of Canterbury was sent for."—p. 161.]

[45] [" At Westminster the 30th of November 1550. This day the duke of Somerset declared to the council that the bishop of Chichester came to him two days past, and shewed to him that he received letters from the king's majesty, with his majesty's hand, and subscribed with the hands of divers lords of the council, the tenor of which here ensueth—

" Right reverend father in God, right trusty and well beloved, we greet you well. And where it is come to our knowledge that being the altars within the more part of the churches of this our realm already upon good and godly occasions taken down, there doth yet remain altars standing in divers other churches, by occasion whereof much variance and contention ariseth among sundry of our subjects, which if good foresight were not had, might perchance engender great hurt and inconvenience; we let you wit that minding to have all occasions of contention taken away, which many times grow by these and such like diversities, and considering that among other things belonging to our royal office and cure, we do account the greatest to be to maintain the common quiet of our realm; we have thought good, by the advice of our council, to require you, and nevertheless specially to charge and command you, for the avoiding of all matters of further contention and strife, about the standing or taking away of the said altars, to give substantial order throughout all your diocese, that with all diligence all the altars in every church or chapel, as well in places exempted as not exempted within your said diocese, be taken down, and in the lieu of them a table set up in some convenient place of the chancel within every such church or chapel, to serve for the ministration of the blessed communion. And to the intent the same may be done without the offence of such our loving subjects as be not yet so well per-

could not in conscience obey it, and prayed to be excused.
Upon that he was summoned to appear before the council, and
there he said, he could not conform himself to their order: for
he thought he followed in that both the scriptures, and the
doctors and fathers of the church; and that he did not perceive
any strength in the six reasons, given by the bishop of London,
to justify the change.   He quoted a passage in Isaiah, which
the archbishop, with the bishop of London, and the rest of the
council, thought not at all to the purpose: so he was ordered
to confer with the archbishop, and the bishops of Ely and
London, and to appear before them on the 4th of December.
When he was again before the council, he entered into a dispute with the archbishop and the bishop of Ely.   They pressed
him to give his reasons for being so positive; he insisted on
those words in the Epistle to the Hebrews, *We have an altar:*
and though they thought it was clear, that by the altar Christ
himself was meant, yet that did not satisfy him.   They also
shewed him from Origen, that the Christians in those days had
no altars: he might call the table an altar if he pleased; so
the ancient writers did: but all this had no effect on him.   A
few more days were given him to consider of the matter: he

[Council
Book, p.
176.]

[p. 177.]

[p. 179.]

[Dec. 8,
Ibid. p.
183 b.]

197

suaded in that behalf as we would
wish, we send unto you herewith
certain considerations gathered and
collected that make for that purpose. To the which and such other
as you shall think meet to be set
forth to persuade the weak to embrace our proceedings in this part,
we pray you cause to be declared
to the people by some discreet
preachers in such places as you
shall think meet, before the taking
down of the said altars, so as both
the weak consciences of others may
be instructed and satisfied as much
as may be; and this our pleasure
the more quietly executed, for the
better doing whereof we require you
to open the foresaid considerations
in that our cathedral church in
your own person, if you conveniently may, or otherwise by your
chancellor, or some other grave
preacher, both there and in such
other market towns and most not-

able places of your diocese, as you
may think most requisite. Given
under our signet, &c.
"According to which letter he said
he could not conform his conscience
to do that he was by the said letter
commanded, and therefore prayed
the said duke he might be excused.
Whereunto the said duke for answer used divers reasons moving
the said bishop to do his duty, *and
in such things to make no conscience*
where no need is.   Nevertheless
the said bishop would not be removed from his former opinion,
and therefore the said duke said he
would make report to the rest of
the council, and so in the end he
prayed the lords of the council this
day that the bishop might be sent
for and shew his mind touching
this cause; which was agreed, and
commandment given for the bishop
to be here to-morrow."

positively answered, he could not obey their order with a good conscience; and rather than do it, he was resolved to suffer the loss of all he had. Two days more were given him; but he was still firm. So, on the 11th of December 1550, he was sent to the Fleet. Further proceedings against him were stopped for many months; in which time it is said that the king himself wrote to him: but all was in vain. So, in September 1551, a commission was given to judge him; and, on the 14th of October, it seems both Heath and he were deprived: for then an order passed in council for seizing the temporalities of both their bishoprics. Letters were written, in June[46] 1552, concerning them to the bishops of Ely and London; the former was to receive Day, and the latter Heath, and to use them as in Christian charity should be most seemly. It seems that both Heath and Day saw the change of doctrine that was preparing, with relation to the sacrament: so they were willing to lay hold on the first colour to break off from any further compliances; for the points they stood upon did not seem of such importance as to suffer deprivation and imprisonment for them[47].

There was at that time a very scandalous venality of all offices and employments, which was so much talked of at the court of France, that the ambassador whom the king had there wrote over an account of it; and it was said, that whereas king Henry had by his endowments made some restitution, yet, for all the wealth they had seized on in chantries and collegiate churches, no schools nor hospitals were yet endowed. Here a very memorable passage in Ridley's life deserves to be remembered. He wrote to Cheke, that he being to give Grindal a prebend in St. Paul's, had received a letter from the council[48]

Marginal notes: [Council Book, p. 184.] [Archæologia, xviii. p. 150.] [Sept. 27. [Oct. 24. Council Book, p. 420.] [June 15, Ibid. p. 575.]

Scandals given by many.

---

46 [" At Grenewiche the 15th of June 1552. A letter to the lord chancellor, signifying unto him that doctor Day is sent to him by the king's majesty's appointment, to be used of his lordship as to Christian charity shall be most seemly; at whose hands his highness doubteth not but he shall receive such Christian advice as shall tend to the glory of God. A like letter to the bishop of London for the receiving of doctor Heth."—

Council Book, p. 575.]
47 [The account of the deprivation of Heath and Day is given at greater length, and more circumstantially, in Strype's Cranmer, ch. xxx. pp. 226—262.]
48 [" At Grenewiche the 23th of June 1550. It was agreed . . . . . . and likewise that William Thomas may have his majesty's interest in the prebend of Cantleurs or Cantlens copse (?) in Poules." Council Book, p. 57.

to stop collation : for the king was to keep that prebend for the furniture of his stable. " Alas, sir," he writes, " this is a " heavy hearing. Is this the fruit of the gospel? Speak, " Mr. Cheke, speak for God's sake, in God's cause, unto whom- " soever you think you may do any good withal : and if you " will not speak, then I beseech you let this my letter speak [49]."

[Council Book, vol. iii. pp. 443, 448.] There was nothing that opened all men's mouths more than a complaint entered in the council-book, made by one Norman against the archbishop of York, that he took his wife, and kept her from him. The council gave such credit to this, that as a letter was written to that archbishop not to come to parliament, so they ordered a letter to be written to sir Thomas Gargrave and Mr. Chaloner to examine the matter. What they did, or what report they made, does not appear to me. Holgate, during all the time he was archbishop of York, was more set on enriching himself than on any thing else. He seemed heartily to concur in the reformation, but he was looked on as a reproach to it, rather than a promoter of it. This might have a share in the censure, that, as was reported, king 198 Edward passed on the bishops in that time ; *Some for sloth, some for ignorance, some for luxury, and some for popery, are unfit for discipline and government.* At this time the anabaptists were again inquired after, and a commission was granted to Cranmer, Thirlby, Cox, and sir Thomas Smith, to inquire after them, and to judge them.

[Strype, Mem. Eccl. ii. p. 414.]

Gardiner is deprived. Now Gardiner's business was brought to a conclusion [50]. On the 23rd of November a committee of the council was appointed

---

" At Westminster the 28th of June 1550. These suits following were declared unto the king's majesty by the whole council, and so granted . . . . That William Thomas shall have the king's majesty's interest in the prebend of Cantleurs or Cantlens copse(?) given to his highness by William Layton, late prebendary there."—p. 62.]

[49] [It appears from the letter which is printed in Coverdale's Letters of the Martyrs that William Thomas, clerk of the council, endeavoured to get the prebendal stall of ' Cantrells' alienated to him and

his heirs. Ridley resisted, but agreed not to give it when it should become vacant, which happened soon afterwards by Layton's death, till he had acquainted the king with the vacancy. In the letter which is dated July 23, 1551, he says that the council, ' no doubt by this ungodly man's means,' had written to forbid any appointment to it.]

[50] [" At Westminster the 23th of November 1550. This day the bishop of Winchester's matter was renewed, and thereupon considering the time of his intimation, was long sithens expired : it was agreed that

to consider how to proceed further against him. On the 14th [Council
of December an order was sent to the lieutenant of the Tower Book, vol.
iii. p. 167]
to carry him to Lambeth on the 16th[51], and after that as often [Dec. 15.
as they required him. The commission to try him was directed Ibid.
p. 186.]
to Cranmer and others. He desired counsel: it was granted;
and his lawyers had free access to him. On the 19th of [Ibid.
January[52] his servants moved in council, that some of that board P.[202.]
might be sworn as his witnesses: they said they would answer
upon their honour, but would not be sworn. And on the 15th [Ibid.
of February, the last mention made of him in the council-book P. 222.]
is in these words: " Forasmuch as the bishop had at all times,
" before the judges of his cause, used himself unreverently to
" the king's majesty, and very slanderously towards his coun-
" cil; and especially yesterday, being the day of the judgment
" given against him, he called the judges heretics and sacra-
" mentaries; these being there as the king's commissioners,
" and of his highness' council, it was ordered that he should be
" removed from his present lodging into a meaner one in the
" Tower, and have but one servant to wait on him: that his

the bishop of Elie, Mr. secretary Peter, doctor Maye and doctor Glynne, all learned in the civil laws, should substantially confer upon the matter, and upon Tuesday next the 25th of this present, to certify unto the council what was to be done duly by the order of the law in this case."—Council Book, p. 167.]

[51] [The 14th of December fell on Sunday, and the lieutenant of the Tower was ordered to bring the bishop on Monday next to Lambeth.]

[52] [" At Westminster the 19th of July 1550. This day the council had access unto his majesty for divers causes, but specially for the bishop of Winchester's matter, who this day was therefore appointed to be before the council. And there having declared unto his highness the circumstance of their proceedings with the bishop, his majesty commanded that if he would this day also stand to his wonted obstinacy, the council should then proceed to

the immediate sequestration of his bishopric and consequently to the intimation.

" Upon this the bishop of Winchester was brought before the council, and there the articles before mentioned read unto him distinctly and with good deliberation. Whereunto he refused either to subscribe or consent, and thereupon both the sequestration and intimation read unto him in form following." Here occurs the form, after which, " Whereunto he answered, that in all things that his majesty would lawfully command him, he was willing and most ready to obey, but forasmuch as there were divers things required of him that his conscience would not bear, therefore he prayed them to have him excused. And hereupon Mr. secretary Peter, by the council's order, proceeded with these words."

Here follows (p. 90) the sequestration.—Council Book, p. 90.]

" books and papers should be taken from him, and that from
" henceforth he should have neither pen, ink, nor paper given
" him, but be sequestered from all conference, and from all
" means that may serve him to practise any ways." Here was
severity upon severity ; which, as it raised him to be depended
on as the head of the popish party, so it must have recommended him to the compassions of all equitable people[53].

[Epistolæ
Tigurinæ.
xxxviii,
p. 51.]

Whether these hard orders were rigorously executed, or
not, does not appear to me.   I find in a letter of Hooper's to
Bullinger, one circumstance relating to Gardiner.   It is without date[54].   In it, as he tells him that Crome did with zeal
oppose their doctrine concerning the sacrament ; but commends
him, as a person of great learning, and a man of a most holy
life ; he tells him also, that Gardiner had a month before sent
him a challenge to a public disputation upon that head ; promising, that if he did not clearly carry away the victory, he
would submit himself to the laws, and would willingly suffer the
cruellest hardships. Hooper accepted the challenge, and a day was
set for them to dispute ; but when the day came near, Gardiner
said, he must be first set at liberty : so all this show of a readiness to maintain the old doctrine vanished to nothing.   Con-

[Ibid.
p. 52.]

,cerning the king, Hooper writes in that same letter, that these
thousand years there had not been any person of his age, who
had such a mixture both of piety and learning, with so true a
judgment as appeared in him.   If he lived, and went on
suitably to these beginnings, he would be the wonder and the
terror of the world.   He took notes of all the sermons he
heard ; and after dinner he asked the young persons that were **199**
bred up with him an account of what they remembered of the
sermon, and went over the whole matter with them.   He wrote
further in this letter, that then they were every day expecting

---

[53] [Gardiner's deprivation has
been more minutely narrated in
Strype's Cranmer, ch. xix. pp. 220
—244.]

[54] [The letter is dated ' Londini,
27 Martii 1550.' The author not
seeing the date at the end, where
there is a long postscript, hastily
inferred that there was none in the
letter, the latter part of which, referring as it does to private matters,
he probably had not read.   It is
addressed, ' *Præclarissimo viro ac
doctissimo D. Henrico Bullingero,
Tigurinæ ecclesiæ pientissimo archi-
episcopo, fidelissimo ac compatri suo
colendissimo.   Tiguri.*]

that the duke of Somerset should be again called to sit in the council

Poynet[55], bishop of Rochester, was translated to Winchester, being nominated to it the 8th of March ; and on the 5th of April he took his oath of homage.   While he was bishop of Rochester he had no house to live in, so he kept his benefice in London.   But it is entered in the council-book, that no bishop after him was to have any benefice besides his bishopric.

A new scene of contention was at this time very unhappily opened.   Hooper, a zealous, a pious, and a learned man, had gone out of England in the latter years of king Henry's reign ; and had lived at Zurich, at a time when all Germany was in a flame on the account of the *Interim*.   Upon that a great question arose among the Germans, concerning the use of things in themselves indifferent.   For a great part of the design of the *Interim* was, to keep up the exterior face of things, as it had been in popery, with the softenings of some other senses put on them.   It was said, " If things were indif-" ferent in themselves, it was lawful, and that it became the " subjects' duty to obey them when commanded."   Many thought that Melancthon himself went in that matter too far. It was visible the design in it was to make the people think the difference was not great between that and popery ; so the rites were ordered to be kept up on purpose to make it easy to draw the people over to popery.   Out of this another question arose ; Whether it was lawful to obey in indifferent things, when it was certain they were enjoined with an ill design ?   Some said, the designs of legislators were not to be inquired into nor judged : and whatever they were, the subjects were still bound to obey.   This created a vast distraction in Germany ; while some obeyed the *Interim*, but many more were firm to

Marginal notes:
[Archæol. xviii. p. 153.]

An account of bishop Hooper.

---

[55] [" At Grenewiche the 11th of May 1550.   Mr. Poynett was appointed bishop of Rochester."— Council Book, p. 31.

" At Westminster the 28th of June 1550.   Upon consideration that Mr. Poynett, now elected bishop of Rochester, hath no house to dwell in, and his living small, it was agreed he should enjoy his benefice *in commendam*, but from henceforth it is decreed that no bishop shall have other benefice than his bishopric only."—Ibid. p. 61.

" At Westminstre the 8th of March 1550.   This day, by the king's majesty's own appointment, doctor Poynet, bishop of Rochester, was appointed and admitted bishop of Winchester."—Ibid. p. 240.]

their principles, and were turned out of all for their disobedience.   Those who submitted were for the most part Lutherans, and carried the name of adiaphorists, from the Greek
word that signifies things indifferent.   The reformed were generally firmer.   Those of Switzerland, particularly at Zurich,
had at this time great apprehensions of a design of introducing
popery, by keeping up an exterior that resembled it.   Of this
I find a very late instance, the year before this, in a letter
that Mont wrote from Strasburg, on the 18th of February

Collect.
Numb. 3.

1548, to Musculus, which will be found in the Collection.

   " When he left Augsburg, there were no changes then
" begun there ; but they expected every day, when the new
" superstitious practices were to be set up.   One of the
" ministers told him, that the magistrates had desired the
" ministers not to forsake them in that time of distress.
" They promised that they would give them timely notice
" when those rites were to be brought in among them.   They
" prayed them likewise to recommend the *Interim* in the
" softest manner, and with the best colours they could.   This
" was refused by the greater number of them, who said, they 200
" could never approve that which was by an unanimous con-
" sent condemned.   He did not doubt but they had heard
" what was done in Saxony.   He wishes the German courage
" and firmness might now appear : that if they could not act
" with their usual courage, they might at least shew their
" courage in suffering.   The duke of Deux-Ponts had left
" Augsburg ; and said, the publishing the *Interim* did not be-
" long to him, but to the bishops.   Those of Bremen had such
" a heavy composition laid on them by the emperor, that they
" said it was not in their power to comply with it, though
" they had a mind to it.   So it was thought this was done on
" design to take their town, as a convenient post for a gar-
" risoned place, to keep that country in order.   He concludes,
" desiring to know what agreement there was, as to these
" matters, in the Helvetic churches."   They were indeed much
inflamed on this occasion ; and very zealous against any compliance with the *Interim*, or the use of the rites prescribed by
it : so Hooper came from Zurich, in the heat of this debate,
and with this tincture upon his mind.

   When he came to Brussels, on the 20th of April 1549, he

wrote a letter to Bullinger, that is in the Collection. " He Collect.
Numb. 4.
" sets forth in it, very tragically, the misery of the Nether-
" lands, under the violent oppressions of the Spaniards. Com-
" plaints were heard in all places of rapes, adulteries, rob-
" beries, and other insolences, every day committed by them :
" so that an hostess of a public house said to him, If she could
" but carry her children in her arms with her, she would
" choose to go and beg from door to door, rather than suffer
" their brutalities every day, as they were forced to do. He
" hoped this would be a warning, to put others on their
" guard.

" The emperor came seldom out of his chamber. Hooper
" had been at the duke of Saxony's house, who had about
" thirty of his servants still attending on him. He designed
" to have talked with Hooper, but the Spaniards hindered it.
" He had no hope of obtaining his liberty, though his health
" was much broken : but he continued firm in his religion, and
" did not despair of things, but hoped religion would be again
" revived. The landgrave was kept at Oudenarde. He was
" both uneasy and inconstant. Sometimes he was ready to
" submit to the emperor, and to go to mass : at other times
" he railed at the emperor ; and at the *Interim ;* (Hooper
" was entertained by Hobby, the English ambassador, from
" whom probably he heard these things ;) he prayed God to
" pity him, for he suffered justly for his treachery. The
" pope's legate was there, and preached all that Lent in his
" own court.

" The pope and the emperor were then in very ill terms.
" The pope pressed the emperor to own the council at Bo-
" logna ; for he was afraid to let it sit again in Trent : but
" the emperor was as positive for their coming back to Trent ;
" and said roundly, he would break with the pope, if that
" were not done. The ambassador told him, that if the em-
201 " peror's confessor were to any degree right set, there might
" be good hope of the emperor : but both he and all his
" ministers were strangely governed, and in a manner driven
" by the confessor. About seven months before this, he had
" left the emperor, because he would not be more severe, and
" would not restore popery entirely in Germany. The em-
" peror had offered him a bishopric in Spain, worth 20,000

" crowns : but he refused it, and said, he would be tied to the
" church, but not to him, unless he would serve the church
" with more zeal. The emperor seemed to design to break
" the peace of Switzerland, and Hooper understood that some
" of Lucerne were then hanging on at court, probably with no
" good design. He wishes they would fear God, lead holy
" lives, and fight bravely ; and so they might expect to be
" protected by God : yet he understood that the emperor was
" troubled that he had meddled so much as he had done in
" matters of religion in Germany : he found that was like to
" cross his other designs, which might have succeeded better,
" if he, had left that matter more at liberty. His army lay
" then near Bremen, but was undertaking nothing. The
" cities there had furnished themselves with stores and pro-
" visions for five years ; and were making no submissions."
This account I thought no digression from my chief design in
writing, since this intelligence came no doubt from the ambassador. Upon Hooper's coming to England, he applied himself much to preaching, and to the explaining the scriptures.
He was much followed, and all churches were crowded where
he preached. He went through the Epistle to Titus, and ten
chapters of the Gospel of St. John. His fame came to court.
Poynet and he were ordered to preach all the Lent at court ;
Hooper [56] on Wednesdays, and Poynet on Fridays : he was
also sent to preach both in Kent and in Essex. At this time
Bullinger wrote to the king, and sent with it a book that he
dedicated to him, which was presented to the king by the
marquis of Northampton ; for an order was made, that none
but privy counsellors might bring books or papers to the king.
The king said to Hooper, that he had read the letter, and
would read Bullinger's book ; and spoke to the marquis of a
present to be sent him : but Hooper told him, he never took
any ; besides, that it was forbidden by the laws of Zurich.
Hooper, in his letters to Bullinger, on the 8th [57] of February
1550, says, the archbishop of Canterbury, the bishops of Rochester, Ely, St. David's, Lincoln, and Bath, were sincerely

[Epistolæ
Tigurinæ,
xxxix.
p. 55.]

[Ibid. xl.
p. 59.]

[Ibid.
xxxvii.
p. 48.]

---

[56] [Hooper's sermons were published this same year in 8vo., with
a dedication to the king and privy
council, by 'Johan Hoper, electe

and sworne Bishoppe of Glocester,'
dated September 6, 1550.]

[57] [The date of this letter is Feb.
5, 1550.]

set on advancing the purity of doctrine, agreeing in all things
with the Helvetic churches.　He commends particularly the
marquis of Dorchester, afterwards duke of Suffolk, and the
earl of Warwick, afterwards duke of Northumberland, who at
that time put on such a show of zeal, that Hooper calls him a
most holy instrument, and the best affected to the word of [Epistolæ
God.　He writes of Cranmer, that he wishes he were not too Tigurinæ, xxxvi.
feeble.　He was at London when the council divided from the p. 46.]
duke of Somerset, but had not meddled in that matter: and Ibid. xxxvii.
he says not a word of it, but that he blesses God the duke of p. 49.]
Somerset was to be set at liberty.　In June, he was named to [July 3. Rymer, xv.
202 be bishop of Gloucester [58]; for he gives an account of it in a p. 240.]
letter to Bullinger, on the 29th of June.　He declined it, as
he writes, both for the oath, which he says was *foul* and *im-* Fœdum et
pious, and by reason of the Aaronical habits.　The king asked, impium. [Epistolæ
what his reasons were?　He told them very freely to him. Tigurinæ, xxxix.
He says of him, that the world never saw such a prince as he p. 55.]
was for his age.　He likewise says, the lady Elizabeth, his
sister, was wonderfully zealous, and very knowing: she read
both Greek and Latin; and few could maintain an argument
against her, particularly in matters of religion.

Among the letters sent me from Zurich, I find some written
upon the occasion of the difficulty that was made in Hooper's
business to Bullinger and Gualter, pressing them very earnestly to write to the king to let fall all the ceremonies: they
tell them, that Ridley, though he stood upon the forms of the
law, yet was very earnest to have Hooper made a bishop.
They seem also to reflect on the bishops for their earnestness
in that matter, as if they were ashamed to have that to be
blamed, to which they themselves had submitted: and they
reflect on Bucer for supporting the matter too much.　Those
of Zurich were more discreet and modest than to interpose in
such a manner.　It would have been too great a presumption
in them to have made any such application; but it seems
Bullinger wrote about it to the king's preceptor, Cox.　I have [Epistolæ
not found his letter: but I find, by Cox's letter to him, that Tigurinæ, ix. p. 80.]
he himself was for proceeding easily in this matter.　He wrote
to him in May, in these words: "I think all things in the

---

[58] ["At Grenewiche the 15th of　tuted bishop of Gloucester." Coun-
May 1550, Mr. Hoper was consti-　cil Book, vol. iii. p. 33.]

" church ought to be pure and simple, removed at the greatest
" distance from the pomps and elements of this world. But,
" in this our church, what can I do in so low a station? I
" can only endeavour to persuade our bishops to be of the
" same mind with myself. This I wish truly, and I commit
" to God the care and conduct of his own work." Of the

[Epistolæ
Tigurinæ,
lix. p. 79.]
[Ibid. cliii.
p. 214.]

king he writes, " Believe me, there appears in him an incred-
" ible beginning of learning, with a zeal for religion, and a
" judgment in affairs almost already ripe." Traheron, at the
same time, writes of him, " We are training up a prince that
" gives the greatest hopes of being a most glorious defender
" of the faith, even to a miracle: for, if God is not so pro-
" voked by our sins as to take him too early from us, we do
" not doubt but that England shall again give the world an-
" other Constantine, or rather one much better than he was."

This matter took up much time, and was managed with
more heat than might have been expected, considering the
circumstances of that reign. He being named to be bishop of
Gloucester [59], was recommended by Dudley to Cranmer, that
he would not charge him with an oath that was (as is expressed) burdenous to his conscience. This was the oath of
supremacy. He next desired to be excused from accepting
the bishopric, or from the ceremonies used in the consecration;
upon which the king writ to Cranmer in August, freeing him
from all dangers and penalties that he might incur by omit-
ting those rites, but left the matter to the archbishop's discretion, without any persuasion or command to omit them.

---

[59] [" At Richemunde the 6th of
October 1550. A letter to the bishop of London, that where there
hath been some difference betwixt
him and the elect bishop of Gloucester upon certain ceremonies belonging to the making of a bishop,
wherein their lordships' desire is
because they would in no wise the
stirring up of controversies betwixt
men of one profession, did send for
him, willing him to cease the occasions hereof, who humbly required that he might for declaration
of his doings, put in writing such
arguments as moved him to be of
the opinion he held; which thing
was granted, and was by their lordships commanded to be at the court
on Sunday next, bringing with him
that he shall for answer have
thought convenient."—p. 140.

" At Richemunde the 7th of October 1550. A letter to Doctor
Cokks, the king's almoner, to repair into Sussex to appease the
people by his good doctrine, which
are now troubled through the seditious preaching of the bishop of
Chichester and others."—p. 140.]

203 The archbishop did not think fit upon that letter to act against the laws. There were several conferences between Ridley and Hooper, not without heat : Hooper maintaining, that if it was not unlawful, yet it was highly inexpedient to use those ceremonies. The council, apprehending the ill effects of controversies between men of the same profession, sent for Hooper, and wished him to let this opposition of his fall. He desired leave to put his reasons in writing ; that was granted him : and when he offered his reasons, they were communicated to Ridley. I gave an account in my former work how honestly and modestly both Bucer and Peter Martyr behaved themselves on this occasion [60]. Peter Martyr mentions Hooper's unseasonable and bitter sermons, which it seems his heat carried him to ; and probably that was the reason that moved the council to command him to keep his house, unless it were to go to the archbishop of Canterbury, or to the bishops of Ely, London, or Lincoln, for the satisfaction of his conscience ; and not to preach or read till he had further license. But he did not obey this order ; he writ a book on the subject, and printed it [61]. This gave more distaste. He also went about and complained of the council; for which, being called before the board, he was committed to the archbishop's custody, to be reformed by him, or to be further punished. The archbishop represented, that he could in no sort work upon him, but that he declared himself for another way of ordination : upon that, he was on the 27th of January committed to the Fleet [62].

[right margin:]
[Council Book, p. 140.]

[Jan. 13. 1551. Archæol xvii p. 151.]

[Ibid. p. 152.]

[60] [See Part ii. p. 153.]

[61] [" A godly Confession and Protestacion of the Christian Fayth, made and set furth by Jhon Hooper, wherein is declared what a Christiā manne is bound to beleue of God, hys King, his neibour and hymselfe. The herte beleueth to justice, confession by the mouth is to saluation, Roma. x. ¶ Imprinted by John Daye ouer Aldersgate. Cum priuilegio ad imprimendum solum. 4to." It was printed also in 12mo this same year. The dedication is dated Dec. 20, 1550.]

[62] [" At Grenewiche the 13th of

January 1551. This day Mr. Hoper, bishop elect of Gloucester, appeared before the council touching his old matter of denial to wear such apparel as other bishops wear, and having been before commanded to keep his house, unless it were to go to the bishop of Canterbury, Ely, London, or Lincoln, for counsel or satisfaction of his conscience in that matter ; and further neither to preach nor read till he had further licence from the council, it appeared both that he had not kept his house, and that he had also written and printed a book, wherein was

[Epistolæ
Tigurinæ,
cclxii.
p. 368.]

Micronius, a minister of the German church at London, in a letter to Bullinger, on the 28th of August 1550, tells him, that the exception that Hooper had to the oath of supremacy was, because the form was *by God, by the saints, and by the holy Gospels*. This he thought impious; and when he was before the council, the king being present, he argued, that God only ought to be appealed to in an oath, for he only knew the thoughts of men. The king was so fully convinced by this, that with his own pen he struck these words out of the oath, saying, that no creature was to be appealed to in an oath. This being cleared, no scruple remained but with relation to the habits. The king and council were inclined to order him to be dispensed with as to these. But Ridley prevailed with the king not to dispense in that matter. The thing was indifferent, and therefore the law ought to be obeyed. This had such an effect, that all Hooper's exceptions were after that heard with great prejudice. Micronius was on Hooper's side as well as Alasco. Ridley had opposed the settling the German church in a different way from the rites of the church of England: but Alasco had prevailed to obtain an entire liberty for them to continue in the same forms of worship and government, in which they had been constituted beyond sea, in which he had been assisted by Cranmer. It is added in that letter, that it was believed that the emperor had sent one over to carry away the lady Mary secretly, but the design was discovered and defeated. To explain this matter of the oath, I shall insert in the Collections the oath of the bishops, as it was practised in king Henry's reign, and con-

Collect.
Numb 5.

contained matter that he should not have written; for the which and for that also he persevered in his former opinion of not wearing the bishops' apparel, he was now committed to the bishop of Canterbury's custody, either there to be reformed, or further to be punished as the obstinacy of his case requireth." Council Book, vol. iii. p. 198.

" At Grenewiche the 27th of January 1551. Upon a letter from the archbishop of Canterbury, that Mr. Hoper cannot be brought to any conformity, but rather persevering in his obstinacy, coveteth to prescribe orders and necessary laws of his head; it was agreed he should be committed to the Fleet.

" A letter to the archbishop of Canterbury to send Mr. Hoper to the Fleet upon the occasion aforesaid.

" A letter to the warden of the Fleet to receive the said Mr. Hoper, and to keep him from conference of any person saving the ministers of that house." Ibid. p. 209.]

tinued to be used to that time, which is on record, and is
among Mr. Rymer's manuscripts. Hooper's matter hung in
204 suspense nine whole months; in which time he seemed positively resolved not to yield, not without severe and indecent
reflections on those who used the habits. Cranmer expressed
a willingness to have yielded to him, but Ridley and Goodrich
stood firm to the law; while many reflected on them, as insisting too much on a thing practised by themselves, as if vainglory and self-love had been their chief motives: they said
they wished that distinction of habits was abolished, but they
thought the breaking through laws was so bad a precedent,
and might have such ill consequences, that they could not
consent to it. Bucer and Peter Martyr expressed their dislike of the habits, but thought the thing was of itself indifferent; so they blamed him for insisting so much on it.
Alasco, on the other hand, encouraged him to continue in his
refusal to submit to the laws in that matter : in conclusion, he
was prevailed on to submit, and was consecrated. This was
written to Bullinger by one of the ministers of the German
church. His standing out so long, and yielding in the end,
lost him much of the popularity, that, to speak freely, he
seemed to be too fond of; yet his great labours in his diocese,
and his patience and constancy during his imprisonment, and
in his last most extreme sufferings, made all good people willing to forget what was amiss, and to return to a just esteem of
what was so truly valuable in him. [Epistolæ Tigurinæ, cxxiv. p. 178, and cclxx. p. 380]

In conclusion, he submitted, and was consecrated according
to the established form, and went into his diocese, which he
found overrun with ignorance and superstition : he applied
himself to his duty with great and indefatigable industry ;
preaching often twice, sometimes thrice in a day, to instruct
the people, and to reform the clergy : he did earnestly wish
that the Articles of Religion, which he knew were under consideration, might be quickly published. He found the greatest
opposition in his diocese rose from the prebendaries of his
church. Of this he made great complaints ; as indeed all the
bishops that were well affected to the reformation found the
greatest opposition in their cathedrals ; though none of them
expressed it so severely as Ferrar, bishop of St. David's, who
wrote to a lord, desiring that he might have leave to defend [March 8, 1551.]

[Fox, vol.
iii. p.175.
Harl.MSS.
Nº. 420.]
himself against those *high-minded, arrogant, stubborn ambitious, covetous canons,* who for private revenge were set
against him: yet on the other hand there were great complaints made of his behaviour in his diocese, as both indiscreet
and contentious.   A petition was sent up to the council in the
name of the inhabitants of his diocese against him, complaining
of his insatiable covetousness, and his daily vexing his poor
tenants and clergy without cause; and indeed his firmness and
sufferings afterwards raised his character more than his conduct in his diocese had done.

[Council
Book, p.
464.]
The last and the most eminent of all the popish clergy that
fell in trouble during this reign, was Tunstall, bishop of Durham.   He was a generous and well-tempered man, learned far
above the common rate.   He retained his old opinion concerning the presence in the sacrament; but he had hitherto submitted, and gone along in all that was done: he had no heat,
nor a spirit of opposition in his temper, yet his opinion was
known.   The true account of his matter has been taken out of
the council-book[63], which has come to light since I wrote my 205
History.   One Ninian Mainvil charged him as consenting to a
conspiracy in the north, for raising a rebellion there: to this
the bishop answered, and Mainvil made replication: the council-book only refers to these, and gives no account of the
bishop's answer.   Mainvil had a letter of the bishop's, which
was his main evidence, upon which the issue of the trial
depended: but that was then wanted; and, as appeared afterwards, the letter was put in the duke of Somerset's hands, and
he still kept it: but whether he did it out of kindness to him,
or to have this as a check to overawe Tunstall, does not
appear.

This letter was found among the duke of Somerset's papers
after his last apprehension: upon which Tunstall was sent for,
and his letter was produced against him.   He could not deny
it to be of his own hand; and, not being able to make any
further answer, he was on the 20th of December sent to the

---

[63] [The first notice of Tunstall is
in the Council Book of May 20th,
1551.   " The bishop of Duresme,
upon the hearing of the matter between him and . . . . and

the dean of Duresme, is committed
to his house."—p. 297.   The next
mention is as related in the text,
p. 464.   See Strype, Mem. Eccles.
ii. p. 367.]

Tower.   Whitehead, dean of Durham [64], and Handmar'sh, Tunstall's chancellor, were accused of the same crime by Mainvil. The dean's death [65] put an end to his trouble, but Tunstall lay in the Tower till queen Mary set him at liberty : and there, in the seventy-seventh year of his age, he wrote his book, asserting the corporal presence of Christ in the sacrament.   It seems the evidence against Tunstall did not at all amount to a consent to a conspiracy, for he was only charged with misprision of treason ; whereas the consenting to it would have been carried further, to high treason itself : but even that must have been by a stretch of his words; since, if his letter had imported that, Cranmer could not have opposed, much less have pro- [Journal tested against the bill attainting him for misprision, if the of Lords, evidence had been clear.   This is confirmed by the opposition p. 418.] made in the house of commons, where the bill fell.   So, since the parliament would not attaint him, a commission was issued out some months after ; and, on the 22nd of September 1552, [Sept. 21, a letter [66] was written to the lord chief justice, signifying to 1551.] him, that there was a commission addressed to him, and to some others, for determining the bishop of Durham's case, with eight letters, and other writings touching the same, which he is required to consider and to hear, and to give order in the matter as soon as the rest of his colleagues were brought together.   He was brought before these commissioners : he desired counsel, and time convenient to make his answer ; both were denied him, as is set forth in the sentence that reversed this.   He was charged as a conspirator against the king and the realm : the commission empowered them to proceed against him for all offences, both according to the ecclesiastical and the

[64] [" At Westminster the 8th of July 1551.   A letter to the dean of Duresme to answer in writing unto such matters as he was charged withal at his being before the council, and to answer in such sort as he will stand to at his peril."—Council Book, vol. iii. p. 341.]

[65] [He was succeeded in the deanery by Robert Horne, who was appointed Nov. 20, 1551.]

[66] [" At Windesor the 21th of Sept. 1551.   A letter unto the chief justice, signifying unto him that there is presently sent to him the commission addressed to him and others for the examination and determination of the bishop of Duresme's case, with also eight letters and other writings touching the same, which he is willed to consider, and proceed to the hearing and ordering of the matter as soon as he may get the rest of his colleagues to him."—Council Book, p. 608.]

temporal laws : he made divers protestations against the several steps of their proceedings ; and at last he appealed from them to the king. The commissioners on the 11th of October deprived him of his bishopric, but did not attaint him of misprision of treason ; for the judgment in that case must have been, the forfeiture of his goods, and imprisonment for life : but he was by order of council on the 31st of October to receive money for his necessities, remaining prisoner in the Tower till further order should be given touching the money and goods lately appertaining to him.

[Council Book, p. 631.]

This was one of the violent effects of the duke of Northum- **206** berland's ambition, who was all this while a concealed papist, as himself declared at his execution. I have laid all these things relating to the deprivation of the bishops that opposed the reformation together, to give a full view of that matter. But now I must look back to some matters that happened while these proceedings went on. There was an information brought to the council of some at Bocking [67], who were irregu-

[Jan. 26, 1551. Council Book, vol. iii. p. 206.]

[67] [The following extracts from the Council Book appear to relate to this matter :

" At Grenewiche the 23th of June 1550. Upon a letter from the lord chancellor touching certain preachers in Essex that used preaching on the workdays, a letter was directed to the bishop of London, declaring the disposition of the people to idleness, and praying him therefore to take order for preaching the holidays only, till a better time of the people's inclination."—p. 57.

" At Grenewiche the 26th of January 1551. A letter to the lord chancellor to send hither the man of Bocking that was examined by him."—p. 205.

" At Grenewiche the 27th of January 1551. Upcharde of Boking was brought before the council, touching a certain assembly that had been made in his house in Christmas last, who confessed that were certain Kentish men to the town to have lodged with good man Cooke. And because Cooke's wife

was in childbed, they came to this Upcharddes house where Cooke was then at dinner, and by Cooke's entreaty there they were lodged. And upon the morrow, which was Sunday, divers of the town about twelve of the clock came in, and there they fell in argument of things of the scripture, specially whether it were necessary to stand or kneel, barehead or covered at prayer. Which at length was concluded in ceremony not to be material, but the heart before God was all that imported, and nothing else. And because it seemed such an assembly, being of sixty persons or more, should mean some great matter, therefore both the said Upcharde, and one Sympson of the same sort, was committed to the Marshalsie till further trial were had, and order taken that letters should be sent both into Essex and Kent for the apprehension of those that are accounted chief of that practice."—p. 206.

" A letter to sir George Norton,

lar in the worship of God; who thought that to stand or to kneel at prayer, or to be covered or bareheaded, was not material, and that the heart only was necessary. When they were brought before the council, they confessed that they met together; sometimes to confer about the scriptures, and that they had refused to receive the communion above two years, as was judged upon very superstitious and erroneous principles; (so it is entered in the council-book;) with divers other evil opinions, worthy of great punishment: five of them were sent to prison, and seven gave bonds to appear when called for: they were required to resort to their ordinaries, if they had any doubt in religion, for resolution from them. Those were probably some of the anabaptists, though that is not objected to them.

The great point that was then most canvassed in the univer-

[Council Book, p. 215.]

knyght, sheriff of Essex, to apprehend certain persons whose names were sent enclosed in a schedule, and to send them hither, that none of them have conference with other. The persons sent for were of those that were assembled for Scripture matters in Bocking, viz.:

John Barrett of Stamphorde, cowherd.
Robert Cooke of Bocking, clothier.
John Eglise of the same, clothier.
Richard Bagge.
Thomas Pygende.
John Kinge.
　　Myxsto.
　　Bonyhill.
Robert Wolmere.

"A like letter to sir Edward Wootton, and sir Thomas Wyat, to apprehend and send up the persons following:

William Sibly of Lamams.
Thomas Yonge of the same.
Nicholas Shetterton of Pluckley.
Thomas Sharpe of Pluckley.
John Lydley of Asheforde.
　　Chidderton of Asheforde.
　　Cole of Maydestone, schoolmaster."—p. 207.

"At Grenewiche the 3rd of February 1551. This day William Sib-

ley and Thomas Yong of Lenham, Nicholas Sheterenden and Thomas Sharpe of Pluckeley, ... Coole of Maydestone, appeared before the council, being of those that assembled at Bokyng in Essex.

"Likewise seven others of Essex appeared the same day, both which being examined, confessed the cause of their assembly to be for talk of scriptures. Not denying but they had refused the communion above two years, upon very superstitious and erroneous purposes, with divers other evil opinions, worthy of great punishment. Whereupon . . . Boneychill . . . . Barrey . . . . Cooke, William Sibley and Nicholas Shitterenden were committed to . . . . .

"Johannes Eglins, Thomas Myxer, Ricardus Blagge, Thomas Piggerell et Johannes King de Bocking in Essex recognoverunt etc. in 40li. &c.

"The condition to appear when they shall be called upon, and to resort to their ordinary for resolution of their opinions, in case they have any doubt in religion. The like recognizance taken of Thomas Sharpe of Plukeley and Nicholas Yong of Lenham."—p. 215.]

sities was the presence in the sacrament. Concerning this, I
have, among the papers sent me from Zurich, a letter of Peter
Martyr's to his friend Bullinger, dated from Oxford the 1st of

Collect.
Numb. 6.

June 1550, which will be found in the Collection. " He ex-
" cuses himself for his slowness in answering his letters by
" reason of the constant labours he was engaged in.   For,
" besides his daily exposition of St. Paul, which might claim his
" whole time, there was a new load brought on him.   He was
" commanded, by an order from the king, to be present at the
" public disputations upon theological matters ; which were
" held once a fortnight.   And in the college, in which he was
" placed, there was a disputation, where he was appointed to
" be present, and to moderate. He was in a perpetual struggle
" with most obstinate adversaries.   The business of religion
" did not go on with the zeal and success to be wished for : yet
" it made a better progress than he had expected four months
" before.   The number of their adversaries was great : they
" had few preachers on their side ; and many of those who
" professed the gospel were guilty of gross vices.   Some, by a
" human policy, were for purging religion, but for altering out-
" ward things as little as might be.   They, being secular men,
" apprehended, that, upon a more visible change, such dis-
" orders would follow as might prove fatal : whereas it was
" evident, that the innumerable corruptions, abuses, and super-
" stitions, that had overrun the church, were such, that it was
" impossible to reform it without bringing matters back to
" those pure fountains, and to the first sound principles of
" religion. The Devil studied to undermine those good designs
" by keeping up still many relics of popery, that by these the
" memory of the old abuses might be preserved, and the return
" to them rendered easier.   On the other hand, they had this
" great comfort, that they had a holy king, full of fervent zeal 207
" for true religion. He writes, that he speaks, in all this tender
" age, with that learning, that prudence, and that gravity,
" that it amazes all people who hear it.   Therefore they were
" all bound to pray God earnestly to preserve him long for the
" good of the church.   There were several of the nobility well
" inclined, and some bishops not of the worst sort, among
" whom the archbishop of Canterbury was the standard-bearer.
" Hooper was lately made a bishop, to the joy of all good men ;

" who was to pass through Oxford in his way to his diocese.
" He believed that he himself had given Bullinger an account
" of his being made a bishop, otherwise he would have wrote
" it.   He also commends Coverdale's labours in Devonshire :
" and adds, that if they could find many such men, it were a
" great happiness.   Alasco, being forced to leave Friezeland
" by reason of the *Interim*, was then about the settling his
" congregation in London.   He was at that time in the arch-
" bishop's house.   The peace with France gave them some
" hopes.   All were under great apprehensions from the pope's
" designs of bringing his council again together : but they
" must still trust in God.   And, after somewhat of their private
" concerns, he desires his prayers for the progress of God's
" word in this kingdom.

" He also, in a letter written on the 6th of August 1551,
" laments the death of the young duke of Suffolk, looking on
" him as the most promising of all the youth in the nation,
" next to the king himself."   After some more on that subject,
he adds this sad word, " *There is no end put to our sins, nor*
" *any measure in sinning*[68].   He commends Hooper's labours
" in his diocese mightily, and wishes that there were many
" more such bishops as he was."

1551. [Epistolæ Tigurinæ, ccxxxiii. p. 326.]

[Ibid. p. 327.]

Upon the death of the two young dukes of Suffolk, Grey,
marquis of Dorchester[69], was made duke of Suffolk.   He had
married their sister, but had no sons by her.   He had three
daughters, of whom the eldest, lady Jane, was esteemed the
wonder of the age.   She had a sweetness in her temper, as
well as a strength of mind, that charmed all who saw her.   She
had a great aptness to learn languages, and an earnest desire
to acquire knowledge.   Her father found out a very extraordinary person to give her the first impressions ; Aylmer, who
was afterwards, in queen Elizabeth's time, advanced to be
bishop of London.   Under his care she made an amazing progress.   He found, it seems, some difficulty in bringing her to
throw off the vanities of dress, and to use a greater simplicity
in it.   So, on the 23rd of December 1552, he wrote to Bullinger, " That the lady Elizabeth was a pattern to all in the
" modesty of her dress ; and yet nobody was prevailed on by
" such an illustrious example to follow it, and, in all this light

[Oct. 10, 1551.]

[Epistolæ Tigurinæ, cxxvii. p. 183.]

---

[68] *Peccatis neque finis neque modus imponitur.*   [69] [This ought to be Dorset.]

" of the gospel, to abstain from wearing gold, or gems, or
" plaiting of hair." He was particularly charged with the
education of lady Jane Grey, whom he calls his scholar : but
it seems he could not prevail in this particular ; so he desires
Bullinger to write his thoughts to her on that head.

[Cap. 11,
Statutes,
vol. iv. p.
111.]

There was nothing done for almost two whole years, pur-208
suant to the act passed in November 1549, for making a new
body of ecclesiastical laws[70]: concerning which, it is not easy
to guess what was the clause in it that gave the bishops so
much offence, that the greatest part of the bench protested
against it. For both the archbishops, and the bishops of Ely,
Durham, Worcester, Westminster, Chichester, Lincoln, Rochester, and St. David's, joined in the protestation. There were
only two clauses that I can imagine could give them this disgust. One is, that only four bishops, and four common lawyers,
were made necessary to be of the number of the thirty-two
persons. The other might be, the limitation of the time to
three years; though that seems designed to make the act have
its effect in a little time. Two years were almost ended before
any steps were made towards the execution of it. On the 6th
of October 1551[71], the council wrote to the lord chancellor, to

[70] [See Part ii. p. 196.]

[71] [" At Hampton Court the 6th
of October 1551. Letter to my lord
chancellor, to make out the king's
letters of commission to the thirty-
two persons here under written,
authorizing them to assemble together and resolve upon the reformation of the canon laws as by
the minute of the said letter at better
length appeareth :

	Bishops.		Divines.
of 8	Canterbury.	Mr. 8	Taylour of Lincolne.
	London.		Cox, almoner.
	Winchester.		Parcar of Cambridge.
	Ely.		Latimer.
	Exeter.		Cooke.
	Gloucester.		Petrus Martir.
	Bath.		Cheeke.
	Rochester.		Joannes Alasco.
	Civilians.		Lawyers.
	Mr. Petre.		Justice Hales.
	Mr. Cecill.		Justice Bromley.
	Sir Thomas Smithe.		Goodrike.
	Taylour of Hadley.		Gosnald.
	Doctour May.		Stamforde.
	Mr. Traheron.		Carrell.
	Doctour Lyell.		Lucas.
8	Mr. Skynner.	8	Brooke, recorder of London.

" Eight of these to rough hew the canon law, the rest to conclude it
afterwards."—Council Book, p. 407.]

make out a commission for thirty-two persons, to reform the ecclesiastical laws. These were, the archbishop, the bishops of London, Winchester, Ely, Exeter, Gloucester, Bath, and Rochester. The eight divines were, Taylor, Cox, Parker, Latimer, Cook, Peter Martyr, Cheke, John Alasco. The eight civilians were, Petre, Cecil, Smith, Taylor of Hadley, May, Traheron, Lyell, Skinner. The eight common lawyers were, Hales, Bromley, Goodrick, Gosnald, Stamford, Caryl, Lucas, Brook.

This it seems brought Peter Martyr from Oxford to London in March 1552. And on the 8th of that month he wrote to Bullinger from Lambeth, being lodged with the archbishop. He tells him, " That the king did earnestly press the bishops, " that, since the papal authority was cast out of this church, " the ecclesiastical laws might be so reformed, that none of the " papal decrees might continue to be of any authority in the " bishops' courts ; and that another body of laws ought to be " compiled for them. He had therefore appointed two and " thirty persons to set about it, of which number he himself " was one. He says, the greater number of them were persons " both eminently learned and truly pious: in this he desires " both their advices and their prayers. This work must be so " prepared as to receive a confirmation in parliament; in which " he foresaw some difficulties." It seems that this number was thought too great to bring any thing to a good conclusion, or these persons had not all the same views; for soon after, on the 9th of November[72] after this, a new commission[73] was or-

[Epistolæ Tigurinæ, ccxxxvi. p. 330.]

[Ibid. p. 331.]

[Wilkins, Conc. vol. iv. p. 69.]

[72] [" At Westminstre the 9th of November 1551. A letter to the lord chancellor to make out a new commission to these eight persons here under named, for the first drawing and ordering of the canon laws, for that some of those other, that were before appointed by the king's majesty, are now by his highness thought meet to be left out, and the commission made to these following:
The archbishop of Canterbury.
The bishop of Ely.
Doctor Cox.
Petre Martir.
Doctor Taylor of Hadley.
Doctor May.
John Lucas.
Richard Goodrick." Council Book, p. 433.]

[73] [The commission is printed at length in Wilkins' Concilia, iv. 69, and is dated November 11. Strype observes (Mem. Eccles. vol. ii. p. 487) that this commission superseded that of October 22, the names of three of the commissioners being altered, the bishop of Ely being here substituted for the bishop of London, May for Traheron, and Goodrick for Gosnald. In Strype's Cranmer, p. 271, the date is Nov. 9.]

[Strype's
Cranmer,
p. 133.]

dered to be made out to eight persons, for preparing the same
work.   These were, the archbishop, the bishop of Ely, doctor
Cox, Peter Martyr, Taylor, May, Lucas, Goodrick.   Strype
tells us, he saw the digest of the ecclesiastical laws written out
by the archbishop's secretary ; the title being prefixed to each
chapter, with an index of the chapters, in the archbishop's own
hand.   In many places there are corrections and additions in
his hand, and some lines are scored out ; some of them were
also revised by Peter Martyr : the seventh chapter in the title
de Præscriptionibus is all written by Peter Martyr.   Several
chapters are added to the first draught, which is probably that **209**
which was prepared in king Henry's time.   There was a later
and more perfect draught of this work prepared for king
Edward, which coming into Fox's hands, he printed it in the
year 1571[74] : the differences between the two draughts, as

[Ibid. p.
134.]

Mr. Strype assures us, are not very material.   But all this was
brought to no conclusion.

The duke
of Somer-
set's last
fall.
[Epistolæ
Tigurinæ,
ccviii. p.
289.]

I find somewhat to be added concerning the duke of Somerset's tragical death, in a letter that one John ab Ulmis, a
Switzer, then in England, wrote from Oxford the 4th of December 1552[75], to Bullinger ; that the duke of Somerset was
censured, as having been too gentle to the lady Mary, in con-
niving at her mass : but, when he proposed the doing that in

[Ibid. p.
290.]

council, the earl of Warwick answered, " The mass is either of
" God or of the Devil : if it is of God, we ought all to go to it ;
" if it is of the Devil, why should it be connived at in any
" person ?"   Yet still the gentleness of the duke of Somerset
made him suffer it to go on.   But now he adds, since the earl
of Warwick had the greatest share in the government, he had
put her priests in prison, and had given strict orders to suffer
no mass to be said in her house.

[Ibid. p.
291.]

He tells one remarkable particular in the duke of Somerset's
trial : " That after he was found guilty of the conspiracy against
" the earl of Warwick, (upon which the people expressed a
" great concern,) the earl of Warwick addressed himself to the

---

[74] [Reformatio legum Ecclesias-
ticarum, ex authoritate primum regis
Henrici 8. inchoata : deinde per
regem Edouardum 6. prouecta, ad-
auctaque in hunc modum, atque

nunc ad pleniorem ipsarum refor-
mationem in lucem ædita.   Londini
ex officina Johannis Daii anno sa-
lutis humanæ, 1571 Mense Aprili.]
[75] [This is a mistake for 1551.]

" duke, and told him, that now, since by the law he was ad-
" judged to die, he, as he had saved him formerly, so he would
" not now be wanting to serve him, how little soever he expected
" it from him.   He desired him therefore to fly to the king's
" mercy, in which he promised he would faithfully serve him.
" Upon this, the duke did petition the king; and it was hoped
" that he would reconcile those two great men, and that by this
" means the duke of Somerset should be preserved."

It seems there was some treaty about his pardon : for though
he was condemned on the 1st of December, he was not executed
till the 22nd of January. What made it to be respited so long,
and yet executed at last, does not appear. It is probable it
was from a management of the duke of Northumberland's,
who, by the delay, did seem to act in his favour, that so he
might be covered from the popular *odium*, which he saw his
death was like to bring upon him; and at the same time, by
the means of some who had credit with the king, he possessed
him with so bad an opinion of the duke of Somerset, that he,
looking on him as an implacable man, capable of black designs,
resolved to let the sentence be executed upon him.

In the same letter he gives an instance of Hooper's impartial
zeal in the discharge of his function in his diocese : that, while
he was censuring some inferior people for their scandalous life,
one said to him, " We poor people must do penance for these
" things ; while great and rich men, as guilty as we, are over-
" looked.   Upon that he said, Name any person, how great
" soever, that was guilty of adultery, so that it could be proved
" against him, and he would leave himself in their hands, to be
" used by them as they pleased, if he did not proceed equally
210 " against all.   So, in a few days, sir Anthony Kingston, a
" great man in those parts, being accused of adultery, he cited
" him into his court.   He for some time refused to appear.
" At last he came ; and, when the bishop was charging his
" sin severely upon him, he gave him very foul language, and
" at last fell to beat him.   This was presently followed so se-
" verely, that he was fined in five hundred pound, and forced
" to submit to do penance."

This raised the bishop's character, as it contributed not a
little to establish his authority in his diocese. He set himself
to do his duty there with so much zeal, that his wife, who was

[Side notes:] Hooper's impartial zeal. [Epistolæ Tigurinæ, p. 291.]

[Epistolæ
Tigurinæ,
xlix. p.69.] a German, wrote to Bullinger, praying him to write to her
husband to take a little more care of himself : for he preached
commonly thrice, sometimes four times in one day. The crowds
of those who came constantly to hear him made him look on
them as persons that were hungering for the word of life. So
she, apprehending that his zeal made him labour beyond his
strength, studied to get others to put some stop to that, which,
it seems, she could not prevail with him so far as to restrain.

About this time the bishops and divines were employed in
the review of the Common Prayer ; but I have met with
nothing new with relation to that matter, save that on the 6th
[May 16.] of May 1551, there was an order of council for preserving
Reg. Exon.
Voysey, [ii.
fol. 121.] peace sent to all the cathedrals, at least to that of Exeter, for
it is in that register[76]. And on the 18th of January there was

---

[76] [" Item XVI[to]. die Mensis
Maii Anno Domini 1551, M[r]. Blaxton recepit apud exon. litteras sequentes.

" Right Reverend Father yn god
right trustie and welbelovide we
grete you welle. And whereas as
yt ys come to our knowlidge that
there be divers lewide and sedicious
persons yn certaine partes of our
realme, that practise and devise the
means to styre upe unlefulle as-
sembles and commotions to the
trubble and unquiett of us our lov-
ynge subjects, forasmoche as we in-
tende to mete with the said practise in tyme, we have thought good
amonge other things that we have
set forthe the purpose to addresse
unto you, as we have donne the like
to all other prelatts of our realme,
for the conteyninge of our subjects
yn quyet and good order, and the
suppression of rebellion yf at anye
tyme anye shulde happen to be
practyside or begonne within our
reallme; wherefore we requyre and
straytly charge to gyve substanciall
order throughout all your Dioces
that within every parishe churche
within the same, the sayde act may
be openly and distinctly red by the

parson or curat to the parochians,
every Sondaye or seconde Sondaie
at the leste, at suche tyme in the
morninge as the assemble of the
saide parochians ys most frequent,
to thende they maye be from tyme
to tyme admonishide of there dew-
ties and of the perell that shalle
ensewe to them that shalle devise
or attempt any thinge contrary to
the saide act And like as we yn
this perillous tyme, thought yt ne-
cessarye for the preservacion of the
common quiett of our reallme to
addresse to you and the rest of our
prelatts these our letters with the
saide act, So our specialle truste ys
that ye for your parte wille se the
same effectually donne and execut-
ide through your Dioces so dewly
with such regarde and care as them-
portance of the case requiritbe,
where of fayle ye not as ye tendre
our pleasure and wille advoyde our
Indignacion. Yeven under our signett at our manor of grenewyche
the sixt of maii the fyve eyre of our
rainge : E. Somerset. T. Cant., R.
Ryche canc., W.Wyltshire, J.War-
wike, E. Clynton, T. Ely, J.Wyng-
feld.

" To the right reverend father yn

a commission issued out for the repressing of heresy, and for [Rymer, observing the Common Prayer. And on the 27th of October, tom. xv. p. 250.]

god our right trustye and welbelovide the Byshipe of Exceter.

" Item XXIIII^{to}. Julii Anno Domini 1551, M^r. Blaxton recepit apud exon. litteras sequentes :

" Right Reverend Father in god right trustie et welbelovide we grete you well, and being not a litell disquietide to see the subjects of this our reallme vexide with the extreme and suddaine plage that daily encreasithe on all, we cannott but lament the peoples wickidnes throught the which the wrathe of god hathe bene thus marveylously provokyd ; for the more we studie for to instructe them in the knowlidge of god and his moste holy worde that consequently they might followe and observe his lawes and presepts, So moche the more busie is the wickide sprite to alienate there harts from all godlines, and his malice hathe so moche prevailide that because the people ar become, as it were open Rebells againste the divine majestie, God after one plage hathe sent another and an other encreasynge it so from one to one tyll at lenght, seinge non other remedie, he hathe throne forthe this moste extreme plage of sodaine deathe ; and because there is none other waie to pacifie his furie and to recover his grace and mercie, but by prayer and amendment of lyf, consideringe the cure and charge comyttide unto you we have thought good, to call upon you to use all diligence possible throught out your hole dyocese aswell by your self as by your good mynisters to perswade the people to resorte more unto the common prayer, [then they have done, and there not onlie to praye with all there harts in the feare of gode as good and faythefull men shulde do,

but also to have a dew regarde unto there levings, and specially to refraine there gredie appetid from that insaciable Serpent of covetuosnes, wherewith moste men are so infectide that it semethe eche one wolde devower an other with out cherite or any other godly respect to the poore, to their neighburs or to there commen wealthe. For the wiche hathe not only poured out this plage that after this liff shall plage them everlastingly, where yn you muste use those persuations that may engender a terror to reduce them from their corrupt noughtines and detestable vices, but as the bodie and membres of a dull or a sicke hede can not be lustie or apt to do welle, So in manie cures of this our realme, aswell the chief as the particuler ministre of the churche have byne bothe so dulle and so feble in dischardinge of their duties that it is not mervaile thought their flocks wander, no knowinge the voyce of their shepard and moche lesse the voyce of their principall and soverainge master we truste ye ar none of those but if ther have bene suche necligence with in your Jurisdiction we exorte et praye you et nevertheles charge and command by the authorite geven us of god to se it reformide, encreasinge also amendement in that, that alredy is welle begonne in such sorte your diligence maie declare you worthie of your vocacion, and thensforth there of yelde unto god an obedient faythefull et fearfull flocke which we wishe to god we maye shortly see Yevon under our signett at our honor of Hampton Court the XVIII of Julii the fift yere of our reinge. E. Somerset, W. Wyltshire, J. Bedford, F.

1552, the council-book mentions also a letter, written to the lord chancellor, to add in the edition of the New Common Prayer Book a declaration touching kneeling at the receiving the communion[76].

The Articles of Religion prepared.

It remains that I give the best account I can of the Articles of Religion. It seemed to be a great want that this was so long delayed, since the old doctrine had still the legal authority of its side. One reason of delaying the publishing them probably was, that the king, in whose name and by whose authority they were to be published, might be so far advanced in years, and out of the time of pupilage, that they might have the more credit, and be of the more weight: for though it was a point settled in law, that the king's authority was at all ages the same, yet the world would still make a difference in their regard to things passed while he was a child, and those things authorized by him when he was in the sixteenth year of his age.

Not passed in convocation.

The first impression of these Articles appeared with a title apt to make one think they had been agreed on in the convocation. It runs thus in English: *Articles which were agreed to in the synod of London, in the year 1552, by the bishops and other godly and learned men, to root out the discord of opinions, and establish the agreement of true religion*[77]. But there is reason to believe that no such articles were offered to the convocation. Weston objected afterwards to Cranmer, that he had set forth a Catechism in the name of the synod in London; and yet, said he, there be fifty, which, witnessing that they were of the number of the convocation, never heard one word of this *Catechism*. And in a long and much laboured 211

Shrewesbury, F. Huntyngdon, T. Darcy, C. Cobham, T. Cheyne, John Gate.

" To the Right Reverend Father in God our right trustie and welbelovide the Bishop of Excetter, and yn his absens to his chancelor."]

[76] [" At Westminster the 27th of October 1552. A letter to the lord chancellor to cause to be signed unto the book of common prayer lately set forth, a certain declaration signed by the king's majesty, and sent unto his lordship, touching the kneeling at the receiving of the communion."— Council Book, p. 630.]

[77] [*Articles* agreed upon by the Bishops and other Learned and Godly men in the last Convocation at London, in the year of our Lord, 1552. To root out the Discord of Opinions, and establish the Agreement of True Religion. Published by the King's Majesties Authority, 1553. Imprinted at London by John Day.]

sermon of Brooks[78], preached at St. Paul's Cross in November [Nov. 12.] 1553, there is an intimation, that makes it indeed probable that the Articles were brought into the upper house of convocation.   For when he complains that they were set forth as allowed by the clergy, he adds, Whereas the convocation without all doubt (for the lower house at least) was never made privy thereto : that reserve seems to make it probable that they were brought into the upper house.   In the first impression of the Articles, the Catechism is printed first before the Articles ; so this is to be understood of that whole book, which is indeed a very small one.

When this was objected to Cranmer, he answered, *I was ignorant of the setting to of that title ; and as soon as I had knowledge thereof, I did not like it.   Therefore, when I complained thereof to the council, it was answered by them, that the book was so entitled, because it was set forth in the time of the convocation.*   In the interrogatories that were afterwards exhibited to him in order to his final censure, the seventh ends thus, *That he did compile, and caused to be set abroad, divers books :* the last part of his answer to that was, *As for the Catechism, the book of Articles, with the other book against Winchester, he grants the same to be his doings.*

It is true, in the first convocation under queen Mary, when the prolocutor charged Philpot with this, that a Catechism was put forth without their consent, he answered on a sudden, that the house had granted an authority to make ecclesiastical laws to certain persons to be appointed by the king's majesty : and what was set forth by them might be well said to be done in the synod of London, although the house had no notice thereof before the promulgation.   But Weston also said, *That the Catechism beareth the title of the last synod before this, although many of them who were then present were never made privy thereof in setting it forth :* so that both Weston and Philpot agree that the book was never brought before the convocation.   In this matter, Philpot, as he could not deny the fact, so he made use of the best answer that then occurred to him, without considering that the convocation had not agreed to any such deputation of thirty-two persons : for that

[78] [Brooks (James) Bp. of Glocester.   Sermon at Paul's Cross in   the first year of queen Mary, on Matth. ix. 18.   London, 1553. 8vo.]

was settled by an act of parliament; nor did the deputation relate to matters of doctrine, but only to the canons and proceedings in the ecclesiastical courts: for as it was a revival of the acts passed in king Henry's time, so it ran in the same strain with them. These evidences make it plain that the Articles of Religion did not pass in convocation. We have Cranmer's own word for it that he drew them, and that he, who was always plain and sincere, did not approve of that deceitful title that was prefixed to them, to impose upon the unwary vulgar. He also owns that they were his doings. One reason that may seem probable for his not offering them to the convocation might be, that he had observed that many made a difference between obeying orders already made, and the consenting beforehand to the making of them: a greater degree of authority and evidence seemed necessary for the one than for the other; besides that the offering things to debate, while it was free to argue on either side of the question, might carry some to engage themselves so far, that they could not 212 after that submit with any decency. This, as far as I can judge, seems to be Cranmer's reason for not offering the Articles to be debated and passed in convocation.

[Strype's Cranmer, Appendix Nᵒ. lxvi. p. 160. Cranmer's Remains, p. 220.]

But published by the king's authority. But now that they were to be published with authority, that was to be done in the king's name: so, a very few days before the king's death, he sent a mandate to Cranmer to publish the Articles, and to cause them to be subscribed: this was done pursuant to the archbishop's motion to the king and council; for he had desired, "That all bishops might have authority " from him to cause all their preachers, archdeacons, deans, " prebendaries, parsons, vicars, curates, with all their clergy, " to subscribe the said Articles: and he trusted that such a " concord and quietness in religion should shortly follow thereon, " as else is not to be looked for in many years. God shall " thereby be glorified, his truth shall be advanced, and your " lordships (for he writes it to the privy-council) shall be re- " warded of him as the setters forward of his true word and " gospel." Dated from Ford the 24th of November. It seems [Oct. 21.] they were prepared some time before that; for on the 20th of October, in the year 1552, the council had written to the six preachers, Harley, Bill, Horne, Grindal, Perne, and Knox[79],

[79] [" At Westminstre the 21th of October 1552. A letter to Mr. Harley,

to consider of some articles then offered to be subscribed by
all preachers, which can be no other than these Articles : but
as this matter was long delayed formerly, so, when it was now
ordered, it was sent about with all the diligence that so important a work required.   The king also directed his orders to
all the archbishop's officers, enjoining them to cause all rectors,
vicars, or those in any ecclesiastical employments, to appear
before the archbishop, to obey and do on the king's part as
shall be signified to them.

The mandate that upon this was sent out by the archbishop's *And sent to*
officers, which is in the Collection, though it is in the king's *the Arch-*
bishop of
name, yet was issued out by Cranmer himself, in execution of *Canter-*
the mandate.   It is mentioned in it, that it was sent to him by *bury.*
Collect.
the king.   It was thus put in the king's name, pursuant to the *Numb. 7.*
act passed in the beginning of this reign, that all process in
the ecclesiastical courts should be in the king's name : but its
being tested by the archbishop, shews it was the act of his
court.   For though there is an exception in that act for the *[Statutes,*
archbishops, yet that only related to what they should act in *vol. iv. p. 4.]*
their provinces as metropolitans, but not to their proceedings
in their particular dioceses; in which it seems they were put
on the same foot with the other bishops.   The king's mandate
to himself is not in any record that I was able to find out.
After the mandate, the execution of it by his officers was certified to him on the 22nd of June, which is in his register, and
is added in the Collection to the mandate.   But probably the
time given them ran further than the king's life : for nothing
further appears to have been done upon it.   The clergy of the
city of London (probably only his peculiars) appeared before
him, and he exhorted them to subscribe the Articles.   No

Mr. Bill, Mr. Horne, Mr. Grindal, Mr. Perne, and Mr. Knox, to
consider certain articles exhibited
to the king's majesty, to be subscribed by all such as shall be admitted to be preachers or ministers
in any part of the realm, and to
make report of their opinions touching the same."——Council Book,
vol. iii. p. 624.
  " At Westminstre the 20th of
November 1552.   A letter to the

Archbishop of Canterbury with the
articles heretofore drawn and delivered by him to the king's majesty
which being since that time considered by certain of his highness' chaplains
and others, are in some part altered
and therefore returned to him to be
considered, so as after the perfect-
ing of them, order may be given for
the putting the same in due execution." ——Council Book, vol. iii.
p. 645.]

mention is made of any one's refusing to do it; but he compelled none to subscribe, which he affirmed in his answer to an interrogatory put to him by queen Mary's commissioners; for he said that he compelled none, but exhorted such to subscribe as were willing to do it, before they did it. It came to Norwich, where Thirlby was bishop, who complied readily with every thing that he was required to do: though by his sudden turn, and his employments in the next reign, it appears that he acted at least against his heart, if not against his conscience.

213

And the
bishop of
Norwich.
Collect.
Numb. 8.
The mandate for Norwich, which will be found in the Collection, bears date the 9th of June, in the 7th year of this reign: and it is not to be doubted but that the like mandates were directed to all the bishops [80], though they do not appear upon record. " It sets forth, that whereas, after a long time
" of darkness, the light was now revealed, to the inestimable
" benefit of the nation; the king thought it his duty to have a
" uniform profession, doctrine, and preaching, for the evading
" dangerous opinions and errors: and therefore he sent him
" certain articles, gathered with great judgment of the greatest
" part of the learned bishops of the kingdom, and sundry
" others of the clergy; which he required and exhorted him
" to sign, and in his preaching to observe, and to cause them
" to be subscribed by all others who do or shall preach or read
" within his diocese: and if any shall not only refuse to sub-
" scribe, but shall preach contrary to them, he is required to
" give notice of it to the king and his council, that further
" order may be given in the matter. And for such persons as

---

[80] [See Strype's Ecclesiastical Memorials, vol. ii. chap. 22. p. 420, where the mandate to the bishop of London extracted from Ridley's Register fol. 297 is printed. He says that he prints it because none of our church historians take notice of it. It is, with a few trifling variations, partly owing to the original transcribers, partly to those who copied from the two registers, the same with that printed in the Collection, No. 8. He also mentions (ibid. p. 521) " twenty letters ·to ———— signifying that the king's majesty hath sent unto every one of them, certain articles for an uniform order to be observed within every church within this realm. Which articles are gathered with great study and by the advice of the greatest learned men of the bishops, &c. dated in May;" and " Fifty-four articles concerning the uniform order to be observed in every church of the realm. A catechism also to be taught to scholars as the ground and foundation of their learning. Dated in May."]

" came to be admitted to any benefice or cure, he was to confer
" with them on these Articles, and to cause them to subscribe
" them, otherwise not to admit them to any such benefice, to
" which they were presented. But if the person was ignorant,
" and did not understand them, pains was to be taken on him
" to instruct him; and six weeks time might be given him to
" examine them by the scriptures: but at the end of six
" weeks, if he did not subscribe them, he was to be rejected.
" Then follows an order for him to receive the Catechism, and
" to give it to all masters of schools, that it may be taught in
" them all; and he is required to make report to the arch-
" bishop of the province, of the obedience given to these
" orders." This order was so readily executed, that about fifty
of the clergy subscribed it. This instrument was examined,
and sent to me by Dr. Tanner, the learned chancellor of
Norwich.

But besides the evidence that appears from the registers And to the university of Cambridge.
of Canterbury and Norwich, I have a further proof that the
Articles of Religion were only promulgated by the king's authority, in an injunction sent to the university of Cambridge,
signed by the bishop of Ely, sir John Cheke, Mayo, and
Wendy, who were the visitors of the university, bearing date
the 1st of June 1553, directed to all the regents and non-
regents; setting forth, that great and long pains had been
taken by the king's authority, and the judgments of good and
learned men, concerning some articles described according to
the title with which they were printed; these being promulgated by the king's authority and delivered to all the bishops,
for the better government of their dioceses, they did commend
them to them, and, by their visitatorial authority, they do enjoin that all doctors and bachelors of divinity, and all doctors
of arts, should publicly before their creation swear to them,
214 and subscribe them; and such as refuse to do it, are to be
denied their degree. To this is added the form of the
oath to be taken. The injunction will be found in the Col- Collect. Numb. 9.
lection.

Thus it appears, by a variety of evidences, that these Arti- Cranmer designed to set up the provincial synods.
cles were not passed in convocation, nor so much as offered to
it. And, as far as can be judged from Cranmer's proceedings,
he intended to put the government of the church in another

method, different from the common way by convocation : and
to set up provincial synods of bishops, to be called as the archbishop saw cause, he having first obtained the king's license
for it. `This appears by the 18th chapter of the Reformation of
the Ecclesiastical Laws, prepared by him; in which it is plain,
that these provincial synods were to be composed only of the
bishops of the province. The convocations now in use by a
long prescription, in which deans, archdeacons, and cathedrals
have an interest, far superior in number to those elected to
represent the clergy, can in no sort pretend to be more than a
part of our civil constitution ; and have no foundation either in
any warrant from scripture, or from the first ages of the
church ; but did arise out of that second model of the church,
set out by Charles the Great, and formed according to the
feudal law ; by which a right of giving subsidies was vested in
all who were possessed of such tenures as qualified them to
contribute towards the supporting of the state.

[May 20.
Wilkins,
Conc. iv.
p. 79.]

As for the Catechism, it was printed with a preface prefixed
to it in the king's name, bearing date the 24th[81] of May, about
seven weeks before his death : in which he sets forth, that it
was drawn by a pious and learned man, (supposed to be bishop
Poynet,) and was given to be revised by some bishops and
other learned men ; he therefore commands all schoolmasters
to teach it.

King Ed-
ward's
scheme of
the succes-
sion.

I come now to set forth the dismal overturning of all that
had been done now in a course of twenty years. King Edward
was for some months under a visible decay : his thoughts were
were much possessed with the apprehensions of the danger religion must be in, if his sister Mary should succeed him. This
set him on contriving a design to hinder that. He seemed to
be against all females' succession to the crown. I have put in

Collect.
Numb. 10.

the Collection a paper that I copied out of a manuscript of the
late Mr. Petyt's, all written in that king's own hand, with this
title : *My Device for the Succession.* " By it the crown was
" to go to the issue male of his own body ; or if he had only
" female issue, to the issue male coming of the issue female :
" next to the issue male of the lady Frances ; then in succes-
" sion to her three daughters, and to their issue male : and if

[81] [The date is from Greenwich, May 20, as it appears in the original
edition.]

" they had only female issue, to the first issue male of any of
" her daughters.　The heir male after eighteen was to enter
" upon the government : but his mother was to govern till he
" was of that age, with the advice of six of that council of
" twenty persons, which he should name by his last will : but
" if the mother of the issue male should not be eighteen, then
" the realm was to be governed by the council, provided that
" after the issue male was of the age of fourteen, all matters
" of importance should be opened to him.　If at his death
" there were no issue male, the lady Frances was to be
215 " governess-regent ; and after her life, her three daughters
" were to be governesses in succession, till an heir male was
" born : and then the mother of that heir male was to be
" governess.　If four of the council should die, the governess
" was ordered, within a month, to summon the whole council,
" to choose four in their stead, in which the governess was to
" have three voices.　But after the death of the governess, the
" council was to choose the new counsellors, till the king was
" fourteen ; and then he was to choose them, but by their
" advice."

It may seem by this, that the king designed this some time
before his death ; while he thought that he himself might have
issue : but he was prevailed on to change a great deal of this
scheme ; especially those clauses, that kept the crown as in an
abeyance till an issue male should be born ; which would have
totally changed the government : so he departed from these
clauses.

This was afterwards put in another form by the judges ; and _Much al-_
that scheme which they prepared was in six several places su- _tered._
perscribed by the king's hand.　Probably it consisted of so
many pages.　I never saw that paper ; but I have put in the
Collection the paper that was subscribed by twenty-four coun- _Collect._
sellors and judges : in which they set forth, " that they had _Numb._ 11.
" often heard the king's earnest desire touching the limitation
" of the succession of the crown, and had seen his device writ-
" ten in his own hand : and after that was copied out, and
" delivered to judges and other learned men, they did sign
" with their hands, seal with their seals, and promise by their
" oaths and honours, to observe every article in that writing,
" and all such other matter, as the king should by his last will

" declare, touching the limitation of the crown ; and never to
" vary from it, but to defend and maintain it to the utmost of
" their power. And they also promised, that they would
" prosecute any of their number, or any other that should
" depart from it, and do their uttermost to see them severely
" punished."

Opposed
long by
Cranmer.
[Strype's
Cranmer,
p. 295.]

I gave an account in my History [82] of the opposition that
Cranmer made to this : but Mr. Strype has discovered more
particulars concerning it. He tells us, " that he argued
" with the king himself once about it, in the hearing of
" the marquis of Northampton and the lord Darcy. He
" desired leave to speak to the king alone about it, that so he
" might be more free with him : but that was not allowed him.
" He hoped, if he had obtained that liberty, he should have
" diverted the king from it. He argued against it in council,
" and pleaded that the lady Mary was legitimate : but some
" lawyers were prevailed on to say, that the king, being in
" possession of the crown, might dispose of it as he pleased.

[Ibid. p.
296.]

" He stood firm, and said, that he could not subscribe it without
" perjury ; having sworn to the observance of king Henry's
" will. Some counsellors said, they had sworn to that will as
" well as he ; and that they had consciences as well as he.
" He said, Every man was to answer to God for his own deeds,
" and not for other men's : he did not take upon him to judge
" any man's conscience but his own. He spake with the judges
" about the matter ; and they agreed, that the king might 216
" settle the succession, notwithstanding king Henry's will : yet
" he remained still unsatisfied, till the king himself required
" him to set his hand to the will ; saying, he hoped he alone
" would not stand out, and be more repugnant to his will than
" all the rest of the council were. This made a great impres-
" sion on him ; it grieved him much : but such was the love
" that he bore to the king, that in conclusion he yielded, and
" signed it."

The pri-
mate of
Ireland
poisoned.

A little before the king's death, a very extraordinary thing
happened in Ireland. I had told in my former work [83], that
Goodacre and Bale were sent over to promote the reformation
in Ireland. The former was made primate of Armagh ; of
whose death there is a report, that has been all along believed

[82] [See Part ii. p. 223.]   [83] [See Part ii. p. 205.]

by his posterity. A reverend and worthy clergyman of Hampshire, not far from Salisbury, (who is the fourth in descent from that primate, they having been all clergymen but one,) told me he had it from his grandfather, who was the primate's grandson ; " That he being invited to a popish lord's house, a " monk there drank to him in a poisoned liquor, on design to " poison him; of which they both died." This I set down from the venerable person's own mouth, as a thing known and believed in the family.

I have no particulars to add[84], neither concerning the death nor the character of that good prince, king Edward ; whose untimely end was looked on by all people as a just judgment of God upon those who pretended to love and promote a reformation, but whose impious and flagitious lives were a reproach to it. The open lewdness in which many lived, without shame or remorse, gave great occasion to their adversaries to say, they were in the right to assert justification by faith without works, since they were, as to every good work, reprobate. Their gross and insatiable scrambling after the goods and wealth, that had been dedicated with good designs, though to superstitious uses, without applying any part of it to the promoting the gospel, the instructing the youth, and relieving the poor, made all people conclude, that it was for robbery, and not for reformation, that their zeal made them so active.

A character of the court in king Edward's time.

I will here give an eminent instance of fraudulent proceedings in the beginning of this reign ; of which the present learned and zealous dean of Norwich[85] was pleased to send me a copious account out of their registers. The prior, when inducted into that dignity, took an oath not to alienate any of their lands ; which was confirmed by injunctions, exhibited to the convent in the royal visitation. But the king, upon certain reasons suggested by the prior and convent, and approved by him, did dispense with that oath ; so that, notwithstanding the oath, they were left at liberty to alienate some lands, set forth in the instrument dated the 1st of April 1538, countersigned by Cromwell. A month after that, on the 2nd of May that year, the church was converted from a prior and convent to a dean and chapter ; and the last prior was made the first dean of the church.

[84] [See Part ii. p. 224.]   [85] [Dr. Humphrey Prideaux.]

But on the 26th of May 1547, in the beginning of king 217 Edward's reign, a letter was sent to that church, signed by the duke of Somerset, Rich the lord chancellor, and six other privy counsellors; pretending, that they designed the advancement of God's glory, and the truest intent of the late king's determination : by which sir Richard Southwell, sir Roger Townshend, and sir William Paston, were authorized to receive a full surrender of the whole chapter; assuring both the dean, and every one of the prebendaries, that there should be no alteration made in their yearly profits ; and that there should be a just contentation given to the residue of the ministers there. A commission was granted on the 27th to these persons, to take the surrender, with articles and instructions annexed to it : which, because probably many others were of the same

Collect. Numb. 12.

sort, are put in the Collection. But, for all this appearance of fair dealing, it being pretended, that this was only designed that the king should be the founder, and that the church should lose nothing by the surrender ; yet when they had made the surrender, in the hope of new letters patents, they could not obtain them : and lands, to the value of two hundred pounds a year, were taken from them. Upon which, that corporation tried, in queen Mary's time, to get a bill to pass, to restore them to the state they were in before they were prevailed on to make the surrender. But the bill did not pass. Perhaps it might be suggested, that it would alarm the nation too much, if any alienation of church lands, how fraudulently soever obtained, were meddled with. I give this as a well-attested instance ; by which it may appear, how things of this kind were obtained and managed, chiefly in the beginnings of this reign. For I am not so much set on justifying every thing

Collier. Eccl. Hist. p. 332. col. 2.

that was done in this reign, as another voluminous writer is on condemning almost every thing done in it, with a particular virulence against the memory of that pious prince. This, from one of another communion, is that which might have been expected ; but it is a little singular, when it comes from one, who says he is of our church.

The bad lives of those who professed the gospel.

The irregular and immoral lives of many of the professors of the gospel, gave their enemies great advantages to say, they ran away from confession, penance, fasting, and prayers, only that they might be under no restraint, but indulge themselves in a licentious and dissolute course of life.   By these things, that were but too visible in some of the more eminent among them, the people were much alienated from them : and as much as they were formerly prejudiced against popery, they grew to have kinder thoughts of it, and to look on all the changes that had been made as designs to enrich some vicious courtiers, and to let in an inundation of vice and wickedness upon the nation. Some of the clergy that promoted the reformation were not without very visible blemishes : some indiscretions, both in their marriages[86] and in their behaviour, contributed not a little to raise a general aversion to them.

218   It is true, there were great and shining lights among them, whose exemplary deportment, continual labours, fervent charity, and constant zeal, both during their lives, and at their deaths, kept up the credit of that work, as much as it was disgraced by others ; but they were *few*, in comparison of the *many bad :* and those of the clergy in whom the old leaven had still a deep root, though they complied in every thing that was imposed on them, seeing that they had lost those perquisites of masses, and other practices, which brought them their chief gains, and saw nothing came in lieu of them, for their subsistence ; they, who in their hearts hated all that they were forced to profess outwardly, did secretly possess such as were influenced by them with an abhorrence of all that was done : and they disposed the nation to be ready to throw it all off.

That which was above all, was, that God was highly dis-   Much la-
honoured by men who pretended zeal for his glory, but with   mented by
their works dishonoured him.   They talked of the purity of   the reform-
                                                              ers.

[86] [At Westminster the 20th day of November 1551. A letter to the archbishop of York to make his indelayed repair hither, and to cause his wife to be here also either as soon as himself, or as shortly after as may be."—Council Book, p.443.

" At Westminster the 23th of November 1551. A letter to the archbishop of Yorke to stay his coming up hither till the parliament.

" A letter to sir Thomas Gargrave Mr. Challonour and doctour Roukesbye, to examine and use such means to understand the circumstances and very truth of the matter between the archbishop of Yorke and one Norman, who claimeth the same bishop's wife to be his, as they shall think may best serve for the knowledge of the same : for the easier understanding of the matter the supplication presented by the said Norman in this behalf is sent unto them, enclosed in the said letter with request to certify hither what they shall have learned in the case."——Council Book, p. 448.]

the gospel, while they were wallowing in all sensuality and uncleanness; pretending to put all their confidence in the merits and sufferings of Christ, while they were crucifying him afresh, and putting him to open shame. In such lamentations as these I find the good men of that time did often vent their sorrows, in their letters to one another, and break out into severe reflections on them. Some did it afterwards abroad in their exile, and others at home in their sufferings. Their only human hope was in the king himself; in whom there appeared such a progress, both in knowledge and zeal, that they expected to see him complete the reformation, and redress those crying abuses, in which the men in power found their account too evidently to expect a remedy from them. They were men, in whose hands things grew every day worse and worse; and whose arrogance and other disorders our chief reformers were forced in some measure to connive at, that they might not provoke them to retard a work, that could in no wise be carried on without their countenance and authority: though they saw the prejudice it brought upon them, to be obliged to apply to, and to make use of such tools, with which the righteous souls of our best reformers were much grieved. They were engaged with men that were ready to pull down, especially when any thing was to be got by it; but were as backward in building up, as they were forward in plucking down. So that they seemed to design to leave all in a great ruin. These were great hindrances to the progress of the reformation, as they were both the burden and the shame of our reformers.

I thought it not amiss to open this as fully as I found it lying before me: and I hope the reader will not only consider this as a part of the history of a former age, but as an admonition to us in the present. If we fall under the disorders and corruptions that then reigned, why should not we expect such a calamity as overtook and overwhelmed them? We may justly look for worse, since we have the advantages of much more light, and many more blessings, as well as many alarming terrors, which have all gone over us without those dismal con- 219 vulsions that we might have looked for: and they have as easily slipped out of our thoughts, as if we had never seen or felt them. To the viciousness of life, and the open immoralities and neglect of religion, that were the sins of the former age, many among us have added a studied impiety, and a laboured opposition to all revealed religion; which some have owned in so barefaced a manner, that perhaps no age of the world can shew any thing like it. If others with secular views have declaimed against this, and put on some show of zeal, how much more of party than of true religion has appeared in it. The divided parties among us have shewed little true regard to religion, and to a course of virtue and piety, which can only give both strength and honour to a church; and this does too plainly appear in many, who talk the most of it, or for it.

Have we of the clergy made the steps that became us, and that were designed in the former age, for throwing out abuses, for regulating the courts, and restoring discipline? While we have for above one hundred and fifty years expressed once a year a faint wish that the primitive discipline were again restored, and yet have not made one step toward it. What a venality of the advowsons to livings do we hear of; and at best the disposing of them goes generally by secular regards, by importunities, obligations, or friendship: and above all, how few of those that labour in the gospel, do labour indeed, and give themselves wholly to it! How much of their time and zeal is employed in things that do not deserve it so well, as the watching over, the instructing, and the building up their flock in their most holy faith! How few do fast and pray, and study to prepare themselves and their people for the evil day, that seems much nearer us than the greatest part are willing to apprehend; that so we may by our intercessions deliver our church and nation from that which is ready to swallow us up; or at least be so fortified and assisted, that we ourselves, and others, by what they see in us, may glorify God in that day of visitation!

I shall conclude this book with one reflection, that may make us hope, that the reformation was under a particular and watchful care of Providence: when the light seemed almost extinguished in one place, it broke out in another; by which, as it was still kept shining somewhere, so there was a sanctuary opened, to which those who were forced to fly from one place, might in their flight find a covert in another from the storm. In the beginning of this reign, by the breaking of the Smal-

The providence of God towards the reformed.

caldic league, by the taking of the elector of Saxony, and the landgrave of Hesse, and by the *Interim*, the reformation seemed to be near extinguished in Germany. In this church it was at that time advanced; and we kindly then received those who were forced to fly hither for shelter. And now, in the year before the death of this good king, there was not only a revival, but a lasting settlement procured in Germany to the reformation there: so that those who fled from hence found a safe and kind harbour in all the places of the empire, to which they were driven by the storm and tempest that arose here. Of which I go next to gather up such gleanings as have come in my way.

220

THE HISTORY

OF

THE REFORMATION

OF

THE CHURCH OF ENGLAND.

PART III.—BOOK V.

*Of what happened during queen Mary's reign, from the
year 1553 to the year 1558.*

AS soon as the queen came to the Tower of London[1], she sent for the lord mayor and the aldermen of the city, and told them, "that though her own conscience was stayed in matters " of religion, yet she meaneth graciously not to compel or " strain other people's consciences, otherwise than God shall, " as she trusteth, put in their hearts a persuasion of the truth." These soft words were not long remembered. Of the progress of the severities in her reign I have a very authentical account before me, in the original council-book[2], that begins on the

The queen's words were soft.
[Aug. 3.]

---

[1] [See Part ii. p. 240.]

[2] [The first council-book of queen Mary is a very small folio, the entries of which begin on July 14, and extend to August 19, 1553. The second book, which is of larger size, commences with August 22, 1553, and ends Dec. 30, 1557. On the first leaf of it the following account is written, dated from the Council Chambers, Whitehall, May 15, 1730: " This book having been for some considerable time in private hands, came lately into the possession of the right honourable Arthur Onslow, esquire, speaker of the honourable house of Commons, and one of his majesty's most honourable privy

17th of August 1553, and goes to the end of the year 1557:
but from that to her death I have not so sure a thread. The
book begins with orders for letters to be written to Coverdale
and Hooper for their undelayed repair to the court: and a
complaint being made of a sermon preached by Fisher, parson
of Amersham, he was ordered to appear the next day, and to
bring the notes of his sermon with him. A parliament was
summoned to meet in November. On the 14th of August the
writ for the convocation was directed to Cranmer. A letter
was soon after written by the queen and council to the bishop
of Norwich, to suffer none to preach without a special license:
the same order was intimated to the lord mayor of London;
and the same was no doubt universally both ordered and executed[3].

On the 20th of August there was an order for guards to
defend the preacher at St. Paul's Cross, occasioned by what
had happened to Bourn. It seems few came to hear the sermons, for the lord mayor was ordered "to make the ancients
" of the companies resort to the sermons, lest the preacher
" should be discouraged by a small audience." On the 23rd
of August Gardiner was declared lord chancellor. Here I
shall set down the appointments of the lord chancellor as they
were settled at that time. There was a privy seal given for
wages and diets, and for the masters in chancery, for 542*l.* 15*s.*
yearly: 50*l.* was ordered for attending on the star-chamber
every term; and, besides that, a salary was given of 300*l.* and
64*l.* for twelve tun of wine[4], and 16*l.* for wax. All these were
granted the 21st of September, but were to commence from

Marginal notes:
[Council Book, vol. ii. p. 1.]
[p. 2.]
[Nov. 12.]
But her proceeding severe.
Rymer, MSS.
[4624. fol. 220. ex pat. 1 Mar. Reg. m. 37.
[fol. 222.]
[fol. 223.]
[fol. 224.]

council, who delivered the same
into this office to be kept amongst
the other records of the Privy Council; and he had a true copy thereof
made out and delivered unto him
by order of the Lords of the Council.—Tho. Beake, Deputy Record
Keeper." The next council-book
goes on into Elizabeth's reign down
to May 7, 1559. The register from
July 16, to Nov. 3, 1553, has been
printed in Haynes' State Papers,
pp. 155–195, and the Harleian MS.
643 contains extracts from the re-

gister, commencing Aug. 1553, and
extending to the end of the reign.
Some passages of this occur in
Archæologia, xviii. pp. 173–185.]
[3] [On the 29th of August letters
patent were issued, authorizing Gardiner to give licenses to preach to
such as he should deem fit, throughout the country, in cathedrals or
parish churches. The patent is
printed in Rymer xv. 337.]
[4] [The original has "twelve tonnes
of wine."]

the 23rd of August. On the 24th of August there was an [Council
221 order sent to the keeper of Newgate to receive and keep John Book, p. 3.]
Melvyn, a Scot, and a very seditious preacher; so he was
called in the warrant. On the same day a letter was written
to the mayor of Canterbury, to set Panton, vicar of St. Dun-
stan's, and one Burden, on the pillory, for seditious words
against the queen; and to take bonds at their discretion for their
good abearing[5]. On the 26th of August a letter was writ to [Ibid. p. 5.]
the mayor of Coventry to apprehend Symonds, a vicar there,
and to send him up with such matter as can be procured to
charge him with; "and to punish at their discretion such slan-
" derous talkers, as by his lewd preaching have had dissolute
" and seditious talk."

Here is a great deal of heat in ten days' time. Cranmer Against
was called before the council in the beginning of August; Hooper,
probably on the account of his signing king Edward's will, and and others.
acting upon it: but since so many of those who had signed it
were then at the council-board, they were perhaps ashamed to
proceed further against him, who had opposed it so much. He
had for that time only a severe reprimand, and was commanded
to keep his house. He was brought again before some of the
queen's commissioners, being cited to appear, and to bring the
inventory of his goods with him. He brought it, but no further proceedings against him are mentioned at that time. On [Council
the 29th of August[6] Hooper appeared before the council. On Book, p. 7.]
the 1st of September[7] he was sent to the Fleet, no regard [p. 9.]
being had to the active zeal that he had expressed in asserting
the queen's right, and against the lady Jane; so sincerely did
he follow the dictates of his conscience, when he could not but
see what consequences it was like to have. On the 2nd[8], order
was given that his servant might attend on him. On the 31st

[5] [Abearing. This word is used
in the council-book. See Introduction, p. xi.]

[6] [The only entry on this day is
" Aug. 29. John Hooper, bishop
of Gloucester, made this day his
personal appearance."]

[7] [" Sept. 1. This day appeared
before the Lords, John Hooper, bishop of Gloucester, and Myles

Coverdale, bishop of Exon, and the
said Hooper for considerations the
Council moving, was sent to the
fleet. And the said Coverdale commanded to attend until the lords'
pleasures be further known."]

[8] [" Sept. 2. A letter to the
warden of the fleet to permit William Dunston to have access to
Hooper his master."]

of August[9], Coverdale appeared before them, and in respect
that he was a foreigner, he was ordered to attend till further
[p. 10.]   order.   On the 2nd of September[10], Saunders, vicar in Coventry, appeared before the council, and a letter was written to
the mayor of Leicester to bring up their vicar.   On the 4th of
[p. 11.]   September[11], Latimer was summoned to appear, and a letter
[p. 12.]   was written to the mayor of Coventry to set Symonds at
liberty, upon his repentance, for a wish he had uttered, wishing
they were hanged that said mass : if he refused to do that, the
mayor was to give notice of it.

[p. 13.]   On the 5th of September a letter was written to sir John
Sydenham, to let the strangers depart, and to give them a
passport.   This related to the congregation of the foreigners
that had settled, in order to set up a manufacture at Glaston-
[p. 16.]   bury.   On the 10th of September a letter of thanks was
ordered for the gentlemen of Cornwall, for their honest proceeding in electing knights for the parliament.   It seems there
was some debate about it with the sheriff; for a letter was
written to him to accept of the election, and not to trouble the
[p. 17.]   county for any alteration.   On the 13th of September it is
entered, that Latimer for his seditious demeanour should be
close prisoner in the Tower, with a servant to attend him.   On
[p. 18.]   the same day, Cranmer was ordered to appear the next day at
[p. 19.]   the star-chamber.   On the 14th, in the star-chamber, Cranmer,
as well for his treason against the queen, as for spreading seditious bills moving tumults, to the disquieting the present 222
state, was sent to the Tower, and referred to justice.   There
are several orders made for restoring all chalices to churches,
together with all other goods belonging to them, though they
[p. 26.]   had been sent into the great wardrobe.   On the 4th of October
the archbishop of York was committed to the Tower for divers
offences ; and Horne, the dean of Durham[12], was summoned

[9] [" Aug. 31. Miles Coverdale,
bishop of Exeter, made this day
personal appearance."   There is
nothing about his being a foreigner
noticed on any council day.

[10] [" Sept. 4. A letter of appearance to Hugh Latymer."]

[11] [" Sept. 4. A letter to the
Mayor and Aldermen of the city of
Coventrye to set Hugh Symondes
priest, at his liberty, in case he do
recant the lewd words that he lately
spake, wishing them hanged that
would say mass. Or if he refuse so
to do, to stay him, and signify hither
to the end the queen's highness'
further pleasure may be known."]

[12] [" At the Star Chamber, Sept.

again and again, but he thought fit to go beyond sea. Nothing
gave more offence than the promoting petitions for retaining
the doctrine and service settled in king Edward's time. Those
of Maidstone [13] were charged with it; and this is on several occa- [p. 49.]
sions mentioned in the council-book : but as the government
was thus set to overthrow all that had been done in king
Edward's time ; so the fierceness of the popish party made
them on many occasions outrun the government. Some of the
clergy continued to perform the daily worship, and to celebrate
the sacrament : more they durst not do in public, all preaching
being forbidden. The people that favoured the reformation
frequented the service with great devotion and zeal : for all
saw what was coming on them : and so they studied to prepare
themselves for it. Some of the ruder multitudes came into
their churches, and disturbed them while they were at their
devotions : they insulted the ministers, and laughed at their
worship ; and there were every where informers with false
stories to charge the more zealous preachers. In many places
the people broke in violently into churches, and set up altars,
and the mass in them, before the parliament met to change
the laws.

The duke of Northumberland [14] shewed that abjectness of The duke of North-
mind, that might have been expected from so insolent a man, umberland
loaded with so much guilt : he begged his life with all possible begs his life, but
meanness, *that he might do penance all the days of his life, if* in vain.
it were in a mousehole. He went to mass in the Tower, and
received the sacrament in the popish manner [15]. He sent for

15. A letter of appearance to
Horne, dean of Durham." Again
at Westminster Oct. 7. " A letter
of appearance eftsones to the dean
of Durham, upon his allegiance.]
  [13] [" At Westminster December
2. William Smythe, of Maydeston,
for his seditious moving of the inhabitants there to the framing of a
supplication for the retaining still
of their new religion, soliciting first
one and since another, was committed to the gatehouse of Westminster, there to be severally kept,
without conference of any other
person." " December 4. William

Smyth of Maideston, in the county
of Kent, yeoman, standeth bound
in recognizance unto the queen's
highness in the sum of £40 for his
good abearing between this and the
feast of Easter next ensuing, and
thereupon is discharged of his imprisonment."]
  [14] [See Part ii. p. 242.]
  [15] [The proceedings of August
21 and 22 in relation to this are as
follows :
  " The 21 of August was by 8 of
the cloke in the morning on the
Towre hylle aboythe ten thousand
men and women for to have seen

Gardiner, and asked him if there was no hope for him to live, and do penance for his sins.   The bishop said, his offence was great, and he would do well to provide for the worst; especially to see that he stood well with God in matters of conscience and religion : for to speak plainly, he said, he thought he must die.   The duke desired he might have a learned priest sent him, for his confession and spiritual comfort.   " For religion, " he said, he could be of no other but of his : he never was of " any other indeed: he complied in king Edward's days only " out of ambition, for which he prayed God to forgive him ; " and he promised that he would declare that at his death." The bishop shed many tears, and seemed to be troubled for him : and, as he reported himself, he pressed the queen so much, that he had almost gained her consent for his life.   But the emperor, who was then designing the marriage, that took effect afterwards, saw what a struggle there might be against that, and what mischief such a man might afterwards do.   So he wrote his advice for his death positively to the queen [16] : and he was executed, and died as he had lived.

Others suffered with him.

Gates and Palmer, who suffered with him, had tried how far **223** the going to mass, and receiving the sacrament in the popish way, could save them : but when they were brought to suffer, Gates confessed, " that he had lived as viciously as any in the " world.   He was a great reader of the scriptures ; but no " man followed them less : he read them only to dispute.   He " exhorted people to consider how they read God's holy word,

the execussyon of the duke of Northumberlånd, for the skaffold was mad rede, and sand and straw was browth, and all the men that longest to the Towre, as Hoyston, Shordyche, Bow, Ratclyff, Lymhouse, Sant Kateryns and the waters of the Towre, and the gard, and shyryffs, offesers, and evere man stand in order with ther holbardes and lanes made, and the hangman was ther, and sodenly they wher commondyd to depart.   And the sam tym after was send for my lord mer and the aldermen and cheyffest of the craftes in London, and dyvers of the consell, and ther was sed mas afor the duke and the rest of the presonars."—Machyn's Diary, p. 42.   " Item the 22ti day of the same monyth, sufferd at Tower-hyll the duke of Northumberlond, sir John Gattes, captayne of the garde before, and sir Thomas Palmer, alle three beheddyd ; and the day before harde masse in the tower and reseved the sacrament in forme of brede."—Grey Friars' Chronicle, p. 83.]

[16] [The trial took place on the 18th, and the execution on the 22nd of August, so that if any such communication took place, it must have been previous to the trial.]

" otherwise it would be but poison to them. Palmer thanked
" God for his affliction, and said, he had learned more in one
" dark corner of the Tower, than he had ever learned formerly :
" he had there come to see God in his works, and in his
" mercies ; and had seen himself a mass of sin, and of all vile-
" ness the vilest." He seemed not daunted with the fear of
death, though he saw two die before him, and the bloody axe
coming to finish the business on himself. I find nothing new
with relation to the session of parliament.

The writ, upon which the convocation was summoned, was *A convoca-tion sum-moned.*
directed to Cranmer, but executed by Bonner, bishop of Lon-
don. Weston was chosen prolocutor : and the queen sent a *[Wilkins, Conc. iv.*
message to them to dispute about religion. I gave formerly [17] *p. 88.]*
an account of that disputation, and can add little to it. The
minutes tell us, that Philips, who was one of the five that
refused to subscribe, did, on the 30th of April, recant and subscribe. It is indeed of little consequence to inquire into the
proceedings of the convocation during this reign ; in which all
the old notions of popery were taken up, even before they
were enacted : though both this convocation and the next were
summoned by the queen's writ, with the title of supreme head
of the church.

There was at this time an infamous slander set about, of the
queen's being with child by Gardiner. The queen's whole
life being innocent as to all such things, that might have made
them to despise such a report, rather than to trace it up :
besides, Gardiner's great age made, that none could believe it.
But the earl of Sussex, in his officious zeal, pursued it through
eight or ten hands : and one at last was indicted for having
reported it ; though such an absurd lie had, perhaps, been
better neglected than so minutely inquired into. In the same
letter that mentions this, the earl of Sussex gives an account of *MSS. Pe-tyt.*
examinations, touching a design for an insurrection, upon the
arrival of the prince of Spain.

The emperor [18] had, on the 21st of December, signed a com- *A treaty of marriage with the prince of Spain.*
mission, empowering the count of Egmont, and others, to treat
a marriage between his son and the queen. Upon their coming
to England, the queen gave a commission, on the 1st of January, to the lord chancellor, and others, to treat with them.

[17] [See Part ii. p. 262.]   [18] [See Part ii. p. 267.]

And prince Philip of Spain did, on the 28th of April, send
from Valladolid full powers to the same effect.   That which
quickened the treaty was, an account of a vast treasure that
was come with the fleet from the West-Indies to Seville;
reckoned to have brought over five millions, as Mason wrote
from Brussels.   He does not denominate the millions, whether
pounds or crowns.   He wishes the half were true.   It was
necessary to have a great treasure in view: for though I never
found any hint of the corrupting of parliament-men before this **224**
time, yet there was now an extraordinary occasion for it; and
they saw where only the treasure to furnish it could be had.
A concurrence of many circumstances seemed to determine all
things for this marriage.   Every thing was agreed to: the
conditions seemed to be of great advantage to the nation.   In

Parte ii. this treaty of marriage, if Cæsar Campana (who wrote Philip's
Libro 6.
[fol. 106.][19] life very copiously) was well informed, Philip himself was extremely disgusted at it: for he desired to be married to a wife
more suited to his own age.   He adds another particular,
" that the nation shewed such an aversion to it, that the count
" of Egmont, with the others sent over to treat about it, saw
" themselves in such danger, that they were forced to fly away,
" that they might avoid it: and a parliament was to be called,
" to approve of the conditions of the treaty."

Wiat's ris- Sir Thomas Wiat[20] was a man that had been oft employed
*ing and
principles.* in embassies, particularly in Spain[21]; where he had made such
observations upon the subtlety and cruelty of the Spaniards,
and of the treatment that such kingdoms and provinces met
with, that came under their yoke, that he could not look on
the misery that his country was like to fall under without a
just concern about it.   He was the duke of Northumberland's
kinsman, yet he would not join in lady Jane's business: and

[19] [La vita del Catholico et Invi-
tissimo Don Filippo Secondo d'Austria Re delle Spagne &c.   Con le
Guerre de suoi Tempi Descritte da
Cesare Campana Nobile Aquilano.
Parte Seconda.   Nelle quale si ha
intiera cognitione de' moti d'arme
in ogni parte del Mondo auuenuti.
dall' Anno MDXLVII. fino al
MDLXVII. All' Illustrissimo &
Excellentiss. Signore, il Sig. Don

Carlo d' Aquino Conte di Marto-
rano & Prencipe di Castiglione.   In
Vicenza, per Pietro Greco & Fra-
telli MDCVIII. 4to. 1605—8.]
[20] [See Part ii. p. 284.]
[21] [The author is here confusing
Wiat with his father sir Thomas,
the poet, who died in the summer
of 1541, and had been ambassador
in Spain in 1537—1539, and afterwards in Flanders.]

before he knew that any others had done it, he proclaimed the
queen at Maidstone; but he did not, upon that, run to her for
thanks, as others did: yet the queen was so sensible of his
loyalty and zeal for her, that she sent her thanks to him by
the earl of Arundel; to whom he appealed, as to this particular, when he was under examination in the Tower. He
had obtained a pass to go beyond sea; but his lady being with
child, he stayed to see the end of that. Nothing set him on to
raise the country as he did, but his love and zeal for the
public. He never pretended that religion was his motive:
many papists joined with him. When he passed by Charing-
Cross, he might have turned to Whitehall, which was but ill
defended; for many of the earl of Pembroke's men came over
to him. This shewed that he meant no harm to the queen's
person. His marching into London was on design to engage
the city to come and join with him in a petition to the queen
against the Spanish match. The queen herself was so satisfied,
as to his good intentions, that she intended to have pardoned
him, had not a message from the prince of Spain determined
her to order his head to be cut off. I suppose there may be
a mistake here; and that it was the emperor, then in Flanders,
and not the prince of Spain, who was yet in Spain, that sent
this advice. He never accused the lady Elizabeth: but being
entangled by questions in one examination, he had said somewhat reflecting on the earl of Devonshire: for this he begged
his pardon. And when he was on the scaffold, he not only
cleared the lady Elizabeth[22], but referred himself with relation
to her innocence, and that she was not privy to their matters,
to the declaration he had made to the council. All this account
concerning him I take from a relation that his son gave after-
225 wards to the lord Burleigh, marked with that lord's hand on
it. It seems the priests at this time understood the interests of
their cause better than others did above an age after: for they

Ex MS.
Petyt.

---

[22] [The following is an extract
from his speech, reported in the
chronicle of queen Jane, and published by the Camden Society, 1850:
"And whereas yt is said and
wysled abroade, that I shoulde accuse my lady Elizabeth's grace, and
my lorde Courtney; yt is not so,
goode people, for I assure you, ney-
ther they nor eny other now yonder
in holde or durance was previe of
my rysing or commotyon before I
began; as I have declared no lesse
to the quene's counsaille. And this
is most true." p. 73. See also MS.
Harl. 559, fol. 53.]

moved the queen to shew a signal act of mercy, and to pardon all that had been engaged in this rising.

Lady Jane Grey executed.

Only it gave a colour to the severity against the lady Jane Grey and her husband. She was the wonder and delight of all that knew her. I have two[23] of her letters in Latin, writ to Bullinger, copied from the originals all in her own hand, written in a pure and unaffected style. She was then entering on the study of the Hebrew, in the method that Bullinger advised her. She expresses in her letters a wonderful respect and submission to him, with a great strain of modesty, and a very singular zeal for religion. There being nothing in those letters that is in any sort historical, I thought it was not proper to put them in my Collection; though one cannot read them, without a particular veneration for the memory of so young and so rare a creature.

Severities against the married clergy.

And now the government, finding all things under their feet, did begin to shew to the whole nation what was to be expected. All that adhered to the reformation were sure to be excluded from all favour: commissions were sent over the whole kingdom, to proceed, as upon other points, so particularly against the married clergy. These came to York, directed to the guardian of the spiritualities in that place: and the dean and chapter were authorized by the queen to act pursuant to their instructions. And they acted as in a vacancy: though the commission to proceed against the archbishop bears date the

[Wilkins, vol. iv. p. 88.]

16th of March; yet, on the 9th of March, they sent out a general citation of the clergy to appear before them on the

Reg. Ebor. Sede Vac. f. 65, 66.

12th of March. They did not indeed begin to deprive any before the 27th of April: and from that day to the 20th of December they deprived one and fifty, of whom several were prebendaries.

I will here insert a short account of the unjust and arbitrary deprivations of the married clergy, that was published by Parker, afterwards archbishop of Canterbury. "What ex-
" amples have they in stories beforetime, that deprivations
" have been thus handled before our days? I will not speak of
" particular cases; where some men have been deprived, never
" convict, no, nor never called: some called, that were fast

---

[23] [Three letters from her to   pp. 3—8, and also in Ellis, ii. 11,
Bullinger are printed in Epistolæ.   181 and elsewhere.]

" locked in prison; and yet they were[24] nevertheless deprived
" immediately.   Some were[25] deprived without the case of
" marriage after their order : some, induced to resign, upon
" promise of pension, and the promise as yet never performed.
" Some, so deprived, that they were spoiled of their wages, for
" the which they served the half-year before; and, not ten
" days before the receipt, sequestered from it. Some, prevented
" from the half-year's receipt, after charges of tenths and
" subsidies[26] paid, and yet not deprived six weeks after. Some,
" deprived of the receipt somewhat before[27] the day, with the
" which their fruits to the queen's majesty should be con-
" tented; and some yet in the like case chargeable hereafter[28],
" if the queen's merciful grace be not informed thereof, by
226 " the[29] mediation of some charitable solicitor."———And a little
after, " there were deprived, or driven away, twelve of sixteen
" thousand, as some writer maketh his account[30]." But there
are good reasons to think, that numbers have been wrong
taken of this.   Among other suggestions, Dr. Tanner has sent
me this; that the diocese of Norwich is reckoned almost an
eighth part of all England; and he finds, there were only
three hundred and thirty-five clergymen deprived on that
account: by this the whole number will fall short of three
thousand.   This, it is true, is but a conjecture; yet it is a very
probable one : and the other account is no way credible.

I shall, to this, only add another short account of the proceedings at that time, published by Aylmer[31], afterwards bishop

Aggra-
vated by
some.
[fol. 6 d.]

---

24 [*they were* om.]
25 [*were* om.]   26 [*subsidie*]
27 [*afore*]   28 [*as I hear say*]
29 [*the* om.]
30 [This passage is not ' a little
after,' but a few pages earlier in the
volume ; " Is thus the honour of
the clergy preserved, to drive out so
many, twelve of sixteen thousand,
as some writer maketh his account,
to so great a peril and an adventure
of getting the livings." fol. 6 d.]
31 [Aylmer (John). An harbor-
owe for faithfull and trewe subiectes
against the late blowne Blaste, concerning the gouernement of Wemen.
Anno 1559. At Strasborowe the 26

of Aprill. 4to. The volume is not
paged or foliated, but the passage
referred to occurs on the back of
signat. O. " In queen Mary's first
days the bishops that were married
were thrust out of the parliament
house before any law, and all married deans and archdeacons out of
the convocation, many put out of
their livings, and other restored
without force of law. If that were
lawful for her, why is it not lawful
for this ? Yea some noblemen and
gentlemen were deprived of those
lands which the king had given
them without tarrying for any law;
lest my lord of Winchester should

of London. "The bishops that were married were thrust out
" of the parliament-house; and all married deans and arch-
" deacons out of the convocation. Many put out of their
" livings, and others restored, without form of law.——Many
" churches were changed, many altars set up, many masses
" said, many dirges sung, before the law was repealed." From
these accounts we may easily believe, that, when the laws were
altered, there was a vigorous and a speedy execution of them.

The queen
writes the
first letter
to king
Philip.

Collect.
Numb. 13.

   After all matters relating to the queen's marriage were
settled, the emperor sent a fleet for the prince of Spain: and
upon that occasion the queen was prevailed on to break through
all forms, and to write the first love-letter to him; of which,
having met with the original, I have put it in the Collection,
as a singularity in such matters. She tells him, " that she
" understanding that the emperor's ambassador was sending
" the bearer to him, though he had not written since their
" alliance had been a treating; yet she, thinking herself
" obliged by the sincere affection that he had for her, con-
" firmed by good effects, and by the letters that he had
" written to the emperor's ambassador, could not restrain her-
" self from letting him know the duty, in which she intended
" to correspond always with him: and she thanked him for all
" his good offices. She acquainted him, that her parliament
" had, without any opposition, agreed to the articles of their
" marriage, and thought them honourable, advantageous, and
" more than reasonable. This gave her an entire confidence,
" that his coming to England should be safe, and agreeable to
" him. She ends, recommending herself most affectionately
" and humbly to his highness, as being his entirely assured,
" and most obliged ally."

Proceed-
ings against
heretics.
[Jan. 21,
p. 66.]

   But, the matter of the marriage being settled, and afterwards
executed, I will now look again into the proceedings of the
council. On the 16th of January[32], one Wotton, called an

have lost his quarter's rent. Many
churches were changed, many altars
set up, many masses said, many
dredges sung, before the law was
repealed; all was done in post-
haste."]

[32] [Two interesting notices in the
Council Book have been omitted

by the author:

" Dec. 17. A letter to the lieutenant of the Tower, willing him at
convenient times, by his discretion,
to suffer the late duke of Northumberland's children to have the liberty of walk within the garden of
the Tower. And also to minister

esquire, was committed to be close prisoner in the Fleet for his obstinate standing against matters of religion.   On the 14th of [Feb. 19,[33] February, letters were written to the lord Rich, and to sir p. 73.] John Wentworth, to punish some in Colchester, Coxall, and other places, who dissuaded people from frequenting such divine service as was then appointed by law to be observed.   Upon this, many were committed, and others put under recognizances to appear.   On the 8th of March[34], an order was sent to the [p. 89]
227 lieutenant of the Tower, to deliver Cranmer, Ridley, and Latimer to sir John Williams, who was to carry them to Oxford. On the 26th of March[35], an order was given to send up Taylor, parson of Hadley; and Askew of West-Hillesly.   Barlow, [p. 97.] bishop of Bath and Wells, was carried beyond sea, by one [p. 107.] Williams, a mariner of Bristol[36]; who, returning to Pembroke-shire, some gentlemen there seized on him, and sent him to London; so he was sent to the Marshalsea, and a letter of thanks was written to those who had seized on him : so careful were they to encourage every officious show of zeal.

But now came on the second convocation in this reign, in A convoca-which all that was done was, that the prolocutor Weston, with tion. some deputed to go along with him, were ordered to go to [Wilkins, vol. iv. p. Oxford, to dispute with the three bishops.   Of which I can 94.]

---

the like favour to the lady Jane and doctor Cranmer, upon suggestion that divers of them be and have been evil at ease in their bodies for want of care."

" Jan. 16. A letter of appearance to Thomas Wotton, esquire." " Jan. 21. This day Thomas Wotton, esquire, for obstinate standing against matters of religion, was committed to the Fleet, to remain there as close prisoner."   " March 4. A letter to the warden of the Fleet, to permit mistress Wotton to repair to her husband, so that she talk with him in the presence of the warden."]

[33] [The mistakes in date frequently arise from the author's carelessness in reading X as V.]

[34] [" March 8. A letter to the lieutenant of the Tower, to deliver to sir John Williams the bodies of the late archbishop of Canterbury, doctor Ridley and Latymer, to be by him conveyed to Oxforde."]

[35] [" A letter to sir Henry Dorell and one Foster, to attach the bodies of doctor Tailor, parson of Hadley, and Henry Askewe of Holesley, and to cause them to be safely sent up hither unto the lords of the council, to answer such matters as at their coming shall be objected against them."

" At St. James' the 22th of April. This day one Williams, maryner, of Bristowe, for conveying Barlo, late bishop of Bathe, over sea, committed to the Marshallsey. A letter of thanks to Mr. Hugan and the rest of the gentlemen of the county of Pembroke, for the sending up of Williams, maryner."]

[Wilkins, vol. iv. p. 94.]

add nothing to the account I formerly gave of it. On the 27th of April, Weston returned and reported the conference or examination of Cranmer, and the two other bishops, attested under the seal of the university; and soon after that they were dismissed; for the parliament met on the 2nd of April, and was dismissed on the 5th of May.

[Council Book, p. 112.] Cranmer's treason pardoned, that he might be burnt.

On the 3rd of May[37], Cranmer, Ridley, and Latimer, being judged obstinate heretics, the judges were asked what the queen might do, since Cranmer was attainted. He was a man dead in law, and not capable of any other censure; and this seems to be the true reason that moved the queen to pardon the treason upon which he was already condemned: for though he was very earnest to obtain a pardon for that, it does not appear that there was any regard had to him in granting it; but, on the contrary, it seems it was resolved that he should be burnt as a heretic: and since that could not be done while he stood condemned of treason, this seems to be the only motive of that mercy, which, in this case, was certainly

[p. 121.]

done out of cruelty. On the 20th of May[38], a servant of the lady Elizabeth's was brought before the council: but there is nothing in particular mentioned, only he was required to attend. There were suspicions of her being concerned in Wiat's rebellion, as appeared in the account given of Wiat himself. It is alleged, that Gardiner studied to suborn false witnesses to charge her with that; and that this went so far, that a warrant

Reply to Parsons, p. 84.

was brought to Bridges, the lieutenant of the Tower, for her execution; but that he would not obey it till he knew the queen's pleasure. Some credit seems due to this, since it was

---

[37] [" At St. James', May 3rd. It was this day ordered by the lords, that the mayor of Oxford should bring in his bill of allowances for the charges of doctor Cranmer, doctor Rydley and Latymer, and should have a warrant for the same. And further it was resolved by their lordships, that the judges and the queen's highness' learned council should be called together, and their opinions demanded what they think in law her highness may do touching the cases of the said Cranmer, Rydley and Latymer, being already by both the universities of Oxforde and Cambridge judged to be obstinate heretics; which matter is the rather to be consulted upon, for that the said Cranmer is already attainted."—Council Book, p. 112.]

[38] [" At St. James', May 20. Henry Carew, one of the ladie Elizabeth's gentlemen, had this day in commandment by the lords to make his continual appearance before them from time to time, being called thereunto."]

published in her reign, and was not contradicted, nor denied, as far as I can find. But it seems to be denied in a declaration set forth many years after by herself when she was queen; which shall be mentioned in its proper place. On the 25th of [p. 123.] May [39], some in Stepney were ordered to be set on the pillory for spreading false news; the ears of one were ordered to be nailed to the pillory, and then cut off. On the 26th of May, [p. 124.] sir Henry Bedingfield was sent with instructions, signed by the queen, for the ordering the lady Elizabeth.

On the 1st of June, an order was sent to the bishop of [p. 127.] London, to send discreet and learned preachers into Essex, to reduce the people there. Bonner seemed to think of no way of reducing any, but by severity and force; so that the council 228 found it necessary to put him in mind of his pastoral care. Orders were then given for the reception of the prince of [June 3, Spain. Some were ordered to be set on a pillory, and their p. 128.] [p. 130.] ears were to be nailed to it, and cut off. The duchess of Northumberland desired that her sons might hear mass in the Tower: this was granted, but order was given that none might speak with them. On the 11th of June, orders were given to [p. 134.] receive the duke of Savoy at Dover. And on the 5th of July, order was given to punish those who were concerned in the imposture, called *The spirit in the wall*. On the 6th [41] of July, [p. 149.]

[39] [" At St. James' the 25th of May 1554. Whereas one Thomas Sandesbourough of Stepneth, labouring man, hath reported certain false and seditious rumours against the queen's highness and the quiet estate of this realm, the said Sandesborough was by order from the lords delivered into the hands of the bailiff of Stepneth for execution of his punishment as hereafter followeth, viz., that to-morrow next, being the 26th of May, they shall openly at Stepney aforesaid nail one of his ears to the pillory, or some post to be set up for that purpose, and having stood so a convenient time, to cut off his ear from his head, to the terror and example of others that would attempt the like. Afterward the said bailiff shall deliver him to the sheriff of London to be committed to Newgate : and also the wife of one Mering of London, sent to the sheriff of London, to be set to-morrow on the pillory for spreading like news; and two wives of Stepney set on the dooking stool for like offence."—p. 123.]

[40] [" At Winchester July 29. This day two treaties of the marriage between the king and queen's highness, sealed with the seal of Spayne, exhibited by the lord privy seal and the lord Fitzwaters, late ambassdors into Spayne, were delivered to the lord treasurer, to be by him kept in the treasury."]

[41] [" At Farneham the 6th of July, 1554. Thomas Birchall, servant to the lady Elizabeth, having spoken sundry lewd and seditious words of

[July 29, p. 153.]

some of the lady Elizabeth's servants were committed for lewd words of the state of the kingdom. On the 24th of July, two treaties for the queen's marriage, made by the lord Fitzwater, who had been ambassador in Spain, were given to the lord treasurer.

The council orders severe proceedings. [p.,161.]

Now the marriage was made, and the jollities on such occasions put some stop to severities : but it was a short one ; for, on the 15th of August, letters were writ to the justices of peace in Sussex, to punish those who railed at the mysteries of Christ's religion. I must observe here once for all, that the letters themselves, writ by the council, are not entered in the book : these would have set out particulars much more clearly than those short entries do : but there were forms[42] of those letters put in a chest, and the council-book refers us often to

[p. 164.]

the letter in the chest. On the 19th of August, letters of thanks are ordered to Tirrell, and others, for their care, ordering them to imprison all such as came not to divine service; and to keep them in prison till they had the comfort of their amendment. Several men and women were imprisoned in

[p. 165.]
[Aug. 22, p. 167.]
[p. 176.]

Huntingdonshire. The 20th of August, mention is made of some in prison for words. On the 21st of August, an order was sent to examine into a conspiracy in Suffolk, by certain lewd persons. On the 16th of September, a letter was ordered to the lord mayor and aldermen of London, to punish the spreaders of false rumours.

The reconciliation with Rome designed.

But now came on the great affair of the reconciling the nation to the see of Rome. The two former parliaments could not be brought up to that ; so the court was willing to accept all that they could be brought to : but when they saw at what they stuck, they were sent home : and some were so weak as to think, that, by yielding in some things, they should give the court such content, as to save the rest. They were willing to return back to that state of religion in which king Henry left

---

the estate of the realm, was this day committed to the Marshalsey."— p. 149.]

[42] [Thus. " At Hampton Court the 24th of August, 1554. A letter to Mr. Wotton, according to the mynute in the council chest."— Council Book, p. 167.

Burnet has omitted the following interesting entry :

" At Hampton Court the 28th of August, 1554. A letter to the lieutenant of the Tower, to permit the ladies, being wives to the late duke of Northumberland his sons, to have free access from time to time to their husbands."]

it ; and did not rightly apprehend that nothing could give the
queen an entire content, but a total reconciliation with the
pope : whereas those who could not come up to this ought to
have. stood firm at first, and not, by giving ground, have encouraged the court to compass their whole design. The queen
was more than ordinary solicitous to get a parliament chosen
to her mind. She wrote a letter to the earl of Sussex ; and
probably she wrote to all those in whom she confided, in the
same strain. It will be found in the Collection. " She had Collect.
Numb. 14
" now summoned a parliament to the 12th of November, in
" which she expected to be assisted by him ; and that he would
" admonish her good subjects, who had a right to elect the
" members, to choose men of the wise, grave, and catholic sort,
" such as indeed meant the true honour of God, and the pro-
229 " sperity of the commonwealth ; which she and the king her
" husband did intend, without the alteration of any particular
" man's possession ; which, among other false rumours, the
" hinderers of her good purposes, and the favourers of heretics,
" did most untruly report. She desired him to come up
" against the feast of All-Saints at the furthest, that she might
" confer with him about those matters that were to be treated
" of in parliament." This is dated the 6th of October ; and
so careful was that lord to merit the continuance of the queen's
confidence, that, on the 14th of October, he wrote to the gentlemen of the county, to reserve their voices for the person
whom he should name : he also wrote to the town of Yarmouth
for a burgess. But now to open more particularly the great
matter that was to be transacted in this parliament.

When the news of the change of government in England, Pole sent
legate for
that end.
and of the queen's intentions, were brought to Rome, it was
not possible to deliberate long who was the properest person
to be sent legate. Pole had so many meritorious characters
on him, that, besides the signification of the queen's desire, no
other person could be thought on. Anthony Harmer has [Specimen
of Errors,
p. 179.].
given the bull upon which he was sent from Rome. It is
dated the 5th of August, 1553, though the queen came not to
London till the 3rd of August : and Commendone, who carried
her message to the pope, was in London on the 23rd ; for he
saw the duke of Northumberland's execution. It seems that
at Rome, upon king Edward's death, they took it for granted,

both that her right would take place, and that she would
reconcile her kingdom again to that see: and therefore the
bull was prepared.   Pole had at that time retired three hundred miles from Rome, to an abbey upon the lake, now called
De Garda : in his absence he was declared legate ; upon which
he wrote a letter to the queen on the 13th of August, which I

Collect.
Numb. 15.
He wrote
to the
queen.

have put in the Collection.

" He begins, expressing his joy at her exaltation, more par-
" ticularly at the manner of it ; which he reckons a singular
" work of an immediate Providence : in which, as indeed the
" subject seemed to allow it, he enlarges very copiously.   And
" since she carried the name of the *blessed Virgin,* he calls on
" her to say the *Magnificat,* applying it to the late provi-
" dences of God towards herself.   He desires her to consider
" what was the beginning of all the miseries that England had
" felt ; it was the king her father's departing from the apo-
" stolic see and the catholic church.   He was a witness to all
" the steps made in that matter.   He had upon all occasions
" asserted both her mother's marriage and her own right ;
" and had done and suffered much on that account.   He was
" therefore now most particularly concerned to know what her
" mind was with relation to religion ; and though he was then
" three hundred miles from Rome, he was named legate, to be
" sent to her, to the emperor, and to the French king ; there-
" fore he sent one to her to know her mind.   He did not doubt
" of it ; for no person owed more to the apostolic see than she
" did, since it was upon her account that so much outrage had
" been done to it.   So, before he would proceed in his legatine
" function, he desired to know her pleasure more particularly."

The
queen's
answer.
Collect.
Numb. 16.

Upon this, she wrote an answer on the 10th of October, 230
which is also in the Collection.   " She thanked him for all the
" kind expressions in his letter ; and in particular for the good
" advice he gave her.   She was full of reverence and obedience
" to the holy see ; but it was a great trouble to her, that she
" could not yet declare her mind openly in that matter.   As
" soon as it was safe for her to do it, she would let him know
" it.   His messenger would tell him all particulars : she was
" then crowned.   She hoped the parliament would repeal all
" the bad laws ; and that she should obtain the pope's pardon
" for all her own faults.   She sends by him her most humble

" thanks to the pope for his clemency to her, and for his readi-
" ness to forget all that is past." With this she sent back
Ormaneto to him. The bull that the pope sent to Pole is all
a rhetorical panegyric upon the queen's coming to the crown,
and on her pious intentions. But bulls being often in a common
form, it is not in it, but in the breves, that we are to seek the
powers, or instructions, given to Pole. There was a part of
cardinal Pole's register conveyed to me, about a year after my
second volume was printed : a short account of the most remarkable things in it was then printed, in a letter directed to
me. The characters of the truth of the papers are visible ;
some of them are in Latin, and some in Italian : and because I
look on this as a matter of great consequence, I will give a very
particular account of them.

The first paper, which will be found in the Collection, is the
breve, that was at first sent him, of the pope's own motion ;
and bears date the 8th of March 1554. By it, " Pole is em-
" powered to receive all heretics, of both sexes and of all ranks,
" even bishops and archbishops, communities as well as single
" persons, of what heresies soever guilty, though relapsed in
" them, upon their true and unfeigned repentance ; and to
" absolve them from all pains and censures, how long soever
" they had continued in their errors, and though their sins
" were reserved immediately to the holy see. And he was
" empowered to pardon all irregularities run into by them, and
" all the bigamies of ecclesiastical persons ; they first relin-
" quishing their wives : notwithstanding which, they might be
" continued in their orders and functions, and might be ca-
" pable of all ecclesiastical promotions ; all infamy being par-
" doned, provided they, with a contrite heart, should sacra-
" mentally confess their sins to any catholic priest, at their
" choice, and submit to such penance as he should enjoin :
" excusing them from all public confession, abjuration, or open
" penance. Absolving all communities from any unlawful
" pactions in favour of others, though confirmed by oaths.
" Empowering him to receive all regulars, and to absolve
" them from the censures of apostasy ; allowing them to possess
" benefices as seculars. Dispensing with the strict observation
" of Lent, as to milk, meat, and eggs ; and even flesh, upon
" the allowance of either the confessor or the physician.

Collect.
Numb. 17
His first
powers.

BURNET, PART III.　　　　　　　　D d

" Giving him authority to suffer such of the clergy, under the
" degree of a bishop, who were married, upon their true con-
" version, to live in that state, so that no scandals were given
" by it : only they were not to minister at the altar, nor to do
" any ecclesiastical function ; but they might lawfully continue 231
" in the married state, the issue being declared lawful.   To
" this is added, a power of uniting of benefices."

Next comes the clause concerning the possessors of ecclesiastical goods.   " He is empowered to agree, transact, and
" discharge them, for all the profits they had wickedly re-
" ceived, and for the moveable goods that they had consumed ;
" *the immoveable goods that have been by them unduly de-*
" *tained, being first restored, if that should seem to be con-*
" *venient to him.*   And whatever should arise out of any such
" agreement, was to be applied to the church, to which such
" goods had belonged, or for the advancement of studies, and
" to schools.   There is likewise a power granted, to delegate
" others under him, for the care and performance of all these
" particulars.   But because he was to go first to Flanders,
" and stay in those parts for some time ; the pope gave him
" authority to execute these powers, even while he was without
" the kingdom, to all persons belonging to it, that should
" apply to him, particularly with relation to all orders unduly
" received ; and to confirm bishops or archbishops, who had
" been promoted by a secular nomination, during the schism,
" and had assisted the former kings, though they had fallen
" into heresy, upon their return to the unity of the church :
" and to provide to metropolitical or cathedral churches such
" persons as should be recommended to him by the queen,
" according to the customs of the kingdom, upon any vacancy :
" and to absolve and reabilitate all clergymen of all ranks,
" notwithstanding their past errors.   All these powers are
" confirmed, with a full *non obstante* to all constitutions what-
" soever."

Cardinal
Pole stop-
ped in
Flanders
by the
emperor.

Here was a great fulness of favour, with relation to all personal things.   When Pole (whose name I write as he himself
did, and not as we usually do) came to Flanders, he was
stopped by the emperor's order till his powers were seen, and
sent to England.   When they were seen, they were considered
as far short of what was expected, and of what seemed neces-

sary for the carrying on the reconciliation quietly through the
nation : so Pole sent Ormaneto to Rome for fuller powers, and
retired to Diligam-abbey, near Brussels.   While he was there,
he heard the news of Philip's arrival in England, and of the
queen's being married to him : upon which he wrote a letter
of congratulation to the bishop of Arras, which is in the
Collection : and on the same day he wrote this acceptable Collect.
piece of news to the cardinal de Monte ; which is also in the Numb. 18.
Collection.   In the postscript to the bishop of Arras, he tells Collect.
him, that Ormaneto was returned with fuller powers.   He Numb. 19.
brought with him two breves.

The first is of no importance to this matter : but because it
was thought to be suppressed on design, by the writer of the
letter directed to me by him that wrote on this subject in king
James' time, it is put in the Collection.   It sets forth, " that Collect.
" he was sent first to the queen of England ; and after that he Numb. 20.
" was constituted *legate à latere*, for mediating a peace between New and
" the emperor and the king of France.   He had also very fuller
" ample powers given him, while he remained in Flanders, powers
232 " with relation to English persons and affairs.   But since, by Pole.
" reason of the schism, and other errors, many cases might
" happen, that wanted a provision from the apostolical see,
" which could not be comprehended within the faculties given
" him : and because it is doubtful, whether he may yet use
" them in the queen's dominions ; and which of them shall be
" made use of, while he is either with the emperor or the king
" of France : the pope gives him full power to make use of all
" faculties sent to him, by himself, or by any other deputed by
" him ; and to do every thing that he shall think will conduce
" to the glory of God, the honour of the holy see, and the
" bringing the queen's dominions to the communion of the
" church, as fully as may be.   And while he remained with
" the emperor, he gave him all the powers of a *legate à latere*,
" for all his dominions : and he gave him the same powers,
" while he should be with the king of France."

The other breve, which is also in the Collection, sets forth, Collect.
" that, upon the hopes of reducing the kingdom of England, Numb. 21.
" that had been torn from the body of the catholic church, to tion to
" an union with it, out of which there is no salvation ; the church
" pope had sent him his *legate à latere*, with all the powers lands.

" that seemed necessary or proper for effecting that work : in
" particular, to agree and transact with the possessors of
" church-goods concerning them. And whereas, by the be-
" ginnings and progress already made, there is good hopes of
" bringing that work to a full perfection ; which will go on the
" easier, the more indulgent and bountiful the pope shews
" himself, with relation to the possessions of those goods : the
" pope therefore, not willing that the recovering that nation,
" and the salvation of so many souls, should be obstructed by
" any worldly regards, in imitation of the good father, who re-
" ceived the returning prodigal, he empowered Pole, in whose
" prudence and dexterity he put an entire confidence, to treat
" with all the possessors or detainers of ecclesiastical goods,
" for whom the queen should intercede ; and to transact and
" compound with them, that they might, without any scruple,
" enjoy and retain the said goods : and to conclude every thing
" that was proper or necessary with relation to them. *Saving*
" *always such things, in which, for the greatness and im-*
" *portance of them, it shall seem fit to you to consult this*
" *holy see, to obtain our approbation and confirmation.*"
Upon which he is fully empowered to proceed, with a full *non*
obstante, bearing date the 28th of June. With these breves,
cardinal de Monte wrote him a letter, in the Roman way, of a
high compliment ; which is in the Collection.

The next letter is from cardinal Morone ; which is likewise
in the Collection. By this it appears, that Pole had gone to
France, upon his legatine commission : and, after the usual
Roman civilities, " he tells him, he had laid his letter before
" the pope, who was beginning to despair of the affairs of
" England : and though the pope had not the patience to read,
" or hear his letter, which was his ordinary custom, yet he
" told him the sum of it ; with which he was satisfied : and 233
" said, he had given no cause, neither to the emperor, nor to
" any other, to use such extravagant words to him. It seems
" Pole had desired to be recalled ; but the Pope said, that
" could not be done. It would be a great disgrace both to the
" pope and to the apostolical see, to the emperor himself, and
" to cardinal Pole ; and a great prejudice to England. But
" he would not write to the emperor upon it : nor was he re-
" solved about the goods of the church ; concerning which he

Collect.
Numb. 22.

Collect.
Numb. 23.

" spoke often very variously. He resolved to write both to
" the queen and to the prince of Spain ; which letters, he
" adds, will be sent by Ormaneto, who is despatched with every
" thing necessary for the business, conform to his desire." The
rest is all compliment ; dated the 13th of July. Then follows
a breve, merely in point of form, extending the former powers,
that were addressed only to the queen, to Philip her husband ;
dated the 10th of July.

Upon this, the emperor being then at Valenciennes, the
cardinal sent Ormaneto thither ; who gave an account of his
audience to Priuli, the legate's great and generous friend,
which will be found in the Collection. The bishop of Arras
told him how much the emperor had the matters of religion at
heart ; and that he would be always ready to promote them.
But when Ormaneto pressed him for a present despatch, he
said they had no news from England since the marriage : and
that before any other step was made, it would be necessary to
know what ply the affairs of that kingdom were like to take.
It was fit to consider, whether the powers of securing the
goods of the church should come from the legate, or from the
king and queen. Then he desired to see the copy of the cardinal's faculties. As to the point of time, Ormaneto said, it
was not fit to lose a moment, since so many souls were en-
dangered by the delay ; and the first coming of the prince of
Spain ought not to be let slip, by which the honour of the
work would be chiefly due to him. As for his faculties, all
things necessary were committed to the cardinal in the amplest
manner ; and more particular resolutions could not be taken
but upon the place. Somewhat further passed between them,
which Ormaneto reserves till he saw the cardinal. The bishop
of Arras promised to lay all before the emperor, and to do all
good offices. The emperor was at that time so well, that he
was often on horseback, to view his army, which had then
marched to St. Amand ; and the two armies were very near
one another. This is dated the last of July.

On the 3rd of August, the bishop of Arras wrote to the
cardinal, " that the emperor received his congratulations on
" the marriage very kindly ; but did not think it was yet
" proper for him to go to England, till they had a perfect
" account of the present state of affairs there. To know that,

All was
laid before
the em-
peror.
Collect.
Numb. 24.
Collect.
Numb. 25.

Yet he was
still put off
by delays.

" he had that day sent an express thither : upon his return,
" he should be able to give him a more positive answer. He
" knew the zeal of the king and queen was such, that they
" would lose no time ; but yet they must proceed with such
" moderation, that the way to a true remedy might not be cut
" off by too much haste." This is in the Collection. The cardinal had a letter from Bartholomew de Miranda, a friar, who 234
(I suppose) was king Philip's confessor, and afterwards archbishop of Toledo, from Winchester, July 28. It is only a letter

Collect.
Numb. 26.
of respect, desiring his commands. The cardinal wrote to the
bishop of Arras on the 5th of August : he sent him the copy of
his faculties, and expressed a great earnestness in his design of
going speedily into England, as soon as the courier sent by the
emperor should return. He shewed himself as impatient of
the delays as in good manners he could well do. This is also
in the Collection.

King Philip stayed at Winchester some days after the marriage : for, on the 4th of August, he sent the count of Horn
over to the emperor from thence ; and by him he wrote a
letter, partly of respect, partly of credit, to the cardinal. To
this the cardinal wrote an answer, which I have put in the

Collect.
Numb. 27.
Collection : though, besides such high compliments as are
usually given to princes, there is nothing particular in it ; only
he still insists earnestly for leave to come over. On the 11th
of August, the bishop of Arras wrote to him, " that he had
" seen the copy of his faculties, and he joins with him in his
" wishes, to see that kingdom restored to its ancient obedience:
" he assures him, the emperor was pressing the despatch of the
" matter, and he did not doubt but that it would be speedily
" accomplished." Pole wrote on the 2nd of September to Soto,
the emperor's confessor, " thanking him for those pressing
" letters that he had written, both to the emperor and to
" duke Alonso d'Aquilara ; with which the legate was so de-
" lighted, that he writes as one in a rapture upon it ; and he
" animates him to persist in that zeal for promoting this great
" work."

The reason
of those
delays.
He was still put off with new delays ; of which, the best
account I can give is, that this being the decisive stroke, there
was a close canvassing over England for the elections to this
parliament. Since nothing can effectually ruin this nation, but

a bad choice; therefore, as it is the constant character of a good ministry, who design nothing but the welfare and happiness of the nation, to leave all men to a due freedom in their elections; so it is the constant distinction of a bad ministry, that have wicked designs, to try all the methods of practice and corruption possible, to carry such an election, that the nation being ill represented by a bad choice, it may be easy to impose any thing on a body of vicious, ignorant, and ill-principled men, who may find their own mercenary account in selling and betraying their country. It appeared in the two former parliaments, who they were that could not bear the returning to their old servitude to the papacy. It was, no doubt, spread over England, that they saw the legate was kept in Flanders, and not suffered yet to come over: this seems the true cause, why his coming was so long put off. It might be likewise an artifice of Gardiner's, to make the difficulties appear the greater, and by that to enhance his own merit the more. It is plain, that till the election was over, and till the pulses of the majority were first tried, it was resolved not to suffer the legate to come over. This seems to be that which he insinuates in his letter to the confessor, when he says, that *the wisdom of the wise has kept the gate so long shut against him.*

235 On the 13th of October, Pole wrote the pope an account of what had passed between him and the bishop of Arras, and the emperor himself: the bishop of Arras, as he writes, came to him, and assured him that the emperor was in the best disposition possible; but it was necessary to come to particulars, to examine all the impediments, and the best methods to put them out of the way. The legate said he had full powers, and desired to know from England what impediments were suggested. He added, this was not a negotiation like that in making a peace, where both sides did conceal their own designs all they could, till they discovered those of the contrary side: here all had but one design, and he was ready to enter into particulars when they pleased. He had an audience of the emperor, none but the nuncio and the bishop of Arras being present. In it, after usual compliments, the impediments proposed were two: the first related to the doctrine, in which there was no abatement to be made, nor indulgence to be showed. The other was concerning the lands; for the

Collect. Numb. 28

usurpers of them, knowing the severity of the ecclesiastical laws, were afraid to return to the obedience of the church.   To this the legate answered, that the pope was resolved to extend his indulgence in this case : first, as to all the mean profits already received, and the censures incurred by that, which was a great point; the pope was willing freely to discharge that entirely : nor did he intend to apply any part of these to himself, or to the apostolical see, as many feared he would; though that might seem reasonable, as a compensation for damages sustained; but he would convert all to the service of God, and to the benefit of the kingdom : and he had such regard to the piety of those princes, that he had empowered him to grant such favours as they should intercede for, and to such persons as they should think worthy to be gratified, and were capable to assist him in the matter of religion.   The emperor understanding all this, thanked the pope very heartily for his favour in that matter : he said he had granted enough ; he excused himself, that, being wholly taken up with the present war, he had no sooner applied himself to consider the matter : now he knew it well : he had already written to England, and he expected a speedy answer from thence, by which he would know the state of affairs there.   He knew, by his own experience in Germany, that this of the church-lands was the point that was most stood on : as to matters of doctrine, he did not believe that they stood much upon that, they neither believing the one nor the other ; yet those lands (or goods) being dedicated to God, he thought it was not fit to yield all up to those who possessed them : he added, that though the legate had told him the whole extent of his powers, yet he would do well not to open that to others.   He then desired to see his faculties.   The legate upon that apprehending this would give a handle to a new delay, said he had already shewed them to the bishop of Arras ; and he told the emperor, what a scandal it would give to the whole world, if the reconciliation should not be settled by this parliament.   The queen did not think fit to press it formerly, till she had received that mighty assistance which was now come to her by her marriage ; yet if this, which ought to have been the beginning and the foundation of all the rest, were delayed any longer, it must **236** give great offence both to God and man.   The emperor said,

regard was to be had to the ill disposition of the people concerned, who had formed in themselves and others an aversion
to the name of obedience, and to a red cap, and a religious
habit. He said, some friars, whom his son had brought with
him out of Spain, were advised to change their habits. They
had not indeed done it, nor was it convenient that they should
do it. He also touched on the ill offices that would be done
them by their enemies abroad, in order to the raising of
tumults : (meaning the French.) The legate answered, if he
must stay till all impediments were removed, that would be
endless. The audience ended with this, that he must have a
little patience, till the secretary whom he had sent into England
should return.

Mason was then the queen's ambassador at the emperor's
court : he in a letter on the 5th of October, writ towards the
end of it (the rest being a long account of the war between the
emperor and the French king) concerning the cardinal, (which
will be found in the Collection,) that he was sent by the pope
on two designs ; the one to mediate a peace between those two
powers ; the other, to mediate a spiritual peace, as he called
it, in the kingdom of England : but seeing no hope of succeeding either in the one or the other, he began to despair : and
if he did not quickly see some appearance of success in the last,
he would go back to Rome a sorrowful man. And here Mason
runs out, either to make his court to the queen or to the legate,
or that he was really possessed with a very high opinion of
him, which seems the more probable, as well as the more
honest motive : he says, " All the world adores him for his
" wisdom, learning, virtue, and godliness. God seems to dwell
" in him ; his conversation, with his other godly qualities, was
" above the ordinary sort of men. It would be a strong heart
" that he would not soften in half an hour's talk."

At this time the cardinal wrote a long letter to king Philip
in Latin : he tells him, he had been now for a year knocking
at the gates of the palace, and nobody opened to him ; though
he is the person that was driven from his country into an exile
of above twenty years' continuance, because he was against
shutting the queen out of that palace, in which he now lived
with her : but he comes with a higher authority, in the name
of the vicar of the great king and shepherd, St. Peter's

[marginal notes]
Cardinal
Pole much
esteemed
by the Eng-
lish ambas-
sador.
Collect.
Numb. 29.

He writes
to king
Philip.
Collect.
Numb. 30.

successor, or rather St. Peter himself; who was so long driven out of England.   Upon this he runs out into a long allegory, taken from St. Peter's being delivered out of prison from Herod's cruel purpose, and coming to the gate of Mary, where though his voice was known, yet he was kept long knocking at the door; Mary not being sure that it was he himself.   He dresses this out with much pomp, and in many words, as a man that had practised eloquence much, and had allowed himself in flights of forced rhetoric; liker indeed to the declamation of a student in rhetoric, than the solemn letter of so great a man on such an occasion.   It is true that this way of writing had been early practised, and had been so long used, even by popes themselves, that these precedents might seem to warrant him to copy after such originals.

The queen sent to bring him over to England. Collect. Numb. 31.

At last the queen sent the lord Paget and lord Hastings to 237 bring him over: their letter upon their coming to the emperor's court is dated from Brussels the 13th of November. In it they give an account of their waiting upon the emperor with the king and queen's compliments.   The emperor had that day received the sacrament, yet they were admitted to audience in the afternoon: he expressed great joy when he heard them give an account how matters were in England, and roused himself up in a cheerful manner, and said, that, among many great benefits, he was bound to thank God for this as a main one; that he now saw England brought back to a good state.   He had seen what the kingdom had once been, and into what calamities it fell afterwards: and now he thanked God for the miracles shewed to the queen, to make her the minister to bring it again to its ancient dignity, wealth, and renown.   He also rejoiced that God had given her so soon such a certain hope of succession: these tidings of the state of her person, with the report of the consent of the noblemen and others touching the cardinal, and their obedience and union with the catholic church, were so pleasant to him, that if he had been half dead, they would have revived him.   He promised them all assistance, as they should come to need it.

From the emperor they went to the cardinal, who welcomed them with great joy, and with expressions full of duty and thankfulness to the queen.   Here they enlarge on his praises: " they call him the man of God, full of godliness and virtue;

" and so eminently humble, that he was contented to come into
" England in such sort as the queen had commanded ; not as
" a legate, but as a cardinal, and an ambassador sent to the
" queen : and they assured the queen, that, touching the
" matter of possessions, all things should pass on the pope's
" behalf, so that every man there shall have cause to be con-
" tented." Pole took leave of the emperor on the 12th ; he
was to set out in slow journeys, his body being then too weak
for great ones ; in six days he was to be at Calais, where they
had ordered every thing to be ready for his transportation.

It seems by this, that the queen reckoned on it, as sure, that
she was with child : though in that, after the hopes of it were
published with too much precipitation, she found herself so
much mistaken, that it was believed the grief and shame of it,
both together, had an ill effect on her health and life. *The queen believed herself to be with child.*

About this time there was a very abusive libel, printed in
the form of a letter, as writ by Bradford to the queen[45] ; in
which it was said, " that it was believed the queen intended to
" give the crown to the king, hoping that then he would keep
" company with her more, and live more chaste, contrary to
" his nature : for peradventure after he was crowned he would
" be content with one whore ; whereas he had then three or
" four in a night : and these not ladies, but common prosti-
" tutes." One John Capstocke, the printer, was discovered ;
he was condemned to be imprisoned, and to have his ears nailed
to the pillory, and cut off ; yet he was pardoned. The consideration is not mentioned ; it may be easily imagined it was
no small one, probably enough it was upon the discovery of
some of those whom they were seeking out for the slaughter[46]. *[Dec. 5, 1557.]* *Rymer, tom. xv. [p. 480.]*

---

[45] [Bradford (John). Copye of
a Letter sent to the Erles of Arundel, Darbie, Shrewsbury and Pembroke, declaring the Nature of
Spaniardes, and discouering the
most detestable Treasons whiche
they haue pretended most falselye
against Englande. Whereunto is
added a tragical Blast of the papistical Trompet for Mayntenaunce
of the Popes Kingdome in Englande,
by T. E. 1555. 16mo.]

[46] [The printer appears to have
been indicted for writing the book,
which in the indictment is entitled,
' The copie of John Brodfordes
Letter to the quene and to the lordes
and estates of the realm of England." The particular libel quoted
in the indictment was worded as
follows :

" Peradventure her grace think-
eth (*innuendo dictam Dominam Reginam*) that the king will kepe her
more companye and love her the
better if she gyve him the crowne :

Cardinal
Pole carries
his powers
beyond the
limits set
him.

238

I have nothing to add[47] to what I wrote formerly with relation to this parliament, and the reconciliation made in it: no doubt Pole, according to the powers in his breve, desired the queen would name such persons, to whom the favour of confirming them in their possessions should be granted; but it seems they durst not venture on any discrimination, lest that should have made the expected persons desperate. So it is evident, that the confirming of all without exception was, if not beyond his powers, yet at least a matter of such importance, that he ought to have consulted the pope upon it, and to have stayed till he had new and special orders to pass it in so full a manner as he did. But still it is plain, by the message sent to Rome, that he made the council at least to apprehend that it was necessary to send thither for a confirmation of what he had done, without any limits, upon powers that were expressly limited, and reserved to a confirmation.

Collect.
Numb. 32.

On the 12th of December, Mason wrote from Brussels: and after he had given in his letter an account of what passed in the diet, upon a letter written to it by the French king; he also writes, " that one of the emperor's council had told him,

Some
preach for
restoring
the abbey-
lands.

" that his master was displeased to hear that a preacher was
" beating the pulpit jollily (I use his own words) for the resti-
" tution of the abbey-lands: upon this he writes, that if it be
" so meant by the prince, and the thing be thought convenient,
" he did his duty; but if it was not so, it was a strange thing,
" that, in a well-ordered commonwealth, a subject should be
" so hardy as to cry thus to the people, to raise storms next
" summer, against what they were then doing in winter: and
" if the thing were to be talked of, it ought to be to the
" prince and council, and not to the people. He reflects on
" the unbridled sermons in the former times, that they were
" much misliked: so he hoped, that in a good government
" that should have been amended. He thought the person
" that preached this might be well put to silence; for he being
" a monk, and having vowed poverty, possessed a deanery and

ye will live chaste contrary to his nature; for peradventure after he were crowned he wolde be contented within one woman, but in the meane space he wold have choice of three or foure in one night to prove

whiche of them he liketh beste, not of ladys and gentlewomen, but of bakers' daughters and such other poore whores."]

[47] [See Part ii. p. 291.]

" three or four benefices.　He tells them he had heard, by the
" report of other ambassadors, that England was now returned
" to the unity of the Christian church.　He should have been
" glad that he might have been able to confirm this by some
" certain knowledge of it ; but it was ordinary for the ambas-
" sadors of England to know the least of all others of the
" matters of their own kingdom."　A custom of a long continuance, of which I have heard great complaints made of a
later date.　On the 25th of December he wrote, that, ac- Paper-
cording to his orders, he had let the emperor know the ap- Office.
prehensions the queen had of the progress of her big belly ;
and that all was quiet, and every thing went on happily in
England.　Upon this the emperor fell into a free discourse
with him of the difference between governing with rigour and
severity ; and the governing in such sort, that both prince and
people might *s'entre entendre et s'entre aimer,* mutually
understand and mutually love one another.　This, as it is at
all times a noble measure of government ; so it was more
necessary to offer such an advice, at a time in which it was
resolved to proceed with an unmerciful rigour against those
239 whom they called heretics.　The queen seemed to be so sure
that she was quick with child, that the privy-council wrote [Nov. 27,
upon it a letter to Bonner, and ordered him to cause *Te* Wilkins,
Conc. vol.
Deum to be sung upon it.　With such a precipitation was this iv. p. 109.
desired piece of news published. from Fox,
iii. 108.]

Some small favour was, at king Philip's desire, shewed to Jan. 18,
some.　The archbishop of York[45] was released, upon a bond 1555.
The arch-
of twenty thousand marks for his good behaviour.　How far bishop of
York set a
he recanted, or complied, does not appear : one thing may be liberty.
reasonably concluded ; that since no more mention is made of
the complaint put in against him, for keeping another man's
wife from him, there is no reason to think there was any truth

---

[45] [" The 18 day of January ....
whent to the Towre my lord chans-
seler and dyvers odur lordes and of
the conselle, and delyvered a number
presonars, as ther names folowes :
ser James a Croft, sir Gorge Har-
per, ser Gawynn Carow, ser Ne-
colas Frogmortun, master Vaghan,
ser Edward Varner, Gybbs, the bys-
shope of Yorke, master Rogers and
dyvers odur presonars, and after
ther was a gret shottyng of gones."
—Machyn's Diary, p. 80.

" At the Tower the 18 of January
1554.　Bound to their good abearing, order and fyne at pleasure, viz.
the late archbishop of Yorke 20,000
marks, &c. &c.——Council Book,
p. 197.]

in it: for there being so particular a zeal then on foot, to disgrace the marriage of the clergy, so flagrant an instance as this, in a man put in so eminent a post, would not have been passed over, if there had been any colour of truth, or proof for

[Council Book, p. 201.]
[Ibid. p. 206 and Archæologia, vol. xviii. p. 181.]

it. On the 27th of January, Hopkins, sheriff of the city of Coventry, was put in the Fleet for ill religion. On the 19th of February, some small regard was had to Miles Coverdale, as being a foreigner; for he was a Dane[49]: he had a passport to go to Denmark, with two servants, without any unlawful let or search.

On the 29th of January, cardinal Pole gave deputed powers to the bishops, to reconcile all persons to the church, pursuant to the first breve he had from the pope; by which the reconciliation was made very easy; every one being left at his liberty to choose his own confessor, who was to enjoin him his penance: upon which the clergy, both regulars and seculars, were to be entirely restored, confirmed in their benefices, and made capable of all further favours: but those who were accused, or condemned for heresy, were only to be restored to the peace of the church, for the quiet of their consciences. All canonical irregularities were also taken off; all public abjurations, or renunciations, were, at discretion, to be either moderated or entirely forgiven; with a power to the bishop to depute such rectors and curates as he shall think fit to absolve and reconcile all lay-persons to the church. That sent to the bishop of Norwich is still upon record, and was collated with the register, and sent me by Dr. Tanner. With this, I have likewise put in

Collect. Numb. 33.
Collect. Numb. 34.

the Collection the method in which it was executed. First, the Articles of the Visitation are in it, in English; then follow rules in Latin, given by the cardinal to all bishops and their officials. The most material of these is, "that all who were "empowered to reconcile persons to the church, were re- "quired to enter into a register the names of all such as they "should receive; that it might appear upon record, who were, "and who were not, reconciled; and to proceed against all

[49] [See above, p. 221. The extract, as given in Archæologia, vol. xviii. p. 181, is as follows: "At Westminster the 19 day of February, anno 1554. A pasporte directed to all maiores, sherifes, bailifes &c. to permite Miles Coverdall to passe from hence towards Denmarke with two of his servants, his bagges and baggages, without any theire unlawfulle lette or serche."]

" such as were not reconciled : in particular, they were to
" insert Thomas Becket's name, and also the pope's, in all their
" offices."

Now came on the burning of heretics. Many had been kept
above a year and a half in prison, when yet there was no law
against them : and now a law was made against them, which
it could not be pretended that they had transgressed. But
articles were objected to them, to which they were by the
ecclesiastical law obliged to make answer : and upon their
240 answers they were condemned. Sampson, in a letter to Calvin, *Letters*
wrote on the 23rd of February, " that Gardiner had ordered *sent from Zurich.*
" fourscore of the prisoners to be brought before him, and had [*Epistolæ*
" tried to prevail on them, both by promises and threatenings, *Tigurinæ, p 112.*]
" to return, as he called it, to the union of the church : but *The re-*
" not one of them yielded, except Barlow, that had been bishop *formers, when tried*
" of Bath and Wells ; and Cardmaker[50], an archdeacon there." *by Gardiner, were*
So this proved ineffectual. How far these yielded does not *firm.*
appear.

It was resolved to begin with Hooper ; against whom both
Gardiner and Bonner had so peculiar an ill-will, that he was
singled out of all the bishops to be the first sacrifice. A copy
of his process and sentence was sent me by Dr. Tanner, which
I have put in the Collection. On the 28th of January, he was *Collect.*
brought before Gardiner in his court in Southwark, and is *Numb. 35.*
called only John Hooper, clerk. Gardiner set forth, " that
" the day before he had been brought before him, and others
" of the privy-council, and exhorted to confess his errors and
" heresies, and to return to the unity of the church ; a pardon
" being offered him for all that was past ; but that his heart
" was so hardened, that he would not accept of it : so he was
" then brought to answer to certain articles ; but he had again
" the offer made him, to be received into the bosom of the
" church, if he desired it. He rejected that ; and, as the acts
" of the court have it, he did impudently break out into some
" blasphemies." The articles that were objected to him were

---

[50] [John Taylor, *alias* Cardmaker,
is mentioned by Strype in Eccles.
Memor. ii. p. 217, as vicar of St.
Bridget's, Fleet Street, in 1550. He
was also chancellor of Wells 1547,
but it does not appear that he was
archdeacon. He is mentioned in
the second part of the History,
p. 313. The writer's words are *ut
puto, archidiacono.*]

three : " 1. That he being a priest, and of a religious order,
" had married a wife, and lived with her ; and did, both by
" preaching and writing, justify and defend that his marriage.
" To which he answered, acknowledging it was true ; and that
" he was still ready to defend it. 2. That persons married
" might, for the cause of fornication or adultery, according to
" the word of God, be so divorced, that they might lawfully
" marry again.   To this he likewise answered, confessing it,
" and saying, that he was ready to defend it, against all who
" would oppose it.   3. That he had publicly taught and main-
" tained, that in the sacrament of the altar the true and natural
" body and blood of Christ are not present under the accidents
" of bread and wine ; so that there is no material bread and
" wine in it."   To which his answer is set down in English
words ; " That the very natural body and blood of Christ is
" not really and substantially in the sacrament of the altar :
" saying also, that the mass was of the Devil, and was an idol."
Gardiner, upon this, ordered him to come again into court the
next day ; and then he did again try, by many persuasions, to
prevail on him : but he continued still obstinate, and said
further, " that marriage was none of the seven sacraments ;
" and if it was a sacrament, he could prove there were seven-
" score sacraments."   After all this, Gardiner gave sentence,
and delivered him over to the secular arm.   Upon which, the
sheriffs of London took him into their hands, as their prisoner :
but it was resolved to send him to Gloucester, there to receive
his crown of martyrdom.   And there was a particular order
sent along with him to Gloucester ; in which he is designed,
" John Hooper, that was called bishop of Worcester and Glou- 241
" cester, who was judged to be a most obstinate, false, de-
" testable heretic, and did still persist obstinate, and refused
" mercy, though it was offered to him : he was sent to be
" burnt at Gloucester, to the example and terror of those
" whom he had seduced.   Order is also given, to call some of
" reputation in that shire, to assist the mayor and the sheriffs
" of that city.   And because this Hooper is, as all heretics are,
" a vainglorious person ; and if he have liberty to speak, he
" may persuade such as he has seduced, to persist in the
" miserable opinions that he hath taught them ; therefore
" strict order is given, that neither at his execution, nor in

Hooper,
the first
bishop that
suffered,
barbarous-
ly used.
Collect.
Numb. 36.

i

" going to the place of it, he be suffered to speak at large;
" but that he be led quietly, and in silence, for avoiding further
" infection." This will be found in the Collection. But though Collect.
his words could not be suffered to be heard, yet the voice of Numb. 36.
his sufferings, which were extremely violent, had probably the
best effect on those who saw both them and his constancy in
them.   He had been above a year and a half in prison, under
much hard usage.   He sent his wife out of England, to deliver
himself from that which might raise too great tenderness in
him, especially if he had seen her ill used, which the wives of
the clergy were in danger of daily.   He wrote several letters
to Bullinger from the prison ; but was so watched, that he
durst not enter into any particulars.   Most of his letters were
recommendations of some who were then flying out of England:
he in them all expressed much constancy and patience : and he
was preparing himself for that, in which he reckoned his imprisonment would soon end.   He had no other prospect, but
of sealing the truth with his blood.   He was very glad, when
he knew his wife had got safe to Frankfort ; where she lived, [Epistolæ
and wrote several letters to Bullinger in a very clean and Tigurinæ,
natural style of Latin : they do chiefly relate to her husband's pp. 68-70
condition.

Among several letters that Hooper wrote, during his im- [Ibid. pp.
prisonment, to Bullinger, I find one that is so full, and shews 64—67.]
so clearly the temper of that holy man in his imprisonment,
that I have put it in the Collection.   He had written several Collect.
letters to him, that it seems fell into ill hands, and so came not Numb. 37.
to Zurich, as they were directed ; as he found by Bullinger's
last letter, that some of his were also intercepted.   " That last
" which he had, was directed to him, to be communicated to
" all his fellow-prisoners : he promised, that he would take
" care to send it round among them.   The wound that the
" papacy had received in England was then entirely healed:
" the pope was now declared the *head of that church.*   The
" prisoners, who had been shut up for a year and a half, were
" daily troubled by the enemies of the gospel : they were kept
" asunder from one another, and treated with all manner of
" indignities; and they were daily threatened with the last
" extremities, which did not terrify them.
" They were so inwardly fortified, that they despised both

" fire and sword. They knew in whom they believed; and
" were sure they were to suffer for well-doing. He desires
" the continuance of their prayers; let God do with them what
" seemed good in his eyes. He sent over to him two books 242
" that he had written, the one of true religion, and the other
" of false religion, which he had dedicated to the parliament,
" as an apology for the reformation. He gives them liberty
" to correct them as they thought fit; and desired, that they
" might be quickly printed; for they were well approved by
" the pious and learned about him. He desires they may not
" be frighted from doing it, by the apprehensions of any harm
" that might happen to himself upon that account: he com-
" mitted himself to God, who was his defence and his guard,
" through Jesus Christ; to whom he had entirely dedicated
" himself. If God would prolong his life, he prayed it might
" be to the glory of his name; but if he would put an end to
" this short and wicked life, which of these soever it pleased
" God to order, his will be done." This is dated from his
prison, the 11th of December, 1554. It appears that Hooper's
wife was a German[51]; so his sending her in time out of England was a just expression of his care of her.

[Council
Book; p.
213.]
[Archæ-
ologia, vol.
xviii. p.
181.]
[Council
Book, p.
222.]
On the 18th of March, some sacrifices being to be made in
Essex, " letters were written by the council to the earl of
" Oxford, and the lord Rich, to be present at the burning of
" those obstinate heretics, that were sent to divers parts of
" that county." And on the 1st of April[52], informations being
brought that there were preachers at work in several parts of
the kingdom, a general order was sent to all sheriffs to seize
on them. When that madman William Thomas, called otherwise Flower, or Branch, was seized on, for wounding a priest
in the church, they found a cloth about his neck, with these

---

[51] [In one of her letters to Bullinger she signs her name Anne
de Tserclas dict. Hopera. Epp. Ti-
gur. xlix. p. 69.]

[52] [The entry in the Council Book
does not bear out the text. " At
Westminster the first of April 1555.
A letter to the sheriff of Kent to
apprehend Thomas Woodgate of
Chedingston, and William May-
narde of Assheridge, who usen in
the said town to preach seditiously
in corners, and to send him under
safe ward hither."
" A letter to the sheriff of Sussex
to apprehend one Holden of Wy-
theam etc. A letter to the sheriff
of Essex to make search for one of
Harwiche, who useth to lead a boy
from place to place with him, and
preacheth seditiously."]

words, *Deum time, idolum fuge;* Fear God, and fly from idolatry[53]. He was seized on by sir Nicholas Hare and sir Thomas Cornwall: they had letters of thanks from the council for their pains. They were ordered first to examine him, then to send him to the bishop of London, to proceed against him for heresy; and to the justices of peace, to punish him for the shedding of blood in the church: and if he persists in his heresy, order is given, that he be executed in the latter end of the week; but that his right hand should be cut off the day before.

On the 16th of May, some persons were named, and their appointments ordered, who should be in readiness to carry the news of the queen's delivery to foreign princes. The lord admiral was appointed to go to the emperor; and was allowed four pound a day, and two hundred pound for equipage. The lord Fitzwater was to go to the French court, and was to have two hundred marks for equipage. Sir Henry Sidney was to go to the king of the Romans, and to have five hundred marks: and Shelley was to carry the news to the king of Portugal, and to have four hundred marks. This was repeated on the 28th of May. The money was ordered to be ready, for the immediate despatch of those envoys. And on the 29th of May, order was given[54], that the persons named should be ready to go

[margin notes:]
[April 15. Council Book, p. 229.]

[Ibid. p. 242.] Persons appointed to carry the news of the queen's being delivered. [Archæologia, vol. xviii. p. 182.] [Council Book, p. 254.]

---

[53] [" At Hampton Court the 15 of April 1555. A letter to sir Nicholas Hare and sir Thomas Cornewalle of thanks for their advertisements touching the vile part of Braunche, praying them to examine him what he meaned in that he ware about his neck, having this wrought thereupon, *Deum time, Idolum fuge,* and where he had the same, and who else he knoweth to wear the like, and to speak to the bishop of London to proceed against him for his heresy according to the laws. And to speak also to the justices of peace of Myddlesex, to proceed in like manner against him for shedding of blood in the church, according to the statute. So that if he persist in his heresy, he may be executed at the furthest by the latter end of this week. And that his right hand be the day before his execution or the same day stricken off." " At Hampton Court the 22 of April 1555. A letter to sir Nicholas Hare, master of the rolls, and other the justices of peace in the county of Middlesex, with the king and queen's highness' writ for the execution of William Flower, *alias* Branche, signifying unto them, that forasmuch as the said Flower's offence was so enorme and heinous, their majesties were further pleased, for the more terrible example, he should, before he were executed, have his right hand stricken off."]

[54] [No notice to this effect anywhere.]

[Council
Book, p.
257.]
when warned.　On the 1st of June [55], a letter was ordered to the bishop of London, to proceed against some, who were suspected to be of evil religion.　And on the 3rd of June, letters were written to the lord Rich to assist at the execution of some **243**

[p. 259.]
heretics at Colchester, Harwich, and Manytree : a letter was also written to the earl of Oxford, to send his servants to attend on the lord Rich at those executions.　It is not easy to guess whether the many letters written upon those occasions were to prevent tumults, because they apprehended the people might rescue those victims out of the sheriff's hands, if he had not been well guarded ; or whether it was to celebrate those triumphs over heresy with much solemnity ; which is commonly done in those countries where the inquisition is received. At the same time entries are made in the council-books of the examinations of several persons for spreading false rumours.

Orders for
torture at
discretion.
[p. 264.]
On the 9th of June, letters were written to the lord North, and others, to put such obstinate persons as would not confess, to the *torture*, and there to order them *at their discretion :* and a letter was written to the lieutenant of the Tower to the same effect.　Whether [56] this pretended obstinacy was a con-

---

[55] [" At Hampton Court the first of June 1555.　A letter to the master of the rolls to receive into his custody one Christopher Carey, and to keep him in his house, without having conference with any person, saving such as he specially trusteth, until Mr. secretary Bourne and Mr. Englefelde shall repair thither for his further examination.　A like letter to the justice of the common pleas, with one John Dee.　A like letter to the bishop of London with one John Fielde."　No offence is specified either here or in the previous minute of letter to the master of the rolls and the chief justice of common pleas.　"A like letter to the warden of the Fleet to receive sir Thomas Benger, and to keep him in safe ward without having conference with any.　Robert Hutton is appointed, being his servant, to attend upon him, and to be shut up with him."]

[56] [The author has omitted a notice in the Council Book which explains this, p. 261.　"At Hampton Court the 5th of June.　A letter to the lord Northe, Mr. secretary Bourne, and the master of the rolls, sir Frauncis Englefelde, sir Richard Reade, and doctor Hughes, authorizing them, or two or three of them at least, to proceed to a further examination of Benger, Carye, Dye, and Felde, upon such points as by their wisdoms they shall gather out of their former confessions touching their lewd and vain practices of calculing and conjuring, presently sent unto them with the said letters, willing and requiring them further as they shall by their examinations perceive any other man or woman touched in these and the like matters, to cause them to be forthwith apprehended and committed, to be further ordered according to justice."]

cealing of heretics, or of the reporters of false news, does not appear: but whatever the matter was, the putting people not yet convict, by that which the civil law called a half proof, (*semiplena probatio*,) to the *torture*, because they were thought obstinate, and would not confess, and the leaving the degree of the torture to the *discretion* of those appointed for their examination, was a great step towards the most rigorous part of the proceedings of inquisitors. On the 12th of June, orders [p. 266.] were given for making out writs for the burning of three persons condemned for heresy in Sussex[57]. On the 13th of [p. 267.] June, letters of thanks were ordered to sir Henry Tyrrell, and Mr. Anthony Browne, for their assisting at the execution of heretics. And on the 15th of June, letters of thanks were [p. 268.] ordered to the earl of Oxford, and the lord Rich, on the same account. On the 17th of June, letters of thanks were written [p. 270.] to those in Cambridge, who had committed some priests to prison: but they are ordered to release them, if thoroughly penitent. And on the 18th of June, a letter was written to [Ibid.] the bishop of London, informing him that four parishes in Essex did still use the English service: he is required to examine into this, and to punish it, and to send some of his chaplains to preach to them.

On that day a letter was written from London to Peter Martyr, telling him that it was given out that the queen had said, she could not be happily delivered till all the heretics then in prison were burned; for she continued still expecting to be delivered: and on the 24th of June, an order was given to have a passport ready for Shelley, that was to carry the news to Portugal. On the 27th of June, letters were written to the lord Rich, to give the queen's thanks to some gentlemen of Rochford in Essex, *for coming so honestly of themselves to Colchester, and other places, to assist the sheriff at executions.* At this time a condition was put in all passports and licenses to

The queen still looked to be delivered of a child. P. Mar. Loci Com. 1626. fol. 769. [Council Book, pp. 272, 3.]

---

57 [" At Hampton Court the 12th of June 1555. A letter to the lord treasurer to cause writs to be made forth to the sheriff of Sussex for the execution of three condemned prisoners for heresy, being ordered to suffer in three several places of the shire, viz. one at Lewes, named Derike, a beer brewer, and the other two at Steynynge and Chichester.

" At Hampton Court the 13th of June. A letter of thanks to sir Henry Tyrrell and Mr. Anthony Browne for assisting the sheriff in the putting of such to execution as were condemned."—p. 267.]

go beyond sea, that they shall avoid all heretics, and all places infected with heresy.

Fox,
p. 1450.
A practice
that gives
suspicion of
ill designs.

I shall here add a passage recorded by Fox, of a declaration that was made to himself, before witnesses, in the year 1568. A woman told him that she lived near Aldersgate, and was delivered of a boy on the 11th of June 1555; and after she **244** had borne it, the lord North and another lord came to her, and desired to have her child from her, with very fair offers, as that her child should be well provided for; so that she should take no care for it, if she would swear that she never knew, or had such a child: and after this some women came to her, of whom one, they said, was to be the rocker. But she would in no case part with her child. This being at the time that the queen seemed to be every day looking for her delivery, may give some suspicions, and puts us in mind of the words of the Preacher, *That which is, is that which has been.* On the

[Council
Book, p.
275.]

30th of June, letters were written to the gentlemen in Kent, to assist the sheriff at the execution of heretics in Rochester, Dartford, and Tunbridge.

[p. 276.]

On the 2nd of July [58], upon an information of a commotion designed in Sussex, the opinion of the judges was asked about it; and some judges were sent to proceed in it according to

Plots pre-
tended.

law. Great occasion was taken from foolish discourses to alarm the nation with the apprehension of plots, and the blame of all was to be cast on the concealed preachers, that were now hid in corners, instructing the people at the peril of their lives: twelve persons were brought up out of Sussex [59], as guilty of a conspiracy; but I find no more of that matter. Bird, that had been bishop of Chester, and was deprived for his marriage, did now think fit to repent; and engaged so far, that Bonner

---

[58] [" At Hampton Court the 2nd of July 1555. A letter to my lord chancellor signifying the receipt of his, and the examination of such as begin anew commotion in Sussex, which are returned unto him, and his lordship desired to know the opinion of the judges and the queen's counsel learned therein, and thereupon to deliver the same to the justices of assize in that county, to the end they may take further order therein according to the laws."—p. 276.]

[59] [" At Hampton Court the 7th of July 1555. A letter to the sheriff of Sussex to assist the justices of assize presently sent down to examine a conspiracy intended at Widhurst in Sussex, and to cause the most discreet justices and gentlemen of that county to be present with them at their sitting."—p. 278.]

made him his suffragan.　He was blind of an eye; and being
appointed to preach before the bishop, he chose those words
for his text, *Thou art Peter:* but whether his conscience
smote him, or his memory failed, he could go no further: so,
instead of matter of triumph upon the apostasy of such a man,
the shame of such a dumb action turned the triumph to the
other side.

On the 9th of July[60], a letter was written to the bishop of
London, directing him, that the three condemned heretics
should be burnt at Uxbridge, Stratford, and Walden: and he
was ordered to proceed against the rest.　At this time Pole
thought it became him to write to Cranmer, to try how far a
piece of highflown rhetoric could work on him; though some
think this letter was written a very little while before Cranmer's
execution: the original is yet extant[61].　It does very little
honour to his memory, being only a declaration against heresy
and schism, against a married clergy, and separation from the
see of Rome, and the rejecting of *transubstantiation.*　In it
all he proves nothing, and argues nothing, but supposes all his
own principles to be true and sure: he inveighs against the
poor prisoner with some seeming tenderness, but with a great
acrimony of style, and in an insulting manner, like one that
knew he might say what he pleased, and that there was no
room for making remarks and answers to so poor an epistle;
which Mr. Le Grand has thought fit to translate into French,
but I do not think it worth the while to put it in the Collection.

On the 14th of July, the archbishop of York was ordered
to appear, but no more is said concerning him[62].　There were

[p. 279.]

*Cardinal
Pole's let-
ter to
Cranmer.
[Harleian
MSS. 417,
p. 49.]*

*[Le Grand,
l. 289.]*

*[Council
Book, p.
281.]*

---

[60] [" At Hampton Court the 9th
of July 1555. A letter to the bishop
of London, signifying unto him that
it is thought convenient the three
persons he wrote of already condemned for heresy, be ordered to
suffer, one of them at Uxbridge,
another at Stratford, and the third
at Walden, and that he shall proceed with the rest not yet condemned according to the order of
the laws, in case they shall be found
wilful to persist in their errors."—
p. 279.]

[61] [It has been printed from the
original among the Harleian MSS.
in the Ecclesiastical History Society's Edition of Strype's Cranmer, vol. iii. pp. 614—644. There
can be no doubt this is the letter
alluded to by the author in the text,
though its contents bear very little
resemblance to his description of
them.]

[62] [" At Hampton Court the 14
of July 1555. A letter of appearance to the late archbishop of Yorke
to be here on Tuesday next."]

[p. 285.]
intimations given of commotions designed at fairs, and orders
were sent to sheriffs and gentlemen to watch them: informa- 245
[p. 291.]
tions were also brought of a conspiracy in Essex and Suffolk,
and of another in Dorsetshire[63]. On the 6th of August, thanks
[p. 296.]
were written to the earl of Oxford and the lord Rich, with the
other justices of peace in Essex, for their diligence; desiring
them to proceed in their examination of the late intended
conspiracy, and to bring the offenders before them: if their
offence was found to be treason, they were to suffer as traitors;
or if their guilt did not rise up to that, they were to order
them to be punished according to the statutes.

[p. 300.]
Ambassa-
dors sent
to the
pope, came
back with
a bull,
On the 28th of August, notice was given to the sheriffs and
justices of peace, that the king was going to Flanders. The
ambassadors sent to Rome did return about the middle of September: and in council, on the 16th of September[64], the bishop

63 ["At Hampton Court the 29th
of July 1555. Letters to the sheriffs
and justices of peace of the counties of Kent, Surrey, Sussex, Essex,
Norfolk, Suffolk, Hertford, Middlesex, Southampton, that where one
repairing hither out of the county
of Dorset, with letters to the lords,
hath reported vainly and lewdly by
the way that a commotion was presently in the said county of Dorset,
to the evil stirring of the people,
they are willed not to credit the
same, but to punish such as be
spreaders of these false rumours,
and nevertheless to have especial
foresight and care to their charge,
according to their former orders and
instructions."—p. 291.

The author has altogether omitted
the following interesting notice:

"At Hampton Court the 30th of
July 1555. A letter to the lord
treasurer with a letter enclosed, sent
to the queen's majesty from father
Elstan, warden of the convent at
Grenewiche, wherein he complaineth
how he and father Peto were beaten
with stones, which were flung at
them by divers lewd persons, as
they passed from London to Grene-
wich on Sunday last. His lordship

is desired to make diligent search
who were the offenders herein, and
to cause the mayor of London to
make a proclamation with promise
of reward to him that will detect the
same, and to speak with the lieutenant of the Tower, and the bailiff
of St. Katheryns, to mark from
henceforth who that disorder themselves unto them, and to apprehend
them and commit them to ward.
His lordship is also desired to speak
with the lord mayor for the speedy
punishment of the late disorders at
the graye freers in London."—p.
292.]

64 ["At Grenewiche the 16th of
September 1555. The bishop of
Elye exhibited this day in the council chamber a bull from the pope's
holiness, bearing date the 7 day of
June 1555, wherein the land of Irelande is erected to the name and
title of a kingdom, which bull was
forthwith delivered by the council
to the bishop of Dublin, to be published in the said realm of Ireland,
and transcripts to be made thereof
throughout the said realm, and afterward to be laid up in the treasury
of the said realm."—p. 304.]

of Ely produced the pope's bull, erecting Ireland into a kingdom ; and bestowing on the crown of England the title of *king
of Ireland*.   This was given to the bishop of Dublin, with an
order to publish it in Ireland : for that insolent pope would
not give them audience upon their powers from the king and
queen of England and Ireland, pretending that none had a
right to assume the title *king*, but as it was derived from him.
So, as a special grace, he conferred that regal title on the
queen, and then admitted them to audience, after he had made
them stay a month waiting for it at Rome.   It seems they
knew the bigotry of the English court too well to dispute this
point: so they yielded it up very tamely, fearing that they
should be disowned, if they had made any opposition to it.
But the main errand they came upon was, to obtain a confirmation of the settlement of the church-lands made in parliament
by cardinal Pole : that was not only flatly refused, but a bull
was published, that in effect repealed it all.

" It begins setting forth what pope Symmachus decreed
" against the alienating of any lands belonging to the church
" upon any pretence whatsoever, or farming out the rights of
" the church : he laid an anathema on all who should be any
" way concerned in such bargains ; and gave an authority to
" any ecclesiastical person to recover all, with the mean profits ;
" and this was to take place in all churches.   Pope Paul the
" Second had likewise condemned all alienations of church
" goods, and all farms of leases beyond the term of three
" years, and had annulled all such agreements, farms, or leases.
" Both the parties, as well the granter as the receiver of such
" leases, were put under excommunication ; and the goods so
" alienated were to revert to the church.   But these prohibi-
" tions notwithstanding, of late years several persons, both of
" the laity and of the clergy, had possessed themselves of
" castles and lands, belonging both to the church of Rome, and
" to other cathedrals, and even to metropolitan churches ; and
" to monasteries, regular houses, and hospitals, under the
" pretence of alienations, to the evident damage of those
" churches and monasteries, without observing the solemnities
" required by law in such cases : and they continue their pos-
" session, by which the incumbents in those churches are great
" sufferers ; and the popes themselves, who were wont to

erecting
Ireland
into a
kingdom.
[p. 304.]
[Archæolo-
gia, vol.
xviii. p.
183.]

See the
Coll. of the
former
books,
Numb. 1.
The pope's
bull for re-
storing all
church-
lands.

" supply the poor who came to Rome out of these lands, are
" no more able to do that, and can scarce maintain themselves 246
" and their families; which turns to the offence of God, the
" reproach of the clergy, and is matter of scandal to the faith-
" ful: therefore the pope of his own motion, upon certain
" knowledge, and by virtue of the plenitude of the apostolic
" power, does annul all the alienations or impropriations, either
" perpetual, or leases to the third, or to a single life, or beyond
" the term of three years; or exchanges and farms of cities,
" or lands, or goods, or rights belonging to the Roman church;
" or to any cathedral, monastery, regular house, or to any
" ecclesiastical benefice, with or without cure; to seculars, or
" regulars; hospitals, and other pious foundations, by whom-
" soever made, though by popes, or by their authority; or by
" the prelates of cathedrals, monasteries, or hospitals; or the
" rectors of churches, though cardinals, that had been made
" without the solemnities required by law, in what form of
" words soever they have been made, though confirmed by
" oath, and established by a long prescription: all these are by
" the apostolic authority rescinded, annulled, and made void,
" and the possessors of such lands are to be compelled by all
" censures, and pecuniary pains, to make satisfaction for all the
" mean profits received, or to be received; and all judges are
" required to give judgment conform to this bull." Dated the
12th of July.

Reflections made on it.   Thus the pope, instead of confirming what the legate had done, did in the most formal terms possible reverse and annul it all. Even papal alienations, or made by the papal authority, are made void. The pretended consent of the convocation is declared null; and all ratifications of what was at first illegally made are annulled. By this also, not only the possessors of church-lands, but all the tenants to any estate belonging to the church, who hold for lives, or years, beyond the term of three years, may see in this bull how that all that they now hold by those tenures is made void. No doubt the ambassadors of England did all that in them lay to have this bull softened, or to have an exception made for England: but that pope was not to be moved, and perhaps he thought he shewed no small favour to England, on the queen's account, in not naming it in this bull; and in not fulminating on the account of

the late settlement. Thus the matter of securing the abbey-
lands by that fraudulent transaction is now pretty apparent.

Pope Paul was in the right in one thing, to press the setting
up courts of inquisition every where, as the only sure method
to extirpate heresy. And it is highly probable that the king,
or his Spanish ministers, made the court of England apprehend,
that torture and inquisition were the only sure courses to root
out heresy. It has appeared already what orders were given
about *torture*, even to use it at *discretion :* but another step
was made, that carried this matter much further.

Instructions had been given, in March 1555, to the justices
of peace to have one or more honest men in every parish
secretly instructed to give information of the behaviour of the
inhabitants amongst or about them. One of these was directed to the earl of Sussex, who acted with a superlative
247 measure of zeal : he wrote, on the 18th of April this year, to
the bishop of Norwich, complaining, that at a town near him
there had been no sepulchre, nor creeping to the cross before
Easter. The day after he wrote that letter, it appears, by
another of his letters, that Ket, who led the insurrection in
Norfolk in king Edward's reign, and whose body was hanged
in chains, had fallen down from the gallows ; and that prophecies were spread about the country, of what should follow when
that should happen. He ordered the body to be hanged up
again, if it was not wasted ; and he imprisoned those that gave
out these prophecies. He went on to greater matters, and
drew up an account of the obedience that the justices had paid
to all the instructions and orders that had been sent them. I
had a volume of his letters in my hands some years ago ; but
I wrote out of it only the answers he returned to the sixth
article, in these words : " It is agreed, that the justices of the
" peace, in every of their limits, shall call secretly before them
" one or two honest and secret persons, or more, by their dis-
" cretions, and such as they shall think good, and command
" them, by oath or otherwise, as the same justice shall think
" good, that they shall secretly learn and search out such
" person and persons as shall evil-behave themselves in the
" church, or idly, or despise openly by words the king's and
" queen's proceedings ; or go about to make or move any stir,
" commotion, or unlawful gathering together of the people ; or

" that tell any lewd or seditious tales, rumours, or news, to
" move or stir any person or persons to rise, stir, or make any
" commotion or insurrection, or to consent to any such intent
" or purpose. And also, that the same persons so to be ap-
" pointed shall declare to the same justices of peace the ill
" behaviour of lewd, disordered persons; whether it shall be
" for using unlawful games, idleness, and such other light
" behaviour of such suspected persons, as shall be in the same
" town, or near thereabouts: and that the same informations
" shall be given secretly to the justices; and the same justices
" shall call such accused persons before them, and examine
" them, without declaring by whom they be accused: and that
" the same justices shall, upon their examination, punish the
" offenders, according as their offences shall appear to them,
" upon the accusement and examination, by their discretion,
" either by open punishment, or by good abearing."

Here was a great step made towards an inquisition; this
being the settled method of that court, to have sworn spies and
informers every where, upon whose secret advertisements
persons are taken up. And the first step in their examination
is, to know of them, for what reason they are brought before
them: upon which, they are tortured, till they tell as much as
the inquisitors desire to know, either against themselves or
others. But they are not suffered to know, neither what is
informed against them, nor who are the informers. Arbitrary
torture, and now secret informers, seem to be two great steps,
made to prepare the nation for an inquisition.

In September, the duchess of Suffolk, who had married **248**
Mr. Bertie, went out of the kingdom without a license; upon
which, a commission was sent into Lincolnshire to take an
account of her estate. On the 19th of September, there was a
paper cast into a house near Fulham, with some intimations
of ill designs in Essex [65]. The master of the house brought it to
the council; upon which they sent orders to that country, to

[Council
Book, p.
305.]

[p. 306.]

---

[65] [" At Grenewiche the 19 of
Sept. 1555. A letter to sir Henry
Tirrell and Anthony Browne, with
a copy enclosed of a seditious bill
lately cast into the house of one
John Smythe of Odam green, in
the parish of Fulham, who brought
the same unto the lords himself for
his own declaration, and knoweth
not who cast it into his house. And
for that the same bill mentioneth
the resort of some lewd fellows in
Essex unto the said Smith, if he
would come among them, the said

see what foundation there was for such suspicions.   Tracy [p. 306.] (probably the son of him concerning whose will there was much ado made in king Henry's time) had been brought before the bishop of Gloucester ; and he, as was informed, behaved himself stubbornly towards him : upon which he was brought before the council, and was required to declare his conformity in matters of religion.   He promised to do it ; and upon that he was sent back to his country.   On the 23rd of September, there was some hopes given of the king's [p. 309.] coming back ; upon which, sir Richard Southwell was sent to attend on him.   On the 9th of October, the governor of Jersey [p. 312.] having examined one Gardiner for speaking some indecent words of the king, desired orders how to proceed against him : upon which he was ordered to proceed according to the statutes, if these took place in that island : but if not, according to the custom of the place.

On the 12th of September [66], Brooks, bishop of Gloucester, who was constituted subdelegate to cardinal Puteo the pope's delegate, to try Cranmer, (it being, it seems, thought indecent that Pole, who was to succeed him, should be his judge,) came to Oxford, with Martin and Story, who were the king and queen's commissioners, to demand justice against Cranmer ; exhibiting articles against him. Cranmer made a long apology for himself.   Among other things, he said, " the loss of his " promotion grieved him not : he thanked God as heartily for " that poor and afflicted state in which he was then, as ever

Cranmer proceeded against.

Mr. Tirrell and Mr. Browne are required to have eye to any such resort, and to use their discretions in meeting betimes with all assemblies about them, and to punish the offenders as they think convenient, and to certify also their doings."

" Richard Tracie, gent., appearing this day before the lords, for that hitherto he had behaved himself very stubbornly towards his ordinary, which is the bishop of Gloucestre, was therefore ordered to repair home into the country, and to declare unto the said bishop his conformity in matters of religion, which he himself hath offered

and promised to do."——Council Book, p. 306.]

[66] [The official despatch of Brooks, bishop of Gloucester, to the cardinal de Puteo, is in the Lambeth Library, MSS. 1136, from which it has been printed in the Oxford edition of Strype's Cranmer, and was again collated for the edition published by the Ecclesiastical History Society, where it may be seen, vol. iii. p. 538. From this document it appears that Martin and Story were at Oxford at the commencement of the process on Monday, Sept. 9.]

" he did for the times of his prosperity. But that which stuck
" closest to him, and created him the greatest sorrow, was, to
" think that all that pains and trouble, that had been taken by
" king Henry and himself for so many years, to retrieve the
" ancient authority of the kings of England, and to vindicate
" the nation from a foreign yoke, and from the baseness and
" infinite inconveniences of crouching to the bishops of Rome,
" should now thus easily be quite undone : and that the king
" and queen should, in their own realm, become his accusers
" before a foreign power. If he had transgressed the law,
" they had sufficient authority to punish him ; and to that he
" would at all times submit himself." They exhibited interrogatories to him ; and he gave his answer to them. In conclusion, they required him to go to Rome, within fourscore
days, to make his answer in person. He said he was most
willing to go, if the king and queen would send him.

On the 16th of October, Ridley and Latimer suffered martyrdom : but Gardiner, who was with impatience waiting for
the news, was, soon after he heard it, struck with an illness, in
which he languished for some time. Pilkington, bishop of
Durham, in a sermon that he preached, said, *he rotted above
ground, so that it was scarce possible to get any to come near* 249
him. He died on the 12th of November. On the 5th of November, orders were given for to dispose of many prisoners.

Cranmer was now to be offered up. Some have thought,
that upon his attainder the see of Canterbury was vacant ; and
indeed, the chapter of Canterbury acted accordingly : but the
papal authority being restored, he was still, according to the
papal law, archbishop, till by a commission from Rome he was
judged an obstinate heretic, and was thereupon deprived.
When the eighty days were out, a mock process was made at
Rome ; in which it was falsely said, that he did not care to
appear ; upon which he was declared contumacious : and then
a formal sentence was given in the pope's name, *as sitting on
the throne of justice, having before his eyes God alone, who is
the righteous Lord, and judgeth the world in righteousness.*
With such specious words was that grossly unrighteous judgment introduced. And upon that, a letter came from Rome,
on the 14th of December, mentioning his being condemned
and deprived, and delivering him over to the secular arm.

The deprivation must have passed some days before : for, on the 11th of December, Pole's bulls were granted ; in which mention is made of the see's being vacant by the deprivation of Cranmer. The writ for burning him mentions his being judged an obstinate heretic by the pope, and deprived by him ; and that he had been degraded by the bishops of London and Ely, by commission from the pope : so on the 24th of February the writ was sealed. I have nothing to add to the sad narration I gave, both of his fall, and of his repentance, and his firm constancy to the last, in that amazing instance of holding his hand in the fire till it was almost burnt away ; of which Thuanus gives a very particular account, so that the truth of the fact cannot be disputed. [Rymer, tom. xv. p. 431.]

[Thuanus, lib. xvii. cap. iii. p. 57·.]

On the 13th of March[67], the privy-council were concerned, when they heard his paper of recantation was printed. Rydall and Copeland, two printers, were required to deliver to Cawood, the queen's printer, the books of his recantation, to be burned by him. One part of his character may be added out of Pole's letter to him. In one place he says, he hears " it was pre-" tended that he forced no man in points of religion, but " behaved himself mildly towards all persons." And in another place he writes, " that it was said his life was unblameable." But though Pole throws that off, as of no importance, yet, upon his mentioning these good characters, it may be depended on that they were true. Ridley, in that noble letter that he wrote to Grindall, when they were every day looking for their crown, says of him, " that he then shewed how well he de-" served the great character of the chief pastor and archbishop [Council Book, p. 385.]

[Letters of the Martyrs, p. 40.]

[67] [" At Grenewiche the 13th of Marche 1555. Willielmus Ryddale et Willielmus Coplande de London prynters recognoverunt se debere Dominis Regi et Reginæ quadraginta libras bonæ et legalis monetæ Angliæ solvendas etc. Et nisi etc. The condition of this recognizance is such, that if the above bound Ryddale and Coplande do deliver forthwith to Mr. Cawoode, the queen's majesty's printer, all such books as they of late printed, containing Cranmer's recantation, to be by the said Cawood burnt, And do also from henceforth print no such book as is already condemned, or made within forty years passed, nor no other thing hereafter to be made, except the same be first seen by some of the council, or allowed by their ordinary. That then this present recognizance to be void or else &c."—Council Book, p. 385.]

" of this church :" to which he adds of Latimer, " that he was
" the ancient and true apostle of Christ to the English nation[68]."
In a word, if it had not been for Cranmer's too feeble compliance in king Henry's time, and this last inexcusable slip, he
might well be proposed as one of the greatest patterns in
history.　And if the excesses to which some opinions had formerly carried men, did in some particulars incline him to the
opposite extremes, this must be reckoned a very pardonable 250
instance of managing the counterpoise without due caution.
He was a pattern of humility, meekness, and charity.　He had
a true and generous contempt of wealth, and of those shows
of greatness that belong to a high station.　His labours in
searching into all ecclesiastical authors, both ancient and
modern, are amazing to those who have seen the vast collections that he writ out, on all matters of divinity, with his own
hand.　But now, after a long course of vexation and contradiction, and, in conclusion, after a long and severe imprisonment, he was put to a cruel death, by persons whom he had
served faithfully and effectually : for he had both served the
queen, and reconciled her to her father ; and he had shewed
a most particular favour to Thirlby, and others who concurred
to finish this tragedy.　I have put all this matter together ;
and now I must look back to public affairs.

Proceed-
ings in con-
vocation.
[Wilkins,
Conc. iv.
p. 120.]　There was a convocation sat with the parliament in October ;
and to the middle of November 1555.　Christopherson was
chosen prolocutor : and after Bonner had confirmed him, he
desired that the lower house would name eight or ten persons,
to hear some secret propositions that were to be made to them
by the king and queen, and by the cardinal, concerning the
public good of the kingdom, and of the church.　They upon
that did choose the prolocutor, and ten more : and to these the
bishop of Ely proposed to offer the queen a subsidy, in return
for the great favour she had shewed the clergy, in forgiving
the first-fruits and tenths, and in restoring to the church all
the impropriations of benefices, that were then, by the suppression of the monasteries, vested in the crown : for all which

---

[68] [Commendo etiam vobis re-
verendissimos patres et concaptivos
meos in Domino, Thomam Cran-
merum, jam vere magni pastoris et
archipræsulis nomine dignissimum
et veteranum illum nostræ gentis
Anglicanæ verum apostolum et
Christi, H. Latimerum.]

the bishop of Ely proposed a subsidy of eight shillings in the pound, to be paid in four years. The last session of the convocation was on the 15th of November ; and a memorandum was inserted in these words : " After this convocation was " begun, there was a national synod ; the clergy of York being " joined with them." For which, the cardinal thought it safe and fit to take out a license under the great seal. The first session was on the 4th of November : and in this the cardinal set himself so zealously to remove many abuses, that Mason wrote, that many of the clergy wished he were in Rome again.

The earl of Devonshire went out of England this summer. As he passed through Flanders, he waited on the emperor ; and, as Mason wrote, he owned that he owed his liberty to him. The queen sent, and offered her mediation between the emperor and the French king : the emperor accepted it ; but with very sharp reflections on the French king.

There was in April a treaty of peace between the emperor and the king of France set on foot : in which the queen was mediator, and sent over both Pole and Gardiner to Calais in order to it. The constable and the cardinal of Lorraine were ordered to come from the court ; but the pope's death made it be thought more necessary to send that cardinal to Rome : what further progress was made in this does not appear to me, 251 for I take it from a letter of Mason's to Vannes, then the queen's ambassador at Venice. It will be found in the Collec- Collect. tion, the original being in Dr. Tanner's hands, who sent me Numb. 38. this copy. By this letter it appears, that Bolls of Cambridge-shire, and sir Peter Mewtas, were then in prison upon suspicion ; but nothing appeared against them. That letter tells us, that the princes of Germany were alarmed upon the cardinal Morone's coming to Augsburg, apprehending probably that he came to disturb the settlement then made in the matters of religion in the empire : but the emperor had sent such powers to his brother Ferdinand, that his coming was like to have no effect. He also tells in that letter, that the dean and prebendaries of Westminster were using all endeavours to hinder the converting that foundation into an abbey : and that Dr. Cole was active in it, affirming that monks had not their institution from Christ, as priests had : but he saw the court was resolved to have no regard to the opposition they made. He adds, that the duke of Alva was still in England, though he had sent his baggage and servants to Calais.

Motions in the diet of the empire. Mason writes news from the diet, that matters of religion had not been quite settled, but all were to continue in the state in which they were then till the next meeting; and it was provided, that all parties should live according to the religion then accepted of them. The emperor seemed resolved not to consent to this. He writes, that the allowance of the marriage of the clergy, and in particular of bishops, had been earnestly demanded, but was utterly refused. On the 28th of October he writes, that two monks of the Charter-house had desired the king's letter that they might return to their house, and at least receive their pension : the king answered, that, as touching their house, since the parliament was then sitting, it was not a proper time to move it; but when he should come to England, he would help them the best he could : and as to their pensions, he ordered Mason to write concerning that to

[Council Book, p. 350.] secretary Petre. On the 7th of January, 1555–6, a letter was written to the mayor and aldermen of Coventry, to choose some catholic grave man for their mayor for that year : a list of three persons was sent to them, and they were required to give their voices for one of them. These were John Fitz-Herbert, Richard Wheeler[69], and one Colman.

Compassion expressed to those who suffered, punished. [p. 356.] On the 14th of January, a letter of a very singular nature was written to the lord mayor and the sheriffs of London, " requiring them to give such substantial order, that when any " obstinate man, condemned by the order of the laws, shall be " delivered to be punished for heresy, that there be a great " number of officers, and other men, appointed to be at the " execution; who may be charged to see such as shall misuse " themselves, either by comforting, aiding, or praising the " offenders; or otherwise use themselves to the ill example of " others, to be apprehended and committed to ward : and " besides, to give commandment that no householder suffer any " of his apprentices, or other servants, to be abroad, other than " such as their master will answer for. And that this order " be always observed in like cases hereafter." Philpot's mar-

[Dec. 18, 1555.] tyrdom had been about a month before this; and he being a

69 [The author has mistaken the name, which is spelt *Whestler* in the larger Council Book, and *Westler* in the smaller.]

man highly esteemed, who went through all his sufferings with
252 heroic courage and Christian constancy, it is probable there
was more than ordinary concern expressed by the people at
his sufferings ; which drew this inhuman letter from the
council ; for they had no sacrifices at that time ready to be
offered.

While these things passed in England, the scene abroad was
considerably altered, by the resignation of Charles the Fifth,
who delivered over his hereditary dominions to his son Philip.
He began that with the dominions derived from the house of
Burgundy ; after that, he resigned up to him the crown of
Spain, and all that belonged to it : upon that, letters were
written to the several states and cities of Spain on the 17th of
January.   These were all in one form : so that which was addressed to the city of Toledo was sent over to the queen, translated out of Spanish into English, which, for the curiosity of
the thing, I have put into the Collection.

Charles the Fifth, the resignation of Spain.

Collect. Numb. 39.

In it, " he tells them, that which he always denied to the
" Germans, that for religion's sake he had enterprised the war
" of Germany, upon the desire he had to reduce those countries
" to the unity of the church ; that so he might procure an
" universal peace to all Christendom, and to assemble and
" assist at a general council, for the reformation of many
" things, that so with the less difficulty he might bring home
" those who had separated themselves, and departed from the
" faith.   This he had brought to a very good point, when the
" French king allured the Germans to a league with him,
" against their oaths and fidelity to the emperor, and so they
" made war on him both by sea and land ; and then the French
" king procured the coming of the Turk's army into Hungary,
" to the great damage of Christendom ; upon which he was
" forced to bring down an army, to the great prejudice of his
" own person, by his being obliged to keep the field so long,
" that it had brought on him painful infirmities : he was upon
" that become so destitute of health, that he was not able in
" his own person to endure the travel, and to use that dili-
" gence that was requisite ; which proved a great hindrance to
" many things, of which he had a deep sense : he wished he
" had taken the resolution he was now taking sooner ; yet he
" could not well do it, by reason of his son's absence ; for it was

" necessary to communicate many things to him. So he took
" order for his marriage, and to bring him over to him ; and
" soon after that he resigned to him all his states, kingdoms,
" and the seigniories of the crown of Castile and Leon, with
" all their appurtenances, which are more amply contained in
" instruments which he had signed of the same date with this
" letter : trusting that he, with his great wisdom and experi-
" ence, of which he had great proof in all that he had hitherto
" handled in his father's name, would now order and defend
" the same with peace and justice. He therefore, having had
" large experience of their loyalty, fidelity, and obedience, did
" not doubt but that they would continue to serve and obey
" him in the same manner and sort as if God had taken him
" into his mercy. Dated at Brussels the 17th of January
" 1556."

Reasons to think he died a protestant.

Soon after that, he retired to the place he had designed to 253
spend the rest of his days in ; and, according to the account
given by my worthy friend Dr. Geddes, there is great reason
to believe, that he applied himself to serious reflections on
religion. No prince knew better than he did, both the corruptions and the practices of the court of Rome, and the
artifices and methods by which two sessions of the council of
Trent had been conducted. He must likewise have understood the grounds upon which both the Lutherans and the
reformed in Germany built their persuasions. He had heard
them often set out ; but the hurry of business, the prepossess-
sion of education, and the views of interest, had prejudiced
him so far against them, that he continued in a most violent
enmity to them : but now that he was at full leisure to bring
all his observations together, and that passion and interest had
no more power over him, there are great presumptions to
believe, that he died persuaded of the doctrines of the reformed religion. Augustin Casal, a canon of the church of
Salamanca, was his preacher, and was esteemed the most
eloquent preacher that Spain ever produced : he was taken up
in the year 1558, and with thirteen more was publicly burnt
at Valladolid, in the year 1559 ; the unfortunate prince Charles,
and his aunt, Donna Juana, then governess, looking on that
barbarous execution. Constantine Pontius, a canon of Seville,
who was his confessor, esteemed a man of great piety and

learning, was likewise taken up by the inquisition for being a protestant: he died in prison, probably enough by the torture the inquisitors put him to; but his bones, with his effigies, were burnt at Seville: so were the bones of the learned Egidius, whom the emperor had named to the bishopric of Tortosa, one of the richest in Spain: and at the same time eighteen were burnt alive for being protestants; of which the History of the Inquisition gives this account, that had not the holy tribunal put a stop to those reformers, the protestant religion had run through Spain like wildfire: people of all degrees, and of both sexes, being wonderfully disposed at that time to have embraced it. And the writer of the Pontifical History[70], who was present at some of those executions, says, that had those learned men been let alone but three months longer, all Spain would have been put into a flame by them.

The most eminent of them all was Bartholomew de Carranza, a Dominican, who had been confessor to king Philip and to queen Mary, and had been by her recommended to the archbishopric of Toledo. He had assisted Charles in the last minutes of his life. He was within a few months after his death, upon suspicion of his being a protestant, first confined by the inquisition to his own palace at Tordelaguna: and after he had been for seven years kept within that confinement, he was carried to Rome, and kept ten years a prisoner in the castle of St. Angelo; and was at last condemned as one suspected of heresy. That great man had been sent by Charles as one of his divines to the council of Trent, where he preached, and wrote a treatise[70] of the personal residence of bishops. These things put together, make it highly probable, that Charles himself was possessed with that doctrine that was so much spread among those who were then most about him. Mezeray[71] tells us, "that, at Philip's arrival in Spain, he

[70] [Carranza (Bartholomæus) de Miranda, archiepiscopus Toletanus. Controversia de necessaria residentia episcoporum pastorumque Tridenti explicata. 8vo. Ven. *ad signum Spei*, 1547: reprinted at Antwerp 1554 in 8vo. and at fol. 176—212, of vol. i. " De Summi Pontificis auctoritate de episcoporum residen-tia et beneficiorum pluralitate gravissimorum auctorum complurium opuscula ad apostolicæ sedis dignitatem majestatemque tuendam spectantia. Venetiis. 1562. 4to.]

[71] [Au mois d'Aoust precedent, le Roy Philippe avoit quitté les Pays-bas, et s'en estoit allé par mer en Espagne, où il choisit sa residence [Abregé Chronologique ou

extraict de l'histoire de Franoe, tom. iii. [p. 990, 1, ed. Par. 1667.]

" caused a great many to be burnt for heretics in his own 254
" presence, both at Seville and at Valladolid, both seculars
" and ecclesiastics, men and women, and in particular the
" effigies of his father's confessor : and if reports may be be-
" lieved, he intended to have made his father's process, and to
" have had his bones burnt for heresy ; being only hindered
" from doing it by this consideration, that if his father was an
" heretic, he had forfeited all his dominions, and by conse-
" quence he had no right to resign them to his son." This
digression will be forgiven me, I hope, both because it belongs
to the main design upon which I write, and since our queen
was queen of Spain when this persecution was first begun.

The me-
thod in
which the
queen put
her affairs.

There are in my hands two papers concerning the method
in which the queen ordered her council to proceed : there is no
date put to them ; but they were written either soon after the
king went beyond sea, or perhaps about this time ; for now
king Philip having the Spanish monarchy put in his hands, and
being engaged in a war with France, the queen had reason to
expect that her dominions might feel the war very sensibly, as
afterwards they did : and so it might seem necessary to put
the administration of her affairs into a good method. One of
these papers is writ in cardinal Pole's own hand, and is a memorial prepared for the queen, of the things that she was to recommend to her council, for she had ordered them to attend on
her.   It is in the Collection.   " First, she was to put them in

Collect.
Numb. 40.

pour le reste de sa vie. Son pere
avoit tendrement chery les Fla-
mands, et s'estoit heureusement
servy de leur conseils et de leurs
armes : mais luy, nourri dans l'air
imperieux d'Espagne, ne pouvoit
s'accommoder avec des peuples
libres qui scavoient prodiguer leurs
biens et leur vie pour leur Prince,
mais non pas les laisser prendre. Il
leur donna pour Gouvernante Mar-
guerite sa sœur naturelle, femme
d'Octave Duc de Parme a laqnelle
il adjoignit pour conseil Antoine Per-
renot de Granvelle cardinal, Franc-
Comtois d'origine, mais hautain et
arrogant comme un Espagnol. A
son arrivée en Espagne il fit brusler
en sa presence à Seville et à Valla

d'Olit, une grande multitude de
ceux qu'on nommoit Lutheriens,
hommes et femmes, gentilhommes
et ecclesiastiques, mesme le fan-
tosme de Constance Ponce, con-
fesseur de Charles V. qui l'avoit
assisté jusqu'à la mort. Il ne faut
pas s'estonner s'il ne craignit point
de ternir la memoire de son pere,
puisque si on en croit quelques-
uns, il voulut luy faire son procés
et brusler ses os pour crime d'he-
resie, et que rien ne l'en empescha
sinon cette consideration que si son
pere avoit esté heretique il estoit
descheu de ses estats, et par conse-
quent n'avoit pas eu droit de les
resigner à son fils.]

" mind of the charge that the king gave them at his departure,
" which was to be rehearsed to them ; and that is, perhaps,
" the following paper : they were still to attend at court, the
" matters they were to treat about being of great weight ; and
" they were to lay such matters as were proposed in council
" before the king, that they might have his pleasure before
" they were to be executed.   They were in particular to know
" the resolution of the council, touching those things that were
" to be proposed in this parliament, and these were to be sent
" to the king that very day : and since the king delayed his
" coming over, they were to consider whether it were not
" better to delay the parliament till Candlemas, if there should
" be no prejudice to her affairs, that money was so long
" wanted ; for there was great need of it at present, for the
" setting out of ships, both for the emperor's passage to Spain,
" and for the king's return, for the payments due at Calais,
" for the debt owing to the merchants, the day of payment
" approaching, and for the debt of Ireland : and she was to ask
" of her council an account concerning all these things ; she
" was likewise to charge them to call in her own debts, as the
" best way to clear what she owed to others : and she was to
" offer them all authority for doing it effectually ; and to
" require them, that at the end of every week she might know
" what came in that week, and what order was taken for the
" rest.   And that all those who have any commission to exe-
" cute any matter, shall at the end of every week inform the
" council what progress they have made that week : and that
" the council should never begin to treat of any matter in the
255 " second week, till they were informed of what was done in the
" former week."   Thus she was to be taught what she was to
say to them : upon which they, who did not know how weak a
woman she was, might imagine that she understood her own
affairs well, and thought much of them : whereas the poor
bigoted woman was only as a machine, made to speak and to act
as she was prompted by those who had the management of
her : for of herself she seemed capable to think of nothing but
how to destroy the heretics, and to extirpate heresy.

The other paper is in Latin, and seems to be that which the
king had left behind him.   It is also in the Collection.   " He Collect.
" named in it a select committee, to whom the special care of Numb. 41

" matters of state, of the revenue, and the weighty affairs of
" the kingdom, were to be referred.   These (in a modern
" term) were the cabinet-council; and the persons were, the
" cardinal, (in all great matters, when he could conveniently
" come,) then the lord chancellor, the lord treasurer, the earl
" of Arundel, the earl of Pembroke, the bishop of Ely, the
" lord Paget, Rochester the comptroller, and Petre the secre-
" tary.   Every one of these was constantly to attend, to de-
" termine in all matters of state and revenue, and to make
" honourable payment of all debts, and to do every thing in
" which the honour and dignity of the crown was concerned.
" They were also earnestly prayed to lay all differences, or
" quarrels among themselves, aside; that so they might
" amicably, and in the fear of God, deliver such things in
" council, as might tend to the glory of God, and the honour
" and good of the crown and kingdom.   And when there is
" occasion for it, they were either to come to the queen, or to
" send some of their body, to inform her of every thing that
" came before them : and at least thrice a week they were to
" give her an account of all their consultations and actings.   In
" particular, they were to consider when the parliament was
" to meet, and what things were to be proposed and done in it,
" and to digest all that in writing.   On Sundays they were to
" communicate such things to the whole council as should be
" thought convenient to be laid before them.   They were to
" take special care for the payment of debts, for the retrench-
" ing of expense, and for the good management of the queen's
" estate, revenues, and customs, and for the administration of
" justice."   Such were the orders laid down : how they were
executed does not appear.

Proceed-
ings
against
heretics.
[Council
Book, p.
361.]

The queen herself never came to council, and the cardinal
very seldom.   Sometimes they were very few that attended at
that board : often not above three or four.   And now I return
to give an account of what I find in the council-book.   On the
19th of January[71], a letter of thanks was ordered to the lord

[71] [" At Grenewiche the 19th of
January 1555.   A letter of thanks
to the lord Willoughby, Mr. Daly-
son, and others the justices of peace
of the county of Lincoln, for their
advertisements, Requiring them to
proceed hereafter with all such as
shall be condemned before them,
according to the order of the laws,
and not to stay any." — Council
Book, vol. ii. p. 361.]

Willoughby, and others in Lincolnshire. At first, upon the condemnation of heretics, notice was given to the council, before the execution, to see if a pardon should be offered them : but they found so few, if any, inclined to accept of it, that they did not think fit to expose the queen's pardon to any further contempt : so those persons are required to proceed thereafter, against all such as should be condemned before 256 them, according to the laws, and not to stay for any order. On the 20th of January[72], letters were written to the sheriffs [Ibid. p. of Warwickshire, Bedfordshire, and Cambridgeshire, ordering 362.] them, that though the prisoners should be acquitted by order of law, yet to detain them in safe custody, till they should hear from the earl of Sussex. On the 14th of February[73], the [Ibid. p. council was alarmed with this, that a stage-play was to be 369.] acted in Shrovetide ; and that many were to run to it : so the lord Rich was ordered to hinder the acting of it, and to examine and report what he could learn concerning it. On the 16th of February[74], there was an order sent to sir Henry Bedingfield, lieutenant of the Tower, to put two to the *torture,* and to *pain*

---

[72] [" At Grenewiche the 20th of January 1555. A letter to the earl of Sussex, of thanks for his travail and advertisements; to whom it is also signified, that, according to his request, letters are sent to the sheriffs of the counties of Warwick, Bedford, and Cambridge, for the proceeding according to the order of the laws with such as are by them apprehended for committing divers robberies in Norfolk. And as touching his desire for to have more justices in the said county of Norfolk, order shall be given therefore at the beginning of the next term."

" Letters to the sheriffs of the said counties of Warwick, Bedford, and Cambridge, to proceed as before, and if any of the said parts shall be acquitted for this their offence by order of the laws, yet are they willed to detain them still in safe custody until they shall hear further of them from the said earl of

Sussex."—Council Book, p. 362.]

[73] [" At Grenewiche the 14th of February 1555. A letter to the lord Riche, that where there is a stage play appointed to be played this Shrofetide, at Hatfeld Bradock in Essex, his lordship is willed to stay the same, and to examine who should be the players, what the effect of the play is, with such other circumstances as he shall think meet, and to signify the same hither."—Council Book, p. 369.]

[74] [" At Grenewiche the 16 of Feb. 1555. A letter to sir Henry Bedingfelde, to receive from sir John Baker the bodies of Burton and Thomas Tailer, and to keep them in safe custody, and to join with the said Mr. Baker in examining of them, and to put them upon the torture, and pain them according to their discretion if they will not confess their offence."—Ibid. p. 370.]

[Ibid. p. 373.]

them at his discretion.   On the 19th of February[75], a letter of thanks was ordered to the lord Rich for stopping the stage-play.   He had put the actors in prison, but he gave a good character of them: so he was ordered to set them at liberty; but to have an eye on all such meetings.   Several inquiries were made at this time after seditious books: many examinations and commitments were made on that account.

[Ibid. p. 405.]

On the 20th of April, one Harrys, a carpenter and gunner at Deptford, was brought before the council, for having said on Maundy-Thursday, " The queen hath this day given a great " alms; and has given that away that should have paid us our " wages.   She hath undone the realm too; for she loveth " another realm better than this."   He confessed the words, but asked pardon, and was dismissed.   It seems, about that

[Ibid. p. 418.]

time they expected the king's coming over: for, on the 1st of June, the lord admiral was ordered to attend on him.   On the

[Ibid. p. 434.]

21st of June, an order was sent to the lieutenant of the Tower, and to a master of requests, to put one to the *torture*, if he thought it convenient.   Information was given to the queen by Wotton, her ambassador in France, that several heretics had fled over to France, and were well received there: in particular, that Henry Dudley (perhaps a son of the duke of Northumberland's) and Christopher Ashton were plotting there

Paper-Office. [April 8, Turnbull's Calendar, p. 220, also April 12, p. 222.]

against the queen.   Upon that, a letter was written to Wotton, to demand that they might be seized on, and sent at her charge to the frontier, to be delivered to her officers.   When the draught of this was brought to her to be signed by her, she with her own hand interlined these words; *considering that when the king my husband and he were enemies, I neither did, nor would have done the like.*

---

[75] [" At Grenewiche the 19 of Feb. 1555.   A letter of thanks to the lord Riche, for his travail in staying the stage play which was appointed to be played this shrove-tide at Hatfelde in Essex: requiring him, for that he noteth the players to be honest householders, and quiet persons, to set them again at liberty, and to have an eye and special care to stop the like occasions of assembling the people together hereafter."—Ibid. p. 373.

" At Grenewiche the seconde of Marche 1555.   A letter to the bishop of London, in answer of his, whereby he is willed to take such order that Poule Barkley, presently remaining in the Fleet, for a seditious letter which he wrote, shall be set at liberty, if he be so penitent for his offence as his lordship writeth."—Ibid. p. 380.]

Wotton wrote over, that the heretics took great advantage from the new war that the pope engaged the French king to make on the king, after a truce for five years had been agreed to, and sworn by both-kings.   But the pope sent a legate to France, to persuade that king to begin the war.   And though the consciences of princes are not apt to be very scrupulous in the observing or breaking their treaties; yet a treaty, made and confirmed by an oath so very lately, it seems, made such an impression on that king, that so great an authority was to be interposed, to give a colour for the breaking it.   Those called heretics took great advantages from this to infuse a 257 horror in people at the papacy, since one who pretended to be the vicar of the Prince of peace became thus an open and a perfidious incendiary.

This of the pope's dispensing with a prince's oath gave so great a distaste every where, that I do not remember an instance in which it was openly put in practice since that time. But the protestant princes of Germany do believe, as one of the greatest of them told me, that the confessors of the princes of that communion have secret faculties to dispense with their breach of faith; which is so much the more dangerous the more secretly it may be managed.   On that ground it was that the prince, who told me this, said, that in all their dealings with princes of that communion, they took their word, but would never put any thing to their oaths: for they knew that the popish princes reckoned they were bound by their word, as they were men, and members of human society; but for their oaths, they reckoned, these being acts of religion, their confessors had it in their breast to tell them how far they were bound to keep them; and when they were absolved from any obligation by them.   But we have seen in our days, to the no small reproach of the reformation, that princes professing it have in an avowed manner shaken off their leagues and alliances, with this short declaration, *That they reckoned themselves freed from them:* as if they had been things of so little force, that they might be departed from at pleasure.

Pole was now in his synod, labouring to bring the clergy to their duty.   On the 13th of December, *The Institution of a Christian Man* was divided in parcels, to be examined by them : and some were appointed to prepare a book of Homilies. On the 16th of December, a translation of the New Testament was ordered, and parcelled out : the *Seven Sacraments* were also treated of.   On the 20th of December, the cardinal sent an order to the prolocutor, to intimate to all the clergy, more particularly to all deans, that they should confirm no leases that had been made of their benefices : this seems to be done in obedience to the pope's bull, formerly mentioned, that condemned all leases for a longer term than three years.   There was offered to them a schedule of some terms that were to be carefully considered in the translation of the New Testament. On the 8th of January, that was again considered : propositions were also made for having schools in all cathedral churches.   Thus Pole found it necessary to give some instruction in the matters of religion to the nation : for an earnest desire of knowledge in these points being once raised and encouraged, it was neither safe nor easy quite to extinguish that, which is so natural to man ; and therefore, instead of discouraging all knowledge, and bringing men to the state of implicit faith, without any sort of inquiry, he chose to give them such a measure of knowledge as might be governed and kept within its own bounds.   There was in this synod a question moved ; what should be done with such of the clergy as should refuse to say or come to mass? but I do not see what was determined upon it.   Nor do I see what reason was given 258 them for another petition to the queen, lords, and commons, for maintaining their liberties and immunities, nor what effect it had.

[Wilkins, Conc. iv. 151.]

Pole prorogued the synod to the 10th of November, and from thence to the 10th of May. The reason given is, because the bishops were in their visitations, which could not be soon ended ; since a large space of time seemed necessary for their taking an exact account of the quantity and quality of all ecclesiastical goods[76]. I suppose this was the procuring terriers of the lands, and inventories of the goods belonging to the

---

[76] Pro certiore bonorum ecclesiasticorum [prædictorum] quantitatis et qualitatis ratione [sine quâ ad perfectam illorum dispositionem devenire non poterat] habendâ, majus temporis spatium requirebatur. —Wilkins, Conc. iv. 151, ex Reg. Bonner, fol. 424.]

churches: for many orders were given out for restoring such plate and furniture, as could be found, that had belonged to any church.

From the 10th of May, Pole prorogued the synod to the 10th of November: the reason given is, for the great want and penury of victuals. For I find the dearth at this time was very great. Wheat was at four marks the quarter; malt at two pound four shillings; pease at two pound five shillings: but the next harvest proving plentiful, it fell as low as it had been high. Wheat was at five shillings, malt at a noble, and rye at three shillings [and] four pence a quarter. A great scarcity of all things.

On the 28th of July[77], the council hearing that some naughty books were sent over, and concealed in the duchess of Suffolk's house, ordered the bishop of Lincoln to search for them, and to send them up. On the 19th of July[78], the council was alarmed with reports of conspiracies in Suffolk and Essex: so they sent orders to inquire about them; and about a zealous man, that went about carrying letters and books over the country, from whence he was called Trudgeover; so he was ordered to be sought for. On the 15th of August, a letter was written to the mayor, jurats, and commons at Rye, to choose one of the queen's servants to be mayor for the ensuing year. [June 28, Council Book, p. 440.]
[Ibid. p. 459.]
[Ibid. p. 480.]

---

[77] ["At Sainte James' the 28th of June 1556. A letter to the bishop of Lincoln, either to repair himself, or to send some trusty person to Grymesthorp, in the county of Lincoln, being the house of the lady Katheryne, duchess of Suffolk, to search for such naughty books as be hidden there, and to send the same hither."]

[78] ["At St. James' the 19th of July 1556. A letter to the justices and commission of oyer and terminer in the county of Suffolk, of thanks for their diligence in the apprehending of certain that went about a conspiracy, whom they are willed diligently to examine to what purpose they conspired, and who were of counsel with them, or privy to their doings, and thereupon to confer with some learned men in those parts, whereunto their offences do weigh in law, and so to proceed with them according to the order of the laws."

"A letter to the earl of Oxforde and the justices in commission of oyer and terminer in Essex, signifying unto them the said intended conspiracy, and willing them therefore to have a more vigilant eye to their charge, and to make diligent search for one that nameth himself Trudgeover, and to apprehend him, for the better searching and apprehending of which lewd person there are joined in commission of oyer and terminer with them sir Henry Doyle, sir John Bruse, knights, and William Foster, esquire."—Council Book, vol. ii. p. 459.]

On the 21st of August, a letter of thanks was ordered for the earl of Sussex, for his diligence in apprehending those who spread about lewd and seditious reports; with whom he is desired to proceed according to the laws: and as for those lewd priests that had been married, and were found still to repair to their women; they tell him, they had written to the bishop of Norwich, to cause them to be apprehended and

[Ibid.
p. 489.]
punished. And a letter was at the same time ordered for the bishop of Norwich to that purpose. On the 23rd of August [79], a letter of thanks was ordered to the lord Darcy, for his apprehending some ill-disposed persons, who used conventicles, and readings, about Harwich. He was to get them to be fined according to their quality, and as he thought fit; and to bind them to appear before the bishop of London: and a letter was ordered to the bishop, either to reduce them to the church, or to order them according to the laws.

[Ibid.
p. 506.]
On the 4th of September, the earl of Sussex had moved, that offenders should be proceeded against by martial law: his zeal is commended; and it was written back to him, " that " these deserved to be so used; but that is not thought best: " they are to be punished as the laws order. But when they " have had their punishment, he shall cause them to be kept 259 " in prison, and in irons, till they know themselves and their

[Ibid.
p. 511.]
" duty." On the 15th of September, a letter of thanks was written to the earl of Sussex, and the justices of Norfolk, for their diligence in punishing one Thomas Long.

Calais in
danger of
falling into
the hands
of the
French.
At this time they were called on to consider of the danger Calais might be in: so a state of the fortifications, and of what was necessary to maintain the place, was laid before the council: but the giving orders in that matter was delayed till the king should come over, of which they were in daily expecta-

[Ibid.
p. 513.]
tion: for on the 17th of September they understood that the emperor, with his two sisters, had embarked on the Tuesday before; and that the king was to come to Calais, and from thence to England. Privy-seals were at this time sent about

---

[79] [" At Croydon the 23th of August 1556. A letter to the bishop of London, that when they shall come before him to travail with them, either to reduce them to the unity of Christ's church, or else otherwise to order them according to the laws in these cases provided."—Council Book, p. 489.]

every where, for a loan of money ; but it came in very slowly.
Some took the privy-seal, but did not pay in the money.　There
was about a thousand privy-seals given out, at one hundred
pound apiece.　On the 6th of October[80], a letter was sent to [Ibid.
Calais, to search for some who had fled from England thither : P. 525.]
it is directed to the earl of Sussex ; which makes it probable
they were heretics : for in that matter his heart was entirely
as the queen's heart was.　On the 7th of October, the lady [Ibid.
Throgmorton was before the council, asking leave to send P. 526.]
some supply to her husband sir Nicholas, who was then in
France : the cardinal had told her, in the presence of the lord
chancellor and others, that for this one time the queen allowed
of it, so it did not exceed forty crowns.　It seems the way of
exchange was much beset, when so small a supply, from so
near a relation, could not be conveyed without such an application.　On the 17th of November, a letter was ordered for the [Ibid.
bishop of London, to receive a companion of him who was P. 540.]
called Trudge-over, to be ordered by him according to law ;
and they complain to him, that a man and a woman of Colchester, that had been sent to him, charged with heresy, were
returned back discharged by him, but were now worse than
they were before.　In another book, that seems to be the
minutes of the council, it is entered, that twenty-four persons
were discharged by him, who were still rank heretics[81].

I find at this time the council was much employed in the [Ibid.
matter of the privy-seals.　Our fleet was then so inconsider- P. 541.]
able, that fourteen thousand pound being ordered to be applied
to the fleet, by the lord treasurer and the lord admiral, both

---

[80] [" At St. James' the 6th of
October 1556.　A letter to the deputy and council of Callaice, willing
them to make diligent search for
one old Botts, Thomas Lincoln,
Nicholas Lincoln, and to apprehend
them and commit them to ward.
And to signify the same hither, to
the end further order may be taken
with them, with a postscript that
they have regard to such persons as
shall loiter and lurk there, having
fled from hence, to commit them
also to ward to order them accordingly.

" A letter to the earl of Sussex,
of thanks for the continuance of his
good diligence and travail, signifying unto him, that as touching the
continuance of the privy watch and
beacons, the same is referred to his
lordship's discretion, either to discharge them or longer to continue
them.　The effect of the former
letter to the deputy and council of
Callaice is also signified unto his
lordship."—Council Book, p. 525.]

[81] [Here the two Council Books
precisely resemble each other, neither taking notice of this fact.]

for repairing, furnishing, and victualling it, they reckoned, that, when that was done, ten thousand pound a year afterwards would answer what was necessary. On the 19th of February, one Christopher Howe was ordered to be proceeded against for some detestable words, not fit to be heard: so it was ordered, that only such parts of them should be opened, as might serve for evidence to the jury. On the 21st, complaints were brought of a jailor who suffered heretics to go freely about. On the 24th, the queen expected hourly to hear of the king's arrival; so the lord admiral and others were ordered to attend on him. An ambassador came at this time from Russia: he landed in the north of Scotland, and was well received, and nobly treated by the lord Wharton; for which, thanks were written to him. Here several orders are entered concerning 260 the lord Stourton and his servants: three of them were ordered to be hanged in chains at Mere.

I had in my former work [82] given a due commendation to that which seemed to me a just firmness in the queen, not to pardon the lord Stourton for so heinous a crime as the murdering father and son in so barbarous a manner. But since I have lived long in Wiltshire, I find there is a different account of this matter in that neighbourhood. The story, as it has been handed down by very old people, is this: The day before the execution was appointed, there was a report set about, that a pardon or a reprieve was coming down; upon which the sheriff came to the earl of Pembroke, who was then at Wilton, for advice. That lord heard the report, and was much troubled at it: so, apprehending some message might come to him from the court, he ordered his gates to be shut somewhat early, and not to be opened till next morning. My lord Stourton's son came down with the order: but since the gates were not to be opened, he rode over to his father, who received the news with great joy. In the night the sheriff left Wilton, and came so secretly to Salisbury, that Stourton knew nothing of it, and believed he was still at Wilton, where he knew he was the night before. But when he was so far gone, that the sheriff knew he could not come back in time to hinder the execution, he brought his men together whom he had ordered to attend on him that day; and so the lord was executed before his son could come back

[82] [See Part ii. p. 350.]

[Ibid.
p. 579.]

[Ibid.
p. 580.]

[Ibid.
p. 582.]

[Ibid.
p. 583.]
[Ibid.
p. 585.]

[Ibid.
p. 594.]
An account
of lord
Stourton's
execution.

with the order to stop it. I set down this story upon a popular report, of which I have had the pedigree vouched to me, by those whose authors, upon the authority of their grandfathers, did give an entire credit to it. So meritorious a man as the lord Stourton was, who had protested against every thing done in king Edward's parliament, had no doubt many intercessors to plead for him in this his extremity. I leave this with my reader as I found it.

On the 20th of March[83], the king came to England. Orders being sent into Kent, that the gentlemen should attend upon him in their best apparel; thanks were afterwards written to them for their readiness in furnishing him with post horses. On the 17th of April[84], proceedings are ordered to be made upon a book that is called lewd and seditious: and the countess of Sussex coming over at this time, and bringing letters which gave some suspicion, she was sent to the Fleet. She had been for some years separated from her husband: she was ordered to be examined strictly; but upon this and many other occasions, particulars are not set forth, and only a general mention is made of the minutes put in the chest. [Council Book. pp. 595, 597.] [Ibid. p. 6c4.] [Ibid. p. 605.]

There is, besides the great council-book, another council-book, which, I suppose, might be the minute book which was perused by my learned friend doctor Kennet, and who communicated to me all the extracts that he had made out of it, and some other manuscripts, which I never saw. It seems, it was apprehended that the French designed a descent in Dorsetshire: so orders were sent to make musters in that county, and to have them in readiness, in case of an invasion or a rebellion: and three hundred men were sent over to Calais, with orders concerning the fortifications[85].

---

[83] [At the foot of the proceedings of this day is entered in the Council Book, '*Reditus Regiæ Majestatis in Angliam.*']

[84] [In both Council Books, a minute of twelve lines, of the 3rd of January 1556, is carefully erased, and in the margin of both is written, ' Put out by order of the lords of the council, at Westminster the 25th of March, 1557.']

[85] [The entry in both Council Books is the same, and is as follows: "At Westminstre the 30 of Maie 1557. A letter to the earl of Oxforde and the lord Riche, of thanks for their diligence in sending over the three hundred men to Callaice. And as for the money by them defrayed, the same is paid to him whom they sent; allowing for every cote iiijs., which is the old rate."—Council Book, p. 621.]

The alarms
oft given
of plots.
[Ibid.
p. 631.]

On the 14th of June, complaint was made of some naughty 261
plays and lewd books. The council was often alarmed with
these plays: but it does not appear whether there was any
thing in the plays with relation to religion or the government;
or whether it was, that they apprehended some mischief from
the concourse of the people that those representations brought
together. One sir Thomas Cawarden was committed to the
Fleet for his misbehaviour to the state: he was ordered to be
kept a close prisoner, with only one servant, since he had
made no manner of submission, and had not acknowledged his
offence: but what this offence was does not appear to me.

[Ibid.
p. 641.]

On the 29th of June, orders were given for sending two thousand men to Calais, with directions to distribute them to the
places about that wanted a reinforcement the most. Eight
hundred and sixty of them were ordered for Guisnes; and a
letter was written to the mayor and jurats of Calais[56], to con-

[Ibid.
p. 642.]

tinue their mayor for another year. On the 3rd of July, the
cardinal made an offer of one hundred men to serve the queen:
he was ordered to levy them immediately, and to send them to

[Ibid.
p. 643.]

Dover. Two hundred foot, and six hundred horse more[57], were
ordered in all haste for Calais: and assurance was given, that
more should quickly follow. There were then great apprehensions of disorders on the borders of Scotland, which were
wholly in the hands of the French[88].

A severe
prosecu-
tion.

Bonner at this time gave the city of London a most dismal
spectacle, a little removed from the city, perhaps for fear of a

[86] [This is a mistake for Rye.]

[87] [" At Westminster the first of
July 1557. A letter to the lord
deputy of Callays, that where he
writeth for a further supplement of
men for the better guarding of the
piers on that side, it is signified
unto him, that 250 men, whereof
200 are footmen, and fifty horsemen, are appointed to be sent over
with all speed from the lord cardinal's grace and the lord warden,
and one hundred harquebutters shall
be also sent from the earl of Pembroke and the other lords appointed
for the wars, putting his lordship
also in remembrance that it was not
intended that he should attempt to
annoy the enemy until the main
force came, but only to stand upon
his guard and defence."—p. 643.]

[88] [From p. 648, which gives the
proceedings of July 11th, 1557, to
p. 659, on which the minutes of
July 27th begin, is lost from the
large Council Book. The smaller
copy of the Council Book supplies
this deficiency (pp. 617—634) as
far as July 26th. Here a leaf is
missing, so that there is omitted
part of the proceedings of July 26th,
and nearly all those of July 28th.
From July 29th the proceedings
are in both Council Books.]

tumult, at Stratford, where thirteen persons, eleven men and two women, were burnt in one fire. He had condemned sixteen to be thus sacrificed : but cardinal Pole heard there was some hope of working on three of them ; so there came an order to put them in his hands : and he, by the 26th of July, prevailed so far on two of them, that a pardon was granted to those two who had been condemned by the bishop of London, but were prevailed on by the cardinal to abjure, (a very extraordinary thing, as is mentioned in the pardon,) and had received them into the communion of the church ; " and had upon that in- " terceded with the king and queen for their pardon, which " they, as true sons of the church, did willingly imitate, and " embraced this occasion of shewing their zeal." I cannot tell what became of the third person whom he had taken out of Bonner's hands.

Cardinal Pole saved two persons.

Rymer MSS. Exemplo licet raris- simo.

But here I must lessen the character of the cardinal's mild-ness towards heretics : for on the 28th of March this year[89] he sent orders to proceed against the heretics in his diocese ; and on the 7th of July he sent a *significavit* of some heretics to be delivered to the secular arm.

[Wilkins, Conc. iv. p. 173.]

[Ibid. p. 174.]

I find likewise, by other evidences, suggested to me by the laborious Mr. Strype, that Pole was not so mild as I had re-presented him. Parker in his British Antiquities, which Strype believes assuredly he can prove that it was written by him ; he calls him *Ecclesiæ Anglicanæ carnifex et flagellum ;* the whip and the executioner of the Church of England : and Calfhill, a canon of Christ-Church in Oxford, in a letter he wrote to Grindal bishop of London, mentions the proceedings of the visitors sent to Oxford by Pole ; who were, Brookes, bishop of Gloucester ; Cole, dean of St. Paul's ; and Ormaneto : he sent them thither, not only to restore the pope's authority, but dili-gently to inquire if there were any who neglected the pope's ceremonies ; and if there were any found that were under the least suspicion, (*levissima suspicio,*) they were without any delay to eject them : he writes, there was nothing eminent in Ormaneto but intolerable insolence ; nothing could be imagined more arrogant than he was. They raged, as he adds, against a great many in the university ; and burned in the market-place an infinite number of Bibles and other books. The like

[Vid. Mem. Eccles. vol. iii. p. 392, and Thua-nus, lib. xvii. p. 577.] [Antiq. Britann. Ecclesiæ, p. 523.]

262

[89] [This should be ' the following year,' 1558.]

severity was practised at Cambridge; of which Mr. Strype promises an account in the Life of Whitgift, now ready for the press.

The nation began to grow every where weary of the cruel executions of so many heretics: the great promoter of these barbarous proceedings was the earl of Sussex. He died in March this year: for his son Thomas, who succeeded to him in his honour, was then deputy of Ireland; and on the 1st of April order was given for a new patent to him by the title of the earl of Sussex.

The nation abhorred this cruelty.
[July 28, 1557.
Council Book, p. 660.]

At one time complaints were brought of the sheriffs of Kent, Essex, Suffolk, and Staffordshire, and of the mayor of Rochester, and the bailiff of Colchester, that when some persons, being condemned for heresy, were delivered to them by their ordinaries, they, instead of proceeding to a present execution, had delayed it: so letters were ordered to them, requiring them to signify what it was that had moved them to stop the usual proceedings. Information was also given of some lewd and seditious words, spoken by some of the queen's household; upon which they were sent to prison: and orders were given to prosecute them. On the 3rd of August, thanks were ordered to be given to sergeant Brown for his proceedings with Trudgeover; and orders were given for the disposing of his head and quarters. On the 7th of August, sir John Butler, sheriff of Essex, was fined ten pound because his deputy had respited the execution of a woman, condemned for heresy, that should have been executed at Colchester; and he was to answer for his deputy's fault. This perhaps is the same with that which was mentioned on the 28th of July. Many were ordered to be proceeded against for writing and spreading lewd and seditious books. It seems the lord Rich continued to give the council notice, before they proceeded to any executions in Essex, and so laid the odium of the severity on the council, for shewing no pity: so, on the 6th[90] of August, they wrote to him to proceed according to law, and not to give them any more trouble on

[Ibid. p. 667.]

[Ibid. p. 670.]

[Ibid. p. 660.]

[Aug. 8, p. 671.]

90 [" At Richemounde the eight of August. A letter to the lord Riche, returning unto him the persons sent by him hither, being apprehended in mistress Parker's house, with whom, and all other that shall be apprehended, he is willed to proceed according to the order of the laws, and the qualities of their offences, and not to trouble this board any more with them."—— Council Book, p. 671.]

those occasions. Complaint was made on the 10th of August [Council Book, p. 673.] of a bad choice that the town of Calais had made of a mayor for the ensuing year, especially in so critical a time. They were told, that, by such an election, they might have their charter to be brought in question. On the 12th of August, [Aug. 11, Ibid. p. 674.] orders were sent to Canterbury to proceed without delay against those who acted there a lewd play that was sent up.

On the 15th of August, the news came of the great defeat given [Ibid. p. 676.] the French at St. Quintin's : so an order was sent to the bishop [A great of London to publish that at St. Paul's Cross. On the 24th of coldness in those matters at Bristol. [Ibid. p. 685.]
263 aldermen of Bristol, requiring them to conform themselves, in frequenting sermons, processions, and other ceremonies, at the cathedral : and not to absent themselves, as they had done of late, nor to expect that the dean and chapter should come with their cross, and in procession, to fetch them out, of the city ; which was a thing unseemly, and out of order. On the 2nd of September, news came of the taking of St. Quintin's ; upon which, an order was sent to the lord mayor of London to have [Ibid. p. 691.] bonfires at night, and to come the next day to high mass. On the 6th[91] of September, an order was sent to the lord mayor [Sept. 5. Ibid. p. 695.] of London to apprehend those who had acted a play, called *A Sack full of News ;* but there was an order sent soon after [Sept. 6, Ibid. p. 696.] to set them at liberty. On the 6th of October, news came that peace was made between the pope and the king ; upon which [Ibid. p. 707.] the council ordered high mass to be at St. Paul's ; and the lord mayor was required to be there, and to have bonfires over the city. The council was for some time wholly taken up with the matter of the loan, and the privy-seals ; and though the government had certain notice of the design of the French upon Calais, yet no parliament was called, by which money, and every thing else that was necessary to the preserving it, could have been furnished. But the spirit of the nation was now much turned ; and compassion began to rise towards these poor people, that were thus sacrificed to the cruelty of the priests and the bigotry of a weak peevish woman, so that they would not venture on calling one, but tried other ineffectual methods of raising money ; which increased the jealousy of the nation more than it added to the queen's treasure.

[91] [The first order is of the 5th of September, the second of the 6th.]

Bonner
called on
by the
council to
be more
severe.
[April 20.]

Bonner was again quickened, by another letter, to proceed against heretics : upon which, he sent down Dr. Chedsey to Colchester ; who, in a letter that he wrote to Bonner, on the 21st of April 1558[92], tells him, that, while he was sitting at Colchester, examining heretics, he received a summons to appear before the council : but he desires that Bonner would make his excuse, since he was on the great work of finding out heretics, anabaptists, and other unruly persons, such as the like was never heard.

[Council
Book of
Mary and
Elizabeth,
p. 130.]

There is also in the minute-book an entry of the letter of the 1st of August 1558[93], written on Bembridge's account ; who, when he was ready to be burnt, offered to recant : upon which the sheriff of Hampshire stayed the execution : for that he was chid ; but a letter was written to the bishop of Winchester, to examine whether his conversion was entire and sincere.

[Council
Book, p.
742.]

And now I have no more light from the Council Book : for that authentic volume goes only to the end of the year 1557 ; the last passage I find in it relating to religion being on the 15th of December[94] : then they wrote a letter to the bishop of London, and sent with it the examination of John Rough, a Scottish minister, whom they had sent to Newgate, and required him to proceed against him according to the laws. It may be perhaps thought that I have taken out of it nothing but what related to proceedings against heretics : but that is because there is scarce any thing else in it ; for I have taken

---

[92] [" At Grenewiche the 20th of Aprill 1558. A letter of appearance to Mr. Doctor Chedsey."—Council Book of Mary and Elizabeth, vol. i. A. 1558–9, p. 80.]

[93] [" At Rychemonde the first of August 1558. A letter to sir Richard Pexsall, knight, sheriff of the county of Hampshire, signifying that the queen's majesty cannot but find it very strange that he hath stayed one Bembrigge from execution, being condemned for heresy ; and therefore he is straightly commanded to cause him to be executed out of hand, and if he still continueth in the catholic faith as he pretendeth, then to suffer him such discreet and learned men as the

bishop of Wynchester shall appoint, who is written unto for this purpose, to have access unto him, and to confer with him, for the better confirmation of him in the catholic faith, and to be present with him also at his death, for the better aiding of him to die God's servant. The said sheriff is also commanded to make his undelayed repair hither immediately after the execution, to answer his doings herein."]

[94] [" At St. James' the 15 of December. A letter to the bishop of London, with the examination enclosed of a Scottisheman, named John Rough, presently sent to Newgate, against whom he is required to proceed by the order of the laws."]

out of it every thing that related to the government, or that
264 was in any sort historical.   But the council knew what it was
that the queen's heart was set on, and what would please her
most; and so they applied their care and diligence chiefly to
that.

There was a strange spirit of cruelty that ran through the
body of the clergy : it was animated by the government, and
shewed itself in so many dismal instances, in all the parts of the
nation, that it struck people with horror.   This, joined with the
intolerable haughtiness of the king, and the shameful loss of
Calais, brought the government under a universal hatred and
contempt.   In a book, corrected, if not written by the lord
Burghley, in queen Elizabeth's time, entitled, *The Executions
for Treason*, the sum of those who suffered in this wretched
reign is thus reckoned : " Four hundred persons suffered pub-
" licly in queen Mary's days, besides those who were secretly
" murdered in prisons : of these, twenty were bishops and dig-
" nified clergymen; sixty were women; children, more than
" forty : some women big with child ; one bore a child in the
" fire, and the child was burnt[95]."

It does not appear that the bishops or clergy shewed any
great inclination to entertain Pole's project for the reformation
of abuses ; or that they were at much pains, in the way of instruction, to reduce the people.   All that I find in this way is,
that Bonner set out an instruction for his diocese in the year

[95] [" The Execution of Justice
in England, for Maintenaunce of
of publique and Christian Peace,
against certeine Stirrers of Sedition,
and Adherents to the Traytours and
Enemies of the Realme, without any
Persecution of them for Questions
of Religion, as is falsely reported
and published by the Fautors and
Fosterers of their Treasons."   The
first edition was published in London Dec. 17, 1583, the second in
the following 14th of January. The
passage in the text is not exact. In
the original it is as follows : " There
were by imprisonment, torments,
famine and fire, of men, women,
maidens and children, almost the
number of four hundred, besides
such as were secretly murdered in
prisons ; and of that number above
twenty that had been archbishops,
bishops, and principal prelates or
officers in the church, lamentably
destroyed, and of women above
threescore, and of children above
forty, and amongst the women,
some great with child, and one out
of whose body the child by fire was
expelled alive, and yet also cruelly
burned ; examples beyond an hea-
then cruelty."   The tract was reprinted in the Harleian Miscellany,
vol. ii. p. 122, and in Somers' Tracts,
vol. i. p. 189.]

1555[96]. The people had heard so much of the Second Commandment, that he did not think fit to leave it quite out, as is done in most catechisms of the church of Rome : but yet he durst not venture on giving it honestly ; therefore, instead of the words, *nor worship them ;* he gave it thus, *nor adore them with God's honour.* Watson, bishop of Lincoln, did, in June 1558[97], put another out for his diocese. It seems he was in a high degree of favour with the cardinal ; since, notwithstanding the zeal he expressed against plurality of benefices in one person, he was allowed to hold the deanery of Durham *in commendam*[98] when he was promoted to Lincoln. The license is in January 1557 ; in which it is said, that the cardinal consented to it.

Paper-Office. [Turnbull's Calendar, p. 292, art. 586.]

[July 2, Ibid p. 320, art. 641.]

The papal provisions in this reign. Rymer.

The first public occasion that the ill-natured pope found to express his displeasure at Pole, was upon the death of Day, bishop of Chichester. The pope would not suffer Christopherson, the new bishop, to be preconized in Pole's name, but did it himself, as Carne wrote over on the 10th of April. Carne after that, on the 15th of June, wrote to the queen, that the pope had ordered cardinal Morone to be imprisoned on the account of religion. Four cardinals were sent to examine him. Carne adds, that he was in high reputation at Rome for his sanctity ; and he believed him a good catholic, and a holy man.

The style in which all the bishops' bulls during this reign did run, was, that the pope, by his apostolical authority, did provide the person to the see, and set him over it. Upon which the bishop so named did renounce every clause in his

---

[96] [Iniunctions geuen in the Visitatiō of Edmunde, Bishop of London. Lond. by John Cawood, 1555. 4to. Besides these there were published in the same year Homelies not onely promised before in his Boke, intituled A necessary Doctrine, but also now of late adioyned &c. Anno 1555. Lond. by John Cawood, 4to. : and 'A profitable and necessary Doctrine with certayne Homelies, adioined thereunto. Lond. in . Ædibus Joannis Cawodi, 1555.' 4to.]

[97] [Holsome and catholyke doctrine concerning the seven sacra-

mentes of Chrystes church, expedient to be knowen of all men, set forth in maner of shorte sermons to bee made to the people. 4to. Lond. by Robert Caly. 1558.]

[98] [He never held the deanery *in commendam,* for Thomas Robertson was appointed to the deanery July 23, 1557, and Watson was consecrated bishop of Lincoln Aug. 15, 1557, having been appointed by papal bull dated March 24, 1557. The patent by which he was made bishop of Lincoln bears date Dec. 24, 1556, and may be seen in Rymer, xv. p. 454.]

bull, that was in any sort prejudicial to the crown : and the renunciation being so made, the custody of the temporalities was given to the bishop elect.   In the bulls, no mention is
265 made either of the queen's recommending nor of the chapter's electing.   Rymer has gathered the bulls for Exeter, Bangor, St. Asaph, Carlisle, Chester, Peterborough, and Lincoln, besides those for Canterbury and York ; and they all run in the style of papal provisions.   Nor does he mention a *congé d'élire*, except for Chester, Winchester, Carlisle, Lincoln, Chichester, and Peterborough.   There is something particular in the restitution of the temporalities of Carlisle to Oglethorp : it is added, [Rymer, that he was to pay four hundred marks.   I do not comprehend xv. p. 446.] what could be the reason of this singularity.

There was another convocation in January 1557–8. Harps- Proceed- field was chosen prolocutor. On the 28th of January, Bonner, ings in con- as the cardinal's commissary, proposed some heads of reforma- [Wilkins, tion ; and the lower house desired leave to offer their proposi- Cono. iv. p. 155.] tions. On the 4th of February, a subsidy was agreed to of [Ibid. p. eight shillings in the pound, to be paid in four years ; and on 156.] the 9th, he told the bishops that the lower house had agreed to it. Complaint was made of a want of priests to serve the [Feb. 18.] cures : in order to remedy this, and to provide a supply for the smaller benefices, it was proposed, 1. That no priest should be taken up to serve in the wars. 2. That the bishops might have authority to unite small benefices, which the priest should serve by turns. 3. That the parishioners of chapels of ease might be obliged to come to the parish church, till curates could be provided. 4. That bishops might be authorized by the pope to ordain *extra tempora*. There was also some consideration had about the furnishing of arms ; and a decree

---

99 [He has printed the congé d'élire, issued 13 March, 1554, to the dean and chapter of Wells, xv. 369, to Lincoln, St. David's, Rochester, Gloucester, Hereford, Chester and Bristol, all of the 19th of March, 1554, pp. 374, 375, of Ely July 10, p. 403, of Norwich Sept. 4, p. 405, of Bristol and of Lichfield Oct. 25, p. 407, of York, 19 Feb. 1555, of Dublin Feb. 22, and of Bangor March 4, p. 415, of Exeter March

11, p. 416, of Chester May 28, 1556, p. 437, of Winchester July 16, p. 441, of Carlisle July 21, p. 441, of Lincoln Dec. 7, of Chichester Dec. 17, and of Peterborough Dec. 26. p. 452.

The papal provision for York, p. 427, 1 Sept. 1555, in Rymer, p. 425, is the first instance in which the Restoration of Temporalities specifies that the pope appointed.]

passed for the provision of them, after the same rate that the laity had agreed to. But then the convocation was prorogued, first to the 11th of November, and then to the 17th; on which day the queen died.

But now to open the state of the nation: Calais, and the places about, were lost; and the nation was so exhausted, that the supporting the government was no easy thing. The persons most in favour with the two kings of France and Spain were two clergymen, the cardinal of Lorraine, and the bishop of Arras, soon after promoted to be a cardinal. They saw, that the continuance of the war made it reasonable on both sides not to put a stop to the progress of heresy; though it had not that effect in England: they therefore, at an interview, projected a peace; that so both kings might be at full leisure to extirpate heresy out of their dominions.

In order to this, France was willing to make great restitutions: only, from the first opening of the treaty, they declared very positively, that they resolved never to part with Calais. A treaty was opened; and the earl of Arundel, the bishop of Ely, and dean Wotton, were sent to treat in the queen's name. I shall here only give the abstract of two papers which I found relating to this matter.

The first is the council's letter to the ambassadors, written on the 8th of November[1]; which is in the Collection. The ambassadors saw no hope of the restoring of Calais; so they had moved the council to lay the matter before the parliament. " It was not thought convenient to break it to the whole 266 " house: it was thought best to begin with the nobility, and " some of the best and gravest sort. But before they made " that step, they thought it necessary to ask the queen's mind: " she thought it was best to lay it first before the king. Upon " which, they sent the ambassadors with a letter to the king; " and resolved to stay till his answer came. They write, that " the queen was still sick and weak: they hoped for her " amendment; but they were driven to fear and mistrust the

[1] [" At the Star Chamber the third of November 1558. A letter to the earl of Arundell, the bushopp of Ely, and Mr. Doctor Wotton, being commissioners with the king's majesty for the treaty of peace with the French, in answer of their letters according to the minute in the council chest."—Council Book, p. 187.

" worst. In a postscript, they tell them they had received
" the ambassadors' letters of the 4th, by which they saw the
" French were resolved not to restore Calais: and that the
" king told them, that his commissioners had almost agreed
" with the French in all other matters; but he would agree to
" nothing, unless the queen was satisfied. The council ordered
" the ambassadors to lay before the king the importance of
" leaving Calais in the hands of the French; and how much it
" would touch the honour of the king and queen, that, so many
" restitutions being to be made on both sides, this alone should
" not be restored. The subjects of this realm would certainly
" be very uneasy at this. The war was begun at the king's
" request, and for his sake. If to other of the king's allies,
" places are to be restored, that were taken from them some
" years ago; what then can be judged, if a peace is concluded
" without this restitution? Yet, on the other hand, if there is
" an agreement in all other matters, (which is like a giving up
" of the point,) much were to be endured for the wealth of
" Christendom. In these matters, the ambassadors were or-
" dered to deal plainly with the king, and to study to know
" his mind; since the French keeping these places might be as
" great prejudice to his low countries as to England. They
" desire a plain and speedy answer, that they might know
" what to offer to the nobility and parliament with relation to
" this matter."

　　The answer to this belongs to this reign; though it was
written on the day after the queen died, signed by the three
ambassadors. It is in the Collection. " They had written Collect.
Numb. 43.
" formerly, that the French king had said he would hazard
" his crown rather than restore Calais: yet for all those high
" words they did not quite despair. The commissioners of
" both kings had broke up their conferences, and returned to
" their masters, to give an account of what they had done, and
" to receive their final orders. The ambassadors believed, that
" if the king insisted positively on the restitution of Calais,
" that this might induce the French to agree to it: whereas,
" if the king and his ministers spoke but faintly of that matter,
" they were sure the French would still refuse to do it. There-
" fore they did not think fit to use any words to the king, to
" make him imagine that the queen or the kingdom would

" consent to a peace without the restoring of Calais : because
" their instructions were express in that point. The king
" continued to say, that he would make no peace, unless the
" queen should be satisfied : so that if she and her council con-
" tinued to insist on that point, they did believe the French 267
" would restore it, rather than lose the view they had of peace.
" And whereas the council wrote to them, that if all other
" things were near agreed, much were to be endured for the
" peace of Christendom ; yet that all others should have resti-
" tution, and that poor England should only bear the loss, was
" hard ; especially so great a loss : and they were so far from
" thinking that the leaving Calais to the French would purchase
" a sure peace, that they thought, on the contrary, that nothing
" shewed more evidently that the French did not intend to
" continue the peace, with England especially, than their keep-
" ing of Calais. The French could easily annoy England on
" the side of Scotland ; the dauphin being then married to the
" queen of Scots : and what the French pretend to by that
" marriage was not unknown to them." (This probably was,
to claim the crown of England upon the queen's death.) " Now
" if the French kept Calais, the English could neither hurt
" their enemies, nor assist their friends, or be assisted by them
" so easily, as when that place was in their hands. England
" would be shut out from the rest of Europe : the very know-
" ledge of the transactions abroad would come late to them,
" and that place would be a scourge for England, as it was
" before Edward the Third took it ; which made him come
" with his son, and but with a small army from Normandy
" into France, and to march through Picardy to besiege it, the
" enemy pursuing him with a greater army : but he fought
" through them, till at last he fought them at Cressy ;
" where, though the French were three to one, yet he totally
" defeated them, and continued the siege till he took it. So
" the French having Scotland on the one hand, and Calais on
" the other, it was easy to apprehend what might follow on
" this. The French would sign any terms with them to keep
" that place. These would be only parchment and wax. They
" knew how many parchments king Francis sealed to king
" Henry ; and the present king to king Edward. They saw
" the effects they had ; and if a war should follow between

" England and France, they were not sure that Spain would
" join with England : whereas now the king could not honour-
" ably make any peace without us; and he himself said he
" would not : so they did not think Christendom should have
" a good peace, if Calais were left to the French ; and it was
" certainly more the interest of England to continue the war
" in conjunction with the king, than to make a peace, letting it
" go, and then be forced to begin a new war, and to have all
" the burden of it lie upon England. All this they thought
" themselves bound to lay before the council. The bishop of
" Ely adds, that he was with the commissioners by the king's
" order; they had not yet agreed concerning the matters of
" Corsica and Siena : the French have likewise demanded the
" restitution of Navarre ; so that some thought the treaty
" would be broken off without concluding in a peace. The
" earl of Arundel adds, that, after they had gone so far in
" their letter, he received a letter from the bishop of Arras,
" dated the 17th, in which he writes thus ; The bishop of Ely
" has told you on what terms we were in this purgatory at his
268 " leaving us. The French told us yesterday that they would
" condescend to every thing rather than yield in the matter of
" Calais, or let that place go out of their hands. And we on
" our part told them, that, without full satisfaction to the
" kingdom of England, we would not treat with them in any
" sort. And we parted so, that there is more appearance of
" a rupture than of a conclusion of the treaty." But after all,
our ambassadors doubted much whether it would break off
only on the account of Calais. If they were in doubt about it,
while the queen was yet alive, it may be easily supposed that
her death put them out of all doubt concerning it.

And now I am come to the conclusion of this inglorious
reign. Campana gives a different account of the immediate
occasion of the queen's death, from what is to be found in
other authors. He tells us, that king Philip, seeing no hope
of issue by her, and that she was in an ill state of health,
designed a marriage between the duke of Savoy and the lady
Elizabeth : the queen had a very bad opinion of her sister,
suspecting she had ill principles in religion. King Philip
thought the duke of Savoy would be a firm friend to him, and
a constant enemy to France. But he could never bring the

A particu-
lar relation
of the oc-
casion of
the queen's
death.
[Campana,
par. ii. lib.
x. fol. 60.]

queen to hearken to this : yet now that she was declining very fast, he sent over the duke of Feria to propose the match to the privy-council, without any regard to the queen, or to the opposition she might make to it. And he ordered him to use all possible means to bring it to a conclusion. The queen resented this highly ; and when she saw it was designed to force her to it, she fell into an extreme melancholy. The privy-council did not entertain the motion : and the queen dying in a few days, an end was put to it : for though I find the duke of Feria was in England upon queen Elizabeth's coming to the crown, it does not appear that he made any proposition of that matter to her. What truth soever may be in this, the nation was now delivered from a severe and unhappy, though short reign : in which superstition and cruelty had the ascendant to such a degree, that it does not appear that there was any one great or good design ever set on foot, either for the wealth or glory of the nation. The poor queen delivered herself up to her peevish and fretful humours, and to her confessor ; and seemed to have no other thoughts, but about the extirpation of heresy and the endowing of monasteries. Even the war, that commonly slackens vigorous proceedings, had not that effect here. Her inexorable hatred of all she accounted heretics was such, that I find but one single instance of a pardon of any condemned of heresy ; and that was upon the cardinal's intercession. God shortened the time of her reign for his elect's sake : and he seemed to have suffered popery to shew itself in its true and natural colours, all over both false and bloody ; even in a female reign, from whence all mildness and gentleness might have been expected ; to give this nation such an evident and demonstrative proof of the barbarous cruelty of that religion, as might raise a lasting abhorrence and detestation of it.

A parallel of queen Mary and queen Elizabeth's reign.

It was visible that the providence of God made a very remarkable difference, in all respects, between this poor short and despised reign, and the glory, the length, and the prosperity of the succeeding reign. So that, as far as we can reason from the outward characters of things, the one was all over mean and black, while the other shined with a superior brightness, to the admiration of all the world. It wanted no foil to set it off, being all over lustre and glory. But if that

269

The news of the queen's coming to the crown no sooner reached Zurich, than all those who had retired thither resolved to return to England.   They had been entertained there both by the magistrates, and the ministers, Bullinger, Gualter, Weidner, Simler, Lavater, Gesner, and all the rest of that body, with a tenderness and affection that engaged them to the end of their lives to make the greatest acknowledgments possible for it.   The first of these was in all respects the chief person of that society, with whom they held the closest correspondence.   Peter Martyr was likewise there, and was treated by them all with a singular respect, even to a submission.   Jewel was first formed by him at Oxford, and so continued to his death in a constant commerce of letters with him, writing always to him by the title of *Father.*   I saw a great volume of those letters as I passed through Zurich in the year 1685[2]; so I was

ad hoc filium gratias Cæsari parenti egisse pro singulari parentis erga se clementiâ et pietate, quod tam præclaro et nobili se matrimonio condecorare et illustrare studeat et hujus benefitii se nunquam immemorem futurum, verum hoc sibi dolere quod pater male fidere sibi in religione videatur, se hoc credere quod ejus majestas credat et quod in Novo Testamento et orthodoxis patribus, traditum sit.   Ad quod Cæsar se clarius et magis dilucidum responsum expetere, nempe quod nunquam à vetere religione deficere velit, post similem responsum priori repetitum Cæsarem intulisse, video et hunc mihi filium corruptum esse, ac tandem filium hujuscemodi juramentum dare recusare.]

[2] [" Among the archives of the dean and chapter, there is a vast collection of letters, written either to Bullinger or by him; they are bound up, and make a great many volumes in folio; and out of these no doubt but one might discover a great many particulars relating to the history of the reformation: for as Bullinger lived long, so he was much esteemed.   He procured a very kind reception to be given to some of our English exiles in queen Mary's reign, in particular to Sandys, afterwards archbishop of York, to Horne, afterwards bishop of Winchester, and to Jewel, bishop of Salisbury.   He gave them lodgings in the Close, and used them with all possible kindness; and as they presented some silver cups to the college, with an inscription acknowledging the kind reception they had found there, which I saw, so they continued to keep a constant correspondence with Bullinger, after the happy reestablishment of the reformation under queen Elizabeth; of which I read almost a whole volume while I was there : most of them contain only the general news, but some were more important, and relate to the disputes then on foot, concerning the habits of the clergy, which gave the first beginnings to our unhappy divisions : and by the letters, of which I read the originals, it appears that the bishops preserved the ancient habits rather in compliance with the queen's inclinations, than out of any liking they had to them; so far they were from liking them, that they plainly expressed their dislike of them. Jewel,

desirous to have the volume sent me : but I found, that, by their rules, that could not be done. I also understood, that there were several letters relating to our affairs, scattered through several other volumes ; so professor Otto did kindly and with much zeal undertake to get them to be copied for me. The person who managed and procured this for me was **272** that pious and learned professor at Geneva, Alphonsus Turretin, born to be a blessing to the state he lives in. He has

in a letter bearing date the 8th of February 1566, wishes that the vestments, together with all the other remnants of popery, might be thrown both out of their churches and out of the minds of the people, and laments the queen's fixedness to them ; so that she would suffer no change to be made. And in January the same year Sandys writes to the same purpose : *Contenditur de vestibus papisticis utendis vel non utendis; dabit Deus his quoque finem.* ' Disputes are now on foot concerning the popish vestments, whether they should be used or not, but God will put an end to those things.' Horne, bishop of Winchester, went further : for, in a letter dated the 16th of July 1565, he writes of the act concerning the habits with great regret, and expresses some hopes that it might be repealed next session of parliament, if the popish party did not hinder it ; and he seems to stand in doubt whether he should conform himself to it or not, upon which he desires Bullinger's advice. And in many letters writ on that subject, it is asserted, that both Cranmer and Ridley intended to procure an act for abolishing the habits, and that they only defended their lawfulness, but not their fitness, and therefore they blamed private persons that refused to obey the laws. Grindal, in a letter dated the 27th of August 1566, writes, that all the bishops who had been beyond sea, had at their return dealt with the queen to let the matter of

the habits fall : but she was so prepossessed, that though they had all endeavoured to divert her from prosecuting that matter, she continued still inflexible. This had made them resolve to submit to the laws, and to wait for a fit opportunity to reverse them. He laments the ill effects of the opposition that some had made to them, which had extremely irritated the queen's spirit, so that she was now much more heated in those matters than formerly : he also thanks Bullinger for the letter that he had writ, justifying the lawful use of the habits, which he says had done great service. Cox, bishop of Ely, in one of his letters, laments the aversion that they found in the parliament to all the propositions that were made for the reformation of abuses. Jewel, in a letter dated the 22nd of May 1559, writes, that the queen refused to be called head of the church, and adds, that that title could not be justly given to any mortal, it being due only to Christ ; and that such titles had been so much abused by antichrist, that they ought not to be any longer continued. On all these passages I will make no reflections here : for I set them down only to shew what was the sense of our chief churchmen at that time concerning those matters which have since engaged us into such warm and angry disputes, and this may be no inconsiderable instruction to one that intends to write the history of that time."–Burnet's Letters, &c., p. 42.]

given the world already, on many occasions, great instances of
his exquisite learning, and of a most penetrating judgment,
having made a vast progress in a few years ; in which a feeble
and tender body, though it is a great clog, that gives his
friends many sad apprehensions, yet cannot keep down an
exalted mind from many performances, that seem to be above
both his years and his strength.   But how valuable soever
these qualities are, yet his zeal for the great things of religion,
and his moderation in lesser matters, together with a sublime
and exalted piety, is that which I observed in him, even when
he was scarce out of childhood, and have, with a continual
joy and delight, seen the advances of it ever since.   This
grateful account of him I owe not so much to his friendship,
(though I owe a great deal to that,) but to his rare and singular worth.   By his means I procured copies of the letters
that our reformers continued to write, chiefly to Peter Martyr,
Bullinger, and Gualter : and with them I have a solemn attestation, under the seal of that noble canton, of their being
true copies, carefully collated with the originals ; which I have
put at the end of the Collection.   If there had not been many
interruptions in the series of those letters, they are so particular, that from them we should have had a clear thread of
the history of that time : but many of them are lost ; and they
are wanting on some of the most critical occasions.   I shall
make the best use of them I can, as far as they lead me.

Horne and Sandys went first to England : so Jewel, who
was following them, writes from Strasburg, on the 26th of January 1559, to Peter Martyr : and adds, " that they were well
" received by the queen ; that many bishoprics were void ;
" Christopherson was certainly dead : that White, whom Mar-
" tyr knew well, had preached the funeral sermon when queen
" Mary was buried ; the text was, *I praised the dead more*
" *than the living :* in which he charged the audience, by all
" means not to suffer any change to be made in religion.   In-
" veighing against the fugitives, that might perhaps return
" into England, he said, whosoever should kill them would do
" a deed acceptable to God.   Upon this he writes, that both
" the marquis of Winchester, and Heath archbishop of York,
" seemed highly displeased at it.   He adds, that Bonner was
" obliged to restore to Ridley's executors all his goods that he

They were
well receiv
ed by the
queen.
Collect.
Numb. 44.

" had violently seized on, and was confined to his house." I
have seen a copy of White's sermon[3]. In it he commends
queen Mary for this, that she would never be called head of
the church : though the falsehood of that is on record, in the
writs that were sealed for above a year after she came to the
crown.   He runs out with great fury against heresy : Geneva
is, in particular, named the seat of it.   He says, queen Mary's
death was like the death of an angel, if they were mortal.   He
insinuates his fears of *flying in the winter, on the sabbath*, or
being with child ; all which he represents as allegorical.   Yet
he has some decent words of the queen ; and says, they were 273
to comfort themselves for the death of one sister in the other
that survived.

Those of
Zurich
advise a
thorough
reforma-
tion.
Collect.
Numb. 45.

Gualter wrote to one Masters, who was the queen's physician, and was well known to him, on the 16th of January.
" He congratulates the happy change of their affairs.   He
" wishes (I translate his words strictly) that they would not
" hearken to the counsels of those men ; who, when they saw
" that popery could not be honestly defended, nor entirely
" retained, would use all artifices to have the outward face of
" religion to remain mixed, uncertain, and doubtful : so that,
" while an evangelical reformation is pretended, those things
" should be obtruded on the church, which will make the re-
" turning back to popery, to superstition, and to idolatry, very
" easy.   I write not these things to you, he adds, as knowing
" that there are any such among you ; but I write, from a fear
" that there may be some such : for we have had the ex-
" perience of this for some years in Germany, and know what
" influence such persons may have.   Their counsels seem to a
" carnal judgment to be full of modesty, and well fitted for
" carrying on an universal agreement : and we may well
" believe, that the common enemy of our salvation will find out

---

[3] [*Sermon preached at the Funeral of Queen Mary*, 13 *Dec.* 1558,
on Eccles. iv. 2.—MS. in the library
sometimes of Richard Smith, se-
condary of the Poultry Compter.
Wood, Ath. Oxon. sub an. 1559.
Now in the British Museum, MS.
Donat. 1578.   See Ayscough's *Catalogue,* i. 8.   It has been printed

from a MS. in the Cotton library in
Strype's Ecclesiastical Memorials,
Appendix, N°. 81, p. 277, but from
a very faulty copy.   A much better
penes me.—Baker.
The copy in the Museum is con-
temporary, consisting of thirteen
folios of a very small 4to. size.]

" proper instruments, by whose means the seeds of popery
" may still remain among you." A little after he writes, " that
" he apprehends, that in the first beginnings, while men may
" study to avoid the giving some small offence, many things
" may be suffered under this colour, that they will be continued
" but for a little while; and yet afterwards, it will scarce be
" possible, by all the endeavours that can be used, to get them
" to be removed, at least not without great strugglings." Dr.
Masters, in answer to this, tells him, he had laid his letter
before the queen, and that she had read it all. He promises
to use his best endeavours for carrying on a sound reformation.
This plainly insinuates their fears of somewhat like what was
designed by the *Interim* in Germany.

[Epistolæ
Tigurinæ,
1558–1602,
Ep. xxv.
p. 33.]

Francis earl of Bedford had gone out of England in queen
Mary's time, and had stayed some time in Zurich: he had expressed a true zeal for the reformation, and a particular regard
for the divines there; of which a letter in the Collection gives
a clear account: and upon that they wrote often to him, and
pressed him vehemently to take care in the first beginnings to
have all things settled upon sure and sound foundations.

The earl
of Bedford
had stayed
some time
at Zurich,
and wrote
to them.
Collect.
Numb. 46.

On the 24th of January the convocation was opened; but
the bishops, in obedience to the queen's proclamation against
preaching, did not think fit to open it with a sermon. Those
who I find are marked as present are, the bishops of London,
Winchester, Lincoln, Worcester, Coventry and Lichfield, and
the abbot of Westminster. These appeared personally; and
the bishops of Ely, Peterborough, and St. Asaph sent their
proxies: but no mention is made of the bishops of Bath and
Wells, St. David's, Llandaff, and Exeter. All the other sees
were then vacant; Canterbury, Salisbury, Norwich, Chichester,
Hereford, Gloucester, Oxford, Bangor, Bristol, and Rochester:
ten in all. Harpsfield was chosen prolocutor. He asked,
What they had to do, and what was to be done, to preserve
religion? The bishops answered, They must pray the queen,
that no new burden might be laid on the clergy in this parliament. This was to prevent the demand of a new subsidy, the
former not being yet paid. In the seventh session the prolocutor offered to the bishops the five articles mentioned in my
History[4]. These they had drawn up for the discharge of

Proceed-
ings in con-
vocation.
[Wilkins,
Conc. iv.
p. 179.]

[Fuller,
lib. xvi.
p. 54.]

[Ibid. p.
55.]

274

[4] [See Part ii. p. 388.]

their consciences, and they desired the bishops to be their leaders in this matter. The bishops received their paper, and promised to offer it next day to the house of lords. In the next session, the prolocutor and clergy came up, and asked the bishops if they had delivered their paper to the house of lords? Bonner answered, that they had delivered it to the lord keeper, the mouth of that house; who, to all appearance, received it kindly, or thankfully, (*gratanter*,) but gave them no answer. The clergy desired the bishops to get an answer from him, or at least to know his pleasure, before their next meeting. In the ninth session the bishops told the clergy, that they had not yet found a fit opportunity to obtain an answer from the house of lords. On the tenth session Bonner told the clergy, that all their articles, except the last, which was, "That the authority of treating and defining, in matters "of the faith, of the sacraments, and of ecclesiastical disci- "pline, belonged to the pastors of the church, and not to the "laity;" were approved by the two universities. After this came only perpetual prorogations from day to day, without any business done, till the ninth of May, in which the convocation was dissolved. So this was the last and feeble struggle that the popish clergy made in convocation.

[Wilkins, Conc iv. p. 180.]

[Ibid. p. 182.]

The bishops stood firm in the house of lords, where there were none of the other side to answer them; few of the temporal lords being very learned. They seemed to triumph there, and hung so upon the wheels, that there was a slow progress made. On the 20th of March, Jewel writes to Peter Martyr, "That after a journey of fifty-one days from the time "he left Zurich, he got to London; where he was amazed to "find the pope's authority was not yet thrown off: masses were "still said; and the bishops continued still insolent. Things "were beginning to mend a little: a public disputation was "then resolved on; and he adds, that the queen spoke with "great esteem of Peter Martyr. The inferior sort of the "populace was both ignorant and perverse. He tells him, "Brookes, bishop of Gloucester, whom he calls an *impure beast*, "was newly dead; and cried out, as he was[5] dying, that he "was damned."

The bishops oppose the reformation in the house of lords.
Collect.
Numb. 47.

[5] [Wood says he died in the beginning of February, about Candlemas in 1559.]

Jewel, in a letter to Bullinger from London on the 22nd of May 1559, which is in the Collection, after great acknowledg- Collect. ments of his obligations to him and to all Zurich, "thanks him Numb. 48. "for quickening them to act with zeal and courage. There "was need of it; for besides those who had been always their "enemies, the deserters, who had left them in the former "reign, were now their most bitter enemies. Besides this, the "Spaniards had corrupted the morals of the nation to a great "degree. They were doing what they could, and all things 275 "were coming into a better state. The queen did very "solemnly refuse to be called head of the church: she thought "that title was only due to Christ. The universities were "strangely corrupted by Soto, and another Spanish monk: it "was scarce credible how much mischief they had done in so "little time. He tells him, that the lord Bedford had asked "him, What would be the most acceptable present that he "could send to him and his brethren? He answered, Nothing "could be so acceptable to them, as his expressing a zeal for "promoting the gospel, and against popery. That lord assured "him, he would do that faithfully: which, as he writes, he "was doing very sincerely. He writes also, how that several "princes were making addresses to the queen for her mar- "riage; but many suspected her inclinations lay to one Pick- "ering, a worthy and pious man, and one of a most noble "figure, as to his person. He refers him for other things to "his letters to Peter Martyr." On the sixth of April, Jewel wrote a particular account of the disputation; which though it is upon the matter the same that is in my History, yet since it is both a confirmation of it, and has some circumstances that are new, I have put it in my Collection. "He tells him that Collect. "Cole treated the reformers with many reproaches and much Numb. 49. "scorn, and called them seditious incendiaries. He delivered "his speech with great emotion, stamping with his feet, and "putting himself as in convulsions. He said, the apostles "divided their work into two provinces, the *western* and the "*eastern*: the first St. Peter and St. Paul had given to them, "where the worship was to be all in Latin; the *eastern* di- "vision fell to the other apostles, where all was to be performed "in Greek. This he introduced with pomp, as a thing certain. "He affirmed, that it was not fit the people should understand

" the public worship; for ignorance was the mother of devo-
" tion. The paper prepared by the reformers was read gravely
" and modestly by Horne: so that all who were present (he
" names the earl of Shrewsbury in particular) acknowledged
" the victory was clearly on their side. By this, and by what
" happened the second day, the popish cause sank much in the
" opinion of the people."

Collect.
Numb. 50.

On the 28th of April, in another letter, which is in the
Collection, he tells Peter Martyr how earnestly the bishops
contended in the house of lords. "Feckenham defended
" monastic orders from the sons of the prophets, and the
" Nazarites among the Jews; and said, Christ and his apo-
" stles were monks. None struggled more vehemently than
" Thirlby. He saw a design at court of seizing on the
" bishops' manors, and assigning parsonages to them instead
" of them : but he laments most of all, that no care was taken
" of schools, or of promoting learning; the universities were
" in a most miserable condition. The earl of Bedford pressed
" the queen to send for Peter Martyr; she said she would do
" it : but as much as Jewel desired to see him, he writes, that
" he would not advise his coming over, if he was not sent for
" with such an earnest and honourable invitation as he de-
" served to have. He saw many of the queen's ministers
" were in hope to enter into the Smalcaldic league; and one
" who had been a bishop possessed them with an opinion, that
" if Martyr were brought over, that would obstruct the other 276
" design : he expresses an ill opinion of that person, but does
" not name him :" it must have been either Barlow, Scory, or
Coverdale, for these were all the bishops of the reformation
that were then alive; Coverdale, as being a Dane[6], is the
likest to have been engaged in the Lutheran opinion. He
concludes his letter, that those who had returned from their
exile were yet in great misery, no care being taken of them.

He com-
plains of
want of

His next is on the 10th of April[7]: "He laments the want
" of zeal and industry in promoting the reformation; far short

---

[6] [Vide Supra, p. 220.]

[7] [This letter, which is dated
April 14, 1559, should have been
mentioned before that of April 28th.
Jewel especially mentions it as his

third letter to Peter Martyr, and
that of the 28th of April as his
fourth. It is the 6th letter in the
first volume of Zurich Letters,
1558-1579, p. 9.]

" of what the papists shewed in queen Mary's time. Then zeal, and an excess of caution.
" every thing was carried on violently, without staying either
" for law or precedent. But now every thing is managed [Epistolæ Tigurinæ, 1558-1579, Ep.vi.p.9.]
" in so slow, so cautious and prudent a manner, as if the word
" of God was not to be received upon his own authority : so
" that, as Christ was thrown out by his enemies, he is now
" kept out by his friends. This caution made that the spirits
" of those that favoured them were sunk, while their enemies
" were much exalted upon it. Yet he acknowledges, that
" though no law was made abrogating the mass, it was in
" many places laid down. The nobility seemed zealous in
" their hatred of popery. The queen had indeed softened her
" mass much ; but there were many things amiss that were
" left in it : if she could be prevailed on to put the crucifix out
" of her chapel, it would give a general encouragement ; she
" was truly pious, but thought it necessary to proceed by law,
" and that it was dangerous to give way to a furious multi-
" tude."

Cox, on the 20th of May, wrote to Weidner, another divine [Epistolæ Tigurinæ, Ep. xi. p. 15.]
of Zurich, whom he calls a venerable old man. " He tells
" him, that they found the short reign of queen Mary had
" such effects in hardening the minds of the people in their
" superstition, that it would not be easy to change the nation.
" Great opposition was made to every good motion by the
" *Scribes* and *Pharisees* in the house of lords ; for there was
" none there that could maintain arguments against the
" bishops : but the divines who were returned from their exile
" were called to preach at court before the queen ; where
" they plainly affirmed that the pope was Antichrist, and that
" their traditions were blasphemies. Some of the nobility
" came every day over to them, and many of the people, but
" not one of the clergy ; they stuck all together as a body
" that was not to be moved. He tells him the event that the
" public disputation had ; and that now king Edward's laws
" were to be revived. Thus, says he, God has regarded the
" low estate we were in, and with his fatherly compassion has
" pitied us, and taken off the cross we lay under. God grant
" these his great and inestimable benefits may never be for-
" gotten by us. But he laments, that, while there was so
" great a harvest, there were so few labourers."

All business was brought to a good conclusion in parliament. The king of France's unlooked-for death had given such a change to the face of affairs abroad, that the queen and her ministers seemed to be animated with more courage than had appeared hitherto.   Of this there is a letter of Jewel's in the Collection.   In the beginning of August, it appears, from another letter in the Collection, that preachers were sent to 277 many different parts.   " Many northern counties were assigned " to Sandys.   Jewel had a large province ; he was to make " a circuit of about seven hundred miles, through Berkshire, " Gloucestershire, Somersetshire, Devonshire, Cornwall, Dor- " setshire, and Wiltshire.   The popish bishops made a very " poor address to the queen, persuading her not to change the " state of religion ; to which she answered very resolutely : " and they, rather than abjure the pope once more, which " they had often done before, were resolved now to relinquish " their bishoprics.   It was plain they had no religion among " them ; yet now they pretended conscience : they were full " of rage ; and one of the artifices they used at that time to " keep the people from receiving the reformation was, the " giving out of prophecies, that this change would be short- " lived : howsoever the queen had courage ; so he thanks God " for the state to which their affairs were then brought. " Matters went well in Scotland : Knox was preaching in " many places of the country, well guarded : the monasteries " were everywhere pulled down, and all the superstitious stuff " that was in them was destroyed.   The young king of France " took among his titles both England and Scotland.   He under- " stood it was designed to make himself bishop of Salisbury ; " but he was positively resolved to decline it."   In the letters sent me from Zurich I find none of Grindal's on this occasion ; but Mr. Strype in his Life has informed the world, that Grindal, when he knew he was designed to be a bishop, wrote to Peter Martyr for his opinion in several matters.   I shall give the substance of his letter.   " He did not approve of the " queen's taking away the estates of the bishoprics, and giving " them parsonages instead of them : he thought this was the " patrimony of the inferior clergy ; so he did not see how " they could be supplied, if these were given to the bishops. " He had also a doubt concerning the popish vestments.   At

Marginal notes:

Collect. Numb. 51.

Collect. Numb. 52.

[Strype's Grindal, p. 29.]

"another time he asked his advice, whether the popish priests,
"upon their changing again, should be received and continued
"in their functions? or whether such of them as had been
"concerned in the late cruelty ought not to be prosecuted for
"that?"

To all this Peter Martyr answered, "That for the taking Peter Mar-
"away the bishops' estates, and giving them parsonages for tyr's ad-
"them, they could neither hinder nor help it; but they ought Grindal.
"out of them to support the clergy that laboured in those
"parishes. For the habits, he confessed he did not love
"them; for while he was a canon in Oxford he never would [Ibid.
"use the surplice. He thought they ought to do what they p. 30.]
"could to get them to be laid aside; but that, if that could
"not be done, he thought he might do more good, even in
"that particular, by submitting to it, and accepting a bishop-
"ric, which might give him an interest to procure a change
"afterwards. As for the popish priests, he advised the for- [Ibid.
"giving all that was past; and the receiving them, according p. 31.]
"to the practice of the primitive church in the return of the
"Arians to the orthodox body. But they were to watch over
"them, and to instruct and examine them with more care."
This answer came too late, for Grindal was consecrated before
278 he got it; but it was no doubt a great satisfaction to him, to
find that a person whom he esteemed so highly approved of
the resolution that he had taken : in which it was probable
Jewel's opinion, of whom they had all a high esteem, might
contribute to settle him ; for though he disliked the use of
those vestments, and treats the insisting so much on it with
great contempt, yet, on the other hand, he blames those who
laid too much weight upon that matter, and so looked on it as
a thing of more importance than truly it was.

They all rejoiced in the happy turn of affairs then in Scotland, the much greater part of that nation declaring themselves
openly and zealously against popery.

Here I shall insert an account concerning Scotland, of what The begin-
happened in the reign of king Henry, but that came not to nings of the
my knowledge till the impression of this volume was advanced tion in the
to the reign of queen Mary. The Scottish nation was so well parliament
disposed towards the reformation, that immediately upon king land.

[Dec. 14, 1542.] James the Fifth's death, which was in December 1541 [b], there appeared a wonderful inclination among them to be better informed in matters of religion. Cardinal Beaton, to prevent this, had got a will to be forged, in the name of the deceased king, constituting him regent: but as that was discovered to be a forgery, so the nobility had no regard to it, but owned the earl of Arran to be the second person in the kingdom; and that he was, next to the young queen and the heirs of her body, the heir of the crown. So they took the oaths of allegiance to the queen as their sovereign, and to the earl of Arran as their governor till the queen was of perfect age: and upon that the cardinal was secured.

[March 12, 1543.] A parliament was summoned to meet in May 1542, in which the regency of the earl of Arran was of new confirmed on the 13th [9] of May; and all the subjects were required to obey him in all things pertaining to that office, conform to the acts formerly made; which were again ratified by that parliament. They also ratified the oaths that had been taken to him by some lords spiritual and temporal; and all who were present were required to confirm these oaths by solemn oaths in full parliament; which they all did by the holding up of their right hands, swearing that they would be true and obedient to the lord governor, and serve him with their persons, kindred, friends, and goods, and no other, during the queen's nonage.

[March 15.] On the 15th of May [10], they ordered an authentic publication to be made of all they had done under the great seal; and they all affixed their seals to the instrument made to confirm this settlement. On the same day a council was named; six of these was the number that was at the least necessary to concur with the governor. The cardinal was not one of them. The archbishop of Glasgow, who was lord chancellor; with the bishops of Aberdeen, Moray, Orkney, Ross, and Brechin;

---

[8] [This date is a mistake for 1542.]

[9] [Parliament met on the 12th of March 1543, and James, earl of Arran, was appointed governor of the kingdom, during the nonage of the queen, on the next day, March 13. Vid. Acta Parl. Scot. vol. ii. p. 411.]

[10] [This is another mistake. The parliament was prorogued by order of the earl of Arran, March 19th. Vid. Acta Parl. Scot. vol. ii. p. 425.]

and the abbots of Dunfermline and Coupar, were for the ecclesiastical state. The earls of Angus, Huntly, Murray, Argyle,
Bothwell, Marshall, Cassillis, and Glencairn ; and the lords
Erskine, Ruthven, Maxwell, Seton, and Methuen, for the nobility ; with some other commoners of the boroughs. After
279 whom, the treasurer, the secretary, the clerk of register, the
justice clerk, and the queen's advocate, are named. It seems
they intended that no peers should be created but with the
concurrence of the parliament : for the governor, with the
advice and consent of the estates of parliament, made the lord
Stewart of Ochiltree a peer, to have vote and place in parliament. In the same record, mention is made of the draught
of an act offered by the lord Maxwell to the lords of the articles, in these words :

It is statute and ordained, that it shal be lawful to all [Acta Parl.
our sovereign lady's lieges, to have the holy writ of the New Scot. ii.
415.]
Testament and the Old, in the vulgar tongue, in Inglis or
Scotts, of a good and tru translation; and that they shall
incurre no crime, for the having, or reding of the same.
Provided always, that no man dispute, or hold opinions,
under the pains contained in the acts of parliament [11].

The lords of articles found this reasonable ; and thought,
that the Bible might be used among all the lieges of the realm,
in our vulgar tongue, of a good, true, and just translation,
because there was no law shewed to the contrary. And therefore they agreed, that none should incur any crime for having
or reading it, nor be accused for it : but added the proviso that
was added to the draught offered to them.

But the archbishop of Glasgow did in his own name, and in The use of
the name of all the prelates of the realm that were present in the scriptures in
parliament when the act came to be read in full parliament, the vulgar
dissent (simpliciter) *to it, as being one of the three estates of* tongue
much op-
the parliament : and they opponed them thereto, unto the posed :
[ibid.]
time that a provincial council might be had of all the clergy
of this realm, to advise and conclude thereupon ; if the same
be necessary to be had in the vulgar tongue, to be used among
the queen's lieges or not ; and thereafter to shew the utter

[11] [This is not an exact copy,   affairs of Church and State in Scot-
either in spelling or as regards the   land, vol. i. p. 89. ed. Edin. 8vo.
words. See Keith's History of the   1844.]

determination that shall be done in that behalf. Upon this he demanded an instrument to be made, according to the forms in that kingdom. But notwithstanding this opposition, the act passed. For in the same record, there is an order entered, as signed by the governor, requiring the clerk of register to cause the acts passed in parliament to be pro-claimed; *and in special, the act made for having the New Testament in vulgar tongue, with certain additions.* In the copy sent me, this bears date the 19th of March, but I believe it should be May; since the matter was not before the parliament till May [12]. I have set down all this matter almost in the words of the record of parliament that was sent me.

But granted.
[Ibid. p. 425.]

In the same record, the instructions are set down that were given to the ambassadors, that were sent to treat concerning the queen's marriage with Edward, then prince of Wales : in which it appears, that they thought it necessary, if their sovereign went out of the kingdom, even after she was of perfect age, yet that the governor of the realm should continue to exercise his authority all the days of his life : and that after his death, the nearest lawful person of the blood should succeed to the said office, by a large and ample commission; of 280 which they order a form to be devised.

The free use of the scriptures was a great step to let the nation look into the nature of the Christian religion : and the clergy foresaw well the consequences that would naturally follow upon it; so it was no wonder that this was opposed so zealously by them. It was a great piece of foresight, to secure the nation, by having a governor with full powers still residing amongst them. In the subsequent treaty with France, there was not that care nor precaution used : but at the conclusion of the marriage, the French proceeded in so perfidious a manner, as to give a warning to all who in future times should treat with that court. For on the 4th of April 1558, (a fortnight before the articles of the marriage were settled, which was on the 19th of April,) the young queen being then but little more than fifteen, a secret act was passed; in which, after she had set forth the ancient alliance between the two crowns, and the honourable entertainment that she had received from the present king of France;

[12] [See notes 9 and 10, p. 478.]

"She, to confirm and establish the affection between the
"two kingdoms, and in order to unite the kingdom of Scot-
"land to the crown of France, in case she should die without
"heirs of her body, had made some dispositions in favour of
"the crown of France, which she intended should have their
"full effect: yet she, by a communication with the deputies
"sent from Scotland, saw into the secret designs of some, who
"were practising to the effect, that, in default of heirs of her
"body, the crown should descend to some lords of the coun-
"try; depriving her by that means, to her great regret, of
"the power of disposing of it. Yet since she could not at that
"time openly oppose them, for certain just causes of fear;
"and considering that she was out of her kingdom, and had
"no strong places in it at her own disposal; and that great
"troubles might arise, if what she was then doing should be
"publicly known; especially considering the present war with
"the kingdom of England: she therefore did protest, that
"what consent or agreement soever she should make to the
"articles and instructions sent over by the states of her
"kingdom, with relation to the succession, in case she
"should die without heirs of her body; she intended still,
"that the disposition then made in favour of the crown of
"France should have its full and entire effect, notwithstand-
"ing any agreement she had made, or should yet make,
"conform to these instructions, as a thing contrary to her
"will and intention." Upon which she demanded an act from
the keeper of the great seal, Bertrandi, who was made a cardinal that year.

A perfidious proceeding of the court of France.

This instrument was signed by her, and by the dauphin;
and is printed in that great collection of the treaties of France,
that was published twenty years ago [13]. It opens a scene of
treachery, that, how much soever the design was suspected,
(as will appear by the paper, of which an account will be given
in the following relation,) yet it was never certainly known,
281 till they themselves have made their own shame thus known

Recueil des Traités, t. ii. p. 510

[13] [Leonard (Frederic). Recueil
des Traitez de Paix, de Treve, de
Neutralité, de Confederation, d'Alliance et de Commerce, faits par
les Rois de France avec tous les
Princes et Potentats de l'Europe,
et autres depuis pres de trois siecles
en six tomes. A Rotterdam chez
Reinier Leers 1693. 4to.]

to the world.   But at that time this was so carefully concealed, that Francis the Second sent a formal obligation under his great seal ; by which he bound himself to the duke of Châtel-herault, to maintain his right of succeeding to the crown of Scotland, in case the queen should die without heirs of her own body.   The original obligation is still preserved in Hamilton.   The queen's secret act was as ill-grounded in law, as it was perfidious in itself: for certainly, what power soever our princes, with the concurrence of their parliaments, have to limit the succession to the crown, our princes themselves cannot, by any private act of their own, alter the succession, or dispose of it at pleasure.   But to return to that which has led me into this digression.

The knowledge of religion, that the free use of the scriptures brought the nation to, had such an effect, that the reformation was every where desired ; and the vices and ignorance of the popish clergy gave all people an aversion to them. This was long connived at even by the queen mother, during her government : but now that she thought all was sure, she threw off the mask, and declared herself an open enemy to those whom she had courted hitherto, and seemed to favour. Upon this there was a great and a sudden turn.   Popery was the object of all men's hatred : the churches were purged from idolatry and superstition : the monasteries were broke into ; and many acts of hot and irregular zeal were complained of in all the corners of the kingdom.

One thing is not a little to the honour of Knox and his followers in that tumultuary reformation, that the multitude was so governed, even amidst all that popular heat, that no blood was shed, and no man was killed in it : which being positively delivered by Lesley[14], bishop of Ross, that must be looked on as a testimony beyond exception.

But since the affairs of Scotland have not hitherto been so clearly represented, as I find them stated in some original papers, that I fell on in the Cotton library ; I will give a full account of them, as far as those papers do guide me.

[14] Nobilium qui hæreseos obstringebantur crimine, humanitas non est reticenda, quod eo tempore paucos catholicos de religionis re mulctarint exilio, pauciores carcere, morte nullos.—Leslæus de Rebus Scot. [lib. x. p. 581. ed. Rom. 1578.]

There is a long representation drawn up, of the breach of faith, and of the violation of their laws, during the government of the queen regent of Scotland : at the end of which, there is a petition to the queen, signed by the great lords of that kingdom, in which both papists and protestants concurred. And in order to obtain that concurrence, the matters of religion are not insisted on; but the continued course of a perfidious and illegal administration is charged on the queen dowager. So that from this it appears, that the war was not begun, nor carried on, upon the account of religion, but upon the pretence of public and national rights. I have put it in the Collection.

Collect. Numb. 53.

" They begin it to shew, that the arms that they were forced
" to fly to was no rebellion. They run the matter back to the
" first proposition for carrying their queen into France : which,
" they say, was obtained, partly by corruption with money,
" partly by authority, and partly by fair promises : yet before
282 " that was agreed to, a treaty was made by the parliament,
" and sworn to, as well as ratified by the great seals of the
" king and dauphin of France, that Scotland should be go-
" verned by their own laws, and by the nobility and people of
" Scotland : that all offices should be given to them ; and, that
" no garrisons of the French should be admitted to settle in
" the kingdom. Great practice was made after that to bring
" the parliament to consent that their queen should marry the
" dauphin : and to obtain that, the succession to the crown was
" declared to belong to the duke of Châtelherault and his
" heirs, after the heirs of the queen's body. New oaths were
" then taken, and charters given under the great seal of
" France, and under their queen and the dauphin's seal, that
" Scotland should be governed by a council of natives : the
" castles were also to be put in sure hands. Duplicates of
" these were lodged in the castle of Edinburgh, and with the
" duke of Châtelherault. Upon this, an embassy was sent to
" France, of two bishops, two earls, and four lords ; and the
" marriage was concluded. They were upon that dealt with,
" to endeavour that the crown of Scotland might be given to
" the dauphin. They refused to undertake that ; and believed
" that it could not be brought about. The word upon that was

" changed. And it was desired only, that the *matrimonial*
" *crown* might be sent him ;" (which was afterwards explained
in the act of parliament that granted it, that he should be
king of Scotland during life.) " The lords were suffered to
" return : but when they came to Dieppe, one bishop, two
" earls, and two lords died in one night. The three that were
" left came home much amazed, believing that the others had
" been poisoned."

Here I must add another particular relating to that deputation. In the council-book that goes from April 1554 to
January 1558, that was cast by and neglected, many leaves
being cut out of it, and was first discovered by a nephew of
mine, whom I desired to search their register for me ; it
appears, that on the 13th of December 1557 there was a tax
laid on the kingdom, to be paid in before Easter, for the
expense of that embassy, of fifteen thousand pounds Scots
money, that is, one thousand two hundred and fifty pound
sterling ; which was to be levied by the same proportion that
all the taxes were then levied ; of which there are several
instances in that book : the one half was levied on the spiritualty ; and two thirds of the other half was on estates in land,
and the other third was levied on the boroughs. This shews
that the estates of the spiritualty were then reckoned by a
settled proportion, the full half of the kingdom. The persons
deputed were, the archbishop of Glasgow, the bishop of Orkney,
and the prior of St. Andrew's, (afterwards earl of Murray ;)
the earls of Cassillis and Rothes, and the lord Fleming ; with
the provost of Edinburgh, and of Montrose. When I wondered
how so small a sum could answer the expense of so great an
embassy, on such an occasion ; he shewed me, that either the
value of money, or, which is the same thing, the value of things
to be purchased by money, is almost incredibly changed now,
in the course of a hundred and sixty years ; of which he **283**
gave me this instance : the tun of wine was then by act of
parliament to be sold at twenty livres ; or, in sterling money,
at one pound thirteen shillings and fourpence ; and in the
retailing it, their pint, which is four English pints, was to be
sold at four farthings, their penny having six farthings ; so
that, reducing this to English measures, three quarts of wine

were to be sold at a penny. This I thought was a small digression which the reader would not be ill pleased to find laid
in his way. To return to the Scotch memorial.

" The queen dowager took two methods to gain her point :
" the one was, to shew favour to all those who had received no
" favour of the duke during his government, because they were
" in the interest of England ; whereas he was at that time in
" the interest of France. The other was, she offered them a
" permission to live according to their conscience in religion :
" in conclusion, the queen dowager brought the parliament to
" give the matrimonial crown to the dauphin ; but with this con-
" dition, that the duke's right should not be impaired by it."

When all this was obtained, the queen forgot all her promises:
" She began with the greatest of the Scottish lords then in
" office, the earl of Huntley, who was then lord chancellor,
" and the duke's particular friend ; she took the great seal
" from him, and gave it to one Rubay, a French advocate : she
" also put the earl of Huntley in prison, and set a great fine on
" him, and left him only the name of chancellor. She made
" another Frenchman comptroller, who had the charge of the
" revenue of the crown : and she put all Scotchmen out of the
" secrets of the council, committing these only to Frenchmen.
" She kept in several places garrisons of Frenchmen, who lived
" on discretion. She gave them no pay. She sent the revenue
" of the crown to France ; and brought over some base money
" that was decried in France, and made it current in Scotland.
" She also set up a mint for coining base money, with which
" she paid the soldiers. She tried to get the castle of Edin-
" burgh into her hands, but that failed her. She gave such
" abbeys as fell void to Frenchmen, as to her brother the car-
" dinal of Guise, and others : and for the space of three years
" she kept all that fell void in her own hands, except such as
" were of any value ; and these she bestowed on Frenchmen.
" Nor did she ever follow the advice of those lords, who, upon
" her first entering upon the government, were named to be of
" the council. Many intercessions were made to her, upon
" these proceedings, by the nobility : sometimes companies of
" them joined together ; and sometimes they applied to her
" more privately, for they foresaw that they could not be
" borne long.

" The queen dowager set herself next to a practice, which
" of all others was both the most dangerous and the most dis-
" honourable, to set aside the duke and his house : pains was
" taken to engage the lord James and other lords in it, who
" had no friendship for the duke ; to whom the queen dowager
" promised that she would bear with their devotion in religion,
" if they would join with her against the duke in favour of the
" French. This encouraged them to do those things by which
" they incurred the censures of the church ; and were by reason 284
" of a law not much known brought in danger of the guilt of
" treason. So process was ordered against them : and upon
" that the queen dowager tempted them to engage in the
" French interest : but that not prevailing, they were declared
" traitors. The rest of the nobility being alarmed at this, the
" queen dowager brought out her French garrisons, and dis-
" posed of their estates, and entered into St. John's town in a
" warlike manner : she changed the magistrates, and left a
" garrison in the town. The whole nation was alarmed at
" this, and were coming together in great numbers. But she
" not having force enough to conquer the nation, sent for the
" duke and the earl of Huntley, and employed them to quiet
" the country ; promising that every thing should be redressed
" in a parliament that should be held next spring, with many
" other more particular promises : upon this assurance these
" lords quieted the country. While this was a doing, the
" duke's eldest son, being then in France, was sent for to
" court ; but he had secret advertisements sent him, that it was
" resolved to proceed against him to the utmost extremity for
" heresy : upon which he kept out of the way, till an order
" was sent to bring him in, dead or alive : upon that he made
" his escape ; but they seized on a younger brother of his, of
" the age of fifteen, and put him in prison.
    " In Scotland the nobility had separated themselves, trusting
" to the faith that the duke had given them, that all things
" should be kept quiet till the parliament. But some com-
" panies coming out of France to Leith, the queen dowager
" ordered that town to be fortified, and put twenty-two ensigns
" of foot, with one troop of horse, in it. The nobility upon
" that charged the duke with breach of faith, who could do no
" more but press the queen to forbear to give such cause of

" jealousy; but all was to no purpose. The town was for-
" tified; all the ammunition she had was carried into it, and
" the French continued still· to be sending over more forces.
" The duke, with the nobility, represented to the queen dowa-
" ger, that it was now plain she designed a conquest : but she
" despised all their requests; for by this time the French
" thought they were so strong, that they reckoned it would be
" a short work to subdue Scotland.   There were but two or
" three mean lords, Bothwell and Seaton, that kept company
" with the queen dowager; yet even these signified to their
" friends, that their hearts were with their countrymen. Upon
" all this, the duke, with the rest of the nobility, and with the
" barons and burgesses of the realm, seeing an imminent
" danger to the whole nation, and no hope of remedy at her
" hands, began deeply to consider the state of the kingdom :
" their sovereign lady was married to a strange prince out of
" the realm, and wholly in the hands of Frenchmen, without
" any council of her own natural people ; and they considered
" the mortality of her husband, or of herself without issue.
" The queen dowager, sister to the house that ruled all in
" France, persisted in ruining the liberties of her daughter the
" queen's subjects, on design to knit that kingdom for ever to
285 " France ; and so to execute the old malice of the French on
" the crown of England, of which they had already assumed
" the title.
      " They upon all these grounds were constrained to consti-
" tute a council for the government of the kingdom, and for
" the use of their sovereign, to whom they had signified the
" suspension of the queen dowager's authority ; maintaining,
" that, being sore oppressed with French power, they had, as
" natural subjects, sufficient strength for that, though they are
" not able to stand against the power of France : but partly
." for the right of their sovereign, and partly for the ancient
" rights of the crown, they have been forced to spend their
" whole substance ; yet they cannot longer preserve them-
" selves from being conquered by the power sent over from
" France, a greater force being promised to be sent next
" spring.   They therefore lay the whole matter before the
" queen of England's ministers, then upon their borders, and
" commit their cause to her protection ; desiring nothing but

" that their country may be preserved from France, to-
" gether with the rights of their sovereign, and of the whole
" nation."

To this they add a petition, " that the numbers of French
" soldiers then within the kingdom might be removed speedily;
" that so they might live quietly, and be suffered to offer to
" the king and queen such articles as were necessary for the
" peace and good government of the kingdom, without altera-
" tion of their ancient liberties :" this was signed by the earl
of Arran, as he was then called, but that was his father's title ;
for he had no higher title in Scotland : the son therefore
signed James Hamilton.   It was also signed by the earls of
Argyle and Glencairn ;   by lord James, afterwards created
earl of Murray ; and by the lords Boyd, Ochiltree, Maxwell,
and Ruthven ; and by a son of the earl of Huntley's, and a son
of the earl of Athol's ; both these families being at that time
papists.   And thus, by the tenor of this whole paper, it
appears that religion was not pretended to be the cause of
the war.

Upon the suspending the authority of the queen regent, I
will here add a particular reflection, which will shew what
archbishop Spotswood's sense was, when he first wrote his
History of that transaction.   He gives an account of the
opinion that Willock and Knox delivered, when they were
called and required to give it, which they did in favour of
that suspension ; for which he censures the opinion itself in
these words : *Howbeit the power of the magistrate be limited,
and their office prescribed by God, and that they may likewise fall into great offences ; yet it is nowhere permitted to
subjects to call their princes in question, or to make insurrection against them : God having reserved the punishment
of princes to himself.*   Yet in a fair manuscript of that history, written with great care, as for the press, this whole
period was first penned quite in another strain : *Allowing the
states of the kingdom a right to restrain their prince, when
he breaks through rules ; only censuring clergymen's meddling in those matters :* this is scored through, but so that it
is still legible ; and Spotswood interlined with his own hand
the alteration ; according to which his book was printed.   This
manuscript belonged to me ; and forty-two years ago I pre- 286

sented it to the duke of Lauderdale, and shewed him that passage, on which he made great reflection. I cannot find out in whose hands that manuscript is fallen; but whosoever has it, will, I hope, justify me in this particular : for though I am not sure as to the words, yet I am very sure they are to this purpose.

* * I have laid out, by all the methods I could think on, for that MS. of archbishop Spotswood's history, that I mention page 285. I once thought I had found it; for I fell on one copy that had belonged to the late duke of Lauderdale; but it was not that which had belonged to me : yet by that I see, that archbishop came gradually, and not all at once, out of his first opinion. For in this MS. there is a material difference in the correction that is in the archbishop's own hand, from the first draught. The first draught is, that princes *may commit offences deserving deprivation:* but the correction is, *They may fall into great offences,* without any more. A little after he had written, *whatsoever may be thought of this opinion;* which imports some doubt concerning it : these words are struck out; but so that they are still legible. A little after that, the MS. has it, that *by an act of council, all the errors committed by the queen regent were reckoned up.* This is softened, by these words inserted after *errors; alleged to have been committed.* Thus it appears, that the archbishop's first notions had carried him to write in a style that wanted great correction, as his thoughts grew into a better digestion, or as his interests carried him to see things in a different light, from that in which they had at first appeared to him. * *

When this representation and petition was brought to the queen, Cecil drew up a state of the matter, which will be found in the Collection; putting this as the question, *Whether* [Collect. *it was meet that England should help Scotland to expel the* Numb. 54. *French or not ?* For the negative he says, " It was against " God's law to aid any subjects against their natural prince " or their ministers : it was also dangerous to do it : for an " aid secretly given would be to no purpose : and an aid pub- " licly given would draw on a war ; and in that case, the " French would come to any composition with the Scots, to " join with them against England : since they will consent to

" any thing, rather than suffer Scotland to be united to the
" crown of England.   He adds, It may also be apprehended,
" that the emperor, the king of Spain, the pope, and the duke
" of Savoy, with the potentates of Italy, will join with the
" French king, rather than suffer these two kingdoms to be
" joined in one manner of religion; and many within both
" kingdoms will not approve of this.   But, in opposition to all
" this, he concludes for assisting the Scots.

" He lays it down for a principle, that it is agreeable to the
" laws of God and of nature, that every prince and state
" should defend itself; not only from perils that are seen,
" but from those that may probably come after : to which he
" adds, that nature and reason teach every person politic, or
" other, to use the same manner of defence that the adversary
" useth of offence.   Upon these grounds he concludes, that
" England might and ought to assist the Scots to keep out the
" French : and so earnest was that great statesman in this
" matter, that he prosecutes it very copiously.

" His first reason is that which the Scots would never
" admit, but he might think it proper to offer it to an English
" council ; that the crown of England had a superiority over
" Scotland, such as the emperor had over Bohemia or Milan.
" He next shews that England must be in great danger from
" the French, if they became the absolute masters of Scotland.
" Upon this he runs out to shew, that the French had been
" long enemies to England ; that they had been false and
" double in all their treaties with them these seven hundred
" years ; and that the last peace was forced from them by
" their poverty.   That France could not be poor above two
" years ; nor could it be long without war ; beside the hatred
" that the house of Guise, who then governed the French
" councils, bore to England.   They call in question the queen's
" title, and set up their own against it : and at the treaty of
" Cambray they set that pretension on foot ; but it was then
" stopped by the wisdom of the constable : yet they used
" means at Rome to get the queen to be declared illegitimate ;
" upon which the bull was brought into France : and at the
" solemnities, in which the king was killed, the arms of Eng- 287
" land and Ireland were joined with the queen of Scots' arms.
" The present embroilment in Scotland is the stop that now

" restrains them from carrying these pretensions further ; but
" as soon as they can, they will certainly set them on foot :
" and the assaulting England by the way of Scotland is so
" easy, that it is not possible to avoid it, but by stopping the
" progress of that conquest. A war by the way of Scotland
" puts France in no danger, though it should miscarry ; but
" England is in the utmost danger, if it should succeed. He
" concludes, That as the matter was of the last importance, so
" no time was to be lost ; since the prejudice, if too long de-
" layed, would be irrecoverable."

What further steps were made in the secret debating of this
point does not appear to me but by the conclusion of the
matter : for the queen sent forces, under the command of the
duke of Norfolk, to the borders of Scotland. What followed
upon that is set out fully in the common historians, and from
them in my former work.

But a copy of the bond of association into which the lords
and others in Scotland entered, (the original of which remains
still in the possession of the duchess of Hamilton,) will set out
more particularly the grounds that they went on. It is in the
Collection : and it sets forth, " that they promised faithfully, Collect.
" and in the presence of God, that they would to the utmost Numb. 55.
" of their power set forward the reformation of religion, ac-
" cording to God's word ; that the true preaching of it might
" have a free passage through the whole kingdom ; together
" with the administration of the sacraments. And that they,
" considering the misbehaviour of the French among them,
" and the intolerable oppression of the poor by their soldiers,
" maintained by the queen dowager, under colour of authority,
" together with the tyranny of their captains, and the mani-
" fest danger of becoming their conquest, to which they were
" then reduced by fortifications on the sea-coast, and other
" attempts ; do promise to join with the queen of England's
" army, then come in to their assistance, for driving out those
" their oppressors, and for recovering their ancient liberty ;
" that so they may be ruled by the laws and customs of their
" country, and by the natives of the kingdom, under the obe-
" dience of the king and queen their sovereign. And they
" promise that they shall hold no private intelligence with
" their enemies, but by the advice of the rest, or at the least

" of five of their number : and that they shall prosecute this
" cause as if it were the cause of every one of them in parti-
" cular, and hold all who withstand it as their enemies ; and
" that they will prosecute them as such, according to the
" orders of the council ; to whom they refer the direction of
" the whole matter, promising in all things to submit to their
" arbitration."

This was first subscribed at Edinburgh on the 27th of April,
in the year 1560; and is signed by the duke of Châtelherault,
the earls of Arran, Huntley, Argyle, Morton, and some others,
whose hands are not legible; and by the lords Saltoun, Ruthven,
Boyd, Ogilvy, Ochiltree, the abbot of Kinloss, and the commendator of Kilwinning : about one hundred and forty more 288
subscribed it. This was the bond that was signed by those
who were at that time at Edinburgh : and it is probable, that
many other bonds of the same nature were signed about the
same time, in other parts of the kingdom ; but they have not
been so carefully preserved as this has been. The earl of
Huntley, though he continued still a papist, signing it, shews,
that either the ill usage he had met with from the queen
dowager had shaken him in his religion, or that provocation
and interest were then stronger in him than his principles. But
I leave my conjectures to go on with the history.

The great
progress of
supersti-
tion in
queen
Mary's
reign.
Collect.
Numb. 56.

On the 2nd of November, Jewel being returned from the
circuit which he was ordered to make, wrote, (in a letter to
Peter Martyr, to be found in the Collection,) " that the people
" were much better disposed to the gospel than it was appre-
" hended they could be : but he adds, that superstition had
" made a most extraordinary progress in queen Mary's short
" reign. The people were made believe they had in many
" places pieces of the true cross, and of the nails with which
" Christ was crucified : so that the cathedral churches were
" dens of robbers ; and none were more violent and obstinate,
" than those who had been before of their body ; as if by that
" they would justify their falling off from them. They had
" turned them all out. Harding went away, and would not
" change again. Smith, who had been a violent opposer of
" Peter Martyr in Oxford, fled towards Scotland; but was
" taken on the borders, and brought back ; and had abjured a
" fifth time, and was then become a violent enemy to the

" papists."   In another letter he tells him, " Smith was mar-
" ried[15]; and that, being hated and despised by all sides, he
" was forced to keep a public house."   Jewel wrote, " that if
" they had more hands matters would go well : but it was
" hard to make a cart go without horses.   He was glad to
" hear Peter Martyr was sent for.   But he owns he had his
" fears still, that though things were begun well, they would
" not end so well.   He adds, *We are islanders in all respects.*
" Oxford wanted him extremely.   The queen was then courted
" both by the king of Sweden and by Charles of Austria."
It was then given out that Sweden was full of mines of gold,
and only wanted skill and industry to work them: but he
writes, " Perhaps the queen meant to marry one nearer at
" hand :" (he gives no other hint in that letter, to let it be
understood of whom he meant: probably it was Pickering ; as
appears in another letter.)   He concludes, " that though reli-
" gion did make a quick progress in Scotland, yet that the
" French did not despair of bringing that kingdom back to
" their obedience, and of restoring their religion in it."

   On the same day he wrote to Simler, who had congratulated
him upon the news they had of his being to be promoted to a
bishopric.   He wrote, " that there was yet nothing but a
" nomination of him.   He adds, We hope our bishops shall be
" pastors, labourers, and watchmen.   And that they may be
" better fitted for this, the great riches of bishoprics are to be
289 " diminished, and to be reduced to a certain mediocrity : that
" so, being delivered from that king-like pomp, and the noisi-
" ness of a courtly family, they may live in greater tranquillity,
" and may have more leisure to take care of Christ's flock with
" due attention."

   On the 5th of November he wrote, " that he found debates
" raised concerning the vestments, which he calls the habit of
" the stage, and wishes they could be freed from it.   He says,
" they were not wanting to so good a cause : but others seemed

Marginal notes:
[Epistolæ Tigurinæ, 1558-1579, Ep. xxxiv. p. 47.]
[Epistolæ Tigurinæ, 1558-1579, Ep. xix. p. 25.]
[Ibid. Ep. xiv. p. 20.]
The revenues of bishops lessened, that they may be more diligent in their duty. [Epistolæ Tigurinæ, 1558-1579, Ep. xxii. p. 29.]
Collect. Numb. 57. Jewel's opinion of the disputes concerning the vestments.

---

[15] [This letter is dated June 1, 1560.   In a previous letter, dated March 20, 1559, he says, " Faber tuus, præclarus scilicet patronus castitatis, deprehensus est in adulterio : et eâ causâ, quod alioqui vix solet fieri, cum Maria adhuc viveret, novo more, nullo exemplo jussus est cedere lectione theologicâ."—Epistolæ Tigurinæ, 1558-1579, Ep. iv. p. 6.]

" to love those things, and to follow the ignorance of some
" priests, who were stupid as logs of wood, having neither spirit,
" learning, nor good life to commend them ; but studied to
" recommend themselves by that comical habit : while no
" care was taken of learning or of breeding up of youth.
" They hoped to strike the eyes of the people with those
" ridiculous trifles.   These are the relics of the Amorites : that
" cannot be denied.   He wishes, that, at some time or other,
" all these may be taken away and extirpated, to the very
" deepest roots.   He complains of a feebleness in the councils :
" they still talked of bringing Martyr over ; but he feared
" that we looked too much towards Saxony to expect that.
" Some among them, he says, were so much set on the matter
" of the habits, as if the Christian religion consisted in gar-
" ments : but we (says he) are not called to the consultations
" concerning that scenical apparel : he could set no value on
" those fopperies.   Some were crying up a golden mediocrity ;
" he was afraid it would prove a leaden one."

Collect.
Numb. 58.

The queen
kept a cru-
cifix in her
chapel.

On the 16th of November he wrote, in a letter to be found
in the Collection, " that the doctrine was every where purely
" preached.   There was in many places too much folly con-
" cerning ceremonies and masks.   The crucifix continued still
" in the queen's chapel.   They all spake freely against it, but
" till then without effect.   There was a secret piece of worldly
" policy in this which he did not like.   He complains of the
" uncertain and island-like state of their affairs : all was loose
" at present.   He did not see in what they would settle ; and
" did not know but he should be obliged to return back to
" Zurich again."

Bishops
conse-
crated.

The em-
peror pro-
poses to
the queen
a match

In December and January the consecration of the bishops
came on.   But here a stop lies in my way.   For some months
the thread of the letters to Zurich, by which I have been
hitherto guided, is discontinued[16].   At this time an ambassador came over from Ferdinand the emperor, with letters dated
the 11th of February 1560[17], proposing a match between his

[16 [For seven letters between that
of Jewel of Nov. 16, 1559, and that
of Feb. 4, 1560, see the Index of
Letters arranged in Chronological
Order in the Second Series of Zurich Letters, 1558–1602, p. xviii.]

[17 [This is a beautifully written
copy, with the seal pasted on the
back of the letter, which is endorsed
*Serenissimæ Principi Dominæ Eli-
sabethæ Reginæ Angliæ et Franciæ
etc. Dominæ Hyberniæ etc. Sorori et*

son, archduke Charles, and the queen.   He had writ of it to her before, but thought fit to follow these letters with a formal embassy.   The originals are yet extant.   The queen wrote an answer in form, and signed it : but it seems that was on some considerations not thought fit to be sent : for the original is in the Paper-Office.   It will be found in the Collection.

" The queen wrote, that, examining her own sentiments in
" that matter very carefully, she did not perceive any inclina-
" tion to change her solitary life ; but found herself more fixed
" to continue still in it. She hoped the emperor would favour-
290 " ably receive, and rightly understand what she wrote to him.
" It might indeed seem strange, considering her age and her
" circumstances : but this was no new resolution, nor taken up
" on the sudden, but was the adhering to an old settled purpose.
" There had been a time in which her accepting some honour-
" able propositions might have delivered her out of very great
" dangers and troubles : on which she would make no other
" reflections, but that neither the fear of danger, nor the desire
" of liberty, could then move her to bring her mind to hearken
" to them. She will not, by a plain refusal, seem to offend
" him ; yet she cannot give occasion, by any of her words, to
" make him think that she accepts of that to which she cannot
" bring her mind and will."   Dated the 5th of January 1559.
Signed, Your Majesty's good sister and cousin, *Elizabeth :*
countersigned, *Rog. Ascham.*

Consanguineæ nostræ Charissimæ, and signed in a very bad hand *Ferdinandus.*

There is no proposal of a match in the letter, but an assurance that the queen's refusal would make no difference in the emperor's disposition towards her. The point of the letter is contained in the following paragraph :

Sed postquam res aliter cecidit, et Serenitas Vestra nunc iterum affirmat nondum etiam in animo suo ad connubium propensionem existere, non restat nobis aliud agendum quam Serenitatis vestræ voluntati acquiescere, neque enim sumus ejus animi, prout et superioribus mensi-

bus Serenitati vestræ scripsimus, quod velimus Serenitatem vestram vehementius aut importunius ad mutandum propositum urgere, eive modum ac legem præscribere quod vitæ genus amplecti debeat. Eâ namque prudentiâ et sapientiâ Serenitatem vestram prædicant ut nulla nos dubitatio teneat Serenitatem vestram ipsammet satis et abunde intelligere, quid sibi et quid Regno suo sit maxime necessarium ac consultum."

The letter, like all the other documents in this volume, is mounted, but is very nearly perfect, having been burnt round the edges, and lost a letter or two here and there.]

A confer-
ence con-
cerning the
queen's
crucifix.
Collect.
Numb. 60.

The first letter of Jewel's, after his consecration, is on the
4th of February 1560. It is in the Collection. He tells Peter
Martyr, " they were then engaged in the question about the
" lawfulness of having images in churches (which he calls *lis*
" *crucularia*). It could scarce be believed to what a degree
" of folly some men, who were thought to have a right judg-
" ment of things, were carried in that matter. There was not
" one of all those whom he knew, that was drawn to be of that
" mind, besides Cox. There was to be a conference concerning
" it the day following. Parker and Cox on the one hand, and
" Grindal and he on the other hand, were to debate it in the
" hearing of some of the council : he could not but laugh within
" himself, when he thought what grave and solid reasonings
" would be brought out on this occasion. He was told, that it
" was resolved on to have crucifixes of silver or tin set up in
" all churches ; and that such as would not obey this would be
" turned out of their bishoprics : if that was true, he would be
" no longer a bishop. White, bishop of Winchester, Oglo-
" thorp of Carlisle, Bayne of Coventry and Lichfield, and

[Epistolæ
Tigurinæ,
1558-1579.
Ep. xxxiv.
p. 48.]

" Tunstall of Durham, were lately dead." In another he
writes, " that Bonner was sent to the Tower, and that he went
" to see some criminals that were kept there, and called them
" his *friends* and *neighbours :* but one of them answered, Go,
" you beast, into hell, and find your *friends* there ; for we are
" none of them. I killed but one man upon a provocation, and
" do truly repent of it ; but you have killed many holy persons,
" of all sorts, without any provocation from them, and are
" hardened in your impenitence [18]."

The zeal
in singing
psalms.

On the 5th of March he writes, " that a change appeared

---

[18] [" Episcopi aliquot Mariani
sunt in turri Londinensi in veteri
hospitio suo ubi antea fuerat sub
Edvardo rege. Quo cum abductus
esset, et in medium jam carcerem
pervenisset, et, ut est homo perur-
banus, et non tantum animo sed
etiam facie ut scis liberali vinctos
quos ibi reperit, officiose salutâsset
et amicos ac socios appellâsset re-
clamavit statim quidam e numero :
" Et egone" inquit " bestia, videor
tibi socius esse tuus ? Abi quo dig-
nus es ad inferos; ibi invenies socios.
Ego unum tantum hominem eumque
inductus aliquâ causâ, occidi : tu
majorum numerum bonorum viro-
rum, martyres Christi, testes atque
assertores veritatis sine causâ occi-
disti : et me quidem facti pœnitet ;
tu vero ita obduruisti, ut nesciam
an possis duci pœnitudine." Hoc
scribo ut scias quo ille loco sit, quem
etiam scelerati homines et malefici
repudient et fugiant, nec ferant so-
cium.]

" now more visibly among the people. Nothing promoted it [Epistolæ
Tigurinæ,
1558–1579,
Ep. xxx.
p. 40.]
" more than the inviting the people to sing psalms. That was
" begun in one church in London, and did quickly spread itself
" not only through the city, but in the neighbouring places :
" sometimes at Paul's Cross there will be six thousand people
" singing together. This was very grievous to the papists :
" the children began to laugh at the priests as they passed in
" the streets ; and the bishops were called *hangmen* to their
" faces. It was said White died of rage. He commends Cecil
" much."

291   Sandys, bishop of Worcester, wrote in a letter on the 1st of Sandys,
bishop of
Worcester,
much of-
fended at
the image
in the
queen's
chapel.
Collect.
Numb. 61.
April 1560, which will be found in the Collection, " that after
" he returned from executing the injunctions, and preaching in
" the north, he was pressed to accept of the bishopric of Wor-
" cester : he saw, if he absolutely refused it, the queen would
" have been highly offended. He found it more truly a burden
" than an honour. The doctrine of the sacrament was pure, to
" which he and his brethren were resolved to adhere firmly
" as long as they lived. There was yet a question concerning
" images : the queen thought that was not contrary to the
" word of God ; and it seemed convenient to have a crucifix,
" with the blessed Virgin and St. John, still in her chapel.
" Some of them could not bear this : we had, says he, accord-
" ing to our injunctions taken away all the images that we
" found in churches, and burned them. We see superstitious
" people plainly worship this idol : upon this he had spoken
" freely to the queen ; with that she was so displeased as to
" threaten to deprive him : she was since that time more soft-
" ened, and the images were removed : but the popish vest-
" ments were still used ; yet he hoped that should not last
" long. He laments much that Peter Martyr was not sent for.
" It was easy to guess what it was that hindered it ; it was
" the pretence of unity that gave occasion to the greatest di-
" visions."

Parkhurst came into England in the end of the year 1559. [Epistolæ
Tigurinæ,
1558–1579,
Ep. xxvi.
p. 34.]
He went to his church of Cleve in Gloucestershire, and kept
out of the way of the court. He writes, that many bishops
would be glad to change conditions with him. He heard he
had been named to a bishopric, but he had dealt earnestly
with some great men to spare him in that : when he came

through London, both Parker and a privy-counsellor had pressed him to accept of one, but he could not resolve on being miserable.

Sampson's exceptions at his being made a bishop. Sampson had been with the other divines at Zurich, and was reckoned by them both a learned and a pious man: while he was coming to England with the rest, he was informed that a bishopric was designed for him; so he wrote while he was on his journey to Peter Martyr for his advice, as will be found in Collect. Numb. 62. the Collection, in this, " whether it was lawful to swear to the " queen, as supreme head of the church under Christ.   He " thought Christ was the sole head of the church, and no such " expression of any inferior head was found in the scripture. " He thought likewise, that the want of discipline made that " a bishop could not do his duty.   Many temporal pressures " lay upon bishops, such as first-fruits and tenths, beside the " expense of their equipage and attendance at court : so that " little was left for the breeding up of youth, for the relief of " the poor, and other more necessary occasions, to make their " ministry acceptable.   The whole method of electing bishops " was totally different from the primitive institution.   The " consent either of the clergy or people was not so much as " asked.   Their superstitious dress seemed likewise unbecom- " ing.   He wrote all this only to him, not that he expected " that a bishopric should be offered him; he prayed God that " it might never happen.   He was resolved to apply himself " to preach, but to avoid having any share in the government 292 " till he saw a full reformation made in all ecclesiastical func- " tions, both as to doctrine and discipline, and with relation to " the goods of the church.   He desires his answer as soon as " was possible."

Peter Martyr answered his letter on the 1st of November[19], but what it was, can only be gathered from Sampson's reply to it: he received it on the 3rd of January, and answered it Collect. Numb. 63. on the 6th, 1560.   It is in the Collection.   " They were then " under sad apprehensions, for which he desires their prayers " in a very solemn manner.   They were afraid lest the truth " of religion should either be overturned, or very much dark-

---

[19] [This is a mistake for Novem- ber 4.   It has been printed from his collected works in the Second   Series of Zurich Letters, 1558–1602. Epist. xiv. p. 19.]

" ened in England. The bishops of Canterbury, London, Ely,
" and Worcester were consecrated: Pilkington was designed for
" Winchester; Bentham for Coventry and Lichfield; and Peter
" Martyr's Jewel for Salisbury.

" Things still stuck with him; he could neither have in-
" gress nor egress: God knew how glad he would be to find
" an egress; let others be bishops, he desired only to be a
" preacher, but no bishop. There was yet a general prohi-
" bition of all preaching : and there was a crucifix on the altar
" still at court, with lights burning before it : and though by
" the queen's order images were removed out of churches all
" the kingdom over, yet the people rejoiced to see this was
" still kept in the queen's chapel. Three bishops officiated at
" this altar; one as priest, another as deacon, and a third as
" subdeacon, all before this idol, in rich copes : and there was
" a sacrament without any sermon. He adds, that injunctions
" were sent to preachers not to use freedom in the reproving
" of vice; so he asks what both Martyr, Bullinger, and Ber-
" nardin thought of this: whether they looked on it as a thing
" indifferent, and what they would advise him to do, if in-
" junctions should be sent out, requiring the like to be done in
" all churches; whether they ought to be obeyed, or if the
" clergy ought not to suffer deprivation rather than obey?
" Some among themselves thought that all this was indif-
" ferent, and so might be obeyed. He understood that the
" queen had a great regard to Bernardin Ochino; so he de-
" sires that he would write to her, to carry on the work of
" God diligently. He solemnly assures them, that she was
" truly a child of God : but princes had not so many friends
" to their souls as they had to their other concerns. He
" wishes they would all write to her; for she understood both
" Italian, Latin, and Greek well. So they might write in any
" language to her : but if they wrote, they must write as of
" their own motion, and not as if any complaints had been
" writ over to them."

On the 13th of May he wrote again, " that a bishopric had He refused
" been offered to him, but that he had refused it : and he de- a bishopric.
" sires Peter Martyr, to whom he wrote, not to censure this Tigurinæ,
" till he knew the whole state of the matter: but he rejoices Ep. xxxii.
" that Parkhurst was made bishop of Norwich." And by his P. 44.]

letter, it seems Norwich was the bishopric that was offered to him. Parkhurst wrote soon after his promotion to Martyr, and assured him there was no danger of setting up Lutheranism in England: only he writes, "We are fighting about "ceremonies, vestments, and matters of no moment [20]."

[Epistolæ Tigurinæ, 1558–1579, Ep. xxxiii. p. 45.]
Jewel wrote to Peter Martyr, on the 22nd of May, that 293 " the church of Salisbury was so struck with thunder, " that there was a clift all down for sixty foot: he was not " got thither; so he could not tell whether foolish people " made judgments upon this, with relation to him, or not. " He writes, that Bonner, Feckenham, Pole, Scory, and Wat-" son were all put in prison for railing at the changes that " were made. The queen expressed great firmness and " courage in maintaining the establishment she had made in " matters of religion. He tells him, that not only Cecil and " Knolles desired to be kindly remembered to him, but Petre " likewise, which perhaps he did not look for."

A peace made in Scotland. [Epistolæ Tigurinæ, 1558–1579, Ep. xxxvi. p. 52.]
On the 17th of July he writes to him, " that there was a " peace made in Scotland, and that the French were sent " away. Scotland was to be governed by a council of twelve " persons; only all greater matters were to be referred to a " parliament. He writes, that the duke of Holstein was come " over to see the queen, and was nobly treated by her, and " made a knight of the garter: the king of Sweden's coming " over was still talked of." After Jewel had been some time in his diocese, he wrote to Gualter on the 2nd of November,

[Ibid. Ep. xx. p. 27.]
1560 [21], " that he now felt what a load government was to " him, who had led his life in the shade, and at study, and " had never turned his thoughts to government; but he would " make up in his diligence what might be otherwise wanting: " the opposition he met with from the rage of the papists was " incredible."

On the 6th of November he wrote, that May, dean of St.
[Aug. 12.] Paul's, who was designed to be archbishop of York, was dead: it does not appear on what views that see was so long kept

---

[20] [There is no letter from Parkhurst to Martyr after his promotion, neither does the expression occur in any other letter written by him, in the Zurich Letters.]

[21] [This should have been 1559. The same view is expressed in a letter of the same date to Josiah Simler. Ep. xxii. p. 29.]

void, after the rest were filled.   Parker was much troubled
at this, and wrote very earnestly about it to Cecil.   The
letter will be found in the Collection.   "There were great
"complaints in the north: the people there were offended to
"see no more care had of them; and for want of instruction
"they were become rude: this was like to have an ill influ-
"ence on the quiet and order of the country.   It was perhaps
"so long delayed for the advantage the queen's exchequer
"made by the vacancy: but if, for want of good instruction,
"the people should grow savage like the Irish, it might run
"to a far greater charge to reduce them.   Why should any
"person hinder the queen's zeal to have her people taught to
"know and to fear God?   If those hitherto named for the
"north were not liked, or not willing to go thither, he pro-
"posed that some of those already placed might be removed
"thither.   And he named Young, bishop of St. David's, for
"York; and the bishop of Rochester, Guest, for Durham:
"and if any suspicions were had of any of their practising to
"the prejudice of their successors, there were precedents used
"in former times to take bishops bound to leave their churches
"in no worse case than they found them.   He had pressed
"them formerly with relation to those vacant sees; he saw
"the matter was still delayed: he would never give over his
"importunity till the thing was done; which he hoped he
"would instantly promote, out of the zeal he bore to souls so
"dear to Christ."

Collect.
Numb. 64.
Parker's
care in the
northern
sees.

294   This he wrote on the 16th of October; so it does not appear if the design for May was then so well fixed as Jewel
apprehended.   The hint in this letter of the practices of
bishops was occasioned by the ruinous leases that the popish
bishops had made; for seeing the change that was designed,
they had by the law at that time so absolute a power over
their estates, having no restraints laid on them but those of
their own canons, that their leases, how mischievous soever to
their successors, were good in law.   The new bishops in many
places had scarce necessary subsistence, or houses left them,
and were to be supported by dignities given them *in commendam:* and it was perhaps suggested, that they, to procure a
little better subsistence to themselves, might be prevailed on to
prolong, or confirm such leases.

The popish
bishops
made great
alienations

See more
of this in
the Annals
of the Re-
formation,
chap. 12.

Collect.
Numb. 65.

Jewel's
Apology
published.

The archbishop's importunity had its effect: for in February thereafter, Young was removed to York; and Pilkington, a learned and zealous man, was made bishop of Durham. And thus the sees of England were filled. Jewel, in a letter soon after to Peter Martyr, in February 1560, which will be found in the Collection, "wishes that all the remnants of former "errors, with all the rubbish, and even the dust that might "yet remain, might be taken away:" he wishes they could have obtained it. It seems by this that their wishes had not prevailed. "The council of Trent was then to be opened "again, but the queen was resolved to take no notice of it. "He gives an account of his Apology that was then set out." This has been so often printed [22], and is so well known, that it is not necessary to enlarge more upon it: as it was one of the first books published in this reign, so it was written with that strength and clearness, that it, together with the defence of it, is still to this day reckoned one of our best books. In that letter he writes of the countess of Lennox, the mother to the lord Darnley, "that she was a more violent papist than even "queen Mary herself. Her son was gone to Scotland, and it "was believed he might marry the queen of Scotland: the "earl of Hertford had a son by the lady Catharine Grey; "some called him a bastard, but others affirmed that they "were married. If that was true, then, according to king "Henry's will, he must be the heir of the crown. But he "adds, *Ah! unhappy we, that cannot know under what* "*prince we are to live!* He complains that schools are for- "saken, and that they were under a great want of preachers. "The few they had were every where well received." He writes in another letter, "that in queen Mary's time, for want "of good instruction, the anabaptists and Arians did much "increase; but now they disappeared every where."

The popish clergy, when they saw no appearance of any new change, did generally comply with the laws then made; but in so untoward a manner, that they made it very visible

---

[22] [Apologia Ecclesiæ Anglicanæ, authore Johanne Juello, episcopo Sarisburiensi. Lond. 1562. 8vo. The Apologie of the Church of England, by John Juell, Bishop of Salisbury. London. 1562. 4to. The original has been often reprinted, and there are several different English transla- lations.]

that what they did was against both their heart and their conscience. This put the bishops on receiving many into orders that were not thoroughly well qualified ; which exposed them to much censure. They thought that, in that necessity, men of good hearts that loved the gospel, though not so learned as might be wished for, were to be brought into the service of 295 the church : but pains was taken, and methods were laid down, to breed up a more knowing race of men, as soon as was possible.

I turn now to shew how the affairs of religion went on, particularly with relation to Scotland ; of which mention was made in some of Jewel's letters.

But before I open this, I will give an account of two instruments sent me from Scotland, that came not to my hands but since the pages 280 and 281 were printed off ; yet they are so important, that, as I have put them in the Collection, so I will *Collect.* give a short account of them here. On the 19th of April, *Numb. 66.* fifteen days after the queen of Scotland had passed that secret fraudulent protestation formerly mentioned, when the articles of the marriage were mutually signed, it was not only provided that the crown of Scotland, in case she should die without children, should descend to the duke of Châtelherault and his heirs, the instrument itself being published in the French Col- *[Recueil* lection ; but the dauphin did, on the same day, set his seal to *des Traités,* a charter, still preserved at Hamilton, setting forth the faith *p. 511.]* and engagements that the king his father had formerly made, to secure to the earl of Arran the succession to the crown of Scotland, in case the queen should die without children ; to which he promises he will pay all obedience. He confirms and ratifies that promise for himself and his successors ; promising in good faith, (*bond fide,*) that in that case he will not only suffer that lord to enjoy that crown, but that he will assist and maintain him in it.

The promise made by his father, king Henry, to which this refers, bears date the 17th day of June, anno 1549 ; and was sent over to Scotland, in order to the getting of queen Mary to be sent to France. By it the king promised, in the word of a king, that in case the queen should die without children, he would assist the earl of Arran in the succession to the crown against all that should oppose him. These instruments I have put in the Collection, as lasting memorials of the fidelity and sincerity of that court; to give a just precaution to posterity in future ages: by which it will appear how little contracts, promises, and public stipulations are to be depended on, where a secret protestation, lodged in a clandestine manner, is set up to make all this void; which, I hope, will not be soon forgotten or neglected.

But to return from this digression, which, though a little out of its place, seemed too important to be omitted.

The French grew weary of carrying on the war in Scotland.
The distraction that France was in made it not easy to them to carry on the war of Scotland, by reason of the charge that the sending forces to so great a distance put them to: whereas it was but a short march to the English to go to the assistance of the lords of Scotland; so they were willing to make up matters the best they could by a treaty. Commissioners were appointed to treat on both sides. In the mean while the queen regent of Scotland died; so Cecil and Wotton, who were employed by the queen in that treaty, apprehending the French might, upon this emergent, study to gain more time, wrote to the queen for positive orders.

Collect. Numb. 67.
A letter was written to them on the 15th of June, signed by 296 five privy counsellors; which is in the Collection, taken from the original. By it, it appears, that this treaty was then a secret, which they saw must soon break out; so the persons employed in Scotland advised the acquainting king Philip with it, because they looked on it as brought very near a total agreement. To this the queen's council agreed. Those in Scotland apprehended that perhaps the French would, upon the regent's death, go away, and leave the kingdom without coming to any agreement. If they should do so, they did order them to advise with the duke of Norfolk, and the lords of Scotland in league with them, how the French may be forthwith expelled the kingdom, without any loss of time: for, by all the advertisements they had, they understood that the French intended to gain time as much as was possible. If the French desired to have some of their colleagues in the town, to assist them in managing the treaty, that was by no means to be granted: but if they desired the assistance of such Scottish men as were of

their faction, and if their friends in Scotland consented to it, that seemed reasonable. The rest of the letter relates to one Parrys, an Irishman.

The treaty, by reason of the weakness of the French force, was soon brought to a conclusion. The French were to be sent away in three weeks. An assembly of the states was to meet, and to settle the affairs of the kingdom : it was to be governed by a council of twelve persons ; of whom the king and queen were to name seven, and the states to choose five : and by these all affairs were to be governed, they being made accountable to the parliament. The last article was, " that " the king and queen should not use the title or arms of Eng- " land and Ireland any more." It was brought to a good end

When matters were brought to a settlement in Scotland, the Scots sent up the earls of Morton and Glencairn to the queen. Their message will best appear from the instructions, which will be found in the Collection, copied from the original, that is still preserved, and in the possession of the duchess of Ha- milton : by which " the estates of parliament, considering how " the two kingdoms lay joined together, and reflecting on the " inconveniences that they and their ancestors had suffered by " continual wars, and on the advantages of a perpetual friend- " ship between them, therefore they did order a proposition of " marriage to be made to the queen of England with the earl " of Arran ; who, after his father, in default of succession of " the queen's body, was the next heir to the crown of Scotland. " And they resolved that an embassy should be appointed to " make the proposition in the honourablest manner that could " be devised. They also order thanks to be given to the queen " for the good-will she has on all occasions expressed for their " kingdom ; which she had particularly declared of late, by " the support she had given them for their relief; by the " means of which they enjoyed their present quiet. And they " were also ordered to move the queen to send strict commands " to her wardens, and other officers on the borders, to suppress " all broken men, and to restrain all thefts." These instruc- tions were appointed to be sealed and subscribed by six of every estate ; and that was to be held as valid as if all the estates had sealed and subscribed them. Collect. Numb. 68.

297

This order of parliament is signed by the archbishop of Signed by the three

estates.
[Acta Parl.
Scot. vol. ii.
p. 606.] St. Andrew's, the bishops of Dunkeld, Galloway, Dumblane, Argyle, and the elect bishop of the Isles: and by as many abbots and priors; the prior of St. Andrew's, afterwards earl of Murray; the abbot of Arbroath, afterwards marquis of Hamilton; the abbots of Newbattle and Culross; the commendator of Kilwinning, and the prior of Lochleven. So many of the ecclesiastical state of both ranks concurring, shews that they rejoiced in the deliverance that they had from the servitude under which the French had almost brought them.

These instructions are also signed by the duke of Châtelherault, who subscribed only *James;* and by the earls of Argyle, Athol, Morton, Crawford, and Sutherland; and by the lords Erskine, Gordon, Saltoun, Hay, Ochiltree, Innermeith, Boyd, Lindsay, Gray, and some others, whose names cannot be read: and by eight provosts of boroughs. But no seals are in this noble instrument; so probably it was an authentic duplicate, that was deposited in that family, to remain as an undoubted proof of the right of succeeding to the crown of Scotland, if the queen had left no issue of her own body.

Collect.
Numb. 69.
The queen
of Eng-
land's an-
swer to it. To this an answer was given, which I have put in the Collection, from the draught of it in Cecil's hand. " The queen " received the hearty thanks that the three estates sent her " very kindly; and was glad the assistance she had given " then, was so well accepted by them. She was so well satis-" fied with the effects it had, that if the like cause should " happen, in which they might need aid from her, she assures " them it shall not be wanting. The queen did perceive the " difference between the benefits bestowed by her father, on " many of the nobility of that nation, which were supposed " to be to the prejudice of the kingdom, and so had not the " success expected; and those they had received from her, " which were directed to the safety of the realm: so the di-" versity in the bestowing them had made this diversity in the " acceptation of them.

" She received that proposition of marriage as a mark of " the good intention of the estates for knitting the kingdoms " in amity; in offering to her the best and choicest person " that they had, though not without danger of the displeasure " of the French king. But the queen was not disposed pre-" sently to marry; though the necessity of the kingdom might

" perhaps constrain her afterwards to it. Yet she desired,
" that the earl of Arran might not forbear to marry on her
" account : but that the amity between the two kingdoms
" might remain firm ; since it was so necessary to their pre-
" servation, though no marriage were made upon it. The
" queen had heard a very good report of the earl of Arran,
" and thought him a noble gentleman of great worth, and did
" not doubt but he would prove to be such. In the last place,
" the queen desired the states would reflect on former prac-
298 " tices among them, and would continue in a good agreement
" among themselves, and not fall into factions. And she con-
" cluded with a promise, that on her part no reasonable thing
" should be neglected, that might tend to the common defence
" of both the realms against any common enemy."

Things went on pursuant to this treaty; to which it was **The death**
not thought the French would have any regard, when their **of Francis the Second**
affairs should be in a better condition. The apprehensions
of that were soon at an end. In December 1560, the union
which that kingdom had with France was totally broke by the
death of Francis the Second : so that Mary queen of Scot- [Dec. 4.]
land had nothing left but her own strength to depend upon.
The treaty of Leith being in all other points executed, the
queen ordered both Throgmorton, her ordinary ambassador in
France, and the earl of Bedford, whom she had sent over
extraordinary, to demand queen Mary's ratification of that
treaty : which I shall open more particularly, because, upon
this occasion, that jealousy was raised between the two queens
that ended so fatally to the one. The queen of Scots used
many shifts to excuse her not doing it.

In a letter of Throgmorton's, of the 16th of April, which
is in the Collection, he tells the queen, " that having pressed **Collect.**
" the queen of Scots to it ; she said, She had not her coun- **Numb. 70.**
" cil about her, particularly the cardinal of Lorraine her
" uncle, by whom she was advised in all her affairs : nor had
" she heard from her council in Scotland. She promised,
" that when she heard from them, and had advised with
" her council about her, she would give an answer that
" should satisfy the queen. But her natural brother, the
" lord James, being come over to her, the queen had com-
" manded Throgmorton to demand again the confirmation of

" the treaty. Upon which, the ambassador sent a gentleman
" to know her pleasure, when he should wait on her, to re-
" ceive it from her hand. This, as he wrote to her, was
" desired by the queen, as a mean to make them live hereafter
" in all love, peace, and amity together. And nothing could
" so demonstrate that queen's intention to entertain this, as
" the establishing that knot of friendship between them, for
" both their quiet and comfort, which was at that time the
" only refuge of them both." Of this he sent the queen his
mistress a copy.

On the 1st of May, Mr. Somer, whom the ambassador had sent
to Nancy, where the queen of Scotland was at that time, came
Collect. back with her answer ; which is in the Collection ; it being the
Numb. 71. only original paper that ever I saw in her hand. Dated from
Nancy, the 22nd of April 1561.

The queen " She writes, she was then leaving that place ; so she could
of Scotland " give no answer till she came to Rheims, where she intended
did not
ratify the " to be at the king's coronation : and she says, that lord
peace. " James was only come to do his duty about her, as his sove-
" reign lady, without any charge or commission whatsoever."
This Throgmorton sent to the queen, together with a letter
from the cardinal of Lorraine to the same purpose, which he 299
Collect. also sent her in a letter, which will be found in the Collection ;
Numb. 72. in which he writes, " that though Somer had used the best
" means he could, to put the Scottish queen in mind of the
" promise she had made to the earl of Bedford, and to Throg-
" morton himself, yet he could get no other answer from her."
The ambassador was ordered by the queen not to be present
at the coronation : so he did not know when or where he
should see her ; for it was said, she did not intend, for some
time, to come into the neighbourhood of Paris : he therefore
proposed to the queen to send a letter of credit by Mr. Somer
to that queen ; and with it to order him to go and demand
her answer. By that queen's discourse with lord James, it
seemed she did not intend to give a plain answer, but still to
shift it off : but he thought the queen insisting on it by a person sent express to stay for an answer, she would be able to
judge from thence what measures she ought to take. The
queen of Scotland had said to the ambassador, that she intended to give lord James a commission, with a charge to look

to the affairs of Scotland during her absence; and he, when
he took leave of her, left one to bring that after him : but
that person was come with letters from that queen, but with
no commission; and he understood by him that she had
changed her mind, and would give no such commission till
she should come to Scotland herself; nor would she dispose
of any thing till then.   This was easily seen to be on design
to let all people understand on what terms they might expect
benefices, grants, or other favours from her.

The true reason why she would not employ lord James was, She is
because she found she could not draw him from his devotion jealous of
lord James.
to the queen, nor from his resolution to observe the late treaty
and league between England and Scotland : and it is added,
that the cardinal of Lorraine saw he could not draw him from
his religion, though he used great persuasions to prevail on
him.   Upon these accounts the ambassador wrote over, " that
" he saw he might be much depended on : so he advises the
" queen to consider him as one that may serve her to good
" purpose, and to use him liberally and honourably.   He had
" made great acknowledgments of the good reception he met
" with as he came through London : so he on many accounts
" deserved to be both well used and much trusted.   The
" queen of Scotland had great expectations from the popish
" party ; and from the earl of Huntley in particular.   He gives
" in that letter an account of a great tumult that had then
" happened at Paris, upon occasion of an assembly of pro-
" testants for worship in a private house, in the suburbs.   The
" rabble met about the house, threatening violence : upon
" which those within, seeing persuasions had no effect, fired
" and killed seven or eight of them.   The court of parliament
" sent an order to suppress the tumult, and disperse the
" multitude.   This was plainly contrary to the edict lately
" made : but the ambassador apprehended that greater dis-
" orders would follow."   And that I may end all this matter
at once,

300   I find in a letter of Jewel's that is in the Collection, that Collect.
the duke of Guise sent to the princes of Germany, to divert Numb. 73.
The duke
them from assisting the prince of Condé ; assuring them, that of Guise
he himself was very moderate in the points of religion, and studied to
divert the
had very favourable thoughts of the Augsburg Confession : he queen from

studied also to persuade the queen, that the war which was
then breaking out in France was not for religion; but was a
conspiracy against the government: which he hoped she as a
queen would not assist.   At the same time the queen of Scotland sent the queen a present of a diamond of value, with
some very fine verses made by Buchanan, then in her court.
She also in her letters vowed a perpetual friendship with her,
and wrote, that she would pass through England.   Yet the
queen saw through all this, and was not diverted by it from
assisting the prince of Condé.   Upon this the duke of Guise
did openly charge all the disorders in France on her, as the
principal author of them: by this the mask was thrown away,
and these jealousies broke out into an open war.   Jewel
wishes the queen had begun it sooner, and that the princes of
Germany would follow her example, now that she was engaged,
and had sent one to engage them likewise.

By that time the queen of Scotland had got by sea into her
kingdom: she alone had her mass, which was put down all the
kingdom over.

There was this year an extraordinary bad season through
every quarter of the year, and perpetual rains.   There was
also much talk of many monstrous births, both by women, and
beasts, hogs, mares, cows, and hens: some births were without
heads, or heads of a strange form; and some without arms or
legs.   Very probably things of that sort were magnified by
those who reported them; and, no doubt, they were made the
presages of some dismal events to be looked for; it being
ordinary in all great changes to enlarge, and even to forge
stories of that sort, on design to alarm people with the apprehensions of some signal judgments to follow after such unusual
warnings.   This last letter being written some time after the
great convocation that settled our reformation, is mentioned
here out of its place, to finish a matter to which I have nothing
here to add.

But now to return to give an account of that famous meeting
of the clergy.   I must first lament that here there is another
total stop in the correspondence with Zurich, that has hitherto
furnished me with so many particulars.   I cannot think but
that there were copious accounts of the progress of matters in
it given to them, if not during the convocation, in which the

bishops were no doubt much employed, yet at least soon after
the prorogation, which was in the beginning of April : but in
all the volume of letters that is sent me, I find not one, either
during their sitting, or after it was ended, till that I mentioned
last, which is of the 14th of August[23]. Being then destitute
of those authentic vouchers, I must gather up what remains
I could find, to give a clear account of the great transactions
then on foot.

The imperfect abstract[24] which I have often vouched gives
us but a very defective account of their proceedings. Their
301 first session was on the 13th of January. Day, provost of [Jan. 12.
Eton, preached. Parker told them, they had now in their Wilkins,
hands an opportunity of reforming all things in the church. p. 232.]
The queen did earnestly desire it, and so did many of the
nobility. He sent them to choose a prolocutor, and recommended Nowel, dean of St. Paul's, to them. They chose him
upon that; and on the 16th of January, Parker exhorted
them to consider against the next session what things wanted
a reformation[25]. On the 19th, he sent for the prolocutor,
who came up with six of the clergy. He said they had before
them some sheets of matters to be offered for a reformation,
which were then referred to be considered by a committee.
He also said, that the articles set forth in a synod at London,
in king Edward's time, were likewise before a committee to
be considered ; and, if need was, to be corrected by them.
On the 20th, the archbishop and bishops were for the space
of three hours consulting secretly about those articles. On
the 22nd, they were again for three hours considering the
same matter. On the 25th they were two hours. And on
the 27th, they were for three hours more upon the same

[23] [No less than nineteen letters,
bearing date from Feb. 7, 1562, to
Aug. 13, 1562, have been published
in 'The Zurich Letters' First and
Second Series, some from the volume which the author saw when
he was at Zurich, some from other
sources, but they do not throw any
light upon the proceedings of this
convocation.]

[24] [The register of this convocation has been destroyed ; see Strype,

Ann. i. 315, but Wilkins gives an
account of it *ex regist. convoc.*]

[25] [' Et tunc dimisso clero infe-
rioris domus, reverendissimus rogavit patres, quod unusquisque eorum
citra proximam sessionem excogitare
velit ea, quæ *in eorum separalibus
dioecesibus* reformatione indigeant,
ac in proximâ sessione in ecclesiâ
collegiatâ D. Petri Westmonasteri-
ensis habendâ proponere dignare-
tur.' Wilkins, Conc. IV. p. 232.]

[Wilkins,
Conc. iv.
p. 233.]
matter. And on the 29th of January, all in the upper house agreed unanimously in settling the Articles of Religion, and they subscribed them.

Some alterations made in the Articles of Religion.
The differences between these Articles, and those set forth by king Edward, are very particularly mentioned in the Collections[26] added to my second volume. The most material is the leaving out that express declaration that was made against the corporal presence of Christ in the sacrament, which I then thought was done in compliance with the opinion prevalent among the people of the popish persuasion, who were strangely possessed with the belief of such a presence : but I am convinced, by the letters sent me from Zurich, that in this, great regard was likewise had to the Lutheran churches, with whom a conjunction was much endeavoured by some : so that perhaps this was one consideration that made it be thought convenient to suppress the definition then made in this matter by the convocation : but it does no way appear to me, whether these words were suppressed by the consent of the convocation ; or whether the queen ordered it to be done, either by a direct command, or by denying to give her assent to that part of the Article.

I must also add, that the homily *against wilful Rebellion,* for that is its true title, was not drawn up till some years after this convocation had settled those Articles ; in which the titles of the homilies are set forth, though it is added in the manuscript to the rest, with the title *against Rebellion.* It is plain, both by the body of the homily and by the prayer at the end of it, that it was penned after the rebellion that was raised by the earls of Northumberland and Westmoreland, many years after this, and while there were wars abroad on the account of religion. This I do not write as disagreeing in any part from the doctrine delivered in that homily, but only as an historian, in order to the setting matters of fact in a true light.

[Wilkins,
Conc. iv.
p. 238.]
But now I go on as the minutes, or rather the abstracts, lead me. When the great matter of the Articles was settled, the bishops of London, Winchester, Lincoln, and Hereford, 302 were appointed to draw articles of discipline. On the 3rd of February, the archbishop and bishops were in a secret conference for the space of three hours. On the 5th of February,

26 [See Part ii. Records, p. 209.]

a committee was appointed to examine the Catechism. Then the prolocutor, with six of the clergy, brought up the Articles of Religion that had been sent by the archbishop to the lower house: many had already subscribed them; but he proposed, that such as had not yet done it might be required either to subscribe them in the lower house, or to do it in the presence of the bishops. Upon this the upper house ordered that the names of those who had not subscribed them might be laid before them next session. On the 10th, the prolocutor, with eight of the clergy, came up and told the bishops that many had subscribed since their last meeting: upon that the bishops renewed their former order.

On the 13th, there was some treaty concerning the subsidy; but on that day, and, it seems, on some days following, there were very warm debates in the lower house, of which I shall give a particular account, from a copy taken from the minutes of the proceedings of the lower house, which will be found in the Collection. On the 13th day, six articles were offered to the house, which follow; first, " that all holydays, except Sun-" days, and the feasts that related to Christ, should be abro-" gated. Second, that in the Common Prayer the minister should " always turn his face towards the people, so as to be heard by " the people, that they might be edified. Third, that the cere-" mony of the cross in baptism may be omitted, as tending to " superstition. Fourth, that forasmuch as divers communicants " were not able to kneel during the time of communion, for age, " sickness, and other infirmities; and some also do supersti-" tiously both kneel and knock; that the order of kneeling may " be left to the discretion of the Ordinary within his jurisdic-" tion. Fifth, that it be sufficient for the minister in time of " saying divine service and ministering the sacraments to use " a surplice; and that no minister say service, or minister the " sacrament, but in a comely garment or habit. The sixth " and last is, that the use of organs be removed." The words are strictly as I took them from the copy of the Journal: but the sense of the fifth is not clear, except we suppose the word *once* to have come after *the minister;* so that it was proposed that it should be sufficient *once* to use the surplice.

Great debates concerning some alterations in the Book of Common Prayer. Collect. Numb. 74. [Wilkins, Conc. iv. p. 240.]

A practice common among papists of knocking on their breasts, saying Culpa mea, at the elevation.

There arose great disputes[27] concerning these propositions;

[27] [Wilkins' account goes no further than this. Strype in his Annals,

some approving, and others rejecting them ; and it was proposed by some, to refer the matter to the archbishop and
bishops. Many protested, that they could in no manner consent to any one of them ; since they were contrary to the
Book of Common Prayer, that was ratified by an act of parliament : nor would they admit of any alteration of the orders,
rules, rites, or regulations, already settled by that book.
There were public disputations between learned men, some
approving, and others condemning the propositions. Thirteen
persons were named as the disputants. In conclusion, the
house was divided, and counted : forty-three voted for the
propositions, and thirty-five voted against them, and that no 303
change should be made in the Book of Common Prayer then
established. But when the proxies were counted, those who
were for the propositions were in all fifty-eight ; and those
who were against them were fifty-nine : so that they were
agreed to by a majority of eight of those who were present,
and who had heard the disputations ; yet those were outvoted
by a majority of one vote, by the proxy of an absent person.
All their names are set down in the paper. One thing observ-
able is, that in this minute it is added, that those who rejected
the Articles seemed to go chiefly on this ground ; that they
were contrary to the authorized Book of Common Prayer : as
if this had been the assuming an authority to alter what was
settled by the legislature. It is not to be imagined, but if the
affirmative vote had prevailed, that it could not be intended to
have any other effect, but to make an address to the parliament, to alter the book in those particulars. I have represented this matter as I found it, and will not make any judgment upon it, either on the one side or the other ; but will
leave that to the reader, and go on with what remains in the
abstract.

But by one
proxy it
was car-
ried, that
none
should
be made.

This debate in the lower house put a stop to the business of
the convocation for six days, in which they only treated of the
subsidy. On the 19th of February, some articles were communicated to the lower house ; and they were ordered to
bring them back, with their observations on them. These

i. p. 315 sqq., gives a full account
from the *Synodus Anglicana* published in 1702, and from the rough
draughts in the handwriting of abp.
Parker, and of bps. Grindal, Sandys,
and Cox.]

seem to relate to benefices and dilapidations. And they were
ordered to inquire how many benefices were then vacant. On
the 22nd, the subsidy was agreed to. On the 24th, the prolocutor being absent, his surrogate, with the clergy, were called
up; and the engrossed bill of subsidy was read to them, and
they all unanimously agreed to it.

On the 26th, a *Book of Discipline* was brought to the upper
house by the prolocutor, with ten of the clergy; to which, as
it was then said, the whole clergy did unanimously consent.
This was referred to the archbishop, with the bishops of London, Winchester, Chichester, Hereford, and Ely. On the 1st
of March, the prolocutor brought up some additional articles,
which they desired might be added to the *Book of Discipline*,
that they had formerly brought up. The archbishop gave
them the book back again; and ordered them to bring it back,
together with the additions they had made to it.

A Book of Discipline offered by the lower house.

On the 3rd of March, the prolocutor brought up the Catechism; to which, he said, the house did unanimously agree:
the considering of it was committed to the bishops of Winchester, Hereford, Lincoln, and Coventry. (This seems to be
the Catechism drawn by Nowel, dean of St. Paul's.) After
that, there was a conference among the bishops for the space of
two hours. On the 5th of March the prolocutor brought up
the *Book of Discipline*, with some additional chapters: one
only is named, *Of Adultery*, with an &c. On the 10th there
was a conference among the bishops for two hours; and on
the 12th for two hours more; and on the 16th for other two
hours; and on the 19th for two hours more. After that,
304 nothing is marked but several prorogations, till the 10th of
April, that the royal writ came for the prorogation. And this
is all that remains of this great convocation.

It does not appear what that *Book of Discipline* was. In
one of the Zurich letters, as shall be told afterwards, it is said,
that some things agreed to in this synod were afterwards suppressed. This, I suppose, relates to that *Book of Discipline*:
but whether this was the reformation of the ecclesiastical laws,
prepared by Cranmer and others; or whether it was modelled
in any other manner, cannot now be certainly known.

But to this account that I have given, I will add some other
particulars that the diligent Mr. Strype has laid together;
[Strype's Annals, i. p. 317.]

referring my reader for a more copious account of them to his
Annals.

" It was designed to have Jewel's Apology joined to the
" Articles : which archbishop Parker intended should be in all
" cathedral and collegiate churches, and also in private houses.

" Degrees of punishment were proposed for all those who
" should preach, write, or speak in derogation or contempt of
" this book ; for the first, second, and third offence.

" It was proposed that all vestments, copes, and surplices
" should be taken away ; that none but ministers should bap-
" tize ; that the table for the sacrament should not stand altar-
" wise ; that organs and curious singing should be removed.

" That godfathers and godmothers should not answer in the
" child's name ; but should recite the Creed, and desire that
" the child may be baptized in that faith. Here on the margin
" Parker writes, *Let this be considered.*

" That none should be married but after the banns have been
" asked for three Sundays or holydays. On the margin Parker
" writes, *Priests solemnizing matrimony without testimonial*
" *of banns to suffer grievous punishment.*

" That the queen and parliament be prayed to renew the
" act for empowering thirty-two persons to gather ecclesiastical
" laws, and to review those appointed in king Edward's time.

" That all peculiar jurisdictions should be extinguished, so
" that the whole diocese be put under the jurisdiction of the
" bishop ; that no appeal shall lie in cases of correction. On
" the margin Parker writes, *Let this be thought on.*

" That in every cathedral a divinity lecture should be read
" thrice a week.

" That the apparel of the clergy should be uniform. That
" no person not in priest's orders shall hold any ecclesiastical
" dignity above a year, if he does not take priest's orders.
" Parker writes, *Too much : and let it be thought on.*

" That none be capable of a dispensation for a plurality of
" benefices with cure of souls, if he is not at least a master of
" arts, and they not beyond twelve miles distance. Parker
" writes, *Let it be considered, whether this ought to be re-*
" *strained to degrees.*

" That if any has two cures, he shall reside constantly on 305
" one, unless at some times to go and preach in the other,

" under the pain of losing the greater benefice.   Parker adds,
" *Let this be thought on.*

" That no patron sell, or assign the next advowson ; and
" that no grant be made of any benefice till it is void.

" That all incumbents or curates shall, on Sundays in the
" afternoon, offer to teach the children of the parish the Cate-
" chism."

The next paper is, of *Remedies for the poverty of ministers'*
livings : but the *remedies,* how good soever, were not found
practicable ; so all this matter was let fall.

With this convocation my design of continuing the History
of the Reformation is now concluded.   And here I once intended to have ended my work : but the letters sent me from
Zurich give me such a full and particular account of the first
unhappy breach that was made in our church, with so many
curious incidents, that I am by these invited to set that matter
out in a clear light, since I have it before me in the letters of
the most eminent of our bishops.

A further continuation of the History, beyond my former work.

There was a great variety of sentiments among our reformers on this point; *Whether it was fit to retain an external*
face of things, near to what had been practised in the times
of popery, or not? The doing that made the people come
easily in to the more real changes that were made in the doctrines, when they saw the outward appearances so little altered :
so this method seemed the safer and the readier way to wean
the people from the fondness they had for a splendid face of
things, by that which was still kept up.   But on the other
hand it was said that this kept up still the inclination in the
people to the former practices : they were by these made to
think that the reformed state of the church did not differ much
from them ; and that they imitated them.   And they apprehended that this outward resemblance made the old root of
popery to live still in their thoughts ; so that if it made them
conform at present more easily to the change that was now
made, it would make it still much the easier for them to fall
back to popery : so, for this very reason, they stood upon it,
and thought it better to put matters in as great an opposition
to the practices of popery as was possible or convenient.

A controversy about the use of things indifferent.

The queen had, in her first injunctions, ordered the clergy to wear seemly garments, and square caps; adding, that this was only for decency, and not to ascribe any worthiness to the garments: but when the *Act of Uniformity* was settled, whereas in the Liturgy passed in the second year of king Edward, *copes* and other garments were ordered to be used; but in the second book, passed in the sixth year of that king, all was laid aside, except the *surplice;* yet the queen, who loved magnificence in every thing, returned back to the rules in king Edward's first book, till other order should be taken therein by the queen. There was likewise a clause put in the 306 *Act of Uniformity*, empowering the queen to *ordain and publish such further ceremonies and rites as might be for the advancement of God's glory, the edifying of his church, and the due reverence of Christ's holy mysteries and sacraments.*

Great diversity in practice.

The matter being thus settled, there followed a great diversity in practice; many conforming themselves in all points to the law; while others did not use either the surplice or the square caps and hoods according to their degree. This visible difference began to give great offence, and to state two parties in the church. The people observed it, and ran into parties upon it. Many forsook their churches of both sides: some, because those habits were used; and some, because they were not used. It is likewise suggested, that the papists insulted, upon this division among the protestants; and said, it was impossible it should be otherwise till all returned to come under one absolute obedience.

The queen wrote to the archbishop of Canterbury to bring all to an uniformity. [Jan. 25, 1565. Lansdowne MS. viii. art. 6. printed in Parker's Correspondence, p. 223.]

Upon this the queen, in January 1564–5, wrote to the archbishop of Canterbury, " reflecting (not without some acrimony " of style) on these diversities; as if they were the effect of " some remissness in him and in the other bishops: requiring " him, that, with the assistance of other bishops commissioned " by her for causes ecclesiastical, he should give strict orders " that all diversities and varieties, both among the clergy and " people, might be reformed and repressed; and that all should " be brought to one manner of uniformity through the whole " kingdom, that so the people might quietly honour and serve " God."

Upon that, some of the bishops met; six in all. Of these,

four were upon the ecclesiastical commission: the archbishop
of Canterbury, the bishops of London[28], Ely, and Rochester :
and with these joined the bishops of Winchester and Lincoln.
They agreed on some rules and orders meet to be observed, not
as equivalent to the word of God, nor as laws that did bind the
conscience, from the nature of the things considered in themselves ; or, as that they did add any efficacy or more holiness
to the public prayers and sacraments ; but as temporary orders,
merely ecclesiastic, and as rules concerning decency, distinction,
and order for the time.

They began with articles of doctrine and preaching : " That
" all preachers should study to preach to edification, and handle
" matters of controversy with sobriety and discretion ; exhort-
" ing people to receive the sacrament frequently, and to continue
" in all obedience to the laws and to the queen's injunctions.
" All former licenses are declared void ; but are to be renewed
" to such as the bishop thought meet for the office ; they paying
" only a groat for the writing.   If any should preach unsound
" doctrine, they were to be denounced to the bishop, but not to
" be contradicted in the church.   All were to be required to
" preach once in three months, either in person or by one in
" their stead.   Such as were not licensed to preach were to read
" the Homilies, or such other necessary doctrine as should be pre-
" scribed.   In the sacrament the principal minister was to wear
" a cope ; but at all other prayers only surplices.   That deans
" and prebendaries should wear a hood in the choir, and preach
" with their hood : all communicants were to receive the sacra-
" ment kneeling.   Then follow rules about tolling the bell when
" people die ; about the altar, the font, and who may be god-
" fathers in baptism.   That no shops be opened on Sundays.
" That bishops shall give notice against the day of giving
" orders, that all men may except against such as are unworthy.
" That none be ordained but within their own diocese, except
" those who have degrees in the university.   Rules follow for
" licenses for archdeacons to appoint curates to get some texts
" of the New Testament by heart ; and at the next synod to
" hear them rehearse them.   Ordinaries were to guard against
" simoniacal practices, and none were to marry within the

Orders set out by the bishops.

307

[28] [The letter to Grindal, bishop
of London, on the subject has been
printed in Parker's Correspondence,
p. 227, from his Register, fol. 253.]

" Levitical degrees. Then follow rules of their wearing ap-
" parel, gowns, and caps; they were to wear no hats but in
" travelling: but those who were deprived might not wear
" them. To this they added a form of subscription to be re-
" quired of all that were to be admitted to any office or cure in
" the church, to this effect; that they should not preach but
" by the bishop's special license; that they should read the
" service distinctly and audibly; that they should keep a
" register book, and use such apparel, specially at prayers, as
" was appointed; that they should endeavour to keep peace
" and quiet in their parishes. That they should every day
" read a chapter in the Old and New Testament, considering it
" well, to the increase of their knowledge; and, in conclusion,
" that they should exercise their office to the honour of God,
" and the quiet of the queen's subjects, and observe an uni-
" formity in all laws and orders already established; and that
" they should use no sort of trade, if their living amounted to
" twenty nobles or upwards."

The proceedings here in England are fully collected by
Mr. Strype; so, as to these, I refer my reader to the account
given by him, which is both full and impartial. I shall only
give the abstracts of the letters that passed in this matter
between our bishops and Bullinger, Gualter, and the other
divines in Zurich. These foreign divines did not officiously,
nor of their own motion, intermeddle in this matter. It began
[Jan. 25.] in January 1564-5; for then the queen wrote to the archbishop, and in March the order was settled by the archbishop
and bishops: but when the bishops saw the opposition that
many were making to this, Sampson and Humphreys being
the most eminent of those who opposed it, who were in great
reputation, particularly in the University of Oxford, where
the one was dean of Christ's Church, and the other was president of Magdalen's, and divinity professor; and they were
much distinguished for their learning, piety, and zeal in re-
Horne, bi- ligion: upon this, Horne, bishop of Winchester, wrote on the
shop of
Winches- 16th of July [29] to Gualter, and stated the matter clearly to
ter, writes him. I have put his letter in the Collection, though it is
to Zurich,
upon these already printed: but I thought it convenient to insert it, since
diversities the letters that are to follow depend upon it.
in practice.

[29 The letter is dated 16 cal. Augusti 1565, which is July 17.]

After he had mentioned some of Gualter's works, he com- Collect.
mends those of Zurich for not being imposed on by the arti- Numb. 75.
fices of the French; in which he hopes those of Berne would
308 follow the example that they had set them.　He comes to the
affairs of England, "where they were still in fear of the
" snares of the papists, who took great advantage, from a
" question lately raised about vestments, to say protestants
" could never agree together.　The act of parliament was
" made before they were in office; so that they had no hand
" in making it: by it the vestments were enacted, but without
" any superstitious conceit about them, the contrary being
" expressly declared.　What was once enacted in parliament
" could not be altered, but by the same authority.　The
" bishops had obeyed the law, thinking the matter to be of its
" nature indifferent: and they had reason to apprehend, that
" if they had deserted their stations upon that account, their
" enemies might have come into their places.　Yet upon this
" there was a division formed among them: some thought
" they ought to suffer themselves to be put from their ministry
" rather than obey the law; others were of a different mind.
" He desires that he would write his opinion of this matter as
" soon as was possible.　They were in hope to procure an
" alteration of the act in the next parliament: but he appre-
" hended there would be a great difficulty in obtaining it, by
" reason of the opposition the papists would give them; for
" they hoped that if many should leave their stations, they
" might find occasions to insinuate themselves again into the
" queen's favour."

It seems he wrote a letter in the same strain to Bullinger, 1565.
as will appear by his answer of the 3rd of November, which
will be found in the Collection.　"He writes, that he had Collect.
" heard of the division among them from others; but not Numb. 76.
Answers
" knowing the whole state of the question, he was not forward from
" to give his opinion till he had his letter.　He laments this thence,
justifying
" unhappy breach among them: he approves their zeal, who those who
obeyed the
" wished to have the church purged from all the dregs of laws.
" popery: on the other hand, he commends their prudence,
" who would not have the church to be forsaken, because of
" the vestments.　The great end of the ministry was edifica-
" tion: and that was not to be abandoned but upon very good

" grounds : especially when the deserting their stations was
" like to make way for much worse things : and that they
" saw either papists or Lutherans would be put in their places,
" and then ceremonies would be out of measure increased.
" No doubt, they had brought many persons of all sorts to
" love the purity of doctrine ; but what a prejudice would it
" be to these to open such a door, by which swarms of abuses
" might creep in among them : this they ought carefully to
" prevent.   As for those who first made those laws, or were
" zealous maintainers of them, he confesses he is not pleased
" with them.   They acted unwisely, if they were truly of the
" reformed side ; but if they were only disguised enemies,
" they were laying snares with ill designs ; yet he thinks
" every thing of that sort ought to be submitted to, rather
" than that they should forsake their ministry : and since it
" was declared that those vestments were to be used without
" any superstitious conceit, he thinks that ought to satisfy
" men's consciences.   But in the mean while he proposes to 309
" them, to press the queen and the nobility to go on and
" complete a reformation, that was so gloriously begun.   He
" knew that in many places questions were at that time moved
" concerning the extent of the magistrate's authority ; he
" wishes these might be every where let alone : certainly
" matters of that nature ought not to be meddled with in
" sermons : there may be an occasion to debate about them
" in parliament, and it may be proper to speak to the queen,
" and to her counsellors, in private about them.   Upon the
" whole matter he concludes, that as on the one hand he
" would be tender in dealing with men of weak consciences ;
" so on the other hand he proposes St. Paul's rule in such
" cases, of *becoming all things to all men :* he circumcised
" Timothy, that he might not give offence to the Jews ;
" though at the same time he condemns those who were im-
" posing the yoke of the Judaical law, as necessary in the
" beginnings of Christianity."

Bullinger
writes to
those who
would not
obey them.

When Sampson and Humphreys understood in what a
strain Bullinger and Gualter had written concerning the vestments, they wrote, on the 16th of February [30], a copious

[30] [These are two distinct letters.   ford, Feb. 9, 1566, and Thomas Samp-
Laurence Humphrey wrote from Ox-   son from London, Feb. 16, 1566.]

account of the grounds on which they founded their refusal
to obey these orders. Their letters came to Bullinger on the
26th of April ; and he answered them on the 1st of May. [1566.]
This will be found in the Collection. " He puts them in Collect.
" mind of Peter Martyr's opinion in a like matter, when he Numb. 77.
" was at Oxford ; to which he could add nothing. He could
" not approve of any persons officiating at an altar on which
" there was a crucifix ; and in a cope on the back of which
" there was a crucifix. He tells them how both he and
" Gualter had answered Horne's letter on the subject : and
" he sent them copies of these letters. He would be ex-
" treme sorry, if these did not give them satisfaction. He
" prayed earnestly to God for them. He had a great dislike
" to all controversies of that sort ; and did not willingly
" meddle in them : he did think that laws might be made
" prescribing *decent* habits to the clergy, which may be re-
" duced to that branch of St. Paul's character of a bishop,
" that he ought to be κόσμιος, which may be rendered *decent*,
" as well as we have it, *of good behaviour*. Nor was this the
" reviving the Levitical law. Every thing is not to be called
" Levitical, because it was practised by the Jews. The apo-
" stles commanded the converts to Christianity to abstain from
" things strangled, and from blood. The maintaining the
" clergy by the tithes came from laws given to Jews ; and
" from them we have the singing of psalms among us : so
" things are not to be rejected because of some conformity
" to the Mosaical institution. Nor can this be called a con-
" formity to popery : nor is every thing practised among
" them to be rejected on that account ; otherwise we must not
" use their churches ; nor pronounce the Creed ; nor use the
" Lord's Prayer ; since all these are used by them. It was
" in this case expressed, in the orders set out lately by them,
" that the habits were not enjoined on the superstitious con-
" ceits of the papists : they were only to be used in obedience
" to the law. It savours too much of a Jewish, or of a mo-
310 " nastic temper, to put religion in such matters. If it is pre-
" tended, that the obeying laws in matters indifferent was the
" giving up our Christian liberty ; that would go a great way
" to the denying all obedience, and might provoke the magis-
" trate to lay yet heavier loads on them. Habits peculiar to

" the clergy was an ancienter practice than popery itself :
" St. John is said to have carried on his head somewhat like
" a mitre ; and mention is made of St. Cyprian's having a
" peculiar garment, called a *dalmatica.* St. Chrysostom
" speaks of their white garments. Tertullian tells us, that
" the heathens converted to Christianity quitted their *toga,*
" the Roman upper garment, and used the *pallium,* or cloak.
" He wishes there were no impositions on the clergy in such
" matters : yet since this was an ancient habit, and was now
" enjoined, without making it a matter of religion ; he wishes
" they would not set too great a value upon it, but yield
" somewhat to the present time ; and that they would consider
" it as a thing indifferent, and not affect to dispute too subtlely
" about it ; but to behave themselves modestly. They had
" put a question to him, Whether any thing may be pre-
" scribed that is not expressed in scripture ? He did not
" approve of laying on a load of such things on people's
" necks ; but some things might be appointed for order and
" discipline. Christ kept the feast of the dedication, though
" appointed by no law of God. If it is said, the things com-
" manded are not necessary, and are of no use, yet they are
" not for that to be condemned, nor are schisms to be raised
" on that account." Many things are again repeated in this
letter that were in his letter to Horne.

That letter was printed in England. A copy of this was sent to Horne ; and both Grindal and he, apprehending the good effect that the printing it might have, in settling the minds of many that were much shaken by the opposition that was made to the orders that had been set out, printed it here[31]. So that it was not necessary for me to put it in the Collection, if I did not intend to lay the chief papers relating to this matter so together, as to set it all in a clear light.

Upon this, Sampson and Humphreys wrote over to Zurich, complaining of the printing of their letter, and carrying their complaints against the constitution of the church much further than to the matter of the vestments : they complain of the

[31] [The judgement of that godly and learned father, H. B., declaring it to be lawfull for the ministers of the Church of Englande to weare the apparell prescribed by the lawes and orders of the same realme ; Engl. Lat. 8vo. London, by W. Seres, 1566.]

music and organs; of making sponsors in baptism answer in
the child's name; of the cross in baptism; of the court of
faculties; and the paying for dispensations; all which will
appear fully in a letter of theirs in the Collection, which they Collect.
wrote to them in July.   " They acknowledge their letter had Numb. 78
" not fully satisfied them : they do not think the prescribing
" habits to the clergy merely a civil thing ; they think St. Paul's
" κόσμος belongs to the ornaments of the mind.   And add,
" How can that habit be thought decent that was brought in
" to dress up the theatrical pomp of popery ? The papists
" gloried in this our imitation of them.   They do approve of
" setting rules concerning order, but that ought not to be
" applied to this, that overturns the peace and quiet of the
" church, in things that are not either necessary or useful ;
" that do not tend to any edification, but serve to recommend
311 " those forms which all do now abhor. The papists themselves
" glory in this, that these habits were brought in by them ;
" for which they vouch Otho's Constitution and the Roman
" Pontifical. They were not against the retaining any thing
" that was good, because it had been abused in popery.

     " They affirm, that in king Edward's time the surplice was
" not universally used nor pressed ; and the copes, then taken
" away, are now to be restored. This is not to extirpate
" popery, but to plant it again ; and, instead of going forward,
" is to go back. It was known how much virtue and religion
" the papists put in the surplice ; and at this day it is held in
" as great esteem as the monks' habits were wont to be. The
" use of it may by degrees bring back the same superstition.
" They did not put religion in habits ; they only opposed those
" that did : and they thought that it gave some authority to
" servitude, to depart from their liberty. They hated conten-
" tion, and were ready to enter into friendly conferences about
" this matter. They do not desert their churches, and leave
" them exposed to wolves ; but, to their great grief, they are
" driven from them. They leave their brethren to stand and
" fall to their own masters ; and desire the same favourable
" forbearance from them, though in vain hitherto. It was by
" other men's persuasion that the queen was irritated against
" them : and now, to support these orders, all that is pre-

" tended is, that they are not unlawful; it is not pretended
" that there is any thing good or expedient in the habits. The
" habits of the clergy are visible marks of their profession.;
" and these ought not to be taken from their enemies.   The
" ancient fathers had their habits ; but not peculiar to bishops,
" nor distinct from the laity.   The instances of St. John and
" Cyprian are singular.   In Tertullian's time the *pallium* was
" the common habit of all Christians.   Chrysostom speaks of
" *white garments*, but with no approbation : he rather finds
" fault with them.   They. had cited Bucer ; but he thought
" that the orders concerning habits, by reason of the abuse of
" them in the Church of England, ought to be taken away, for
" a fuller declaration of their abhorrence of Antichrist, for
" asserting the Christian liberty, and for removing all occasions
" of contention.   They were far from any design of making a
" schism, or of quarrelling.   They will not condemn things
" indifferent as unlawful : they wish the occasion of the con-
" tention were removed, that the remembrance of it might be
" for ever buried.   They who condemned the papal pride
" could not like a tyranny in a free church.   They wish there
" might be a free synod to settle this matter ; in which things
" should not be carried according to the mind of one or two
" persons.   The matter now in debate had never been settled
" by any general decree of a council, or of any reformed
" church.   They acknowledge the doctrine of this church was
" now pure ; and why should there be any defect in any part
" of our worship ? Why should we borrow any thing from
" popery ? Why should they not agree in rites, as well as in
" doctrine, with the other reformed churches ? They had a
" good opinion of their bishops, and bore with their state and
" pomp; they once bore the same cross with them, and preached 312
" the same Christ with them : why are they now turned out of
" their benefices, and some put in prison, only for habits ?
" Why are they publicly defamed ? The bishops had printed
" the private letter that they had written to them, without
" their knowledge or consent. The bishops do now stand upon
" it, as if the cause were their own.   But to let them see that
" the dispute was not only about a cap, they sent them an
" abstract of some other things, to which they wish some

" remedy could be found ;" (which is in the Collection ;) " and Collect.
" conclude with some prayers to God, to quiet those dissen- Numb. 79.
" sions, and to send forth labourers into his vineyard."

To this I have joined the answer that Bullinger and Gualter Collect.
wrote to them.   In it they tell them, " that they did not Numb. 80.
" expect that their letters should fully satisfy them : they only answer to
" wrote their opinion to them because they desired it.   They Sampson.
" were heartily sorry to find that they could not acquiesce in
" it.   They would engage no further in that matter : they
" could answer their arguments, but they would give no occa-
" sion to endless disputations.   They thought it would be more
" expedient to submit to those habits, and to continue in the
" church, than, by refusing to use them, to be forced to leave
" their churches.   They went no further, and did not approve
" of any popish defilements or superstitions.   Nor did they in
" any sort enter into those other matters, of which they do now
" complain, and of which they knew nothing before.   These
" were matters of much greater consequence than either the
" surplices or the copes : so that it was to be hoped, that the
" letter they had written about the habits could not be stretched
" to these matters.   There was nothing left to them, but to
" commend them to God, and to pray that he would quiet this
" unhappy dissension among them, and give his church the
" blessings of peace.   They only desire them to remember that
" the ministers of the gospel ought not only to hold fast the
" truth, but likewise to be prudent stewards, having a due
" regard to the times, bearing many things with patience and
" charity, and so maintain the peace of the church : and not to
" prejudice it by an over-eager or morose temper ; nor think
" it enough that they had a good design ; but they must pursue
" it by prudent methods."

Bullinger and Gualter, seeing the division like to be carried They wrote
much further than the matter of the vestments, thought the to the earl
best office that they could do their friends, was to write to the of Bedford.
earl of Bedford ; being well assured of his zeal in the matters
of religion.   They wrote to him on the 11th of September that
year : the letter will be found in the Collection.   They tell Collect.
him, " that when they first heard of the contention raised Numb. 81.
" about the vestments, they were afraid it might have a further
" progress.   They, being desired, did give their opinion freely

" in the matter : and thought that, for things of so little im-
" portance, it was not fit for the clergy to desert their stations,
" and to leave them to be filled perhaps by wolves and de- 313
" ceivers. They were sorry to find that their fears of the
" mischief that might follow on this contention were but too
" well grounded.   They hear, that not only the vestments are
" complained of, but that many other things are excepted to,
" that plainly savour of popery.   They are also sorry that the
" private letter which they wrote should have been printed ;
" and that their judgment of the vestments was extended to
" other things, of which they could in no sort approve : so that
" their opinion in one particular is made use of, to cast a load
" on persons, for whom they should rather have compassion in
" their sufferings than study to aggravate them.   It gave
" them a very sensible grief to see the church of England,
" scarce got out of the hands of their bloody enemies, now like
" to be pulled down by their intestine broils.   So, having an
" entire confidence in his good affection to the gospel, they
" pray him to intercede with the queen and the nobility, in the
" parliament that was soon to meet, for their brethren that
" were then suffering ; who deserved that great regard should
" be had to them, and that their faults should be forgiven
" them.   It had appeared what true zeal they had for religion ;
" since the only thing about which they were so solicitous was
" that religion should be purged from all the dregs of popery.
" This cause in general was such, that those who promoted it
" proved themselves to be worthy of the highest dignity.
" Princes were to be nursing fathers to the church : then they
" perform that office truly when they not only rescue her out
" of the hands of her enemies, but take care that the spouse of
" Christ be not any way stained with the false paint of super-
" stition, or render herself suspected, by having any rites
" unbecoming the Christian simplicity.   They do therefore
" earnestly pray him, that as he has hitherto shewed his zeal
" in the cause of the gospel, so he will at this time exert him-
" self ; and employ all the interest he has in the queen, and in
" the nobility, that the Church of England, so happily re-
" formed, to the admiration of the whole world, may not be
" stained with any of the defilements or remnants of popery.
" This will look like a giddiness in them : it will offend the

" weak among them, and give great scandal to their neigh-
" bours, both in France and in Scotland, who are yet under
" the cross.   The very papists will justify their tyrannical im-
" positions by what is done now among them.   They lay all
" this before him with the more confidence, knowing his zeal
" as they do."   They also wrote in the same strain to Grindal
and Horne, as will be found in the Collection.

When Grindal and Horne understood that those of Zurich
were not pleased with the printing of their letter; of which
they wrote to them, and sent with it the paper, in which were
put the heads of those other things in the constitution of this
church, to which they excepted ; they both, jointly, wrote
answer to them, in one letter to Bullinger and Gualter, on the
6th of February ; which will be found in the Collection.

314   " They tell them, they had printed their letter, but had
" suppressed the names of those to whom it was directed.   It
" had the good effect that they expected from it : for it had
" satisfied and settled the minds of many, who were upon the
" point of leaving their churches; and even the most trouble-
" some were so far wrought on by it, that they were silent,
" and less violent in their opposition than they had formerly
" been.   Some few were turned out, but they were not of the
" more learned sort ; except Sampson, who, they acknowledge,
" was both pious and learned.   Humphreys, and other learned
" men, were still continued in their stations.   The letter that
" they had printed related only to that particular upon which
" it was written, and could not be applied to any thing else :
" nor was there any other question then on foot : so that it
" was a calumny to say, that their opinion was asked about
" any other matter.   The noise and the complaints, that some
" had made, had very much provoked the queen and many of
" the nobility against them.   The papists triumphed upon it,
" and hoped to come in again, and to fill the places, which
" were made void upon their deserting their stations.   They
" do solemnly attest the great God, that this dissension was
" not raised by any fault of theirs ; and that it did not lie at
" their door that those vestments were not quite taken away.
" They may take their oaths upon it, that they had used all
" possible means in that matter ; and had, with the utmost
" earnestness, and the most sincere diligence, laboured to

Collect.
Numb. 82.

Collect.
Numb. 83.
Grindal
and
Horne's
letter,
shewing
their un-
easiness in
many
things.

BURNET, PART III.   M m

" obtain that which their brethren desired, and which they
" themselves wished for. But since they could not do what
" willingly they would do, they must be content with doing
" what they could do.

" As to the other particulars complained of, they plainly
" write, they did not approve of that figured music, together
" with the use of organs, that was continued in cathedrals.
" They enlarge on many other particulars, and set forth the
" method of convocations. They did in no sort approve of
" women's baptizing. They gave way, till God should send
" better times, to the form of making the sponsors in baptism
" answer in the child's name; for which St. Austin's authority
" was pretended: but they did openly declare, that they
" thought it was not convenient. Nor did they approve of using
" the cross in baptism; though the words spoken when it was
" made did plainly shew, there was no superstitious conceit
" kept up by the use of it. They also suffered the posture of
" kneeling in the sacrament, with the due caution with which
" it was enjoined, that was set down in king Edward's book,
" declaring the reason for which that posture was still con-
" tinued. For the abuses of their courts, though they cannot
" correct them entirely, yet they did openly inveigh against
" them; which they would continue still to do, till they should
" be sent back to hell, from whence they came. Every man
" had full freedom to declare his mind as to all these abuses:
" they had laboured in the last parliament all they could to
" purge out all errors and abuses; which, though it had not
" then the desired effect, yet they would not give over their
" endeavours to bring it to a happy conclusion: and this they 315
" would do, as they desired the continuance of their friendship
" and brotherly love."

[Epistolæ
Tigurinæ,
1558–1579,
Ep. lxviii.
p. 90.]
The others still insisted; and Sampson in a letter from
Oxford[32] the 9th of February, 1565–6, to Bullinger, reduces
the questions concerning the habits to seven heads. First, If
a habit different in form and colour from the laity ought to be
enjoined to the clergy? Secondly, If the Mosaical ceremonies

---

[32] [This letter is from Laurence
Humphrey, not from Sampson, who
wrote another on the same subject
to Bullinger, Feb. 16, 1566. It is
one of those alluded to in the note
to p. 309, and therefore is wrongly
placed here by the author.]

may be brought into the Christian church? Thirdly, If it is lawful to conform to papists in habits and outward rites, and if it is fitting to borrow ceremonies from that corrupt church? Fourthly, If the using a peculiar priestly habit is merely a civil matter, and if it does not savour of monkery, popery, and Judaism? Fifthly, If those who have hitherto used their liberty, may with a good conscience, upon the account of the queen's mandate, involve themselves and the church again in a yoke of bondage? Sixthly, If the popish clerical habit can be called a thing that is indifferent? And the seventh is, If they ought to use these habits, rather than desert their stations? To these he begs him to send as soon as may be a full and copious answer.

A few days after this, Jewel wrote to Bullinger, (in the letter that is in the Collection[33],) " that he was so attacked " by many different hands, that it took him wholly up to pre- " pare answers to them. He was not in the house of lords " during the last parliament, in which there was a great heat " for a whole month concerning the succession to the crown : " but the queen would suffer no declaration to be made " in that matter, though it was most vehemently pressed, " there appearing on both sides a great deal of earnestness. " The queen thought any such declaration would turn the " eyes of the nation too much towards the rising sun. He " says, the controversy about the vestments had raised great " heats. The queen was fixed, and could not be wrought on " to let any change be made. Some of their brethren were " so eager in disputing about that matter, as if the whole " business of religion was concerned in it. They leave their " stations and churches, rather than yield a little. Nor were " they at all moved from their stiffness by the most learned " letters that he and Gualter had written to them on that " subject; nor by all the advices of their friends. He thanks " God that they had no other, nor more important debates then " among them. Cheyney, bishop of Gloucester, did indeed " in parliament profess himself openly to be a Lutheran; but " he was not like to have many followers."

In a letter of his, that is also in the Collection, written to

Marginal notes: Jewel's sense of those matters. Collect. Numb. 84

Collect. Numb. 85.

[33] [This letter is of Feb. 24, 1567, and so a whole year after the letter last mentioned.]

M m 2

Bullinger on the 1st of March, 1565, he writes, " that he was
" overwhelmed with the books that the papists had written
" against him, and was by that means engaged in a profound
" course of study.   He tells him how cardinal Granvelle had
" intended to cut off the intercourse between England and the
" Netherlands; hoping by that means to provoke the English
" to break out into tumults : but the design turned upon him-
" self; for the English resolving to settle their trade and
" staple at Embden, the people of Flanders could not bear
" that.   The pope had sent one to Ireland to raise a flame in
" that island.   But the pope's agent, who was an Irishman,
" was taken, and sent over a prisoner to England.   In Scot- 316
" land the queen only had her mass, all the nation being
" averse to it."

Reflections
on this
matter.

By Grindal and Horne's letters it appears, that they had
no other zeal in this matter, but to preserve the church in the
queen's favour, and in obedience to the laws : yet in letters
that were upon this occasion written to Zurich, (a part of one

Collect.
Numb. 86.

is in the Collection,) by some others that adhered to Sampson,
they let them know, that both Parker the archbishop, and
Grindal and Horne, were too much sharpened in this matter ;
therefore they pray them to use their endeavours to soften
them more towards their brethren : but they acknowledge
that Pilkington of Durham, Sandys of Worcester, and Parkhurst of Norwich, had by their moderation made good all
their promises ; so they deserved that thanks should be given
them : they desire further, that they would write to them all
to proceed more mildly, and to endeavour to get those dregs
of popery to be removed ; and that they would tolerate, at

Other let-
terswritten
to Zurich
by some
bishops.
[July 20,
1573.
Epistolæ
Tigurinæ,
1558–1579,
Ep. cx.
p. 167.]

least connive at, those who did not approve them.   I find Pilkington complains in a letter to Gualter, " that the disputes
" which began about the vestments, were carried much further,
" even to the whole constitution.   Pious people lamented ;
" atheists laughed at it; and the papists blew the coals, and
" were full of hopes upon it.   The blame of all was cast on
" the bishops.   He adds, I confess we suffer many things
" against our hearts, groaning under them : we cannot take
" them away, though we were ever so much set on it.   We
" are under authority, and can innovate nothing without the
" queen ; nor can we alter the laws : the only thing that is

" left to our choice is, whether we will bear these things, or
" break the peace of the church."

Parkhurst in one letter writes, " Many good people are
" pleased with all that is done; but there are some things
" that do not please me."   And in another he writes, " Mat-
" ters of religion go on well : there are but a very few things
" that I dare find fault with.   That which grieved him most
" was, that the lives of those who professed the gospel were
" so very contrary to it.   The gospel was never preached
" among them more faithfully, and with more zeal : he prays,
" God grant us his Spirit that we may walk in the Spirit, and
" mortify the works of the flesh."   The last letter that those Collect.
of Zurich wrote on this subject was on the 26th of August, Numb. 87.
1567 [34], directed to the bishops of London, Winchester, and
Norwich.   " They express their grief that some learned men
" were deprived : they hear daily that some of those that had
" given good proofs of themselves in the Marian persecution
" were now not only turned out, but imprisoned : they hear
" that in Ireland many that have the same scruples are yet
" kept out of all trouble by the queen's order, upon the inter-
" cession of their bishops : which makes it probable, that the
" like favour might be obtained in England, if the bishops
" would intercede with her majesty for it ; which may the
" rather be expected, since the bishops themselves acknow-
" ledge, that it were better for the church that these cere-
" monies were all laid aside ; and affirm, that they had often
" moved in parliament that they might be taken away, that so
317 " the church might be more pure and less burdened.   There-
" fore they do not doubt but that they, out of their piety, will
" endeavour to procure favour to their brethren, to which
" they do very earnestly, but yet decently and modestly, press
" them."   Cox, bishop of Ely, who I do not find meddled
much in these controversies, has in a letter to Gualter some
very sad expressions ; for which there is too much occasion at
all times.   " When I consider the sins that do every where
" abound, and the neglect and contempt of the word of God,
" I am struck with horror, and tremble to think what God
" will do with us.   We have some discipline among us with

[34] [This date is six years earlier than that of the last letter mentioned.]

" relation to men's lives, such as it is ; but if any man would
" go about to persuade our nobility to submit their necks to
" that yoke, he may as well venture to pull the hairs out of a
" lion's beard."

Sandys was of the same mind : he lamented the occasion of
this dispute, and hoped to see an end put to it. In a letter
[Epistolæ to Bullinger from Worcester, dated the 3rd of January 1566,
Tigurinæ, he writes thus : " The true religion of Christ is now settled
1558–1579,
Ep. lxvi. " among us, which is the most valuable of all things. The
p 86.] " gospel is no more shut up, but is freely preached ; and for
" other things, we need not be much concerned about them.
" There is some small dispute concerning the popish vest-
" ments, whether they ought to be used or not ? But God will
" put an end to these things [35]."

Of the af- A few days after that, Jewel, in a letter, dated the 8th of
fairs of February 1566, to Bullinger, (a part of it is in the Collection,
Scotland.
Collect. the rest of it relates to the books he was then writing in de-
Numb. 88. fence of his Apology,) tells him, " that the queen seemed fixed
" in her resolution not to marry : he expresses his great con-
" cern that the heat raised on the account of the *surplice* was
" not extinguished. He writes, that the affairs of Scotland
" were not in a quiet state : some of the chief of the nobility
" had retired into England ; others fortified themselves in
" their castles, and were as in a state of war with the papists.
" The queen, though an obstinate papist, yet does not seem
" resolved what course she had best take ; for in matters of
" religion the greatest part both of the nobility and people
" were against her ; and their number did daily increase.
" The king of Spain sent lately an Italian abbot thither with
" Spanish gold. He was a subtle and crafty man, and did
" so far gain not only on the queen, but on the king, that
" though he had hitherto gone to sermons, and had no mass,
" yet upon the assurance of a rich ship that was expected
" within a day, he presently ordered mass to be said in his
" church ; while Knox in the very next church was preaching
" against idolatry, and the whole papal tyranny, with greater
" zeal than ordinary : but the Spanish ship was furiously

[35] Contenditur aliquantulum de vestibus papisticis utendis vel non
utendis ; dabit Deus his quoque finem.

" shattered by a storm, and was cast on the coast of England;
" so that weak king would find what he had gained by his
" going to mass." Sampson and Humphreys wrote a long
and particular answer to the letter that Grindal and Horne
wrote to Bullinger ; but that runs into a tedious controversy, with which the divines of Zurich wrote that they
would meddle no more in those matters : so I do not think
fit to insert it.

318   " They complain that the archbishop had contributed to
" buy an organ for Canterbury, which was no sign of his
" disliking it. They complain that many were put in prison
" because they would not provide godfathers and godmothers
" for baptizing their children : they say the convocation signi-
" fied little ; for many things were agreed to in the convoca-
" tion in the year 1562, that would have tended to the great
" good of the church, but were suppressed : for nothing was
" of force but as the queen and the archbishop consented.
" And in the last convocation, a very learned man that be-
" longed to the bishop of Norwich proposed somewhat relating
" to the vestments : to whom a bishop said, What have you
" to do in those matters ? We began them, and we will end
" them.   He answered the bishop, This matter has been
" hitherto laid wholly on the queen, but now you take it on
" yourselves.   They also in another paper set forth, that in
" queen Mary's days, when the church of England was broken
" and dispersed, a body of protestants formed themselves into
" a church at London, and had their ministers and deacons,
" and continued through all her reign, though many of them
" were burned : but that, after queen Mary's death, the exiles
" were recalled, and the prisoners were set at liberty ; only
" this church that had continued all the while in the midst of
" the flame was now extinguished.   In another letter he as-
" sures Simler there was no danger of Lutheranism ; only we
" are now fighting among ourselves about ceremonies, vest-
" ments, and matters of no importance.   That matter has
" somewhat shaken men of weak minds : I wish that all, even
" the smallest remnants of popery could be wholly put, not only
" out of our churches, but chiefly out of the minds of all peo-
" ple ; but the queen at this time cannot bear any alteration
" in religion."

I shall carry this matter no farther, having gone beyond what I had at first proposed by the importance of these papers, that give so clear and so true an account of the beginnings of those unhappy disputes, of which we have seen and do still feel the unhappy consequences. In these we clearly see what was the sense of the most eminent and the most learned of our reformers in those matters. They continued their correspondence with Zurich as long as those great men lived with whom they had lodged in their great distress, and to whom they had been so singularly obliged, that they were ready always to acknowledge it, and were often sending presents to them.

The queen of Scots marries the lord Darnley.In Scotland things were running into great disorder. The queen, as she liked the person of the lord Darnley, and perhaps the better, because he seemed to be of a soft and gentle temper, and easy to be governed ; so her faithfullest counsellors concurred in advising the marriage. He was the next heir to the crown of England after the queen : for though the queen dowager of Scotland, that was Henry the Eighth's sister, having married the earl of Angus, after king James the Fourth was killed ; but falling to be in ill terms with him, either found or suborned witnesses (as it was given out) to prove upon him a precontract in words of the present time, by which she obtained a sentence dissolving that marriage : yet the daughter she had borne to him was declared legiti- 319 mate, in the bull that confirmed the sentence, declaring that marriage dissolved, the original of which I saw : the reason given is, because she was born of the mother's part *bonâ fide.* Lord Darnley being thus descended, and born within the kingdom of England, might have been a dangerous competitor for that crown, especially if he should fortify himself by a prudent marriage, and a good conduct in England : so it was certainly good advice given the queen, since she liked his person, to secure her right to that succession by this marriage. When she married him she declared him king, and put his name on the coin after her own. The qualities of his mind did not answer the gracefulness of his person : for sometimes he was in all things compliant to the queen ; but that lasted not long. She had such an affable and obliging air, which her education in the court of France had much improved, that it was not easy to resist it. At first she seemed so indifferent as to the matters of religion, that the minds of the nation were much quieted, when they concluded that she continued to be a papist more from principles of honour and interest than from her own persuasion.

But they came to have other thoughts of her when she began to express more zeal in those matters. Her kindred by her mother pushed her on ; and she was animated both from the court of France, and from Rome, to restore the popish religion : on these hopes she set her gates open to all that desired to come to her mass, and had many masses every day in her chapel. The body of the Scottish nation did not easily bear with the mass, which the queen had at first privately in her court for herself, and for a very small number of servants, who were of her own religion. In the parliament in the year 1563, a petition was offered by the noblemen, and the superintendents, and ministers of the reformed religion, which will be found in the Collection, setting forth, That whereas in the last convention of the kirk, that was held at Edinburgh in June last, some were sent to the queen with certain articles, to which they desired answer ; and though the queen had answered them in part, yet she referred the farther answer to the present parliament : so a full answer was now prayed. And whereas in the parliament held in July 1560, it was enacted, that the mass, and all papistry should be put out of the realm, and Christ's religion should be universally received ; and that the queen, by divers proclamations, has approved Christ's religion, which she found publicly received at her arrival, in particular at Dundee, on the 15th of September last, in which the king and queen did, both by act of council and by proclamation, promise that in this present parliament she would establish the religion of Christ, and abolish all laws and constitutions contrary to the same ; upon which they desired, that the premises might be considered : and so they laid before the parliament the articles which they had laid before the queen and her council, together with her answer and the reply made to it by the kirk.

In the articles they demand first, That the papistical mass, with all idolatry, and the pope's jurisdiction, might be abolished, not only in the subjects, but in the queen's own person : and

She shews more zeal in her religion.

Collect. Numb. 89.

The demands of the reformed.

that the true religion might be ratified through the whole 320 kingdom, as well in the queen's person, as in the subjects : and that the people might be required to resort on Sundays to prayers and preaching, as they were before to the idolatrous mass. Secondly, that provision may be made for the ministers' maintenance ; and that such as are admitted into the ministry may have their livings assigned them where they labour, or in parts adjacent; and that they may not be put to crave them of others : and that the benefices then vacant, or that have been vacant since March *anno* 1558, or that shall become vacant, be given to learned persons, able to preach God's word, upon their trial and admission by the superintendents. And that no bishopric, abbey, or other ecclesiastical benefice, having many churches annexed to it, be given to any one man : but that the churches may be severally disposed of, so that every man may serve at his own church; and that glebes and manses be assigned to them, that they may reside at their churches, and discharge their consciences in them ; and that the churches may be kept in due repair. Thirdly, That none may have charge of souls, or be put in colleges or universities, or publicly instruct the youth, but such as are tried by the superintendents and the visitors of the churches, and are admitted by them. Fourthly, That lands founded for hospitals may be restored to the use of the poor ; and that all rents and profits belonging to any order of friars be applied to the poor, and for schools in towns. Fifthly, That horrid crimes, blasphemy, sorcery, adultery, incest, and murder, with many other crimes that are reckoned up, may be severely punished ; and that some order may be taken for the ease of the labourers of the ground, concerning the reasonable payment of their tithes, and in the letting of them.

The queen's answer to them.

To this the queen answered, " That as she did not think that " there was any impiety in the mass, so she hoped her subjects " would not press her to receive any religion against her own " conscience, which would throw her into a perpetual unquiet- " ness, by the remorse of her conscience. She would never " leave the religion in which she had been brought up. And " it would be further a great prejudice to her, in that, by her " so doing, she should lose the friendship of the king of France, " the ancient ally of this kingdom, and of other princes, from

" whom she may find great supports : so she will not in an
" instant put herself in hazard of losing all her friends.   And
" since she has not yet pressed, nor means she hereafter to
" press, the conscience of any man, but leaves them to worship
" God according to their persuasion, she hopes they will not
" press her to offend her own conscience.   But when the par-
" liament meets, her majesty will consent to every thing that
" the three estates shall agree upon ; and she renews the as-
" surance she had given, that men's lives or estates shall be in
" no hazard for any cause of religion."

   As to the second article, " The queen thought it not reason-
" able that she should deprive herself of so great a part of the
" patrimony of the crown, by putting the patronage of bene-
321 " fices out of her hands ; for her own necessity required the
" keeping them in her own hands : yet she was contented to
" assign what might serve for the reasonable sustentation of the
" ministers. She referred the other articles to the parliament."

   To this answer the kirk replied, " That the firmness she
" expressed to the mass gave no small grief to her good sub-
" jects.   Their religion was no other than that which Christ
" revealed, and his apostles preached ; which differed from
" the impiety of the Turks, the blasphemy of the Jews, and
" the vain superstition of the papists."   And upon that, as
they run out into a high commendation of their religion, so
" they require the queen, in the name of God, to embrace the
" means by which she may be persuaded to the truth : which
" they offered presently to her, by the preaching of God's
" word, and by public disputation against the adversaries of
" it, whensoever she thought it expedient.   And as for the
" mass, they undertook to prove it to be a mass of impiety,
" from the beginning to the end.   As for the prejudice that
" the queen thinks would follow on her changing her religion,
" by dissolving the alliance she is in with the king of France,
" and other foreign princes ; they answer, that the true reli-
" gion is the undoubted means to keep up a perfect confederacy
" with him, who is the *King of kings*, and who has the hearts
" of all princes in his hands ; which ought to be more valued
" than all other confederacies whatsoever."

   As to the second article ; " They did not intend to defraud
" her of the patronages ; but only, that persons presented to

" benefices should be tried and examined by the learned men
" of the kirk, or the superintendents appointed for that end.
" But as the presentations belong to her, so collation upon
" them belongs to the church ; and the patrons may not pre-
" sent without trial and examination : which if they might do,
" must bring great ignorance and disorder into the church.
" And it was far against all good conscience for the queen to
" retain a good part of the benefices in her own hands. This
" was so contrary both to all divine and human laws, that they
" were unwilling to open up that whole matter to her. And
" therefore they beg she would consider, that though the
" patronage of benefices belonged to her, yet the retention
" of them in her own hands, and the not giving them to qua-
" lified persons, is ungodly, and contrary to all order, and
" ruinous to the souls of the people. They were desirous to
" have her necessities relieved : but they add, that the tithes
" are the patrimony of the church ; out of which, in the first
" place, those who serve in the ministry ought to be relieved,
" the churches ought to be repaired, and the youth instructed.
" They concluded with thanks for her willingness to have the
" ministers provided for : and they pray, that a special con-
" descending on particulars may be thought on."

But all these petitions were still put off : and the queen, by
her practice among the nobility, began to divide them into
factions ; and plainly said, when these petitions were read to
Spotswood. [pp. 190 sqq.] her, that *she would do nothing in prejudice of the religion
that she professed :* and in wrath told them, *She hoped,
before a year was expired, to have the mass, and the catholic* 322
religion professed through the whole kingdom. And she
managed the parliament so dextrously, that neither was the
treaty of Leith, nor the settlement of religion made in the
parliament 1560, so much as named, much less confirmed. In
this parliament some small provision was made for the ministers ; and acts were made against sorcery and adultery, that
they should be punished by death. There was indeed an act
of oblivion passed for all that was done from the 6th of March
1558, to the 1st of September 1561 : but the parliament of
the year 1560 came to be looked on as an illegal assembly :
so that upon this a great alarm was given to the whole body
of the reformed in that kingdom ; and the jealousy was in-

creased by the queen's marrying the lord Darnley. He had
been bred up a strict papist, but now pretended to be a protestant; yet as he was all the while suspected of favouring the
religion he was bred up in, so he quickly returned to the open
profession of it. This gave occasion to another petition in a
bolder strain, in which the body of the reformed set forth,
" that the true religion was established in that nation ; that
" the mass, and all the idolatry and tyrannical usurpations of
" the pope, were suppressed, and that they were going on to
" a perfect reformation: but that all had been stopped now
" for the space of four years. That upon her arrival, that
" idol the mass was again set up, and men were put in offices,
" to which they had no right. From such beginnings, they
" saw what they might look for : yet, in hope that God would
" mollify the queen's heart, and out of their desire to maintain
" the public peace, they had long expected to see what answer
" would be made to their petitions. But they saw things grow
" daily worse and worse. The queen's gates were then set
" open, in contempt of proclamations set out by herself to the
" contrary. The patrimony of the church was bestowed on
" unworthy persons : their ministers were reduced to great
" poverty, and put to much trouble. Vices of all sorts
" abounded universally : they therefore prayed the queen to
·" think of redressing these matters, and to answer their other
" petitions; assuring her of all due obedience to her laws and
" authority. They also pray, that she would give them no
" occasion to think that she intended the subversion of the
" true religion, and the destruction of those who professed it :
" for they assure her, they would never be subject to that
" Roman Antichrist, nor suffer (as far as it lay in their power
" to hinder it) any branches of his usurped authority to have
" place within the realm." This, which is in the Collection, Collect.
prevailed no more than their other petitions had done. Numb. 90.

   -    I will add to this a few particulars relating to the affairs
ʻof Scotland, as they are set forth in some of these letters that
were sent me from Zurich. Parkhurst, bishop of Norwich, in
a letter to Bullinger, (which is in the Collection,) writes in the Collect.
year 1566, " that in March last, an Italian, called signor Numb. 91.
" David, (whom he charges as skilled in necromancy,) who
" was in great favour with the queen, was dragged out of her

" room, and stabbed by many hands ; and adds, that an 323
" abbot was then so wounded, that though he escaped, yet he
" died of his wounds soon after : and that one Black, a Do-
" minican, in great esteem among the papists, was also killed
" in the court. And upon all that disorder, while the privy-
" council was sitting, the lords escaped with their lives. Since
" that time, the queen had brought forth a prince ; she was
" reconciled to her husband, and had called home her brother,
" and the lords that were of the reformed side : but though
" the queen had borne her son ten weeks before he wrote, yet
" all that while he was not baptized ; for she intended to do it
" with pomp, and many masses in the great church, though
" the inhabitants of Edinburgh were resolved to hinder that :
" they apprehended she would bring over a force from France :
" he concludes with a prayer, not very evangelical, that *God*
" *would either convert, or confound her.* There are circum-
" stances in this letter, of some others killed with signor David,
" that I have found no where else."

About the same time, Grindal wrote likewise a letter to
Bullinger, which is also in the Collection ; in which he thanks
him for the letters he had written over concerning the controversy about the habits. He writes, " that it was not credible
" that a question about things of no moment should have
" raised so great a disturbance as this had done : many, both
" of the ministers and the people, were designing to withdraw
" from them, and to set up separate meetings ; but most of
" them were now come to a better mind. He acknowledges
" their wise and good letters had contributed much towards
" that : yet some continued still in their former resolutions.
" It were an easy thing to reconcile them to the queen, if
" they could be brought to change their mind : but till that
" was done, it was not in their power to effect it. The bishops
" upon their return, and before they were consecrated, had
" endeavoured all they could to get those things removed that
" gave occasion to the present dispute : but in that they could
" not prevail, neither with the queen nor with the parliament.
" So they, upon consulting among themselves, came to a reso-
" lution, not to desert their churches for the sake of a few
" rites that were not unlawful, since the doctrine was entire
" and pure ; in which they agreed in all things with them of

" Zurich. They saw the good effects of these their resolu-
" tions: and those unseasonable contentions about things in-
" different did not edify, but tear the churches.

" From their own affairs he turns to those of Scotland;
" where, he writes, things were in no good state. They still
" retained the profession of the truth; but the queen endea-
" voured by all means to extirpate it: she had lately ordered
" six or seven masses to be said every day in her chapel, and
" admitted all that pleased, to come to them: whereas at first
" she was contented with one private mass, to which no
" Scotchman was admitted. And whereas it was provided
" that the ministers should be maintained out of the revenues
" of the church; she had now for three years stopped all
" payments. There were no public changes yet made; both
" the nobility and the people continued very firm; of whom
" he reckons the earl of Murray the chief. He understood
324 " that the queen was in very ill terms with her husband on
" this account. There was one David, an Italian, recom-
" mended to her by the cardinal of Lorraine, who governed
" all the councils there, and was secretary of state. The king,
" finding he had no regard to him, grew uneasy at it; and
" being young and rash, he entered into a conspiracy with
" some of the nobility, and some of his court: so the Italian
" was dragged out of the queen's presence, notwithstanding
" her earnest entreaties to save him; and he was no sooner
" out, than many ran their daggers into him; so he was mur-
" dered without any cause declared. This horrid crime stuck
" deep in the queen's heart; so that, though she had borne a
" son to him, she could never forgive him."

The dismal fate of that unfortunate queen is so tender a
point, that I will say nothing of it, but in the words of others.
There is a letter of Grindal's to Bullinger, dated the 21st of
June 1567. All in that letter which relates to this matter is
in the Collection; in which these words will be found: " Scot- Collect.
" land is fallen into new troubles; for their late king Henry, Numb. 93.
" on the 10th of February, was found dead in a garden near
" his lodgings. It is not yet agreed how he died. Some say,
" that a few barrels of gunpowder, being on design laid under
" the chamber in which he lay, these being kindled, the house
" was blown up, and so he was thrown out into that garden.

" Others say, that in the night he was dragged out of his
" chamber and strangled, and that then the house was blown
" up.　The earl of Bothwell was generally thought the author
" of this murder.　He also procured, by the authority of the
" archbishop of St. Andrew's, a divorce from his lawful wife:
" and on the 15th of May last the queen had married him,
" and created him duke of Orkney.　Almost all the nobility
" had left the court before this marriage, when they saw that
" no inquiry was made into the king's murder : they had a
" meeting at Stirling, where it appeared, by clear evidences,
" that the murder was committed by Bothwell : so an army
" was brought together on design to seize on him, but he
" made his escape ; and it was not then known whither he
" was gone.　Some say, the queen was besieged in a certain
" castle ; and others say, she was made a prisoner in the
" castle of Edinburgh, as having been conscious to the murder
" of her husband.　But whatsoever may be in this, that in-
" famous marriage must end tragically.　With this he con-
" cludes that matter, promising him a more particular account
" when the certainty of it was better understood."

To this I will add another relation, that may be more certainly depended on.　Cardinal Laurea, whom the pope had
sent to be his nuncio in Scotland, may be supposed to have
had the best information that he could procure from those
of her party, and of her religion, and he would certainly have
put the best face possible on that matter ; especially after her
tragical fate, which raised an universal disposition in all people to think as well of her as was possible ; but chiefly among
those of that religion : so that I know no relation of that affair
that can be so certainly depended on, (making still some
allowances for the softenings of a partial writer,) as that which
we find in that cardinal's Life, which was written by the abbot 325
of Pignerol, and was printed at Bologna in the year 1599 ; in
which he gives this account of this whole matter.

Pope Pius the Fifth sent Laurea to be his nuncio in Scotland, to assist and encourage the queen in her zeal : he sent
by him twenty thousand crowns to her, as an earnest of further supplies ; and wrote to her with his own hand, recommending his nuncio to her.　The nuncio came to Paris in the
dogdays, and brought him who writes his life along with him

to be his secretary. He received letters from the queen of Scots by the hands of the archbishop of Glasgow, who was then her ambassador in France : by these she expressed her desires that he might come to Scotland as soon as might be ; but wished him to delay coming till he should hear from her once more, that she might have all things prepared for his reception. He upon that wrote to her in a very vehement style, pressing her to zeal and fortitude of mind, in carrying on the restoring the catholic religion in her kingdom : with that he sent her over four thousand crowns, and sent one Edmund Hay, a Jesuit, and a man of a cunning and penetrating temper, to be a secret assistant to her : in particular, he pressed her either to punish, or at least to disgrace Lethington, who he believed set on all the tumults, and was a determined heretic, and a favourer of the earl of Murray.

Con has printed these letters [36]. Pius the Fifth's letter bears date the 16th of June, 1566. In it " he recommends " his nuncio to her confidence, who was then bishop of Mon- " dovi, (Montis Regalis,) and promises all possible assistance " to her, in her design of bringing back her kingdom to the " obedience of the holy see." Queen Mary's answer bears date the 9th of October that year from Edinburgh : " she " in it acknowledges the pope's favour and bounty to her ; " she adds some high expressions of her sense of the pope's " zeal and piety, and promises to treat his nuncio with all " respect and confidence. She tells him, that she had borne " a son ; and that she had brought her nobility, though not " without much difficulty, to consent that he should be publicly " baptized after the manner of the catholic church. She pro- " mises to bring him up in that religion : and she hoped this " should prove a good beginning of restoring the right use of " the sacraments in her dominions." The pope seemed much pleased with this beginning of his pontificate ; and in his answer, on the 22nd of January following, he congratulates the birth and baptism " of her son, and prays that it may have a " good effect."

Marginal notes: Life of queen Mary, printed at Rome, an. 1624. [p. 168.] [Ibid. p. 173.] [Ibid. p. 178.]

[36] [Vita Mariæ Stuartæ Scotiæ Reginæ, Dotariæ Galliæ, Angliæ et Hiberniæ Hæredis, *Scriptore* Georgio Conæo Scoto, ad Urbanum VIII. Pont. Max. Romæ apud Joannem Paulum Gellium MDCXXIV. Superiorum Permissu.]

Three months passed before Laurea had any intimation from the queen concerning his coming over : upon which he sent the bishop of Dunblane, who was then at Paris, with copious advices to that queen, and continued to press her very earnestly by his letters to admit of his coming over : the substance of all which is set forth in his Life. He tells us further, " that the queen held a convention of the estates, and had " obtained two things of them, not without difficulty : the one " was, that her child should be baptized according to the rites " of the Roman church ; and the other was, that the pope's " nuncio should be admitted with due respect."   Upon this 326 the nuncio designed to go to Antwerp, thinking that the navigation would be safer from thence than from Calais.   But then he adds, " that such a barbarous and impious crime was com- " mitted in Scotland, that it gave a horror to think of it, much " more to write of it."   Of what follows in that Life I will add a verbal translation.

" The king, as was said, had the small-pox ; upon which, " that the contagion might not endanger the queen, he retired " to a house at some distance from the palace.   As he began " to recover he was often visited by her : one day they supped " together, and after much discourse, and that they had di- " verted themselves till it was late, the queen pretended she " could not stay with him all night, for one of her maids of " honour being married that day she must, according to the " custom of former queens, see the bride put to bed.   She was " scarce gone, when some gunpowder, that was secretly laid " under the house, was fired, so that the whole house was " blown up, and the king killed : though some said, that he " was not blown up ; but that, hearing some noise of armed " men, he had got out by a back-door into a neighbouring " garden, and that he and one of his servants were strangled " before the house was blown up.   It is certain that the king's " dead body was found in that garden, with no other hurt, but " that about his neck a blackness appeared all round it.   When " this base murder was known, all people were struck with " horror : some spoke severely of the queen herself; libels " were published upon it ; and some having discovered that " Bothwell was the author of this horrid murder, they charged " him, as being not only an assassinate, but a cruel hangman.

" It being on such occasions ordinary for people to search into
" and to discover such things.

" Bothwell, though a heretic, had been always zealous for
" the queen, and faithful to her ; and he had lately with great
" courage rescued her out of a danger she was in from a very
" great sedition: besides that, the queen loved him *desperately*;
" therefore he, in hope to be married to the queen, first di-
" vorced his wife, as if upon adultery that might be so done,
" that he might marry another wife, and then he cruelly con-
" trived the murdering the king. The queen, after she had
" borne down some very wicked reports concerning herself and
" Bothwell, being afraid of some tumult, that might have been
" fatal to them, thought fit to leave Edinburgh. So she carried
" her son with her to Stirling, a place of defence ; having laid
" (as is probable) a design with Bothwell how matters were to
" be managed. A few days after, she pretended to go out a
" hunting ; then Bothwell with two hundred horse seemed to
" surprise her, and to seize her by force. But the queen
" coming back with him to the castle, presently made him
" duke of Orkney, and declared him her husband. That
" marriage did neither prove happy nor lasting ; it being a
" conjunction that had nothing of the matrimonial dignity in
" it, but had sprung from a partnership in an unworthy crime.
" Murray was then out of Scotland ; but he had left Lethington
" among others behind him, who were to raise new quarrels
327 " and tumults upon every occasion. It was easy to Lethington
" to work up the minds of the people, who were universally
" enraged against the queen and Bothwell, to a great flame :
" therefore a tumultuary army being in haste brought together
" at Edinburgh, they marched towards Stirling. But when
" the queen heard that, she, with a few women, and some of
" her court, went to them. They received her with due
" respect : and being asked, why they came thither armed ;
" they answered, they came only to punish Bothwell for the
" crimes committed by him, both in the base and cruel murder
" of the king, and in the force he had put on her person. The
" queen justified Bothwell ; and said, he had done nothing but
" by her consent. This did provoke them to such a degree of
" indignation, that they cried all out with one voice, *Then,*
" *madam, you shall be our prisoner :* and without more delay

" they imprisoned her in a castle within an island in Lochleven;
" appointing only one footman and two ordinary women to
" attend upon her."

Thus the pope's nuncio understood this matter.   There are
some inconsiderable circumstances in this relation wrong told ;
yet the main of the story agreeing with other relations, shews
how falsely this matter has been since that time represented,
not only by writers in the Church of Rome, but by many
among ourselves, to put better colours on this odious business.
To this (that I may end all this unhappy matter at once, without adding any reflections on it, or telling what were the censures that passed on this occasion ; of which I have a great
variety on both sides by me, in books printed very near that
time) I shall only add another very important passage, that is
in the Life of that cardinal, relating to the testament which
that queen wrote with her own hand in French the day before
she was beheaded.   In it " she expressed her constant zeal for
" the catholic religion ; and provided, that if the prince her
" son did not renounce the false and heretical persuasion which
" he had drunk in, the inheritance of the crown of England
" should never descend to him, but should devolve from him to
" Philip king of Spain.   When this original will was brought
" to the cardinal, he examined it with great care ; that so it
" might appear that it was truly her last will, and that it
" ought to be acknowledged as such.   He compared it with
" the letters he had formerly received from that queen : and
" not only he himself, but one Lewis Owen, an Englishman,
" (bishop of Casana,) then at Rome, whom the writer calls a
" pious and a most honest man, signed and attested it.   The
" will being thus confirmed, and as it were fortified by a public
" authority, he delivered it to the count of Olivares, the king
" of Spain's ambassador, that it might be faithfully transmitted
" to that king himself."   I have put the words of the author
of that life, in the language in which he wrote it, in the Collection ; so that the reader may compare the translation I have
given with the original.   I leave this dismal relation as I found
it in these vouchers, without any further canvassing of that
black affair ; which was followed by a train of very extraordinary transactions.

The Scottish nation, both papists and protestants, concurred 328

[margin left: p. 72.]

*[margin left: Collect.
Numb. 94.]*

in the new settlement; of which I shall give a particular account from an authentic proof lately found in Scotland, and now kept in the library of the college of Glasgow : it is the first bond of association that was entered into, upon the resignation of the crown, which the queen was prevailed on to make ; (by force, as she afterwards declared, when she made her escape out of the prison with which she was threatened :) she sent it by the lord Lindsay (ancestor to the earl of Crawford) and the lord Ruthven, afterwards made earl of Gowrie. This bears date at Edinburgh the 24th of July, 1567. By it, she resigned the crown to her son ; and during his infancy she named the earl of Murray to be regent; who was then in France, and did not come to Scotland, at least he did not sign this bond before the 22nd of August. But in the council-book, on the 25th of July, the bond itself is entered on record : and the council removing to Stirling on the 29th of July, the queen's resignation was presented, and received by the earls of Morton, Athol, Glencairn, Mar, Menteith, the master of Grame, the lord Home, and the bishop of Orkney, in the name of the three estates : and the earl of Morton taking the coronation oath in the name of the prince, he was anointed and crowned by the bishop of Orkney : who did indeed little honour to this ceremony; for he, a few days before, had performed the nuptial ceremonies between the queen and the earl of Bothwell. Upon all this, the bond (which is in the Collection) was made Collect. to this purpose : " That whereas the queen, being weary of Numb. 95. " the pains and travail of government, and desiring that in her " lifetime her son might be placed in the kingdom, and be " obeyed by all her subjects, had resigned the crown in favour " of her son : they therefore promised, and bound themselves " to assist their king, in setting him on the throne, and putting " the crown on his head ; and that they should give their " oaths of homage, with all dutiful obedience, to him, as " became true subjects, and should concur in establishing him " in his kingdom, and resist all such as should oppose it."

This was made up in some sheets of vellum ; and there are above two hundred hands of the most eminent families of that kingdom set to that bond. Twenty-five of these were then earls and lords ; and there are fifteen others, whose families are since that time advanced to be of the nobility. The noblemen arc, the earl of Murray, (who signs *James Regent,*) the earls of Huntley, Argyle, Athol, Morton, Mar, Glencairn, Errol, Buchan; the lords Graham, Home, Ruthven, Sanquhar, Glams, Lindsay, Carlisle, Borthwick, Innermeith, Ochiltree, Semple, Methuen, Cathcart, Grey, Ross, Lovat, and the master of Montrose: for earls' sons were then so designed. The noble families, whose ancestors signed this bond, are Buccleugh, Queensbury, Athol, Roxburgh, Annandale, Galloway, Findlater, Panmure, Dalhousie, Leven, Stair, Kenmure, Jedburgh, Cranston, Kircudbright.

Collect.
Numb. 96. Besides those who subscribed the first bond, there was a second bond (that is likewise in the Collection) entered into in April 1569; " by which they did not only acknowledge the " king's authority, but likewise (during the king's minority) 329 " the authority of the earl of Murray, as regent; renouncing " all other authority. And they swear to observe this bond; " in which if they failed, they are contented to be counted " false, perjured, and defamed for ever." This, besides many of those who signed the former bond, was signed by the earls of Crawford and Cassillis, and the lords Saltoun, Ogilvie, Oliphant, and the ancestors of the earls of Seaforth and Southesk, and of the lord Duffus. And in a subsequent bond, signed to the earl of Morton when he was regent, there are five other lords who signed it: the earl of Angus, ancestor to the duke of Douglas, the lords Levingston, Drummond, Boyd, and Hoy of Yester, the ancestors of the earls of Linlithgow, Perth, and Kilmarnock, and of the marquis of Tweeddale.

Papists
joined with
protest-
ants. These were for the greatest part protestants: but there were many papists that joined with them. The earl of Huntley, ancestor to the present duke of Gordon, was the head of the popish party. The earl of Athol, whose name was Stuart, and whose family is since extinct in the male line, protested against the reformation in parliament, and had assisted at the baptism of the young king, in the popish manner. And besides these, the lords Oliphant, Grey, Semple, Maxwell, and Borthwick, were still papists. Thus, as the war against the queen regent (eight years before) was engaged in on national grounds, this great revolution of that kingdom seems to have proceeded, as to the civil part, upon the same principles. So that whatsoever was done in this matter, was done, not upon the grounds of the reformation, but upon national grounds, and pretended precedents and laws: in all which the queen of England had secretly a great hand, how much soever it was disguised or denied.

The interest of state was clearly of her side : for the house of Guise, that began to form great projects in France, laid a main part of their scheme in the design of advancing the unfortunate queen of Scotland to the crown of England: and in the view of that succession, many plots were formed to destroy that glorious queen. They also practised upon the king her son, as soon as he was capable of being wrought on, by the duke of Lennox, and others ; whom they employed about him, to keep him in a dependence on them. They assured him, he should still be king of Scotland ; their design being, that if their practices against queen Elizabeth had succeeded, his mother should have left Scotland to him, when she was advanced to the crown of England. They did likewise engage him to continue unmarried : though he, being the only person of his family, it was otherwise very reasonable to marry him soon. Yet they durst not venture on a popish match till their great design on the crown of France had succeeded : and they would by no means suffer him to marry into a protestant family.

They kept him so much in their management, that the queen of England, and her wise council, understanding all this practice, raised those jealousies of his religion, and made such discoveries of that secret correspondence he was in with the house of Guise, that to this all the troubles that the kirk gave him were chiefly owing. The leaders among them knew, from the intelligence sent them by the court of England, more than they thought fit to own, or than could be well proved. This was the true cause of all that peevish opposition that he met with from the ministers there; which is copiously set forth by archbishop Spotswood. But either he knew not, or did not think fit to set that out, as the effect of the jealousy raised by the court of England, on the account of the confidence, in which he was engaged with the house of Guise.

But as these practices had a fatal conclusion with relation to the unfortunate queen Mary, after her long imprisonment, so when upon the murder of the duke of Guise, and the successes in the beginning of Henry the Fourth of France's reign,

The reasons that moved queen Elizabeth to be jealous of the king of Scotland.

330

The effects that this had.

all those projects of that ambitious and persecuting house were at an end; the king of Scotland married to a daughter of Denmark, and continued still after that in a confidence with the queen of England, which secured to him the succession to that crown.

In giving this short view, which I thought important, and in which I was instructed by many papers that I have seen, I have run a great way beyond my design; which was only to open the first settlement of the reformation in the isle of Great Britain, now happily by her late majesty united into one kingdom: so that nothing remains to be written in pursuance of that. Only, since upon some public occasions, I have referred to a declaration of queen Elizabeth's, (by which she owned and justified the assistance that she gave to the subjects, both of Scotland, and in the Netherlands, in the necessary defence, to which the illegal cruelty of their governors forced them;) and since I have been challenged to publish it, not without insinuations that it was a forgery; I have thought it proper to conclude my Collection of Records with that declaration; that so a paper of such importance may be preserved, and may be more generally read.

Collect.
Numb. 97.

The con-
clusion.

I now conclude this work; in which, as I have faithfully set out everything, according to the materials and vouchers with which I was furnished, so I have used all proper means to procure the best information that I could. It remains, that I leave this to posterity, as the authentic history of a series of great transactions, honestly (though often feebly) conducted, with good intentions, and happy beginnings, though not carried on to the perfection that was designed and wished for.

The *proviso* that had passed in king Henry the Eighth's time, that continued all the canon-law then received in England, till a code of ecclesiastical laws was prepared, which though attempted, and well composed, was never settled; has fixed among us many gross abuses, besides the dilatory forms of those courts, which make all proceedings in them both slow and chargeable. This has in a great measure enervated all church-discipline. A faint wish, that is read on Ash-Wednesday, intimates a desire of reviving the ancient discipline; yet no progress has been made to render that more effectual.

331 The exemptions settled by the papal authority do put many
parts of this church in a very disjointed state; while in some
places the laity, and in many others presbyters, exercise episcopal jurisdiction, independent on their bishops; in contradiction to their principles, while they assert a divine right for
settling the government of the church in bishops, and yet
practise episcopal authority in the virtue of an act of parliament, that provisionally confirmed those papal invasions of the
episcopal power; which is plainly that, which by a modern
name is called Erastianism, and is so severely censured by
some who yet practise it; since whatsoever is done under the
pretence of law, against the divine appointment, can go under
no better name, than the highest and worst degree of Erastianism.

The abbots, with the devouring monasteries, had swallowed
up a great part of that which was the true patrimony of the
church : these houses being suppressed, unlimited grants were
made of their lands, without reserved provisions for the subsistence of those who were to serve at the altar; this has put
a great part of our clergy under crying necessities; and though
the noble bounty of the late queen has settled funds for their
relief, the good effect of that comes on but slowly : yet it is
some comfort to think, that within an age there will be an
ample provision for all that serve in the church; and upon
that prospect we may hope that many abuses will be then
quite abolished.

But with all these defects, we must rejoice in this, that our
doctrine is pure and uncorrupted; that our worship is truly a
reasonable service, freed from idolatry and superstition; and
that the main lines of our church government agree to the
first constitution of the churches by the apostles : so that,
upon the grounds laid down by St. John, all may *hold fellowship with us, since we hold fellowship with the Father, and
with the Son Jesus Christ.*

May we all adhere firmly to the *doctrine of the apostles,*
and continue in *their fellowship, in sacraments and prayers,*
suitably to the rules laid down by them; contending earnestly
for the faith delivered by them to the saints, the first Christians ! *And may all who believe in God be careful to maintain good works for necessary uses ;* which are both *good and*

*profitable unto men; avoiding foolish questions and conten-
tions, for they are unprofitable and vain!*

May we all continue to recommend our doctrine and church
by a holy and exemplary deportment, *shining as lights, and
walking worthy of God, who has called us to his kingdom
and glory;* improving all the advantages that we have, and
bearing with all the defects that we labour under, using our
best endeavours to have them redressed; yet still keeping the
unity of the Spirit in the bond of peace; waiting for such a
glorious conjuncture as may restore every thing among us to
a primitive purity and splendour : which God may perhaps
grant to the prayers of those who call on him night and day
for it.

But if we never see so happy a time upon earth, we know,
if we continue watchful, and *faithful to the death,* we shall
arrive at last at a blessed society, of *innumerable companies
of angels,* and *the spirits of just men made perfect;* of whom
is composed *the general assembly and church of the first-born,
who are written in heaven, who see and enjoy God for ever.*
In the view of directing myself and others thither, I have
written, and now I do conclude this work.

CONTENTS

OF THE

THIRD PART OF THE HISTORY.

[The pages referred to are those of the first folio edition, as printed in the inner margin of this edition.]

BOOK I.

Of matters that happened in the time comprehended in the First Book of the History of the Reformation.

BOOK II.

Of matters that happened during the time comprehended in the Second
Book of the History of the Reformation.

BOOK III.

*Of what happened during the time comprehended in the Third Book
of the History of the Reformation, from the year* 1535 *to
king Henry's death, anno* 1546–7.

BOOK IV.

Of what happened during the reign of king Edward the Sixth, from the year 1547 to the year 1553.

BOOK V.

*Of what happened during queen Mary's reign, from the year
1553 to the year 1558.*

BOOK VI.

Of the beginnings of queen Elizabeth's reign.